WILLIAM ALLEN WHITE'S
AMERICA

WILLIAM ALLEN WHITE'S

AMERICA

by WALTER JOHNSON

HENRY HOLT AND COMPANY

NEW YORK

To My Mother
a lifelong Republican

CONTENTS

PART I

THE END OF THE FRONTIER ERA

1. NATIVE AMERICAN   3
2. COLLEGE DAYS IN KANSAS   31
3. YOUNG CONSERVATIVE   47
4. BIG-CITY JOURNALISM   63
5. COUNTRY EDITOR   78

PART II

REACTION AND REFORM

6. THE MC KINLEY YEARS   103
7. EXPANDING HORIZONS   123
8. FULL-BLOWN PROGRESSIVE   148
9. INSURGENT YEARS   170
10. BULL MOOSE DAYS   199
11. SMALL-TOWN JOURNALISM, 1897-1914   226

PART III

WAR AND PEACE

12. WAR IN EUROPE   251
13. HENRY AND ME   274

CONTENTS

14. A KANSAN AT THE PEACE CONFERENCE 292

15. THE REPUBLICANS AND THE PEACE 314

PART IV

NORMALCY AND REFORM

16. THE HARDING ERA 339

17. A KANSAN IN BABYLON 375

18. THE CRASH OF BABYLON 401

19. THE REBIRTH OF THE PROGRESSIVE MOVEMENT 432

20. CONSERVATIVE LIBERAL 452

21. SPOKESMAN FOR THE GRASS ROOTS 475

PART V

A KANSAN LOOKS AT THE WORLD

22. BETWEEN TWO WARS 503

23. AID TO THE ALLIES 526

24. A FIRST-CLASS FUNERAL 558

NOTES 577

ACKNOWLEDGMENTS 607

BIBLIOGRAPHICAL STATEMENT 611

INDEX 615

PART I

THE END
OF THE FRONTIER ERA

NATIVE AMERICAN

"THIS ends the Emporia dateline over the nation," a neighbor of William Allen White's remarked on January 31, 1944, the day they buried their famous small-town editor. Up and down Emporia's Commercial Street, the townfolks gathered in groups to talk over in hushed tones the news to which small-town dailies and major metropolitan papers were devoting columns of space. The Emporia *Gazette* office was swamped with messages of condolence from the great and from the humble; from White's neighbors all over America—from the President of the United States and from the colored Girl Reserves of the Emporia High School. As *The New York Times* remarked, White's ". . . neighbors lived all along the great American Street that runs from sea to sea."

"The Lord must have loved Bill White to send such perfect weather," everyone said on the day of the funeral. Wherever anyone went in Emporia, friends told anecdotes of the man. Bob Roberts, to whom White had referred in editorials over the years as his favorite undertaker, recalled: "Every time he saw me in the Emporia *Gazette* office he pretended to get mad, and he always said, 'Get out, you; I'm not ready for you yet.' Well," added Roberts sadly, "I got him in the end."

Emporia's public schools, stores, and public offices closed at noon that day. Wherever one went one found the sign: "Closed today because of the funeral of William Allen White." While both local people and out-of-town visitors called at the White

3

home, there came into the *Gazette* office over the Associated Press wire eulogy after eulogy from the American press. "A great stillness is on the State," observed the Topeka *State Journal;* White's old friends on the Kansas City *Star* declared that "Kansas and the nation will not be the same with William Allen White gone." Few people could be found in Emporia or in the nation to disagree with the comment of the Oklahoma City *Times:* "The death of William Allen White takes away one of the truly great Americans of this age. . . ."

It was remarkable that the death of a small-town newspaper editor should attract so much attention. Most country editors lived and died without obtaining more than a brief obituary column from other papers. William Allen White, however, had become the best-known and most often quoted country journalist in the United States. He was better known to most Americans than even the editors of great metropolitan newspapers.

By the time of his death, White had become a symbol to many people of the tolerance, sanity, and greatness of small-town America. His town of Emporia, located on the Santa Fe Railroad between Topeka and Wichita, with a population just under fifteen thousand, its two main business streets, its railroad station, its grain elevators, its two colleges, its county building, its small stores and local industries, and its petty quarrels and rivalries, was not unlike other midwestern prairie towns. Yet from this rather typical community, William Allen White vaulted into a position of national power and prominence. In 1895, in an age when his generation was being lured to the city, White had reversed the process by leaving the Kansas City *Star* to launch his career as editor of the Emporia *Gazette.* From the vantage point of small-town Kansas, Bill White gained for himself a position of influence in American affairs which he probably never could have attained in the big city. For all his warmth and charm, White was basically a shrewd and canny human being, and he had realized that he was unusual in his generation by refusing to leave Emporia for high-salaried positions in the big cities.

Although White gained fame for refusing to desert his small town, he was more than a provincial Kansan. He was as much at home in sophisticated New York circles as he was in the parlors of Emporia. His unpolished and unpretentious beliefs were so blended with cosmopolitan ideas that he was something of a composite American. Within the last twenty-odd years of his life, he became the folk hero of the middle class. Consciously he assumed the role of defender, interpreter, and philosopher of this great dominant element in American society. The things he had to say seemed to satisfy the longings and desires of the middle class for stability in a world of increasing chaos. He was a successful man who had remained in the small town and there had become great. To the small-town dweller who cast sidelong glances at the glamour of the big city, White was assurance enough that small-town life was more rewarding and more desirable. To the city dweller who looked back with nostalgia to the town or village of his youth, White was a symbol of the simplicity, neighborliness, and common sense of main-street America.

The American middle class grasped for the symbolism offered by William Allen White. He seemed to be pertinent proof, in their minds, that greatness was essentially small-townishness. He was to them a living vindication of their way of life, which was subjected to attack after attack for being smug, shallow and provincial. With a splendid sense of humor and with full knowledge of the failings of his small-town midwestern life, he used his facile pen to explain the aspirations and problems of his group to the rest of America. To the middle class, White seemed to be a mellow, sane, and common-sense spokesman.

Yet the Emporia editor was not an original or creative thinker. He was no great iconoclast, no revolutionary, no risky radical. Had he been such, he would not have become a folk hero. He was only slightly less confused than his neighbors from coast to coast about the major problems facing American life. But he did seem to them to be an interpreter who spoke from a small-town, agrarian area in such judicious and clear terms that he offered understanding and insight into their problems. He was no thinker who spoke in vague phrases beyond their comprehension. Instead, he spoke in vigorous, forceful, simple terms. Nor was he ever too far in advance of prevailing middle-class opinion. He was extremely careful to take no action that would be so far ahead of the main

5

current of thought that it might alienate his ever-increasing following.

Through a long lifetime William Allen White exerted an influence on public affairs far greater than that of his contemporaries in small-town journalism. Partly through circumstances and partly through remarkable planning, he commanded in American society a position out of all proportion to the circulation—seven thousand copies a day—of his newspaper. His comments on national and international affairs were eagerly awaited and repeated by innumerable Americans. He was looked upon as the source of information about grass-roots America, and he seldom failed to respond with witty, folksy comments on the changing scene. His comments were not brilliant, incisive interpretations, but they did appeal to many as helpful common-sense judgments on the problems of life.

The large crowd that gathered from all over Kansas and the nation to attend William Allen White's funeral on that January day in 1944 was a graphic demonstration of the position this country editor had achieved in American life. Many of those at the funeral realized that White's lifetime had paralleled the growth of the United States from a small rural nation of thirty-odd million people to a highly industralized society of one hundred and forty millions. He had been born in 1868, a year before the first railroad spanned the American continent. He died during a war when robot bombs and airplanes had remade the world into a mere neighborhood, but into a terrifying neighborhood rather than the friendly small-town neighborhood that White had glorified. In the year that he was born, pioneer settlers were rolling across the plains of Kansas in their prairie schooners, peopling the last great American frontier; in the year that he died, descendants of these frontiersmen were fighting on the world-wide battlefields of the second great war in a generation.

White was an observer and interpreter of most of the changes that transformed America from 1868 to 1944. He was also an active participant in many of them. As a child in the small town of El Dorado, Kansas, he caught a fleeting glimpse of the picturesque Indian and cowboy frontiers. He watched blue-coated Civil War veterans plow up the prairie sod and turn Kansas into a farming community. As a boy he saw the fringe-topped surreys appear on the streets of El Dorado, and he watched the telephone and electric lights come to his state. He also saw a trickle of the millions of immigrants who were pouring in from the Old World, seeking the golden land of opportunity. As a youngster he saw the farmers' fields wither under the drought and their crops disappear before the blight of grasshoppers. As he grew older, he noticed how the G.A.R. veterans controlled the Republican party and dominated the politics of the state.

As a youth in his early twenties, he opposed the Populist farmers' militant protest against their lot in a rapidly developing industrialized and urban society. In 1896, the year after he had purchased the Emporia *Gazette*, he gained his first nation-wide audience with his slashing attack on William Jennings Bryan, the Democrats, and the Populists, in his biting editorial "What's the Matter With Kansas?" Two years later he watched the youthful nation, now an industrial force to be reckoned with in world affairs, emerge on the international scene as a great imperial power after its defeat of the decayed Spanish Empire. He lent support to the enthusiasm for the "white man's burden" that helped extend America's sphere of influence in the Far East, in the Pacific islands, and in the Caribbean.

From 1901 to 1909, White was a confidant and publicist of President Theodore Roosevelt. He played an important part in the Progressive movement by popularizing the aims of the Progressives in articles for *McClure's Magazine*, the *Saturday Evening Post*, and the *American Magazine* at a time when American magazines had a powerful influence on the public. He managed the campaigns of progressive Republican candidates in his own state. In 1912, he bolted the Republican party and helped Theodore Roosevelt launch the Bull Moose party.

Five years later, he watched his America take its place on the side of the Allied powers fighting the threat of militaristic Germany. He witnessed something of the war at first hand as an observer in France for the American Red Cross. As a reporter at the Peace Conference he watched the traditions and forces of the Allied world mold the Versailles Treaty, and he saw Woodrow Wilson fight for and create the League of Nations. Back home by the summer of 1919, White talked for the ratification of the peace treaty and for American entrance into the League. To his horror, he saw small hatreds and partisan blindness wrecking America's participation in the first real attempt at world peace through collective security.

During the 1920's, he saw America embark upon a policy of isolation in international affairs and reaction in domestic politics. Both trends he opposed without success in his pungent editorials and magazine articles. Under Presidents Warren G. Harding and Calvin Coolidge, whose candidacies he had supported, he realized that the captains of industry whom he had opposed in prewar America, were securing immense political and economic power. He watched the country turn dangerously nationalistic. He saw citizens of recent immigrant backgrounds, immigrants who had helped make America's extraordinary development possible, persecuted by the Ku Klux Klan. He fought such bigotry through his editorials and by running for governor of Kansas on an anti-Klan program in 1924. Three years later the Emporia editor helped to launch Herbert Hoover's boom for the presidency, and took an active part in the 1928 campaign.

During the first year of a depression that disrupted the fundamental roots and concepts of American life, White went to the Republic of Haiti as a member of the President's Commission to investigate the American occupation of the island republic. The report that he helped write made a forceful contribution to a shift in America's Latin-America policy to that of the Good Neighbor.

Out of the depths of the depression, he saw in 1933 a new progressive-minded administration take charge of the nation. He eagerly supported, except at election time, many of the New Deal laws designed to make monopoly capitalism serve the American people. While these hopeful developments were occurring, through visits to Europe and the Far East he observed the ominous rise of Adolf Hitler in Germany; he heard Benito Mussolini's boast that he would re-establish the Old Roman Empire; and he saw Japanese aggressions in North China designed to secure ultimate domination of the Far East.

In September, 1939, he saw the world plunged into another great conflict. Realizing that America's security depended upon a victory for the Allies, he helped found and actively led the Committee to Defend America by Aiding the Allies. Under his leadership the committee rallied the American people behind a program of action that helped keep Great Britain fighting while America launched her own preparations for a war that was inevitable. He died a little more than a year and a half before the successful conclusion of the war. By the time of his death, however, he was convinced that the Allied cause would triumph over that of the Axis.

Perhaps no other person during the seventy-six years from 1868 to 1944 quite so completely reflected the expansion and development of America in its many phases as did the man who by the last twenty years of his life was affectionately referred to as the Sage of Emporia. He was part of the unfolding of the American nation, part of a folk saga unprecedented in world history. Through his editorials, letters, novels, biographies, and magazine articles, he described the changing America from the point of view of the middle class, the farmer, and small-town America. With his death, this America lost its most vocal spokesman. "Here was, first of all, an American—American in the best and strongest tradition of this country," reflected the New York *Herald Tribune*. "William Allen White was a real power in the land. His career, the respect and affection in which he was held, were the best of all possible answers to the doubts which cynics have directed at the American people."

*   *   *

An important aspect of White's charm was his understanding of human beings. He learned to know human nature in his early days in El Dorado. He grew up in a society of middle-class pioneer people. It was in these El Dorado days that he acquired a belief in the dignity of his fellow men and an unshakable faith in their basic decency and friendliness. After White's death, the St. Louis *Post-Dispatch* caught this quality in the man when it declared that "There was a wonderful kindliness and neighborliness about White, typical of American wilderness days when men in trouble or in want had to lean upon one another."

Although William Allen White had been born in Emporia on February 10, 1868, his father in 1870 moved his family to the

9

more pioneer town of El Dorado some sixty miles southwest of Emporia. It was a tough town during Will White's early child-hood. Shootings, lynchings, wild-riding cowboys, open gambling, and flourishing saloons were part of life in this frontier town. As a boy, White remembered that he and his companions used to hunt unusual bottles and corks behind the saloons. "We boys also knew," he recalled, "there was a gambling room over the saloon, and that across the alley there was a house, with drawn shutters, which, when we were out at night, we could stone with impunity if we could run fast enough to escape being caught." El Dorado filled up with settlers so rapidly in the 1870's, however, that the wide-open frontier aspects of life quickly disappeared.

The town, too, was occasionally visited by Indians, and the visible remains of their civilization were to be seen on every hand. Indian legends haunted the rocks, caves, streams, and ravines where Will White played as a child. But El Dorado had no serious Indian troubles. "The reason we never had any real Indian prob-lems," White once jestingly remarked, "was that the Indians, after seeing Kansas, decided to let the white men have it since Kansas would cause them more trouble than the Indians ever could."

As a growing boy, Will White was a dumpy, freckle-faced, redheaded lad, built along horizontal rather than perpendicular lines. He had an impish, puckish note in his make-up, which he never lost. "Everybody liked him," a schoolmate remembered in 1907. "He was so good-natured they could not do otherwise." In many ways he was a cocky person as well as an impish one. This same schoolmate was puzzled when trying to explain William Allen White's success as a newspaper editor and writer. She could recall no marks of genius on Will as a boy, but he had been a per-sistent and cocksure individual. "I smile even now at the memory of him," wrote this schoolmate, "coming partly onto the stage, red-headed, freckle-faced, with prominent ears, his hands behind his back, his head well up in the air, and a broad grin suffusing his countenance, the very picture of self-confidence— He always did things in a manner that seems to say: 'Behold this is I.' In all his appearances in public and the statements he made there was the air of 'I' about him, but as to any distinguishing marks of genius if he ever had them no one discovered the fact."

During the first few years in El Dorado, the Whites lived in a little frame house on South Main Street, which also served Will's father, a frontier doctor, as a drug and general store. His stationery in 1871 offered the following goods for sale:

Dr. Allen White, Pharmaceutist, wholesale and Retail Druggist, Wholesale and Retail Dealer in Paints, Oil, Window Glass, Perfumery, Toilet Articles, Books, Stationery, Pure Liquors, etc.

Recollecting these early days, son Will described the store as the kind of drugstore "with the big red bottle in one window on one side of the door and the big green bottle, or blue, in the window at the other side of the door; the regular old-fashioned drugstore with a little soda fountain with about six syrups and 'Don't care' for the leftovers, a sort of combined flavor." One day druggist White, finding one of his customers lying drunk near the store, doused the drunk with two buckets of water despite the protests of some of his neighbors, explaining, "This is a free country and a man has got a right to water his own whiskey."

In 1874, Dr. White sold his drugstore and bought a farm seven miles north of El Dorado. Having been born and reared on a farm in Ohio, he had an irresistible desire to go back to the pioneer life of his childhood. In an area where farmhouses were now of clapboard construction, he insisted on building a log cabin with a huge fireplace and rafters, from which hung dried pumpkins, sage, and onions. He had a rail fence built around the farm, and hired a number of men to work it for him. Old Doc White, as he was known to his neighbors, was so fat and clumsy that he wasn't of much use himself on the farm. As Will remembered his father, "he was kindly, jolly, enterprising and hard-working, a roly-poly little man . . . about five feet six with a whiskbroom beard on his chin . . ." A fellow resident of El Dorado described Doc White as being "five feet one way and 220 pounds all over," and declared that "he hated to get up and sit down often, but when on his feet and in motion he moved briskly for one of his size." Son Will was to be built according to the same specifications.

The Whites didn't remain on the farm very long. No hired girl would work there, and the hired men were too much for Mrs. White to handle. Finally, Will's mother rebelled, and the Whites moved back to town. As her son recalled later, "Men were supposed to run their own homes in those days—but not men who married my mother." Back in town, Doc White built a large house with broad verandas. He enjoyed company so much that finally the Whites decided to turn it into a hotel; they called it the White House.

"Drummers" en route to Wichita and western Kansas frequented the White House and brought news of the outside world. Old Doc White thoroughly enjoyed the role of host and loved to furnish a good table, something that the William Allen Whites became noted for as well. Roly-poly Will and his roly-poly father frequently went to market, where Doc White would pick out, as Will recalled, "fine thick sirloins and porterhouse steaks, and tall, fat rib roasts and bring them home to his guests whom he fed and roomed at $2.00 a day. . . . I think he lost money every day he kept the hotel open and I think that was his chief pride in life."

While his mother complained that they were going to end up in the poorhouse, the only real economy old Doc would practice was to keep his high-priced "five-cent" tobacco in a silver case in his hip pocket and to carry plug tobacco in his coat pocket for strangers who wanted to "borrow" a chaw. Finally Mary Ann White put her foot down and the hotel closed, to the great disappointment of Doc White. Even though he was losing money operating it, he was making enough money out of real estate so that it really did not matter.

Doc White enlivened life in the drab little town on the Kansas prairie. Quite conspicuous in his white panama hat, white pleated shirt, and nankeens, he attracted attention when he walked down the main street whistling and clicking his cane on the wooden sidewalks. When he came into a store or house, "his entrance never was orderly; never blustering but always gay, conspicuous—an entrance!" Perhaps from his father Will White learned the technique of attracting attention, of being good company and colorful copy for newspapermen in search of a story.

* * *

Will's father had been an early settler of Kansas. Many times young Will heard the story of the western migration of the White family from his father's lips. Dr. Allen White was a restless pioneer descendant of stock that traced its roots back to a middle-class Englishman who had joined the great Puritan migration to Massachusetts in the 1630's. Until the turn of the nineteenth century, the White family lived in Raynham, Massachusetts, tilling their land, working as carpenters and mechanics, and serving in public office. William Allen White's grandfather, John White, early in the nineteenth century, began the westward movement of the White family. After ten years in New York State, he settled permanently near Norwalk in northern Ohio, where Will's father, Allen White, was born in 1819.

Young Allen White, after attending a one-room country school, spent a few weeks at Columbus, Ohio, acquiring a sketchy medical training and a few medical books and instruments. He settled down in the northwest corner of Ohio at the town of Delta, where he farmed a bit, practiced some medicine, and tended a store. In 1845, at the age of twenty-six, he married his first wife, a widow, Mrs. Elizabeth Kitts. Mrs. Kitts was considerably older than Allen White, and they never had any children. Will's mother, Mary A. White, his father's second wife, never would discuss her husband's first marriage with her son.

Nine years after this first marriage, in 1854, Allen White completed the pilgrimage of his family by selling his property and moving west to the newly opened territory of Kansas. Throughout his lifetime Will's father followed the frontier maxim that "It's good for a man to be shifty in a new country." This, of course, meant beating the other fellow to the opportunities that were awaiting exploitation in the frontier area. Ohio by 1854 had close to two million people, and it undoubtedly seemed easier to Allen White to get ahead in the newer West than in the more complex society of Ohio.

Allen White not only took a restless spirit with him to Kansas, but as the son of the New England stock he carried with him Puritan ideas of individualism blended with social responsibility. Although Will's father objected to the antislavery agitation of the day, he was a reformer for woman's rights and for prohibition. His son was to be decidedly influenced by such Puritan ideas as the social responsibility for evil. He came to believe that no one could understand the meaning of Kansas without understanding the ardent reforming spirit of the state in terms of New England Puritanism. Although many other influences affected the state, he always attributed its major characteristics to New England Puritanism. In 1916, the Emporia editor declared, for instance, that "the glory of Kansas is that she is as a state the sole legatee and custodian of the New England conscience."

William Allen White always believed that his native state had been founded by Puritans with the supreme purpose of eradicating injustice and creating a Puritan civilization based upon reason and justice. He so thoroughly convinced himself of this theory that, when a study of the state's population revealed that proportionally few New Englanders had settled there, he nevertheless declared in the introduction to the book that Kansas was the product of New England!

There is no doubt that William Allen White's Kansas was different. It had a tremendous reforming instinct. The state was extremely hostile to any variation from its pattern. Kansans were reformers, intolerant of other people's ways, because they considered themselves to be a chosen people entrusted with creating God's Holy Commonwealth on earth. Believing that they had this special mission, they organized fervent crusades like prohibition, Populism, and Progressivism against evils that appeared to be manmade.

Kansans had too much faith that they were carrying on God's work to be tolerant of those whose views differed from theirs. They were, William Allen White once explained to the rest of the nation, a "moral people in so far as morals consist in obedience to the legally expressed will of the majority with no very great patience for the vagaries of protesting minorities . . . a people neighbor-bound by ties of duty, by a sense of obligation, by a belief in the social compact, in the value of the herd, in the destiny of the race. All these social totems are concentrated in the idea of God in the Kansas heart. We are a deeply religious people. Time was when they used to say in Kansas that the Republican party and the Methodist Church were the spiritual forces that controlled the State. 'Ad astra per aspera,' to the stars by the hard ways, is the state motto and kindly note the 'hard ways.' Ours is no easy approach to grace, no royal road to happiness, no backstairs to beneficence. There is no earthly trail paralleling the primrose path in which one can avoid the wrath of God and the lady next door. Life and liberty are indeed highly esteemed in Kansas; but the pursuit of happiness only upon conditions set forth in the Ten Commandments, the Golden Rule, and their interpretation by the Kansas statutes . . . Deep in our hearts is the obsessed fanaticism of John Brown. Joy is an incident, not the business of life."

Kansas was unique from the very first year it was opened to settlers. By the time Dr. and Mrs. Allen White reached the new territory Kansas already was suffering from more than the normal amount of frontier violence. The American Civil War was looming on the horizon, and antislavery forces in New England saw Kansas as a place to wage battle against slavery. Funds were raised and a small band of settlers were sent across the country to people Kansas for freedom. Missourians, who in normal western custom viewed Kansas as their particular domain since it lay just to the west of them, resented any "forced" immigration into the territory. Armed Missourians raided free-state settlers and secured control of the territorial government. Soon Kansas was a battleground, and "Bleeding Kansas" became a symbol of the coming struggle between the North and the South.

The violence of Bleeding Kansas did not please Allen White. He was no abolitionist. He was in Kansas to make a living, not to fight over the question of slavery. After a few months in Kansas, the Whites left for a four-year stay in Texas. All that son Will ever knew about his father's experiences in Texas was that he did not like the cooking. In 1859, the Whites returned to Kansas, where they settled in the little town of Americus some eleven miles northeast of Emporia. The next year, when the town of Emporia won the county seat away from Americus, Dr. Allen White settled in Emporia.

The Civil War years must have been trying for Will's father. He was not in favor of the war. He was an adamant Copperhead Democrat who preached the need of a compromise peace between the sections. To adhere to such views in Kansas stirred emotions turbulently in an area that had just gone through years of civil strife itself. Possibly it was just a prank, or it might have been because of his views, that twice his buggy was pushed into the Neosho River and the taps removed from the buggy's axles.

* * *

From his mother William Allen White heard a different story of western settlement, but also in its way a story typical of the growing, expanding American continent. His mother often related to her only child the tale of how her parents, Thomas and Ann Kelly Hatton, had migrated from Ireland to the province of Quebec, where Will's mother, Mary Ann Hatton, had been born on January 3, 1830, in a wilderness log cabin. Early in her childhood her parents moved their large family across the border to Oswego, New York. While growing up in Oswego, Mary Ann Hatton saw the first railroad come into the town and heard the first woman preacher who occupied a pulpit in Oswego. Very often she went to hear Susan B. Anthony preach the doctrine of woman's rights and herself became a lifelong advocate of woman suffrage and equality for women. She instilled in her son Will a reforming instinct for these measures, as well as a firm belief in prohibition.

Mary Ann Hatton's parents were dead by the time she was sixteen, and she went to live with foster parents, who soon moved to Illinois. These foster parents, Mr. and Mrs. Robert Wright, were ardent Congregationalists; they interested Will's mother in the little Congregational college at Galesburg, Illinois. "She must have been very happy there," William Allen White once wrote, "for as a child I learned of the glories of Knox College, and it came to be a place of high adventure to me, a sort of port of dreams."

The 1850's were exciting days at Knox. The college, founded by a band of New England preachers to carry on Puritan ways in the heart of the Illinois prairies, was a powerful center of abolitionism. In this environment of abolition and frontier religious revivals, Mary Ann Hatton became an ardent antislavery advocate, as well as a devoted follower of the new Republican party. In the revivals in which she participated while at Knox, the evangelical preachers taught their converts that their duty as Christians was to rid the nation of such sins as slavery. The Kingdom of Heaven could be had on earth, the preachers declared, provided slavery was removed from the face of the land.

By the time she left her early environment for Kansas, Mary Ann Hatton was a strong-willed, powerful reformer. She was to implant in her son much of her own Puritan fervor of social responsibility for the ills of the world. That he was his brother's keeper, William Allen White was to hear many times in his youth. He was also to hear a great deal about the martyred President, Abraham Lincoln. In 1858, his mother had thrilled to Lincoln's words when she heard him debate with Stephen A. Douglas at Galesburg. When the Civil War broke out, it was in her mind a great crusade for freedom. She reportedly wept because she had no one to send to the Union Army.

In 1865, Mary Ann Hatton left Illinois for Emporia, Kansas, to study at the new normal school that had just been opened in the town. Unable to find employment in Emporia to help defray her expenses, Mary Ann Hatton secured a teaching post at Council Grove, a town thirty miles northwest of Emporia, to which her foster parents had moved from the East. Council Grove was a tough outfitting station on the busy Santa Fe trail to the southwest. It was a town booming with blacksmiths, harness makers, repair shops, saloons, dance halls, rough and hardy mule skinners, Indian traders, and Indians from a nearby reservation. Reminiscing about these early days in Council Grove, one person wrote: "It was unsafe to leave the house without arms, and they were carried in the field while following the plow or while working in the woods. There was constant danger of Indian raids and massacre."

Mary Ann Hatton's abolitionist sentiments involved her in grave trouble in Council Grove, a town which had no sympathy for the freed Negro. Negroes were not permitted to attend the Council Grove school, but on her first day she allowed a Negro child in her class. After all, she must have reasoned, this country boasts of its democracy and equalitarian doctrines. Why, then, should the Negroes be denied equal privileges with other Americans? But she had not taken into account the great gap between American ideals and American practices. Immediately, irate parents removed children from her classroom. Mary Ann Hatton finally had to submit and exclude Negroes from her school, but she created such a furor that the community finally provided a separate school for the Negroes. All her life she was a dominating personality, a fighter for what she considered right. Her son once observed, "My mother was the type of woman known as a 'captain'—a masterful person who had her own ideas, and being purebred Irish wanted to make her own views prevail."

In 1866, Mary Ann Hatton met Dr. Allen White. About the time of their first meeting, Dr. White's first wife, then living at Americus, Kansas, secured a divorce on the grounds that he had been "wilfully absent from the plaintiff for more than one year past without any cause or justification therefor. . . ." The following year, when Dr. White proposed to Mary Ann Hatton, he succinctly observed, "My History pertaining to domestic relations are not as prepossessing as I would desire by no means." On April 15, 1867, they were married in Michigan, where Mary had gone to take care of a very sick sister. Their son often remarked that it was a strange courtship and marriage. His parents were so different in their ages and points of view that he wondered many times how they had remained together. Dr. White was forty-eight and Mary Ann Hatton was thirty-seven. Their only child to survive infancy, William Allen White, was born on February 10, 1868.

His parents were both unusual people. They were to provide him in his early training with wide differences in background, point of view, and temperament. His father was an easygoing human being who enjoyed other human beings. Although for many years a frontier wanderer, in later life he showed his Yankee shrewdness by amassing considerable money for that day in Kansas. His mother was a stern, firm, serious soul who taught her son the importance of hard work. She was a person of tremendous purpose. "She was more of the dour Irish," her son once wrote, "or black Irish who have a small sense of humor. . . . From my Irish grandmother, Ann Kelly of Dublin, I have my sense of humor. Family tradition says that she was a blithe and merry soul. My grandfather, Thomas Hatton, her husband, was a peasant weaver who gave my mother her purpose and her strength."

Politically, William Allen White's parents were at opposite poles. His father was a loyal Democrat, his mother an aggressive Republican. Son Will was to be influenced politically more by his mother than by his father. His mother loved to wrangle over politics and enjoyed a heated political discussion. His father refused to discuss politics with her and only laughed when she became excited and overheated.

The two of them also had different conceptions of pioneer life. Dr. White looked upon the frontier as a zone of immense opportunity and challenge where one could escape the rigidity of an older society. Here one could strike out on his own and earn his own place in the world regardless of the wealth and social position of his family. To Mary Ann White, the frontier was a grim, bleak existence devoid of any of the intellectual and social graces so important to a woman who loved education and culture. Her view of pioneer life corresponded to the bitter, grim picture that Ed Howe was to paint so unforgettably in his book *The Story of a Country Town*.

Mary Ann White was quick-witted, quick-tempered, and volatile. Dr. Allen White was easygoing, romantic, and slow to anger. Many times he was too tenderhearted to collect his bills, but in the expanding economy of the day he nevertheless accumulated a good deal of money.

William Allen White showed a definite mixture of many of the traits of his parents. He was quick-witted, a lover of a good battle, volatile and romantic over many issues. He also enjoyed human beings, and there was a disarming naïveté about him, but beneath this surface impression he was an extremely shrewd and practical human being. White was a mixture of Irish romanticism, Yankee shrewdness, and good midwestern common sense. "He had the smile of a roguish little boy, with dimples complete; the broad noble brow of a philosopher and statesman; the eyes of a poet and the shrewd determined mouth of the politician, businessman, newspaper editor . . . ," Edna Ferber observed in her autobiography, *A Peculiar Treasure*.

*   *   *

William Allen White had a vivid recollection of his mother reading to him as a child during long winter evenings. She laid in her son the foundation of a real literary and cultural appreciation. "Night after night," he once wrote, "I remember as a child, sitting in the chair, looking up to her while she read Dickens and George Eliot, Trollope, Charles Reed, and the Victorian English novels. My father, I remember, used to growl a good deal at the performance, and claimed that if my mother read to me so much I would never get so I would read for myself. But his prediction was sadly wrong. It was to those nights of reading and to the books that my mother had always about the house that I owe whatever I have of a love for good reading."

Other books that thrilled young Will were *Tom Sawyer, Children of the Abbey, Arabian Nights, Little Women, Gulliver's Travels, Robinson Crusoe, Wit and Humor, Scottish Chiefs, Tom Brown*, and *The Circuit Rider*. As a young lad, Will White read also the *Youth's Companion* and once in a while saw the colored cartoons of Thomas Nast, America's favorite cartoonist, in *Harper's Weekly*, in which Nast carried on an unceasing war against Tammany Hall of New York and the general corruption of politicians.

His family inspired Will with a lifelong interest in music. One Sunday afternoon, while Dr. and Mrs. White and Will were sitting in the shade of the cottonwoods along the banks of the Walnut River, his father whittled a whistle for the boy. After the whistle came a cornstalk fiddle, a pumpkin-reed pipe, a jew's-harp, a comb, a guitar, a mandolin, and an accordion; and finally Will began to learn to peck out tunes on a small portable organ.

The first money Will White ever earned came from playing the organ for country dances. In addition to White at the organ, the orchestra included a blind fiddler and a cornettist. Part of White's task in this orchestra was to call off the dances. "Most of our playing," he later recalled, "was by ear and we were expected to play every tune we had ever heard. We had no notes. Why should a real musician bother with notes?" Among the dances that he called off were the quadrilles and the Virginia reel. The favorite pieces that this orchestra was called on to play included the *Cornflower Waltz, Sweet Violets, Flower from My Angel Mother's Grave, When the Leaves Begin to Turn*, and *Genevieve*. To his organ playing Will added a little singing in the moonlight. He and half a dozen other boys organized a Screech Owl Club, and "went out howling under the moon like the precocious pups

we were," he later wrote. "What fearful noises w
made, singing 'The fox is on the hill, I hear him how
'When the Leaves Begin to Turn.' "

Through the course of his early years in El Do
White saw at first hand nature's best efforts to driv
of Kansas. In 1871, El Dorado was completely destroy
nado. Two years later a terrible drought ruined the
following year millions of grasshoppers darkened t
remembered how the men and women watched the s
vainly hoping for an end to the shimmering clouds o
saw the grasshoppers strip the fields of their crops, e
and then just sit around working their jaws. Prairie fi
quently menaced the young community of El Dor
sionally," White recalled, "a prairie fire came roarin
side of the hill from the town, and the boys rushed
the schoolroom, without waiting for dismissal, to jo
fighting fire. Sometimes they soaked their homemade
coats in the rain barrels hauled to the scene on
whacked the little blazes that ran before the flames li
the dry grass, blistered their chubby faces, and retu
school vain and tired boy heroes to boast of their ac

Yet, in spite of nature's devastating efforts, Kansas fi
settlers in White's youth. Hundreds of thousands of y
veterans and their wives poured into Kansas. From 36
in 1870—the year the Whites settled in El Dorado—
panded its population to 1,428,108 by 1890. During
White's lifetime, Kansas was to be relatively stable, i
population to just 1,801,028 people by 1940.

Young White watched thousands of "mover" v
through El Dorado on their way to people western
these pioneers left eastern and central Kansas, the
moved out of the prairie plains into the arid, high pl
up to the Rockies. They left the country of the long
with its usually adequate rainfall and timber, for the
grass with its scanty rainfall and flat, timberless plain
toward the horizon. The White family never lived i
grass country. El Dorado was in the heart of central
Emporia was on the fringe of eastern Kansas in the blu

country. In all that William Allen White was to write explaining Kansas to the rest of the nation, he seldom spoke for western Kansas. He spoke for the Kansas of mixed farms, the more prosperous Kansas. Writing in the 1890's about the different sections of Kansas, White remarked: "Eastern Kansas is a finished community like New York or Pennsylvania. Central Kansas is finished, but not quite paid for; and Western Kansas, the only place where there is any suffering from drouth or crop failures, is a new country—old only in a pluck which is slowly conquering the desert."

The prairie, the woods, and the Walnut River taught Will White as much as did his formal education in the classroom. He and his playmates, Sumpter Smith, Matt Long, Al Ewing, Charlie and Ed Harvey, trapped and hunted in the woods, rowed, fished, and swam in the Walnut River in the days before erosion had made the stream excessively muddy. They cut stick horses and kept "stick horse livery stables in the woods under paw-paw bushes with grapevines hanging down." An old-time citizen of El Dorado recalled: "We remember him riding his stick horse and screaming out his orders to the boys of Boyville." The boys played in the pokeberry patch and made red ink out of the berries. "Lord! how it used to smell," White once remembered; "I can smell it yet." The birds and the animals were part of his childhood experience.

While the Whites lived on a farm, Will had his regular chores. He learned how to milk the cows and feed the hogs and saw wood. In the hayloft he learned the ways of acrobatics, turning flipflops and swinging on homemade trapezes. This was the life that White was to describe in nostalgic terms in his book about boys, *The Court of Boyville* (1899). These stories reveal the boy Will White was and the boy he had longed to be. He wanted to be "Piggy Pennington," the king of Boyville; a free, unhampered, natural, athletic young fellow. Actually, however, he was the "Mealy Jones" of Boyville, a boy whose mother made him wear shoes when the other boys went barefoot, who was forbidden to swim in the river and to fight with the other boys, and who was too roly-poly to be a good athlete. Undoubtedly, young Will occasionally violated his mother's injunctions against swimming

and fighting, but it was not until his college days and shortly thereafter that he seems to have thrown off his mother's domination and struck out to be a free and unfettered person. "He never resented the tricks his companions played upon him, though they were many," reminisced an old schoolmate in 1907. "They said he was a coward when it came to a fight; and, knowing this, the boys were always trying to get him into a corner and compel him to stand or run. . . . I have often wondered if the boy was afraid of the physical discomfiture of a fist fight or of incurring the displeasure of his mother, who prohibited him from fighting."

Although Will White as a boy was good-natured and could be gay and frivolous, he could also be serious-minded. Time after time, one of his teachers recalled, he would "be seen sauntering off by himself, hands in his pockets. . . ." With grownups, he was frequently bashful and shy. Later in life he advised a young mother to have her children "perform on every occasion possible, so they won't be company shy. Why, I was so bashful when I was a youngster I was miserable . . ." When a fellow newspaperman, Jay E. House, met White in 1892, he observed: "He was a fat boy then, cherubic as to countenance, and with a diffident, embarrassed manner. He talked volubly enough in an odd, effusive, staccato sort of way without much regard to punctuation marks. But somehow he reminded one of a bashful boy, who, after much urging, had gone over to a neighbor's for Sunday dinner and found a house full of strange company." Perhaps as part of an innate shyness, White, throughout his lifetime, was filled with nervous tension. He would get all choked up inside, and then let it off by writing such beautiful editorials as the one to his dead daughter, Mary White—or such scathing editorials as "What's the Matter With Kansas?"

* * *

As a growing boy, White participated in many frontier revivals and camp meetings, which were the scene of hell-fire, emotionalized religion. The preachers, well trained in the art of arousing the hysterical qualities of their audience, created an atmosphere in which the exultation and frenzy of some listeners reached such a high pitch that they would bark or scream, while others would faint or go into a trance. When White was once asked to name his favorite hymn, he remarked, "I suppose through the years the hymn that has remained with me most tenaciously is an old camp meeting song. The chorus runs:

> I shall arise and go to Jesus
> He will receive me in his arms.
> In the arms of my dear Jesus,
> Oh, there are ten thousand charms.

"I heard it as a boy at camp meetings. Camp meetings fifty years ago were the survival of the sylvan orgies of the ancients. A camp meeting in those days was an emotional outbreak. Noise and action distinguished a camp meeting. The preacher was the leader in the hullabaloo, and as the spiritual temperature rose, people seemed to lose their control, and I first realized as a boy the fundamental psychological facts of life. That emotions are dangerous, for at the camp meetings of my boyhood there was always a love-making obbligato in the brush around the camp meeting . . . And even as a boy emerging from childhood I got the potency of that hymn as a rouser of romance and religion at the same time." This emotionalized religion left a heavy imprint on American life. The Methodist Church, for instance, was the principal force behind Kansas prohibition, and the later Populist and Progressive movements had a powerful revivalistic religious quality in their make-up.

The Whites were not church members in El Dorado, probably because there was no Congregational church. The revivalistic Christian, Methodist, and Baptist churches were probably too emotional for their more intellectual religious tastes. Will, however, made the rounds of the camp meetings more as a matter of entertainment and romance than from a sense of religious obligation. It wasn't until after he had become a father that he joined a church—the Congregational—in Emporia. Attendance at Sunday school by young White also was largely a social affair. He regularly went to the Baptist school in the morning, the Presbyterian at noon, and the Methodist in the afternoon. The boys and girls received cards for good attendance, and these cards became a commodity to trade for marbles, chalk, and walnuts. Attending three

Sunday schools also made it possible to meet "three separate Dulcineas" and, he added, "get three separate and delicious eye shocks, and anoint himself unctuously with the belief that he was a good and pious youth." Out of his Sunday-school experience, however, he gained a great deal of Biblical lore, which was later in life to appear in his speeches and writings.

From time to time, Will's boyhood was enlivened by a trip to Wichita or the state capital, Topeka. On these visits to Wichita, the Whites stayed with Marsh Murdock, the founder of the Wichita *Eagle*, and the brother of Bent Murdock, editor of the *Walnut Valley Times*. Wichita was the big circus town for central Kansas, and Will was a first-rate circus fan. On these trips he became a friend of redheaded Vic Murdock, Marsh's son; this friendship ripened into the closest type of personal and political intimacy throughout a lifetime.

Politics drew the Whites to Topeka. During White's boyhood politics got into his blood, and ever after it was to occupy a large share of his time. While his father was alive, Will was a good Democrat. In 1876, during the Tilden-Hayes race for the presidency, he wore a scarf with Tilden's name embroidered on it. This lone Democrat in their school was a challenge to the young Republican patriots; one boy grabbed one end of the scarf and another grabbed the other end and began to choke this rash young Democrat. The screams of Will's childhood sweetheart, Lila Heaton, attracted the attention of some older boys, who rescued him from a martyr's death. Many times Will drove around Butler County with his father, who was vainly trying to organize a strong unit of the Democratic party in a hopelessly Republican county. Doc White and several other Democrats subsidized the *Butler County Democrat* to counteract the Republican sentiments of the *Walnut Valley Times*. At the age of ten, Will White went to work for the *Democrat* as a printer's devil, but this first experience in newspaperwork lasted only four or five days. At the time of his death in 1882, Doc White was mayor of El Dorado. In local politics, however, the badge of Republican or Democrat meant little. His election was a reward for being an outstanding booster for the town.

Although his father was a Democrat and his mother a Republican, the parents agreed heartily on two vital Kansas issues. They were both prohibitionists and supporters of woman suffrage. Susan B. Anthony stayed at the White house in both Emporia and El Dorado, and Will recalled that he "was scared of her. She seemed fierce and carnivorous—the kind that ate little boys alive." Doc White was particularly indignant at the Republican party for granting the Negro, just out of slavery, the franchise and withholding it from women.

White always suspected political disappointment as the cause of his father's death. The Democratic State Convention, meeting at Emporia, on August 30, 1882, denounced the prohibition law passed the year before as the "cause of neighborhood quarrels, contentions, and strife, of fraud, corruption, perjury, and violence. . . ." It was a serious blow to Doc White to have his party denounce prohibition. He died on October 4, 1882.

After the death of his father, Will White quickly lost any sense of kinship with the Democratic party. His mother's "black" Republicanism filled his mind. But it was more than his mother's influence. After all, he was a shrewd, practical young fellow. Why be a Democrat—a member of the minority party in Kansas? Why butt your head against a stone wall? Kansas politics were dominated by the Republicans. The thousands upon thousands of Civil War veterans who had poured into Kansas in the sixties and seventies made it a solidly Republican state. Furthermore, wasn't the Republican party the party that had saved the Union and won the Civil War? Wasn't the Democratic party in control of the sinful cities and recent immigrant groups?

It wasn't long before Will White accepted, as his mother and millions of Americans already had, the belief that the Republican party was the party of God. It was the only party to which decent, hard-working people could belong. It was the patriotic party, whereas the Democrats had been the party of treason during the war. Most Kansans were in complete agreement with the frontier preacher who used to tell his congregation that "Hell was peopled by two kinds of folks—those who didn't read the Bible and those who voted Democratic." Brand Whitlock said of Ohio—and in Kansas the situation was even more extreme—"It was natural to be a Republican; it was more than that, it was inevitable that one should be a Republican; it was not a matter of intellectual choice, it was a process of biological selection . . . It was a fundamental and self-evident thing, like life, and liberty, and the pursuit of happiness, or like the flag, or the federal judiciary. It was elemental, like gravity, the sun, the stars, the ocean. It was merely a synonym for patriotism, another name for the nation . . . It was inconceivable that any self-respecting person should be a Democrat."

In White's lifetime, from 1868 to 1944, the Democrats were able to elect only five governors of Kansas, several United States senators, and about a dozen congressmen. The Democrats seldom captured any of the county offices, and these were the backbone of any party. If you wanted to have influence in Kansas, White reasoned, you had to be a Republican. It might be all right philosophically to be a rugged independent, but if you wanted political power in Kansas it was foolish to be anything but a Republican. The Republican party, however, was to have its difficulties in retaining control of Kansas. In 1882, for instance, the Democrats captured the governorship because a third party, the Greenback-Labor party, took enough votes from the Republicans to permit the election of the Democrat. Generally the Democrats were able to win in Kansas only when a third party took votes away from the Republicans or when the Republicans split asunder, as in 1912.

During William Allen White's youth, Kansas and the nation were in a state of political ferment. Both Republican and Democratic parties were closely allied to the rising industrial forces. The industrialization of the country in the late nineteenth century greatly altered life in towns like El Dorado. Small-town gristmills, carriage shops, and slaughtering establishments could not compete with factories whose goods were shipped in on the newly constructed railroads. Self-sufficiency gave way to interdependence. Technological improvements, too, quickly altered the appearance of small-town America. In less than a decade after Allen White's death, the town of El Dorado installed a water system and telephones and was voting bonds for electric lights.

The Republican party was the political expression of this new industrialism. Before the Civil War the farmers of the South and West had controlled the nation through the Democratic party.

The war split the southern and western farmers and enabled the industrial forces of the East to gain control of politics. Afterward the western farmers, swayed by the emotional appeal of "Vote as you shot," remained loyal to the Republican party and refused to vote with their rural allies in the South. The bulk of the western farmers, with great disdain for their own best interests, supported government bounties for the industrial forces, such as the protective tariff, when as an economic group dependent on foreign trade they had everything to lose by such a course. But clever appeals to their patriotism and the association of the Republican party with divinity were too much for them; they could not probe beneath the surface and see the underlying economic issues.

Ruthless exploitation of the natural and human resources of America dominated the last forty years of the nineteenth century. As Vernon L. Parrington, another citizen of Emporia, Kansas, pointed out in his *Main Currents in American Thought*, a great barbecue was spread before the nation. The industrialists ate the best portions of the feast, and the farmers and industrial workers got the crumbs and paid the bill. But very few farmers and workers understood the situation. They were unable to see the bill because on all sides they witnessed immense material progress. The population of the country increased from thirty millions in 1860 to seventy-five millions by 1900. Railroad mileage developed by leaps and bounds, and manufacturing plants sprang up with breathtaking speed. Furthermore, the mantle of progress was thrown about the exploitation of the day. America was so busy conquering a continent that no vision of the wreckage was possible to most people. "They threw themselves blindly into the Impossible, and accomplished the Unbelievable," noted Ole Rölvaag in *Giants in the Earth*. "If anyone succumbed in the struggle—and that happened often—another would come and take his place. Youth was in the race: the unknown, the untried, the unheard-of, was in the air; people caught it, were intoxicated by it, threw themselves away, and laughed at the cost."

With freedom from government regulation, the new industrial figures demonstrated what untrammeled enterprise could do in the way of exploitation. These industrialists also through their agents made sure that no policies were adopted that were hostile to their rugged individualism. By 1900, small business had lost dominance to big business. Large corporations had crushed out competition and replaced it with monopoly. Here and there, however, during the last years of the nineteenth century, individuals and groups raised their voices in protest. But these critics of America's "Gilded Age" had a difficult time. The people to whom they were speaking were unable to see that the industrial forces were using the state and federal governments to gain favors, and that they were buying and selling the governments for their own ends. To restrict such practices, these critics advocated the development of the powers of the government to curb the predatory rich. But the people refused to support their pleas until the progressive days after 1900.

During the seventies and eighties, small protest groups were organized under the name of Antimonopoly, Independent, Labor, Reform, and Greenback parties. They felt that democracy meant equality of opportunity for all, and certainly not the right of a few to amass great wealth and build gigantic corporations. These small third parties objected to the national banking system, which left control of the money of the nation in the hands of a few private financiers; they advocated regulation of the railroads; and the direct election of United States senators by the people and not by legislatures dominated by the railroads. In Kansas in 1882, the Greenback-Labor party declared: "We are opposed to all monopolies, and are in favor of equal rights, equal burdens, equal taxation and equal benefits for all, with special privileges for none." Under another name, Populist party, these protestors were to increase their numbers and capture the Kansas governorship twice during the nineties.

It was in this political climate of increasing protest that William Allen White was to become a Republican. In spite of exploitation by the industrial barons, the Republican party was able to retain control of rural Kansas most of the time. By being a Republican, and a good one throughout his lifetime except from 1912 to 1916 when he fought for the Bull Moose party, White always maintained that he was able to exert more influence for the good of the state and the nation from within the party than from the outside. For many years he scorned the protests of the Greenbackers and Populists but after his own ideas had matured during Theodore Roosevelt's administration, he tried to carry out many of their demands through the Republican party. Until his views did mature, however, he unwittingly used his talents to help the forces of concentrated wealth retain control of the Republican party, Kansas, and the nation.

Before White became too deeply involved in the politics of Kansas, he was to have a taste of college education. In 1884, at the age of sixteen, he graduated from the El Dorado high school. "As a schoolboy, his experience was not unusual. He was bright and quick in his studies," one of his teachers recalled. "At that time, no one would have thought of him as likely to become a writer of anything. He was not especially apt in composition. He would write some droll things, but he made no serious attempt at good writing. He may have composed stories in the privacy of his room, or rhymed to the moon in his lonely walks, but these gave him no facility in his daily work. The essay that he wrote for graduation cost him many a weary sigh, and he had a very nervous and perspiring time in reading it to the public one May evening in 1884." Although White never became a good public speaker, he made up for it by developing an excellent, sparkling literary style. In high school and college he devoted five years to studying rhetoric. "It was the best course I had," he once said. "I learned how to put words together." Very early in life he had wanted to become a writer. He worked arduously to develop the pungent style that was to bring him fame. "I believe the secret of his success in the field of letters," a schoolmate reminisced in 1907, "is due to the fact that he set his aim and never lost sight of it."

CHAPTER 2

COLLEGE DAYS IN KANSAS

"I DON'T know exactly how to start a diary and as this is my first offense I trust any little errors may be overlooked," young White wrote early in 1885 while he was attending the year-old Presbyterian College of Emporia. White studied at this college from September, 1884, to May, 1885, and from January to May, 1886. The diary that he kept for only a few months reveals that he was lonely in Emporia and dissatisfied with the training he was receiving. The diary demonstrates also that he was an introspective young man, subjecting himself to a great deal of self-criticism. Although he appeared on the surface to be merely a fat, wisecracking, good-humored youngster, actually he was a serious-minded boy who underwent many doubts about himself and his future. "I have had a very gloomy day and a very queer Sunday," he noted one day, and a week later added, "I wish this measly relic was in Halifax or somewhere. Saturday I forgot to make an entry. Nothing happened that day only I had the blues bad. . . ."

Although he did not enjoy his course work, he did revel in the new friendships that he made. He roomed at the home of Mrs. Harriet Jones and struck up a lifelong acquaintance with her son Robert. Another good friend was James Barnett, who later became professor of political science at the University of Oregon. The Parrington boys, Vernon and John, also were excellent companions. White met also Vernon L. Kellogg, son of Lyman B. Kellogg, president of the Emporia Normal School, who persuaded White to attend the University of Kansas in 1886.

The diary which Robert Jones kept in the fall of 1884 reveals that he and White frequently went swimming and boating on the Neosho River. "Cloudy day but White & I went to the river early this morning took dinner along & built a great big fire & laid down upon the bank to read. Had a fine time of it. Didn't get back until dark," Jones noted on October 25. During November the two boys heard campaign orators extol the virtues of the rival presidential candidates, James G. Blaine and Grover Cleveland. On November 1, the Jones diary records in a disdainful Republican spirit their visit to a Democratic rally, where they heard "an old Whiskey Crank Democrat. Didn't do anything like the Republicans did. Very small sort of affair all around." When news of Cleveland's narrow victory reached Emporia, Bob Jones with consummate brevity wrote, "I feel disappointed."

White's own diary shows that he was an omnivorous reader even though his classwork did not challenge him much. He read Mark Twain's *Life on the Mississippi*, which elicited the comment, "like it very much," "found it comparatively interesting." Ralph Waldo Emerson's *Essays* attracted his earnest attention. On January 10, 1885, he wrote: "I am reading Emerson's Essays. I like them as far as I've gone very much but find it *very* deep." Four days later he added: "Read also some of Emerson's Essay on Self Reliance liked it very much."

He read widely in the Bible. "i am reading the new Testament and Emerson's Essays like both," he noted on January 14. "Would like to be able to read the New Testament understandingly probably will before I quit . . . I read several chapters in the Testament this evening very good." In February, White heard a lecture on Charles Dickens. "It was grand indeed . . ." he told his diary. "I think myself Dickens is one of the greatest geniuses the world has ever produced. (I say because genius is immortal.)" Many years later, in 1934, William Allen White remarked about these early, creative influences in his life:

So I would say if anything made me, it was Emerson and Whitman plus Dickens, plus the King James Version, with the realistic contemporary writers in the nineties leading me on. But the faith of my life has been Emersonian. I am still an Emersonian plus what might be called the Biblical philosophy, the realism of the Proverbs, the altruism of Jesus which of course were Emerson's sources somewhat. Probably I have learned nothing since my twenties and have merely elaborated the Emersonian-Nazarenean philosophy.

It was during these months at the College of Emporia that Will White bought and read Ed Howe's *The Story of a Country Town.* "I like it very much," he noted. While a student at the University of Kansas, White was to make a pilgrimage to Atchison to see cynical, pessimistic Ed Howe who had written this truly great and bitterly realistic book about a prairie community. Howe wrote of people as White knew them from his own experience in El Dorado. The book made sense to him. Writing some years later about Ed Howe, now a good friend, White stated: "E. W. Howe is the most remarkable man Kansas or the Middle West has produced. Moreover, he has written the greatest novel ever written in or about Kansas or the Middle West. His 'Story of a Country Town' is one of the ten best novels written in America."

Young White reveled in weighty arguments with his friends. "Bob Jones and I had quite a discussion this aft.," he recorded on January 14, 1885; "Subj. Definition of Knowledge. I held that knowledge was implanted at birth and developed by exercise. He opposed with no other definition, simply opposed." White devoted a great deal of time to writing original prose and poetry. "Spent . . . the evening talking to Kellogg," he recorded in his diary. "Kellogg is a 'daisy kid' in every way. I read him M [illegible] and various other 'efforts.'" When White was made librarian of a college library society, he wrote: "I delivered a neat little inauguration speech and covered myself with glory (!)." The next week, after listening to a paper written by two other members of the society, he indignantly observed: "I thought the paper was a fraud . . . They copied a piece about a cat from Bill Nye I think. It makes me mad to see anyone copy."

* * *

As his freshman year drew to a close in May, 1885, White decided to return to El Dorado to work, so that his mother would not have to support him any longer. T. P. Fulton, political friend

33

of his father and editor of the weekly *Butler County Democrat*, offered him a job as printer's devil. In addition to the boss and White, there were three other workers in the shop. White learned how to set type, make up the forms, and feed the big press and work the job press. "The one thought-producing implement" that T. P. Fulton had in the office, White recalled, "was a square box, about two feet square, filled with sawdust and sand, where the editor spat as he wrote. He couldn't write without spitting, and I never thought he could spit without writing."

White learned an extraordinary amount on the *Democrat* as to what a lack of newspaper ethics really entailed. He once wrote: "Well, those were the days, in 1885, when we had some advertising in the newspapers, but it was mostly Democratic advertisers, or, if it was a Republican advertiser, it was a Republican whom the editor knew something about. We didn't sell advertising in the sense that we gave our number of subscribers and would say that a thousand subscribers is worth so many cents. We went out and got it partly by panhandling and partly by putting a gun into his ribs. It was a nice blend between mendicancy and mendacity." White, also, saw the suppression of unfavorable news about the editor's friends. He later wrote about this experience:

When I was a young fellow in my teens, working in a printing office, one night the town banker's wife caught her husband coming out of the back door of the millinery store where the pretty milliner lived. A big scene was staged. Everyone in town knew about it. And T. P. Fulton, the editor, didn't print a word of it. Old Joe, the foreman, and I were sitting around the big open-doored monkey stove in the office the following Saturday night, waiting for "T.P." to show up and pay us off. Old Joe was spitting tobacco juice on the coals and . . . I asked:

"Joe, do you suppose the banker paid 'T.P.' to keep it out? How much do you think he got?"

Joe chewed for a while and spat amberly into the glowing coals and answered:

"Willie, 'T.P.' didn't get nary a red cent."

We sat in silence for a while and Joe spat again.

"You know, Willie, when 'T.P.' first come here and started this paper, 'T.P.' was just like us folks. But now, he's got to thinkin' like a God damned banker. They don't have to buy him!"

White worked twelve hours a day for the sum of $1.50 a week, when he could collect it from the editor. Fulton was always in financial trouble, and when he went fishing, which was often, White and the other employees would go out and collect debts owed by subscribers and advertisers and thus piece together their wages. While setting type, Will White met a young printer, Ewing Herbert, who soon became his very close friend. Herbert once recalled that in order to impress his friend with his own ability as a printer he asked White if he had ever seen type lice. White replied in the negative and as "he was nearsighted," he "bent very close, at my suggestion, to see the almost invisible insects. As I slapped the type together and saw the dirty water streaming from his face I did not laugh according to plans and specifications. The joke had lost its flavor on the instant and I felt hearty contempt for myself . . . I begged his pardon and implored him to squirt water in my face—yes, throw a bucketful on my person. He called my bluff and all I asked and more. It was a mad afternoon we had of it, for when the water buckets had been emptied we flung the sponge and towels at each other so long as they held together."

It was while working on the *Democrat* that White first met Henry J. Allen, who came to town selling books. Later they met again when Allen was a student at Baker University and White was at the University of Kansas. After college days, they became close political allies. It was politics that made it possible for Will White to move up in the newspaper profession from printer's devil to cub reporting. Fulton left one day in August for Washington to persuade the new Cleveland administration to award the local postmaster's job to him, a deserving Democrat. Fulton said, "Willie, you go out on the street and pick up some locals. You know how to do that." White replied, "Yes, sir," even though he hadn't had any previous experience. For the next six months, until he returned to the College of Emporia for the second term, he took notes on local affairs and carelessly set them into type without writing them out beforehand. Good writing and the exact choice of words, which later were to mark his editorials and articles, were not part of his equipment on the *Democrat*.

White's first attempt at reform through the press came in the issue of October 22, 1885. A few doors from the newspaper office the town's chief gambler had his headquarters. This character owned a red-wheeled buggy in which he took out a girl whom the cub reporter wanted to cultivate. The editorial on October 22, written by White, declared that "El Dorado has a few gambling holes that should receive the attention of the proper officers. We heard a man say, who we think is posted, that there are no less than a half dozen poker rooms in this place, and the most of them are being run in apparently open defiance of the laws. It is a blot on the fair name of our thriving city that should be rubbed out, and the guilty parties brought to justice."

The reaction to the item demonstrated the vigor and lustiness of early newspaperwork. The town marshal ignored the challenge, but the gambler for four long days searched for the reporter, as White later wrote, "to get a chance to kick our base of supplies in our subconsciousness, and only a fleet and earnest pair of young feet kept the gambler from achieving his end. Incidentally, he got the girl. Which taught us a lesson about the gratitude of republics."

In January, 1886, Will's mother insisted upon further education, and he dutifully returned to Emporia, where this time he roomed with Ewing Herbert, now also attending the college. But the tang of newspaperwork was in White's blood. After school hours he set type in the office of the Emporia *News*, where Herbert was working as a reporter. The *News* at this time was edited by Frank MacLennan, soon to acquire the Topeka *State Journal* and make it a recognized force in state affairs. White remembered him on the *News* as an "indefatigable worker. He lived, ate and slept on the job. And part of his job was making friends. No Emporia editor that I have known in all these fifty years had more friends than Frank MacLennan."

One day Ewing Herbert left for Topeka to represent the College of Emporia at the state oratorical conference, and White took over the duties of the local reporter. This post White held until the semester ended and he returned to spend the summer at El Dorado. By this time he had decided against returning to the college. His close friend Vernon Kellogg, who had just spent a year studying at the better equipped State University at Lawrence, persuaded White to enter K.U., as it was popularly known, in the fall of 1886. "Vernon Kellogg lured me here," White once told a K.U. audience, "lured me with beautiful tales of the social life of the University, which interested me vastly more than the academic life."

*   *   *

K.U. was twenty years old when White enrolled as a student. The town of Lawrence, some thirty miles from the eastern border of the state, was beautifully located in a valley among rolling hills and ridges. The campus was situated on a high hill, Mount Oread, overlooking the town. While White was there, the university had a student body of about five hundred, and three main buildings. In his day, the student body lived in the homes of the townspeople, and his mother moved to Lawrence to be with him during his three and a half years at the university.

These were important years for White. He made lifelong friendships with men and women who eventually became distinguished leaders of Kansas and national life, and he met a group of faculty members who opened new vistas to him. From the standpoint of an education, K.U. meant three or four excellent teachers to White. He idolized James H. Canfield, professor of history, sociology, and economics. Later Canfield became chancellor of the University of Nebraska, president of Ohio State University, and librarian at Columbia University; and his daughter, Dorothy Canfield Fisher, gained fame as a novelist. "He was known as Jimmie," White once wrote. "Dorothy and her brother James used to come on the Hill for him often and take him home, and they went swinging down the Hill together. He was a gorgeous father who romped and played with his children like a great New Foundland brother."

White spent many hours with Canfield in discussion of social and economic problems. Canfield was a rebel. In Republican Kansas he was independent politically and a passionate exponent of free trade. Time after time, irate Republicans tried to force the university to fire him for his attempts at destroying the smug views of his students. No wonder many Kansans considered him a dangerous radical when he allowed his students to write papers on such subjects as "American Communism," "The Distribution of Wealth in the United States," "The Ethical Relation of Capital and Labor," and "Railroads, Their Management and Control."

Canfield's social and economic views had no immediate influence on White. It was not until after the turn of the twentieth century that he agreed with many of Canfield's ideas. Politically, however, Canfield did influence White. White has written that it was at K.U. that he really decided to become a Republican. Canfield encouraged him in this course because, he told White, it was hopeless to be a Democrat in Kansas; Canfield himself had been an independent and got nowhere politically. According to Dorothy Canfield Fisher, "That red-headed, quick-witted, mandolin-playing young Will White enchanted this Vermont-New York professor by being not only intensely American, but intensely Kansas."

Three teachers quite markedly influenced White's literary career. Arthur Canfield, brother of James and a poet and inspiring teacher of good literature, W. H. Carruth, poet and professor of German, and A. R. Marsh, professor of rhetoric and English literature, were the center of an intense interest in poetry. These men spurred White on to write verse. He was class poet and fraternity poet, and he wrote the words of the class song for graduation in 1890. He and a fellow student, T. F. Doran, collected and published an anthology of university poetry, but modestly did not include any of their own. A column that White was writing for the El Dorado *Republican* did contain, on June 28, 1887, a sample of the type of poetry he was composing:

O what shall we do on the Fourth of July, said the youth to the maiden fair. O we'll take down the hammock and quickly hie, to the home of the chigger and dark green fly, where through leafy bowers the breezes sigh, and dream of our love out there. O what shall we do on the Fourth of July said a youngster free from care.

O we'll fill up our systems with green apple pie and purchase toy pistols and then we'll try to blow out our souls to their homes in the sky, to sing with the angels fair. O what shall we do on the Fourth of July, the old codgers ask in despair. O we'll get a jug of Old Red

Eye, and a gallon or two of rock and rye, and go out where there is nobody nigh, and get on a great old tear. O what shall we do on the glorious Fourth, said the editor weary and tired. We'll stay at home in this day of mirth and boom the town for all 'tis worth. O we'll raise the price of our city's worth, although the boom's expired.

White once recalled that on the day he arrived at the University of Kansas he was dressed like a country hick in a Prince Albert coat and a wide-brimmed hat, with a large bull's head stickpin in his necktie. A fellow freshman has noted, "He was then a freckle-faced kid, always with a genial smile, and pretty cocksure of himself." Another fellow student remembered him "as a round-faced, happy-go-lucky urchin . . . full of laughter and good will to mankind." Helen Sutliff, his "steady" college girl, proudly wrote her sister after seeing White act in a college play: "He was fine I assure you. New talents are cropping out in that boy all the time."

Vernon Kellogg took charge of White at K.U. and introduced him to his fraternity brothers. As White recalled this experience, "Vernon had notions, or at least he was an ambitious and optimistic man, and he had a theory that he could steer me into the Phi Delta Theta fraternity. I was a terrible dose for those boys. It took Vernon over five months to beat down the black balls which accumulated into a pyramid every time my name was suggested." Kellogg won out, and White became a loyal Phi Delt. Among the members of the fraternity who became White's intimate friends was Walter Armstrong, later general manager of the western branch of the Union Pacific Railroad. Another was Fred Funston, known to the boys as Timmy, who joined the Cuban revolutionary army in 1896, fought in the Philippine Islands against the Spanish and Aguinaldo's forces, and emerged as a general in the United States Army.

Many years later Funston wrote that his first impression of White was unfavorable. "He was fat, freckle-faced and flippant," Funston stated, "and wrote 'pieces' for the El Dorado *Republican*, which when copied in the Lawrence papers made cold waves chase themselves up and down the spines of the faculty and other proper folk. I made a mental prediction in those early days that White would come to some bad end. . . ." When Funston was gaining fame for his exploits in the Philippines, White wrote that in college, "He was a round-faced fellow full of fun and of the type that instructors yearn to strangle, for the levity that he bred in the classroom. . . . On festal occasions Funston grew melancholy and felt called upon to go forth without hilarity and ribaldry, but in terrible earnest, and tear up the board sidewalks of the town of Lawrence because he deemed their presence dangerous to the public welfare."

Two other close fraternity friends were Edward C. and William L. Franklin, destined to take their places respectively among the leading American chemists and physicists. Fraternity lines were not rigid at K.U. in those days; White also formed close friendships with other fraternity and nonfraternity boys. There was Herbert S. Hadley, later a college professor and chancellor of Washington University and Republican governor of Missouri; Edwin E. Slosson, editor of the *Independent*, director of Science Service at Washington, D.C., and an interpreter of science to the public; and Henry E. Riggs, later dean of the Engineering School at the University of Michigan and president of the American Society of Engineers. An acquaintance of White's at K.U., later to become a close friend, was William E. Borah.

Borah was older than most of the other students and was an extremely serious member of the university community. "My general impression of him at the time was that he was an earnest person. I was not. I was frivolous," White once declared. "If he noticed me it was because I made him grin . . . I should say that his outstanding qualities were a studious habit, an obvious indifference to the opinions of others, a desire to get on in the classroom rather than on the campus, not exactly a grind, but a man who had years to make up and a purpose to attain, one of those older students in a group, like a big New Foundland dog among smaller and more agile pups, who is good natured so long as he is not disturbed."

When Paul Jones, publisher of the Lyons [Kansas] *News*, once observed that White, Borah, and Funston had the common quality of honesty, White replied: "I think the thing we all had, and Funston more than any of us, was a tremendous desire to be free.

Looking back in those days [at K.U.] it was obvious that we all were battling against conventions . . . we were militant in our letch to be free . . . I was back in a lot of freshman work and had my junior and senior work, just as irregular educationally as I have been politically. And it was because I didn't subscribe, I didn't conform . . . Our meeting place was in the classes of James H. Canfield . . . and he was a free man who preached freedom and nurtured independent thinking and made us more or less rebels, all of us . . . let's say that it was the love of freedom, the thing called independence, that we got out of K.U."

White certainly did not conform as a student. When he enrolled as a freshman he was so thoroughly disgusted with his work at the College of Emporia that he did not claim any credits. Since he had some college work, however, the authorities allowed him to take some advanced courses. He cut across accepted lines and took many advanced social science courses. He also regularly cut classes which he disliked and spent the time in the library, reading the books stored away in the stacks. By the time he was a junior and a senior, he had such mixed-up credits that the university catalogue didn't know how to classify him. The catalogue took the easy way out and just omitted his name as a student. Solid geometry proved to be his downfall. Even after taking the final examination three times, he did not pass this required freshman course.

White was too busy with extracurricular activities to become an outstanding student. He made A's in two rhetoric and one history course, C's in two mathematics and one Latin course, failed in solid geometry, and made B's in all his other courses. Because of his failure to pass solid geometry, he did not receive a degree. His mother was brokenhearted, and in later years he himself became disturbed over the matter. In 1934, he wrote the registrar of K.U.: "Sometime, when you have nothing else to do, look up and see how many hours I would need for the purposes of graduation. I might be able to take some correspondence work and make up my old A.B. degree in my declining years." Six years later, in a gay mood, he wrote Paul Jones: "On my eightieth birthday I may go back and challenge the University to give me my degree and toddle across the stage with a cane, waving my false teeth defiantly at the Faculty to show that I am a scholar if not a gentleman."

* * *

Journalism and campus, town, and state politics occupied most of William Allen White's time at K.U. Fraternities competed with other fraternities and with nonfraternity students for control of college publications. Vernon Kellogg was the master political strategist of the campus. "In college politics," White later wrote, "he and I worked together, he furnishing the brains and I the legs, and we rather bossed things for two or three years . . . making combinations of fraternity and non-fraternity men, controlling a lot of college honors that grow out of college politics." White learned the knack of political bargaining and the need of maneuvering his opponents into a position where trades could be made between factions to unite them on a candidate or on a purpose. This was to be invaluable training for the rest of his career. He could make a political deal with the best of his contemporaries, and through college politics he established friendships with men like Charles F. Scott, Philip P. Campbell, and W. Y. Morgan, who were to become influential figures in Kansas politics. White observed correctly that "The University of the Eighties turned loose a Bund of politicians who dominated Kansas for a generation. The sheer momentum of University politics carried us well into the new century."

During his three and a half years at college, White held many journalistic posts. One year he was business manager of the *University Review*, and another year, business manager of the *University Times*. He was editor of the college annual, *Helianthus*, in 1889. In his freshman year he was a local reporter for the *University Courier*. His previous newspaper training on the El Dorado and Emporia papers made him valuable to these amateur college papers. The *University Courier*, on February 15, 1887, admitted White's value by stating: "White, one of our local chasers, has been very busy this week with his lessons, hence the general absence of 'goaks' in this issue." The signed articles that appeared over the name Will A. White attracted state-wide attention. The

Iola *Register* observed that he has "already done some of the brightest work the Lawrence papers have ever shown."

By now White was putting care into his composition. He was writing and rewriting his material in order to express himself in a crisp, flowing style. No longer was he setting his material up in type, composing as he went along. His style had begun to lose any pompous, flowery note. The importance of simple, direct, understandable style had been impressed upon him by Bent Murdock of the El Dorado *Republican.* During the summers of 1886 and 1887, White reported for the *Republican,* and he learned from "Uncle Bent" that simplicity was more desirable than flamboyancy in newspaper writing. On the death of Samuel J. Tilden in August, 1886, he had written an editorial in an extremely verbose style. One of its sentences asserted: "His name will be enshrined in the hearts of his countrymen and carved deep in the tablets of fame after the echo of other names heralded with tocsin of war and bloody passion will have died away and are lost forever." He found Mr. and Mrs. Murdock laughing at this sentence, and reading the vain, pompous phrases with great delight. "It taught me a lesson," he later wrote, "and that was that Mr. Murdock's style, simple, direct, and above all understandable, is the only kind of writing that really pays." A fellow student at K.U., Irving Morse, recalled visiting White frequently in his room, and seeing "a large book of Synonyms and Antonyms on his table. . . . I noticed particularly that it was 'finger-marked' as if it had been in daily use. After Will became famous as a writer I saw that there was a connection; he had studied the meaning of the words he used so carefully that he knew the exact shade of meaning each word conveyed."

White wrote many short stories and book reviews for the *University Review.* In one review, he pointed out that it was ominous that no Kansas author's books were published by a leading publishing house. This fact led him to ask his reading audience, "Are we second rate people? Is there a 'Kansas Literature'? If so is it worthy of serious notice? If so why has it not received something besides local attention? . . . At any rate the Kansan can say to those who speak heresy regarding things Kansan: 'We may not have a Kansas literature, with anything distinctively Kansas in it worthy of outside notice. All this may be true; but then we are ahead of you of Missouri, Nebraska, Iowa, Michigan and ,the rest; we have something we are proud to call a State literature, a Kansas literature; and we have a coterie of writers, who, if they are not well known elsewhere, are read, and in a few cases have become classics in the region of country lying between the meridians 94 deg., 38 min. and 102 deg. of W. Lon., and between the parallels 37 deg. and 40 deg. N. lat., as the geographies put it.' " Soon White himself was to become a nationally recognized Kansas writer and through his articles, editorials, and letters was to help popularize other Kansas authors, such as Eugene Ware and Ed Howe.

Newspaperwork off the campus attracted White more than did college journalism. Vernon Kellogg, editing the Lawrence *Journal*, persuaded White to take charge of the local page, and for a time he also wrote editorials for the Lawrence *Tribune*. White always recalled with relish one story that he wrote about a Lawrence wedding. "It was a pretty good society item even if I do say so," he commented. "I told all about the wedding and what the bride wore, but at the end I wrote: 'The happy couple will continue to live at No. —— on —— Street.' That was a mistake that kept me off the main street and running up and down alleys for weeks trying to gather news. That 'happy' couple would have killed me if they had ever caught me."

By this time White was a hidebound Republican, and he soon found himself in a rather bitter feud with Pete Foley's daily Democratic paper. One day White wrote the following item for the *Journal:* "It is said that the Democrat 'Yoomerist' appreciates his own jokes, and laughs heartily when he reads them to his friends. This may be a good thing for the debilitated system of the Democrat's Funny Fellow but it must be a severe strain on the silken ties of friendship." In one attack White went too far. He charged that Foley started an editorial that was finished by the printer's devil and, White added, "Out of respect to the intelligence of the 'devil' it is nothing more than fair to say that the article reads as though Pete had done the big end of the literary labor." Foley's answer was to charge into the *Journal*'s office with a baseball bat, but White talked him out of using it.

It is not surprising that irate citizens frequently tried to beat up this fat, redheaded, cocky college boy editor. Tension was particularly high during the county campaign of 1889. Two Republicans, not nominated for posts by the county convention, bolted the party and ran as independents. White immediately assailed them as traitors.

The Lawrence *Journal* was always involved in partisan politics. Its owner held a job with the railroads, and consequently the paper adopted a correct political attitude. White was right in the midst of Republican party caucuses and election scraps. During these days he first met Joseph L. Bristow, district clerk of the county, whose campaign for United States senator he managed in 1908. Another, later political ally whom he met while working on the Lawrence paper was Arthur Capper, who came to Lawrence to report K.U. commencements for the Topeka *Capital*.

White reported his first Kansas Republican convention in 1888. Here he saw figures like Senators John J. Ingalls and Preston B. Plumb, who had been leaders of the Grand Old Party since the days of "Bleeding Kansas." At that convention White heard an ex-soldier, Lew Hanbeck, deliver a patriotic speech on the battle of Lookout Mountain. The speech should have inspired any faltering souls with undying love for the party that had saved the Union. The Republican party was having its troubles retaining control of Kansas. A drought had hit the farms, and the farmers were beginning to organize a Farmers' Alliance for political action. Kansas was also feeling the impact of organized labor. Strikes were occurring among the coal miners, railroad workers, and smelting and refinery workers. Traffic on the Missouri Pacific Railroad was halted, several trains were damaged, and shop machinery was destroyed.

Vast economic and social changes were sweeping Kansas and the country. A greedy America was at work exploiting and reaping great wealth for those in control of the new giant corporations. Everywhere under the cry of freedom for the individual, a good old frontier agrarian belief, powerful corporations were increasing their dominance over American life. And the pioneer economic situation that made the unregulated individual possible gave way to an economic collectivism dominated by the impersonal corporation. But even though the agrarian situation that produced the unregulated individual passed away, corporation lawyers cleverly talked in terms of "freedom of enterprise" in order to checkmate demands of the Farmers' Alliance and the Knights of Labor for governmental control of powerful, unprincipled corporations. Although White was aware of the gathering chorus of criticism of the Republican party's support of plutocratic forces, he dismissed these protests as the outbursts of demagogues.

By January, 1890, when White left K.U. to embark upon a career of journalism, he was an extremely clever writer, but he had only a superficial awareness of the social forces that were molding his state and nation. For the next decade he was to lend his agile pen to the support of those forces which were exploiting the American people and jeopardizing the future of American democracy. Although he knew human beings, he had no profound awareness of the world of ideas. Emerson's social philosophy, Walt Whitman's militant democratic aspirations, and Professor James Canfield's encouragement of independent thinking failed to provoke White into challenging the established order of things. His superficiality at the age of twenty-one was sternly criticized by Vernon Kellogg. White wrote to a college friend, Jennie Sutliff, on January 21, 1891: "I got a letter from K——g today; he thinks I am conceited and says I am too much inclined to be 'smart' and take a snapshot judgment of men and things. He thinks I ought to outgrow it. Possibly he is right. I wonder if the world doesn't really revolve around me and if I have been going on all these years with this sorry impression of the matter. C'est possible."

CHAPTER 3

YOUNG CONSERVATIVE

"WILL WHITE is making for himself quite a reputation, both as a philosopher and poet, on the El Dorado *Republican* . . ." the *University Review* reported in April, 1890. It was natural that White should have decided upon a journalistic career. He was a clever writer. He enjoyed describing people and their doings. Newspaperwork was a way to state and national fame. What young American hadn't thrilled at the writings of Charles A. Dana, Horace Greeley, "Marse" Henry Watterson, and James Gordon Bennett? Editors, too, were powerful figures in the political world. Both Kansas senators—John J. Ingalls and Preston B. Plumb—had been pioneer journalists. Since Kansas editors dominated the politics of that state, what better profession could an ambitious young redheaded fellow desire?

Young Will White knew the great Kansas editors of the eighties either through their papers, which came over the exchange desk of the journals he had worked on, or through personal acquaintance. Kansas journalism had started out under a baptism of fire during the days of "Bleeding Kansas." Both sides in this struggle had their papers, and their editors who carried Colt's horse pistols. These editors wrote in abusive language and sometimes died with their boots on. As late as the nineties, Kansas editors were still masters of invective even though by then they seldom shot their rivals.

White regularly read the papers of D. R. Anthony, Marsh Murdock, Sol Miller, F. P. Baker, J. K. Hudson, and John A. Martin. The feuds carried on by these editors and their derisive, vilifying language greatly attracted and impressed White. He, too, was to be a master of vituperative language when he described the Populists, William Jennings Bryan, and later the Ku Klux Klan. The color and dash of Kansas journalism was a natural outlet for William Allen White's own emotional, romantic spirit. Furthermore, newspaperwork afforded an opportunity to persuade, lecture, and lead people. How, then, could he fail to enter a field that offered free sway to colorful expression and was so teeming with possibilities of leadership and fame?

When White left K.U. in January, 1890, the Kansas City *Times* noted: " 'Billy' White, a Kansas University grad, poet, paragrapher and hustler, is the new associate editor of the El Dorado Republican." Bent Murdock, editor of the *Republican,* who was serving in the Kansas Senate, hired White to run the paper for him; White did so for twenty-one months. It was his job to write local news, solicit advertising, take care of job printing, hire and fire the other employees, buy the newsprint, and, when there were no editorials from Murdock, write them himself. White always believed that Murdock was the best editorial writer he had ever known. He carefully studied Murdock's straightforward, simple, and forceful style and was so successful in copying it that many papers attributed the editorials to Murdock.

This period of training in imitation of Murdock's style, White once wrote, "was one of the most profitable years I ever had in my life. . . . I remember one of the happiest moments of that time was my joy at having what I had written, quoted under his name." Murdock was highly amused when White's editorials were mistaken for his own. Now and then he would squint out of his glasses at White and observe, "You seem to be raisin' hell, I notice." After White had written one particularly good article, Murdock sidled up to the associate editor's desk and said, "Well, Mistofer, you think you have done it, don't you?" After grunting a bit he added, "Old [Senator] Plumb says you are all right. He says your piece is a daisy. Thinks it is like your father." Squinting over his glasses some more, he muttered, "Old Doc White."

White used his freedom on the *Republican* to experiment in short stories, poetry, and essays. Under the pen name of Elder Twiggs, a cracker-barrel philosopher, he wrote essays with such challenging titles as "The Demon Rum," "Dudes," "Holiness and the End of the World," "Platonic Love Attachments," and "Old Maid in Love." Much of his writing was based on El Dorado and its citizens. One writer later expressed bewilderment that White was able to make so much copy out of such a humdrum, commonplace Kansas town.

White regularly sat in the Butler County Republican conventions and many times traveled to Topeka to visit the legislature. One month he saved all his salary and bought a Prince Albert coat, gray pants, patent leather shoes, white spats, and a broad black stetson hat, and swanked around Topeka. Victor Murdock recalled traveling on the train to Topeka once in 1890 with his good friend Will White and talking politics all the way. When the train arrived at Topeka, a lady on the seat just in front of them arose majestically, turned to them, snorted "Thank goodness," and stomped away.

One of White's earliest political speeches, entitled "The Foreign Relations of Kansas," was delivered at a Young Republican club during his days on the *Republican*. "Strictly speaking there are but two of the major powers with which she enters into close diplomatic combination," White amusingly asserted. "There are indeed minor ports and outlying provinces to which she sends her soldiers in time of war and her consuls and her tradesmen in time of peace; such for instance are the seaports of hell—Texas and Missouri, but the two great principalities Kansans recognize; the two places where her heroes muster and her statesmen long to tarry; the two centers where the song of home sweet home falls on the Kansan ear . . . and the rasping whir of the grasshopper wakes no homesick yearning in the Kansan's breast, are the Kingdom of Heaven and Washington, D.C. To these and these only Kansas lowers her flag and in their boundaries Kansans feel a congeniality of the atmosphere." White closed this brief speech with ringing praise for the House of Representatives: ". . . still 'tis true today as it was in the beginning so it shall ever after, that it is better to be door keeper in the House of Representatives than to dwell in the tents with the wicked."

Life did not, however, consist only of business and politics. The young editor frequently hired a horse and buggy on pleasant Sunday afternoons and took some attractive young lady for a ride over the surrounding prairies. On moonlight nights he serenaded his choice of the moment with his mandolin. As he remembered, he "fell desperately in love every six months and added the interest to his note every 90 days." One acutely embarrassing event occurred at a dance one evening in the El Dorado opera house. White had never learned to dance very well, and he was prancing high, wide, and handsome when suddenly, awkward as a cow, he stepped through a lady's dress up to her knee and petticoats. He was "ashamed beyond words," and, after hours of anguish, the next day in a gesture of retribution sent her a box of American beauty roses.

While he was working on the *Republican*, White struck up a friendship with the writer Albert Bigelow Paine, who then lived at Fort Scott, Kansas. After some correspondence, they decided to publish a book of their poetry, but White insisted that the project be kept secret since he was not sure how long it would take him to complete his verses. "I am not lazy," he explained to Paine, "but I have a severe & complicated case of chronic hereditary inertia and a malignant form of procrastination (don't know that I've spelled that word right)." Furthermore, he had an acute fear of his own inadequacy and inferiority as a writer. "I shall publish a book some time," he told Paine, "when I get rich enough to corner all the copies of Shakespeare & the Real Live Poets on the market & force my own works on the public; but until then I shall be content to figure in the newspaper corners." He refused to send Paine any of the verses that he had written in college because, he declared, "I am afraid you would think more of me if you didn't examine my work closely."

When Paine praised his work, White was inspired to devote much of his time in the next two years to completing his share of the poetry book. The following verses are typical of the kind of poetry that he was writing:

WOMANHOOD

I kissed her baby, and its hazel eyes
  Beamed through my soul, where, in a dim recess,
  There is a pictured face on which distress
Plays hide and seek with hope; a tear-drop dries,
Warmed by her parting smile; again she tries
  To reach me with a zephyr-blown caress.
  This, I in anguish had called "Faithlessness"
And pricked it on my heart with poisoned dyes.

The baby's lips were sweet with drowsy wine
  Pressed out of dreams, by fragrant mem'ry stirred.
  I drank my fill and yielded to its mood.
And when I woke the picture still was mine;
  (By baby lips the title had been blurred,)
  And underneath was written, "Womanhood."

After working a year on the *Republican*, White began to medi-
tate over his future course. He wrote to a college friend: "I got
your letter last night. Read it over several times—very unusual
letter that gets read once clear through by me. I *am* in a pickle
about what to do and get pickleder and pickleder every day. This
is what in tragic and dramatic language we would call my encis.
I am now to decide whether I am to be a literary man pure and
simple: a city journalist with a department or a country editor
with a local political influence and a predilection toward poetry.
If I could do what I want to do I should write poetry, novels—
especially novels—(and especially poetry) and have say three
thousand a year to live on. That's my ideal of a successful man. I
don't know that I care to be a Great Man and have people standing around in one crowd abusing me and another crowd wanting
to see me."

This letter was a remarkable outline of his future career. Although in 1891 he thought he had to choose between a literary
and a newspaper career, he was soon to discover that he could mix
the two. As editor of the Emporia *Gazette* he learned that he could
use the small-town editorship as a steppingstone to national fame.
National fame and a profitable literary career, he found, were
much easier to achieve from the vantage point of Emporia, Kansas,

than from a big-city newspaper. Fame could be obtained by staying in the small town provided one was alert and took full advantage of all opportunities. A purely literary career, White realized, would cut him off from the main current of American life. But as editor of a small-town paper, which did not require his full energies, he could be free to write and, at the same time, dip into politics and help mold the forces that were shaping his state and nation.

White's newspaperwork on the El Dorado *Republican* in 1890 and 1891 plunged him directly into political turmoil and strife. Kansas was the storm center of the new Populist, or People's, party. The Populists thundered in unequivocal terms against exploitation by industrial America. Their movement was a mixture of anger over hard times and the privileges granted to the capitalists, and an honest desire to fight for a democracy in which equality of opportunity could exist. The party hated the growing power of wealth in the hands of the few. Monopoly in railroads and communications they wanted to check by government ownership and operation. They advocated the graduated income tax to check the accumulation of wealth. They did not propose to return to a laissez-faire system, in which the government kept hands off economic matters. Instead they demanded that the government step in and regulate the economic order in the interest of all the people. The Populists desired an increase in government ownership and control, not to achieve state socialism but to strengthen the position of small business. They saw the chief danger to American democracy in the destruction of free enterprise by the irresponsible, antisocial private monopoly system based on governmental favors. Where free enterprise would not degenerate into private monopoly, the Populists wanted the fullest freedom for free enterprise.

Kansas became the whirlwind of the Populist crusade for a more democratic society. Kansas deeply felt the heavy hand of exploitation by railroads, warehouses, and mortgage companies. By 1890, the Kansas farmer was in a difficult situation. The late seventies and eighties had been boom years. The farmers, believing that utopia was just around the corner, had heavily mortgaged their farms to make improvements. Towns and counties had voted bonds to subsidize the construction of railroads. Land values were boosted, "false front" buildings were constructed, and "paper" towns were surveyed. But in 1887 the drought hit Kansas and the boom collapsed. For the next ten years the Kansas farmer had a difficult struggle to maintain himself. The continuing drought led T. A. McNeal, Kansas newspaper editor, to state: "I have seen it dry, so dry that you had to prime the mourners at a funeral so they could shed tears for the departed." Many left the state for more promising areas. The general panic and depression that afflicted the United States from 1893 to 1896 only increased the despair in Kansas.

Central Kansas, where El Dorado was located, suffered the most disastrous effects of the collapse. Here the expansion of the boom years had been most extreme. The subsequent collapse witnessed a great exodus of people from this region. The farmers who remained suffered under a heavy debt obligation. In 1890, in some of the counties of Central Kansas, three-fourths of all the farms were mortgaged. After 1888 the Kansas farmers realized that they suffered from the limited amount of money in circulation. They had to pay extremely high interest rates on loans, and they were sure that there was a definite connection between the shortage of money and the low prices paid for farm produce. It was no wonder that when the Populist party was launched in 1890 it should clamor for a government-controlled currency to meet the needs of an expanding economy and demand an increase in the supply of currency through the free and unlimited coinage of silver at a ratio to gold of 16 to 1.

Another problem was the lack of storage facilities. At harvesttime the farmer had to dump his goods on a low-price market and then watch the warehouse operators hold the produce until the price rose. The rates charged by railroads, too, seemed excessively high. Charges that railroads, through monopoly agreements, fixed excessively high rates led the Populists to advocate government ownership and operation of the railroads. The Populists denounced the railroads also for entering politics and giving politicians free passes. State conventions and state legislatures were frequently bought and sold by the railroads for the purpose of lowering taxes and blocking railroad regulation. When the Populists captured control of the governorship of Kansas in 1892, colorful Jerry

Simpson, with a great deal of justification, told a crowd in front of the Statehouse: "Fellow citizens, we have come today to remove the seat of the government of Kansas from the Santa Fe offices, back to the Statehouse where it belongs."

Although White was a bitter foe of the Populists, he did realize that their appeal had behind it a deep religious quality. The Populists looked upon the bankers and industrialists as immoral, unchristian forces that were preventing the achievement of the Holy Commonwealth in the United States. The Populists came out of the same camp-meeting revival background that had produced abolition and prohibition in Kansas. "It was a fanaticism like the crusades," White once wrote. "Indeed the delusion that was working on the people took the form of religious frenzy. Sacred hymns were torn from their pious tunes to give place to words which deified the cause and made gold—and all its symbols, capital, wealth, plutocracy—diabolical . . . They sang their barbaric unrhythmic jargon, with something of the same mad faith that inspired the martyrs going to the stake. Far into the night the voices rose, women's voices, children's voices, the voices of old men, of youths and of maidens rose on the ebbing prairie breezes as the crusaders of the revolution rode home, praising the people's will as though it were God's will and cursing wealth for its iniquity."

White's editorial attacks on the Populists were so severe that the Populists burned the 22-year-old editor in effigy, boycotted the El Dorado *Republican*, and launched their own paper. In editorial after editorial, White denounced the Populists as un-American for advocating governmental control of monopoly. Actually, the Populists were not un-American. White was simply accepting in an uncritical fashion the symbols and slogans of the industrial forces, without showing any insight into the dangers to democracy inherent in these beliefs.

White regularly charged that the Populist leaders were unsuccessful people who turned to politics when they could not succeed in other fields. America in White's youth had a hearty contempt for anyone who was not a material success. Many of the Populists were unsuccessful farmers, lawyers, and merchants. How, reasoned White, could a young, respectable newspaper editor have any sympathy for such people? Later, when he himself advocated many of the Populist reforms that he had once ridiculed, he justified his position by declaring that these demands were no longer being advocated by wild-eyed reformers and unsuccessful people, for under Theodore Roosevelt "Populism shaved its whiskers, washed its shirt, put on a derby and moved up into the middle of the class—the upper middle class." Reform was all right, apparently, if it was in safe, clean, and prosperous hands. Few of the Populists, of course, actually were fanatics. They simply had an insight into the needs of the time that White did not have. He could not conceive that anything was basically wrong with a country which had made such great material progress as America had made.

One old-time Populist wrote White in 1912 that he heartily approved of White's support of Theodore Roosevelt's independent candidacy. The Populist recalled overhearing White and Fred Funston in the *Republican* office many years before. "It seemed to me," White's correspondent wrote, "that the greater percentage of words they used were oaths, and I wanted so much to take those young men and wash out their mouths." White immediately replied: "I have your letter of October 7 before me. It brings up the memory of the fellow I was twenty years ago and it is not on the whole a very pleasant memory. I was a pretty disreputable pup and considerable of a smart-aleck. I realize that I must have been highly offensive to a lot of decent fellows."

White's cocksure attitude and smug assumption that the nation was safe only if it was in control of the Republican party led him to write a short, satirical story, "The Regeneration of Colonel Hucks," for the September 4, 1891, issue of the El Dorado *Republican*. It was the story of Colonel William Hucks, who left the Grand Old Republican party to join the Populists, but who by 1891 saw the true light again and was back in the Republican fold. It was replete with neat references to patriotism and to the divinity of the Republican party. When Colonel Hucks, for instance, told his wife that he had decided to attend the Republican convention at Topeka, White adroitly wrote: "And 'Mother,' whose father had 'fit with old Grant,' and whose brother had died at Shiloh, and whose faith in the war party had known no wavering, though her voice had been quiet for a year or so, only smiled and said, 'I

am glad to hear you are going, William, for you do need the rest.' "
The next day, as the colonel drove out the gate on his way to the
convention, he was whistling "John Brown's Body." At the convention Colonel Hucks shook hands with Senator Preston B.
Plumb and heard patriotic speeches about the Civil War. White
concluded this excessive appeal to Civil War memories and emotions by writing:

As he drove into his front yard that night he noticed the old regi-
mental flag waving over the door. Inside of the house, he observed
that "Mother" had brought out the pictures of Grant and Sherman
and Lincoln, which she had put away the year before. They were
hanging in the best room with little Link's [their son's] faded blue
soldier-cap in the center of the group.
"Did you have a nice time at Topeky, William?"
"Yes, Mother," and after a pause he added, as he looked at the little
cap and the old flag, which now and then floated in through the door,
"and say, Mother, 'his soul goes marching on.' "

This story was reprinted by other Republican papers, and Senator Preston B. Plumb had the State Central Committee circulate
it as campaign literature. It was designed to appeal to people's
emotions, not their reason. White himself was convinced of the
moral basis of the Republican party. It was much easier for him
as a defender of Republicanism, to play on past memories than
to attempt to dispute the Populist attacks on the evils of monopoly.
Furthermore, he wanted to get ahead and the way to accomplish
this was by strict party regularity and not by any critical investigation of the social and economic issues of the day.

* * *

The publication of "The Regeneration of Colonel Hucks"
brought Will A. White, as he was then known, to the attention
of the Kansas City papers. Both the Kansas City *Star* and the
Kansas City *Journal* offered him editorial positions at the salary
of $25 a week. Like so many rural, small-town boys, White was
irresistibly drawn to the big city. Here one could earn more
money and have a much broader cultural and intellectual life than
in a small town. But the incident that was to make White unique

in his generation was that after four years in the big city he returned to spend the rest of his life in the small town. In October, 1891, White and his mother moved to Kansas City where, at the age of twenty-three, he took a position on Colonel Van Horn's *Journal*. He preferred the *Journal* to the *Star* because the *Journal* was a "sound" Republican paper. The *Star*, on the other hand, would desert the Republican column if the Democrats nominated a better candidate.

For five months White wrote editorials for the *Journal*. He was quickly disillusioned. He discovered that it was so "soundly" Republican that it never would criticize the party and the party's alliance with the seekers of privilege. The *Journal*'s editorials were devoted to the welfare of special-interest groups. White later described the paper as follows: "The *Journal*, which was Republican in politics, sang softly as the organ of commerce and business progress, and spoke even in that remote day for the railroads and the banks."

White might hate the Populists, but he honestly considered himself to be a Lincolnesque type of Republican, interested in the Republican party as the party of the people and not the party of the selfish rich. Through a long career, White fought to make the Republican party a servant of middle-class America. He broke many lances against business domination of the party. The great tragedy of White's life was that the "malefactors of great wealth" were able to use his type of midwestern liberalism as window dressing to disguise their own firm control of the party. For all the liberalism that the rural Middle West gave the Republican party, the party machinery was in the powerful grasp of other hands.

After five months in Kansas City, White asked to be transferred to Topeka as the *Journal*'s Kansas reporter. From March to September, 1892, he was in the thick of Kansas politics. The Populists were gathering strength for another assault on the two major parties. They had succeeded in defeating Senator John J. Ingalls in 1891 and in sending William Peffer, one of their own followers, to the United States Senate. In 1892, they captured control of the governorship and won five out of the seven Congressional seats. Because of conflicting election returns, control of the lower house of the Kansas legislature, however, was in dispute between the Republicans and the Populists. Both parties tried to organize the lower house, and an exciting legislative war ensued. Eventually the State Supreme Court, controlled by Republicans, recognized the Republican-dominated house as the legal one. John Fiske, a New England lecturer and writer, visited Topeka during this legislative war and wrote home: "Before leaving Wednesday took a drive through the town: there was a rumpus going on at the State House, and considerable of a crowd here and there in the streets. . . . Too much politics to the square mile in Kansas. Republican and Populist legislatures exchanging blows. Kansas is the most forlorn, Godforsaken country I ever set my eyes on: Laurence [sic] and Topeka are not much better than Lewiston, Maine."

With other young Republicans like Ewing Herbert, Harry Frost, and Charles M. Harger, White launched the Kansas Day Club on January 29, 1892. White served as president of their first meeting and made the chief speech. These young Republicans were out to defeat the Populists by instilling new blood and life in the Republican party. Among the future leaders of the party at the dinner were Chester I. Long, Charles Curtis, and Charles F. Scott.

By 1892, White had shifted his own strategy in attacking the Populists. Instead of appealing to old Civil War prejudices as he had done in "The Regeneration of Colonel Hucks," he now urged the Republican party to emphasize that the Populists were too inexperienced to handle governmental problems. "During the next five years," he asserted in July, 1892, "the vast producing empire of the West is going to take the first steps toward a commercial supremacy which will be acknowledged before the end of the first decade of the coming century. In taking those steps it will be necessary to trample upon many traditions of railroad transportation. The railroad corporations of the country may be depended upon to oppose any changes in the present order of things. It is probable that legislation will have to force what the manifest exigencies of trade demand. If this legislation comes from inexperienced hands, it will have to be done over again, and the great West will suffer by the delay." He therefore urged the Republican party to contrast the experienced nature of its candidates with the inexperience of the Populists. There was no doubt that White believed some governmental control of the railroads was necessary, but he felt that the Populists were too ungentlemanly, too fanatical, too extreme, and too inexperienced to be trusted with this task.

Hanging around the lobby of the Copeland Hotel at Topeka, White learned the traditions of the old-time Republican politicians. He participated in "smoke-filled" meetings and caucuses. Later his short stories in *Stratagems and Spoils* (1901) were to reek with the reality of American politics. The major lesson he learned and recorded was that "There is much scandalous talk by scantily informed people about the corruption of politics. The truth of the matter is: That politicians are about as honest in their business as storekeepers are in their business, or lawyers are in their business, or bankers or preachers, or day laborers, or farmers, or college professors, are in their own callings. . . . The county convention of Douglas County, Kansas, or of Kings County, New York, is operated on a moral plane about as high as the faculty politics of the average University, or as that of the Church politics of the various religious organizations."

* * *

While working on the *Journal*, White retained his intimate friendship with Ewing Herbert and Fred Funston. Herbert was editing a paper at Hiawatha, Kansas, and Funston was working with White on the *Journal*. When White later wrote an attack on excessive drinking, he recalled: "Fred Funston and I started shimmeying down the primrose path together as young newspapermen working on the Kansas City Journal. . . . Fred never stopped. And boy, he was the funniest man I ever knew with three drinks under his belt. He couldn't carry anything—not even a baked apple—without getting riotous. I know he was funny because I used to stay sober just to enjoy him." Then White continued: "But for the grace of God and the wife who caught me young and treated me rough, I would have been in New York right now an old man cashing out on a Hearst contract, living with my third wife and seventh woman, six years back with my debts and folks would have said, 'You know, if old Bill would have just let liquor alone he would have been a hell of a newspaperman.'"

During 1892 and the early part of 1893, White wrote a great deal of poetry and sent it to Albert Bigelow Paine for their forthcoming book. In order to test the quality of the verses, he and Ewing Herbert organized their own Chautauqua lecture circuit. Herbert lectured on literature and White would read his poetry. On January 22, 1892, he wrote to Paine: "Herbert and I have been having a great time. We took the town of Effingham, all right, and made our little old $5 apiece, and they turned around and offered us $10 to come again at any time we wanted to. We have since had an offer from Emporia, and our rate is $25 a night net for the two and we pay our expenses. We are going right about planning a trip. Herbert has arranged for Lincoln Center, and Atchison. We are trying to fix up Clay Center, Salina, and Abilene, all on the U.P. and Iola, Eureka, Winfield and Wellington on the Mo. Pacific . . . We don't anticipate the earth but in addition to the flat rate, we make the provisional that for each twenty-five dollars above the gross amount of $60, we get a $10 rake off. That is square . . . In the various towns we are corresponding with schools and Epworth Leagues, and it is not overestimating it to presume that 200 people should come at an average price of 35 cents." White closed this letter to Paine with the admonition "keep sober and as Lydia E. Pinkham says: Yours for Health—." Not all their lecture engagements turned out too successfully. Once at Belton, Missouri, it rained so hard that only six people appeared. As a result, White and Herbert did not have enough money to pay their fare back to Kansas City and had to ride in a freight car, narrowly averting arrest as tramps.

Some of his early poetic efforts White sent to *Harper's* and the *Century*, but they were rejected. Sometimes a wave of pessimism would sweep over him, and he would write to Paine: "I have about given up the idea that I can write poetry worth a dam; and I am of the impression that if I ever get in the Temple of Fame it will be as a 'valley' or something. I can do a certain kind of prose in a peculiarly mock simple vein, very fairly; but that is so easily imitated that I am sure that it will never make me great. I have an ambition to some day write a novel; it will be a western novel of my own idea; I only know about the west, and when I know about it thoroughly, I shall tell what I know." In 1909, he was to publish his first book-length western novel, *A Certain Rich Man*, which over the years sold close to three hundred thousand copies. His prose, not his poetry, brought him the fame that he so greatly desired and had worked so hard to achieve.

Continuing his speculation to Paine about his writing, White added on March 3, 1892: "I am not much on plots and I believe in the Howells idea—the stories have all been told; my hero shall not however marry my heroine and I propose to show how much happier they shall all live 'ever afterward' if they are not married than they would be if the conventional ending were imagined. I have not enough ideas for two books and shall never try a second and fail; there are some things that the experience of others teaches us: The fatality of the second novel is one of those things." He apparently did not recall this youthful bit of wisdom, for in 1918 he published a second novel, *In the Heart of a Fool*, that never attracted much attention.

*   *   *

In the middle of June, 1892, White left the Kansas City *Journal* in a rage. He and a coworker, Tom Norton, were covering the Populist State Convention at Wichita. Sockless Jerry Simpson, whom White had characterized as the "Sockless Socrates of the Kansas Desert," liked White and gave him an exclusive story, which he sent to Kansas City in time to make the state-wide mail edition for June 16, 1892; whereas the stories filed hours later by the Kansas City *Star* and Topeka *Capital* reporters failed to reach their destination in time for this strategic edition.

Of course White and Norton lorded it over their rivals on the basis of this scoop. But they were heartbroken the following morning when they bought the mail edition at Newton while on the way back to Kansas City. Their story wasn't on the front page, or the second page, or the editorial page. They finally discovered it buried on the market page with the core of the story cut out. Immediately the other reporters began to jeer and tease White and Norton. As the train clicked off the miles to Kansas City, White and Norton became angrier and angrier at the telegraph editor, who, having a grudge against them, had deliberately sabotaged their story.

That night they reached the *Journal* office and bearded the editor in his office. "We went into his office," White recalled, "and locked the door and turned the key and proceeded to call him all the dirty fighting names we could think of and dared him to fight either of us, whichever he would pick, and promised that the other would go outside and stay out until the fight was over. But he just grinned at us; then we tried with all kinds of physical indignities to incite him to fight, but couldn't. Whereupon we walked downstairs, three flights to the business office, asked for our time, drew our money and quit. I didn't have the sign or sight of a job, but it was one of the proudest moments of my life, that I had the nerve to do just that. And Tom was Irish too."

White referred to this incident later in life and declared: ". . . when I walked out of his room after chucking my job, I had a deep consolation like that of a great faith that had been justified. But it wasn't sheer impulse, however the moment's drama may have flowed upon a rising tide of passion. If I seem impulsive in politics, it is because I am acting as a sentimentalist rather than as a hard-boiled realist. I am a sentimentalist and make no bones about it, and always shall be; not because I am proud of it but because I am made that way. I believe in the nobility of man and the Divine purpose of God which of course is pure sentiment but on the other hand, what do the realists know about it any more than I do? And I am happy following my own courage."

CHAPTER 4

BIG-CITY JOURNALISM

"I THINK I owe more to you and the influence of the Star than I owe to any other one influence outside of family," White wrote Colonel William R. Nelson, publisher of the Kansas City *Star*, on November 11, 1904. White worked on the *Star* from September, 1892, to June, 1895. The files of the Emporia *Gazette* and White's correspondence reveal the immense influence of Nelson's *Star*.

Colonel Nelson taught White to submerge the editor's activities in his paper. As a result, the *Gazette* readers seldom knew of White's own undertakings. Although his editorials reflected his beliefs, they failed to describe how the editor was working to carry out those beliefs. Although he became the confidant of presidents, governors, and congressmen, his neighbors did not learn of these things in the pages of the home-town paper. For years he trained his reporters and editors not to mention his name except when he gave specific permission. He once observed: "I have seen many editors kill themselves with their communities by talking about themselves too much. I came to the *Gazette* with that lesson already learned."

The *Star* under Nelson was primarily a local paper devoted to local news and service. It carried on a continual campaign for better housing, parks and playgrounds; and it exposed loan sharks, medical quacks, and political corruption. William Allen White made the *Gazette* the same type of paper. Although White's editorials on national affairs readily attracted outside attention, the

63

bulk of his editorial writing was devoted to local matters and people; it praised the flowers of a neighbor, denounced an inveterate drunkard, urged the town to build more streets and to plant more trees, or encouraged investment in local industries. The *Star*'s experience taught White that a good local paper should take the leadership in civic betterment; that it should have courage and make a stand for decent things. "The editor must be something of a preacher, something of a teacher, something of an autocrat," White once told his readers, and added: "The editor must be guide, philosopher, and friend to all—the rich as well as the poor." The *Gazette* assumed militant leadership in county and state politics, and led in fights to build such agencies as the local Y.M.C.A. and Y.W.C.A.

On the *Star*, White learned that it required courage to run a militant newspaper. In 1893, the *Star* launched a crusade against political corruption, and charged that the present political machine "stands in the way of every salutary project in Kansas City, and that it must be wiped out before any substantial results can be accomplished in the direction of public improvements and municipal reform." One day an angry political boss stormed into the *Star* office and attempted to kill Nelson. White wrote of this episode:

I remember one day we were all sitting there at work. The telegraph editor's office and the editorial writers and the Colonel and the managing editor were all on one floor. I was hitting it up at my typewriter along about half past nine or ten in the morning when I heard an uproar across the hall in the Colonel's room. Then I heard the unmistakeable bang bang and a fall, and we all ran and there was a fellow in to lick the editor, and there was the dear old Colonel on the floor. So I got there just as the managing editor, Tommy Johnston, who was about six feet two, and the telegraph editor, who was a little taller than I, and the city editor, Ralph Stout, who weighed about 240 pounds, arrived, and we gathered up the man, a fellow named Joe Davenport. Each took a handle. I remember I had an arm and Stout had a leg and Tommy Johnston had a leg, and Pipsey had another arm. We carried him down the hall to one of those double stairways and one, two, three, and down he went. I being the youngest, being twenty-three at the time, scrambled down, met him on the landing and as he gathered himself up, he pulled out a large gun. I was in the War and saw some large guns, but I never saw such a gun as that . . . He poked it under my nose and I was on the landing, leading down into the main office.

On this side was the city editor's office, on that side was the business office. I first thought I would crawl into the gun. But I had another thought and I put my hand on the railing and jumped over it, and as I jumped over it, I said, "Excuse me, Mr. Davenport," and as I looked over I saw old Campbell, the live stock editor in the city desk. He had a gun and had a bead on Davenport, so if Davenport had killed me, I knew that my redeemer lived and that I would be avenged, which didn't do me much good.

But I landed right in the midst of a white-headed boy, not Gus, but one of Gus's brothers in the circulation department, who didn't know much about the show. I landed right on his desk and he was the only fellow who had any real trouble out of the thing, for they had to bring him to.

While he was working on the *Star*, Editor White learned also that a newspaper should not suppress news because it might be unfavorable to certain advertisers and subscribers. "The only excuse an editor has for being," he wrote in the *Gazette* for October 12, 1903, "is that his paper shall print the news. The question that comes to every man running a newspaper is: What is news? That he must settle for himself, and having found a rule must stick as closely to it as possible. When an editor begins monkeying with his conscience, stretching his rule to shield his friends or to punish his enemies, he is lost. He becomes wobbly, and has no anchor and no direction. Every day matters come up in every community, big or little that are disagreeable to print. Nasty stories are always afloat. Gossip is always in the air . . . It is a safe rule to follow, that gossip may be ignored, no matter how loudly it buzzes, till it becomes a matter of court record. Then it may not be left out of the paper. . . . That it seems to the Gazette is the fair way to treat unsavory matters."

One aspect of White's career that irritated and confused his standpat readers was his willingness to change his mind and to support measures he had only recently opposed. Colonel Nelson's policy always had been that the *Star* was at perfect liberty to change its editorial position in the light of new facts. White learned this lesson thoroughly. When the Topeka *Capital* once observed, "The Emporia Gazette is the best loved paper in Kansas because its editor never looks in yesterday's files to see if what he proposes to write today is consistent," White's reply was as follows:

Isn't it the very truth? Of all the cowards, of all the wobbly pussyfooters, the man who is afraid of his own record is the worst. The thing that should govern a man is not what he has said but the truth as he sees it. A man who ignores the truth because he once failed to see the truth is probably a fool and never saw the truth. For facts change and with changing facts come changing conclusions. Yesterday's truth is tomorrow's error. Only the man who is wise enough to know this has a hold on the truth. Consistency is a paste jewel that only cheap men cherish.

Colonel Nelson believed also that newspaper editors should not run for political office. White's friend Ed Howe once observed that to get your newspaper competitor "in politics is equal to getting him in jail." Only once did White run for political office, although he mingled thoroughly in politics.

However, it was not only in the field of ideas that Colonel Nelson influenced White's newspaper career. The *Gazette* was to follow some of the make-up policies of the *Star*. Pursuing the *Star*'s lead, the *Gazette*, after a few years, stopped advertising harmful patent medicines and quack remedies. Scareheads were not allowed in the *Star* nor in the *Gazette*. No concessions to yellow journalism—red type, flaming letters, gaudy pictures—were made in either paper. While Nelson never admitted comic strips, White reluctantly admitted them after vigorous insistence from his staff.

Colonel Nelson was not the sole powerful influence White met in the *Star* office. Above White in the *Star* hierarchy were James B. Runnion, Thomas W. Johnston, Jr., and Alexander Butts. When White published *Stratagems and Spoils* (1901), he dedicated it "To the Kansas City Star, An Honest Newspaper, And To William R. Nelson, James B. Runnion, Thomas W. Johnston, Jr., And Alexander Butts Who Made It . . ." Among White's intimate fellow writers and reporters were Noble L. Prentis,

Ralph Stout, and Rosewell Field. White shared a small office with Prentis, who, then in his late fifties, made a deep impression on young White. Prentis at this time was known through Kansas for his historical sketches and feature stories, some of which have been reprinted in *Kansas Miscellanies*. White once wrote of Prentis's influence: "He took me to raise by hand, and weaned me, as it were, on his own bottle, and I loved him as boy loves his father." Alexander Butts, Rosewell M. Field, Prentis, and White wrote the editorials for the *Star*. Butts and Field, like Prentis, were much older than White. White spent a large share of his time talking and learning from these older men. "We all loved to talk," White said later. "We probably talked too much. I know Noble and I did. And Ros, when he got his work done, was a great visitor. The deadline for editorials was eleven o'clock in the morning. So between eleven o'clock and lunch we used to have great powwows, all of us. I, in my twenties, was a kind of a big-pawed, rangy pup who must have amused the elders greatly."

Colonel Nelson believed that his editorial writers should spend a large amount of time studying particular problems of interest to the city. He assigned White to investigate the problem of private versus municipally owned gas. Coming to the conclusion that the private company was charging the consumers too high rates, the *Star*, with White writing the editorials, launched a campaign which resulted in lowering the gas rate. While White was gathering information about the gas company, for the first time in his life he came up against the problem of industrial unemployment, poor housing, and slums. Always he had lived in small rural towns in which large industries and dependent workers did not exist. Now he was living in a rapidly growing city of some 132,000 people, thousands of whom worked as laborers for the swiftly developing railroads, packing houses, and stockyards. Slum conditions were prevalent in Kansas City. The *Star* agitated for better housing, and White wrote reams of editorial copy attacking the owners of slum property. One editorial denounced these landlords as "stingy speculators in real estate, who are holding on for a ride and who do not wish to improve their property." One of White's articles on slum housing aroused the real estate owners; they marched into the *Star* office and unsuccessfully demanded that the story be retracted. Another of his stories exposed the nauseating conditions of the stockyards and cost the *Star* a big advertising contract. After this occurrence, Tommy Johnston, the managing editor, told White: "Bill, you can raise more hell in three innocent looking lines imbedded in a thousand-word story than any man I ever knew. You will drive me to drink."

In one feature story for the *Star* on April 20, 1894, realizing that the great West had filled up with people and that the frontier had disappeared before his own eyes, White observed rather superficially: "Fifty years ago the times fairly bubbled with adventure. . . . The opportunities open to a man who would be a hero today are few. The battles of the century have been fought; the lands are all discovered, and nearly all settled. . . . No great problem rises before the people . . . youth that is venturesome and daring, has to sit by the register and warm its blood by the second handed heat of books or stories timed to the click of a crutch." White's generation was to have an overwhelming number of problems despite his boundless optimism. He and his generation were to be called upon to try to adjust the American structure of private capitalism to the service of the people; to solve problems of unemployment and exploitation; and to arrange America's relations with a world of neighbors through the troublous times of two great world conflicts. It was his generation that would have to meet and try to solve the various problems that had been neglected while America spread westward, conquered the last frontier, and built an industrial civilization.

For three years—from September, 1892, to June, 1895—White witnessed at first hand some of the problems created by the development of large-scale corporations and the impersonal machine age. It was not until Theodore Roosevelt's presidency, however, that he showed any critical understanding of these problems. As a reporter, White did observe that thousands of people were thrown out of work in the nineties through no fault of their own. They wanted to work but could find no work. Never before had White seen such a situation. In the America from which he came, poverty and unemployment were not yet serious problems because at least a living could be made from the land. In 1895, White returned to small-town America and for the rest of his life was its spokesman. His America, far different from urban America where thousands of people were piled indiscriminately upon one another, was a personal world where life centered in contacts with fellow human beings. In this America the human being was not dwarfed by the machine; he was a real person and he had dignity. White's world was a friendly world in which neighbors shared their joys and sorrows.

"It is a lot better to run a paper in a country town than in a city," White editorialized in the Emporia *Gazette* on May 25, 1899. "W. R. Nelson has run the Kansas City Star—the best paper in the West—for twenty years and spring goes and comes without the least sign to him that he is appreciated. This morning Mrs. J. T. Alexander brought the Gazette a mess of new peas and miscellaneous garden truck, and John C. Wood, who runs a mighty handy grocery store across the street from the office, sent over some home grown strawberries as big as a baby's fist. What's the use of talking about the city? It's more fun to live in Emporia and be neighborly . . ." White knew the small-town businessman and farmer from personal contact. He was to become for urban America an interpreter of what "grass-roots" America was thinking and desiring. Naturally, living in the friendly small-town world, White would adopt a more kindly and optimistic view of the major problems and their solutions than would some of his contemporaries who were living in the midst of the chaos of industrial-urban life.

*   *   *

In April, 1894, Colonel Nelson launched the Sunday edition of the *Star*, for which his editorial writers now had to turn in feature stories. White did a great deal of traveling in Kansas to interview political personalities for feature articles. He wrote pieces about Populist Governor Lewelling, Senator Preston B. Plumb, and the Republican boss of Kansas, Cy Leland. Leland was a personal friend of White's and whenever it was possible White gave him a boost in the *Star*. White also wrote short stories and poems for the paper. Some of the short stories were later reprinted in his first book, *The Real Issue* (1896), and some of his poems had already appeared in his and Paine's *Rhymes By Two Friends* (1893).

Rhymes By Two Friends had been a long time appearing. It was not published until over three years had elapsed from the time White and Paine had first planned the venture. White had a hearty dislike for much of the poetry that was then appearing. He charged that it was too academic; that it was "ethereal, unreal, often unintelligible, and too frequently inane, expressive of no common brotherhood, acknowledging aristocracy, appealing to a class, and promulgating theories of unusual (not to say freakish) mental and emotional development." He advocated that poetry be written "of the joys of earth . . . of human things, plainly, simply, and with directness . . . every line for every man. . . ." Although White was hardly a spectacular success as a poet, he did practice what he preached. His verses were of everyday things and everyday people and their commonplace doings.

Albert Bigelow Paine had their joint effort published by a printer, M. L. Izor, of Fort Scott, Kansas, where Paine was then living. The poets were in frequent correspondence over the book, and occasionally Mr. and Mrs. Paine joined Will White and his sweetheart Sallie Lindsay in Kansas City for a little social life. During the fall of 1891, White had been attracted to a frail, dark-eyed, vivacious, 21-year-old schoolteacher in Kansas City, Kansas, who had written some short stories for a Chicago paper. White's college friend, Walter Armstrong, knew Sallie Lindsay and made a date for him. After the first meeting, Armstrong's services were no longer required. White did not, however, assiduously cultivate Sallie Lindsay's affection until after he had returned to Kansas City from Topeka in September, 1892, to work for the *Star*.

On November 25, 1892, White wrote Paine: "I have been wondering of late how the great work on our chef d'oeuvre is getting on. So I thought I would take my typewriter in hand and write you a few lines to let you know that I am feeling well and hope you are the same. . . . Rose Field's new book is out today. I am told that it has some good Kansas stories in it. I don't think, however, that Field can write about Kansas. He is not of the people. Come up old man and let's go somewhere together . . . Sallie Lindsay told me to tell you howdy when I wrote."

Over a considerable number of months, White discussed with Paine his project of embarking upon the editorship of his own paper. White wanted to be his own boss, to receive the proper credit and recognition for a job well done. Even though the *Star* was a free newspaper and the staff was a constant stimulus to a young newspaperman, it was not like having his own paper in a town where everybody knew the editor and looked up to him as a leader and molder of public opinion. When Paine suggested one possible paper to White, he replied: "The principal objection to taking hold of the Monitor scheme is that the book keper [*sic*] would be a virtual partner in the concern. He would own so nearly half the stock that he would feel that his job is safe. I can't have any human being on earth around who feels that his job is safe. And more than that I want to fire him and hire a girl. Kill the book-keeper and I'll take the snap."

White's impending marriage to Sallie Lindsay brought a temporary halt to negotiations for his own paper. When White first met Sallie, she recalled, he was "a country lad with a come hither look in his eyes." "Sallie just came along," White once wrote, "held out her apron and kicked the tree, and I fell in it. I never had a chance." At the time that Will met Sallie, her father, originally from Kentucky, was working in the Kansas City stockyards. At the age of sixteen Sallie had started to teach school in Kansas City in order to remedy the serious financial condition of her large family.

Will and Sallie were married at her home on April 27, 1893. On February 27, 1930, while he was away on a diplomatic mission for President Herbert Hoover, White wrote Mrs. White: "My Beloved. This is the twenty-seventh; and we were looking over houses in Penn Valley 37 years ago today. All day it has been with me through all the strange things of the day—37 years ago, when we looked forward to only two months of waiting. And oh how worthwhile it has been. You have made life so lovely, so fine, so happy for me." Mrs. White was to play a significant role in her husband's career. Most of what he wrote for national magazines and book publication was carefully edited by Sallie. In the early days, she worked arduously on the *Gazette* to make that enterprise a success, and in later years always kept in touch with the paper and frequently wrote stories or tipped off the staff about a news item.

The White-Lindsay marriage attracted widespread comment in the press. "Will A. White . . . one of the young men whom Emporia claims as 'her boys,' is to be married Thursday morning to Miss Sallie Lindsay," an Emporia paper noted. "Will White has become a household word among the newspaper readers of Kansas, and he is attaining a high rank in literary work of all kinds. The many friends who know him personally and through his sketches and poems will wish him every good fortune and extend to Mr. and Mrs. White very hearty congratulations." The Topeka *Lance* observed: "Will White's marriage to Sallie Lindsay of Kansas City, Kan., is calling forth all the pretty speeches imaginable from the Kansas press." The Bolton [Missouri] *Leader* commented: "Mr. White is . . . gifted in the art of embellishing . . . ideas in rhyme or cadence of the most beautiful or in style of the most poignant and pointed. In harmonious keeping with his many other marks of wisdom, he was married . . . to Miss Sallie Lindsay."

The Whites planned to spend their honeymoon in Colorado, in hope that the mountain air would improve Mrs. White's frail health. On their way west, they stopped off at Emporia to visit A. H. Plumb and other old friends, and then spent two weeks at the Montezuma Hotel at Las Vegas, New Mexico. While they were at Las Vegas, Albert Bigelow Paine wrote White, proposing that they all leave for New York City to pursue literary careers. While White was thinking over this scheme, he wrote Paine: "My wife is getting on very nicely out here in this country. We are going to Santa Fe and from there to Manitou and from there to Moraine, Colorado." At Moraine Park, where they rented a furnished cabin for five dollars for the season, they were joined by Will's mother and Sallie's brother Milton.

From Colorado, White wrote Paine on May 24, 1893, concerning the New York proposition: "You see it's this way Paine: I'm out after Sallie's health; I think we are on the road to secure it. She is doing nicely. BUT until I am sure just how she is going to be I don't want to lay any definite plans for the future. I know you are anxious old man and I understand the reason for your anxiety. But I cannot deceive you, and as I do not want to stand in your road I think you had better go ahead with your plans without me.

If it is so in the fall that I can trot along and join you—well and good. If not—God bless you."

These weeks in Colorado were filled with reading proofs and inserting last-minute changes in *Rhymes By Two Friends*. One day White told Paine: "It seems to me in looking over my stuff that it is mostly rot and that I will cut a poor figure in the book." When Paine, however, informed him that James Whitcomb Riley had praised his poetry, White replied: "I am very much pleased— you who know my vainity [*sic*] know how much—that Riley should have seen and admired my stuff."

The panic and depression in the summer of 1893 wrecked the Whites' summer vacation and ended any thought of their going East with Albert Bigelow Paine. They had placed their savings in a bank at Manitou, and it was wiped out when the bank closed. At the same time, the *Star* was retrenching its staff and wired White that he was no longer employed. Later White recalled: "We were two of the sickest-looking newlyweds you ever saw, but before we could decide what to do we got another telegram from the *Star*. One of the older editorial writers was stricken with a heart attack and the *Star* not only wired me to come back but sent money for me to travel on. I had only enough for one ticket, so I left Mrs. White out there until I could send for her and I hurried back to work before they changed their mind again."

Shortly after returning to Kansas City, White put the finishing touches on his poems in *Rhymes By Two Friends*. He made a great many last-minute changes that must have been exasperating to Paine and the printer. Just before the book was released, White wrote Paine: "Now that the book is all up kindly send me a completed form, that I may look over the whole thing and be prepared for the shock. You can go ahead with the index as you think best ONLY I want to see Ewing's [Herbert] preface. Make the title page simple and let me see proof. . . . I really feel that I ought to be prepared for the worst, and your man was *so* negligent about sending proofs and SO much more negligent about correcting them when he did send them that I want to get my heart hardened to my ill-shapen offspring or I might disown them in the shock of a public meeting. *Don't* neglect this."

After seeing the completed book, White demanded additional

changes. The printer made the changes since White insisted: "I couldn't let the book go out with my authority if they are not made." The printer hoped to make money out of the book, and the two authors were interested in attracting the attention of the eastern press to their literary efforts. Each author was to receive a hundred copies, and the remaining three hundred copies Izor was to sell to pay for printing expenses and for his own labor. As the work on the book progressed, it was necessary for Paine to lend Izor money to bring the work to completion. When the book was released, Paine sent the authors' two hundred copies to papers for review purposes. This disrupted his friendship with White. Paine later wrote: "That was my mistake. White had counted—and with good enough reason, no doubt—on getting his hundred copies, to do with as he pleased. But we were very good friends, and I presumed—overpresumed—on that friendship." White was furious at Paine's distribution of his hundred copies. For a long time they were very cool to each other. Years later, for instance, White refused to write to Paine for a copy of the book desired by a close friend, and he would not write to Paine to congratulate him on his biography of Mark Twain. When White began to mellow, however, he and Paine renewed their friendship. On August 3, 1917, White wrote Paine: "I spent Sunday with your Mark Twain. It is a beautiful book. You have made a great and lasting monument to you and your friend. I am very proud of you." Some years later he told Paine: "No one has watched your career with more pride and affection than Sallie and I. You have made your place in the literature of your generation and left a fine, fair name."

Although it is still rumored in Kansas that White tried to buy all existing copies of *Rhymes By Two Friends,* he always denied the tale. This was the only volume of poetry he published, but occasionally he turned back to writing verses. One of his friends observed in 1897: "His principal work in the future will undoubtedly be in the line of prose. He says he has taken 'the cure' for poetry, but its entire success may be doubted. He has lived close to Nature, and she has whispered many things and we shall expect him some time to tell us in Nature's own rhythmic way."

* * *

White's life in Kansas City was light and gay, befitting his twenty-odd years of age. To a prospective biographer, he once wrote: "I didn't think much of the way you handled the Kansas City episode. It was just a little bit stiff and not quite gay enough, not quite derisive enough as a young squirt. Also keep that attitude in your head. I was such with no discount." Band concerts, operatic performances, and the legitimate theater were regularly attended by the Whites. White retained his consuming interest in music, particularly that of Brahms, Beethoven, and Tchaikowsky, and developed a lifelong love for the stage. Although he enjoyed life in Kansas City, he was restless. On the *Star* he was working hard at writing feature stories and editorials, but he wasn't getting ahead fast enough. When his request for a salary raise to $35 a week was turned down, he began again to think of buying his own paper and building a career in which he could gain recognition. He had watched the older men on the paper and noticed how the paper used them and lived on them and how they died without a byline.

White had no desire for such anonymity. He had a passion to be famous. When he discussed with Sallie the idea of buying a country paper, he justified the step by saying that as long as he remained on the *Star* he would "never be known for having written such and such a story. The *Star* would get all the credit." Then he significantly added: "I want the public to know that Will A. White wrote that piece." White had courage and was willing to take a chance. He was confident of his ability to cut loose from the *Star* and make a success of his own paper. Sallie was fully aware of the confidence he had in himself. Three years earlier, in 1892, a *Star* reporter had told Sallie that one of their top editorial writers was leaving. The next evening she relayed the information to Will, who had just left the *Journal.* He immediately said that he was going right down to the *Star* to apply for the post. Sallie gasped at Will's calm assurance that he could replace this experienced editorial writer, but he did get the job and he made a success of it. In 1895, when they were discussing acquiring their own paper, she agreed that her husband's desire to become known outweighed the benefits of living in Kansas City.

White realized, too, that it was easier to gain a position of influence in a small town than in Kansas City. When Florence Finch Kelly, the well-known newspaperwoman, stopped off in Kansas City in 1895, she had a long discussion with White as to the "relative attractions of the city and the country newspaper field and young Mr. White said decisively that he did not intend to stay in city work, that he was going to buy a country newspaper of his own just as soon as he could and be a country editor. I wanted to know why and he replied: 'Well, I want to live and work some place where I can sit down with the mayor on the edge of the sidewalk and we can let our feet hang off and can discuss local politics and the state of the nation and what we must do to be saved till it's time to go home to dinner.'" White told his colleagues on the *Star* that he wanted more time to "slosh around." A big city paper that required the editor's full time did not interest him. He wanted a small paper which, when it was on its feet, would require only a portion of his efforts. The rest of the time he could devote to writing articles and books, and to mixing in politics.

White debated some time as to whether he would buy W. Y. Morgan's Emporia *Gazette* or the Atchison *Champion*, while Professor W. H. Carruth extolled the assets of owning a paper at Lawrence. "I deliberately picked a College town when I set out to leave the Star," he once wrote. "I tried to buy the Lawrence Journal, the Manhattan Mercury, and the Ottawa Republican. Bill Morgan was the only fellow that I could outtalk. I came to a College town because I knew I wouldn't last two years in a town like Atchison, or Pittsburg, or Parsons, or Coffeyville, and a larger town irked me then and it wearies me now. The virtues of Emporia are not the Gazette's virtues, Heaven knows, but the good points of a College town with a first class railroad division which increases its business every year. But that is the kind of a town I picked when I wasn't much older than Ed Howe when he picked Atchison. He wanted a booze-fighting, hell-raising, he-man town with hair on its chest and cardamon seeds on its breath. And he got it, and look at it."

White had to borrow $3,000 to buy the *Gazette*. He sent his good friend Ewing Herbert to Emporia to negotiate a loan from Major Calvin B. Hood, the town banker. Hood lent White $750, and White borrowed $1,000 from Governor E. N. Morrill, $1,000 from the estate of Senator Preston B. Plumb, and $250 from George Plumb. Will's mother put up sufficient security to back the loans. White's newspaper reporting and association with Kansas Republican politicians had led to a close friendship with E. N. Morrill. The Plumbs were old friends of the White family, and the dead senator had been much impressed with Will's ability as a newspaperman. In five years' time, White repaid the loans with royalties from *The Real Issue* (1896), *The Court of Boyville* (1899), and the small earnings of the *Gazette*.

On June 1, 1895, the Kansas City *Star* announced White's departure from the paper and declared: "No man of his years is more generally known throughout Kansas, and his location in that state at the head of a well-established newspaper will cause universal satisfaction among his friends. He is heartily in love with his profession, he is intensely loyal to Kansas, he enjoys an acquaintance which will be serviceable to him in the highest degree, and the good wishes which he carries with him to his new field of labor are more than likely to be realized."

CHAPTER 5

COUNTRY EDITOR

"WHITE had that fine rambunctious independence characteristic of a vanishing, if not vanished America, before the age of the Machine began to stifle individualism and the desire of men to be their own bosses," the St. Louis *Post-Dispatch* remarked on January 30, 1944. From June, 1895, until his death forty-nine years later, William Allen White was his own boss. To a remarkable degree, relying on his own ability and talent, he shaped his career through five decades of stress and strain for America and for the world. Amazingly enough, in the first editorial that he ever wrote for the Emporia *Gazette*, he sketched his future path through life; and he followed it rather consistently although, of course, his ideas matured greatly over a lifetime.

"In the first place," White wrote in his opening editorial on June 3, 1895, "the new editor hopes to live here until he is the old editor, until some of the visions which rise before him as he dreams shall come true. He hopes always to sign 'from Emporia' after his name, when he is abroad, and he trusts that he may so endear himself to the people that they will be as proud of the first words of the signature as he is of the last words." "From Emporia" suggests that even this early White planned to spend a great deal of time away from Emporia. "You aren't 'from Emporia' when you're in it," Lewis Gannett has pointed out, and then has observed: "Will White must have had it in mind even then to be what he became, a world citizen from Emporia." White

78

was aware that constant references to him as a simple country editor would attract more attention than the publicity he might secure if he became a city newspaperman. It was unique to be a famous country editor and refuse offers to leave for the big city. "From Emporia" gave him a vantage point of influence with the American people that never could be secured in New York City or Chicago. Distinguished men "from New York" and "from Chicago" were plentiful but not "from Emporia."

As Chester Rowell, long-time editor of the Fresno [California] *Republican* and intimate friend of White's, detected, "White used the small-town angle for all that it was worth." However, although the Whites lived in Emporia many months of each year, they nevertheless burned the rails and highways out of Emporia with great frequency. They were far from provincial Emporians although they always happily signed the register as "from Emporia." Lewis Gannett once related the following story, which contains keen insight into White's life:

One long evening on the lawn behind his house in Emporia, Will White lay, as usual, in the hammock, looking rather like a watermelon with legs attached, talking about his newspaper. I accused him of having invented himself, of creating his own character as the shrewd, kindly, country editor. He was really, I said, a sophisticated city guy. He tried to tell me that his paper was no better than a dozen other Kansas county-seat papers, and the next morning he took me over to the office, and showed me the exchanges to prove it. They were good country papers, often good imitations of "The Emporia Gazette." But nobody read them in New York, or even in St. Louis; and everybody knew "The Emporia Gazette." Partly that was because Will White must have been born with more salt in him than most babies; also, partly because he was the New Yorker in Emporia as well as the Emporian when he came to New York. New York is full of small-town boys trying their best to forget that they are small-town boys. Will White made a career out of remembering it, but he remembered it with a city perspective.

White announced to Emporia in his first editorial that he was a Republican and would support that party's candidates first, last, and all the time. "There will be no bolting," he declared, "no sulking, no 'holier than thou' business about . . . politics—but politics is so little. No one man in ten cares for politics more than two weeks in a year. In this paper, while the politics will be straight, it will not be obtrusive. It will be confined to the editorial page—where the gentle reader may venture at his peril. The main thing is to have this paper represent the average thought of the best people of Emporia and Lyon County in all their varied interests."

This cherubic, apple-faced, 27-year-old editor had no easy road ahead. The *Gazette*, housed in a little one-room office, was hardly more than junk. Although the county contained 20,000 people, the *Gazette*'s circulation was only 485. The paper comprised a Cranston cylinder press with a water motor, four or five cases of type, a couple of make-up stones, and some miscellaneous printing materials. The value of these physical assets was $750—the rest of the purchase price of the *Gazette* was listed as "goodwill."

The payroll the first week totaled $45. White, who had arrived in town with a working capital of just $1.50, later observed that he never knew how he met that first payroll. The second week's payroll proved to be very easy. That week politicians announced their candidacies for county offices with paid advertisements. During the sluggish months of July and August, however, the editor had to borrow $120 from the bank to keep the paper going, but by September the *Gazette* was getting on its feet. White brought to the *Gazette* one major asset. In his previous newspaper training he had learned to perform all the varied functions of a newspaper office. He was able to set type, put the paper to press, feed the press, kick the jobber, set the advertising, take charge of the circulation, deliver the paper, solicit subscribers, and run the bank account. Technological improvements were to come so fast in the newspaper industry, however, that by 1935 he was to write: "Today, after 50 years in the business, I go into the back room of the *Gazette* office and instead of being familiar with every process and being able to do every mechanical thing necessary to print the *Gazette*, I can do practically nothing, though my hands retain their one-time printer's skill. But nothing in the *Gazette* office is done today as it was done 40 years ago. The type is set by machinery, the forms are not locked up as they were. Instead of being printed from type on sheets fed into a press, the *Gazette* is not printed from type, but from tubular, stereotyped plates from a continuous roll of paper. Four processes to which I am almost a stranger, now follow the copy from the printer to the reader." Furthermore, White observed that the amount of capital needed by 1935 to buy the equipment for a small country daily was so large that an industrious young lad without capital found it almost impossible to acquire his own paper. This, of course, was to have grave implications for democracy, since newspaper ownership was to be increasingly concentrated in the hands of fewer and fewer people of wealth.

Shortly after White had acquired the *Gazette*, he brought his boyhood chum, Lew Smucker, to the paper as business manager. In July, 1895, he added a young lady, Laura M. French, as a printer. From 1903 to 1919, Miss French was to serve as city editor and relieve White of many of the details of the paper so that he could devote his time to writing. When he bought the paper, he acquired Walter Hughes, who was doing odds and ends and serving as the foreman's first assistant. Walt Hughes helped to build the *Gazette* and served as business manager from the first decade of the twentieth century until his death in 1932. The foreman of the *Gazette* in 1895 was big, black-haired Jack McGinley, a two-fisted Irishman, whom White had to send away for the Keeley cure several times.

Arthur D. Read, a *Gazette* carrier from 1897 to 1903, has described the struggling paper during the early years in these words: "The office which held Mr. White, the business manager and the one, or sometimes two reporters, and toward evening six or eight carriers, was a very crowded place. Mr. White had an old-fashioned table sort of a desk always covered several inches deep with letters and exchanges. As the pile thickened, they slid off on the floor and it was, therefore, covered about a foot deep. I suppose at times this was all cleared out, but I can never remember otherwise. The window [it was the show window of an old store building] was always piled high with papers of all sorts and was a favorite lounging place for the carriers, who would rough house and read the papers. . . . At times, Mr. White would get pretty well worn out and would beseech us in agonizing tones to get out and give him a little room, and would also promise that in the 'new building,' he would have a spare room for us with plenty of room and nurses to take care of us."

White worked with great zeal to make the *Gazette* a success. He introduced a number of innovations. Every Monday he ran a column of church news. He won over the children of the town by devoting a column a week to them. One Emporia girl demonstrated White's appeal to the youth when she said in 1902: "The thing I like about White is that he takes an interest in the young people and stands by them. He is the friend of every boy and girl in this town." Around Thanksgiving time in 1895, he ran a series of articles by ministers, lawyers, businessmen, and teachers as to why Emporia should be thankful. On October 4, White had run James Whitcomb Riley's "When the Frost Is On the Punkin," and every fall thereafter this poem was reprinted. Special editions frequently appeared celebrating Emporia's industries, homes, and thriving tradesmen. On June 4, 1895, he announced to his readers: "You will observe that there is no editorial in today's paper. It will be that way lots of times. When there is nothing to say there will be nothing said." Although the *Gazette* was to become justly famed for its sparkling editorials, in the first years many a day passed without any editorial's being printed.

In the first Saturday issue, June 8, 1895, White started to print some of his own short stories and poems. During the course of the next year he also ran in serial form Arthur Conan Doyle's Sherlock Holmes stories, *A Study in Scarlet* and *The Sign of the Four*; Bret Harte's *Young Robin Grey*; Thomas Hardy's *The Spectre of the Real*; and Rudyard Kipling's *The Undertakers*. Two weeks after he took over the paper, Mrs. White began to write a regular society column.

To give the paper broader appeal, White began to pay for telegraphic news of outside events. His rival, the *Republican*, simply copied the day-old news from the Kansas City *Star*, but White offered the town up-to-date news. When he launched this service he warned his fellow townspeople: "The dispatches which appeared in the *Gazette* last night came over the Postal Union wire and cost the editor a neat little sum of money. If the people of Emporia want them they can have them. But they must pay for them. The merchants of this town have talked about having a paper with bonafide dispatches. If they will pay for such a paper, a reasonable amount, they can have it."

Before long, the *Gazette*'s advertising and circulation started to increase in a gratifying fashion. On June 3, 1896, summarizing the year's activity, White announced that he had three hundred new subscribers, owed no outstanding debts over thirty days old, had paid off $214 in notes, and had installed a $600 job department. "This office," he declared, "is a paying institution. It is here to stay. If you want to get on the band wagon, bring your work here."

At this time White was working sixteen hours a day to make the *Gazette* a success. He showed rare and shrewd business ability in launching a paper in a town against the old, firmly entrenched *Republican*. His intimate contacts with Republican politicians had aided him immensely. Immediately after buying the *Gazette*, he won the city printing away from C. V. Eskridge's *Republican*. Against the City Council's award of the printing to White, Eskridge brought three unsuccessful injunctions, which prompted White to state that: "The taxpayers have paid for three injunction suits growing out of this man's greed. . . . The records of Mr. Avery, Mr. Thomas, Mr. Evans, Mr. Davis and Mr. Jones as business men and citizens place them above the slanders of a defeated and disgruntled editor . . ." Tom Evans, the Republican sheriff, also induced the county commissioners to give the *Gazette* the county's printing.

After the fall election of 1895 had put the Populists in charge of the County Commission, in spite of White's savage editorial attacks on that party, White still received county business, largely through the efforts of P. F. Yearout. The money from the official business undoubtedly tided the *Gazette* over financial pitfalls during the first few years. White revealed his indebtedness to Yearout by writing to a state official in 1900: "Mr. P. F. Yearout, editor of 'The Emporia Times' has applied to you or will apply to you for the printing of the constitutional amendment. If you give this out to any Populist paper in Kansas, I think it would pay to oblige Yearout. He is a particularly decent populist editor, and he runs a paper that is not a 'fly up the creek,' blackmailing sheet but is a decent, plain paper, and one that has a business standing in this community. When I first came here Yearout helped me by getting the Populist county commissioners to give the printing of the official ballot to me . . . and I have always wanted to return that favor. If you could give Yearout a whack at it it would be an obligation to me, and would also be advertising the amendment in a paper which has a good circulation in Lyon and Greenwood Counties; also it would not hurt your standing a bit."

Another source of income came to White after the inauguration of President McKinley. Cy Leland, powerful Kansas Republican and close friend of White's, sent the *Gazette* the Pension Office printing which was worth approximately a thousand dollars a year.

For the first four years the *Republican* was a severe opponent of the *Gazette*. The *Republican* had welcomed White's advent into the town's journalism by stating: "It is reported that W. A. White has purchased the *Gazette*, a paper published in this city, and will take charge the 1st of June. Next." The "Next," implying that White wouldn't last long, never took place. Instead, C. V. Eskridge found his paper falling by the wayside, and committed suicide. "It was the case of the young bull horning the old bull out of the herd," White once observed, "and I expect I was cruel and should realize it. I know how I dread the approach of the young bull."

Referring to the *Gazette* as a "Willie—Willie silly—Billy paper," the *Republican* charged on July 31, 1895: "The Gazette is not a newspaper. In representing itself as such it could be prosecuted for obtaining money under false pretenses. It has no excuse for living." The following day White replied to this attack by pointing out that, while the *Republican* used space to attack him, the *Gazette* was printing news. "A long array of shimmering dancing gems of thought about the editor of the Gazette gleamed forth from the first column of the Republican's 'choice reading' page last evening," commented White. "The subject is an interesting one but the chances are that the subscribers of that paper would much prefer the welcome news that the military board decided yesterday afternoon to hold the state militia encampment at Emporia this year. That piece of news was published exclusively in the Gazette last evening." When White secured the city printing, C. V. Eskridge's rage poured forth like floodwaters. "Silly Willie," screamed the *Republican,* on August 20, 1895, "or the Gazette, or the editor of the Gazette, or whatever you may choose to call this arrogant, egotistical, bombastic, trashy, insignificant combination of aliases, says . . . We do the city printing free of charge to the taxpayers . . . maybe not mad, but 'gone crazy.' Of course, he did not have far to go; but, it is very evident that he got there."

For several months White answered these attacks in kind, but after the second or third month he ignored the *Republican.* He realized that he could win more subscribers by improving the quality of the paper than by quarreling with his competitor. At one point, when Eskridge had a very able writer on his staff, White got the writer out of town by securing him a better position on a Topeka paper. A little polite blackmail finally forced Eskridge to cease his attacks on the editor of the *Gazette.* White once wrote: "Governor Eskridge's love affair with the lady at Fourth and Constitution ran along well into the middle nineties. One time he took a mean crack at me about something and I printed a two-lined item in the Gazette indicating that I knew about it and the old man shut up tighter than a clam and never said an unkind thing about me after that."

The row between the *Gazette* and the *Republican* divided the town of Emporia for a number of years. After Eskridge died, those opposed to White raised money and brought in innumerable editors to run rival papers. White often said that "after a few good funerals my path was easier in Emporia." Since, as he also said, there were three things no one could do to the satisfaction of everyone—"poke a fire, mind a baby and run a newspaper"—his enemies were continually launching rival papers. By 1907, White had seen fourteen men fail in their efforts and six papers discontinue publication. When one daily competitor closed its doors, White editorialized:

Editor Phillips, late editor, owner and publisher of the Emporia Daily and Weekly "Democrat," has left for parts unknown, probably to the horror and consternation of the parts, and certainly for the general betterment of this community. Far be it from this paper to say aught that would cast an unwarranted aspersion upon an earnest though unfortunate gentleman. It is not the purpose of the Gazette

85

to be sensational nor to exaggerate interesting facts. But as a matter of news and stated in the precise terms of scientific description, without coloring the statement by loose vernacular, the simple homely truth demands that it be said of Phillips that he was, is and will be while he lives on this easy old earth, the most picturesque, unique, original, shameless, deliberate, conscienceless, malicious and indefatigable dead beat that ever pressed the sidewalks of Commercial street with his velvety feline feet. It is but just to him to add he was not a harsh or irascible man. He did not exact tribute with either club or gun or buzz saw. He had the soft, self-deprecatory, insinuating voice of a cooing dove; and he glided into his machinations with the gentle, noiseless, hypnotic sinuosity of a rubber-tired rattlesnake. He was as bland as a sunrise and as deadly as a pestilence.

Not only did he have the face to charge for a total circulation of 150 copies, advertising rates that would make reputable editors blush whose papers circulated by the thousand; but Editor Phillips actually got those rates. Earth was a wilderness of suckers for him. He put the marks of his easy touch all over the town and when advertisers were coy he cut their advertisements from other papers, charged up the account, waited till the store keeper was out and traded out the amount of his account and twice as much besides. Rebuffs and insult rebounded from him without denting his pachyderm complacency, nor rubbing the creamed and mantled waters of his stagnant moral sense.

Poor old Phillips, he has left us. We may never look upon his like again—thank heaven—until the sulphurous blazes of perdition illuminate the job lot in the deepest part of the seventh pit.

Editor White was plunged into politics from the very day he bought the paper. A county election was on, and White advocated the election of the straight Republican ticket. He praised the Republicans as orderly and businesslike, and charged that the Populist-Democrat fusion party was composed of disorderly people. Very smugly he stated: "The only wise laws that have been put on the statute books of the nation in twenty-five long years have been Republican laws." When the Populist Emporia *Times* had the temerity to assert that the Republican party was the party of vested interests and had no principles, White replied: "To talk of principle in company like the Times and its organization of place seekers, would be like reading the Sermon on the Mount in the den of the Forty thieves." Overlooking the unemployment of the industrial cities and the distress of farm groups, he asserted just before the county elections that "peace and fair prosperity prevail in Kansas. . . . The thing to do now is to be happy. There is every reason why the people should rejoice. We have begun to enter into the kingdom."

In spite of White's arduous efforts, the fusion ticket of Democrats and Populists carried the county election. This defeat was just one of many White was to suffer over the years. Frequently, when he was "making" senators, congressmen, and governors he could not carry his home town and county for his candidates. White attributed the 1895 defeat to the voters' objection to having the Republican party run by professional politicians. What the party needed, he asserted, was leadership by merchants, substantial farmers, and professional people. It should be run by middle-class citizens, not by party hacks. From 1895 to his death, White continually preached that the Republican party was basically the party of middle-class America. Yet he came to recognize that the party was dominated by politicians who served the interests of the industrial and financial plutocracy of the country. By remaining with the Republican party, he and the rest of middle-class America gave those interests a means of achieving political domination under the guise of being a party of the people.

In 1895, White was by no means so firm a defender of the established order of vested business as his political editorials in support of the Republican party might have implied. He felt that some governmental regulation of business was desirable, provided of course it came from the safe and sane Republican party. Although he had asserted during the campaign that all was well with society, he actually knew better. Before the heat of the campaign overwhelmed him, he had written a splendid editorial expressing the despair and plight of farmers in drought-ridden Kansas:

There came through Emporia yesterday two old-fashioned "mover wagons," headed east. The stock in the caravan would invoice four horses, very poor and very tired, one mule, more disheartened than the horses, and one sad-eyed dog, that had probably been compelled to rustle his own precarious living for many a long and weary day. A few farm implements of the simpler sort were loaded in the wagon, but nothing that had wheels was moving except the two wagons. All the rest of the impedimenta had been left upon the battlefield, and these poor stragglers, defeated, but not conquered, were fleeing to another field, to try the fight again. These movers were from western Kansas— from one of those counties near the Colorado line which holds a charter from the state to officiate as the very worst, most desolate, God-forsaken, man-deserted spot on the sad old earth. They had come from that wilderness only after a ten years' hard, vicious fight, a fight which had left its scars on their faces, had bent their bodies, had taken the elasticity from their steps, and left them crippled to enter the battle anew. For ten years they had been fighting the elements. They had seen it stop raining for months at a time. They had heard the fury of the winter wind as it came whining across the short burned grass and cut the flesh from their children huddling in the corner. These movers have strained their eyes watching through the long summer days for the rain that never came. They have seen that big cloud roll up from the southwest about one o'clock in the afternoon, hover over the land, and stumble away with a few thumps of thunder as the sun went down. They have tossed through hot nights wild with worry, and have arisen only to find their worst nightmares grazing in reality on the brown stubble in front of their sun-warped doors. They had such high hopes when they went out there; they are so desolate now—no, not now, for now they are in the land of corn and honey. They have come out of the wilderness, back to the land of promise. They are now in God's own country down on the Neosho, with their wife's folks, and the taste of apple butter and good corn bread and fresh meat and pie—pieplant pie like mother used to make—gladdened their shrunken palates last night; and real cream, curdling on their coffee saucers last night for supper, was a sight so rich and strange that it lingered in their dreams, wherein they walked beside the still waters, and lay down in green pastures.

The year 1896 centered largely in politics for the 28-year-old editor. He covered the Republican National Convention at St. Louis for the *Gazette* and the Kansas City *World*. With Ed Howe of the Atchison *Globe*, he saw the sights of the old river town. "St. Louis stinks," he wrote home. "There is a peculiar sour smell about the place that goes through everything. It is the smell you find in hotels after they have been running a number of years. It is a cooking smell, and it makes the head ache. Ed Howe, who has been across the ocean, says it is like the smell that comes from the steam kitchen when you are sea sick. The next day Howe and White visited the Union Market. "It is the best I ever saw," White commented. "Chicago cannot equal it. They have watermelons for sale and cantelopes [sic] and every kind of fish. The meat looks good and the vegetables are clean. Howe bought a lot of truck and we took an armload of it into a restaurant near by and made them serve it. That tickled the waiter girl to death, and we could see her going around whispering it to all the other girls. Then they smiled and looked at us and pretty soon the cook stuck his head out from behind the door and the cashier wandered by and looked us over. We didn't mind. There were two of us and we could laugh back. If he or I had been alone we would have been too mortified to take our eyes from the table."

White could find little enthusiasm in the Republican convention to relate to his readers. The convention, dominated by Cleveland businessman Mark Hanna, nominated Governor William McKinley of Ohio on the first ballot. "Reporters who have attended national conventions for a generation say that this is the most listless convention they ever reported," White commented. "There is no life in it. The applause is hollow; the enthusiasm is dreary and the delegates sit like hogs in a car and know nothing about anything."

The Democratic convention, which met three weeks later in Chicago, was far more dramatic. With his stirring "Cross of Gold" speech, William Jennings Bryan captured the Democratic nomination. Although White did not attend this convention, he recognized the fact that Bryan's speech had electrified the nation, and he captured the emotional quality of Bryan's appeal when he later observed: "Through the nerve of the telegraph that speech thrilled a continent, and for a day a nation was in a state of mental and moral catalepsy. If the election had been held that July day, Bryan would have been chosen President. Indeed, all his opponents did in the three months following his speech was to arouse the people from their trance. It took much shaking up to break the spell, much marching of the patient up and down the land under torches and to martial music to revive him and restore him to his natural faculties."

Thirty-six-year-old William Jennings Bryan voiced the protests of the older rural America against the dominance of the new industrial-urban order. He was the Great Commoner. He talked as farmers talked, and he voiced all their distrust of new ways and new wealth, all "their hatred of privilege and corruption in politics for private gain, their contempt for the new aristocracy which revealed itself in city ways; their feeling that honest toil should give prosperity. He had called America back to old principles and doctrines—principles and doctrines as old as Jackson and Jefferson. He had launched another democratic revolt just as Lincoln had done in 1860." Bryan fused the economic discontent of the Populists, their hatred of debts, mortgages and high freight rates, with the old Jeffersonian ideal of the need of equality of opportunity to maintain a democratic society.

Bryan's bitter campaign of 1896 marked the close of the frontier era in American history. Up to this time, a fairly democratic society had maintained itself because of the country's unlimited natural resources. All that was needed was freedom for the individual to exploit these resources. But by the 1890's, pioneer America had been replaced by industrial America. Freedom for the individual under industrialism often meant exploitation of others, and it was this freedom and exploitation that had produced the slums, the poverty, and the unemployment of the heartbreaking years from 1893 to 1896. Bryan realized that if American democracy was to continue the government must step in and regulate the free individual for the benefit of the many. The government would have to plan to ensure freedom and equality for its citizens.

William Allen White and millions of middle-class people like him failed to comprehend the true meaning of the Bryan revolt of 1896. Imbued with the frontier belief in the free individual, they felt that any governmental regulation of business was un-American. They did not see that democracy could be preserved under industrialism only if the predatory were curbed by the government. On July 31, 1896, an editorial in the Emporia *Gazette* boldly stated that the Democratic-Populist ticket meant the destruction of the American way of life. "In this American government," asserted White, "paternalism plays no part. It is every man for himself. It is free for all, and in the end the keenest, most frugal, and most industrious win." A few days later he stated that the issue was "Shall American institutions, as they have been since the beginning, stand, or shall they be changed? . . . The American idea is today in the balance. The Republicans are upholding it. The Populists and their allies are denouncing it. The election will sustain Americanism or it will plant Socialism." During the heat of the Bryan campaign, White even temporarily forgot that he himself had advocated some limited governmental controls in the past.

*   *   *

In Emporia, White wrangled all that summer and fall with Vernon L. Parrington, who was then teaching at the College of Emporia. Parrington did his best to show White that the rise of urban industrialism had altered the American scene and thus required new ideas and thoughts to meet the changed situation. Many years later White admitted that Parrington had been right. "He knew the eternal justice of it," White once wrote; "he was right and I was wrong. He just had a better brain than I, that was all." White's support of McKinley, the representative of the new industrial forces, was typical of millions of small-town middle-class people. They supported Mark Hanna's candidate and considered McKinley the hope of democracy against Bryan, the "dangerous un-American demagogue." Actually, there was no more traditional American than Bryan. His forebears were pioneers, typical Americans. Of them Bryan once wrote: "There is not among them so far as I know, one of great wealth or political or social prominence, but so far as I have been able to learn they were honest, industrious, Christian, moral, religious people—not a black sheep in the flock, not a drunkard, not one for whose life I would have to apologize." Bryan grew up in Illinois and attended a small western denominational college. Afterward he moved to Nebraska and practiced law. Bryan's great appeal was that he fused democratic aspirations, deep Christian principles, and the farmers' bitterness over their loss of prestige in American life and their failure to prosper.

Although he lived in a rural area, White could not feel that the

91

reforms advocated by Bryan and the Populists were sound, because they were not being advocated by "safe and sane" business people. When White stated that the Democratic party, once the party of treason, was now "a menace to good government" and threatened "the overthrow of the American idea," the Democrats and Populists organized huge protest parades through Emporia's streets. They carried large signs on which White was depicted as a jackass. They threatened to run him out of town unless the attacks ceased, but White defied them and outfought them.

One day in August, as White was walking along an Emporia street, fifteen or twenty Populists stopped him and began to argue the merits of the campaign. The thermometer that August morning stood at 107, and the town had been baking for several months under the Kansas sun. With wheat selling at 40 cents a bushel, butter at 10 cents a pound, eggs at 6 cents a dozen, and chickens at 8 cents a pound, it was little wonder that these farmers were Bryan lovers. The red-faced editor was in no mood to debate the campaign in the stifling heat, but the crowd insisted. White became so angry that his words got stuck and all he could do was sputter. Finally he broke away and stalked to the *Gazette* office with a number of thoughts sizzling in his angry brain. When he reached the office, the editorial page needed more copy. He looked at his watch and noticed that he had just a few minutes before he must catch the train for Colorado, where he had been called by the illness of Mrs. White. Rigid with indignation, he sat down and wrote "What's the Matter With Kansas?" Shortly before this editorial was written, Eugene Ware had been in town to see White and had filled him with figures to prove that the Populists were responsible for the state's loss of population and capital.

When the editorial appeared, White was in Colorado. His staff did not approve of the diatribe against the Populists. Jack McGinley, the foreman, held up running the editorial for several days and finally turned it over to Laura M. French, saying, "Here, set this damned thing! I don't like it, I think it will hurt the paper, but I guess it will have to go." Miss French, a thoroughgoing Bryan follower, burned with anger as she set the editorial from White's sprawling, handwritten original. The editorial quoted

Ware's figures to prove that the Populists were driving people and money out of Kansas. In bold and picturesque language it ridiculed the Bryan demands. Instead of the satire he had used in "The Regeneration of Colonel Hucks," this editorial was replete with vigorous, sarcastic language. Blaming the Populists entirely for the sorry plight of Kansas, White asserted:

. . . Go east and you hear them laugh at Kansas, go west and they sneer at her, go south and they "cuss" her, go north and they have forgotten her. Go to any intelligent people gathered anywhere on the globe, and you will find the Kansas man on the defensive. The newspaper columns and magazines once devoted to praise of her, to boastful facts and startling figures concerning her resources, are now filled with cartoons, jibes and Pefferian speeches. Kansas just naturally isn't in it. She has traded places with Arkansas and Timbuctoo.

What's the matter with Kansas?

We all know; yet here we are at it again. We have an old moss-back Jacksonian who snorts and howls because there is a bathtub in the statehouse; we are running that old jay for governor. We have another shabby, wild-eyed, rattle-brained fanatic who has said openly in a dozen speeches that "the rights of the user are paramount to the rights of the owner"; we are running him for chief justice, so that capital will come tumbling over itself to get into the state. We have raked the old ash heap of failure in the state and found an old human hoop skirt who has failed as a business man, who has failed as an editor, who has failed as a preacher, and we are going to run him for congressman-at-large. He will help the looks of the Kansas delegation at Washington. Then we have discovered a kid without a law practice and have decided to run him for attorney-general. Then for fear some hint that the state had become respectable might percolate through the civilized portions of the nation, we have decided to send three or four harpies out lecturing, telling the people that Kansas is raising hell and letting the corn go to weeds.

Oh, this is a state to be proud of! We are a people who can hold up our heads! What we need is not more money, but less capital, fewer white shirts and brains, fewer men with business judgment, and more of those fellows who boast that they are "just ordinary clod hoppers, but they know more in a minute about finance than John Sherman"; we need more men who are "posted," who can bellow about the crime of '73, who hate prosperity, and who think because a man believes in national honor, he is a tool of Wall Street . . . We need several thousand gibbering idiots to scream about the "Great Red Dragon" of Lombard Street. We don't need population, we don't need wealth, we don't need well-dressed men on the streets, we don't need cities in the fertile prairies; you bet we don't! What we are after is the money power. Because we have become poorer and ornrier and meaner than a spavined, distempered mule, we, the people of Kansas, propose to kick; we don't care to build up, we wish to tear down. . . .

Give the prosperous man the dickens! Legislate the thriftless man into ease, whack the stuffing out of the creditors . . .

Whoop it up for the ragged trousers; put the lazy, greasy fizzle who can't pay his debts on the altar, and bow down and worship him. Let the state ideal be high. What we need is not the respect of our fellow men, but the chance to get something for nothing. . . .

There was nothing original in "What's the Matter With Kansas?" except the clever phrases and White's unique manner of expressing ideas already held by millions of others. "I have had all that in my system for two years," he told the publishers of his forthcoming book, "and it did me good to get rid of it." Had the editorial uttered new and original thoughts, it would not have attracted attention. But since it repeated in an adroit fashion the unexpressed views of many middle-class people, it caught on at once.

Paul Morton, third vice-president of the Santa Fe Railroad, was so greatly impressed with the editorial that he sent it to H. H. Kohlsaat, publisher of the Chicago *Times-Herald* and the *Evening Post*. Kohlsaat reprinted "What's the Matter With Kansas?" and told his readers: "This is one of the most bitterly ironical arraignments of the shiftless spirit that has handicapped that rich state. . . . It is couched in language so bold yet picturesque as to seem the utterance of a wit in whom the bitterness of reality cannot wholly suppress mirth over the imbecility that has caused it." The New York *Sun* reprinted it from the Chicago papers, and Mark Hanna had the Republican campaign committee circulate it in pamphlet form. Easterners welcomed the editorial, since it supplied them with the simple explanation that Bryan and the Populists were fanatics and demagogues. Instead of having to concern themselves with the basic issues of the campaign, they could now quote this Kansas editorial as proof that it was really just a simple choice between decent and orderly Republicans and unsuccessful and rabble-rousing Democrats.

Publisher Kohlsaat wrote White during the campaign that his article had attracted more attention than any other item of campaign propaganda. White was immensely flattered when his political idol, Speaker of the House of Representatives Thomas B. Reed, wrote him on September 17, 1896:

DEAR SIR:
Would you have the goodness to present to the author of "The Matter With Kansas" my personal thanks. I have not seen as much sense in one column in a dozen years.

Very truly,

T. B. REED

Joseph W. Babcock, chairman of the Republican Congressional Committee, wrote White on September 22, asking for the price of a quantity of reprints for circulation in the campaign. H. L. Nelson, editor of *Harper's Weekly*, wrote White: "I have read with a great deal of pleasure your editorial of August 16 on 'What's Wrong With Kansas?' and I wish to congratulate you on the admirable stand that you have taken in your state, and to express my great satisfaction with the literary merit of your editorial."

The editorial made White famous. Hereafter newspapers all over the country were to quote his editorials and speeches on politics and a variety of other subjects. Magazines like *McClure's*, *Scribner's*, and the *Saturday Evening Post* were soon to call on him for short stories and articles. He was now, at the age of twenty-eight, a nationally recognized figure, and from 1896 to his death in 1944, he was to continue to increase significantly his position of influence and prestige with the American people.

Although McKinley defeated Bryan by half a million votes, Bryan carried the South and trans-Mississippi states like Kansas and Nebraska. When Kansas went for Bryan and the entire Democratic-Populist ticket, the Emporia *Gazette* for November 6, 1896, announced the results with the following headline:

HERE IS THE SICKENING TRUTH

KANSAS HAS GONE POPULIST—EVERYTHING FROM DOG CATCHER TO GOVERNOR

THE MOST CRUSHING AND OVERWHELMING REPUBLICAN DEFEAT KANSAS EVER SAW

THE STATE NOW A CURSE

HONEST MEN ALL OVER THE NATION JEER KANSAS AND SCORN HER AS A TAINTED, FOUL, SHAMEFUL THING, AND THE POPULISTS ARE HAPPY OVER THE CRIME THEY HAVE DONE

White's colorful and pithy style in "What's the Matter With Kansas?" was not a haphazard occurrence that could not be repeated. Over the years he produced editorials, articles, and books which demonstrated that he had a style of his own. He was a prolific writer. For the two years preceding "What's the Matter With Kansas?" he had spent his evenings writing and rewriting short stories about Kansas life. These he added to some of his stories which had already appeared in the *Star*, and sent them to the Way and Williams publishing company in Chicago. The Whites had high hopes for Will's literary career. When Sallie was visiting her family in Kansas City in the spring of 1896, she mentioned to her husband the difficult time her mother always had had financially, and said, "You will save me from it won't you, when you write your great book? . . ."

A few weeks after young White had sent his manuscript to the publishers, and had received no word as to their decision, he sat down and wrote them in his scrawling long hand:

Does the sea give up its dead? What has become of the "1001 choice gems of thought" that I sent you once in the dear dead past? If you are holding them for storage or freight charges kindly send me a notice on blank no 438797 and I will remit. If however there is any "show" for the thoughts let me know; I am willing to make the pilgrimage to Chicago if you believe that a conference would be of any value to either of us.

You must not think that I am too impatient, you may have stories of your own some day.

By September 15, 1896, White was more than concerned over the delay of Way and Williams to reach a final decision on his book. "Can you 'report progress' on the stories I sent you March second?" he inquired. "I do not wish to seem impatient but when one is a young man five long weary months is a terrible stretch of time to be away from one's manuscripts. . . . It is hot weather but I feel that it is my duty to ask you to take some certain and immediate action in this matter." When the book was finally published in November, under the title *The Real Issue*, it revealed White as a realistic interpreter of Kansas life. He had lived through grasshoppers, droughts, cyclones, and booms and, as a result, sympathetically but graphically described these Kansas conditions. The stories were good folksy tales about plain men and women. They were filled with descriptive anecdotes about everyday life in small-town Kansas. A number of the stories dealt with life on the high plains of Western Kansas. One particular story, "A Story of the Highlands," told how a woman went mad from the constant sun in summer and the biting winds in winter. White thus described the solitude, loneliness, and grimness of this woman's life: "The even line of the horizon is seldom marred. The silence of such a scene gnaws the glamour from the heart. Men become harsh and hard; women grow withered and sodden under its blighting power. The song of wood birds is not heard; even the mournful plaint of the meadow lark loses its sentiment, where the dreary clanking drone of the windmill is the one song which really brings good tidings with it."

The publication of *The Real Issue* established White as a leading realistic writer of the farm country. When Hamlin Garland, the foremost realistic novelist of the rural West, praised *The Real Issue*, White replied: "Your kind note of the 7th came today and made me happy. You do not understand how I cherish your encouraging words. Your ideals have been mine and your work my model for many years. Before I knew your books, I was influenced by Mr. Howells and I am yet under the charm of his genius. I wish you could call his attention to my work. It would seem impudent in me. A word of criticism now from him (privately) would help me I believe. . . ."

The Real Issue was highly acclaimed by book reviewers. The *Dial*, a literary magazine published in Chicago, hailed the book as "truthful studies of Kansas life, with occasional touches of humor and a heavy burden of pathos. The general effect is almost as sombre as that produced by Mr. Howe's 'Story of a Country Town.' . . ." "The book will come as the voice of a new writer, whose note sounds clear and strong above the murmur of the day's mediocrity," noted the Kansas City *Star*. ". . . Taking up the book, one instantly recognizes its literary value, feels the manner, realizes the clearness, the expressiveness of these unpretentious pages. . . . For the young writer there can be only the warmest congratulations, and from his early readers, a hail as he passes onward."

Life, the old humor weekly, welcomed *The Real Issue* by stating: "It is a pleasure to find that Mr. White has just as original ideas about story writing as he has exhibited in editorials . . . If the despair of Kansas is in Mr. White's stories, so also is the aggressive hopefulness and good sense that will ultimately be its salvation." After praising White's "vigorous" and "picturesque style," *Life* concluded: "The humor of the whole proceeding is delicate and fine. Kansas may contain the 'most picturesque lot of cranks on God's green earth'—but there is a man among them who can write a short story when he isn't sloshing around among the Populists."

The book caught on quickly; within a month Way and Williams were printing a second edition. "What's the Matter With Kansas?" provided an excellent springboard for selling the book, and both White and his publisher made the most of the situation. White displayed business acumen in the many letters he wrote his publishers concerning the advertising and distribution of the book. After one letter of instructions to Way and Williams, he added: "You must not think I am assuming too much but I know you have so many things to do that I feel bold to give you the benefit of my imagination." Regularly he criticized the publishers for not advertising the book properly, and one letter was appropriately closed with the statement: "Scream when you have had enough."

White obtained approximately $2,000 from this book. He actually earned more, but his publishers failed in 1898. By that time, money was pouring in from magazine articles, and he took a small settlement and dropped the matter. Shortly after the book was published, S. S. McClure, the ablest magazine editor of his day, paid White $300 for the privilege of reprinting two of the stories in *McClure's Magazine*. From this time on, White's articles were avidly sought by eastern magazines, and by the turn of the century he was quoting his own terms to these magazines.

White had selected Way and Williams as his publishers since Chicago in the middle nineties had a thriving literary and publishing life. Way and Williams were noted for the excellent format and typography of their books. "I am partial to your firm," White wrote them on June 2, 1896, "because being something of a printer, I like your style. If I am to have a book I want a handsome book." In addition to Way and Williams, Stone and Kimball (later just Herbert S. Stone & Company) were making Chicago a significant publishing center. These two houses not only were publishing internationally famous authors, but were concentrating on books about the Middle West by local writers. Books by Hamlin Garland, George Ade, and Eugene Field strengthened the lists of these Chicago publishers. Out of Chicago, too, came two significant literary magazines, the *Dial* and the *Chap-Book*. A Midwesterner like White was naturally attracted to this literary renaissance in the metropolis of his section.

Through his publisher, Chauncey Williams, White was soon to meet such important midwestern writers as Brand Whitlock, Opie Read, George Ade, Finley Peter Dunne, Octave Thanet, James Whitcomb Riley, Booth Tarkington, and Ray Stannard Baker. Chicago literary critics quickly welcomed White to their circle. "A new American star has arisen in the literary firmament. A western star, if one may draw sectional lines," remarked one Chicago paper. ". . . It is gratifying to western people, who feel that they are not provincial on all things—not 'half baked,' as some eastern scholar has beautifully put it—to be able to extend a sincere welcome to such a sturdy young writer as William Allen White."

PART II

REACTION AND REFORM

CHAPTER 6

THE McKINLEY YEARS

"THE hard-headed editor of the Emporia *Gazette* is giving the people of Kansas many good chunks of common sense," declared the Republican New York *Tribune* on January 13, 1897, after reading one of William Allen White's attacks on the Populist party.

White was rewarded for this and for his many other scathing editorials on the Populists by being invited by Mark Hanna to speak at the Lincoln Day banquet of the Ohio Republicans in 1897. White told the powerful old-guard leaders that for six or seven years Kansas had been under the spell of demagogues. Even the Kansas Republicans, White charged, had been led by demagogues who had tried to outpromise the Populists, and as a result "the State platform was often more of a fly trap than a declaration of Republican principles . . . these political economists of the soft soap school would stand proudly on a platform recommending moonshine as a legal tender, endorsing astrology, declaring for bluegrass and the barefoot cure, pledging the party to vegetarianism, and whooping it up for the free and unlimited coinage of flapdoodle." But, White added, the campaign of 1896 had clarified the Kansas political scene. When the national Republican party adopted a strongly conservative platform, the Kansas Republicans who had been toying with Populist ideas left the party. "That is why," he stated to his audience, "I came so far to tell you that Kansas is all right . . . In this great fight before the American people for the preservation of American institutions, gentlemen, you may depend on Kansas."

His audience burst forth into peals of laughter when the 29-year-old Kansas editor began to ridicule the Populists in his own sprightly style. "Of late," White asserted, "a new delusion has spread through the country to the effect that the Populists are off the reservation, killing plutocrats out of season and contrary to law. These things being prevalent belief, make the streetcar horses laugh till their sides hurt when they see a man from Kansas. That is unfair. Kansas is a little queer at times, but so is Indiana and Illinois, for that matter. But just because four or five Kansas congressmen have the lumpy-jaw you should not infer that we grow tails and run wild with the buffalo."

Following the speech Mark Hanna insisted that White visit President-elect McKinley at Canton, since illness had prevented McKinley from attending the meeting. Out of respect for Hanna White went. He always had a warm spot in his heart for Mark Hanna. Even after White became a Progressive and knew that the Hanna type of businessman was corrupting politics, he set Hanna aside in a niche, not to be touched or criticized. White, of course, was grateful to Hanna for the lift Hanna had given to his career. Through Hanna's recognition White had emerged as a national figure before the age of thirty. Furthermore, White liked Mark Hanna as a person. Hanna was intensely human. "As a man," White has written, "he enjoyed a good joke, a good fellow, or a good dinner; and liked all three served, if possible, at the same table . . . Hanna had a cash-register conscience; he was never a man of attenuated ideals."

White refused to call on McKinley until Hanna gave him the following letter of introduction:

Hon. Wm. McKinley
MY DEAR SIR:
This will introduce Mr. W. A. White (who wrote What's the Matter with Kansas). I have a great admiration for this young man and bespeak for him your Kind Consideration. He wants no office.
Sincerely yours
M. A. HANNA

The White-McKinley meeting was not a success. Four years later when White was gathering material for an article on McKinley, he wrote his old teacher James Canfield: "You know I am handicapped in writing about McKinley, because I never liked his style of man. He was not robust enough for my style of beauty . . . The red corpuscles were all gone out of his blood." As White and his publisher, Chauncey L. Williams, who had accompanied White to Ohio to help him publicize *The Real Issue*, were ushered into McKinley's office, the President-elect read a card and called "Mr. White." The editor stepped forward and McKinley shook his hand and remarked, "I am happy to meet you and greet you." After McKinley had repeated the performance with Williams, the two were ushered out. When they reached the outdoors, White scooped up a handful of snow and rubbed Williams's hand with it, observing that it was necessary "to take out the frostbite." McKinley's cold reception, however, failed to depress the natural buoyancy of White. He and Williams hurried to a photographer's shop for several tintypes. To accompany these pictures, White wrote the following verse:

CANTON AND CLEVELAND

These faces young and comely are not smiling they are bent
In those uncanny postures by a frigid President.
His heart is ice, his hand is stone, his meditations grow
In forms of grotesque hoar frost and his dreams are drifted snow.
And when these two lads struck the blast of his cold storage cheer
They took the train for Cleveland and they got the glad hand here.

After his return home from Ohio in mid-February, White busied himself with editing the *Gazette*, opposing the Populists in a county election, and writing short stories for *McClure's Magazine*. Every evening after a full day's work on the paper, White wrote stories about boyhood. He had on hand a number of manuscripts that he had written in the past and had been unable to publish, but such was his growing concern with his writings that he refused to sell them, even now that his fame made it possible. "I have got some old things," he wrote Paul Lemperly of Cleveland, "but they don't seem to be good for anything, and I don't want to send them out. McClure's wanted to buy them, but I would not sell them because they were so rotten." Before White sent his completed stories to *McClure's*, Sallie White read them aloud to Mr. and Mrs. Robert L. Jones for criticism, and the stories, also, were sent to an English teacher at the Emporia Normal School for correction.

"Just now I am working like a horse," he wrote Chauncey L. Williams on April Fool's Day. Three weeks before, he had written Williams in a restless mood:

My Dear Good Old Man;

There you are up in the city a sweatin' and a cussin' and damnin' the whole universe, with the cars a clanging way down at the bottom of the big brown devil's gulch of a street below you and the feathery steaming smoke blurin' good sunlight around you. There you are surrounded by the machines and the contrivance man has made, and the hollowness and emptiness of it all throbbing like a drumbeat in your ears, and here I am sitting at my little old desk, the door of my office opening on the street and the spring ebbing and flowing on the soft breath that flutters in, bearing the purring noises of the quiet rural street—wooden sounds not harsh and clanky—but muffled by the gentle life that moves about me. And I want to come up to be with you and you want to come down and be with me. It is strange the unrest that sometimes—always I guess—possesses us.

I know that you must often feel tired of the eternal chink of your chains—so do I. There are times when I want to quit the whole business of life and go fishing forever and ever. The fact that while we live there can never be a perfect holiday, that there must be always that hell-hound of business yelping over the hill behind us on the trail, always after us always forcing us on, is our curse even if it is our blessing.

Someday maybe we will get two hills and a vale ahead of the beast and have a day off. Someday maybe this summer we'll go where there are green field and sunning brooks, where there are skies and mountains—the latest home of the Gods before they left the world. Maybe we will find some old god who has lost his pack and commune with him in the blackness of the great untrailed forest where the tall ferns are, and where the waters among the rocks call and call and call for some sore heart to come and drink the healing balm of their sweet laughter. That spot I know; I wish we were there now. It would be good . . .

In June, 1897, the Whites' peaceful but busy existence was shattered by the news that President McKinley was about to appoint the *Gazette* editor as postmaster of Emporia. Quickly the Whites packed their bags and went to Washington. After convincing Mark Hanna that he did not want the post, White visited in the capital and started acquaintanceships with Elihu Root, Thomas B. Reed, and Henry Cabot Lodge.

One day, after an introduction from the Kansas congressman, Charles Curtis, White had lunch with Assistant Secretary of the Navy Theodore Roosevelt. Roosevelt was an admirer of White's *The Real Issue,* and he was subscribing to the Emporia *Gazette.* "I have held through a generation my first flash of Theodore Roosevelt," White said in 1934, ". . . a tallish, yet stockily built man, physically hard and rugged, obviously fighting down the young moon crescent of his vest; quick speaking, forthright, a dynamo of energy, given to gestures and grimaces, letting his voice run its full gamut from base to falsetto. He seemed spiritually to be dancing in the exuberance of a deep physical joy of life."

White was tremendously impressed with this man Roosevelt, just ten years older than himself. They were to be on intimate terms for a lifetime, and White never really recovered from the impact of Theodore Roosevelt on his own personality. "I hope some genius somewhere will be able to gather from those of us who still live, something immortal to put into the pages of history, this unique and splendid, this superb spirit and personality, call it what you will, combination of qualities that was Theodore Roosevelt," declared White in 1936. "To me he seemed as nearly a perfect man as any I have known. He was not perfect, not more than 85 per cent, with a slight discount off for that, but most of them don't run over 30."

The two men had natural attractions for each other. They both had a flair for publicity and a love for the glamour of the spotlight. They both were rather superficial thinkers but, at the same time, they were charming human beings. They both enjoyed a good political fight and dearly loved to wrangle with their opponents. Both had youth and vigor. Roosevelt was vigorous in his physical life as well as in his writing; White, scorning exercise, was vigorous in his writing. White was such a prolific writer that he well might be called the "Theodore Roosevelt of American literature."

The youthful Kansas editor brought into Theodore Roosevelt's life the sparkling, vivacious, freshness of the West, which Roosevelt loved so much from his own travels in that region. Roosevelt's friendship maintained White in continued national prominence. It is really not astonishing that Roosevelt captured White's admiration in 1897, since, when he became president, he captured the admiration of middle-class America. Roosevelt swept like a meteor across the American panorama. Roosevelt the great showman, with his jutting teeth, his pince-nez, his famous scowl, and his constant chatter about the strenuous life, won for himself a position of tremendous prestige that faded somewhat, however, after his death.

In 1897 Roosevelt's mind was stirring and grappling with some of the problems created by the rise of industrial America. He told White in their initial meeting that when he was police commissioner of New York City he had begun to realize that the government had to see that justice existed between corporations and its workers and between corporations and the consuming public. He also explained to White that Mark Hanna was in politics to protect his industrial empire from the passage of laws that would force him to serve the public. Roosevelt showed the bewildered Kansan that ruthless plutocratic business forces were responsible for corrupt politics. "It was a shock," recalled White. "I was a young protagonist of the divine rule of plutocracy. I think I called it 'brains'! He shattered the foundations of my political ideals. As they crumbled then and there, politically, I put his heel on my neck and I became his man."

*   *   *

While in the East on this trip, the Whites spent some time in New York City visiting S. S. McClure and the managing editor of *McClure's Magazine*, John S. Phillips. During part of their visit, Ida M. Tarbell, feature writer for the magazine, took charge of the Emporia visitors. She once recalled that White was "a little city-shy then, or wanted us to think so. As I was one of the official entertainers of the group, it occasionally fell to me to 'take him by the hand,' as he put it, and show him the town. I could have hardly had a more delightful experience. He judged New York by Kansas standards, and New York usually suffered. His affection and loyalty for his state, his appreciation and understanding of everything that she does—wise and foolish—the incomparable journalistic style in which he presents her are what has made him so valuable a national citizen."

White also met *McClure's* able art editor, Auguste F. Jaccacci, or Jac, "the finest of them all," commented White to Mrs. T. W. Johnston of the Kansas City *Star* upon his return to Emporia in July. On subsequent visits in the next two years he was to start deep friendship with Lincoln Steffens and Ray Stannard Baker, who by that time had joined *McClure's* brilliant staff. The New York visit also afforded White the long-desired opportunity of spending some time with William Dean Howells, early prophet of realism in American fiction.

Back home in Emporia for the rest of the summer of 1897, White plunged into the writing of feature articles for *McClure's* and *Scribner's*. But his literary career was constantly being interrupted by politics. A county election was at hand, and White threw himself wholeheartedly into the task of defeating the Populist ticket.

In the midst of his fight to save the county, he was overjoyed to receive from Theodore Roosevelt a copy of Roosevelt's little book *American Ideals*. The letter that accompanied the book was even more flattering. "I don't know anyone," declared Roosevelt, "who has fought more valiantly or more faithfully than you have fought to bring about the realization of some of these ideals."

The world that had produced those ideals of White's was changing rapidly that fall of 1897. Trouble with Spain over her colony of Cuba was looming on the horizon. Shortly before war came, the Whites, in company with Chauncey L. Williams, made a trip to Clover Bend, Arkansas, to visit midwestern storyteller Alice French, known to the literary world as Octave Thanet. "I remember that Mrs. White and I visited her for several days at Thanford, a plantation near Clover Bend, Arkansas," White once recalled. "It was my first visit to the south and I marveled at the beauty of it and the strangeness of it all. The house at Thanford in those days was a large, frame dwelling, tastefully, even to my eyes then, splendidly furnished. Miss French set a marvelous table. I shall never forget the culinary climax of the visit which was roast pig stuffed with nuts and apricots; such food as would make a Lucullan feast seem like hog and hominy . . . I remember hearing of the sinking of the Maine while we were there, the beginning of the new era. We sat about a log fire and talked of many things; the 'ships and sealing wax' out of which the new era was about to be built. . . ."

The opening of the war with Spain in April, 1898, brought the United States upon the world scene as a great international power, but many of its citizens accepted this new position with extreme reluctance. Ever since Cuba had revolted against Spain in 1895, the editor of the Emporia *Gazette* had denounced any suggestion of American intervention. "The people of Cuba are Mongrels with no capacity for self government," he asserted on December 28, 1896. "If they throw off the tyranny of Spain, they would have a tyrant of their own. They are a yellow-legged, knife-sticking, treacherous outfit, and the people of the United States have nothing in common with them." After the sinking of the *Maine* in Havana harbor and before America declared war on Spain, White editorialized: "As between Cuba and Spain there is little choice. Both crowds are yellow-legged, garlic-eating, dagger-sticking, treacherous crowds . . . It is folly to spill good Saxon blood for that kind of vermin. . . ."

When White's college friend Fred Funston, who had fought with the Cuban army, spoke in Emporia on March 24, 1898, to arouse sympathy for the revolutionists, White still remained hostile to any aid to Cuba. In April, however, when war finally came, White made the best of the situation. He had opposed the war, but now he felt that it was his patriotic duty to support it. Editorially, he stated on April 27: "War is good for the sorrow that it brings. Whom the Lord loveth He chasteneth. And war, that tears women's hearts and men's limbs, war, that feeds on the flesh of the young men, war, with its tragic gaiety, is good; it is one of God's weapons for fighting the devil in man. Therefore we welcome God's chastening hand. We bow beneath the rod and smile back to Heaven . . ." "This is terrible . . ." White observed many years later.

America went to war in a gay, lighthearted spirit. Editor White expressed the popular feeling of the time in an article for the July, 1898, *McClure's* when he wrote: "Populists stopped watching the money power, Republicans ceased troubling themselves over repudiation, Democrats forgot the deficit. A simple but great emotion, that of patriotic joy, was stirring the people, and they moved as men move under stress of strong passion."

During the course of the war European powers, except Great Britain, were hostile toward the United States. Great Britain encouraged American expansion at Spain's expense, and there was some talk of an Anglo-American alliance. White was opposed to such a step. "All that we need," he declared, "is to keep out of other people's quarrels and to keep our hands off other people's property."

Although most Americans went to war to free the Cubans, this nation emerged from the conflict with an overseas empire. When the United States acquired the Philippines, it became a Pacific power. White thoroughly believed in the superiority of Anglo-Saxon peoples, but he did not want his country to acquire these islands. Finally, he bowed to what seemed inevitable and editorialized on March 20, 1899: that "Only Anglo-Saxons can govern themselves . . . It is the Anglo-Saxon's manifest destiny to go forth as a world conqueror. He will take possession of all the islands of the sea. He will exterminate the peoples he cannot subjugate. This is what fate holds for the chosen people. It is so written. Those who would protest will find their objections overruled. It is to be."

White did not adopt this new attitude of the inevitability of American expansion, an attitude which was sweeping through the entire country, without great reluctance. "What is to be will be . . ." he observed. "And yet thousands of people cannot help longing for the old order. They cannot but feel that something good has gone, and that this promiscuous throwing about of the boundaries of the world, this widening of duties, this deepening of responsibilities brings a hardship with it and a loss of the old-time individual freedom." At best, the 31-year-old editor was a reluctant expansionist. There seemed to be no other way out. He had to bow before destiny, but he could feel remorse for the simple days of the past before the United States acquired world responsibilities.

* * *

The Spanish-American War, in White's opinion, produced one constructive result. It elevated Rough Rider Theodore Roosevelt to the governorship of New York. "No other American since Lincoln has furnished as much common sense in his public utterances as Theodore Roosevelt," White declared in the *Gazette* on September 24, 1898. "He should be made governor of New York and president of the United States." On June 23, 1899, when Governor Roosevelt traveled through Kansas en route to Las Vegas to attend a reunion of the Rough Riders, he invited White to ride on the train with him part of the way. "There is very much that I have to talk over with you," he wrote White. "As you know, you have got the ideas of Americanism after which I am striving . . . And if you have got any more men of the stamp of yourself and Funston, for Heaven's sake bring them along with you to the train." White introduced many Kansas editors to the governor and had the train stop at Emporia for a ten-minute platform appearance.

At White's suggestion, the Kansas press gave Roosevelt's tour excellent publicity, and White proved himself a real prophet by editorializing on June 26: "There is no man in America today whose personality is rooted deeper in the hearts of the people than Theodore Roosevelt. He is more than a presidential possibility in 1904: He is a presidential probability for that year . . . He is the coming American of the earth's twentieth century—a fitting type of a promising epoch." Then, revealing his practical bent, White sent Roosevelt a batch of clippings from the Kansas papers and urged him to write a personal note to each editor.

From Roosevelt came a warm letter thanking him for the clippings and stating: "I cannot tell you how much impressed I was by the rugged look of power in the Kansas man whom I met along the line of the railroad. What a splendid type it is! I can see their faces now. Our country is a pretty good country after all!" As to a presidential boom, he observed, "I am not out for presidential honors at present. I am trying to be a middling good Governor . . ." At this point a Boston newspaperman urged White to organize Kansas for Roosevelt in 1900, but White pointed out that, since President McKinley had a powerful hold on the party organization, it was best to wait until 1904 for Roosevelt.

Just after Roosevelt's Kansas trip, White left for Chicago to visit Chauncey L. Williams and arrange for Doubleday and McClure's publishing firm to buy *The Real Issue* from the now defunct Way and Williams. One day he visited a golf course with Williams and wrote to Mrs. White: "I was down to the golf club this morning and the 'caddies' were the only human beings whom I could really talk to. They seem to take me into fellowship and appreciate my view of the situation thoroughly. I was introduced to any number of fellows who were very brown and very sweaty and very much out of breath, but they talked a strange gibberish and I could not make them understand even the sign language. . . ."

When the negotiations were completed with Doubleday and McClure, White hurried home to Emporia to write three additional boyhood stories for *McClure's Magazine* and to prepare all the stories for book publication that fall. "I cannot tell you the satisfaction that I take in knowing that we are going to have some more of your Boyville stories," wrote Ida M. Tarbell, "they have been one of the joys of my life for the past two years . . ."

Every morning at four, White arose and worked on this assignment. He was not only completing these stories and running the paper, but he was doing his best to elect the county Republican ticket and attending meetings of the Republican State Central Committee, building a new office building, moving into a new house, writing two stories for *Scribner's Magazine*, and running a street fair in Emporia. As he wrote to Charles F. Scott of the Iola *Register*, "I belong to the burdened and oppressed laboring classes."

The White-sponsored street fair was held September 28-30, 1899. For two months before the fair, the *Gazette* publicized it by carrying front-page stories about the gala attractions to be offered the public. Through his friendship with Paul Morton of the Santa Fe, he arranged for excursion trains to run from various parts of the state. Through Republican boss Cy Leland, he made arrangements for Indians to be present from one of the reservations. Working with the Young Men's Business Association, White raised money from Emporia merchants and citizens to underwrite the expenses. From his contacts with *McClure's Magazine*, he arranged for the first automobile seen in Kansas to be shipped for the fair from Chicago. When the Emporia *Republican* urged farmers to stay away from White's fair, the *Gazette* stated that the fair was really a town institution, and that the *Republican*'s opposition wouldn't hurt: "That paper has neither prestige, influence nor subscribers."

The street fair was an immense success. There was a farmers' parade, a flower parade, a colored-baby show, a cakewalk for the children, innumerable booths for farm products and town merchants' wares, and amusements. The climax of the three-day celebration was a parade in which the automobile was driven through Emporia's streets. Tremendous crowds turned out to see their first horseless carriage driven by E. H. Brown of Chicago. In the car with Brown were Governor W. E. Stanley, a Pottawatomie Indian chief, and William Allen White. "A crowd, the like of which never before had filled the town," the town historian wrote, "came on the big day to see with their own eyes this wonderful vehicle." The success of the fair was a crowning personal triumph for the young editor who had been in Emporia only four years. By now he had outstripped his competitors and was a powerful factor in local and state affairs.

Only one incident marred the street fair. As one newspaper reported it:

. . . Needless to say it was a great success—the best Emporia ever saw. There was one feature, however, that did not "come off" as advertised. It was the colored-baby show. Everything promised well until the last moment. The babies—fifty of them—with their mothers were on the stage in spick-and-span dresses, the judges were taking notes, the band was playing soft airs and Editor White's face wore the smile usually reserved for subscribers who call to pay a year in advance.

At this critical juncture some godless farmhand away back in the crowd of 500 spectators began to whistle "All Coons Look Alike to

Me." Instantly the audience took up the refrain and before the band could get in its work there was a combined whistling and vocal concerto that completely broke up the baby show. The judges retired to the rear of the stage to smother their risibilities, the band broke away from its leader to swell the popular air and Editor White's jaw fell six inches.

When the music seceded the mothers on the platform decided it was time to quit. In a towering rage they hastily threw shawls over the heads of their babies and with one accord filed off the stage, shaking a fist at poor White as they descended the ladder. . . .

A month after the successful street fair, Doubleday and McClure published White's second book of short stories, *The Court of Boyville*. By the opening of the new year, forty-five hundred copies had been sold. When the publishers suggested that they would push *The Court of Boyville* and his first book, *The Real Issue*, by inserting "What's the Matter With Kansas?" in the latter volume, White was enraged. "Nothing could displease me more," he wrote his publishers. ". . . If I have any rights, title, interest or alimony in that book, allow me once now, for all and forever, to undo any hint or suggestion of using "What's the Matter With Kansas" in it . . . for Heaven's sake let the dead past bury its dead. . . ."

The Court of Boyville was a nostalgic picture of his childhood days in El Dorado. It was very similar to what he was to write many years later in his autobiography. In *The Court of Boyville* he depicted all the pathos of boyhood against a background consisting of barns, the open prairie, and virgin woods. A superintendent of schools from Russell, Kansas, rather unwisely assailed White's book and urged that it be suppressed because he ". . . made a hero out of the 'toughest boy in town' and a fool out of the polite, well-dressed and well-behaved boy." The Kansas City *World* reported that immediately innumerable teachers rallied to White's defense "and made it warm for his traducer."

White had been over three years writing the sketches that appeared in *The Court of Boyville*. "It is the biggest job that I have tackled yet," he had confided to Chauncey L. Williams on November 30, 1897. Some critics have felt that White would have become a leading American literary figure in the Mark Twain tradition had he continued to produce stories of the Boyville type. He was busy, however, not in just one career but in three. In addition to literary work, he was running the *Gazette*, and he was also devoting large amounts of time to politics. He once wrote to such a critic and observed that ". . . probably I would have written more books, if I had not been interested in Kansas politics. But at that I think much of my health and happiness is due to the fact that I have carried my eggs in three or four baskets. . . ."

The completion of *The Court of Boyville* had been delayed by White's political career and by the writing he was doing for various magazines. A few months before *The Court of Boyville* was published, he had started to write a series of fictionalized articles on politics for *Scribner's Magazine*. The first appeared in June, 1899, and the second was published that November. White was now in the position where he could ask as much as three hundred dollars for such a story. He wrote three more for *Scribner's* over the next two years, and all five were published in book form in 1901 under the title of *Stratagems and Spoils*.

"The Man on Horseback," which appeared in the November, 1899, *Scribner's* was the story of a powerful businessman who defied the people and forced his streetcar franchises through a city council after he had corrupted it with bribes. "I think the 'Man on Horseback' almost your strongest bit of work," wrote Governor Roosevelt. "There is a certain iron grimness about the tragedy with its mixture of the sordid and the sublime that made a very deep impression on me . . ." William Dean Howells, who came to Emporia to lecture on November 9, said that the story "seemed to me so perfect in its way that I should not have known how to better it."

Howells's visit to Emporia was a gala day for the Whites. They held a dinner in his honor and had Mr. and Mrs. Victor Murdock of the Wichita *Eagle*, Alexander Butts of the *Star*, and Miss Louise Jones and Miss Martha Wooster of the English department at the Emporia Normal School as their guests. As White once related the story of the dinner:

A brand new spic and span hired girl had come that day for the occasion. It was her first town job. She lived over by Reading and probably her folks had to tie her to get shoes on her. The idea was to serve the dinner in courses, soup, the quail, a salad mixed at the table, and a mince pie—it being in November; then coffee and candy, raisins, nuts and things. The new girl stood by and batted her eyes and said "yes," as she listened to the instructions. The quails went into the oven just before the guests were called, so all hands sat down and the soup came on all right.

The talk was pretty good. Victor Murdock and Alex Butts were good single-handed dinner table talkers and never let chattery cross talk break up the dinner. Mr. Howells also was putting out his line— a good one! Then suddenly, in the door with the quails came Mrs. J. M. McCown, who lived near-by and unbeknownst to the hostess had poked her nose in the kitchen to see how things were going, as two or three other neighbors had just before dinner. Mrs. "Mac" found the new girl with her hat on and her bundle in her hand, just about ready to jump. Answering an inquiry the new girl said "My God, I can't do it. I have got it all mixed up. I don't know which goes when." So Mrs. McCown took a look in the oven and assumed command of the regiment. When she appeared with the quail she gave the hostess a wink and the host a dirty look, indicating he should keep his mouth shut, and the dinner went on.

After the mince pie was served with the cheese, Mrs. McCown was invited to sit down and from that minute all went merry as a marriage bell. Whereupon Mrs. "Mac" explained what had happened in the kitchen, and that final course was the best of the evening. And how Howells enjoyed it! How Alex Butts threw his head back and laughed, and Victor had to be told three times, he enjoyed the story so much.

Since that day men who were to be president and men who had been president have sat around that oval table. Major generals, cabinet officers, powerful politicians, literary pundits and J. P. Morgan's family have poked their pink toes under it. But no one ever sat there of whom the host and hostess stood in such awe then and since, the greatest man of them all.

Two days after the dinner in Howells's honor, White was extremely flattered to receive a letter from the editor of the *Saturday Evening Post* asking him to write for its editorial page. White turned the offer down saying: "I have kind of gotten in a rut, here in Emporia, running a country daily by day, and writing short stories by night, so that I do not believe that I can think of anything interesting to the readers of the 'Post' . . ." More than likely this was not the real reason for rejecting the offer. He probably did not want to tie himself down to regular editorials for fear he would run out of ideas and produce a dull and turgid column. For this very reason he was to refuse other enticing offers of this type in years to come. When he had nothing to say, no editorials appeared in the *Gazette,* but he wouldn't be able to do this if he wrote a column for someone else. He was a man of moods and wrote his best editorials when inspired by some impressive man or dynamic event. He could write in different styles reflecting his feeling at the moment. These moods he translated into such simple, easy Kansas vernacular that the words seemed to dance across the page.

* * *

White's writing at the turn of the century was beginning to display more maturity and to reflect the growing clamor for the regulation of trusts and monopolies. He himself was developing a deeper insight into life and was beginning to understand that there was need of reform in American society. "The Gazette is not afraid of the trust bogie," declared White on February 26, 1900, "but when any corporation develops the greed of a beast, it forfeits consideration of man." White was warm in his commendation when Governor Roosevelt asserted that "It is well to remember on the one hand that the adoption of what is reasonable in the demands of the reformers is the surest way to prevent the adoption of what is unreasonable. . . ."

The governor thanked White for his praise and observed that ". . . you are among the men whose good opinion I crave and desire to earn by my actions. I rank you with, for instance, Judge Taft of Cincinnati and Jim Garfield of Cleveland, and with the men whom I am trying to get around me here, men of high ideals who strive to achieve those ideals in a practical way, men who want to count for decency and not merely prattle as to why others do not so count. . . ." Of White's fictionalized political story in the current *Scribner's,* "The Mercy of Death," dealing with a United States senator who used his office to make killings on the stock market and inner trades with business forces in return for favorable votes in the Senate, Roosevelt wrote: "The study is something unique and it is of really tremendous force. I do not know when I have ever seen anything like it. I would like to have it distributed as a tract among certain people I know!"

The approaching presidential and state elections occupied much of White's time during the spring and summer of 1900. When the Bryan Democrats urged the direct election of United States senators, White's reply revealed that he was not yet a progressive thinker. "The election of senators by a direct vote of the people," charged White, "will elevate men to the Senate who are as cheap as the men elected governors. Any cheap screw can be a governor." Furthermore, the convention system of selecting candidates was immune from reformers' influence and amenable to financial interests, which was desirable, White asserted, since the latter represented the highest intelligence. The next editorial stated that J. R. Burton of Topeka was in Washington lobbying for some Indian lands in which he was financially interested. Burton was to be elected Republican senator the following year by the state legislature; yet White's mind was still so fuzzy that he did not see that the boss-dominated convention and state legislature was the mechanism through which special interests secured control of United States senators.

When rumors reached Kansas in May, 1900, that Governor Roosevelt was to be run for the vice-presidency, White wrote him: "I most sincerely hope that circumstances will keep you out of that. I cannot think of anything that would be more inept than to put you among the Mummies for the next four years. It seems to me that your work is in New York State . . ." But White did not take into account Republican boss Thomas Platt of New York. In order to get Roosevelt out of New York politics and kill him politically, Platt maneuvered the Republican convention into nominating Roosevelt as vice-president. How could Platt have foreseen that an assassin's bullet would raise that "madman" Roosevelt to the presidency? When Roosevelt received the nomination, White with greater omniscience than he realized told the Rough Rider: "Providence has a bigger work for you than I can imagine, and so with an implicit faith in Providence, and a firm belief in

Republican victory, I desire to congratulate you upon your place upon the Republican ticket. . . ."

White had been planning to cover the Republican convention for McClure's newspaper syndicate, but the birth of a son, William Lindsay White, on June 17 kept him at home. "He is our first born that has lived," White wrote, "and he is a strong little ten pounder. His name is Bill and anyone who calls him Willie or Will is going to be put out on the first ballot." Sallie White had been very ill just before the birth of her son. As Will wrote an old Kansas City friend, ". . . my wife has gone down into the Valley of the Great Shadow and has come up and is getting well and strong."

From June to November, 1900, the *Gazette* carried the Republican ticket at its masthead. Enthusiastic praise was forthcoming for McKinley and Roosevelt, Governor Stanley, and the entire state ticket. When Democratic orators denounced the Republican party as the party of imperialism, White, who once himself had been opposed to overseas empire, replied: "The White man's might has made right for three thousand years. It is in every deed or conveyance or legal instrument in the civilized world, and it's not going to change for Mr. Bryan."

Just before the campaign drew to a close, the November *McClure's Magazine* appeared with a sketch of Mark Hanna by the *Gazette* editor. It was a superficial portrait at best. There was no hint that Hanna had entered politics in order to obtain franchises and privileges for his business activities. Instead, with the soft spot that White always had for Hanna, Hanna was depicted as the most representative American of his day. "No better evidence may be found today that the United States has a representative government than is found in the dominance of Hanna in the majority political party in this nation," wrote White. "Hanna is a representative American. He is the American average. . . . Mr. Bryan, emotional, fanatic, raw, represents American movements when mob spirit rages; but Hanna, with his apparent faults, which he does not deny, nor his friends try to conceal, and with his undeniable virtues—thrift, industry, practical sense, a cash-register conscience, fidelity, love of truth—with his efficiency—and that covereth a multitude of sins—with his sense of humor, that anchors him to sanity, Hanna is a walking, breathing, living body of the American spirit."

After the Republican victory that November, the Whites visited New York City to gather material for further sketches of American politicians for *McClure's Magazine*. While they were in New York, White was offered a fabulous salary to remain there and write for *McClure's*. The Associated Press dispatch for November 30 stated that White was going to sell the *Gazette* and work in the East. The story, however, mentioned that White had denied the authenticity of the dispatch. The following day the Kansas City *Star* ran an editorial entitled "William Allen White and Kansas," pointing out that White did not have to deny the dispatch since, "It is safe to say that Mr. White will live in Kansas all of his days, and die there . . . He is a Kansan through and through . . . The vigor and pungency of his style have been assimilated from the vitalizing Kansas air . . . Great is Kansas, and William Allen White is its prophet."

Forty years later White, reminiscing over the incident, wrote: "That was in 1900 and the young man just turning 30 with quite a shock of rusty-copper-bronze hair, who, at the time, weighed about 227 pounds stripped for the ring, is now baldish, 185, neat, red-eyed, a bit toddly, well into his seventies and he has stayed put all these years." Had White followed the trek of the other young midwestern writers to the East, he never would have become the eloquent spokesman of small-town America. Money he would have had, but he never could have gained the widespread reverence that his name commanded during the last fifteen or twenty years of his life. When he bought the *Gazette* he decided that small-town journalism was his way to fame. Although *McClure's* might offer great financial return, it did not present as sure a road as the *Gazette* to prestige, influence, and power in American life.

After White's death, Dorothy Canfield Fisher remembered the joy with which her father, James Canfield, welcomed White's refusal to stay in New York. "I can still see my father, gray-haired by this time, as he (literally) threw his hat into the air with a shout of relief when the Will Whites, having immensely enjoyed their stay in the city as much-feted lions, bought their tickets back to Emporia, Kansas," wrote Mrs. Fisher. "It had been assumed that the small-town man would shake the provincial dust from his feet as soon as a good chance offered, and go to live in some great center. 'Center of what?' the Whites asked the world with a mocking laugh, settling down to stay where they belonged."

During 1901, White was to reject other remunerative offers. John Brisbane Walker, editor of the *Cosmopolitan*, first offered him $5,000 a year to write a monthly feature for the magazine. "I am frank to say that the prospect of getting up an article every month," White replied, "whether it rains or not, appalls me and I would not undertake it for ten times five thousand dollars." Then Walker, through a go-between, offered him $3,000 more to work for the *Cosmopolitan*. "I assume that this would take me out of Kansas," White replied, "and of course I could not go out of Kansas for eight thousand or ten thousand or twice ten thousand. . . . It may jar your opinion of my common sense to know that I turned down a salary of three hundred dollars a week to go to Washington and act as correspondent . . . The 'Gazette' and Emporia furnish me that recreation and the life that I like. They give me an independence that money could not buy."

Shortly after this offer was rejected, S. S. McClure urged him to come East and run a new magazine that McClure was planning, at any salary suitable beginning with ten thousand a year. "Mrs. White whose advice is vital and has good common sense," wrote her husband, "believes that my place in the world for some time to come, is here in Emporia." Years later he explained these refusals to Mark Sullivan by saying ". . . that I would rather live in a country town and be absolutely free to make my own particular kind of a damn fool and to water my own lawn with a 35 foot hose, than to dwell in the tents of the wicked as a court jester . . ."

CHAPTER 7

EXPANDING HORIZONS

"THE EDITOR must be something of a preacher, something of a teacher, something of an autocrat," William Allen White declared on January 26, 1901. "He must take a 'side' in everything. Nothing fails so rapidly as a cowardly paper, unless it is a paper that confuses courage with noise . . ." No one could question White's courage. He was a rugged fighter who tried to execute his editorial preaching by concrete political action. Although many of his views may have been superficial in 1901, they were customarily expressed in a colorful and unique fashion.

Throughout the early months of 1901, White devoted much of his activity to working with Republican State Chairman David Mulvane and recently elected Senator J. R. Burton to secure patronage appointments from Mark Hanna. Although the *Gazette* editor had opposed Burton's election, he wrote to Hanna: "I am trying to work with Mulvane and Mr. Burton and with the Republican organization in this state, despite the fact that I was for the other fellow and have not changed my opinion the slightest about the successful man. However, it would always seem to me that more good can be done by working with the successful man for decency, than kicking against him in indecency. That is why you will probably find me on their side whenever I can serve the interests of decent politics." When Hanna praised White's "political adaptability," White's reply demonstrated his belief in the importance of party organization, and in the workaday world attitude that "if you can't lick 'em, join 'em." "I hope as you say my work 'under the new environment' will indeed prove effective," he told Hanna. "I have not changed my opinion about Burton in the slightest . . . But I am working with him because it has always seemed to me that the fellow who wants the decent thing in politics can get it more certainly by working with the undesirable man who happens to be in power, than by deserting him and letting him spend his power on the bad man in politics."

White thoroughly believed in the process of building a strong party through awarding jobs to deserving workers. To Assistant Postmaster General Joseph L. Bristow, old Kansas newspaper friend, White wrote on April 16, 1901, urging the removal of a local postmaster because the incumbent during the last campaign "when we needed him . . . and were in a mighty rough shape . . . was neither fish, flesh, fowl nor good red herring." When the reappointment of the United States district attorney for Kansas came up, White, eager to help the incumbent, wrote Vice-President Roosevelt for a letter of introduction to Attorney General Philander C. Knox. Roosevelt was only too happy to comply, and his high regard for the 33-year-old editor was to be seen in the sentence he wrote to Knox, saying that there were few men "whom I more cordially respect than I do Mr. White."

White was intensely busy during these months in his two other careers: running the *Gazette* and writing magazine articles. S. S. McClure was pleased with the biographical sketches of current political leaders that White had been writing for his magazine. "Use your skill on topics of the day, or stories of big personalities," McClure told Hamlin Garland, "and you'll make a place for yourself, as Miss Tarbell and William Allen White have done."

The *Saturday Evening Post*, too, began to claim a portion of White's literary production. When Major General Frederick Funston, with a small group of volunteers, hacked his way for three weeks through tropical jungles and captured the Philippine insurgent leader, Emilio Aguinaldo, White celebrated this exploit in a *Post* story. After the completion of this article, White was so engrossed in politics and in running the paper that he told George H. Lorimer, editor of the *Post*, "Don't you crowd me with any ·

more work. I am going to be as busy as a bird pup from now until the middle of October . . ." but he added in a P.S., "My wife who is boss has read this letter— She says to add that if you really want me to do anything else that I'll do it. So probably I will."

Through a hot Kansas summer that burned up the crops, White devoted a large share of his time to the writing of a series of fiction stories for the *Post,* thus demonstrating the importance of Sallie in his decisions. Late in July, White traveled to the rapidly growing Oklahoma Territory, where two million acres of Apache, Kiowa and Comanche land had just been thrown open to white settlers. He was on a *Post* assignment gathering material on one of the last great land rushes in American development. As early as June, wagons had been bringing people to the borders of the new country. The mecca of the land-hungry pilgrims was Lawton, seat of the government land office. White watched as twenty-five thousand people poured into Lawton in the first week of August and built a city of tents. "The crowd that tramped the sod streets of the tented town . . . was an American crowd," wrote White. ". . . It was of the Northland and of the South. Probably never in the world will so many Texas people meet so many Kansas people. Iowa and Arkansas bunked together. Michigan neighbored with Alabama . . . The next generation in the new country, and all over Oklahoma, in fact, where this blending of American types and manners and morals is in progress, will be a wonderful one."

The Kansas editor, who had grown up in the pioneer town of El Dorado, was struck by the lack of a frontier society at Lawton. "If there is any frontier in America," he observed, "it should be found at Lawton. But the Lawton crowd revealed the fact that the West is gone. The gentleman with the fringed leather trousers, who used to ride into the saloon, light his cigar with a five-dollar bill, and then back out with an ardent impulse to plant a crop for the coroner, was not present at Lawton . . . The crowd was a shirt-waist crowd; men wore cuffs, said 'there' instead of 'thar,' ate with their forks, and at night put on pajamas when they went to bed under the big tents that were called hotels . . '. The only men who carried revolvers were the deputy sheriffs . . . The crowd passed quietly into local government. . . ."

*　　*　　*

A few days after his return from Oklahoma, Vice-President Roosevelt wired White to join him at Colorado Springs to discuss Roosevelt's possibilities for the presidential nomination in 1904. One highly amusing and relatively upsetting incident occurred for White during their meeting. White mentioned that he had never scratched the Republican ticket. Roosevelt turned to him, clicked his teeth, scowled and asked, "Is that a boast or a confession?" Then Roosevelt quickly added, "I've scratched the Republican ticket a dozen times and if I live I'll keep on scratching it a dozen times more."

Roosevelt was dreaming of the presidency early in 1901. He already had promises of support from Massachusetts and Illinois. He was now in Colorado to attend a dinner where he was pledged the Colorado delegation. White was with Roosevelt at this dinner, and was asked by the Vice-President to assist in lining up Kansas and Missouri for 1904. When White returned to Emporia, he wrote Cy Leland on August 15, 1901: "Roosevelt wants to see you . . . He wants the friendship of our fellows, and I believe he is a square man and if he wins, will show his appreciation of that friendship in a substantial and manly way."

Three or four days after sending this letter, White went to Topeka to see Leland, and then he wrote to Roosevelt that Leland "believes that no man in the world can come into Kansas and organize the state against you. Leland (as you probably know) handled Kansas for McKinley, when as he says, there was not half the sentiment for McKinley that there is for you now." White added that he and Leland agreed that if New York, Pennsylvania, and Ohio came out for Roosevelt, the nomination was assured. "Leland and I can use our influence with Mr. Hanna in Ohio," White offered. But could the support of Matthew Quay of Pennsylvania and Thomas Platt of New York be counted on? The situation in Missouri was clearly favorable to Roosevelt, White said in the same letter, since he had just talked with the leaders of the party at Kansas City, and they had agreed that the sentiment was overwhelmingly for Roosevelt. "This seems to be kind of a popular uprising like the crusades," White happily told Roosevelt; but he shrewdly added, "Still I am a great believer in the power of money and the legitimate use of it in a campaign. Kansas and Missouri and probably Colorado will not need any but there will be other states where money can be used legitimately by honest men and square decent fellows . . . I would be glad to undertake the job of passing the hat in Kansas."

When Roosevelt received White's letter raising the question of Quay, Platt, and Hanna, he told White that Hanna seemed friendly and that Platt had promised to support him but, "When it comes to Quay, I am really at a loss what to say . . . there are certain things which he has done of which . . . I cannot in any way approve . . ." Immediately, White wrote back: ". . . if I could feel in some way that I had been a truly serious factor in making so good and honest a man president . . . I would have all the pride a soldier has. . . . No one can abhor more than I, dirty politics. . . . So I think, perhaps you have mistaken what I meant in my letter, when I referred to Hanna and to Platt and to Quay. I believe that these men can be made your friends without the sacrifice of the least one of your political ideals or of your personal honor. . . ."

In the midst of these negotiations for the presidency, William McKinley was shot by an anarchist. After visiting McKinley on September 7, the day after the shooting, Roosevelt wrote White that fortunately the President was out of danger. The crime, he observed, was a fearful comment on the teachings of yellow journalism and on the anarchists. White's editorial reaction to the shooting revealed a growing belief that action must be taken to curb exploitation by the captains of industry. "For half a century the greed of the great captains of industry has been almost untrammeled," he charged. White added that he held this group responsible for importing European laborers who had no conception of American ideals and who, therefore, turned to force to solve their problems. A few days after the crime, White traveled to the East to report the western political situation to Theodore Roosevelt and to gather material for further magazine articles.

While in Washington waiting for Roosevelt to return from

McKinley's sickbed, White visited Charles G. Dawes, comptroller of the currency. Roosevelt had given him the following letter of introduction to Dawes: "This is to introduce to you Mr. William Allen White, of Emporia, Kansas. I have spoken to you about him. He is just the salt of the earth, and whatever he says can be relied upon absolutely. He is one of the very few men whom I will absolutely guarantee."

On September 13, 1901, McKinley's condition became very serious, and the following day he died. Roosevelt's ascendancy to the presidential office disturbed the business world. Although he moved cautiously at first, his administration was to launch an attempt to curb the predatory forces. The McKinley administration had been the benevolent handmaiden of plutocracy; the Roosevelt administration was to become the leader of the progressive forces that in September, 1901, were waiting in the wings for their cue to emerge and dominate the stage.

The progressive forces demanded that the federal government regulate industry, finance, and transportation in the interest of the people. Public control of economic forces, they declared, was the only way to retain a liberal democracy in an industrialized society. The progressives built on the groundwork laid by the Populist party and William Jennings Bryan. When William Allen White was frequently asked why he was advocating such reforms since he had opposed them a decade before, he replied that after 1901, reforms could be supported because they were promulgated by successful men, not by "long-haired reformers." White and the rest of the progressives were perfectly willing to admit that they were building upon the agitation of the Populists, and as White aptly described the situation, "The Insurgents caught the Populists in swimming and stole all of their clothing except the frayed underdraws of free silver."

Theodore Roosevelt stirred public opinion and dramatized the progressive cause. He popularized the belief that the greed and lust of the "malefactors of great wealth" must be curbed by the government. "We are engaged," he declared in 1912, "in one of the great battles of the age-long contest waged against privilege on behalf of the common welfare." Roosevelt clarified issues that were obscure to William Allen White and millions of other Americans. Under Roosevelt's imaginative leadership, middle-class America began to realize that equality of opportunity was necessary to preserve freedom in the machine age. "The movement was no longer the cry of the oppressed, but the demand of the aspiring," White later wrote. "It was no longer indignant, it was constructive. Liberalism in that day represented not so much the attack of the have-nots upon the haves as the vision of a just and righteous relation between men; a plan to readjust obvious inequities by governmental agencies."

From 1901 to 1917, Editor White played an ever-increasing role in progressive activities, but at no time was he ever far in advance of the thinking and desires of the average American. He was no scout for social reform like John P. Altgeld, Eugene Debs, or Robert M. LaFollette. He was no profound student of social affairs charting broad new paths to follow. He was just a little ahead of his own middle class, and thus he always remained respectable in their eyes, never lost their confidence, and generally was able to capture their support for a candidate or for an issue. He was a true Rooseveltian—colorful, dramatic, warm and friendly, but with no deep insight into issues, seldom probing beneath the surface, and no dangerous radical although the conservative Republicans thought otherwise.

White's intimate relationship with Roosevelt and the many articles he was to write about the President increased White's own national prominence. White was with Roosevelt the first night that the new President spent in Washington. In addition to White, the party included Nicholas Murray Butler, of Columbia University, and Captain Cowles, and his wife Anna Roosevelt. Recalling this evening, White remarked years later: "I remember that Captain Cowles had little to say. The two Roosevelts, the Colonel and his sister, made the talk. I was shy, over-awed, and tremendously impressed. Professor Butler was keenly observant, appreciative of the scene . . . I remember I sat on the edge of my chair, pop-eyed with wonder, as the young President plunged into the discussion of his plans, of his hopes, of his fears, with a kind of dynamic, burning candor that amazed me even though I had seen him several times in action during the four years of our friendship. But now he was President, and it seemed that he should be different. But he was absolutely unchanged. The Captain sat in a deep chair by the unlit grate in the little parlor, watching us wordlessly, occasionally grunting approval, or sniffing his doubt . . . The Captain was not impressed. His eyes began to blink. . . ."

One rather startling and dramatic statement came from Roosevelt. "The young President began to project his imagination into the years," White recalled. " 'But,' he cried, 'my great difficulty, my serious problem will meet me when I leave the White House. Supposing I stay there seven years. Supposing I have a second term, I shall still be young in my early fifties on the shelf, retired, out of it. I know that I can make a fairly good fist of it as President, given a certain amount of luck. But imagine me as an ex-President, dedicating buildings and making commencement speeches, occasionally perhaps the chairman of some convention!' We two youngsters began to protest. There we could say something. A clatter of young voices arose. To us it was a great night, a memorable occasion." But then White happened to look at Captain Cowles. "He had folded his hands across his abdomen. His eyes were closed. His rhythmic breathing told the story. What was this young brother-in-law to him? Not a President, but a pest. Brothers-in-law are always brothers-in-law. Young brothers-in-law are just obstreperous young brothers-in-law when a Captain is in his sixties and is sailing through calm water."

White was in and out of the new President's office during those September days that he was in Washington. All sorts of reformers and newspapermen were crowding Roosevelt's office to find out his plans. Lincoln Steffens has written that one evening the President grabbed White and him and took them for an hour's walk through the streets. "With his feet, his fists, his face and with free words he laughed at his luck," wrote Steffens. "He laughed at the rage of Boss Platt and at the tragic disappointment of Mark Hanna . . . He described what he would do if an assassin attacked him . . . It would have frightened the assassin to see and hear what it was T.R. would have done to him; it may have filled Bill

White with terror; what I sensed was the passionate thrill the President was actually finding in the assassination of his assassin."

* * *

In October, 1901, after White returned to Emporia, Scribner's published his third book, *Stratagems and Spoils*. In these stories White burlesqued the Populists and declared that the only hope for a better society was better individuals. Passing laws would not solve problems, White declared since ". . . human nature which is at the bottom of our ills can't be changed at the next meeting of the legislature. . . . Reform must come from the individual. It is a matter of slow growth. It is not accomplished by enactment of a resolution. . . . No reform can be accomplished, no lasting good may result from a wave of emotion which has jealousy of the poor for the rich and envy of the strong for the weak for its impulse."

All the knowledge White had gained about political conventions and meetings, the history of the Populists, and the danger of corrupt politicians he packed into this book. To meet the problems facing America, White merely advocated the election of good men to office. Legislative reform of business was not an important objective, he maintained. The stories in this book had been written over the period from 1899 to 1901. They represented the conservative White rather than the progressive person he was becoming by the time the book was published. Although the stories were hostile to government control of industry, White, by the fall of 1901, under the influence of Roosevelt, was expounding the need of curbing predatory business forces.

William Dean Howells praised the relentless realism of *Stratagems and Spoils* and said that it formed "a substantial body of political fiction, such as we have so long sighed for . . ." Theodore Roosevelt told Mrs. William E. Borah that he considered the book to be "the best political story ever written," and the Kansas City *Star*, on November 10, 1901, commented: "A Western writer has been expressing Western life, intimately and with sanity . . . he is writing absorbing and truthful stories of life in the West."

On his return to Emporia that fall, White discovered that his friendship with Roosevelt had enhanced his prestige and power in Kansas politics. He discovered, he soon wrote the President, that the entire state thought he was to be "the Mark Hanna in the White House." Actually he did recommend a number of appointments to Roosevelt, but the President did not always accept the recommendations. White failed most notably to secure a post for his old friend Cy Leland. Almost every day from the middle of October to early in 1902, White urged the appointment on Roosevelt. Leland was a hard political boss through whom the railroads, utilities, and packing houses worked to prevent state regulation. As long as a man was loyal to Leland, he did not care what the man represented. He once told Charles Sessions of the Topeka *Capital* that he didn't mind if a man was a "son of a bitch" provided he was "his son of a bitch."

Theodore Roosevelt informed White that powerful people had questioned Leland's honesty. White immediately observed: "He is a blunt man with primitive passions, who is a good hater and a loyal friend. I have never heard of any scandal connected with his name . . . I cannot believe there is anything crooked with Leland and if there was, I would not ask you to appoint him." White held Senator Burton of Kansas responsible for blocking Leland, and told Roosevelt that Burton had the heart of a harlot and was for sale to the highest bidder. Roosevelt was aware of Burton's failings, but, as he wrote White, decent men like Professor James H. Canfield also were opposed to Leland. Roosevelt added that he didn't mind appointing someone whom a senator opposed, but the appointment had to be a man of principle, "because if a fight comes I want to be dead sure my man is white—not, perchance, gray." That Leland might be on the gray side was unwittingly admitted by Leland himself, when he told White that the reason Professor Canfield was against him was that he had forced the State Board of Regents to fire Canfield from K.U. "because of *free trade* proclivities and his Democratic teachings." White explained to his old teacher that the real reason he felt obligated to Leland was that Leland had agreed to help White organize Kansas for Roosevelt the past summer when Roosevelt, as vice-president, was planning for 1904. "Now if I would desert Leland in this situation," White stated, "*believing* him *as I do* to be an *honest* man, I would be a pretty lowdown pup."

During the first week in December, White was in Washington futilely trying to persuade Roosevelt to make the appointment. A short time later, when Leland urged him to go see Roosevelt again, White wisely replied: "Now talking with Roosevelt often does no good, because he does all the talking. But when you can write to him and he can't talk back, you get a chance to put in more." White's loyalty to Leland did not adversely affect Roosevelt's admiration for the Emporia editor. When a Kansas opponent of White's denounced his advocacy of Leland, Roosevelt was quick to rally to White's defense. "I thank you for your letter," Roosevelt wrote, "but don't you think that the implied reflection on White is a little rough? He seems to me to be about as square a man as one could desire."

In the midst of this political fight, White found himself the subject of an attack on another front. Eight days before Christmas, he received a telegram saying that Senator Thomas Platt was going to sue him for libel for his article on Platt in the current *McClure's*. The telegram also informed him that Platt had told Roosevelt: "I will get that fellow's scalp if it is the last thing I ever do." White wired this statement to John S. Phillips on December 17, 1901, and observed: "However I shall sleep well tonight and have no fear that if he does get my scalp, LePage's liquid glue which is advertised in McClure's Magazine, will stick my scalp on again."

The Platt article was filled with blistering phrases from White's agile pen. Platt was described as having an "itch for power," as "intriguing with both sides" in a fight, as being "implacable" and "ravening for revenge," and as being "merely a magnified type of hundreds of earthworms boring beneath the roots of local self-government . . . burrowing silently yet with incalculable power, loosening the soil, sagging foundations . . ." White accused Platt of taking money from corporations and in return guaranteeing them favorable laws by the New York legislature. White also described how Governor Roosevelt had blocked a dishonest appointment that Platt desired. As a senator, White asserted, Platt was a small figure, and "holds men by fear rather than by fealty . . . He has the dry, purple-pink parchment skin of senility . . ."

Platt charged that the "so-called biography" "was made of a

tissue of lies" and that there was "malice in every line of it." Immediately, White was again in the spotlight of the national stage. Platt's threatened libel suit, however, did not seem to bother him. He wrote Scribner's that they should capitalize on all the free advertising in the papers about his name and push *Stratagems and Spoils*. "It seems to me," he wrote his publishers on December 20, 1901, "that if you could get a window downtown in New York, where old man Platt wouldn't throw rocks at it, we could clean up a thousand or so copies while the scrap is on. I am not as you observe, a modest wood violet by a mossy stone . . ."

Since White and Roosevelt were so intimate, Platt suspected that the President had given White some of the inside information used in the sketch. Roosevelt actually had helped White on the article by arranging an appointment for him with Platt. Platt warned Roosevelt that no man who was White's friend could also be his friend. When Platt left the White House, after this interview, he told reporters that White would never enter the White House again. When White heard that Platt suspected Roosevelt of giving him information, he wrote to the President's secretary denying that Roosevelt ever had said anything to him about Platt. Knowing, however, Theodore Roosevelt's voluble tongue and his lack of caution in describing people, there is little doubt that he had supplied his good friend with many intimate details and many savory phrases.

A good row like that developing over the Platt story was relished by White. He wrote A. F. Jaccacci at *McClure's* not to worry, since "no twelve human beings could be found who would give Platt a character. . . ." Roosevelt wasn't particularly disturbed either over Platt's insinuations. He told White that "you need not bother about the incident at all. It was only a crumpled rose-leaf in a bed that contains much more serious obstacles to sleep—although I find it pretty comfortable anyhow!" The controversy attracted widespread newspaper comment. The New York *World*, on December 19, carried two cartoons by Powers depicting Platt dressed as an Indian and armed with a hatchet on the war path looking for White. The cartoons so pleased the Emporia editor that he had the originals framed and hung in his office, and he wrote the *World* in good Roosevelt language: "They were bully.

Where did he get . . . my Adonis-like shape." Platt, however, had his defenders. After he dropped the libel suit, the Boston *Journal* praised him and asserted: "Mr. Platt did well to cool off and await some worthier target. Why should he take Mr. William Allen White seriously? Mr. White is an odd sort of a humorist; that's all."

Senator Albert Beveridge of Indiana thought the Platt article was "marvelous," and he told George Lorimer of the *Saturday Evening Post:* "I was so captivated that I immediately sat down and wrote him a letter of appreciation." Beveridge then urged Lorimer to persuade White to run for the Senate. "If I ever get to know him in a personal way," Beveridge promised, "I shall jab him fuller of this with the hypodermic syringe of suggestion than the cocaine fiend fills himself with dope." From this time on White and Beveridge were close friends, although White was never lured into running for the Senate.

Thomas Platt never went through with his threatened libel suit. Although he had told reporters, "I intend to use all my money, all my power, to bring about the punishment of this man who has so maliciously attacked me," when *McClure's* staff let him know through a mutual acquaintance that they would welcome the suit, and that they had a great deal more material on his past, the suit was not heard of again. The fitting climax to the Platt incident came under President Roosevelt's guidance. While White was visiting him at the White House the following summer, Roosevelt decided to have some fun at Platt's expense. Roosevelt was sure that Platt didn't remember White's face, and, of course, Roosevelt was quite aware that Platt had told reporters that White never would be admitted to the White House again. Roosevelt seated White in his office and said: "Platt will be in pretty soon. He won't know you. I won't introduce you, but I thought you would like it." White sat through the interview and Platt was completely unaware of his identity. When Platt left, Roosevelt burst out laughing, and White conspicuously walked out of the office past the newspaper reporters just to make sure they saw him in the White House.

* * *

In the first weeks of the new year, while the Platt suit was pending, White worked as hard as ever editing the *Gazette*, writing additional magazine articles, and participating in Republican party politics. In the midst of writing an article on Senator Ben Tillman, he broke down. Ever since 1895 he had been moving at a killing pace. After working all day to build the paper into the leading journal in the town, he would stay up all hours of the night writing articles and books. During the third week in January, his nerves went to pieces. On January 21, 1902, he wrote to Ed Howe that he had to leave Kansas for a rest and asked Howe to announce it in the Atchison *Globe* rather than have it appear first in the *Gazette*.

Sallie White went with her husband first to Colorado, then to California, and finally to Catalina Island. For two months he was so nervous and exhausted that he could not even read newspapers or his letters. While the Whites were away, they left the *Gazette* in the capable hands of Walt Hughes, the business manager, and Laura M. French, the city editor. Not until late spring was White recovered enough to return home. Even as late as July 23, he wrote John S. Phillips: "I haven't been very well this summer, that is to say I haven't been strong."

When White returned to Emporia, he found a battle raging over the appointment of the local postmaster. He and Major Hood, town banker, had opposed the nominee of Senator Burton and the local congressman, J. M. Miller, their factional opponents within the Republican party. Roosevelt had told White on January 31, 1902, that he would not make the Burton appointment, and that "if any change is made . . . it will only be for someone who is entirely satisfactory to the patrons of the office, and especially to yourself." By June, Roosevelt was greatly embarrassed by the situation, since he had accepted other congressmen's recommendations for post offices but not Miller's. "I wish I could see you on here soon," he wrote White. Several weeks later Roosevelt informed Miller that his recommendation could not be appointed and that some other name had to be submitted.

From 1908 to 1916, when White was bucking the Republican machine group, this post-office fight was used by his foes in an attempt to discredit him. It was charged that the successful candidate paid White $1,200 to get the position, but White denied it, and there is no evidence to dispute his statement. Another charge that his opponents were to bring against him was that he was politically dishonest. In 1899, White had bought a lot for the *Gazette* building adjacent to an empty government lot. The government had acquired this land in 1891 for the construction of a post-office building, but the depression ended the project. When good times returned, the government began to erect public buildings again. White immediately pushed Emporia's need for a building, and he wrote the chairman of the Congressional Committee in a joking mood that he would even support his political foe, Congressman Miller, if the building was authorized. When he fought Miller's campaign for re-election, Miller charged that White had promised to support him in return for the post office. This, declared White, was "a perfectly absurd twisting of facts into an untruth," but his own humorous bent and his gift of expression had lent itself to this misinterpretation. Throughout his life, White had a penchant for writing in a humorous mood things which his political enemies were able to twist and make appear sinister. He was continually involving himself in hot water because of his flippant and impish style.

White's close relationship with the President in 1902 was demonstrated by this post-office appointment and by the two articles that he wrote publicizing Theodore Roosevelt's work in the presidency. Although there is no direct evidence, there is every indication that Roosevelt inspired these articles and was relying on White's writing ability to sell his administration to the people. "Roosevelt is the hero of the average man," declared White in an article for the *Saturday Evening Post* for October 4, 1902. "There are well-known bands or gangs of nomadic financial marauders strolling over the American stock markets with no more moral sense than pirates," added White. "They are drunk with the power that crass wealth gives them over American civilization . . . New laws are required to bring these brutes to the halter." Obviously, Roosevelt was the man to curb these monopolists, since he was "looming up as the great national leader, bigger than any party, the epitome of his times, the great American."

White was now conscious of the need of curbing the "malefactors of great wealth." At about the same time that he came to this realization, his good friends on *McClure's Magazine* stumbled on muckraking. The issue of October, 1902, printed an article by Claude Wetmore and Lincoln Steffens on "Tweed Days in St. Louis" and in November one by Ida M. Tarbell on the "History of the Standard Oil." In January, 1903, the magazine carried articles by Steffens, Tarbell, and Ray Stannard Baker, exposing the corruption to be found in business and politics. The public response to these exposures was so great that other magazines entered the field, and by 1904 the major magazines were all making ringing attacks upon the abuses and evils of American life. The most sensational development of the progressive movement had been launched.

Lincoln Steffens, the greatest of the muckrakers, wrote a series on city governments and pointed out that the source of bad government was not the politician but the businessman who corrupted the politician in order to obtain favors. While he was exposing corruption in the cities, he wrote *McClure's:* "If we take up the states, I would prefer to wait for William Allen White to write the articles . . ." Actually, White never wrote muckraking articles. He probably was not constitutionally equipped to write the type of exposé articles that were capturing the public imagination. White's romantic, optimistic nature did not lend itself to the rather gloomy, hopeless attitude taken by many of the muckrakers as they unearthed the magnitude of business and political corruption. He did, however, learn a great deal from his muckraking friends, and there is little doubt that they opened his eyes to the immediate need of regulating business if democratic society was to survive.

The muckrakers exposed many evils that Theodore Roosevelt promptly took action upon, and there is no question but that their work made the task of enacting progressive laws easier. Roosevelt, however, was frequently irritated at the muckrakers' constant hammerings and denounced them for seeing only the filth of society. One day, to cheer him up, Finley Peter Dunne informed the President: "William Allen White has promised to take up the 'merry sunshine' work in a more serious and effective fashion, and

I look to him to save our countrymen from the suicide which is the logical consequence of believing all we read now-a-days."

In February, 1903, while *McClure's* staff was gathering material for further muckraking articles, the Whites traveled to Washington, where White obtained information for a series of political articles in the *Saturday Evening Post*. In these articles White praised Roosevelt's launching of antitrust suits against monopolies, and asserted that the President was "an attorney for the people" struggling against Wall Street domination of the country. Roosevelt was honest, brave, and wise, added White. He would lead the fight of the people against the barons of high finance.

Through most of 1903 White carried on a voluminous correspondence with the President over an investigation of frauds in the Post Office Department, and Kansas Senator Burton's connections with these frauds. He told the state's newly elected senator, Chester I. Long: "I have but one reason for being in politics and that is to wipe from the name of Kansas the smut-pot of 'Burton in the Senate.' " White wrote Senator Henry Cabot Lodge that unless Roosevelt forced an investigation of postal affairs in Kansas, the Postmaster General would try to forget the entire affair. "The time may come," he advised Lodge, "when you may be told that the sentiment in the West favors covering this business up for the good of the party. This is not the truth. The good of the party out here demands vigorous prosecution of every man who is guilty of fraud . . . I am writing this frankly to you, because I know that you have the President's confidence." Lodge immediately sent the letter to Roosevelt, observing that, "I think you think I have been too much worried about the Post Office matter. White's letter will show you how the situation seemed to him."

After the postal frauds prosecution was set in motion, White gathered material to demonstrate that Senator Burton should be indicted for fraudulent activities. At the same time he persuaded Roosevelt not to appoint a railroad lobbyist, Charles Blood Smith, to a federal judgeship in Kansas. Smith had the backing of both Kansas senators, but White wrote Roosevelt that "His habits are not those of a gentleman, and as a judge he would merely reflect the Wall Street railroad combine. It would be a crime to appoint him." On the basis of White's information, Roosevelt investigated the situation and agreed that White was correct. Then Roosevelt indignantly stated that had he made the Smith appointment it would have been a lasting stain on his administration.

During the spring and early summer of 1904, White's efforts to link Senator Burton with fraudulent activities and his advocacy of the investigation of corruption in the Post Office Department bore fruit. In addition to White, many other people had urged an investigation of postal affairs, and on March 7, 1903, Roosevelt appointed Joseph L. Bristow, fourth assistant postmaster, to do the work. Bristow had already gained a great deal of prestige by unearthing frauds in the American postal service during the occupation of Cuba following the Spanish-American War. It took courage on Roosevelt's part to launch the investigation. Many Republican congressmen were closely associated with the postal officials accused of grafting. These officials, through their control of rural free delivery routes and salaries and allowances, had freely granted patronage to the congressmen. Naturally these officials, in order to protect themselves, worked through the congressmen to try to kill the investigation. Roosevelt was warned that an exposé might endanger the party's chance in 1904.

White consistently urged Roosevelt to back Bristow's investigation, and insisted that it would help Roosevelt in 1904 rather than kill his chances for election. Working with Bristow and the President, White sent them every scrap of information he could gather on the postal situation and on Senator Burton. In March, 1904, Burton was convicted of a felony in connection with his official position. White could take a great deal of satisfaction in the conviction. At the beginning of Roosevelt's term of office, he had warned him to beware of Burton. Furthermore, White had turned over to federal authorities some of the information that led to Burton's conviction.

About the same time that Burton was sentenced, Joseph L. Bristow presented his official report that led to seventy-four indictments, including the indictment of men as high up in the postal service as August W. Machens, general superintendent of the free-delivery system. Bristow sent his close friend White a copy of his report and, in the crusading fashion that was later to characterize his term in the Senate, told White: "This report that stirred up

Congress so much, in fact, did not amount to so much after all. The real animus behind most of these members is their friendship for Beavers and Machen . . . Some of the men who stormed about this alleged 'Bristow Report' are probably mad because Machen was indicted and convicted. I do not intend to pay any attention to the storm and fury, but go ahead and attend to my business and let results take care of themselves. I have done nothing but what was right and am willing to stand by my record."

When politicians favorable to the indicted postal officials tried to imply all types of corruption and chicanery on Bristow's part, White wrote a long letter to the President revealing the ridiculous nature of the charges. This letter was apparently effective, since White soon after heard from a friend in Washington that "your letter to the president regarding Bristow certainly turned a trick . . . the things said were sufficient to send the Kansas Bunch in run to cover."

White celebrated the convictions of Burton and the crooked postal authorities by writing an article for the September, 1904, *McClure's*. The article was timed to assist Roosevelt's bid for election, and to strengthen his hand with the public against the politicians in case any more investigations were necessary. White praised Roosevelt for giving the country a moral uplift, for having the courage to buck politicians within his own party, and for pushing the Bristow investigation to completion. In the case of the Burton conviction, White stated: "He is the first President of the United States who has pushed a case against a crooked United States senator . . . A man whom one class of thieves hate all thieves will fear; that is why Roosevelt is regarded as an unsafe man in certain business circles, where business methods and traditions license acts which, scraped of the veneer of high finance, are mere stealing."

* * *

The political bug that Roosevelt had planted in White's mind several years before, as to the absurdity of always supporting the straight Republican ticket, began to bite White in the summer of 1904. On July 20, he wrote a militant editorial urging the people of Missouri to elect Joseph Folk, the Democratic candidate, to the governorship of that state. Folk had achieved nation-wide publicity as a result of his investigations of corrupt politicians in St. Louis and of the businessmen who had corrupted these politicians. White, several months before his endorsement of Folk, had visited St. Louis and met Folk. He was greatly impressed with the man, particularly since Folk had helped unearth some material on Burton.

White's editorial bluntly stated that all the corruptors of politics would be against Folk. Therefore, it was the duty of every decent Republican to vote for Folk. Observing that he himself was a good Republican, White declared: "But there are sometimes considerations in politics greater than party—considerations of honest government. Honest government is the first thing required in this nation. Honest men in office honestly earning their salaries and giving the people full value received for their taxes—these considerations are more important than Republican victory or Democratic victory . . . Parties are means for good government and not its ends. A citizen should not 'belong' to a party, in the sense that the party's action and organization should bind him with a silly prejudice to vote for what his good sense and his conscience tell him is wrong merely to conform to party regularity . . . It is a question above party, and if a similar situation existed in Kansas, the Gazette would be for the Democratic nominee with all the vigor it could command. It is better to be a bolter to a party than a traitor to a state."

White had advanced a long way in his thinking on party regularity from the days just past, when he had scorched anyone for leaving the Republican party to join the Populists. In this editorial, he was also foreshadowing his own bolt from the Republican party in 1912. The editorial on Folk attracted nation-wide attention. The New York *World*, for instance, on July 25 editorialized: "In William Allen White, Mr. Folk has found a champion, who it seems to us, represents about as high a type of civic and journalistic responsibility as the country affords. Each is worthy of the other. The Gazette editorial has been generally reproduced and favorably commented upon."

White's support of Folk seems to have helped his election materially, since White's K.U. classmate, Herbert Hadley, Republican candidate for attorney general in Missouri, wrote to White protesting his support of Folk. White also indirectly aided Folk by supplying some information to Samuel Hopkins Adams for his article on the Missouri campaign printed in *Collier's Weekly*. White told Adams that Roosevelt had expressed to him the wish that Folk be elected. "If I had poked him up a little further," White wrote on November 9, 1904, "I think I could have got him to advise me to write an inspired letter saying so. When you get the 'Rough Rider' in an inspired mood he is a great man to be inspired but on the other hand when he thinks it over calmly and deliberately his inspiration cools and he is not so badly inspired as he was . . . Don't you know that I used to think that McKinley psychologically had no private life. He was a statue in a park. On the other hand I think that Roosevelt has no public life. He is constantly parading around in his pajamas, which are becoming enough in their place but which frequently give people a shock. . . ."

During the last week in June, White attended the Chicago convention, where Theodore Roosevelt was chosen as the Republican presidential candidate. Roosevelt's nomination had been a certainty for over a year. According to White, Roosevelt made the politicians take a back seat at the convention. "The people are for Roosevelt," asserted White, "and the politicians know it and obey." The reason Roosevelt was strong with the people, declared the Emporia editor, was that he would fight graft and was determined to check wealthy corporations from buying political favors. "He is driving the money changers out of the temple," White added.

From Chicago, White traveled to St. Louis to report the Democratic convention. A story that was to be widely circulated after White had become a folk hero to middle-class America was that while attending a Democratic convention—it could have been any from 1904 to 1940—he was called upon to deliver the invocation. He was supposed to have refused with the comment: "I don't want God to know I am here." "Nothing like it ever happened," White once explained. "But I am always glad to see it. It puts my best foot forward."

The Democrats at their 1904 convention bowed to conservatism. Bryan, with his advanced stand on government regulation of business, had carried the party to defeat twice. He was, therefore, shelved by the convention for Judge Alton B. Parker of New York. Parker's nomination was based on the hope that Wall Street bankers would turn to him and away from the potentially dangerous Roosevelt. But this did not occur. White, in his reports of the convention, was extremely friendly to the defeated Bryan. Instead of denouncing Bryan as a dangerous demagogue as he had done in 1896 and 1900, White stated that Bryan in defeat was the hero of the convention, a dramatic figure. "He has lived cleanly, and has acted fairly and squarely according to his lights," wrote White. "He quit like a gentleman, with his colors flying . . . Whatever his enemies may say of him, they must admire the pluck which he showed at the last."

This changing attitude toward Bryan, and White's own realization that Bryan had been an advance agent in the progressive movement that Roosevelt was now leading, demonstrate that White's thoughts on the social order had matured greatly over the past three years. He was growing more tolerant toward advanced social thinkers. He was revealing that he could learn and grow with the years and that he could change his mind.

* * *

The Emporia editor was not exclusively concerned with politics that summer of 1904, since his second child, Mary White, was born that June. Mrs. White and the baby were so sick all that summer that they finally went to Colorado to improve their health. White remained in Kansas, where he threw himself with great vigor into the political campaign. White joined a Kansas group known as the "Boss Busters," who nominated E. W. Hoch for governor over the wishes of Republican bosses like Cy Leland. White made many speeches, in addition to his editorials, for the entire Republican ticket. Although he might advise people in other states not to vote the straight ticket, home in Kansas there was little question in his mind that the Republican ticket was far superior in every way to the slate of its opponent.

The Emporia *Gazette*, with a daily circulation of two thousand copies by 1904, was *the* political organ of Lyon County. But in addition, in view of White's commanding position with Theodore Roosevelt and his growing influence through his magazine articles, any editorial that appeared in the *Gazette* was likely to be reprinted in papers all over the country. As a result, White at the age of thirty-six was far more significant in national affairs than most small-town editors ever became in their entire lifetime.

White's growing political power in Kansas was buttressed by the support he had from the Kansas City *Star*. Throughout his career, White and the editors of this paper, many of them his intimate friends, were significant powers in Kansas politics. Whenever White wanted to publicize a desirable candidate, the pages of the *Star* were open to him. From 1906 to 1914, he was to make full use of the *Star* in his attempts to build a progressive Kansas. The *Star*'s circulation, blanketing Kansas, western Missouri, and parts of the other surrounding states, reveals something of its significance. In 1905, for instance, the morning edition had 123,000 circulation and the afternoon had 130,000, while the weekly edition had 247,000.

Near the close of the 1904 campaign, White insisted that the election of Roosevelt was necessary for the honest enforcement of the antitrust laws. "The problems facing the country," he charged, "which demand adjustment are problems concerning the equitable distribution of the wealth piling up in this country . . . When a man owns more than a million he is using the surplus to promote great deals, in which there are unfair profits. These profits come out of some one—partly out of the laborers at the factory, partly out of the general public. This is wrong." When a friend objected to such statements, White replied: "A man once sent me a special delivery letter to tell me that I was a damn fool. I wired him to save his money next time and let the information come by freight as I had made the discovery he was so keen to get to me many years before."

White hailed the election of Theodore Roosevelt on November 8 as a personal triumph for the President. He had now led the Republican party away from the issues of the nineties, away "from the consideration of problems that concern the accumulation of national wealth toward problems that concern its equitable distribution," declared White. Roosevelt's triumph, added the

Emporia editor, meant an endorsement of his policy of curbing predatory businessmen. The trust problem, however, asserted White, could be solved only by "a sane, conservative, unselfish nation." The people, he insisted, must not attack the trusts filled with hate, malice, and greed. These words were so close to Roosevelt's own attitude that they were probably a paraphrase of a conversation White had had with the President on the trust problem.

Roosevelt approached the trust problem in a cautious and conservative fashion. He was so cautious that, in spite of the prosecutions he did launch, the trusts were more firmly entrenched when he left office than when he entered. Roosevelt, after all, was the head of the party of big business. He had to move slowly, or thought he did. He differentiated between good and bad trusts, and pointed out that he was opposed only to evil trusts. With no broad underlying social philosophy behind the Roosevelt attitude, the trusts continued to spawn and to exert powerful political influence in spite of the progressive attempt at trust regulation.

White, always a good Rooseveltian, insisted in an article in the *Saturday Evening Post*, for December 3, 1904, that the Republican party must now be reorganized as the Roosevelt party designed to tackle the trust problem. Roosevelt was high in his praise of White's statements. "The great point is," Roosevelt told White, "that I have been able to give direction and guidance to the forces which were demanding, sometimes inarticulately, although often with more sound and fury than was necessary, that the government should effectively shape the policy that I have clumsily called a 'square deal'!"

The problems of trust regulation and the organization of the Republican party as the liberal party of the country were driven momentarily from White's mind just after Roosevelt's election by a striking example of the pitfalls of county journalism. For days White's editorial column hammered at a citizen of Emporia, William Meffert, for operating an illegal saloon. Then, on November 18, the following item appeared in the paper:

Last evening at dusk as the editor of the Gazette was starting for home, a few yards from the office door he met Mrs. Delta Meffert, divorced wife of William Meffert, of whom mention was made in these columns recently. She was accompanied by a lady friend, and as the Gazette man started to pass, Mrs. Meffert pulled from her cloak a small but effective looking whip. The editor of the paper side-stepped and did what every true gent would do; ran forty yards like a white-head back to the office by the back door.

That calm dispassionate communion which a man holds with a situation in the sixteenth part of a second convinced the man in question that when a lady challenges a gent to an athletic contest of any kind, he cannot win a sparring match with any grace, nor be the victor in a wrestling match with a lady with any credit at all; but that a foot race is the one event in the sporting calendar in which any gent may vie his prowess with any lady. And how he did win! Shooting the chutes, leaping the gap, or looping the loop are clumsy, dilatory tactics, compared with the way that fat old codger hiked the hike around to the back door of the office.

A number of eastern newspapers carried the story, but stated that White actually had been whipped for abusing a lady. He was disturbed and upset by what he considered unfavorable national publicity. He felt that the Kansas state treasurer, Tom Kelly, whom he had been attacking as an embezzler, had circulated the story to the papers in order to discredit him. White immediately wrote to a wide variety of people, including Bliss Perry, editor of the *Atlantic Monthly;* Theodore Roosevelt; Elihu Root; James H. Canfield; Nicholas Murray Butler; Senator Henry Cabot Lodge; R. J. Collier and Norman Hapgood of *Collier's Weekly;* and George Lorimer of the *Saturday Evening Post,* denying the accuracy of the story and explaining that a political enemy had falsified the details. George Lorimer, whose home White had recently visited, ended the incident by writing White in a spirit of levity. "Fie, fie! and then tut, tut! How could you do it?" asked Lorimer. "I cannot say that it was entirely unexpected, for ever since I saw the fatal beauty of your figure, its majestic curves covered with those purple pajamas, I have feared that if anyone outside the immediate family heard about them you would either be pinched or chased."

CHAPTER 8

FULL-BLOWN PROGRESSIVE

"THE COMING of spring in this latitude," William Allen White declared in the Emporia *Gazette* on March 1, 1905, "is one of the beautiful things in nature . . . The air is full of an 'ethereal softness' . . . Everywhere men and women are making newer and larger plans for broader and better life and easier living. Spring is a mood as well as a season. It starts the roots of new hopes and aspirations in the mind . . . Only things and souls that are dead fail to begin life anew in the spring."

The spring of 1905 saw the complete blossoming of the Emporia editor as a militant and ardent spokesman for the progressive cause. "No one doubts but that municipal ownership of street railroads, gas, water, lights, and power will be as prevalent in America twenty years from now as any political custom," he told his neighbors on April 10. White, in his accustomed vigorous manner, threw his support behind a bill before the Kansas legislature to prohibit the railroads from issuing passes to politicians. Even though White as an editor had railroad passes in his pocket, he also advocated the abolition of passes to newspapermen. "The worst drawback to a real railroad man who is hustling," he asserted, "is the fellow with a pass who blackmails the railroads."

During these early months of 1905, the Emporia editor was proving of invaluable assistance to Mark Sullivan, enterprising young journalist, who was conducting an investigation of patent medicine frauds. Patent medicine firms followed the practice of inserting in their advertising agreements with newspapers the provision that the companies could cancel their advertisements any time that material detrimental to their interests appeared in the paper. Such a provision, of course, prevented any mention of the current magazine exposés of patent medicine frauds or any discussion of pending legislation to regulate the industry. White, who had refused to sign such contracts, sent Sullivan original copies of the contracts for reprinting in *Collier's Weekly*.

The complete degree to which White had abandoned his old ideas of laissez faire was illustrated in his support of a state-owned oil refinery. Kansas oil producers were suffering from high rates charged by the Standard Oil Company's monopolistic control of refineries. White backed Governor E. W. Hoch's proposal to establish a state refinery as the only way of securing reasonable rates.

Ida M. Tarbell, whose articles on the Standard Oil Company in *McClure's Magazine* made her the leading authority on that monopoly's tactics, came to Kansas to investigate the situation. White put her in touch with Governor Hoch and other prominent figures backing the state refinery. When Standard Oil tried to check the state's action by advertisements in the Kansas papers, White refused to accept their advertisements. "I do not wish to be a Pharisee in this matter," he told Standard Oil, "and yet it seems to me that in view of the stand that the state of Kansas as a state has taken in regard to Standard, it would not be right for me as a citizen to take the other side."

After the state had created its refinery, White observed that this action was aimed at all unfair monopoly. "It is only as Kansas is America in miniature," he asserted, "that she is called to act against this economic wickedness. . . . It is only a homely manifestation of the American love of equality." White was confident by 1905 that government planning and regulation were not necessarily steps toward tyranny. "The fact that the surrender to the state of many of the things of life which individuals have hitherto enjoyed, has proved harmful to the Latin races, proves nothing as to the American people," he told the citizens of Kansas. "They have an extra supply of individualism, of love of personal liberty, and will guard the liberties they surrender as closely as those that they hold."

It was White's confident expectation that the United States would demonstrate to the rest of the world that individual freedom could be retained while at the same time the government regulated the forces of greed and exploitation. He was also confident that the money power was actually being driven out of politics by a moral awakening of the American people. The Golden Rule, he argued in an article for the *Atlantic Monthly*, must be applied to American life. It was not, however, he pointed out, just a problem of curbing the predatory traits of big business. Every small businessman and every good middle-class citizen who exploited the poor had to cease their immoral practices as well. The greatest injustice in American life, he charged, was the unstable condition of industrial workers. The government, White insisted, must intervene "and proclaim a man's right to work, and to be paid for his work well enough so that he may grow mentally and morally to a stature sufficiently large and strong to do his duty as a citizen of this republic. . . . The test of our life today, of our engines of government, will be found in the way they lead the strong man to a righteous appreciation of his duty toward the weak."

* * *

White's writings during the next few years were a decisive indication that he had now acquired a deeper insight into the problems created by the rise of an industrial civilization. With his ability to express himself in pungent, sparkling language, he now plunged into the task of explaining the progressive cause to his middle-class audience. Most of his writing had to be done in the heat of the political battle. He seldom had more than two or three months' intervals when he could escape from running campaigns or plotting legislative strategy.

The only political post that he accepted during these progressive years came to him in March, 1905, when Governor Hoch appointed him to the Board of Regents of the University of Kansas. For the next seven years, in the midst of an already crowded career, he took an active interest in the affairs of the university. "Of course I am grateful," he told the governor on March 7, 1905. "It is the only job in Kansas that I ever wanted, and the only one that I would take. But man alive—Emporia is full of statesmen who really want something and who are just as capable as I am to fill the places they desire, and they think I have legged for this job. . . . But that doesn't bother me particularly, but here is something that does bother me. You have hampered my influence for you. . . . As a member of your administration even in a small capacity, I am stopped from saying anything that will carry any real weight with the people. . . . Perhaps I can do more good as a regent of the University than I can in the *Gazette*. Sincerely I hope so. It was kind and generous and thoughtful of you, and from the bottom of my heart I thank you for what you did. . . ."

White thoroughly enjoyed his years as a regent. When he joined the board, the university was under the vigorous leadership of Chancellor Frank Strong. According to White, Strong seemed, as White worked with him on university problems, "the embodiment of all that is expressed by the words gentle, kindly, courageous, wise and honest, both intellectually and emotionally." Under Strong, the university was transformed from a small western college into a full-grown university with well-developed graduate and professional schools. Attendance increased by leaps and bounds, and new buildings spawned on the campus. Over the years, White proved of extreme value to Chancellor Strong in dealing with Governors Hoch and Stubbs and by securing favorable publicity for K.U. from his newspaper friends.

During the spring and summer of 1905, while White was editing the paper and participating in his first Board of Regents' meetings, he was also busily writing sketches about small-town life for a forthcoming book. "It is a country town tale centering around a printing office. We think it is good," he wrote a friend on the Kansas City *Star*. Shortly before the Fourth of July, 1905, the Whites stole away from the Kansas heat to spend the summer in Colorado, where White could escape from political activities and from the routine of the *Gazette* office. Back in Emporia late that fall, White completed the book, *In Our Town,* and then, just after the turn of the new year, the Whites left Emporia to join Ida M. Tarbell for a two months' vacation in California.

Shortly before leaving town, White noticed the following item in the Leavenworth *Times:* "Look out for some heavy editorials shortly. We have pasted a picture of editor of The Emporia Gazette before our desk for inspiration." Immediately, the 38-year-old editor sat down and wrote an editorial saturated with his rich sense of humor:

Whatever may be said of the face of the editor of this paper—which, to use a typographical expression, is 96 point extended—it has never been used for inspiration. It has been successfully used in cases of sluggish liver; a number of gentlemen in Emporia whose circulation is impaired used it successfully to start heart action; it flushes the face, quickens the breath, loosens the vocabulary, increases the temperature. It is a familiar object at the note counter of the bank every ninety days, and is good at the various grocery stores around town for thirty days' credit. As a face it is not a startling success. It lacks expression. It looks like a rear view of Cupid taken from another exposure. Other faces have more in them; this face has nothing but features in it, and they are a job lot representing Grecian, Gothic and Irish architecture. If the editor of the *Leavenworth Times* gets any inspiration out of that face he is welcome to it, but he is likely to lose a lot of valuable time trying. A better way would be to take a slug of Leavenworth's justly celebrated and popular laughing water with a dash of bitters and a jigger of one thing and another in it.

Soon after the Whites had returned from California in March, 1906, McClure, Phillips & Company published White's fourth book of short stories, *In Our Town*. Of all his fiction, *In Our Town*, a sensitive and humorous treatment of small-town life, still makes enjoyable reading after the era that produced the book has passed away. His works like *Stratagems and Spoils* are dull reading, but *In Our Town* has certain qualities that transcend time limitations. Mark Twain was alert to this quality in the book when he wrote White, shortly after its publication: "Howells told me that 'In Our Town' was a charming book, and indeed it is. All of it is delightful when read to one's self, parts of it can score finely when subjected to the most exacting of tests—the reading aloud. Pages 197-216 are of that grade—I have tried them a couple of times on the family—and pages 212-216 are qualified to fetch any house of any country, caste or color, endowed with those riches which are denied to no nation on the planet—humor and feeling. Talk again—the country is listening."

There was no hint of the satirical note that Sinclair Lewis was later to apply to small-town America in *Main Street* and *Babbitt*. White's book, instead, was a folksy, pleasant, and enchanting tale of small-town America at its very best. The other side of this America, with its bitter frustration, its boredom, and its venomous gossip, was not to be found in White's book. The Los Angeles *Herald* observed: "It is 'Boyville' grown up; better because more skillfully and deftly done; riper, because 'Bill' is a bigger boy now than he was five years ago, and more human. No writer today handles the small town life to compare with White, and this is the best book he has yet done."

Once, when White read that he might have been a great writer had he left politics and newspaperwork alone, he observed: "If I had devoted my life to writing I would probably have been about where Booth Tarkington is now—maybe! Well, at that, I think I have had as much fun as Booth Tarkington. I think I will leave about as much of my personality in the history and institutions of my country as Booth . . . I don't regret that I came out of the cloister and have lived my life in my own way."

There is no doubt that something of the mellow note that was to make White such a delightful and incomparable person during the last twenty-odd years of his life pervaded the pages of *In Our Town*. The mellow quality of the book is evident in the opening page:

Ours is a little town in that part of the country called the West by those who live east of the Alleghenies, and referred to lovingly as "back East" by those who dwell west of the Rockies. It is a country town where, as the song goes, "you know everybody and they all know you," and the country newspaper office is the social clearing-house.

When a man has published a paper in a country community for many years, he knows his town and its people, their strength and their weakness, their joys and their sorrows, their failings and their prosperity—or if he does not know these things, he is on the road to failure, for this knowledge must be the spirit of his paper. The country editor and his reporters sooner or later pass upon everything that interests their town.

While *In Our Town* was receiving glowing reviews, White plunged again into the political situation in Kansas. He launched a relentless attack on the practice of issuing railroad passes to politicians. "So long as the railroads are in politics, they must not object to the people running the railroads," he wrote a Santa Fe official in April 5, 1906. "The railroads cannot name senators, pack state conventions, run legislatures and boss politics generally with passes, and then successfully maintain that they are private concerns doing a private business." A few months after this letter, he informed the Santa Fe officials that he would no longer accept passes in return for free advertising in the *Gazette*.

White was disturbed at Governor Hoch's failure to push action against the railroads. "I mix a great deal with the people of Emporia," he wrote Hoch on May 6, 1906, "and know what they think. I know that those who were most loyal to you a few years ago, are not loyal now. I know they think you have failed in many things where they believed you might have succeeded. . . . It is so easy to sit down and write a letter to the governor telling him a lot of nice things, and I want you to know that it is mighty hard to write what I am writing, but I think you ought to know it. I think you ought to know there is a great big revolt on in Kansas that cannot be sniffed or scorned away, against the domination of the railroad in local politics. . . ."

Several weeks later he warned Hoch that the opposition to his leadership "is not among the irresponsible, but among the conservative farmers and business men . . . The people feel that you have considered the good of the Republican party first and the good of the state second. What the Republicans of Kansas want to feel is that they have a governor who would gladly send the Republican party straight to hell, if the interests of the people of Kansas and the enforcement of the laws of Kansas demand it." Then he added that the people considered Hoch a figurehead for the machine bosses like Cy Leland, David Mulvane, and Morton Albaugh. "You must cut loose and be master of the situation," he told Hoch. "The simple truth is that unless you do something to change the situation, the major part of the Republican ticket will go down, and I fear you will go with it." To another friend, he declared: "This is a very unhappy situation in Kansas for Republicans, and probably none of them is more unhappy than I am. A lot of fellows do not like to vote the Democratic ticket, and yet as the situation stands now, and unless it changes materially, there will be nothing left to do for a man who is frank and honest with himself."

When White was attacked by some Republican papers for criticizing Governor Hoch for certain actions and praising him for others, White answered that "when a man needs praise he will get it from the Gazette, and when he needs blame he will get it from the Gazette . . . When the party does a worthy thing, the Gazette praises it; when the party sneaks and sells out to the boodlers—the Gazette says so, and is not mealy-mouthed about it. For he is the best partisan who exposes the rogues who try to capture his party, and he is the worst patriot who allows his party's interests to weigh more heavily than his country's. . . ." Arthur Capper's Topeka *Capital* praised White's attitude, and declared: "Old Bill White is taking the fire out of the standpat, mole-eyed party organs and not batting an eye under their broadsides. It is such papers as the Emporia Gazette that make a party worth its salt as a representative of honest, faithful government. If the Republican party pulls away from its unconscionable tricksters and fixers and bosses, it will be due to the Emporia Gazette style of truth-telling Republicanism."

White's habit of criticizing the Republican party, which continued from this period until his death, created consternation in the ranks of the regular, bitter-end party members. The actual fact that he supported the party at election time did not soothe their irritation over what they considered his unreliability and irresponsibility. "Snort" Brown summed up their attitude toward White many years later in the Atchison *Globe*, which White reprinted with great glee in the *Gazette*:

William Allen White is the most unique character in America.

One day he is the most lovable man in the nation, and the next day he is the most asinine, and it is all due to the fact that he has worms . . . There are times when Mr. White writes in a manner scintillating and titillating, and with all wisdom. Then is when we love him.

Then comes the onrush of worms!

The hideous worms!

The worms that drive men crazy, and make them drivel, and leak at the nose and the mouth, and jibber and jabber childishly, idiotically and nonsensically.

And then is when William Allen White writes the stuff that breaks the hearts of communities. Then it is when he casts aside the graces, and becomes brutish. Then it is when we cannot love William Allen White.

But we do pity William when we cannot love him. And Atchison must assume the same attitude. . . .

Atchison must drag out the mantle of charity in this case, and be kind to the fat old man who, on account of worms, does not know what he does.

Instead of kicking Bill White, Atchison should pray for him, for he is very much in need of prayer, for worms are as bad as devils. . . .

Poor Bill Allen White!

How his innards do rumble!

How distorted his face!

How distracted his mind!

Our great heart goes out to him!

Worms are hell!

They sure is!

In May, 1906, White told his readers that the Kansas Republican party needed a Moses to lead it out of the jungle of machine domination. When Charles Curtis's candidacy for the senatorial post about to be vacated by Burton was advocated by the party bosses, White charged that Curtis and Burton were two of a kind backed by the railroad interests. "Everyone knows," White declared, "that Curtis is a professional politician without an ideal and without any breadth of view, and that he is ignorant of the great world outside of politics."

Although a number of local conservative Republicans disliked the increasingly progressive tone of the *Gazette*, there was little they could do about it. Some of them tried to establish a safe and sane Republican paper that summer, but the *Gazette* was so firmly entrenched that they were unable to persuade the local merchants to buy advertising space in this new journal. The *Gazette*, by this time, had a daily circulation of 2,476 copies and went into 95 per cent of the Emporia homes and 85 per cent of the homes in the surrounding country. "The Gazette," wrote White, "pays me $4,000 a year because the mass of the people believe in it, even if the politicians down here don't like it. Local support is my strong suit."

When the Republican state convention that summer, dominated by railroad attorneys, issued a platform without a statement in favor of an antipass law or the direct primary, a group of more progressive Republicans, led by White; W. R. Stubbs, speaker of the Kansas House of Representatives; J. S. George, president of the Kansas Shippers Association; and George Plumb, president of the Kansas Live Stock Growers Association, organized a campaign to secure people's signatures to petitions demanding the antipass law and the direct primary. White persuaded Senator Robert M. LaFollette, who as governor of Wisconsin had successfully curbed the power of the railroads in the politics of that state, to come to Kansas and speak in his eloquent fashion for the growing progressive movement. "We are beginning this fight under great odds," White wrote LaFollette on July 6, 1906. "But the example of your wonderful fight stimulates us and encourages us, and your presence with us for a day will be of inestimable value to us."

After LaFollette's visit, White urged the Kansas City *Star* to send a reporter through the state, writing articles on the progressive revolt within the Republican party's ranks. "LaFollette came to Kansas, and talked all kinds of hot news stuff," he told the *Star*. ". . . It has gone all over the state, and the people are quoting LaFollette. It is a big movement, which may quiet down before the election, but it is certainly worth handling." In Topeka, sparked by W. R. Stubbs and Joseph L. Bristow, a Square Deal League was organized that summer from members of the legislature who opposed both corporation control of politics and Charles Curtis's bid for the senatorship.

White kept President Roosevelt well informed concerning the growing schism in the party in Kansas. He had been so busy with his writing and with state politics, however, that he had not seen the President for many months. "I do wish you would get here some time about a month hence, or some time when I can really see you and talk over matters. I miss you," Roosevelt had written the Emporia editor on April 12, 1906. Just before Secretary of War William Howard Taft spoke in Kansas late that summer for the state and Congressional Republican ticket, White wrote Roosevelt: "I am immensely interested in him. . . . If Secretary Taft learns the Kansas language as you learned it eight years ago, Kansas will be for him, but he must be mighty 'keerful' as there is the devil to pay and no pitch out here this year." Roosevelt wrote back: "Of course I am not going to try to nominate any man. Personally you know how highly I think of Secretary Taft, but I am not going to take a hand in his nomination, for it is none of my business." But, as has been pointed out, Roosevelt had trouble taking Roosevelt's advice, because in the same letter he went on to observe: "I am sure Kansas will like him. He would be an ideal President. He is the kind of broad-gauge American that Kansas ought to like."

In this exchange of letters White also told Roosevelt that he did not enjoy the rumors that Roosevelt would be a candidate in 1908. "I have it in mind," declared White, "to write this kind of an article: Talk of President Roosevelt for a second term in 1908 is unfortunate; first because it assumes him insincere, and second because the country should not have him for president during the next term. He has been president or will have been president in March, 1909, for seven years and a half. During that time he has led the country in lines of civic righteousness further than any American leader has led it, but also more closely. If we are to get any real benefit from that leadership, we should not lean on it. We should begin to try at least to walk alone. Four more years of Roosevelt might make us too dependent upon him, because essentially whatever real good he has done, must be as a permanent influence upon American political and social life. And if seven years of President Roosevelt can't permanently impress that influence on the people—eleven years will only make us flabbier and flabbier; for the fault is in the people." The President immediately replied that White should write the article, since those were his views as well.

The campaign that fall found White unhappy. He felt that the Republican state ticket was not progressive enough for his tastes, but, on the other hand, he did not want the Democrats to come into power. Although he had declared in May that, unless the boodlers and bosses were removed from control of the Republican party, the people should vote Democratic, by election time he refused to carry out his own advice. Instead, he supported the straight Republican ticket, but without any apparent enthusiasm. His justification was that by not bolting the party he could build a progressively minded wing that could seize power from the reactionaries after the election. Furthermore, he always contended that the Democratic party was hopeless in Kansas, and that it would only be wasted effort to support its candidates. During the campaign, White was a leading member of the Square Deal League, or Republican Voters' League, as it was formally known. This league devoted its efforts to supporting those Republican legislative candidates who were for an antipass law, a direct primary, and an equitable railroad regulatory law.

That White was not enamored of the Republican campaign was clearly indicated by his spending a number of weeks in the East during September and October. He was there consulting with some of his old friends who had just taken control of the *American Magazine*, hoping to make it the great organ of a progressive democracy. Ida M. Tarbell, John S. Phillips, Albert Boyden, Lincoln Steffens, and Ray Stannard Baker all left *McClure's* to launch the *American Magazine* on its new path. White and Finley Peter Dunne joined the *American* staff as editorial associates. White's advice to the group was not to make their new magazine too serious. "It seems to me," he wrote John S. Phillips on July 6, 1906, "the great danger before you is that of being too purposeful. People will expect the pale drawn face; the set lips and a general line of emotional insanity. You should fool 'em. Give 'em something like 'Pigs is Pigs.' From the prospectus they will judge that you are going to produce a 'Thin red line of heroes,' and instead of which you should have the sharp claque of the slap stick and the rattle of broken glass down the sky-light to indicate the course of the Dutchman's journey."

Ray Stannard Baker remembered White, during their *American Magazine* days, as coming to New York every once in a while with Mrs. White and offering fresh suggestions for stories and articles for the magazine. "He had the reputation of being a humorist," Baker has written. "He was that and much more, for his pictures of life were full of affection and understanding." White wrote an article for the first issue of the magazine under its new editors, and Norman Hapgood of *Collier's* introduced him to the readers of the *American Magazine* by declaring: "Among American writers of our day we know none characterized more surely by rightness and health of spirit than William Allen White of Emporia, Kansas. None sees the world more justly in its true proportions, as it is. None, therefore, is more kind, more charitable, with gentler humor, or in more every-day fashion entirely wise. He can, with this wisdom, amiability and amusement that are his, do things that stiffer spirits find impossible . . . In his freshness, in the openness of his manner and the breeziness of his words, there is much that we are proud to call American."

White's article, "The Partnership of Society," was a competent analysis of the meaning of the progressive movement. He stated that there were two spirits in every man—the altruistic and the egoistic—and that "the problem of this generation and the next and the next is to civilize the conscienceless devil of malicious greed out of the hearts of men." Through a lifetime he was to maintain this belief and repeat it in almost identical words in his little volume *The Changing West* (1939). He denounced those members of society who became so enamored of money that they forgot their duty of service to mankind. Toward these men, White maintained, the old Puritan doctrine that "every man is his brother's keeper" must be applied. "That is an A-1 article," Theodore Roosevelt wrote him, "and I am delighted with it. To plagiarize from your letter to me about my Harrisburg speech, I feel as if I could have written it myself—perhaps I should be more accurate in saying that I feel as I ought to have written it myself. By George, I would like to have that article circulated as a tract!"

That fall White also wrote a series of three articles for *Collier's* on the theme "What's the Matter with America?" These articles were devoted to an exposition of the desirability of substituting the direct primary system for the convention method of nominating candidates for office. White went into great detail as to the manner in which special privilege groups like the railroads dominated party conventions and selected candidates favorable to their interests. The direct primary, he declared, was necessary to clean out control by vested interests. What was needed was more democracy in our system. Return the government to the people, and let the people elect their own candidates.

After White had returned to Emporia in November, 1906, he began to speculate concerning his own reversal of point of view during the past few years. He had come a long way since he had denounced the Populists as rattlebrained fanatics for stating that "the rights of the user are paramount to the rights of the owner." He himself now thoroughly believed that declaration. In an editorial to the home folks, on December 14, White admitted that the Populists had been correct, but that they were "out too early in the season" and their "views got frost bitten." White was thoroughly in step with the majority of the American people. The bulk of the middle class had voted against Bryan's "dangerous views" in 1896, and then had voted for Theodore Roosevelt in 1904 because he advocated just such measures! As White observed in his editorial, "This is a funny world. About all we can do is to move with it, and grow with it. Those who do not move are dead in the shell."

*　　*　　*

The closing weeks of 1906 and the opening days of the new year found Editor White busily engaged in trying to prevent the state legislature from sending Charles Curtis to the United States Senate. "Fighting Bob" LaFollette's visit during the preceding campaign had aroused the people against railroad domination of politics. Building on the foundation that LaFollette had laid, White, W. R. Stubbs, Henry J. Allen, and Joseph L. Bristow now tried to prevent Curtis's election by labeling him a railroad senator. Bristow was the candidate of this progressive Republican group. White wrote Roosevelt, in the midst of the fight: "Here in Kansas I find every single general attorney of every railroad in the State, and every single newspaper that has ever been suspected of railroad alignment, solidly tied up with the Senatorial candidacy of Charles Curtis . . . anything you can do to keep hands off the Kansas fight, merely occupying a seat at the ringside, will be most heartily appreciated."

The bosses of the Republican party outmaneuvered the progressives in the legislature and Curtis was elected. White adopted a practical view of the situation. He realized that until the direct primary replaced the convention system and United States senators were elected directly by the people, the bosses in the pay of vested interests would always win in a convention fight. The people had to be educated to the need of a direct primary. "Would you join sixty or a hundred fellows in Kansas who would go up against this outfit unselfishly, and without so much a desire to win as to educate the people?" he asked a number of his newspaper and political friends on March 18, 1907. "The time is ripe. The Republican party must be the party of the people, and the fellows who make it so this year and next and next and next, even though they get a baptism of fire in the meantime, will be serving their country as surely as though they went into battle."

Still battling against the railroads, White was instrumental in bringing about the adoption by the Kansas Publishers Association of an unequivocal resolution requesting the passage of a state anti-pass law. He told President Roosevelt that if railroad manipulators like Harriman and Gould would stop meddling in state politics the people would deal fairly with the railroads. And he added: "The local attorneys for railroads who corrupt local government are many of them educated by state taxes at the state law schools. These men are of a caste and culture which makes their harlotry particularly shameful and scandalously mercenary."

While White was spearheading the progressive attempt to curb the railroads in Kansas, his old friend, Victor Murdock, newly elected congressman, was attempting to push additional federal legislation to check their power. The railroad lobby defeated Murdock's efforts, but only after a brisk fight, during which White urged the President, Senator LaFollette, and Norman Hapgood of *Collier's* to come to Murdock's assistance.

White devoted most of his efforts in the spring of 1907 to planning the progressive Republican campaign of 1908. He had learned from bitter political experience that the time to prepare for a campaign was after the conclusion of the last campaign and not six weeks before election day. After innumerable conferences and letters, White succeeded in persuading W. R. Stubbs to run for governor and Joseph L. Bristow to run for United States senator. Stubbs, who wanted to run for the Senate himself, was told by White that he was the only gubernatorial candidate who could defeat the machine. With Stubbs as governor, dominating the legislature, White was certain that the incumbent Senator Chester I. Long could be defeated. It was some time before Stubbs withdrew from the senatorial race for the governorship, and at times White was indignant at Stubbs' refusal to listen to his advice. "Stubbs is a mule," he wrote a mutual friend, "and a balky mule at that, a good draft horse withal, and a hard worker, but essentially a mule, a blamed stubborn untamed kicking balky-mule."

When the progressive Republicans held a conference to plan their antirailroad campaign, they also agreed to secure a LaFollette delegate for the presidential nomination in 1908, if LaFollette wanted them to do this. White reported this decision to Senator LaFollette but advised him that he would strengthen himself for the future if he waived such support and threw it instead to William Howard Taft. White's view of LaFollette in 1907 was extremely revealing as to his own economic and social attitudes. He felt that LaFollette was too radical, too far out in front of middle-class opinion, but, on the other hand, useful as a firebrand who could stir the people out of their apathy.

After helping launch the progressive Republican campaign for 1908, White took his family to spend the summer of 1907 in Colorado, where he intended to concentrate on the writing of a long progressive novel, *A Certain Rich Man.* In July, however, his writing was interrupted by a serious request from his old friend William E. Borah, newly elected senator from Idaho. During the previous March, the officers of a lumber company and their attorney, Borah, had been indicted by a federal grand jury for timber frauds. Back of the indictment was the Republican machine of Idaho, whose leaders wanted to end Borah's political career because they could not control him.

Borah wrote White in July that his enemies were in charge of enforcing the federal law in Idaho, and he feared that he would not be given a fair trial. Borah asked White to intercede with Roosevelt to ensure a fair trial. After corresponding with the President, White hurried to Oyster Bay to present Borah's view of the case. At a meeting with Roosevelt and Attorney General Charles J. Bonaparte, White asked that the government drop the entire proceedings against Borah. Roosevelt and Bonaparte refused to do this, but they did agree that a special prosecutor should be sent to Idaho to conduct the trial. At the subsequent trial it took the jury just fourteen minutes to decide that Borah was not guilty.

"I have always felt that the best single day's work I ever did in my life," White wrote Borah ten years later, "was that day I put in for you down at Oyster Bay." Borah's gratitude to White for preventing an unfair trial that might have destroyed his career was revealed in a letter written to White in 1935. "Will, in all the vicissitudes of the last forty years," Borah observed, "there has been laid up in my memory an affectionate and unselfish act upon your part which will never be forgotten as long as I live. In a crucial situation you came effectively to my support. It was of tremendous moment to me at the time and it had much to do with my entire work thereafter. I have never said a great deal about it to you and I have sometimes wondered if you knew how much I appreciated it. But I did appreciate it and I do still think of it beyond any words of mine to express."

After Roosevelt had promised that a special prosecutor would try Borah, White hastened back to Colorado to work on his novel. By the time the White family returned to Emporia in the autumn of 1907, White had completed the first draft of the book. He had no intention of rushing into print with it, since he wanted to spend ample time on its revision. The completion of the novel, however, was delayed by the demands of the campaign of 1908. To help the progressive forces in Missouri, White wrote an editorial supporting the candidacy of Missouri's Democratic governor, Joseph Folk, for United States senator. He also did his best to secure Folk favorable publicity in *Collier's* and from the pen of Lincoln Steffens. "You can be of great help," Folk told him, "and I appreciate what you have done and are doing."

In national politics White vigorously backed President Roosevelt's choice of William Howard Taft for the Republican presidential nomination. Early in February, Mr. and Mrs. White spent a day on a train with Taft while they were en route to Washington. Before White interviewed the Secretary of War for a preconvention article, he had written Taft: "I hardly need tell that I desire to make the article as helpful to you and our common cause of progressive Republicanism, as it may be said honestly." Before this article was written, the Whites had lunched at the White House with the Roosevelts and British Ambassador James Bryce and Mrs. Bryce, and White talked over the article on Taft with the President. Roosevelt scowled at him and remarked: "And now, you old boulevardier, don't hold the knife edge of your balance so perfectly poised in this piece that your readers won't see your bias."

The article, "Taft, A Hewer of Wood," which appeared in the May, 1908, *American Magazine*, fulfilled Roosevelt's request. White portrayed Taft as the epitome of the common man. "Taft belongs to that class of Americans," White declared, "who when occasion requires can hook up their wives' dresses in the back and lace their own shoes." Taft's sympathy, White wrote, was with the average man and against organized greed. Taft was not a man of initiative, but he would work hard and carry on Roosevelt's unfinished policies. "The times demand not a man bearing promises of new things," stated White, "but a man who can finish the things begun. Such a man is Taft, a hewer of wood, who has no ambition to link his name with new measures, but who, with a steady hand, and a heart always kind and a mind always generously just, can clean off the desk."

Kansas politics that year found Editor White more involved in candidates and issues than ever before. Governor Hoch had persuaded the legislature to adopt a direct primary law in January, 1908, and a preference primary system for candidates for the United States Senate. The people could express their wishes on the senatorial situation, and the legislature was morally obligated to elect their choice. This rather awkward system prevailed in many states during these progressive years until the Constitution was amended in 1913 to permit the direct election of senators.

White played a leading role in pushing W. R. Stubbs' candidacy for governor in the Republican primary and Joseph L. Bristow's bid for the Senate. As early as January, White predicted that Stubbs would capture the nomination and be elected governor, but he wasn't too sure of Bristow's chances. Bristow's primary opponent was the incumbent Senator Chester I. Long. White spared no efforts in unearthing Long's record in the Senate and impaling him as the servant of vested interests. White's editorials against Long were readily carried in such powerful papers as the Kansas City *Star*, the Topeka *Capital*, the Wichita *Beacon*, and the Wichita *Eagle*. White wrote Congressman Victor Murdock on March 18, 1908, that Senator Long had just been in Kansas, and had "queered himself by talking of 'Tahft.' Kansas simply will not stand for 'Tahft,' and if Long persists in speaking a foreign tongue he may as well resign."

As election day approached, the Bristow campaign bogged down. White was quite aware of the trouble. Bristow was "too righteous." He lacked color. Urging the Kansas City *Star* to help him give Bristow some glamour, White stated: "The people have acquired an unreasoning prejudice against Bristow. They do not think he is crooked; they do not believe he is tied up to any interests, but they do believe he is 'cold' and that is a worse sin than dishonesty. Given a good warm campaign for Bristow by the Star, and he can win." White was devastatingly frank with Bristow. After encouraging him by saying that he was negotiating with millionaire Charles Crane of Chicago for a loan to finance the campaign, he told Bristow that he did not put enough life into his speeches and, as a result, his campaign was dead. Comparing Bristow with Senator Albert Beveridge of Indiana, White wrote some years later: "Beveridge was a trotting horse. Joe Bristow was a Clydesdale with whiskers on his feet, built for draft and general purposes. Or to change the figure, Beveridge was a geared up speedster, a show car. Joe was a truck, but he always brought it home full of bacon."

"You have been writing some wonderful stuff about Senator Long," one of Bristow's aids wrote White on May 27, 1908, "and it must be having a wonderful influence in the country. It is unanswerable. . . . Can you keep up your gait? . . . You must. . . . Your work is going to do the business." In addition to his widely copied editorials on Bristow's behalf, White raised money and helped organize county groups to turn out the vote for Bristow and Stubbs. White's major attack on Long was based on

Long's record of voting against most of the Roosevelt measures and generally siding with reactionary Senator Nelson Aldrich of Rhode Island. White persuaded Norman Hapgood to carry an article in *Collier's* for July 11, 1908, linking Long with Aldrich. Inspired by White, Hapgood stated that Long was trying "to make Kansas a great conservative stronghold—a sort of Western Rhode Island."

Near the close of the Bristow campaign, the Emporia editor wrote a widely circulated pamphlet, "The Case of Mr. Bristow," and listed thirty-five reasons why Long should be defeated. Senator Long decided that the best way to answer White's charges was a campaign rally in Emporia with White in attendance. "My plan would be to pay little attention to Bristow," Long confided to a supporter, "but to picture White as the leader of my opposition, calling attention to the fact that he is not only Bristow's press agent, but also his manager." A few days later, Long told W. Y. Morgan, who had sold the Emporia *Gazette* to White thirteen years before: "I am willing to risk my return to the Senate on the answer to White's attack. . . . It is one of the most unfair dishonest articles ever published anywhere about any person."

As an old friend of Long's, White attended the rally at which Long followed his plan of attacking White and ignoring Bristow. When White heard Long prove that three of the thirty-five charges against him were incorrect, the Emporia editor withdrew those three. "I admire Senator Long's courage," White wrote a friend after the Emporia meeting, "and I think that he is a good citizen in everything except his belief that Wall Street is right and the people are wrong . . . while he may be a good father and a kind husband, and a generous friend he is not the kind of a man to represent Kansas in the United States Senate." On August 1, White brought Fighting Bob LaFollette to Emporia to speak at a huge rally in Bristow's behalf. LaFollette's militant and colorful presence had a part in White's plan to build up Bristow in the eyes of the Kansas people. A. L. Shultz, of the Topeka *State Journal*, has remarked that White cleverly created the illusion that Bristow was against sin. The fact that Cy Leland was running for governor on the same ticket as Long made White's task easier.

The primary results that August were a smashing victory for

Stubbs and Bristow. Both the Kansas City *Star* and the Wichita *Eagle* declared that White deserved the major credit for this resounding progressive success. The Emporia editor hailed the election returns as a vivid indication that the West was for the "Roosevelt policies." But he knew that without the direct primary the progressives could not have won. He wrote to Senator Borah in Idaho and to Judge Ben Lindsey, who was gaining fame for his juvenile court in Denver, that the only hope of defeating machine rule in those two states was through the primary system. "The only thing a free senator can hope for is the primary," White declared.

White was happy over the Republican ticket that fall. His two friends, Bristow and Stubbs, headed the state ticket and William Howard Taft was the presidential candidate. White had reported the Republican convention at Chicago the past June for a string of thirty papers. Before the nominations, Charles Curtis had given White a tip that James Sherman would be nominated for the vice-presidency. "Charley, of course, had the dirty low-down from the four-minute eggs in Congress and in Wall Street, so far as that goes," White recalled. "He gave me the tip without strings—possibly as a kite-flying enterprise. Anyway I used it and beat the world. My pride in that beat still thrills me."

Although the convention nominated Taft for the presidency on the first ballot, powerful reactionary forces watered down the platform and made sure that a statement denouncing the use of injunctions in labor disputes was not adopted. These same forces nominated James Sherman, a conservative New York politician, for the vice-presidency. "The reactionaries had captured many vital objectives at Chicago in the warm June of 1908," Taft's biographer has observed. "They had not yet captured William Howard Taft but they would do that, too, in the end." White, of course, hailed the Republican platform as being based on the Golden Rule and the Square Deal. The people, asserted White, ran the convention. He apparently was so happy over Taft's nomination that he failed to notice the success of the conservative Republicans in the proceedings.

As early as August, White was able to inform President Roosevelt that the Middle West was for Taft and not for William

Jennings Bryan. "There is no Bryan enthusiasm in Kansas," he wrote Roosevelt on August 15. "Their state ticket is impossible and their congressional ticket is absurd." Since the Republican ticket was having few difficulties, White devoted most of his time that autumn to revising his novel, *A Certain Rich Man*. The *Gazette* was in such a flourishing and prosperous condition that he hardly went near the office. He even hired Walt Mason, later to achieve national fame for his folksy rhymes, to write the editorials. This led to an amusing but highly disturbing incident for White. Mason, a reactionary Republican, wrote an editorial attacking Roosevelt as a rascal. White did not see the editorial until the paper had been distributed. In great haste he wrote Roosevelt: "I am hurt worse than you are. Think of the thousands of men who like you read that fling at the squarest man in the land, and despise me for writing it."

White's prediction that the Republican party would sweep Kansas and the Middle West was fulfilled on November 3. In a spirit of jubilation, White wrote Governor-elect Stubbs: "I shall not waste any time in telling you how happy I am at the results of the election. . . . I want to state right here and now, before you take your office, that I am at your service in any way in which you may need me. I do not care for any office. I do not care whom you appoint to any office. Patronage does not interest me . . . I wish that you would feel free to consult me, to send me on errands, to ask my help and to use my newspaper freely in matters of principle and policy; upon issues and upon the broad questions of right and wrong. I have no desire in the world to be known for my power at the pie counter, but I would like to help some in making Kansas the foremost state in the United States, in the matter of liberal laws and wise policies."

CHAPTER 9

INSURGENT YEARS

"I HAVE been reading in the Associated Press reports . . . today about the closing days of your administration, and my memory goes back to that first night in Washington at Captain Cowles'," the Emporia editor wrote Theodore Roosevelt in March, 1909. "How much water has gone under the bridge since then! How well have you kept the faith. How true you have been to all you hoped and believed in that night. Of all the things you have done —and you have done so many—the best, it seems to me, is that you have lived so clean and so decently through it all that you have come out with the illusion of youth and of strength and of a righteous faith."

There was no doubt that in 1909 Theodore Roosevelt was White's ideal statesman. Although Roosevelt had successfully dramatized the progressive cause, he had done nothing to alter the basic evils in American life and he had failed to place control of the Republican party in progressive hands. In spite of this, thirty years after Roosevelt had left the White House he was still, in White's eyes, the greatest statesman the nation had seen since Abraham Lincoln. "There was a man!" declared White. "Of all the figures whom I have known in public and private life, he was most lovable. I did not say admirable, for he demanded affection or nothing. Theodore Roosevelt was virile—a hickory man reinforced with steel, wide in his interests, catholic in his tastes, a statesman always ready to compromise on unessentials and never afraid of a fight."

Although White was never to be as close to any subsequent president as he had been to Theodore Roosevelt, his prestige and power with the American people continued to grow in such a fashion that on many occasions he was to be a significant force in molding governmental policy. Harry Kemp, "The Tramp Poet of Kansas," who visited White during these years when he was a militant supporter of the Roosevelt administration, has left a penetrating description of the Emporia editor as he entered his forty-first year. Using the name Osageville for Emporia; Jarvis Alexander Mackworth for William Allen White; Ally Merton for Brock Pemberton; and Minnie for Sallie White, Kemp wrote:

I found myself on the usual long one-street called Main Street, in the prosperous little city of Osageville. It was Sunday. A corner loiterer directed me to Jarvis Alexander Mackworth's house.

A habitation of sequestered quiet . . . as I stood before the door I heard the sunrise song of Rossini's *Wilhelm Tell* . . . a Red Seal record . . . accompanied by the slow, dreamy following of a piano's tinkle . . . like harp sounds or remote, flowing water.

I halted, under a charm. I waited till the melody was at an end before I knocked. A small, pale-faced pretty little woman answered.

"Does Mr. Jarvis Mackworth live here?"

"Yes. Come in. We have been expecting you. You are the poet, aren't you?"

"Yes, I am the poet."

"You're a good walker . . . we didn't expect you before Monday or Tuesday. . . . Jarvis, here's the poet-boy from the university."

My host, unseen within, turned off another Red Seal record he had just started, again to the accompaniment of the piano . . . Kreisler's *Caprice Viennois* . . . Jarvis Alexander Mackworth came forth like a leisurely duck, waddling. He was very, very fat. He extended me a plump, white hand . . . a slack handshake . . . but not an unhearty one, rather a grip of easy welcome.

A kind, rubicund, moon-round face, full of large blue eyes smiling a gentle and kindly welcome . . . if the face of Shelley's father, plump and methodic-oracular, could have been joined to the wild, shining ecstasy of Shelley's countenance itself—you would have had Mackworth's face before its time. I never beheld such spirituality in a fat man. His stoutness was not unpleasing.

"My boy . . . come in . . . my God, you're all wet . . . you look frail, too." A pity shone in his eyes. "Minnie, call up Ally Merton . . ." turning to me, "I have, as you can see, no clothes to fit you . . . but Ally might have . . . he's about your size, but he carries a trifle more meat on his bones . . .

"Come in and dry yourself before the fire till he gets over."

We sat before the gas-fire of artificial logs.

"Minnie, will you make a cup of tea for this—poor boy," and he lowered his voice at the last two words, realizing that I was hearing, too.

"Yes, Jarv!"

I sat at the table in the dining room. Jarvis Alexander Mackworth sat on the piano-stool, again playing the piano in rhythm rather than in accompaniment with the records . . . it was Caruso now . . .

"A glorious voice, isn't it, young man?" Mackworth asked, as I ate voraciously of the cold roast set before me . . . of the delicious white bread and fresh dairy butter, just from the churn of some neighboring farmer.

"I know nothing much about music," he continued, "—just appreciate it . . . —seems to me that's what we need now, more than anything else—appreciation of the arts—I like to sit here and pick out the melodies on the piano as the tune runs on. It inspires me. The precious people, the aesthetic upstarts, make fun of Edison and his 'canned music,' as they call it . . . but I say Edison is one of the great forces for culture in America today. Everybody can't go to New York, London, Paris, Bayreuth . . . not to Chicago even . . .

"Beauty must come to Osageville, since Osageville cannot come to Beauty."

I was charmed.

"Mr. Mackworth, you are a great man," I said.

The same month that Theodore Roosevelt left the presidency, Will and Sallie White, with Bill, Mary, and Will's mother sailed from New York for a tour of Europe. This was the first time any of them had been out of the United States. They were to thrill to the wonders in the Old World culture. They visited a Europe that was basking in the dying light of the quiet and peace of the late Victorian world. Forces underneath the current of daily events were already gathering that were to launch upon society the catastrophe of recurring wars, fascism, race hatred, and the denial of the Christian ethical code. The United States was to be directly affected by these new forces, and its own internal affairs were to be profoundly dominated by Old World strife and controversy. But there was none of this grim future apparent during the Whites' trip in 1909. Europe, then, seemed a remote place, delightful to visit, but a continent whose troubles could be disregarded by America.

The Whites carried with them to Europe letters of introduction from President Taft to American diplomats stating that ". . . Mr. White is a journalist of national reputation, and a warm friend of mine . . . Any attention or courtesy shown to Mr. White and his family I shall highly appreciate." The Whites' first stop was at the Madeira Islands, where the lilacs were already in bloom. They disembarked at Naples and spent some time touring Italy. While in Rome the Whites visited the graves of Keats and Shelley. Later White wrote poet Harry Kemp: "You will smile probably, but when you were with us most was in Rome; for it was in Rome that we were much with Keats, and to us you seem a kindred spirit. We visited the Keats memorial and saw the little room where he died—a most miserable death, railing at the materialism of a cold world. . . . In the main part of the cemetery . . . Shelley's heart lies buried. It is indeed a peaceful beautiful spot. It seems full of the joy of death." From Italy they went sightseeing through the mountains of Switzerland and from there into Germany. They spent three weeks in Paris in June, and then five weeks in England, and ten days in Ireland.

While in England, White visited Thomas Hardy and Henry James. "I went on a pilgrimage to James' home," he wrote a friend. "He lives at Rye in Sussex, most charmingly in an old though modest house with a little walled garden back of it. The garden and the house and Henry James are all one. We had a luncheon and a long talk under a great spreading tree in the garden and then a walk and a visit to an old church, a pitch down a steep cobble-stone street past antique shops and old old people . . . Personally Mr. James impresses one as being as kind as Mr. Howells but braver and therefore more likely to be just. He is of a middle height, highdomed, stocky though not chubby; and he has lived alone so much and written so much that he fumbles through the whole basket of his conversational vocabulary for the exact word to use in most ordinary matters. So he creaks when he talks. But he talks well and is altogether a joy." Of English poet Thomas Hardy, White observed: ". . . he is a modest soft-voiced self-deprecatory man thinned and more serious than Noble Prentis, but no more assertive. He wears his clothes as an afterthought, and has a scrubby wayward little moustache of blond gray that has had its own way too long to be taken in hand now. . . . He is a dear."

While they were reveling in their European trip, Macmillan published White's novel, *A Certain Rich Man*. It was not until they were aboard the SS *Celtic* on their way home that they received their first intimation as to the reception of the book. Recalling the scene years later, White wrote:

. . . After she pulled out of Queenstown we went on deck. There the deck crowd was sprawled about in chairs, and one man was reading a copy of the *New York Times*. Looking over his shoulder two Emporians saw in the *Times* a half page advertisement that made their eyes bug out. It was a proclamation declaring that *A Certain Rich Man* was in its "fourth large printing"—and it had been out but three weeks. We had left the manuscript with the publishers when we sailed, read the proof in Europe and in the joy of our first European journey had all but forgotten the book. And there it jumped out of the advertisement at us—a success. That we knew. Hand in hand, two youngsters, one in his first forties, the other in her late thirties, went to the cabin, and without a word burst into tears. And the two little children could not understand what the sobbing was about.

For eight days we read and reread that advertisement, and gloated. The children played on the deck and won prizes and even grandma—aged seventy-nine, and a captain of a woman—realized what the advertisement meant. The *Celtic* has carried many a cargo since then of rich cargo and precious freight. But never before nor since has the fair fine old ship pounding her life out today on the rocks carried so much joy as she bore out of Queenstown that August passage long ago.

The reviewers were enthusiastic over the book. "Mr. White has made the nearest approach yet to the great American novel, so long looked for," declared the *Graphic*, and *The New York Times* stated that it ". . . holds the mirror up to more that is truly native and characteristic in American life than has been reflected by any other storyteller who has essayed the task." A year after publication, when the novel was still selling very well, *Craftsman* maintained that "Everybody knows this book; because everyone who reads it goes immediately and urges all his friends to do the same, for it grips the very roots of American life and shows the beginnings and growth of the great social and industrial problems that we are grappling with today."

Twenty-five thousand copies of the book were bought during the first month of publication. Over the years it was to sell close to three hundred thousand copies. *A Certain Rich Man* contained in novelized form all of White's progressive beliefs. The book opened amidst the events leading to the Civil War and carried the main character, John Barclay, through that conflict and into the settling and building of the Middle West after the war. John Barclay developed into a shrewd lawyer, greedily amassing a great fortune. By 1900, through his stock manipulations, Barclay was one of the most powerful men in the nation. He had helped transform America and his own Middle West from a rural to an industrial society. He had achieved all this at a tremendous price, however. In order to build his power, he had ruthlessly corrupted politics to secure favorable legislation for his interests and had adulterated the products that his firms sold the people. White frequently moralized over Barclay's actions. "That boy—that boy— that boy! Isn't he selling his soul to the devil by bits?" asked one of White's characters. "A little chunk goes every day. And oh, my dear, my dear . . . what profiteth a man if he gain the whole world, and loses his soul?"

Finally, the progressive crusade caught up with John Barclay's greed. In spite of his money and power he could not check the growing spirit of social responsibility in the minds of the public. At this point, Barclay had a religious experience and felt the spirit of God. He gave up all his ill-gotten gains and ended his own life by trying to save a drowning woman. White closed the novel with this message: "The more we give in this world, the more we take from it; and the more we keep for ourselves, the less we take."

The book grew out of White's own experience of having seen his frontier society molded into the grasping greedy capitalism of the Gilded Age. As he was writing it, he became aware that he was telling the old Biblical story of the Prodigal Son in an American setting. The use of the progressive movement afforded White an opportunity to describe the new forces at work curbing an unrestricted capitalism, and to bring about the conversion of his character, John Barclay. A later critic, John Chamberlain, contended that the conversion of Barclay was the one incredible aspect of the novel. Chamberlain believed also that White had no sufficient comprehension of the need for altering social and economic institutions before evil men could be curbed. *A Certain Rich Man* did lack any penetrating insight into the need for environmental change. When a reader of the book in 1910 criticized him for not seeing that the system and not the individual had to be changed, White replied: "I believe that the great combat of the twentieth century is to be the combat between democracy and capital and I am feeling my way slowly into a position upon this question . . . You must not blame me if I cannot go the full length that you do, but, as the fellow said, 'It is something to be on the way!'"

White received an immense amount of fan mail as a result of the novel. From this time until his death, his correspondence became increasingly voluminous. Theodore Roosevelt, on safari in Africa, sent a long handwritten letter to the Emporian. "I like it immensely, not merely as a novel (though from the standpoint of simple enjoyment it is tenfold worth reading) but because it is a real, and very effective, tract for the times . . ." declared Roosevelt. "I profoundly agree with the fundamental teaching of your book. It represents the major part of what I struggled for, what I had closest at heart, what I strove to accomplish, as President." Fellow progressives, Joseph Bristow and James R. Garfield, praised the novel as a great book for the times and Professor William Lyon Phelps of Yale University told White: "It is a true work of realistic art: it tells the truth and at the same time, shows a strong moral grasp of life."

When the Whites reached home late that August, the town of Emporia turned out en masse to welcome them. Mrs. White's mother in Kansas City had been told by the Emporia citizenry to make sure that the Whites boarded one particular train. It happened to be a slow train, and White didn't want to take it but his mother-in-law was adamant. As the train pulled into Emporia, the White family saw a band, a huge crowd, and many flags and banners at the station. As the train stopped, they read on the banners "The Conquering Hero Comes," "In Our Town Once Again," "The Real Issue," "The Homecoming of Colonel Hucks," and "What's the Matter With Kansas, Hey Bill?" As White stepped off the train to a clamor of voices, a special edition of the Joplin *News Herald*, edited by a former *Gazette* reporter, was pushed into White's hands. The entire front page was devoted to White, with one headline reading "Back to Empory in all her glory. Back to the busted garden hose."

The Whites were bundled into a hack and driven to Humboldt Park, preceded by the band and surrounded by the townfolks. There they were greeted by a number of out-of-town friends including Victor Murdock, Fred Trigg, Alex Butts, Marsh and Bent Murdock, W. Y. Morgan, and Charles F. Scott. The home folks and some of the visitors then put on a program based on *A Certain Rich Man.* A quartet led by Mrs. Robert L. Jones sang "Home Again from a Foreign Shore" and "Ever of Thee I Am Fondly Singing." In the middle of the entertainment, White turned to his wife, held his hat under her chin, and said, "Boys, she can't hold it in any more." The homecoming celebration attracted widespread newspaper comment, and Ida M. Tarbell, a frequent Emporia visitor, wrote to White: "I have never read anything lovelier in my life than the account of your homecoming. We all wept over it. Aren't you glad you staid by Emporia?"

*   *   *

By the time that the Whites returned from their European trip, a major fight was being waged between progressive and standpat Republicans. In the spring of 1909, Taft had called a special session of Congress to redeem the Republican party's pledge of a downward revision of the tariff. The Payne-Aldrich tariff that was passed over the protests of progressive Senators LaFollette, Bristow, Beveridge, Cummins, and Dolliver raised instead of lowered rates. When Taft failed to veto the bill, the progressives began to charge that Taft was trying to destroy Theodore Roosevelt's policies.

A second battle that was under way at that time was the struggle in the House of Representatives against the dictatorial power of Speaker Joe Cannon. Among the leaders of the attack on Cannon's powers were Victor Murdock and E. H. Madison of Kansas, George Norris of Nebraska, John M. Nelson of Wisconsin, and C. A. Lindbergh of Minnesota. The Republican revolt against Taft from 1909 to 1912 centered particularly in the rural states of Kansas, Nebraska, Minnesota, Wisconsin, and Iowa. These were the states in which Bryan and the Populists had had a strong following. The leaders of this insurgent movement were agrarian or small-town men, like William Allen White, who had a deep faith in the idealism of the common man, a profound distrust of big cities, and an abiding confidence in agriculture as the backbone of the nation. The insurgent movement against Taft was only one phase of the broader progressive movement, but as Louis Post shrewdly observed in the *Public* magazine, "The insurgents were Progressives who meant it."

White was immediately embroiled in the progressive schism with Taft. W. R. Nelson of the *Star*, incensed at the Payne-Aldrich tariff, wrote White on August 17, 1909, that "Bristow was great. He and Murdock are our heroes now. When you undertook to bring Bristow out for Long's place I had no notion that he had a look-in, or if he were to be elected that he would so soon become a national figure . . . And Murdock is another comer. By aggressiveness, independence and capacity as an organizer he has made himself the leader in the fight on Cannonism and Cannon. . . . The most encouraging feature of the situation is the group of Insurgents in the House and Senate. They are the real stuff." With powerful papers like the Kansas City *Star* backing the insurgent forces, public opinion in Kansas and surrounding states rallied to the fight against the Payne-Aldrich tariff and Speaker Cannon.

After President Taft defended the tariff bill in a speech in Minnesota in September, 1909, White reported that the West was hostile. "We feel," he wrote, "and feel strongly, that the President has turned his back upon that strong element of conscientious independent open-minded Americanism, voted by the insurgent Senators . . . Perhaps the President will work out all right. But he should not make speeches in the West. They don't understand his temperament . . . I like Mr. Taft, and earnestly and sincerely I wish to see him succeed. But he seems to be off on the wrong foot, and those of us who have been stepped on feel hurt."

During the closing months of 1909, White met many times with Governor Stubbs, Senator Bristow, Henry J. Allen, and other Kansas progressives to plan campaigns for progressive Republicans in every Congressional district in the state. "With Stubbs at the head, Bristow *really helping,* your typewriter going all the time, we will clean this state up from top to bottom . . ." one progressive wrote White on October 19, 1909. A fellow newspaperman, T. A. McNeal, told White: "I have a very great admiration for you Bill. I think that you are one of the smartest men I have ever known and I think that you are honest and helping to fight the battle of the ages; the battle against graft and selfishness and greed . . . You have in my judgment grown wonderfully within the past few years and today I regard you as the strongest single force in the State of Kansas. . . ."

While the interparty fight between the progressives and the standpatters was developing in 1909, White publicized the progressive position by writing a series of articles for the *American Magazine* entitled "The Old Order Changeth." The articles reflected a confident optimism on White's part that private capital was going to be controlled and that vested interests would no longer have power in politics.

White described the manner by which special privilege groups had moved into politics and bought control of legislators. With the advent of the progressive movement, however, he felt that the country was moving toward democracy and away from domination by a financial oligarchy. He then described a number of progressive laws and urged all states to adopt them. The secret ballot, publicity for campaign expenses, the direct primary, the initiative, the referendum, and the recall he hailed as steps toward a better democracy. The detailed information as to the success of these measures in certain states White secured in lengthy correspondence with such progressive figures as Robert Lincoln O'Brien of the Boston *Herald*, George L. Record of New Jersey, Brand Whitlock, mayor of Toledo, and Tom Johnson, mayor of Cleveland.

Although some progressives advocated laws to prevent the federal judiciary from declaring acts of Congress unconstitutional, White would not support curbs on the Supreme Court. He felt that only the Supreme Court should have the power to declare a law unconstitutional. White admitted that the federal courts had been the organs of the financial and business forces in the past, but he maintained that judges were human and that in time they would carry out the will of the people. The Supreme Court's power should not be clipped, he thought, because the court was a great bulwark against unwise public clamor, while it would gradually accept well-developed public attitudes. "And the slowness of the courts to respond to public sentiment," he wrote, "is one of the real—though at times amply disguised—blessings of this government . . . whatever the people aspire to earnestly unselfishly, persistently, they may have as the law of the land."

The Emporia editor was definitely convinced that the Supreme Court would lose its reactionary character and never again strike down legislation that was carefully drawn and really desired by the people. To White, as to middle-class America, there was a certain halo of sanctity about the Supreme Court. Although realistically he might have to admit that the court was destroying progressive laws, his emotional attitude was such that he could sanction no step to limit its power.

After the articles had appeared in the *American Magazine*, they were released in book form under the same title—*The Old Order Changeth*—early in 1910. White added a concluding chapter that revealed not only his own essential conservative nature but his heartfelt optimism. He declared that the standpatters and financial groups were foolish to resist control by the people, since the movement was basically sound and was conducted by successful men, not by rattlebrained radicals. He proved, however, to be a wishful thinker when he wrote John S. Phillips that without question the people were successfully regulating capital and that Phillips should "break the news gently to the followers of Karl Marks [sic] . . . 'Babylon is fallen, is fallen . . .'"

* * *

Future editor and writer and spokesman for grass-roots America—William Allen White in 1873. (*Courtesy of Paul Chandler.*)

Sallie Lindsay White at the time of her marriage to William Allen White. *(Courtesy of Paul Chandler.)*

William Allen White about the time he bought the *Gazette.* *(Courtesy of Laura M. French.)*

Mrs. White, Bill, and Mary. *(Courtesy of Laura M. French.)*

William Allen White and William Dean Howells. *(Courtesy of Laura M. French.)*

Ed Howe and William Allen White at the turn of the century.
(Courtesy of Laura M. French.)

Brock Pemberton, Edna Ferber, and William Allen White

"THIS WAY, JUMBO!"

—By Jerry Doyle.

(A cartoon by Jerry Doyle. Courtesy of Philadelphia Record, *Friday, April 5, 1935.)*

(Courtesy of Rollin Kirby, New York World-Telegram, Thursday, March 28, 1935.)

White talking with a young member of the *Gazette* staff.
(Photograph from Walter Johnson.)

Cartoons during the 1936 election campaign show a contradictory day in White's life. At the left he is greeting Franklin D. Roosevelt at the station in Emporia. At the right, he is drafting an anti-New Deal editorial for the *Gazette*. *(Courtesy of the University Library, University of Kansas.)*

Henry J. Allen and William Allen White at the Republican convention in 1936. *(Courtesy of Henry J. Allen.)*

White and La Guardia talk with Harold L. Ickes before the latter's speech to the American Civil Liberties Union in New York, December 8, 1937. In sending an autographed copy of this picture to Ickes, who had requested it, White later wrote: "I'm not quite sure whether it's faith, hope and charity, or the world, the flesh, and the devil. Or perhaps the lineal descendents of the three witches who put the kibosh on Macbeth." *(Press Association, Inc.)*

Brock Pemberton, William Allen White, and H. A. Bruno. White is receiving the 1940 award of the National Association of Accredited Publicity Directors for "the most distinguished service in the whole field of public opinion promotion." White's annotations comment unflatteringly on his own likeness. (*Courtesy of National Association of Public Relations Counsel, Inc.*)

White, Wendell L. Willkie, and Harold E. Stassen confer during Willkie's campaign as Republican presidential candidate in 1940. *(Press Association, Inc.)*

The desk of a man with three careers—editor, writer, man of politics. William Allen White is shown at work here in his office in the *Gazette* building. *(Courtesy of Paul Chandler.)*

"I've lived a swell life," William Allen White said on his seventieth birthday in 1938. *(Press Association, Inc.)*

Mrs. White is greeted on her seventy-first birthday. (*Courtesy of Paul Chandler.*)

In 1943, at his beloved summer home near Estes Park, Colorado, William Allen White had time once more to look into the mountains. (*Wide World Photo.*)

During the opening months of 1910, the Emporia editor was the leader of the bitter fight against the pro-Cannon congressmen in Kansas. To one friend White confided: ". . . we are now facing the crises of this country in which there are on the one hand politicians and those who finance the politicians, the great organizations which receive special privileges, and on the other hand all good citizens of every creed and caste politically and socially. It is a lot of fun to fight on the side of the folks and I believe eventually it will be a winning fight."

On February 3, White wrote President Taft, warning him that the people were supporting the insurgent cause against Speaker Cannon and Senator Aldrich. Unless the insurgents were successful, White stated, the people would elect a Democratic Congress that fall. "If you will just let the insurgents alone they will come home like little Bo-peep's sheep," White told the President. "They are not against your administration . . . But they will not work with Senator Aldrich and Mr. Cannon . . . The movement distinctly is not against you; it is not against your program. But it is against the leadership you are compelled to recognize. We propose to try to change that leadership by sending men back to Congress who will not submit to it—hence insurgents." Realizing the difficult position the President was in, he added: "The leadership of the party remains under the present status with Senator Aldrich and Mr. Cannon. You are more or less bound to take their advice, and of course their advice is for discipline . . . I believe in your program. But I am supposed to be against you because I am putting up a congressional delegation that will put skids under five out of the seven Kansas Congressmen, and replace them with men who are like Murdock and Madison and Bristow . . . It is a puzzle . . ."

In the latter part of March the insurgent Republicans combined with a number of Democrats to exclude Speaker Cannon from the Committee on Rules. The removal of Cannon from that committee was hailed as a great victory by the insurgents. The Kansas City *Times* saw in it ". . . the heaviest single blow that could have been dealt to the form of autocratic misgovernment called Cannonism." Joseph Bristow wrote White that Victor Murdock, the leader of the fight, had shown remarkable decision and courage. "It is a great fight and a great victory," White told Murdock on March 22, 1910, "and everyone in Kansas is very proud of you."

The growing suspicion felt by White and other insurgents that Taft was gradually repudiating Roosevelt's policies was heightened in 1910 by the Pinchot-Ballinger controversy. Gifford Pinchot, chief of the United States Forest Service and close friend of Roosevelt, supported charges that Ballinger, Taft's secretary of the interior, was guilty of land frauds and was hostile to conservation. Taft dismissed Pinchot for insubordination. Although a subsequent Congressional investigation supported Taft and Ballinger, the insurgents were convinced that Taft had now deserted the progressive cause.

The repercussions of the Pinchot-Ballinger controversy in Kansas were extreme. Victor Murdock had written White on December 27, 1909, prophesying that "the Pinchot-Ballinger business is going to be red-hot and formed into a pivot upon which all events will turn." When Pinchot was forced to resign, White editorially hailed him as a "thoroughbred" and vigorously criticized the President. Although Taft actually was not hostile to conservation, his part in the Pinchot-Ballinger controversy gave the country that impression. White joined a Publishers' Conservation League to promote the Roosevelt-Pinchot conservation policies along with such influential publishers as W. R. Nelson of the Kansas City *Star*; H. H. Kohlsaat of the Chicago *Record-Herald*; Fremont Older of the San Francisco *Bulletin*; and E. A. Van Valkenberg of the Philadelphia *North American*.

During this controversy, Senator Bristow told White that he was convinced that Taft was willing to do everything he could to destroy the insurgents. White, analyzing the public's attitude toward Taft, declared that there was a "distinct loss of confidence in the President. The people believe he has failed them. The people regard with suspicion anything that he advocates . . . They believe that he can be fooled, and he takes things from designing men without looking at them." In real sorrow, White wrote to one friend: "What a sad thing it is—the slumping of public confidence in the President. I believe it has come because he has made the mistake of compromising on essential things rather than upon unessentials. Mr. Roosevelt was a great compromiser. He was the

most successful trader that has been in the White House for many
years. Yet he never traded any fundamental right. And President
Taft does not understand that it is not his trading that the people
object to, but the kind of trading he is doing."

* * *

All was not politics in White's life, of course, during the winter
and spring of 1910. He was out of town for several days just before his forty-second birthday on February 10, 1910, and was due
home the evening of that day. Mrs. White planned a big birthday
dinner and surprise party for him at the old Whitley Hotel. From
the lobby of this hotel, a wide stairway rose to the second floor.
In the broad corridors running north and south from the head of
the stairway, long tables were set. That night all the *Gazette* staff
and their families were seated at the tables, waiting for White
to come.

When White left the train in Emporia, he took a cab. Before
he could tell the driver to take him straight home, the driver said:
"Mr. White, a man at the Whitley Hotel wants to see you, and
asked me to bring you there before you go home." White protested that he didn't want to go anywhere except home, and that
he wasn't going to meet any man at the Whitley. "But the man
said it was important that you come there," the driver insisted.
"What kind of a game is this you're trying to put up on me, I'd
like to know. I tell you I'm not going to the Whitley Hotel," declared White. It would only take a few minutes, the driver said,
and he would stay right there to take White home. "Be sure you
wait," White said as he left the cab at the hotel.

Inside the hotel, White looked for the man who was supposed
to be waiting for him. "The man who wants to see you is upstairs,"
Colonel Whitley explained. "Go right on up." "But I won't," said
White. "What are you trying to put over on me, anyhow?" But
the colonel assured him it was all right, that there really was some
important business upstairs that he should get in on. So, finally
and with many protests, White started up the stairs. At the head
of the stairs stood Mrs. White. She called "Happy birthday" to
him, and the guests all echoed her greeting. For this occasion the

fat poet, Walt Mason, had written as place cards, "Gaffer White," one of his prose poems:

Gaffer White, Solemn Reflections Inspired by his Forty-second Birthday, Thursday, February tenth, 1910.

Gaffer White is old and gray,
And he totters on his way,
Crooning old, forgotten hymns—
Mark his weak and trembling limbs!
Seated in his inglemook,
With his snuffbox and his book,
Dreaming of the vanished years,
Smiling gently through his tears!
Bowed his back, his knees are sprung—
But his heart is always young!

Gaffer White has wandered far,
Where the rocks and brambles are;
He has seen the world grow old;
He has seen men's feet grow cold!
After facing many a blast
He is living in the past,
Old and bent and withered now,
With the snow upon his brow,
With the crow's feet 'neath his eyes,
And his bosom rent with sighs;
With his sinews all unstrung—
But his heart is always young!

A few days after his birthday party, White went East to visit in New York and Washington. While in New York, he delivered a lecture on "The Literature of Agitation" before a Columbia University audience. He also had time for meetings with his magazine and newspaper friends. One day he had lunch with Ida Tarbell, John S. Phillips, John Graham Brooks, Anne Morgan, and Brand Whitlock at a beautiful, colonial mansion once inhabited by Washington Irving. "We had a good time," Whitlock recalled. In Washington for just one day, White visited with Bristow and Murdock and talked over the forthcoming state and Congressional primary campaign. White had not been back in Emporia many days before Mrs. J. P. Morgan and her daughter Anne stopped off to pay the Whites a visit. "She is a bully person," Ida Tarbell wrote White about Anne, "and she thinks you are a bully person." Shortly after the Morgans' visit, a conductor on the Santa Fe Railroad wrote White: "The papers had quite a little to say about your entertaining Mrs. and Miss Morgan. Emporia is certainly getting to be universally talked about and people going through on the trains inquire is this the home of William Allen White. You are certainly a notorious person outside of Kansas and the Kansas *Idol* outside of the Ring Politicians."

Late in May, 1910, White returned to New York again, this time to receive an honorary Master of Arts degree at the Columbia University commencement. It was while standing in line at the commencement proceedings that he started a lifelong friendship with Dr. Will Mayo. "Around us were a lot of notables whose faces we recognized," White once recalled. "But we were put side by side and we looked at each other like a couple of dogs for a minute, and finally Dr. Mayo said to me, 'I don't know what I am doing here.' And I said, 'You have got nothing on me, neither do I.' And then we both grinned and he said, 'Who are you?' And I said, 'To tell you the truth I am just a country editor from a little town in Kansas called Emporia and my name's White.' He grinned and said, 'Well, all right, I am just a country doctor from a little town in Minnesota called Rochester and my name's Mayo!' "

While at Columbia, Editor White delivered a talk, "A Theory of Spiritual Progress," before the university's Phi Beta Kappa Society. It was typical progressive talk fused with basic Christian principles. According to White, modern civilization would endure only as long as brotherhood and goodwill were at its foundations. "Whoever would achieve any worthy thing," he declared, "must found it upon the common law of kindness known as righteousness . . . Only until a man has got out of himself, until his effort is for others, until, in short, he is out of the eternal grind and in the wider cycle of kindness, may a man really achieve." When White sent a copy of this speech to his old teacher, W. H. Carruth, the latter told him: "I am thankful for you and for your manful stand for your ideals. God bless you."

While in New York, White dined with Henry Watterson of

the Louisville *Courier-Journal* and Charles Dana Gibson, creator of the Gibson Girl, and Mrs. Gibson. He also attended a dinner at which Judge Gary of the steel trust and a number of other important financiers and industrialists, to his surprise, criticized President Taft's policies. In Washington, he had lunch with Taft at the White House. They talked about everything but politics. "It was all very queer and very amusing," he wrote Henry Haskell of the *Star* on June 6, 1910. To another newspaperman he reported: "We talked for two hours about the nebular hypothesis, the dynamic forces of living matter, the general theory of pragmatism and the esoteric cure for bots. I thought you would like to know how two intellectual giants pass their time."

Several weeks after White's conversation with Taft, Theodore Roosevelt landed in New York after more than a year abroad. White welcomed the Rough Rider home by writing him a long letter. "It seems good to have you with us again," he told the Colonel. "We need you in our business. The American people are terribly sentimental; it seems to me that they are the most sentimental people in the world; that is they will do more for what seems the larger good, for the intelligently unselfish end, than any other people. And they have had a year or so without an appeal to that side of their natures from those in high places. That is the whole trouble with President Taft. His appeal has been to the head, not to the hearts of the people." Then, taking note of a growing movement to run Roosevelt for president in 1912, White said: "But—and this is the second proposition—we do not need you for president. I am against that movement . . . We need your voice sounded in such a way that no one will suspect that ambition is moving you. We need your influence as an unselfish leader working with the people as one of them, not as their ruler. We need a brother and not a master nor a servant. . . ."

The crucial problem at the moment, he told Roosevelt, was the reviving of the Republican party. The party's alliance with aggrandized wealth must be everlastingly smashed, and the people must be in firm control of the party. "Your job," White explained to Roosevelt, "is to work with the people to capture control of the Republican party." "They have a right to expect you to serve them," White added, "in this higher service, this more unselfish and more practical service without reward and without official honor. Of course you may depend upon me. In any event in any program I am for you, and shall be with you."

Shortly after this letter was written, White hurried to Denver to help progressive Republicans Edward P. Costigan and Judge Ben Lindsey launch a powerful interparty attack on the reactionary Colorado Republicans, who were backed by the big power and mining interests. White told the Colorado progressives ". . . that the Republican party had always been the reform party and that its history was a record of successful insurgency! Obviously the progressives were the true Republicans." After White's visit, Judge Ben Lindsey declared that his speech "gave us a big boost. His coming was the very best thing that has happened in years and I am glad to report to you that the Insurgent movement has taken on new life . . . 'Bill Allen' made a splendid impression here. He thinks he is not much of a talker, but his kind of talk is just the stuff we need. It made a more powerful impression than the finest sky-scraping oration that has ever been delivered at a Republican gathering in this state."

When White returned home, he editorially denounced any steps toward the formation of a third party. As he told his allies on the Kansas City *Star*, the insurgent Republicans were in a strategic position to capture the party machinery that autumn in much of the Middle West. A bolt from the party at this time would only weaken their cause. Colonel Nelson, however, was pessimistic about any good coming out of the Republican party and felt that a new party would be required to express progressive principles. White replied that he didn't completely disagree, but that before thinking in such terms they should see if the insurgents could capture control of the Republican party in the forthcoming election. If a split was to come, he told the *Star*, he expected it would take place in 1912.

The month of July found White thoroughly immersed in the insurgent primary campaign for control of the Congressional nominations and in Governor Stubbs' campaign for renomination. That White was a significant power in Kansas politics was evident from the widespread manner in which the various candidates circulated his endorsements. When Richard J. Hopkins, for instance, decided to run for lieutenant governor, he wrote White: "I realize fully the strength of an endorsement by you." As the executive in the campaign, White sent Joseph Bristow and Victor Murdock to those places where the insurgent ticket needed most help. The publications that he issued underlined the pro-Cannon stand of most of the incumbent congressmen and was of great value in bringing about a favorable election result.

White's leadership of the insurgent cause, however, brought him into conflict with some of his oldest friends. He opposed, for example, Congressman Charles F. Scott. He told Scott that "the difference between the insurgents and the Cannon Republicans is fundamental. They believe in the growing rights of men, you believe in the growing rights of property. The thing has got to be fought out in the Republican party and we will see who owns the party, the people or the corporations. I have absolutely no personal feeling in this matter except one of exceeding sadness that I am compelled to line up against a friend, but I do it without a quiver as I should expect my friends to line up against me when we differ in matters of fundamental principle."

The primary election was immensely successful for the insurgents. They captured six out of the eight Congressional nominations, and Stubbs was renominated by a large majority. A Missouri bank president wrote White: "It was a great victory: Shake. You have done the Nation, the State and the party a great service." The machine Republicans, for their part, were aware that White was their chief opponent in the insurgent camp. A year before, when White had criticized them in the state legislature for blocking progressive legislation, one of their number introduced the following resolution:

"Whereas, it appears from a statement of the present managing director of the Republican party in Kansas, William Allen White, that the said party is insolvent . . . be it Resolved, that the said party file a petition in voluntary bankruptcy . . . and the unlawful, spurious and forged promissory notes issued by the said self-elected managing director be repudiated and the party restored to a solvent condition."

*   *   *

The Congressional and state campaigns in the fall of 1910 fully demonstrated White's national prestige and importance. He was not only a figure in Kansas politics, but his support and advice were eagerly sought by Indiana, Colorado, and California progressives. White's endorsement of Hiram Johnson's candidacy for governor in California was hailed by the chairman of the Republican State Central Committee as "the best expression and argument we have had yet." White also came to the aid of Senator Beveridge's campaign for re-election in Indiana with an endorsement and an article in the October issue of the *American Magazine*. Beveridge immediately wrote White: "It is out of the question to thank you sufficiently—the word 'thanks' doesn't at all express my gratitude. . . ." Beveridge, however, was defeated that fall in the Democratic landslide that swept his state.

In the campaign in Kansas, White enlisted the support of the American Federation of Labor for the Republican ticket. "We know the work you are doing is bringing results," the Kansas head of the A.F.L. wrote, "and are only too glad to co-operate with you in any and all public questions." With suggestions from Governor Stubbs, Senator Bristow, and Congressman Murdock, White wrote the Republican state platform, incorporating in it planks for the initiative, the referendum, the recall, and the short ballot. The platform also denounced the Payne-Aldrich tariff, demanded the strict enforcement of the antitrust law, and called for constitutional amendments to provide for the direct election of United States senators and to permit the levying of an income tax. The platform closed with the following declaration inserted by the Emporia editor: "We send our greeting to Theodore Roosevelt, the new world's champion of the rights of man in the world-old contest between rising humanity and the encroachments of special privilege. And as Republicans we stand ready to enlist under his banner in the fight for human rights. . . ."

The platform was adopted by the state convention over the protests of the machine Republicans. White told one of these standpatters: "This movement has been growing in the Republican party for six years . . . It will not stop until it controls the National Republican convention." Old Populists and Socialists now began to write White and in a spirit of fun reproach him for supporting their demands. Socialist Henry Vincent of Girard, Kansas, for instance, wrote White: "Dear Comrade! Pardon the liberty, but why should I hesitate. You certainly have a *red card* by this time! Since you have left us only Woman Suffrage and the old subtreasury from the Populist Platforms of 20 years ago." White explained to Vincent: "The chief objection I have to you Socialists is that you are so cocksure that you are right and that all the rest of us are scoundrels. I am reasonably sure that we are all more or less scoundrels."

On election day the Republican ticket swept Kansas in spite of the general Democratic success in most of the other states. Kansas sent a full Republican Congressional delegation to Washington, although Congress was to be controlled by the Democrats. "You are the backbone of the Republican party in this State . . ." the chairman of the Republican State Central Committee wrote White. White interpreted the election as an indication that the people would vote Republican only if the candidates and platforms were progressive in spirit. To Colonel Roosevelt, who was indecisive and apt to compromise, White wrote that "where the ultra radicals were in control . . . we held our own against the tide . . . I'm writing you this that you may see that the ultra radical position is the only one that fairly and squarely was endorsed by the people in normally Republican states at this election. Every straddler in the West got licked . . . Now don't get it up your nose that I think you are a straddler, because I don't think you are a straddler at all . . . But a lot of fellows out here did try to straddle and they did get licked . . . It will pay any radical leader to make a square toed stand by his convictions stated in their *ultimate* form and go down discredited, rather than to compromise on a halfway declaration." Actually, White was convinced by this time that Roosevelt's besetting sin was his willingness to compromise with the Old Guard. "He thinks," White wrote Mark Sullivan on November 23, 1910, "that compromise is the only thing and he is going to be everlastingly crucified by the American people unless he gets this compromise idea out of his head."

White was still thoroughly opposed to any suggestion that Roosevelt should run for the presidency in 1912. White was convinced that he would be of more value to the country as a preacher of righteousness and director of thought than as president. Possibly by 1916, when the country had learned to walk in progressive paths without Roosevelt's leadership, the time would be ripe for Roosevelt to run again. But for the progressive Republicans to work for Roosevelt's candidacy in 1910 would weaken the movement and make it seem a one-man affair. To anyone who inquired, White stated that he was for either Albert Beveridge or Robert M. LaFollette in 1912.

White was just as forthright in his letters to Colonel Roosevelt that he should not run in 1912. Roosevelt assured him that he did not want the office. But, Roosevelt added: "It is possible that circumstances might arise when it would be unpatriotic of me, when it would represent going back on my principles and my friends, to refuse to be President." After reading this statement, White observed sadly but wisely that Roosevelt "feels that his duty may call him for which I am sorry."

In January, 1911, White assisted Senators Robert M. LaFollette, Jonathan Bourne, and Joseph L. Bristow in launching the National Progressive Republican League. During the course of that year, the league crystallized sentiment in favor of LaFollette for president in 1912. When Theodore Roosevelt criticized the league for being too extreme, White publicized the league's cause and rebuked Roosevelt in a friendly tone in an article called "The Progressive Hen and the Insurgent Ducklings" in the *American Magazine* for January, 1911. According to White, Colonel Roosevelt was the Progressive Hen who had hatched the Insurgent Ducklings, but "they will go into the water, even though she fusses about it, and she cautiously avoids the water even though they love it."

Senator LaFollette was hailed in the article as a highly constructive statesman. "No other American statesman," White wrote, "in fifteen years has affected the state governments of so large an area of the American Republic as LaFollette has." LaFollette was immensely pleased with White's praise.

During the opening months of 1911, Joseph L. Bristow and Victor Murdock kept White informed as to political developments in Washington. Both of them were convinced that Taft on the Republican ticket would assure a Democratic victory. White agreed with this interpretation, but he was in a quandary. By January, 1911, he had been convinced that Senator LaFollette was not well enough known to be able to win in 1912. Colonel Roosevelt, on the other hand, was the most popular candidate the progressives could run, but White still felt that he should not be a candidate.

While the insurgent Republicans were attempting to capture control of their party's machinery, a new progressive star of promise appeared in New Jersey. Democratic Governor Woodrow Wilson, formerly president of Princeton University, was inaugurating laws that were bringing New Jersey into the forefront of the progressive states. "I heard Wilson make a speech last night," Albert Boyden of the *American Magazine* wrote White on January 6, 1911, ". . . All your friends, Miss Tarbell, Anne Morgan, quite a bunch, went over from here, and all were crazy over Wilson. Baker saw Teddy the other day. He got the idea that Teddy thought Wilson had an awfully good chance in 1912." White himself warmly praised Wilson in an editorial on April 18, 1911, and predicted that he would be a future candidate for president. To Fred Trigg of the *Star*, White prophesied that Wilson could carry Kansas against Taft with great ease, and that the Republican party all over the Middle West would be thoroughly defeated unless the state leaders cut loose from Taft.

* * *

Kansas politics gave White great concern in 1911. He was determined that the legislature should carry out the Republican platform pledges for the initiative, the referendum, and the recall. He went to Topeka a number of times to exert pressure on the members of that body. He wrote innumerable letters to influential labor leaders, lawyers, and editors suggesting that they help persuade their state senator and representative to vote for these measures. Governor Stubbs and Senator Bristow threw their support behind these bills, but in the State Senate the standpat Republicans defeated the proposals in late February.

White also devoted a great deal of time to planning the progressive Republican campaign for governor in the 1912 primary. After extended correspondence and frequent consultations with

Governor Stubbs, Senator Bristow, Congressman Murdock, and Henry Allen, it was agreed that Congressman Ed Madison would be the strongest candidate. White wrote Madison that it was his duty to run for that office. "You are the one man in Kansas who can insure Kansas to the Republicans next year," White told him. Madison was reluctant to run for governor and wrote White partly in jest, although his statement contained a large amount of truth, that White was "playing the role of the Kansas 'King' maker."

Arthur Capper of the Topeka *Capital* finally decided to run for the governorship himself. White tried to dissuade him by telling him that an editor should not run for office. "The Capital is as permanent as an institution in this state," White told Capper on April 19, 1911. "It has done more than any other one force in this state to bring us up to our present progressive standard and during the next four years, it seems to me we cannot well afford to have the influence of the Capital crippled, as necessarily it must be crippled if you run for Governor." But, White added, "please, above everything, do not take this as a bucket of cold water on your boom. It is simply the misgivings of a friend who wants to point out every discouragement before it is too late, so that you can have the whole ground before you when you act and when you do act you may depend upon me to do all that I can to help you."

White continued to have misgivings about Capper's candidacy. He was afraid Capper would be defeated and thus forever be lost to the progressive cause. When, however, Capper announced his candidacy in June, 1911, White editorially supported him. "I would rather have your approval than that of anyone else in the state," Capper wrote White, "and your editorial is simply fine. It will do more to boost the proposition than anything else."

Shortly after the endorsement of Capper, the Whites left Emporia for a summer in the Colorado mountains. White had been occupied with politics for so long that he wanted a chance to get away and devote his time to literary pursuits. Just before leaving for Colorado he even considered selling the *Gazette*. He offered the paper for sale for $50,000. "I must either be an editor or an author," he told a close friend. "I am going to be an author . . .

With the Gazette off my shoulders I could write two or three good novels. I have my vanity of course. I believe those novels would do more permanent good than my work on the newspaper . . . I have only twenty years more of kick in me, and I feel that the best will not be forthcoming from the newspaper business. For even if the Gazette didn't need me all the time, to be editor of the Gazette would keep me in politics, and politics is taking too much of my time . . . I want to back out of the game and let the sovereign squats do their own squatting. There are plenty of men who can do that work. And I seem to have my own peculiar job. I someway feel I am wrapping my one little old talent in a napkin. Instead of which I wish to hang my banner on the outer wall."

Had William Allen White disposed of the *Gazette* and retired from the hurly-burly of everyday affairs, he undoubtedly would have written many more books. On the other hand, he never would have attained the prestige and power that he had with so many average Americans during the last twenty years of his life. He had this power largely because he did remain in Emporia as the small-town editor. Had he left Emporia, he would have cut himself off from his roots. He would never have become the weighty inter-preter of the small town to urban America that he became by re-maining as editor of the *Gazette*. Without the Emporia dateline, he would have become just one more literary figure devoid of the attributes that were to make him a folk hero.

Just before White returned from Colorado in the autumn of 1911, he was the principal speaker at a meeting of the Colorado Progressive Republicans. He helped the progressives establish a county and precinct organization for the entire state for the pur-pose of sending a progressive delegation to the Republican con-vention the next year. "The meeting was large and full of enthusi-asm," he wrote Theodore Roosevelt in October 18, 1911, "and I feel sure that if Colorado could have a direct vote on presidential nominees Taft would not stand any more show than a rabbit of getting the Colorado delegation . . . I tried out the names of Taft, Roosevelt, and LaFollette and Taft did not get a 'hand' and they lifted the roof for you and LaFollette."

By October, 1911, White was convinced that Colonel Roosevelt would be nominated by the Republican convention the following summer. Taft was such a political liability that the Emporia editor thought even the machine people would drop him in favor of Roosevelt. "I think you might just as well prepare for the fireworks because it is coming," White told Roosevelt on November 16, 1911. "You can't stave it off, and while up to the present time I have been very excitedly against your being a standing candidate for 1912 . . . I am not altogether sure that it will not be about the best we can do to let the fireworks do their work." The Rough Rider quickly replied to White's statement by remarking: "I do most emphatically feel that I have a right to expect every friend of mine to do everything in his power to prevent any movement looking toward my nomination." Roosevelt may have expected, but he did not require, his friends to follow this course of action. Furthermore, he wrote Henry Cabot Lodge on December 13, 1911: "I told them . . . that I certainly should not definitely state that if it did come in the form of a duty I would refuse to perform the duty."

Although Senator Bristow was opposed to any move toward Roosevelt, White told him on December 28, 1911: "We can and will nominate Roosevelt. And while I believe it is all right for Senator LaFollette to keep up the fight, and so long as he is in the fight I shall support him, yet I believe his chances for nomination are so remote as to be negligible."

A rather amusing incident that involved Roosevelt and White took place that December. A Kansas farmer wrote Governor Stubbs that his fifteenth child had just been born, and he had run out of names. Could the governor help him out? Stubbs suggested either Theodore Roosevelt or William Allen White. The old farmer gratefully wrote back that he had combined the suggestions and named the baby Theodore Allen White, "as he had as high regard for one as the other, and could not discriminate between them." When Roosevelt heard the story, he wrote White: "I think the name of that baby unquestionably fixes the names for the presidential and vice-presidential candidates to be nominated by the People's Party next June."

On January 8, 1912, Governor Stubbs publicly backed Roosevelt's candidacy. White in the *Gazette* on the same day advocated the nomination of LaFollette "believing that he will represent progressive ideas better in the presidency than Colonel Roosevelt." Actually, White was convinced that LaFollette did not have a chance of defeating Taft for the nomination, whereas sentiment was developing in an overwhelming manner for Roosevelt. "I am satisfied," he wrote Bristow, "that unless the drift changes nothing can stop the nomination of Roosevelt." White wrote to Roosevelt on January 16, 1912: "I won't fuss with you for a minute about your presidential boom, but I want to quarrel with you about the style of writing you are dropping into. You remember years ago how we used to fuss about McKinley's long, involved sentences that didn't get anywhere. They had a tendency to fatigue the reader. I am afraid you are going to fall into that habit yourself. I have taken your article in this week's Outlook and have marked up a lot of the sentences to show you what I mean. It seems to me that you are developing a nervous rather than a lucid style. You seem to be in a hurry to get it said and out of your way . . . You have an immense fund of ideas and they come crowding in on you, but what you want to do is to take a club and bat them off; end your sentence and then reach out and get another idea and put it down in another sentence."

In order to test progressive sentiment between Roosevelt and LaFollette, White wrote to every county chairman of the Republican party in the state and to key Republican editors. Their response only served to convince him that Kansas was overwhelmingly for Roosevelt. He told LaFollette's manager on January 22, 1912: "The fellows out here are for Roosevelt. It is not that they are against LaFollette, but against Taft and find it easier to nominate Roosevelt. If Senator LaFollette is coming to Kansas, I should be glad to do everything I can to promote his trip. I should be glad to look after his advertising, engage the various halls and do everything I could to promote his candidacy." Victor Murdock reported to White that from Washington it seemed clear that the Roosevelt campaign had shattered the LaFollette boom. Senator Bristow was not pleased with the growing sentiment for Roosevelt, since he felt that Roosevelt was too much of a compromiser and was unable to see the issues clearly. "LaFollette's superiority over Roosevelt," declared Bristow, "and all the rest of these progressive leaders is in the fact that he has definite and specific notions as to what ought to be done to correct the evils which exist."

During January, 1912, as Theodore Roosevelt played a game of watchful waiting, Gifford Pinchot, Medill McCormick of Chicago, Frank A. Munsey, owner of the New York *Press*, and George W. Perkins, Wall Street banker, carefully nurtured the Roosevelt boom. Although he made no official announcement that he was a candidate, by the middle of January Roosevelt was out for the nomination. Progressives like Bristow and White remained aloof from this movement until February 2, 1912. On that day, Senator LaFollette suffered a breakdown while addressing a publishers' dinner in Philadelphia. He was worn out by his campaign exertions, his daughter was about to undergo a serious operation, and his nerves were on edge because of the growing Roosevelt boom. Senator Bristow was shocked by LaFollette's collapse, and wrote White a long letter describing it as a terrifying spectacle. On the basis of LaFollette's breakdown, White, Bristow, and many other progressives left LaFollette for Roosevelt. Actually, LaFollette's health was not seriously impaired, but his collapse at the dinner gave White and many others the reason or the excuse for climbing on the Roosevelt band wagon. Although White had been for LaFollette, he had also been convinced for some time that Taft could defeat the Wisconsin senator. Since White was shrewd and calculating in politics, why should he remain with a hopeless cause? "It is not that LaFollette is not in many ways better equipped than Roosevelt," he told a friend of LaFollette's. "The whole thing lies in the fact that the prestige of the Ex-Presidency was a powerful weapon in this contest."

LaFollette and his supporters became extremely bitter toward Theodore Roosevelt's candidacy. They charged that Roosevelt had used LaFollette to test progressive sentiment, and when it was clear that the country was progressively minded, Roosevelt had stepped into the race. The Emporia editor, however, denied that Roosevelt had treated LaFollette in an unfair fashion. "I have known the relations between LaFollette and Roosevelt pretty well," White declared, "and do not believe Roosevelt in any way betrayed LaFollette. LaFollette demonstrated that he could not win so Roosevelt went in as the only available man."

For the next four years White was to devote the major share of his time to Roosevelt's political destinies. He was to take a Roosevelt delegation to the 1912 convention, and then bolt the party when Taft received the nomination. He was to organize Kansas for the Bull Moose party that year and try to keep that party alive until the election of 1916. In 1916, he was to see all his hopes for a progressive political movement shattered by Roosevelt's refusal to run again on the third-party ticket. Yet White never really could criticize his old friend nor fail to rally to his banner whenever Colonel Roosevelt sounded the call.

"No normal man can come in personal contact with White and withhold from him a tremendous liking and admiration," commented one Kansas newspaperman on White's Bull Moose activities from 1912 to 1916. "He is a good friend and a good hater. Give him his choice of running his fat legs off for a friend or heaving a brick at an enemy and he would hesitate. In the end he would do the errand for his friend, but he would hurry it along in order that he might also have time to heave the brick. Of all the star performers in the Bull Moose crowd, White probably is the only man whose enlistment in the cause cannot be traced to ulterior motives. . . . He has no axe to grind and such surgical operations as he desires to perform on those in politics at whom his gorge rises could be performed as well in one party as in another."

CHAPTER 10

BULL MOOSE DAYS

"AMONG those who play the game of politics, there is a division of opinion as to whether Bill is a fool or a hero," Kansas newspaperman Jay House remarked in 1914. "The writer's notion is that Bill's chief affliction is the temperament of a genius, and that due to this affliction he does a lot of fool things, but that at the core he is a very sound and estimable public citizen whose impulses are prompted by the highest motives . . . It is only when Bill sits down in front of a typewriter that he goes crazy . . . In his more impulsive moments his feelings overpower him and he temporarily succumbs to his emotions. Some of his editorial writing on the Emporia Gazette is so jaundiced and unfair, so palpably misrepresentative of facts, that it stirs even his friends to anger. But it doesn't mean that Bill intends to be unfair. It merely means that he has again fallen a victim to his emotions."

Although the Emporia editor's opponents charged that his political activities for Roosevelt in 1912 were based on pure emotionalism, White insisted that the progress of the country demanded a revolt from the machine control of the Republican party. Early in February, 1912, White was in Washington conferring with James Garfield, Gifford Pinchot, Victor Murdock, and Jonathan Bourne over Roosevelt's candidacy for the Republican nomination. Bourne insisted that the group should warn the Old Guard in a public statement that they would bolt the party unless Colonel Roosevelt was nominated. Otherwise, he argued, the machine Republicans would ignore the progressives. The group failed to act on Bourne's proposal, but after Taft did win the nomination they bolted. Had Bourne's recommendation been followed, the Republican convention might well have been forced to act in a different fashion.

Back in Kansas, White, Governor Stubbs, and Arthur Capper established a Roosevelt headquarters and launched such a vigorous campaign that they captured a Roosevelt delegation to the national convention. As the result of constant entreaties from other progressives, White ran and was elected Republican national committeeman over reactionary David Mulvane. "I wish to be on that National Committee four years from now when we will probably have the problem of reorganizing the Republican party . . ." he told a supporter. "I believe that our party must be definitely either liberal or else definitely reactionary. I believe that it cannot be liberal unless it is prepared to go into the last ditch and fight for principle, time and again putting up platforms and candidates, with only secondary regard for temporary victories. . . . I may not have large influence, but I am at least going to do my best and I believe my time will come three or four years from now." When White left the Republican party that summer to bolt with Theodore Roosevelt, he resigned his National Committee post and ended any chance of influencing the party toward more liberal ways. When he returned to the party fold in 1916, it was without the power that he once had had. From 1916 to his death, he was to serve as liberal midwestern window dressing for a party that was far from progressively minded.

In order to publicize Roosevelt's cause to the nation, White wrote an article for the May, 1912, *American Magazine* charging Taft with betraying Roosevelt to the reactionaries. "If ever an obligation rested upon a man to redeem another man's pledge," declared White, "that obligation was upon Mr. Taft when he went to the White House." White was convinced that he was only expressing the feelings of the average Middle Westerner when he wrote that sentence.

On June 10, White left for Chicago to help James R. Garfield and Gifford Pinchot organize the Roosevelt forces for the fight in the Republican convention. He was there not only to assist

Roosevelt as national committeeman from Kansas, but also to report the convention for the George Matthew Adams newspaper syndicate.

As the convention opened there was the spirit of no compromise between the rival Roosevelt-Taft factions. There seemed to be no doubt that Roosevelt was the choice of the average Republican voter in view of his smashing victories in those states that had presidential primaries. Most states, however, selected their delegates by conventions, and these delegates were for Taft. Roosevelt charged that many of the convention delegates had been dishonestly elected. The Republican National Committee, firmly in control of the Taft forces, dismissed Roosevelt's charge of fraud, which led Roosevelt to assert: "There is no form of rascality which the Taft men have not resorted to."

On June 15, Roosevelt arrived in Chicago to assist his supporters in the convention fight. "It is a fight against theft," he announced, "and the thieves will not win." When newspapermen asked him if he was ready for the fight, his reply inspired the emblem of the third party that he was soon to lead: "I'm feeling like a Bull Moose!"

Would Roosevelt bolt if he failed to receive the nomination? Elihu Root believed he would. White, who was with Roosevelt in the Congress Hotel almost constantly during the three days before the convention assembled, has denied that Roosevelt planned a bolt if he was not nominated. Talk was in the air that a compromise candidate, Governor Herbert Hadley, for instance, should be nominated to smooth the party rift. According to White, Roosevelt was opposed to any nomination until the "fraudulent" Taft delegates were purged.

"Do you remember those nights of the conference when you and I and a score of others gathered around Roosevelt and we talked over the strategy of the next day?" White wrote Frank Knox on January 9, 1920. "I remember particularly one day in which Deneen [Illinois senator] was up for consideration. He wanted a compromise and the Colonel blew up and said that he would not stand for any compromise until the roll was purged." White also wrote Henry J. Allen, who had been a leader of the Roosevelt forces on the floor of the convention, on March 22,

1940: "What Roosevelt did was to tell everybody, Hadley included, that he would not consent to any nomination unless the rolls were purged and if the rolls were purged, he declared, as you know, time and again that he would accept any nomination, even Taft's." Although Roosevelt may have said this during the pressure of the preconvention days, earlier Roosevelt had warned that "I won't stand it for a moment if the discredited bosses and politicians . . . decide against me."

On June 14, White wired his wife that he had been busy all day working on the proposed Republican platform with Amos and Gifford Pinchot, James R. Garfield, Frank Munsey, Medill McCormick, and Hiram Johnson. Roosevelt himself had not yet arrived in Chicago but the inner Roosevelt group had decided on their action. White stated that if the Taft delegates from Texas and Washington—convention-selected delegates—were seated, they would bolt the party. Roosevelt rallies were conducted day and night at the Congress Hotel, and twenty thousand people flocked to the auditorium to hear the Rough Rider speak just before the convention opened. In a spirit of religious frenzy, the followers of Roosevelt sang "Onward, Christian Soldiers." Roosevelt told his cheering audience: "Our cause is the cause of justice for all in the interest of all . . . We fight in honorable fashion for the good of mankind; fearless of the future; unheeding of our individual fates; with unflinching hearts and undimmed eyes; we stand at Armageddon, and we battle for the Lord." Henry Pringle, biographer of both Roosevelt and Taft, has written: "It was magnificent. It was epic, even if nobody knew where Armageddon was, exactly, and why the Lord had suddenly become an opponent of William Howard Taft."

The convention opened on June 18 in the Chicago Coliseum. A Credentials Committee, sympathetic to Taft, backed up the Republican National Committee in accepting Taft delegates and barring Roosevelt delegates whenever there were two sets of delegates from one state. Governor Hadley, floor leader of the Roosevelt forces, denounced this as "naked theft." When the galleries tried to stampede the convention for the nomination of Roosevelt, the Taft forces held firm. Seeing that everything was lost, the Roosevelt forces stood up and walked out of the hall. William

Allen White resigned his recently elected national committeeman-
ship to go with Roosevelt, and charged that Taft's nomination "was
accomplished by fraud so gross that to call him the nominee of the
Republican party is to be guilty of a grotesque joke."

Not all the progressive Republicans walked out of the Republican party. Senator LaFollette, bitter at Roosevelt and believing
that he was not a true progressive, supported Taft. So did Senator
Borah. Governor Hadley refused to bolt, because the Missouri
Republican organization was progressive. A bolt would only turn
it over to the reactionaries. Hadley tried not to support Taft, but
finally a month before the election he had to come out for him.
It might have been wiser in Kansas and other states had Hadley's
strategy been followed. By resigning his national committeeman
post, White played into the hands of the Kansas machine. David
Mulvane, whom he had defeated for that post, explained the machine strategy of staying with Taft, even though Taft was sure
to be defeated, by saying: "We can't elect Taft, but we are going
to hold on to this organization and when we get back four years
from now we will have it and not those d—— insurgents."

A number of progressive-minded men—Ray Stannard Baker,
Charles Crane, Norman Hapgood, Louis Brandeis—were to support the Democratic nominee, Woodrow Wilson. Wilson's idealism appealed to them. Furthermore, they were suspicious not only
of Roosevelt's devotion to real progressivism but of that of certain
of his supporters. Close to Roosevelt's throne were George W.
Perkins, J. P. Morgan partner, and Frank W. Munsey, millionaire
publisher. "If we're not careful," Albert Beveridge warned, "we'll
be labeled as a Wall Street promotion." Later White and some of
the other progressives, who gaily followed Roosevelt in 1912,
were to become suspicious of these men too. White was to be sure
that Perkins, for instance, deliberately wrecked the Progressive
party in 1916 and he was to write a scathing editorial at the time
of Munsey's death.

* * *

After the nomination of Taft, White hurried to Baltimore to
report the Democratic convention. With a split in the Republican
party, the Democrats faced victory for the first time since 1892.

It took the Democrats forty-six ballots, however, to nominate Woodrow Wilson. White declared that the Democratic party was inherently a reactionary party, because any party "that hesitates five days in nominating a man like Wilson is not to be trusted to carry out the progressive policies that he stands for . . . By all the rules of common sense and political wisdom Wilson should have been nominated on the first ballot."

Since White was not involved in political maneuvering at the Democratic convention, he had time to enjoy the company of the other people working for the George M. Adams syndicate. Adams had hired White to handle political dispatches while Edna Ferber, budding young author, and George Fitch, author of *My Demon Motorboat*, were to write human interest stories. Cartoonists "Ding" Darling and Harry Webster completed "Adams' trained seals." Adams rented a house for his group and every day White and Edna Ferber went shopping for food in Baltimore's outdoor market. One day they decided to hold a huge breakfast for other newspapermen. White and "The divine Edna," as he was to call her over a lifetime, bought everything in sight—fish, flesh, fowl, fruit, vegetables. As Edna Ferber has described it:

No one in history, including Henry the Eighth at the height of his gustatory powers, ever sat down to such a breakfast. There were no courses and no particular routine. It was all there in Gargantuan profusion. A kind of awe crept into the faces of the visiting correspondents. There were oranges, peaches, grapefruit. There were bacon and eggs for the unimaginative; soft-shelled crabs, succulent and sweet; fried chicken, lamb chops, stewed fresh huckleberries (no one knows why. We merely had seen them in the market, bursting black giant huckleberries, and Bill had breathed something about their being elegant with hot popovers). There were waffles with syrup or preserves, little hot biscuits and big hot popovers. Steaming coffee in urns and pitchers of cream. The fat cook kept bringing in fresh supplies. A kind of glaze came into the eyes of the breakfasters. Presently even the cook saw that the famished scribes were replete. At a piled-up platter they only shook their heads, groaning, speechless.

From Baltimore White went home for a few days, but by August 5 he was back in Chicago to help form the Progressive, or Bull Moose, party and report the proceedings for his syndicate.

The convention of this new party was reminiscent of Populist days, with its camp-meeting revival flavor. "I can't make fun of this convention," one reporter wired his newspaper. "This is a religion." Millionaires George Perkins, Oscar Straus, and Frank Munsey mixed with college professors Charles E. Merriam and George W. Kirchwey. "Bill" Flinn, Pennsylvania machine boss, mingled with left-wingers Ben B. Lindsey, affectionately referred to as the "bull mouse" by Roosevelt; Jane Addams, of Hull House; and Walter Weyl, author of *The New Democracy*.

For five feverish days the inner group of the new party labored over the platform. White played an important role, particularly in the protective tariff plank that was adopted and in securing a statement repudiating the Payne-Aldrich tariff. White also led in the withdrawal of a resolution favoring a temperance plank because this threatened to divide the party. The inner conflict within the new party that was to break out openly after 1912, was plainly evident during the platform proceedings. The more radical Progressives were suspicious of Wall Streeter George W. Perkins. Amos and Gifford Pinchot wanted a powerful antitrust plank, but Perkins killed it. Gifford Pinchot and Perkins could not stand each other. Finally, Theodore Roosevelt put them into separate rooms and ran back and forth between the rooms telling them what the group was deciding on the platform. Roosevelt finally persuaded them not to blow up until after the election.

At one point the platform committee met continuously for twenty-four hours at the Congress Hotel. White was so exhausted that he stretched out on a couch, and, when the time came to vote, he would raise a pudgy white hand to signify approval or disapproval. Since George Perkins was raising the money for the new party, he had a controlling influence on the platform. He not only prevented a powerful antitrust plank, but as Chester Rowell, California Progressive, later recalled to White's mind, Perkins changed "a certain plank back into the bad English in which he had written it from the good English into which you had transformed it."

At the convention, George Perkins was made chairman of the executive committee. William Allen White nominated him for this position on August 6. Soon White was to fight with Perkins over party matters, but he never really broke with Perkins the way the Pinchots and other more progressively minded men did. When, in 1914, the party fight between Perkins and the left-wing group was out in the open, White favored Perkins. He told him: "My attitude in the matter of your connection with the committee was stated rather fully in my remarks nominating you for your present position. . . . I have had no occasion to change my views since that time. This does not mean that I have agreed entirely with every position you have taken, but it does mean that I have felt that you were sincerely in this fight." Years after the passing of the Progressive party, when White had realized that Perkins had been the leader in wrecking the party, he declared that he had voted against the nomination of Perkins as chairman of the Executive Committee in August, 1912, but the facts do not bear this out.

The Progressive convention was hardly dominated by radicals, although White hailed it as a radical meeting. Albert Beveridge, keynote speaker, delivered a talk replete with catchy phrases. "We stand for a nobler America, we are against the interests; we are for the workingman; and we are against bosses," he declared in the course of the talk. But Beveridge revealed that no "wild-eyed" radicals who might destroy Big Business were running the new party. The new party would "try to make little business big, and all business honest, instead of striving to make Big Business little, and yet letting it remain dishonest." Reform in order to preserve was the basic premise of the Progressive party. Beveridge made it clear in this address that the fundamental structure of American economic life should not be changed. "Looking back on Albert," White wrote Claude Bowers on July 11, 1932, "after an intimacy of nearly thirty years, I am persuaded that he just didn't happen, that I dreamed him. Earth doesn't hold such contradictions, such spiritual grotesques, such elemental spirits all twisted and woven into one as appeared in Albert."

After Theodore Roosevelt was nominated, the fervent supporters of the Bull Moose crusade hurried home to build a grass-roots organization for the new party. From the outset they had their difficulties. Why, asked progressives like Norman Hapgood and Louis Brandeis, do we need your party when Woodrow Wilson is a proved progressive? The liberalism of Wilson and his progressive platform definitely wrecked the new party's chances of success. The followers of Wilson charged that the Bull Moose party was just a vehicle for the personal ambition of Theodore Roosevelt. This White vehemently denied. "I think you fellows overemphasize Roosevelt," White wrote John S. Phillips on August 20, 1912. "He is a mere incident to this new party. . . . The Progressive party is here to stay as the definitely radical party of this Nation and if any man tries to divert it to his personal ends so much the worse for that man . . . I am satisfied it is going to have a place, perhaps not a winning place, but a definite place in American politics for the next thirty years . . . a great stirring movement in our country, a movement to change the environment of poverty so that whatever of poverty is due to environment may be removed. . . ." Actually, Roosevelt seemed to confirm the suspicion that he was in the new party for personal reasons, when he wrecked the party by refusing to be its candidate in 1916.

White returned to Emporia to establish Kansas headquarters for the campaign, which he was to direct as Progressive national committeeman from that state. When he circulated campaign material for Roosevelt and asked for financial support, he sometimes was charged with hypocrisy in talking of the need of curbing great wealth. "If I am correctly informed," wrote the Democratic national committeeman from Kansas, "you have J. Pierpont Morgan who through his leading satellite, Mr. Perkins, is financing the Roosevelt campaign, and Perkins means the United Steel crowd; the Wall Street money trust; the tobacco trust; the Standard Oil Crowd; and their kindred interests that have dominated this government for a quarter of a century. The real truth is, you, representing Mr. Roosevelt, are not fighting for the people any more than Mr. Stanley representing Mr. Taft is fighting for the people. You both represent enormous wealth."

Actually, although White did not realize it, this letter was sound. But White was so enamored of Theodore Roosevelt that he was unable to understand the real controlling influences behind Mr. Roosevelt's campaign. Furthermore, White, reared in Republican Kansas, could not join the Democratic party. His only alternative was the third party. Although White stated regularly during the campaign that the Progressive party was the truly radical party, the Democratic party platform was in some ways more liberal. When faced with the problem of trying to persuade people to vote for Roosevelt and not Wilson, White adopted the device of declaring that, although Governor Wilson was a tested progressive, he would never be able to persuade the Democratic party to follow him. The Democratic party was inherently reactionary, charged White, because of the big city bosses and the Solid South that formed powerful units within the party. As president, Wilson could never lead these two elements to support progressive principles. This charge, made many times in 1912, 1932, and 1936, against the Democratic party is interesting in the light of history. Under Woodrow Wilson and Franklin D. Roosevelt, although these elements were in the party, more progressive legislation was enacted than had been enacted by all the Republican administrations.

* * *

White's family spent the summer of 1912 in Moraine Park, Colorado, where they had just purchased a cabin close to that of White's old K.U. classmate, W. E. Higgins, now teaching at the university. For years until his death, White was to spend many summers here, recuperating from his arduous activities and concentrating on his writing. Here, too, Bill and Mary were to grow up acquiring a love for fishing, hiking, horseback riding, and for the rugged beauty of the Rockies. Towering Longs Peak was a source of never-failing wonders. From the Whites' cabin one could see the mountains as they changed color during the summer days. Here was a splendid opportunity to escape from the problems of a complex society.

The campaign of 1912, however, was so exacting that White had time for only one week in his new cabin before he returned to Emporia to run the Kansas campaign. One amusing incident occurred when White sent out a circular asking for funds. Some irate Republicans sent him five dollars in Confederate currency and wrote: "We beg to hand you herewith $5.00 of the same kind of money they used from 1860 to 1865 in an attempt to destroy the Republican party. . . . We give you this money freely and hope the present leaders of the progressive movement will at most be no more successful than the Insurgents were during the days of the Late Unpleasantness." In the primary campaign that August for senator, governor, and other state offices the Progressives—Stubbs, Capper, and others—ran in the Republican primary and captured the nominations. With progressive Republicans running for the important offices, the Bull Moosers did not run a separate state ticket. Instead they requested everyone to vote for Stubbs for senator and Capper for governor, but to vote for Roosevelt for president in the Independent column on the ballot. This was done with Roosevelt's approval. It, however, acquired a great deal of publicity to make sure that people did not vote the straight Republican ticket, and thus inadvertently vote for Taft.

Much of the money that White raised as chairman of the campaign went into publications explaining how the voter should mark the ballot. While White was running the Progressive campaign and also doing his best for Capper and Stubbs, Sallie White was taking a leading role in the fight for woman suffrage. Outside of voting for Roosevelt, White urged everyone to vote the straight Republican ticket. His articles advocating the election of Stubbs and Capper were carried in the Kansas City *Star*, Topeka *Capital*, Wichita *Eagle*, and Wichita *Beacon*. He personally sent an immense number of letters to influential people in behalf of these two candidates. Nationally, White wrote a regular article for the Chicago *Tribune* syndicate and a weekly feature for the official Bull Moose publication edited by Will Irwin.

White raised about twelve thousand dollars in Kansas for the campaign. This was hardly sufficient to meet the needs, but he refused to accept any money from George Perkins. The Perkins influence in the campaign, he later admitted, hurt Roosevelt. White was widely denounced by the machine Republicans as the new boss of Kansas politics. "He, White, has undertaken to fix the standard," wrote one candidate that White was opposing. "No man is a progressive Republican unless he thinks just as White thinks and does, or agrees to do, just as White does."

Although the Bull Moosers might sing "Onward, Christian Soldiers," victory was not in the air. Roosevelt was weary and his speeches were not very effective. On Sunday, September 22, he stopped off at Emporia to rest for the day. With White he attended the little Dutch Reformed church. That afternoon White took the campaigner for a ride in a carriage drawn by his bedraggled horse, Old Tom. In shame many people offered their cars, but White insisted on Old Tom. The next day the Ottawa [Kansas] *Herald* stated: "Colonel Roosevelt wanted a 'day of rest' Sunday, and Emporia proceeded to give him a ride behind Old Tom. Old Tom, by the way, is one of the most restful horses you ever saw."

Early in October, White was convinced that Taft did not have a chance in the Middle West. It was a stiff fight between Roosevelt and Wilson. "I should say that Kansas will be for Roosevelt by a considerable majority," he predicted, "yet, if I wake up the morning after the election and read that Kansas went for Wilson, I shall not insist upon the official count." On election night White remained at the *Gazette* office watching the returns until he saw those from Americus township. Then he told the assembled Bull-Moosers: "Fellows, the colonel is beaten. When the most typical American township in America goes for Wilson, that's the way the country's going—as goes Americus, so goes the West."

In Kansas, the Democrats defeated Stubbs for senator, and after several weeks of doubt Hodges defeated Capper for governor by twenty-odd votes. White firmly believed that the only reason for the defeat of Stubbs and Capper was that the machine Republicans had deserted them and had voted Democratic. This convinced White that a separate Progressive party organization had to be launched in Kansas. There was no point in staying in the Republican party, defeating the machine candidates in the primary only to witness the machine Republicans support the Democrats. The thing to do, he reasoned, was to have three separate slates of candidates, which would ensure that machine Republicans would vote for their own choice and not for the Democrats.

A week after election, Roosevelt wrote White: "No man has waged a gamer and more efficient fight for the Progressive Cause than you have. Our task must now be to try to put the organization in permanent form. I hope that you in Kansas will be able to do this without much trouble." The Emporia editor assured Roosevelt that the Kansas Progressives were completing their organization. By this time, however, the rift between Perkins and the Pinchots had broken out in the open. Amos Pinchot urged Roosevelt to oust Perkins and make the party truly radical. As long as Perkins was chairman of the Executive Committee, the party could not dedicate itself to economic justice. Roosevelt, however, declared that the party had to remain practical. Although White felt that Perkins had tried to attract too much publicity for himself during the campaign, he agreed with Roosevelt. "He has done first class work and moreover he should be continued exactly where he is," White wrote Roosevelt. ". . . Anyone who could possibly object to Perkins now maintaining a position similar to that he occupied during the campaign . . . is it seems to me if not seeing red, at least is seeing a pink afterglow that does not exist."

White was shrewd enough to realize that the future of his party depended chiefly on the success or failure of the Wilson administration. "I have no question of the sincerity of Mr. Wilson," White explained to Roosevelt. "I also believe that he is a man of considerable more than ordinary capacity for accomplishing the task before him. . . . But I think he is going to fail. The failure therefore of a man of unquestioned Progressive sympathy and above the average of intellectual and political capacity will everlastingly prove that there is no hope in either of the old parties."

With every expectation that Wilson would fail to make the Democratic party progressive, White led the Kansas Progressives into launching a state organization in order that they would be ready for victory in 1914. Just how enthusiastic Colonel Roosevelt was on the continuation of this party is shrouded in doubt. Although he had stated just after the election that the party should be continued, several months later he told a friend: "The fight is over. We are beaten. There is only one thing to do and that is to go back to the Republican party. You can't hold a party like the Progressive party together . . . there are no loaves and fishes."

When White proceeded to organize the Kansas wing of the party in December, 1912, an irate Republican inquired of him: "What's the Matter With Kansas? . . . Ever read The Regeneration of Col. Hucks? Good story. Read it. Then come on back home. We need you. The lot is full of weeds and the woods pasture needs a new fence."

White's vigorous, unceasing political work over the past year had taken its toll. He was extremely tired and feeble by December. Mrs. White, too, had been ill for several months. On doctor's orders the entire family left Emporia in early January, 1913, to spend the winter resting at La Jolla, California. To Vernon Kellogg, now teaching at Stanford University, White wrote: "I am going to bring my novel out and work on it at odd times and I hope to have considerable time. I have not even touched it within the last year I have been so busy with politics. But I think the game has been worth while."

*   *   *

Before leaving for California, White resigned from the Board of Regents of the University of Kansas. He told Governor Stubbs that, since he and Mrs. White had to go to California for their health, he would be unable to aid in drafting the university's budget and fighting to get it through the legislature. White had thoroughly enjoyed his years as a K.U. regent. This experience, in addition to his own expanding progressive beliefs, gave him a number of well-developed ideas concerning education. It was his firm conviction that the schools were the mainspring of democracy. "If we are to solve the problem of the century—the restriction of ignorance and greed in our business organization," he declared, "we must solve it in the schoolhouse rather than in the legislature or in the courtroom." He was alarmed, however, over the number of teen-age boys and girls who were not in school. This, he held, was dangerous for democracy. The three-fifths of our population which never went beyond the sixth grade were the "skeletons in our national closet." If they should unite politically, they could wreak a terrible vengeance on the nation. Since many students left school because of family financial reasons, White asserted that the state should give the family what the child would have earned and keep the child in school.

The spread of the direct primary, the initiative, the referendum, and the recall necessitated increased education for the people. "These democratic forms," he told a leading educator, "require something more than the sixth grade and the good Lord knows that right here in Kansas we are trying to work out the problem

in fear and trembling . . . There are just enough fairly well educated people in a state like Kansas now to overthrow what may
be called the benevolent despotism of commerce in our politics
and so far as the immediate future (that is to say three or four
years or so) is concerned, we are able to replace it with some sort
of a make-shift State or federal control and State or federal regulation, but the problem of the future is going to come when the
deposed despots get on their feet and control the weapons of
democracy. Then we must have an educated, righteous public
opinion that cannot come out of the sixth grade and must come
out of the High School and the College."

Education, White wrote in an article for the November, 1911,
Craftsman, must develop leadership in men. It must teach the people how to select the leaders who will serve the social commonwealth. "The public schools as they stand," he declared, "do not
produce the citizenship needed for the work ahead of the country." The progressive movement for a better democracy necessitated the teaching of a wider social morality by the schools. The
schools must inculcate, he insisted, a sense of public service and a
feeling for social justice if democracy was to succeed.

White was disturbed as regent by the small number of students
attending the Kansas colleges. Somehow college attendance had
to be made more attractive to high school graduates. Democracy
could not continue without a trained citizenry. The emphasis in
American education on more buildings and bigger and better football teams rather than on preparing citizens for democracy angered
White. "It is not, according to my notion important that we turn
out two hundred and fifty students graduated from the course,"
he wrote fellow regent Scott Hopkins, on June 7, 1907. "But it is
important it seems to me that we should turn out two hundred
and fifty young men and women who will help to make Kansas
a cleaner, decenter, more livable state—more livable in that its
citizens see the folly of piling up unnecessary riches, and see the
wisdom of neighborly kindness and gentility toward one another.
We have come out of the nineteenth [century] loaded with material things . . . and all the club-footed gods have been at work
piling up wealth; but piling it up inequitably. Only institutions
like ours can breed a public sentiment that will make men and

women wise with kindness and charity, who may attack that pile of wealth, and distribute it fairly among the people of the next generation and the next. But if our boys and girls hear on state occasions from the head of our state university, nothing but glorification of our crass material progress as a state and as a state university, what in Heaven's name are they to care whether the inheritance of the nineteenth century is spiritualized in equitable laws and customs growing out of gentle Christlike hearts."

Thirty years after this letter, White was still firmly convinced that education should train people for service in a democratic civilization. He wrote President W. H. Cowley of Hamilton College that "it seems to me that the first, last, and all important job of the American college is to teach youth how to live in a democracy; how to live competently; how to co-operate intelligently; how to understand the ethical requirements for happy living in a free country. It is so easy for a college to produce a go-getter. A go-getter with a college degree three times out of five is a social and political liability to his country. As a nation we are over-developing an acquisitive race. It is the job of the college to pare the nails of the predatory individuals and give them some kind of social understanding, some kind of ethical responsibility, some kind of democratic common sense which will not make them dreamers, will not make them lazy and inconsequential but will train, direct, and give purpose to their natural egoistic traits and talents so that they will not be turned loose in our democracy cultural morons, ethical nitwits, social pariahs."

As K.U. regent, White was extremely valuable as a liaison between the university and the politicians. The Kansas farmers clamoring for lower taxes were a constant threat that the legislature might at any time curb the K.U. appropriations. The university already had such a low salary scale that it was always in danger of losing its best faculty members to other institutions. White served Chancellor Strong, particularly, as a liaison with Governor Stubbs. On problems of appropriations and appointments to the Board of Regents, Strong funneled suggestions through White to Stubbs. When White thought of resigning as regent, after he was chosen Republican national committeeman from Kansas in May, 1912, his old teacher W. H. Carruth wrote him: "For the love of God don't talk about getting off the Board of Regents. You're worth more there than you are on the National Committee, though I'm glad to see a really good boss get up there." And Chancellor Strong told him: "You have been a great safeguard to us."

White vehemently denied any intimation that the Board of Regents, during his years of service, used K.U. as a political football. "I have been on the Board six years," he wrote one critic. ". . . During all that time I have never known one single member of the Board to suggest the employment of anyone from janitor to Chancellor . . . I have never known the politics of any of the hundred men we have hired as instructors during the time of my service . . . We would no more think of a man's politics or his factional alignments when hiring him than we would think of considering his religion or the color of his hair." Interesting, in the light of this statement, was White's urging upon Chancellor Strong the appointment of any young man to the economics department who would appeal to the quickening social conscience of the people. "It would be a grand thing," he told Strong, "if we could get a young teacher who would develop into a man like Richard Ely of Wisconsin and who would stay with us for years to come and keep us alike from the faults of demagogy and from the selfishness of that ultra conservatism which has a clutch upon progress."

White's views on academic freedom were quite broad by the time he became a regent. Before the progressive movement had engulfed him, however, this had not been true. In 1899, when a commencement speaker at the Kansas State Agricultural College had declared that "the salvation of a . . . man's soul may depend on his attitude toward the subject of municipal franchises, or toward the tax assessment of railroad property," White had asserted: "These are the doctrines which the Christian fathers and mothers of Kansas are sending their children to imbibe. The graduate from such a curriculum would be little better than a moral and social outcast, unfit to associate with respectable men. If Kansas is bound to put up with this sort of education, she had far better stay in ignorance and burn her colleges to the ground."

Years later, during the Spanish Civil War in 1938, when a K.U. student lost his life fighting Franco's Fascists, the good respectable

Red-baiters of Kansas tried to push a bill through the legislature to investigate alleged Communist activities at K.U. White led a press attack on this proposed investigation and declared: "The boy who died in Spain had a right to go there if he wanted to. . . . If the teachers of K.U. taught him that this world is not the best possible world and that it should be improved and that many solutions were offered to the troubled world for its wrongs—Fascism, Communism, democracy and anarchy—and if the professors explained carefully each of these offerings, they were within their individual rights and they were doing their exact duty as teachers—no more, no less."

One aspect of life at K.U. which infuriated White was college football. If he could have smashed it as a sport, he would have been elated. Alumni sentiment was against such a move, however. White, therefore, worked to alter certain rules and to abolish paid coaches. He persuaded the K.U. Board of Regents to propose these reforms to the Missouri Valley Conference, but to no avail. White was also opposed to the annual K.U.-University of Missouri game's being played at Kansas City because this tended to professionalize a college sport and place it in the hands of undesirable elements.

After White left the K.U. Board of Regents, Kansas reorganized its educational structure and created one Board of Regents to supervise all the state's institutions of higher learning. From the days of Arthur Capper's governorship, every governor but one asked White to serve on this overall board. But he told a K.U. audience: "I live in a town where there is a state educational institution. And, while I might not be accredited to that institution, if they ever begin appointing members on the Board of Regents from any town that has a state institution, our Board of Regents will blow up, because when you get one appointed from a town that has an educational institution—Pittsburg, Emporia, Hays, Manhattan, Lawrence—then every town will insist on having a member from its town. And the Board of Regents will be a board of nine little vice-chancellors. And that's what you will have. So to every governor who broached that to me, I have breathed that great truth into his heart, that he must never, under any circumstances, appoint anybody from any one of these towns or he will have a vice-chancellor or a vice-president from every institution down on its main street." White's fear was that a local regent would tend to become the real head of the institution. When a Democratic governor failed to get him to change his mind on such an appointment, the governor wittily but correctly observed that he had a number of good men from the various college towns whom he would like to appoint if it were not for "Bill White's law." "I have at least added that much service to the State of Kansas since I have retired from the board," remarked White.

When White left the K.U. Board of Regents in 1912, W. H. Carruth told him: "It is needless to say how sorry we are to lose you from the Board. You have been one of the gentlest and most helpful of rulers. I want to 'place on file' my appreciation of your long and devoted and useful service to the University." A year after he had severed connections with the board, Chancellor Strong wrote him: "I miss very greatly your wise counsel and support."

* * *

Until the middle of May, 1913, the Whites thoroughly enjoyed their five months' rest at La Jolla, California. White was able, in his freedom from politics and from editing the *Gazette*, to rewrite his book, *In The Heart of A Fool*, completely from cover to cover. Late in May, White ceased work on it and made five speeches to help the California Progressive party. Present at his talk in San Francisco was Governor Hiram Johnson, Roosevelt's running mate the past year. "Johnson is very strong out there," White wrote George Perkins a few weeks later. "He can have anything he wants." White had the opportunity of spending some time with two Progressives whom he admired immensely—Chester H. Rowell, editor of the Fresno *Republican*, and Myer Lissner, prominent figure in the organization of the California Progressive party. Rowell and White were not dissimilar. Both were constructed along horizontal lines. Both were small-town journalists who built their papers into commanding influence. White told Perkins that Rowell would make an ideal political candidate; as to Myer Lissner: "I think he is the most dependable Progressive worker on the west coast. He is capable, conscientious and courageous."

En route home, White spoke at a state-wide Progressive affair in Arizona, where he discussed the party's chances with Dwight Heard. On his return to Emporia, he wrote Colonel Roosevelt: "I find the Progressive sentiment in those states stronger than it was before the election. In Kansas, I think matters are in splendid shape." Remaining less than three weeks in Emporia, the Whites spent the summer at their cabin in Moraine Park, Colorado. White again devoted full time to his new novel.

In the middle of September, 1913, when the Whites had returned home, the Emporia editor was once more embroiled in politics. The Bull Moosers were having a difficult time maintaining their organization. It was a herculean task to keep the people politically excited during a nonelection year. But even more unsettling to the Progressive party was Woodrow Wilson's progressive attitude and his success in pushing laws through Congress. White was acutely conscious of the problem created by Wilson's progressive administration. "We might as well be entirely frank," he editorialized on November 5, 1913. "This is a waiting game. So long as the Democratic party continues its present progressive leadership there is no chance for the Progressives, and so far as that goes, we don't care for the offices while the Democrats carry out the principles of the Progressive platform." Then he added rather wishfully: "On the other hand, when the Democratic patronage gives out, probably the progressive leadership will begin to crumble . . . Then when the progressive leadership of Democracy fails, the Progressive party will be in a position to offer a decent home to the progressive Democrats." Rabid Progressive party members vehemently objected to White's praise of Wilson. Henry J. Allen told White: "I wish you would quit delivering rhapsodies on Wilson. It doesn't seem to me that it helps us any."

The New York *Evening Post* took White to task for praising the administration of Democratic Governor Hodges. His praise, declared the *Post*, was "utterly subversive of true Progressive Progress." Through all this criticism White serenely went ahead trying to hold the Kansas Progressive party together. He urged George Perkins to transfer the headquarters of the party to the Middle West, where the party's strength actually existed. For a lifetime White tried to explain to his eastern friends the importance of the Middle West in American life. Twenty-seven years after White endeavored to center the headquarters of the Bull Moose party in his area, he sought to do the same for the Committee to Defend America by Aiding the Allies. But such was the peculiar provincial quality of his New York friends and associates that the soundness of his advice was ignored both times.

"We are a middle-class, western movement," he wrote Medill McCormick of the Chicago *Tribune* on December 29, 1913, "and we haven't very much show to get anywhere in the East and South. . . . I think it is highly important that we should organize ourselves, recognizing these important facts, and Chicago is the place to operate from." White told Roosevelt, just before the latter sailed for South America, that the party should continue and that he must run in 1916 or else the party would disappear. Aboard ship, Roosevelt wrote White: "My present feeling is that I will not even accept the Progressive nomination."

As the year 1913 drew to a close, White was eulogistic in his praise of Woodrow Wilson even though Wilson's success threatened to wreck the Progressive party. "What a fine, level-headed president he is making!" he declared. "Really, the Progressives do not care who gets the Progressive things done just so they are done, and President Wilson certainly is doing a fine job of getting many Progressive things done."

*　　*　　*

Most of White's time in 1914 was devoted to politics, although he did write an article on prohibition that raised a storm about his head. White was a rabid prohibitionist. From time to time he had written editorials praising the lack of liquor in Kansas. He actually believed that Kansas was dry because it had a prohibition law. Fellow newspaperman Jay House asked him after one such editorial: "Why write rot? . . . No crowd of 150 men ever went out for a ride in Kansas without beer under the seat. . . . If you believe your editorial on the matter reflects the attitude of Kansas toward booze you are an unsuspecting innocent and any gold-brick artist could sell you goods . . . The last legislature swam in booze . . . Kansas hospitality is based on beer. There is beer in half the cellars and under practically every automobile seat.

And you, in your innocence, sit down and write an editorial saying booze is remote from the Kansas consciousness. Pish tush! Also, fie, fie! Good lord, Man! Get your eyes open."

White preferred not to believe this description of Kansas. He devoted his first magazine article in a year or more to the subject of Kansas and prohibition. He stated that Kansas was absolutely dry in all but five counties, and that the bootlegger was a negligible figure. White, then, charged that states which permitted liquor had more insane, more poor, more morally decayed people, and more murders and other forms of crime than a dry state. Immediately, this statement was challenged by the secretary of the Brewers' Association in an article in the *Saturday Evening Post* in July. Statistics were advanced to show that Kansas had more insane, more chronic alcoholics, lower church membership, and more criminals than Indiana and a number of other wet states. Pamphlets and news releases were issued demonstrating that nonprohibition states were better off than Kansas.

White's source for the statement that Kansas had fewer insane and criminals than wet states was a speech by Arthur Capper. He now frantically wrote to the state health officer, Dr. S. J. Crumbine, for figures to defend himself. When he had gathered his material, he launched his counterattack on liquor in the *Post* of November 14, 1914. White admitted that his figures had been wrong on insane and criminals, but he declared that all the rest of his indictments were accurate. Then he quoted letters from Governor Hodges and a number of Kansas bankers to prove that Kansas was better off without liquor. "Their statements," asserted the Emporian, "are worth carloads of statistics."

Politically, 1914 was a discouraging year for White and the Progressive party. In Kansas, both Arthur Capper and Senator Bristow decided to run in the Republican primary for governor and senator, respectively. White, unhappily, had to oppose both his old friends because he felt that it was hopeless to re-enter the Republican party unless the reactionary bosses were removed from power. Bristow and Capper, on the other hand, maintained that all the Progressive party achieved was the splitting of the normal Republican vote and the resulting election of Democrats. "If the progressives will remain in the Republican [party] and work in the future as we have in the past, we will dominate in Kansas . . ." Senator Bristow wrote a friend on May 4, 1914. "But if they go into a side show and organize a third party and divide up our strength, you can readily see it will put us to a disadvantage. The third party movement in Kansas is the most unfortunate and unjustifiable of any political movement I have ever known."

White's answer was that even if the Progressives returned to the Republican fold and nominated the candidates, the reactionary Republicans would desert these candidates as they had done in 1912. You could not trust the machine Republicans. White warned Bristow that he would be defeated if he ran in the Republican primary against Charles Curtis, because very few of his progressive supporters would vote in the Republican primary. When Bristow was defeated by Curtis, he was bitter and blamed his defeat on White's insistence on running a third party. He charged that White and the Kansas City *Star* had deliberately misrepresented his position, and he wrote one person: "I have more resentment toward Will White than anybody else." In advising this same person about buying a newspaper, Bristow observed: "The Emporia *Times* might be made a success as a Republican paper, but you would have to fight pretty hard against Will White. He has lots of money and an established prestige, and he is a genius as a writer, and while people hate him and have contempt for him they always read what he has to say."

To inspire the faltering Progressive party, White brought Raymond Robins of Chicago and Albert Beveridge of Indiana to Kansas to speak at their meeting in February, 1914. He also helped to persuade Henry J. Allen to run for governor and Victor Murdock to run for senator on the Bull Moose ticket. By the summer of 1914, White noted that there was a lack of interest in politics that augured ill for their party. He had predicted in April that the European "war now pending is liable to change the entire aspect of things in Kansas and it may be possible that it will change it in the United States." When the war broke out that summer, it naturally took the minds of the people off domestic politics and made the position of the third party even more nearly hopeless than it already was.

Nationally, White recommended that the Bull Moosers should advocate the government ownership of railroads. They must be more radical than the two old parties if they were to have a significant role in national politics. "I suppose the war is not going to do us any good," he wrote George Perkins on April 25, 1914, "but it does not seem to me that anything does us very much good. We seem to be lying rather restlessly in the lap of the Gods and whenever we turn the wrong way we get spanked. Which, on the whole, is rather inconsiderate of the Gods for I can't help feeling that we are a good child." Perkins and Roosevelt, however, refused to countenance support for government ownership of railroads.

That summer the long-standing feud between George W. Perkins and Gifford and Amos Pinchot broke into the open. White adopted a cautious attitude toward the fight. He realized that the Progressive party needed more dramatic and forthright leadership than Perkins could offer. But, as he wrote Roosevelt on June 14, 1914: "I don't believe that Perkins should be incontinently fired; he has served the party conscientiously and with all his heart. But I do believe another type of man should be at the head of the national organization. . . ." Roosevelt quickly replied that Perkins had been essential for the party, and that the party would disappear if it favored men like Amos Pinchot.

In the midst of the campaign that fall, White had to leave Kansas to take Mrs. White to the Mayo Clinic for an operation. He was back in time to witness the overwhelming defeat of the Progressive candidates. Arthur Capper defeated Henry J. Allen for governor and Charles Curtis defeated Victor Murdock for the Senate. Allen was to come back politically and be elected governor in 1918, but Victor Murdock was never to run for office again. Woodrow Wilson appointed him to the Federal Trade Commission, a post which he held until 1924. As George Norris has written, Victor Murdock was "a man of great ability . . . he was honest and extremely courageous. . . . His work was outstanding and difficult."

The decisive defeat of the Progressive party in 1914 left William Allen White bewildered. "So far as politics are concerned," he told his former reporter Roy Bailey, "I am going to sit on the fence for a little while and watch the procession go by." Colonel

Roosevelt wrote White that he intended to continue to fight for the cause of 1912, but that he would not take the lead in party affairs. White's attitude as expressed to the Rough Rider was that the Progressive party was "spiritually weary" and "sapped dry." "We need emotional rest," he wrote on December 15, 1914. The policy he recommended was that of maintaining the organization and then "tie up the boat and wait for the tide." The trouble with the party was that they were not reaching out to the average citizen. They had the support of teachers, successful small businessmen, and young lawyers and doctors, but the farmer and the worker had not been attracted by the party's call.

Publicly White declared, in an article for the December 19, 1914, *Saturday Evening Post:* "Practically the only thing really proved by the recent elections about the Progressive Party is that it is, as it stands, a middle-class party. It polled its best strength in the home wards of the smaller towns—towns of from five thousand to fifty thousand inhabitants. . . . The Progressive idea is essentially for sane-thinking men and women. It is evolutionary not revolutionary; but veal kidneys will not grasp it." Sooner or later, he asserted, progressives still within the ranks of the old parties would see the folly of their ways and would join the sole progressive party. Looking to the future—and he was more optimistic in this article than in his private correspondence—he prophesied that the Progressive party would thrive because the Progressives "are crusaders, and a temporary defeat does not stop them or dampen their enthusiasm."

Political defeat failed to embitter White. With his keen sense of humor, he delivered the following poem before the Saturday Night Literary Club of Topeka a short time after the Progressive failure at the polls:

HOPE BEYOND

I

There are more or less tears being silently shed,
    Bemoaning us three;
And more or less written and more or less said,
Assuming that we are all more or less dead—
    Victor and Henry and me.

II

Now I have arisen to say it aint so,
    Concerning us three.
We're very much hitched to the earth here below;
Our wings haven't sprouted and we shall not go;
We're still here to kick at the old status quo,
    Henry and Victor and me.

III

It's true we are out on the end of the limb,
    All of us three.
It's true that our chances to climb down are slim;
And also, our chance to go upward is dim;
But the scenery's splendid up where we have climb—
    Victor and Henry and me.

IV

The Society's good and the weather is calm,
    For all of us three.
And each of us feels as serene as a clam;
If politics skids, or a wheel slips a kam
Oh, what do we care—not a tinker's red dam;
    Henry nor Victor, nor me.

V

We're naturally touched by your tribute of tears,
    Is each of us three.
But do not give way to your anguish or fears;
We're fuller of ginger than two-year-old steers,
And aint been so happy for seventeen years,
    Victor and Henry and me.
        Because you see
        By Geemunee,
        We're free—per se,
        Victor and Henry and me.

VI

My moral conclusion, must make it clear why,
    In naming us three,
It had to be "me" when it should have been "I"

It's that we Bull Moosers are so mortal shy,
We wished to avoid, even rhyming with pie—
So it's Henry and Victor and Me!

The campaign of 1914 was to be the last election the Progressive party would participate in as a separate and distinct party. The outbreak of World War I tended to take the minds of the people away from internal problems. The broad progressive movement itself, although the Wilson administration did pass some forward-looking laws from 1914 to 1916, was checked by American entrance into the war. After the war, reaction moved into power and the progressives were unsuccessful in their attempts to control either the Republican or the Democratic party. Muckrakers like Lincoln Steffens, writing during the period of conservative Republican ascendancy from 1920 to 1932, seriously questioned the achievements of the prewar progressivism, and felt that it had all been in vain. William Allen White, who lived to see the resurgence of progressivism under the New Deal, adopted the attitude that Franklin D. Roosevelt's reforms would have been severely handicapped without the groundwork laid by the prewar progressive movement.

In White's eyes, the prewar progressives had accomplished a great deal in their attack on the bulwarks of special privilege. "It seems to me," he wrote Charles Edward Russell on November 22, 1933, "we have pushed the enemy back a long ways. The younger generation does not know how far forward it was. It is one of the major blessings of God that human nature always provides a good fight for the righteous in every generation. New imperfections, new weaknesses make new wickedness which always must be assailed, and thank God the fight always will be good."

CHAPTER 11

SMALL-TOWN JOURNALISM, 1897-1914

WHEN two runaway Emporia boys were apprehended by the police of Kansas City in 1913 and questioned as to their reason for leaving Emporia, the older boy stated thoughtfully: "Well, there's nothing there but William Allen White, and we got tired of hearing of him." Long before this event, Emporia was known to the outside world as the home of Bill White. His political success on the national and state scene and his ability to write editorials that sparkled with excellent prose and pungent phrases had made him the leading citizen of the town within a few years from the day he had acquired the *Gazette* on borrowed money. White's great asset was his ability to express himself in a distinctive editorial style. "Taking the hide off somebody" was his particular delight. "We're all beefeaters, especially Bill White," an Emporian told Sam Blythe in 1907, "and that's what makes him the first-class fighting man he is . . . He's a good deal of an idealist, but he can dream and fight at the same time, which, I take it, is a good mixture for any man. He does things and says things in his paper that make us hopping mad, but nobody accuses him of doing anything for any motive except that of his own conscience. He gets preachy, and that makes some others tired. Still, he's a vital force in Kansas, and Kansas knows it. Besides . . . what bully stories he can write! How I wish he would write more of them and let somebody else do the preaching."

The Emporia editor remarked in 1926 that the years from 1895 to World War I were "the most fruitful and happy years of my life." A considerable portion of the money that he received from his countless magazine articles and books was spent in improving the *Gazette*, constructing an office building, and buying a home for his family. For all of White's belief that small-town papers which devoted themselves to local news and local color would be a success, he had to pour a share of his outside earnings into the *Gazette*. If he had spent his full time running the paper, he un-doubtedly could have earned a moderate yearly income. But to travel as extensively as he did, to take vacations in Colorado, to own a comfortable home and entertain out-of-town guests with great frequency necessitated a far larger income than the *Gazette* could have produced. The twentieth century trend toward more and more expensive machinery for the back shop, too, required a larger sum of money than an ordinary Emporia editor might have had at hand. The purchase of such machinery would have forced most editors to borrow from the banks, but White had sufficient outside income to free himself from any bank control of the paper.

By 1904 the *Gazette*, now the principal paper of Lyon County, had a circulation of 2,000 daily and 2,000 weekly copies. Six years later, when White was in the thick of the progressive fight, the paper reached a 3,000 circulation. After the failure of the Emporia *Republican*, no other daily was able to threaten White's newspaper supremacy. Not only did White have money coming in from out-side writing, but he was a hard-working, shrewd newspaperman. "Look at that face, pink and white, fat and sweet, as featureless and innocent as a baby's bottom!" remarked a town enemy in 1899. "But, by God, don't let that fool you!"

During the bitter days of the insurgent revolt against Taft, White's political enemies, both in Emporia and in the state, backed a rival paper, the Emporia *Journal*. On January 16, 1909, the fol-lowing editorial appeared in the *Gazette:*

There is something sad in the announcement of the Emporia Daily Journal that it has printed its "last copy." Because, on the whole, Em-poria has never had a more sincere, conscientious attempt to establish an independent, uncontrolled daily newspaper than this. Editor Mickey has done his best, and his best has had this immense advantage over the best of many predecessors—it has been clean, honest, and unprejudiced. No one controlled him. And his inability to make it go carries with it no stigma of failure. He has fought a manly fight, and in so far as one wins who maintains his integrity, he has won. But those who tempted him into this venture by telling him what marvelous success he might achieve fighting the Gazette deserve censure for their treachery. They abandoned him cruelly. They gave no support to his venture. They saw him spending his own good money and offered no help. They should bear whatever of opprobrium attaches to his failure—not he; for his is no failure. He was talked into a foolish venture by men with axes to grind. They found an honest man, and they left him to find out their perfidy. . . .

White became convinced from his own experience with these papers backed by his political enemies that a newspaper did not succeed upon "its political beliefs, but upon its ability to get reliable news quickly to the people." White always discouraged his progressive friends from launching a paper "as a political and not as a business venture." When a paper was the only daily in a given town, White firmly believed that its news columns should be opened equally to both sides in a controversy. During an important election over a streetcar franchise in 1911, White adopted the policy of giving space one day to one side and the next day to the other side as the only way of being fair to the community.

Although White believed that the news columns should present all sides of a question, he was absolutely convinced that the editorial page should have a definite point of view. At a time when many American papers were starting to neglect their editorial page, White gave his editorials the very best writing he could command. His expressive, vigorous language frequently stirred the wrath of his opponents. In 1899, for instance, a gentleman named Severy, failing to secure the Republican nomination for mayor, ran as an independent. White turned his scathing editorial pen on the man, and one day as he passed Severy, Severy struck him on the back of the head with a heavy cane and knocked him to the ground. As White rose from the ground, a bystander called him a coward, and White struck this fellow in the face. The crowd that quickly gathered broke up the fight and White and Severy were taken into court for fighting and using abusive and indecent language. Severy pleaded guilty, and his fine was paid through a subscription circulated by White's enemies. White was acquitted of any guilt in the affair. When Severy tried to claim, however, that White was facing him when he struck, White noted in an editorial: "Without desiring to question the veracity of the two gentlemen who swore that Severy was standing in front of W. A. White when he struck the blow that felled him, the Gazette desires to offer in evidence, as exhibit 'A' one head, size 7⅜ with a large bump directly on the back, and one $35 suit of clothes with mud down the front and not a spot behind, as exhibit 'B.' " Although other Kansas editors expressed sorrow over the incident, the rival *Republican* announced that it was just what White deserved, since the *Gazette* was "too free in its criticism of persons and things." Then Severy was presented with a new cane in the *Republican* office! Such physical mishaps as the Severy affair, however, never tempered the vigorous language used by White in his editorials.

When he first started his career in country-town journalism, papers were usually owned by a particular economic group and the editor simply served as its mouthpiece. White, always seeking individual freedom, was wary of placing himself in such a position. Although he had had to borrow money to buy the *Gazette*, his outside earnings soon freed him from any responsibility to Emporia's wealthy for the *Gazette*'s editorial position. For the rest of his lifetime, he carried out the following editorial creed: "What we want, and what we shall have, is the royal American privilege of living and dying in a country town, running a country newspaper, saying what we please when we please, how we please and to whom we please." At about the turn of the century, White was offered all the printing of a great railroad. "It would have made me independently rich," White recalled. But he knew that by taking it he would have lost his freedom. He would rather work hard at editing and writing and be free to speak his mind than to eat the "exotic food" of the plutocrats and have to execute their policies.

White was extremely sensitive to any attempts at influencing his editorial policy. When there was a fight between two telephone companies in Emporia, one company tried to use an intermediary to secure a favorable editorial. In a state of indignation, White wrote the company on May 25, 1900, that ". . . if you have any communication to make regarding the policy of the Gazette, or its editorial announcements, kindly make them directly to me, and not to some other party in this town who you may fancy has some influence with me . . . It is particularly annoying to me, and it must be very annoying to anyone else, to assume that anyone is responsible for anything in the Gazette except the man who owns it."

White not only believed that an editor should be teacher, preacher, philosopher, and friend to all, but he told his readers that no honest newspaperman should truckle to his constituency. When the readers were wrong on a question, the editor should say so and not take the easy way out of agreeing with them. "Every paper that amounts to anything makes people violently angry" was his firm conviction. When he was asked in 1903 to analyze why his paper was a success, he observed: "It seems to me that the essence of success in a newspaper is wisely directed courage. All the struggles I have had have been due to mistakes I make in temporizing with evil. Whenever the Gazette has been brave and fair it has been easy enough to get money to pay off Saturday night, but when the Gazette has acted the demagogue, it has been hard work to make the paper go. Character is the one essential to running a successful newspaper, whether the success is financial or political. The best epigram ever made about a newspaper was made by the late Secretary of Agriculture Sterling Morton who said: 'A newspaper's foes are its assets and its friends its liabilities.' It is the man who wants you to keep something out that eats the vitality out of the bank account."

Consistency in editorial opinion was no virtue to White. He was never reluctant to change a point of view when new facts appeared. What he desired was to reflect the events of the day in the light of the truth as he understood the truth. But, as he so often demonstrated, "The Gazette has no policy today that it will not abandon tomorrow if the facts change upon which yesterday's stand was taken."

White could write editorials in many moods. A fellow Emporian was once quoted as saying, "Bill, you know, considers himself a sort of moral regenerator for the town, the state, the Republican party and the nation at times, and when he is in one of those moods he makes the fur fly . . . You get different lights on Bill White. Sometimes you think he takes himself so seriously that it must be painful to him, and at other times he seems to be as frivolous as one of our society buds. Once in a while he writes an essay that is so solemn and so full of high lights and uplifts that you think he has taken a running jump and landed in a pulpit somewhere, and then he sets the town to grinning and guessing with a paragraph like this one I found on the first page of today's Gazette: 'An Emporia man and an Emporia young woman are giving considerable attention to the same vacant house. Their friends are looking every morning in the mails for the invitations.' "

* * *

White frequently used the device of printing a rumor about himself, and then editorializing on the subject. On April 8, 1905, he remarked that there was a rumor that he kept liquor in his cellar. "This is a malicious and unspeakable falsehood," White declared. "The liquor is kept in the pantry, between the dining room and the kitchen. Why not tell the truth? It is also alleged that the editor of *The Gazette* has the gout, caused by high living. Yesterday for dinner he had home-picked sour-dock, mustard, dandelion, horse-radish and beet-top greens, boiled bacon, and potatoes, corn bread and onions. Would you call that high living? Another lie nailed!"

A suggestion from Kansas Bull Moosers that he run for governor prompted the following editorial on January 13, 1914:

A number of Progressives at Lakin, more kind than considerate, yesterday resoluted in favor of this man White, of Emporia, for governor. They wanted him to run as a Progressive candidate. To which the *Gazette* says no—a thousand times no. For we are on to that man White, and without wishing to speak disrespectfully of a fellow townsman, who, so far as we know, may be at least outwardly decent in the simpler relations of life—perhaps he pays his debts when it is convenient, and he may be kind to his family, though that's not to his credit, for who wouldn't be—and he may have kept out of jail, one way or another, for some time; without, as we say, desiring to speak disrespectfully of this man, we know that he's not the man either to run for governor or, if such a grotesque thing could be imagined, to serve as governor.

He can't make a speech. He has a lot of radical convictions which he sometimes comes into the *Gazette* office and exploits, and which are dangerous. He has been jawing politicians for twenty years until he is a common scold, and he has set up his so-called ideals so high that the Angel Gabriel himself couldn't give the performance that this man White would have to advertise on the bills.

So, in the words of the poet, nix on Willyum Allen. The *Gazette's* nose is hard and cold on the proposition to make him governor. He is a four-flusher, a ring-tailed, rip-snorting hell-raiser, and a grandstander. He makes a big noise. He yips and kyoodles around a good deal, but he is everlastingly and preeminently N. G. as a gubernatorial timber— full of knots, warts, woodpecker holes, and rotten spots. He would have the enmity of more men who have walked the plank politically than any other man in Kansas, and his candidacy would issue an irrevocable charter in Kansas for the Progressive party to be the official minority report world without end. Men and women would be trampled to death at seven o'clock election mornings, trying to get at the polls to cast the first vote against him, and at night perfectly good citizens, kind fathers and indulgent husbands, would risk a jail sentence to get in at least ten votes against him as repeaters. It may be that the Progressive party needs a goat, but the demand doesn't require a Billygoat! Now is the time for all good men to come to the aid of the party. But this man White is a shoulder-galled, sore-backed, hamstrung, wind-broken, string-halted, stump-sucking old stager who, in addition to being no good for draft and general purposes, has the political bots, blind-staggers, heaves, pink eye and epizootic. Moreover, he is locoed and has other defects. . . .

This editorial prompted the *Literary Digest* to remark that "William Allen White, the well-known Kansas institution, acted wisely when he defeated himself recently for the Progressive nomination for governor."

White was not only a superb editorial writer, but he was a shrewd businessman. Gradually, as his earnings increased, he delegated more and more responsibility to his staff, but at all times he was aware of what was taking place in the various parts of the office. His business acumen was revealed when he constructed a new building for the *Gazette* on the lot next to where the government planned eventually to build a post office. This would give the *Gazette* a vantage point for collecting news and make its office-building space a desirable location for rental purposes.

"The country newspaper," White once wrote in *Harper's Monthly*, "is the incarnation of the town spirit . . . the newspaper is in a measure the will of the town, and the town's character is displayed with sad realism in the town's newspapers. A newspaper is as honest as its town, as intelligent as its town, as kind as its town, as brave as its town." The *Gazette* was primarily a local paper. Although it carried Associated Press dispatches, the bulk of the paper was devoted to local happenings. But this did not mean printing malicious gossip and scandal. White had nothing but scorn for yellow journalism, with its scare headlines and vivid articles on the seamy side of life, which was then flowering in the big urban centers under the guidance of William Randolph Hearst. An honest editor, White believed, should not print malicious gossip until it was a matter of court record. Vile stories should be handled in such a way that they could be read aloud in the family circle.

"The news is what the newspapers play up," White declared in an editorial. "Moreover, the newspapers should be regulated. Some day the people will appoint or elect or hire town managers, and their duty, among other things, will be to go after the newspapers. Details of murder, hangings, suicides, sex crimes, highway robberies, burglaries, and crimes of violence generally should be suppressed under the police power of the state . . . Newspapers could quit if they would. The community should make them quit, and some day the good sense of the people will organize and go after the newspapers just as it has gone after offenders in other walks of life." One phase of the new yellow journalism that White abhorred was the growth of comic strips. He was to keep them out of his paper until after World War I. He proved himself a poor prophet in 1909, however, when he declared: "In a year or two they will be as rare as the shin-plasters of half a century ago."

Anyone who objected to the policy of the *Gazette* was encouraged to express his views in a column entitled "The Wailing Place." But White would not publish unsigned communications or those which stirred religious or racial hatreds. He refused a diatribe against the Catholic Church because, as he informed his correspondent, "The Catholic Church in Emporia I do not regard as a serious menace . . . I do not believe in stirring up religious feeling in an otherwise quiet community, when the community life does not seem to justify it."

White enjoyed nothing better than deflating Emporia's pompous citizenry. Shortly after he acquired the *Gazette*, he decided to drop the term "professor" because every teacher wanted the title. There was one teacher at the Normal School who raised a rumpus with White because the term wasn't used any longer before his name. White was unrelenting. Then, when the Spanish-American War came, this teacher organized a company at the Normal and became a captain. At this point, White began to refer to him as the professor, rather than as the captain, which made the teacher furious.

White demanded simplicity in style from all his reporters. The *Gazette* style book written by Laura M. French, the city editor, listed as positive "don'ts" such phrases as "at death's door"; "on the sick list"; "joined in holy wedlock"; "departed this life"; "tokens of respect"; and, "the last sad rites." Another important don't for all *Gazette* employees was "Don't use Mr. White's name —say the Gazette, or cut it out altogether if you can't say Gazette. You might lose your job otherwise."

As White's social viewpoint broadened, he began to alter the type of advertising that he would publish in his paper. Around 1909, for instance, he began to drop patent medicine advertisements. A year earlier he had defended such advertising, but by 1909 he was declaring that "I should like to see the whole patent medicine business wiped off the earth." Peruna, lemon extract, and Hostetter's Bitters were among those barred from the *Gazette*. By 1912, White was informing the American Tobacco Company that he would no longer accept their advertising either if it continued to carry such phrases as "Now is the time to learn to chew if you are ever going to." It was such attitudes as these, actually costing White the loss of considerable income, that led the Wichita *Eagle* to remark: "If at times he seems to take it upon himself to be a sort of public conscience, it is because he holds himself to stern standards, and would have in others what he demands of himself."

White's editorial outpourings as well as his news columns were devoted to making the *Gazette* a local-interest paper. Although his comments on national affairs attracted widespread attention, he was apt to write many more editorials about local people and events. A wide variety of items was touched on in these articles. Sometimes he would praise the flowers of a citizen or tell his readers how to prepare this or that food. When one family lost their little daughter in 1903, he wrote a touching editorial, declaring that "there is something in the death of a little child, something in its infinite pathos that makes all human creatures mourn. Because in every heart that is not a dead heart, calloused to all joy or sorrow, some little child is enshrined—either dead or living— and so child love is the one universal emotion of the soul, and child death is the saddest thing in all the world."

When families celebrated wedding anniversaries or contributed in some way to the betterment of the town, they were sure to have a *Gazette* editorial devoted to them. These editorials praising the virtues of his neighbors White considered "the best form of editorial expression . . . It teaches the writer to formulate his understanding of what are fundamental virtues in men. . . . It brings the community to a realizing sense of the worth and value of its citizens. And habitually practiced for a generation, it cements to a paper, friendships which are as much a part of its capital assets as its machinery."

Typical of the cementing type of editorial that he wrote was one praising the Welsh community in Emporia. "The Welsh people of this community," he declared, "have lived here for over a generation. They have been the best single strain of blood in our Emporia life . . . they are the salt of the earth, and Emporia is a better, clearer, kindlier town because it is the home of these people."

Frequently, the editorial column became "preachy." He enjoyed nothing quite so much as telling the women of the town how to cook. Baked beans properly cooked, he believed, were a feast worthy of the gods. But those housewives who substituted canned beans for the home-cooked variety, he asserted, "should be loaded into a patrol wagon and taken to jail . . . Canned beans are clammy and tasteless . . . Beans are no good unless they are cooked at home, in an oven, with a real fire in the stove."

Every once in a while the editor of the *Gazette* would launch a crusade to clean up the town. In 1897, he sallied forth against the "joints" that were selling bootleg liquor. He printed a list of these spots and then wrote: "Day after day the joints sell liquor here—each day getting a little bolder, and the Law and Order League snores on in the sweet unconsciousness of its dreams . . . There is talk of a public meeting to discuss ways and means for closing these joints . . . Will the ministers whose wealthy church members rent buildings for saloons dare to come to this meeting and denounce this business?" A few days later he sarcastically asserted: "Let's have the joints and then we can have some variety in town. An occasional murder—a nice, interesting wife murder that will give us something to talk about . . . Let's have the joints. They are illegal. Their presence violates the law. The dignity of the courts is torn down. Mob law is encouraged. Lawbreaking in other lines is stimulated . . ."

In his editorial writing White could shift with the greatest of ease from a didactic mood to a hilarious mood. As a result, his editorial column varied from day to day according to the spirit of the editor. After preaching the need of social responsibility and the importance of supporting progressive political measures for days at a time, he would suddenly write an editorial like the following: "A new dress, called the lamp-shade dress, is headed this way. It looks like a horror. . . . Yet . . . it isn't what a woman wears; it's what she is that drives us crazy. . . . Put rings in her nose, stripe her forehead, scar her face, or put her in the plug hat of the simple child of the forest, and she still remains the most wonderful thing our blessed Lord ever made."

*   *   *

As early as the first decade of the twentieth century, White was being looked upon by many as the spokesman of small-town midwestern America. Feature articles about the Emporia editor began to appear in urban papers and nation-wide magazines, and his views on a variety of subjects were reprinted with regularity. All these tendencies were greatly increased in the years between the two World Wars, but they had started long before 1914. An article in the New York *Sun* on October 20, 1910, hailed White as being "as much a part of Kansas as her cornstalks and sunflowers," and observed: "He thinks Kansas is the real United States, and had rather be the mouthpiece of Kansas' thought . . . than to be the richest man in the State or an United States Senator." By remaining in the small town, when his generation were flocking to the city, he eventually became not only the spokesman for Kansas but for much of the Middle West. He always maintained that the reason he stayed in Emporia was that people were more sociable and friendly there than elsewhere. Emporia was a personal world where neighbors' joys and sorrows were shared with others. Furthermore, class lines were not hard and fast as in the big city. In Emporia the town carpenter had influence with the banker, but, White asked, "Does the Bronx plasterer have influence with J. P. Morgan?"

A man who lived a life with real neighbors, White believed, would take more with him at death than the man who lived in a metropolitan center filled with strangers. Moreover, he once wrote that "what we can't see is how a man who can have one hundred feet of lawn and a kitchen garden to sprinkle with hose every evening after work, can permit himself to be locked up in a long row of five and six story cell-houses, with nothing to distinguish one cell-house from the other but the number on the front door."

Although White received many fabulous offers—as high as $25,000 a year from the Chicago *Tribune*—to desert country journalism for big-city newspapers, he chose to remain in Emporia. Had he gone to New York or Chicago, he would have been only one of a number of good newspaper editors. But by remaining as editor of the *Gazette* he was unique. Here was a man, people began to think, who refused to succumb to the fleshpots of the wicked city. Mark Sullivan expressed this feeling when he wrote that "from the point of view of national well-being, a thousand young William Allen Whites in a thousand Emporias would serve America well."

For all of White's enjoyment of his neighbors in Emporia, the White family spent a great deal of time away from that town even before 1914. After the *Gazette* was on its feet financially, the

Whites were able to leave town for long intervals and turn the paper over to the capable staff they had assembled. The *Gazette* actually served as a training center for many future editors. Among the young *Gazette* reporters who later went on to their own papers were Roy Bailey, editor of the Salina *Journal;* Rolla Clymer, editor of the El Dorado *Times;* Oscar Stauffer, operator of a chain of papers including the Topeka *State Journal;* and John Redmond, editor of the Burlington *Republican*. Charles M. Vernon, one of White's favorites, later became manager of the Los Angeles office of the Associated Press and Burge McFall became a leading Associated Press correspondent during World War I.

White's "boys," although many of them disagreed with his political views, were always fond of their ex-boss. Roy Bailey wrote him on February 15, 1928:

DEAR "FATHER" WHITE:

One of the fine things about the graduates of the "Gazette school of Journalism" is that no matter how much they may disagree with their professor, who taught them what they know, they always remain loyal to him, and never allow a difference of opinion to interfere with their personal affections. . . .

Oscar Stauffer, whom White helped secure a post on the Kansas City *Star,* told him: "Whether I ever amount to anything more than a pimple it is to you I owe that little. You were better to me than I deserved a hundred times." Walt Mason once remarked: "It is the sincere belief of those who work, year in and year out, with Will White, that the world does not hold a bigger or finer man. Some of those who work with him don't agree with him on many things, and every once in a while they hold indignation meetings and pass resolutions to the effect that he is off his trolley."

White was extremely patient in teaching his young reporters how to handle the news and how to write in simple but effective language. Calvin Lambert, who started as a reporter on the *Gazette* in 1909, recalled: "I never knew a man who had more patience with his employees. The Gazette always had a flock of cub reporters, usually students, and of course they made many mistakes and wrote abominably. He never fired a reporter, and encouraged each of them in his work. However, at all times, Mr. White was The Boss, and when errors appeared in the paper, he didn't hesitate to call us down. Sometimes he stopped the press to correct errors and we never repeated that particular blunder again. . . . As a cub reporter I once had a hectic love affair. One afternoon Mr. White called into the newsroom: 'Where's Cal?' Another reporter explained that I had gone to the Santa Fe Station to see my girl go through. Several days later Mr. White again called for me and was informed that I again had gone to the station to see my girl go through. 'My Gawd,' said the Boss, with a twinkle in his eye, 'that girl must be going through in sections.' "

Brock Pemberton went from the *Gazette* into New York City journalism and later became famous as a Broadway producer. Brock was almost a member of the White family since his mother was the sister of Bent Murdock of the El Dorado *Republican* and Marsh Murdock of the Wichita *Eagle*. He worked as a reporter on the *Gazette* while attending college and after he graduated. He left for New York in 1910. Using a letter of introduction from White to Franklin P. Adams, columnist for the New York *Mail*, Pemberton secured a post on that paper.

Three people assumed the responsibility of running the *Gazette* when the Whites were out of town—Laura French, Walter Hughes, and Walt Mason. When White purchased the paper, Hughes, a boy of seventeen, was working as the printer's devil. Over the years, White relied more and more on him, making him business manager of the paper from 1907 until his death in 1932. Laura French, who came to the *Gazette* a few weeks after White had acquired it, served as city editor from 1903 to 1919. She had charge of training the cub reporters and watching the style of the paper. White once referred to her as "the best newspaper woman that I ever knew, who trained all the boys whom we have produced that were worthwhile."

The third principal member of the *Gazette* staff, Walt Mason, became well known to the outside world. Mason was a newspaper legend before he settled down on the *Gazette*. White referred to him variously as "the poet laureate of American democracy" and "the Homer of modern America, and particularly of Middle-Western America, the America of the country town." Walt Mason's folksy prose poems were widely read by pre-World War I America. Mason's addiction to liquor had cost him job after job until the time he started work on the *Gazette*. He had tramped all over the West writing columns, doing all sorts of work for a handout, never lasting more than a month or two at a job. "For when he got drunk," White observed, "boy he got drunk! And he literally God damned himself out of a job by quarreling with his boss whoever it was." In 1907, when Mason left a Nebraska town to take the Keeley cure, one citizen observed that "the town let its most distinguished citizen go without regret."

While he was at the Keeley Institute, he read an article by White. "It was a good article," Mason wrote later, "so full of humor and kindliness that I thought he was a man who might understand." Immediately, Mason wrote White: "I have taken all of the post-graduate work that Dr. Keeley's well-known institution has to offer, and have tried noble resolves and found myself buying sealskin sacks for the brewer's daughter. I have tried everything but a prohibition town and I want to come to Emporia for my board and keep." The Whites happened to be in Colorado when the letter came, but White told Mason to go to Emporia and help out around the paper until he returned.

Walt Mason worked on the *Gazette* as no other man ever worked. He turned in so much stuff that the printers could not run it all. Gradually, as he conquered his craving for liquor, he began to pay off the debts he had accumulated over the years. He brought to the *Gazette* indomitable energy, a gift for rhyming, and absolute business honesty. He had a difficult struggle to keep away from liquor the first year or two. Every once in a while he would tell White that he was going to Kansas City. White would then call a friend on the *Star* and ask him to meet Walt's train and stay with him all the time to make sure that he did not get drunk. Mason later gratefully wrote: "Had it not been for the cheery sympathy of Mr. White in those dreary days, I'd have given up trying."

On October 26, 1907, when the Whites were out of town, the front page needed more copy for the star head. Laura French asked Mason if he couldn't fill the space. Ten minutes later he handed her a prose rhyme:

FAIR WEATHER SUNDAY

Let us all proceed tomorrow,
humbly to the house of prayer.
The prediction from Chicago
says the weather will be fair.
After rain that saved the wheat
crop, comes the genial smiling
sun; let us seek the sanctuary
when the long week's work is
done. When the weather clerk
is certain that the Sabbath will
be fair, there is no excuse for
staying from the house of Praise
and Prayer.—WALT MASON.

This verse evoked such favorable comment that he wrote more verses for the next week's issues. When White returned, he was overjoyed in spite of the fact that he had once laid down a rule against poetry appearing in the *Gazette*. Mason wrote his rhymes without reflection and without hesitation. White encouraged him by stating: "No other man in all this western country has done such good work as you have in the past year. You have got the real stuff in you." During 1908, White persuaded George M. Adams to syndicate Mason's rhymes. Before long not only was he composing his syndicated poems, but he was writing a daily short story for the Chicago *Daily News*, a book review page for the Kansas City *Star*, and reams of material for the *Gazette*. Adams also published several books of Mason's poems, and by 1920 he had acquired enough money to retire to California, where he continued writing rhymes until his death in 1939.

*   *   *

As part of the role of a country editor, White was always a

booster for Emporia. With an acute sense of responsibility, he told his readers on February 27, 1911:

. . . Those who have lived during the half century now passed, put something here besides houses and streets and trees and material things. They put practical work in politics, in religion, in education, in business, in the social organization to make this a good town. Emporia did not just grow. To have a clean town meant a fight, every day in the year for someone; it meant sacrifice for scores of men and women— sacrifice of time and money and health and strength. To have all these schools and churches meant that thousands gave freely and in a great faith without material results in sight, that we who now enjoy what we have, might reap when we have not sown.

This town is the child of many prayers. This town is the ideal realized only after those who dreamed the ideal, laid them down to rest with the dream still a dream. This town is the fruit of great aspiration, and we who live here now, have a debt to posterity that we can pay only by still achieving, still pursuing; we must learn to labor and to wait, even as they learned it who built here on this townsite when it was a raw upland prairie. It is well to think on these things.

When the Hutchinson [Kansas] *News* once scornfully referred to Emporia as a town dominated by petticoats, White quickly turned the charge to Emporia's credit by saying that this meant that the town had no saloons, no town drunkards, no riotous living, and no whisky paupers to support. He took the lead in raising money for community projects. Although not a member of the Methodist Church, he helped the congregation buy an organ. He headed many drives to raise funds for the Y.M.C.A. One day when Secretary of the Treasury William G. McAdoo stopped in Emporia, White persuaded him to speak at a luncheon to raise money for the "Y." "Hell," said McAdoo, ". . . I'll go, but I wouldn't do it for anyone else but Old Bill White." Not only did he make a speech, but he gave a hundred dollars to the campaign. The College of Emporia also received money from White and many times he secured bequests for the college from outside sources. White served as the first president of the Current Club, a men's discussion group launched in 1900, and he was also a significant figure in the Chamber of Commerce and the Rotary Club.

White was a vigorous proponent of the doctrine of "Buy Emporia Goods." On January 20, 1897, he urged: "Eat nothing but biscuits made from Emporia flour. . . . Eat nothing but Emporia bacon and ham, and Lyon county eggs. . . . Put on an Emporia overcoat over an Emporia suit of clothes. If the money spent in Kansas City for cheap tailoring were spent here, thirty tailors would find work here who now live in the big city." Fifteen years later he urged a dry goods store to buy printing from him because when they bought outside that money was forever lost to Emporia. Until his death the slogan "Buy Emporia Goods" appeared from time to time in the *Gazette*. Yet during the last twenty-odd years of his life he knew that world trade was necessary for American and world prosperity, and although he advocated the lowering of protective tariffs by all nations, with delightful inconsistency he urged all Emporians to buy only Emporia-made goods!

"Personally White is the most unattractive man in Emporia— and that is saying much!" one person remarked in 1909. "You see him as he comes rolling down the street on his way to the *Gazette* office, and you wonder that he ever did anything but sit in the shade of a tree, and drink lemonade. His clothes look as if they had been planned and cut out by the town tinner. His hat is the most impossible structure in the world. His face is the ordinary fat man's face, and is usually covered with a short stubble of sandy beard, and a sheepish smile. There is a half suppressed twinkle in his eye that suggests an overgrown boy. . . . Altogether, you would say that the man was made of putty, were it not for a certain firmness about the jaw indicating that there is steel beneath this flabby exterior, and plenty of it, too. . . ."

During these years before the first great war, White used to wear pants that had been patched and a battered hat that was jammed down on his head of sandy hair. Assuming a completely democratic attitude, he and the family drove about in an old rickety two-seated rig drawn by their feeble horse, Old Tom, when they could easily have afforded an automobile. The tramp poet, Harry Kemp, observed: "Whether this exterior appearance . . . was sincere or affected in him I never could quite tell. I am almost inclined to believe it was not done for effect. . . . If it was an affectation, his personal attitude toward the people with whom he came into contact was not—in his office everybody loved him, and worked for him with that easy efficiency that comes of good will and respect."

Whenever White was out of town, Mrs. White took charge of the *Gazette*. "Mrs. White is of medium height, slight, dark-eyed and sympathetic, intensely interested in her husband's work and of great assistance to him," declared the Buffalo *Express*, on December 28, 1901. Sallie White carefully watched for news items and wrote them herself or telephoned them to a reporter. During the first year or two of son Bill's life, she frequently deposited Bill in a wastebasket while she worked in the office. An old-time carrier boy once recalled that whenever White left town Mrs. White made "us step lively and toe the mark."

In 1900, the Whites revealed their growing affluence by buying "Red Rocks," a fine house that had been built of red stone shipped from the Garden of the Gods in Colorado. They remodeled and improved the house and lived in it for the rest of their lives. After a serious fire in 1920, the house was rebuilt along broad and comfortable lines partially designed by Frank Lloyd Wright. Famous for their hospitality, the Whites had a highly amusing experience during their second year in Emporia. In 1896, when Congressman Charles Curtis visited Emporia, they had him to dinner. White later recalled the following incident:

We were running our house on $5 a week in those days and Sallie budgeted everything. So she bought a chicken, cooked it, removed all the bones, placed it in a crock and covered it with melted cheese and cracker crumbs—oh, yes, and with mushrooms. Those mushrooms—Ah! We debated quite a while over whether we should buy a 75-cent can or a 35-cent can. I wanted the 75-cent can; Sallie's will was her way and we compromised on the cheaper assortment. Even at that it meant I had to go without a couple of 10-cent shaves to pay for this delicacy. Well, sir, Congressman Curtis came. Sallie and I were quite proud. Pretty soon I could see she was trying to catch my eye. She nodded her head toward the congressman's plate. I looked. Ye gods! There he was—deftly removing the mushrooms from his portion of chicken, placing the discarded fleshy fungi on the side of his plate—mushrooms for which I must sacrifice two shaves that week! The next noon when I got home from the office Sallie met me at the kitchen door. She saw the look on my face. "Yes," she said, "I've retrieved the mushrooms—they're waiting for you."

People with national and international reputations visited the Whites in Emporia, and the townspeople became accustomed to seeing Edna Ferber, Ida M. Tarbell, and Anne Morgan walking the streets of the town. "When your world is awry and hope dead and vitality low and the appetite gone," Edna Ferber once wrote, "there is no ocean trip, no month in the country, no known drug equal to the reviving quality of twenty-four hours spent on the front porch or in the sitting room of the Whites' house in Emporia." John S. Phillips of *McClure's Magazine* and later the *American Magazine* recalled: "I once said to the novelist W. D. Howells . . . that my wife and I had been visiting the Whites in Emporia and that I did not know any more delightful place to visit in this country. Howells replied: I do not know any pleasanter place to visit in the world."

The Whites' two children, Bill and Mary, were as different as the Kansas prairies and the Rocky Mountains. Bill, as a boy, was shy, quiet, and retiring. He grew up in the *Gazette* office, and very early took a route to deliver papers. In 1910, when White heard that Ed Howe's son Gene was now working on his father's paper, the Emporia editor wrote Gene: "I shall be mighty proud when my boy, Bill, gets that far along. I don't think Bill will be worth very much. He is a good boy and that is the trouble. He is too good a boy and does not make me any trouble and I am afraid he won't make anybody else any trouble."

Mary, four years younger than Bill, was a vigorous tomboy. As a baby she had been so frail that her parents encouraged her to be an outdoor girl. She soon became a wild, carefree horseback rider. White wrote Franklin P. Adams on December 8, 1914: "Mary has not sold her pony yet. She was out riding on it the other day and some people came along with an automobile and honked and made a loud noise and the pony sidestepped and threw her off. She got up . . . and they came back and making a loud noise and honking and the pony bucked her off again. Her mother asked, 'Well, Mary, didn't they stop and see what was the mat-

245

ter?' And Mary said, 'No, Mother, but what could you expect? They were riding in a Ford!' Otherwise Mary is real well." Mary was not a warm, affectionate child like Bill. When she would enter the *Gazette* office, her father would say, "Give your old father a kiss," but she would refuse. Bill was their grandmother's favorite. Madame White would place the two children in their rockers and she would sit in hers and read the classics to them by the hour.

The White home was a pleasant place to relax after a hard day at the *Gazette* office or after a hard day of writing articles and books. Playing with the children, listening to Mrs. White read aloud, or pounding on the piano were the chief sources of diversion. Once when visiting George Lorimer of the *Saturday Evening Post*, White became fascinated with Lorimer's phonograph-record collection. He himself began to collect records, and developed the lifelong habit of relaxing by playing the records and accompanying them on the piano. During the bitter fight between Roosevelt and Taft in 1912, White wrote his old friend and political opponent, Charles F. Scott: "And finally, brethren, have you got a phonograph, a Victor? You ought to have one and you ought to get a twelve-inch record called 'Schubert's Unfinished Symphony' and then when you come home at night after reading a paper like the Gazette that puts you out of sorts . . . put that old symphony on the machine and click it off . . . It will do you a power of good. I am probably as intense in my convictions as anyone and probably a little more uncharitable than I should be . . . but when I get out home and get the old phonograph to going and run out Wagner's big, beautiful pieces, I seem to get away from the cares that infest the day, and whatever corrosion of worry and weariness that may infect my innards seems to pass."

* * *

White, of course, was more than just an ordinary country editor. His consummate skill as an editorial writer, his amazing energy in producing a remarkable and varied number of magazine articles and books, and his active political career in local, state, and national politics, helped to distinguish him from other country editors. After the defeat of the Kansas Bull Moose ticket in 1914, an opponent of William Allen White's dedicated a poem to him, which reveals something of the respect the people of Kansas had for their nationally known editor:

> We have known you many years,
>   Allen White;
> Read you through both smiles and tears,
>   Allen White;
> You're a treat in every line,
> But in politics you shine—
> In defeat you are sublime,
>   Allen White.
>
> When your man is counted out,
>   Allen White,
> You don't tear your hair and shout,
>   Allen White,
> There has no one heard you yell
> That the country's gone to hell;
> Rome, for you, has never fell,
>   Allen White.

PART III

WAR AND PEACE

CHAPTER 12

WAR IN EUROPE

"GOD save us all from war," White declared in April, 1914, as
he realized that a conflict in Europe would take the eyes of the
American people off the Bull Moose party and off the broader
progressive movement, and focus attention instead on the problems of war. Yet, although White was aware that war in Europe
would affect the United States, like most Americans he had only a
dim understanding of the forces that brought war in the summer
of 1914. He was stunned, and he was genuinely neutral at first
through complete unfamiliarity with the issues at stake.

Like most Americans, the Emporia editor had not realized that
the United States was now a great world power. Instead, he still
thought that the country was the relatively isolated, growing nation of the nineteenth century. Although President Theodore
Roosevelt had been aware that a conflict in Europe or in the Far
East would affect the security of America, his views made little
impression on his stalwart supporter from Emporia. Seldom was
Roosevelt's foreign policy mentioned in the many laudatory articles and editorials that poured from White's pen. When Roosevelt, for instance, exerted pressure in 1903 to solve the German-
British blockade of Venezuela, White was uninterested. "Everyone in this town," he declared, "is busy and earning money and
saving it. Everyone is engaged in honest work and is looking after
his own family. The Gazette contends that this is better than
bothering with Venezuela."

White and his America did not care about "international relations." Few Americans, and certainly not Editor White, understood the importance of the European balance of power to America's peace and security, and few realized that Great Britain had contributed to American security during the nineteenth century by preventing any one European nation from becoming so powerful that it threatened world peace. Germany by 1914, however, had upset the balance of power, but few Americans understood at the time the war broke out that a German victory would be a threat to the security of the United States. White reflected this attitude when he declared in the *Gazette* on August 29, 1914, that there was no difference between the warring powers.

Gradually, as the American public recovered from the initial impact of the war, an underlying sympathy for the Allied cause manifested itself. Ties of language, literature, law, and customs bound the nation to England, and France and England with their democratic governments were much closer to American institutions than German autocracy and militarism. From the vantage point of mid-America, during the opening weeks of the conflict White viewed the war as a grave annoyance. "I certainly feel that the President has gone further than any other Democrat could have gone along the road toward real progress in this country," he wrote Joseph Tumulty on September 4, 1914. "How sad it is that the war is taking the national attention away from justice."

When Germany violated Belgian soil, however, White started to abandon his neutral position and from that time on increasingly favored the Allied cause. He served on a state-wide committee for Belgian relief and was in charge of securing contributions of flour from seven counties. The Belgians "could have gone into the German empire and could have made their country great," White noted on October 3, 1914. "But they gave their lives—and are helping to save the world. It is the choice between the philosophies of Nietzsche and of Jesus of Nazareth."

* * *

"As a citizen, I feel it my duty to let you know that the feeling of people in this vicinity is very strongly against using German barbarities as justification for entering the world war," White wired President Wilson after the sinking of the *Lusitania* on May 7, 1915. "Properly we should make known our horror at the ruthless savage cruelty of these acts, but it seems to me in this time of world madness we should retain our sanity. Running amuck with the rest of the world will accomplish nothing for humanity's ultimate gain."

Despite the clamor for war which followed the *Lusitania* incident, Woodrow Wilson knew that the country was not ready for war. He sent a note to Germany demanding a disavowal of the sinking, reparations, and a pledge against recurrence of undeclared submarine warfare. When White editorially praised Wilson's policy, the President wrote him: "I cannot let your editorial headed 'The President' pass without expressing to you my deep appreciation of its generous attitude and assuring you that such things go a long way to keep me in heart and steady my hand." To a Washington friend, White observed on May 18, 1915: "I hope that you agree with me that President Wilson is doing splendidly in the foreign situation. I find myself in the attitude of endorsing him against my will."

About the time the *Lusitania* was sunk, White wrote an article for the *Metropolitan Magazine*, which expressed his opinion, held in the early weeks of the war, that there was no difference between the belligerents. "We are in a day of confusion," he asserted. "In America the pall of the great European war has put fear into the heart of the people . . . Today human cattle are led to slaughter, more wantonly than ever they were led to slaughter in the darkest days of barbarism—and for no principle, for no contention over fundamental right or wrong."

White was soon to regret his failure to differentiate between the Allies and the Central Powers. As the war continued, he began to realize that Germany, Austria and Turkey were autocratic powers and that their success would endanger America's security. On February 10, 1916, he wrote Gifford Pinchot: "I was most unfortunate in my Metropolitan article. I had no idea of giving the impression that I was not lined up right on this situation. I am so anti-German that you can toast pretzels on my hair."

In August, 1915, while in Colorado, White received a long letter from Colonel Roosevelt denouncing President Wilson as a great influence for evil because of his refusal to take a more belligerent stand toward Germany. Wilson's actions, Roosevelt felt, were humiliating to the national honor of the United States. Immediately, White told the Rough Rider that he was no pacifist but that he did not believe the United States should rush into the war. White declared that he wanted a strong foreign policy, but he did not blame Wilson for not getting us into war, since the country was not prepared to fight.

* * *

By the fall of 1915, the Emporia editor realized that the war was having a pervasive influence in the Middle West. Although he disliked the Navy League and big business support of preparedness for the country, he felt that steps needed to be taken toward defense. He believed, however, that the Bull Moose party should declare itself "in favor of socialization through government ownership of the manufactory of ammunition, arms, battleships and what might be called defensible steel."

It was during 1915 that White realized that isolationism was an unsound policy for the United States to follow in the future. As a powerful nation, it must assume its share of the responsibility for maintaining world peace. Following a lifelong practice of joining organizations to make his private sentiment function as public opinion, he became a vice-president of the League to Enforce Peace. The purpose of this organization was to provide machinery to replace slaughter as the means of settling future international disputes. White told Ralph Stout of the Kansas City *Star:* "I am greatly interested in the League to Enforce Peace. . . . It seems to me the way to help peace is to prepare for it and join all other good people who are willing to prepare for peace by fighting for it."

When White was asked in January, 1916, to express his opinion as to the terms of peace, it was obvious that he had traveled a long way in his thinking from the editorials he had written in August of 1914. There should be no peace in Europe, he observed, until Germany had learned that there was something else in the world besides militarism, and "that there is a God in Israel, and that might does not make right." Furthermore, he stated:

The German System of order and obedience has produced great talent, but order and obedience does not produce genius, and genius after all, directs the world; moves it forward, releases those new springs of life that move men forward. Talent does not move men forward. Talent merely keeps men in a groove. Talent provides for efficiency, but not for forward moving changes, and until the ever-lasting daylights are knocked out of order and obedience, and a more democratic system established, a system that will give men elbow room for growth and for those sudden expansions of men into genius that moves the world forward, I for one, hope for no peace. . . .

When reactionaries pointed to the powerful central government of Germany and declared that the American progressives were seeking the same end, White was quick to denounce their statement. Although he believed that a strong centralized government was necessary to curb the menace of capitalistic exploitation, he did not feel that the central government should become a "strong overbearing state socialism" as in Germany. This type of organization did not allow enough free play and elbow room for the individual to rise and fall upon his own merit and initiative. The democratic state that regulated monopoly in the interest of freedom for the many, rather than the autocratic state that stifled men's initiative, was White's ideal. As he wrote to one opponent of the positive democratic state, freedom could be attained only through planning.

* * *

During the fall of 1915, Germany agreed to stop unrestricted submarine warfare out of fear that the United States would break off diplomatic relations. In February, 1916, however, Germany once more resorted to this type of warfare. Wilson quickly warned Germany that unless she abandoned this warfare the United States would break off diplomatic relations. These were trying days for the President. Not only was Wilson faced with forces clamoring for war, but a more serious problem to the administration was the many citizens who charged that Wilson's diplomatic policy of holding Germany to an accountability for violation of American neutral rights and honor was too warlike. In March, 1916, these isolationists or pacifists tried to push through Congress a bill that would have forbidden American citizens from traveling on armed belligerent ships—a right recognized by international law. Wilson opposed this bill because he felt that no nation should surrender its rights. White backed Wilson's attitude and wired his congressman, Dudley Doolittle: "I most earnestly hope that you can support whatever move preliminary or direct may be before the House unequivocally standing by the president's position. It would be a tremendous mistake for his party and a crime for his country to hamstring the president by an equivocal move at this time." On March 7, the House voted to table the resolution and Doolittle told White: "I took the liberty to make industrious use of your expressions by direct quotation where it counted; your telegram figured in two hundred and seventy-six affirmative votes materially. That is the exact truth."

White's considered judgment, at this point, was that the United States had to present a strong, courageous front to the family of nations. "I think that Wilson is in the main right in his diplomatic policy," White declared, "and I cannot help but feel that the Republicans and some of the Democrats are playing politics with a national issue." Furthermore, he reiterated his belief that the government should acquire ownership of all munitions plants. Under the impact of war he had also altered his opposition to a large standing army. By 1916 he believed that the country should have an army of at least a half to a million men.

On May 4, 1916, Germany temporarily lessened the tension with the United States by agreeing not to sink merchant vessels without warning provided the United States would make the Allies ease their blockade. This was a momentary victory for President Wilson, but only as long as Germany was willing to wait upon American protests to the Allies. The minute Germany decided that unrestricted submarine warfare was worth more than American neutrality, Woodrow Wilson would have to ask for a declaration of war. White caught something of the inevitability of war for the United States in his editorial about Germany's note of May 4. "Naturally, the country that would send out the submarine, and advertise its attack on a liner like the *Lusitania* will not quit until force makes that country quit," he declared on May 6, 1916. "The force may be from within—through revolution

—or it may be from without, in the cordon of the civilized powers drawing a fatal noose at Germany's throat. But force is the one word German imperialism understands, and in the name of civilization, it may be necessary to use force."

*   *   *

Although the Emporia editor was increasingly disturbed by the war, the bulk of his editorials in 1915 and 1916 were written about domestic problems. It was in his private letters that he revealed more concern over the war than in his published editorials and articles. The two years before America's entrance into the war were busy ones for White. He wrote a great many articles for national magazines and played an important role in Progressive party politics. In spite of the grim war raging in Europe, he opened the year 1915 in a gay and carefree fashion by writing a poem about Ida M. Tarbell:

> To I. M. T.
> (on looking
> at her
> portrait)
> Oh I have
> saw the
> Jungfrau
> and once I
> seen a bust, of
> Jove a-frowning
> at mankind—
> more terrible than
> just. Oh I have
> cited Jeffries' and
> Jim Corbett's fear-
> some mugs; and
> glimpsed Pike's Peak
> and Roosevelt and all the
> other pugs. And I have blinked
> in wonder at the Mona Lisa's
> smile; and once I gawked
> at Venus, late of Milo
> for a while. But oh I never

seen such grim, peculiar
sphinx-like grace, in all of
them as Ider M. wear
in her fighting face.

During the early months of 1915, White wrote for the *Saturday Evening Post* and for *Collier's* a series of fictionalized short stories that were published in the following year in book form as *God's Puppets*. This book was quite similar to the political stories *Stratagems and Spoils*, which he had published fifteen years before. His purpose in *God's Puppets* was to smash selfishness in its various forms. The first story was aimed at sex selfishness; the second at money selfishness; the third at personal vanity; and the fourth at political vanity. The fifth and last story, as he wrote to Frank Lloyd Wright, "was a mere sugar coating to leave a pleasant taste in the mouth after the pill had been administered."

When John Reed, soon to become the hero of American radicals, read the first story in the *Saturday Evening Post*, he wrote White: "How on earth did the Post consent? I have a theory that it was so damned transcendentally well done that they couldn't refuse . . . The way you stuck to life . . . It's true, dispassionate life, how well understood, how deeply sympathetically interpreted!" "I think those stories are the strongest things you have done," Theodore Roosevelt wrote White on April 4, 1916. The *Nation*, however, was unfavorably impressed with the book. "Bankers seem to be Mr. White's special prey," the reviewer charged. "On the evidence of his stories, a foreigner would be justified in concluding that American banking is an affair both hazardous and corrupt."

During 1915 White did his best to keep the public interested in the Progressive party. It was an exceedingly difficult task, what with the war and Wilson's progressive legislation. White admitted the hopelessness of his assignment when he wrote to Raymond Robins, Illinois Progressive, on January 16, 1915:

. . . I am going down with the ship even if I am the captain and cook of the Nancy Brig, the crew and the officers too. This is no particular hardship, indeed it is so easy that I fancy that I am indulging myself in a vice. It would be like running my finger down my throat to affiliate with either the Republicans or the Democrats as they stand today. I like Bryan and I like Wilson, although my liking has been more or less tempered very recently, but still it is strong enough to hold if it was not for states rights, Tammany and the Solid South, and the general mossbackism of the present Democratic leadership. When I left the Republican Party I banged the door after me so hard and then threw rocks at the house so continuously ever since, that I suspect there would be more or less strychnine in the veal if I were to attempt the prodigal son, which is far from my present desires.

White gathered information from people all over the country concerning the Republican party, which convinced him that "the Republican party is lapsing pretty hopelessly into a reactionary status." When Senator Borah launched an attempt from within to make the Republican party progressive, White sagely observed: "It recalls Bishop Potter's fight for a model saloon. He couldn't get a model saloon so long as he kept whisky in it, and when he put out the whisky it no longer was a saloon."

In May, 1915, White wrote George Perkins that the Progressive party should plan to run a national ticket the following year even though it was perfectly apparent that it would be defeated. "I cannot help feeling that Colonel Roosevelt is headed back to the Republican party," he remarked, "and, of course, I am sorry that he is heading that way." If the choice in 1916 were "between Wilson and any reactionary Republican or as between Wilson and any Republican who is now considered seriously for the place, I would choose Wilson" he told Perkins. This, of course, was a year and a half before election time. When Gifford Pinchot inquired as to the future of their party, White replied: "My own feeling very strongly is that it is hopeless to go into the Republican party and folly to go into the Democratic party. After that I am not sure. The Independent is a mule, who gets nowhere before or after the fact. And yet, I don't see very much else to do except to be independent. I am for the government ownership of railroads, and I am for prohibition and woman suffrage."

The Whites spent the summer of 1915 in Colorado far away from the distractions of politics and newspaperwork. White devoted his time to what appeared to be an interminable revision of his progressive novel, *In The Heart of A Fool*, which he had been writing for the past five years. Shortly after they returned to Emporia in September, White visited Indiana to gather material for a sketch of his old friend James Whitcomb Riley. Then he and Sallie spent November in New York City visiting friends and attending many dinners and plays. "I had never met Mrs. White before," Hamlin Garland wrote in his diary after a dinner with the Whites, "and I found in her something wistful and lovely. William was wholly admirable in his care of her." Former *Gazette* reporter Brock Pemberton attended a literary luncheon with White during this trip East. This was the period when women were just beginning to smoke cigarettes, although it was still illegal for anybody to sell or give away cigarettes in Kansas. White's female luncheon companion turned to him at one point and remarked, "Isn't it a shame that women are not allowed to smoke publicly with men." "Well, you might try chewing and spitting in your hat," replied White, with a merry twinkle in his impish blue eyes.

When the Whites had returned to Emporia after this New York visit, White wrote Franklin P. Adams that as they got aboard the train he had asked Sallie, "Now, next to the children, what would you rather have than anything else, when you get home?" "Well," she replied, "you say first." "Veal stew and dumplings"; and she said "Neck of mutton with currie." Then, he told Adams: "We were tired of rich food. We wanted to get down to 15 cent shoulder cuts—boils with carrots and rice and peppers, and the short and simple groceries of the poor . . . Also we wanted to get home where the newspapers printed something . . . The love stories of the great papers running in connection with their crime's department, didn't get us. We couldn't find things in the New York papers the way we can find them in the Star and the Gazette."

* * *

On January 10, 1916, White attended a meeting of the Progressive National Committee in Chicago. A declaration of principles, prepared by Chester H. Rowell, E. A. Van Valkenburg, Herbert Knox Smith, William H. Childs, and White, was adopted without dissent. The significant part of the declaration was that, if the Republicans adopted a platform and selected a candidate acceptable to the Progressives, the Progressives would unite with the Republicans. "We will lay aside partisanship and prejudice. But we will never surrender those principles for which we stand and have stood. We will follow only a leader whom we know stands for them and is able to put them through," asserted the declaration.

Just before attending this meeting, White had reached the conclusion that every effort should be made to unite the two parties, but only on the Progressive's terms. If the Republicans would adopt a progressive platform and nominate Supreme Court Justice Charles Evans Hughes, White had no doubt that the Progressives would endorse him. After the Progressive conference, White was shrewd enough politically to know that the Republicans would adopt a progressive platform and nominate an acceptable candidate only if they were sure that otherwise the Progressives would run their own candidate. If the Republicans were confident that the Progressives would do nothing in 1916, then they would make no concessions to the Progressive point of view. Therefore, he urged George Perkins, as chairman of the Executive Committee, to file a full set of Progressive presidential electors before the June conventions and have a candidate file his nomination papers in every Congressional district. "These two things," he told Perkins on January 25, 1916, "would put the fear of God into the hearts of the Republicans as no other action we might take would do. It would lift our convention into a strong position, for with electors and congressmen ready to run, the Republicans could smell the powder in our guns without any trouble."

He explained the strategy to a Kansas supporter: "We have extended an automatic, ten cylinder, hair-trigger, quick-firing olive branch to our friends, which they can accept courteously or it will blast their heads off . . . if the Republicans have got the guts to go up against the buzz saw and nominate either Roosevelt or Hughes on an unequivocal platform demanding an American policy at home and an American policy abroad, we will meet them on that basis . . . If the Republicans equivocate upon the platform or candidates, the Bull Moosers will nominate a presidential candidate and will go through with him." If the Bull Moosers had to run a candidate, White expected that it would be Theodore

Roosevelt. When Justice Hughes continued to assert that he was not a candidate, White told Republicans: "If Hughes would make a square-toed avowal of his principles and let us know where he stands, we could rally behind him, but you cannot rally around a deaf and dumb asylum."

During the first week in June, 1916, White hurried to Chicago to report the simultaneous meetings of the Republican and Progressive conventions. As Progressive national committeeman from Kansas, White also was there to exert his influence on the policy of his party. There were some seven or eight hundred Bull Moose delegates at the convention who wanted to nominate Theodore Roosevelt and go home, "leaving the Republicans to 'take it or leave it.'" George Perkins willed otherwise. According to Harold Ickes, Editor White, Gifford Pinchot, Ickes himself, and a number of other more determined Bull Moosers realized that Perkins was deliberately preventing the nomination of Roosevelt until after the Republicans had nominated their candidate. White and his group wanted to nominate Roosevelt first, since this would force the Republicans to nominate him too, or know that by nominating their own candidate they were going down to certain defeat.

On Thursday of the Progressive convention, White, Pinchot, Ickes, James R. Garfield, and Victor Murdock decided to place Roosevelt's name in nomination in spite of Perkins. But Perkins got wind of their plan. When Garfield rose to place Roosevelt's name in nomination, and just as Raymond Robins, the chairman of the convention, was about to recognize Garfield, Perkins grabbed Robins's coattail and distracted him. Amidst the confusion created by this action, Garfield sat down and Perkins had someone else take the floor, and the golden opportunity passed. White was sure that if Roosevelt had been nominated that day and the convention had adjourned, he would have had a difficult time declining the nomination. Furthermore, if he had been nominated, White doubted that Hughes would have run on the Republican ticket. If the contest had been between Wilson and Roosevelt, White declared years later, Roosevelt would have won and the future history of the country would have been quite different.

On Friday, the day after Perkins had thwarted their plans, White called Colonel Roosevelt at Oyster Bay over the private wire in Perkins's room. Roosevelt vociferously demanded why White had not called him during the past few days. White said that he had hesitated about using Perkins's private phone, and the Colonel roared back: "It isn't his private phone. I had it put in with the explicit understanding that you and Jim Garfield, Hiram Johnson and Gifford Pinchot were to use it as freely as anyone else and none of you have called me up." White then told him that Perkins had never told them they were free to use the phone, "and then I think the Colonel began to tumble to the fact that he was in bondage" to Perkins, White later wrote Harold Ickes.

After this exchange between Roosevelt and White, the Rough Rider asked what kind of convention it was. When White described the delegates as middle-class business and professional men, Roosevelt was quite surprised because Perkins had told him that "it was made up of the lunatic fringe of his party—of the ragtail and bobbed tailed." Roosevelt then told White that he would not accept the nomination. White argued but to no avail. Roosevelt next stated that he would like to recommend Henry Cabot Lodge to the convention for nomination. As White wrote some time later in an unpublished biography of Roosevelt:

"Who," says I.
"Lodge," says he.
"Gosh," says I, with all the scorning enthusiasm of an ardent nature.
"Lodge," I repeated. "They will hoot you out of the party, out of their hearts for such a suggestion," said I.

Then White realized that the Colonel had been receiving "poisoned" advice from Perkins as to the temper of the Progressive convention. White made one last effort with Roosevelt.

"Don't send Lodge's name to the Convention. It will undo all the fine things you have ever stood for."
"It is too late," he said. "It has gone out to the press an hour ago."

On Saturday, Gifford Pinchot, Chester Rowell, Henry Allen, Victor Murdock, Donald R. Richberg, Bainbridge Colby, Matthew Hale, Harold Ickes, and White decided to nominate Roosevelt before the Republican convention nominated their candidate. They were now convinced that Perkins's strategy was to keep them from naming a candidate until after the Republicans had nominated. Then he would recommend that they not put up a candidate of their own, since three candidates would mean the re-election of President Wilson.

That afternoon, just before the Republicans nominated Charles Evans Hughes, the Progressives, over Perkins's protest, nominated Theodore Roosevelt. Then, as White has vividly described the scene:

For some unaccountable reason, the telegram, which had come to the Convention telling the Convention that Roosevelt could not be its candidate, was not read. In the exuberance of the hour a campaign fund was raised . . . Then late in the afternoon came the letter. It was horrible. I have never seen wrath and disillusion sweep over a crowd as they swept over the faces of the men gathered in that great Convention. I sat in the box, a national committeeman box, with a crowd of the Colonel's friends and they say that my eyes were brimming.

That night, when White was in the seclusion of his room, he started "thinking of the shame of it, thinking how ingloriously our great leader and beloved friend had sacrificed himself; how badly he had been handled; what a miserable anti-climatic mess had been made of what might have been fairly heroic. I was full to the bursting point with sorrow. I picked up the receiver, called for long distance, and across six hundred miles, having got Mrs. White on the phone, let out a blat like a wounded calf and bawled five minutes into the telephone."

White was brokenhearted. He wanted to keep the Progressive party alive even though it did mean the re-election of Wilson. He felt that by 1920 the Republican party would have petered out and the Democrats would have become the conservative party. This would have left the Progressive party as the truly forward-looking party. There was no doubt that White, Ickes, Pinchot, and their group felt that the party had been betrayed by George Perkins. Theodore Roosevelt, however, was partially responsible for the failure of the party since he entrusted his destiny to Perkins rather than to his old progressive friends.

Many years later, White told Claude Bowers: "I have a notion

that the healthiest movement in American politics for two generations was the Bull Moose movement, and Perkins plus a Wall
Street coterie plus Roosevelt's weariness of the flesh wrecked it."
When Harold Ickes decided to write his article, "Who Killed the
Progressive Party?" White assisted him because "the truth is most
important. For the failure of that movement in 1916 was one of
the tragedies in American history. The progressive movement had
to submerge in the war. And after the war it was conquered by
the reaction that inevitably follows war, being jammed up it broke
loose with the depression. An ordinary evolutionary movement
such as went on in Scandinavia and Holland for twenty years
would have been vastly better for the United States and the world
and it is of some importance to know why the progressive movement was wrecked in 1916."

* * *

After the tragedy of the Progressive convention, most of the
Bull Moose leaders followed Roosevelt in supporting Hughes; a
minority went over to Wilson. White told Victor Murdock late
in June that he felt as though he had had his face blown off. To
another Kansas friend he confessed: "I am weak and weary, sick
and sore. I am without star or compass politically and am up in the
air and a mile west." Then he revealed something of the impact
of the war on the progressive movement by adding: "The whole
trouble with our humanitarian platform, as I see it at the moment,
is that it hit war. Kaiser Bill blew it up. You cannot get humanitarian progress on the first page when humanitarian retrogression
is occupying the headlines. You cannot get people interested in
minimum wages and laws for hours of service and equitable railroad rates in the face of the news from Verdun."

After the Progressive convention, White reported the renomination of President Wilson at the Democratic convention in St. Louis.
Covering this convention, he declared, was his "idea of a seden-
tary pursuit." While there he wrote Colonel Roosevelt, with no
trace of bitterness over his refusal to be a candidate: "I read in the
paper this morning that you are ill, and I hasten to write to let you
know how anxious I am for your speedy recovery. Politics after
all are such a small segment of life, and the big splendid things of

life outside of politics and beyond it, mean so much more than the differences of politics . . . that any menace to your well-being touches me far more deeply and quickly than the things that may happen to your political fortunes. I shall count among my permanent assets, gathered in the journey upon this planet for whatever further stage of the journey may lie ahead, the joyous satisfaction I have had in your friendship."

Although *Everybody's Magazine* for March, 1916, had reported that William Allen White "looks out on the world from kind, twinkly eyes," there was very little gaiety in White's heart during the 1916 campaign. He confided to Henry Haskell of the *Star* on September 27: "I couldn't write anything about this campaign to save my soul. I don't know what I believe myself and I have no courage to tell other people what they should believe . . . the self-starter in my tear ducts doesn't work. The dry ducts just creak and groan and don't produce any moisture." Nevertheless, White carried the Republican ticket at the *Gazette*'s masthead throughout the campaign.

It was a drab campaign. The Democrats praised the progressive achievements of Wilson's New Freedom and adopted the slogan "He kept us out of war." Candidate Hughes talked vaguely of standing for "the firm and unflinching maintenance of all the rights of American citizens on land and sea." Roosevelt, however, was not vague. He stormed the country for Hughes because, as he wrote White, "I felt that Wilson's re-election would be a damage to the moral fiber of the American people." On October 5, Norman Hapgood wired White, urging him to support Wilson; but White refused. The reason, he explained, was that he was supporting the Republican state and county tickets in order that he would once again have power in the party's ranks in Kansas.

Finally, in late October, White bestirred himself for Hughes. At the insistence of Colonel Roosevelt, who stopped off in Emporia, White wrote an article for the New York *World*. This Roosevelt-inspired piece was designed to win Progressives to Hughes. It declared that Roosevelt was supporting Hughes only on the basis that he would destroy the Republican party of Taft, Cannon, and Aldrich. "The Progressives voting for Hughes from top to bottom honestly believe that Hughes will make the reactionaries surrender," wrote White.

After the Colonel left Emporia, White again lapsed into an indifferent mood. He declared on October 24 that he was supporting the Republican ticket "with all the energy of an ardent nature reacting upon the soporific influence of this dreary campaign." "As the election draws near my hope for an earthquake which will destroy us all, becomes more and more ardent," he wrote a friend on November 1.

The Republicans were too confident of victory. They ignored the Progressive party leaders, assuming that the Progressives would vote Republican. Hughes, while campaigning in California, snubbed Hiram Johnson, and as a result Hughes lost that state by a narrow margin. California's electoral vote was just enough to give Wilson a majority in the electoral college. After the election, White conceded that the bulk of the Progressives who had voted for Wilson had done so because Hughes had been afraid of speaking out for progressive laws for fear of losing his conservative Republican backing.

What the West had wanted from Hughes was fiery leadership. Instead, "He talked tariff like Mark Hanna. He talked of industrial affairs like McKinley . . . He gave the Progressives of the West the impression that he was one of those good men in politics—a kind of business man's candidate . . . always hovering around the status quo like a sick kitten around a hot brick!" White explained in an article in *Collier's* for December 16, 1916. The western Progressives had voted for Wilson because they preferred a president surrounded by progressive Democrats to one surrounded by the errand boys of Wall Street and plutocratic interests in general. Furthermore, the Republican National Committee had revealed no understanding of midwestern opinion. "What a lot of dubs they were in the New York headquarters . . ." White wrote Henry J. Allen. "I wonder if they knew whether Kansas was a breakfast food or a drug."

White was hardly downcast over the election since he never really had had any enthusiasm for Hughes. The political future, however, puzzled him. He confided to Theodore Roosevelt that he never could be a Democrat. He could be a Republican, true, under certain circumstances. Or, although this now seemed remote, he would be willing to help reorganize the Progressive party. Theodore Roosevelt, however, was thinking in terms of remolding the Republicans. He told Governor Lowden of Illinois: "What I most desire is that you shall help bring the Republicans far enough forward to enable us to lead the progressives far enough back to keep a substantial alignment."

White publicly warned the Republican party in his *Collier's* article for December 16, 1916, that if the Republicans wanted to come back into power they would have to retire the Old Guard reactionaries and put progressive Republicans in charge of the party. "Two smashing national defeats under their leadership should be enough to justify their retirement," declared White. He proved to be a poor prophet. Capitalizing on the reaction that followed the war, the Old Guard elected Warren G. Harding, wallowed in a decade of Babylonian debauchery, and then dumped the country into a great depression.

In early December, 1916, White traveled to Chicago to confer with Harold Ickes, Gifford Pinchot, James Garfield, and Chester Rowell as to their next move. They agreed to call a national conference of Progressives and Progressive-Republicans for the following March. At that conference they planned to demand six seats on the Republican National Executive Committee. Some time after this meeting, the *Nation* remarked that "the first emergence from the wreck of the Progressive party, in good order and undiminished as to zeal for the future, appears to be William Allen White, the pink cherubic blond who had so large a share in building of the top-heavy structure."

*   *   *

White closed the year 1916 with little regret. He wrote in the *Gazette:* "As a nation we are rich with blood money. Our prosperity has come from the suffering and tragedy of other nations. We have built up our own wealth on the lives of others. Our prosperity is cursed and tainted. Some day we shall have our own fiddler to remunerate. 'Vengeance is mine, saith the Lord, I will repay!' And he has a little bill against this United States. The year will not be a proud year in our history . . . It will be known in the future as the sad old, mad old, bad old year of 1916, and the year when our God was our belly and we minded earthly things!"

The Emporia editor opened the new year with the receipt of a vitriolic letter from Theodore Roosevelt. Roosevelt did not agree with White that the Middle West had voted for Wilson because Hughes was not progressive enough for their tastes. Roosevelt charged that the Middle West voted for Wilson because of the slogan "He kept us out of war." "This is yellow, my friend!" Roosevelt wrote, "plain yellow! They didn't mind his having put us into war with Haiti and San Domingo (and twice in Mexico); these were little wars in which only people for whom they didn't care were killed; what they meant was that they objected solely to wars in which their own comfort and skins were endangered. They had no ethical feeling, one way or the other, about it; they weren't concerned with honor or justice or self-respect; they were concerned with the safety of their own carcasses. Now such conduct is yellow." Roosevelt closed this handwritten letter by drawing three bats and a belfry with this inscription: "Unsuccessful effort to draw bats from the belfry of W. A. White."

White stoutheartedly denied that the Middle West had voted for Wilson because of the slogan. In fact, he wired Roosevelt that he, Roosevelt, could have carried the Middle West if he had been the candidate. The West was not for peace at any price. This statement pleased the Colonel immensely. "I am, as an American, very greatly relieved," he told White, "to be able to believe that the real fact was that the West fixed its eyes on Hughes' pussyfooting and lack of vision, and on the machine and reactionary support of him, and voted against him on these counts, and only incidentally for Wilson."

Shortly after the election, tension between the United States and Germany reached the danger point. On February 1, 1917, Germany once more resorted to unrestricted submarine warfare. Germany was aware that a resumption of this type of warfare would probably bring the United States into the war. But Germany had now decided that submarine warfare was worth more than American neutrality. Now, since he considered Germany's actions to be a threat to the honor and security of the United States, President Wilson severed relations.

White's analysis of the attitude of the Middle West, two months before America entered the war, was revealed in a letter to James Bryce, former British ambassador to the United States and author of *The American Commonwealth*. According to White:

The West as I read it is strongly pro-Ally, but the war is not a first page story in the West. A score of things interest the West more than the war interests the West. . . . The Republicans made a vast mistake in trying to make a campaign out of foreign policy. You can't stage it. It doesn't get across in a country where balance of power lies at least a thousand miles from any border . . . In the present state of daze and confusion following the suspension of diplomatic relations, I should say that the crying need of the times is leadership in America. There is no strong voice to which the people will listen. Colonel Roosevelt was crucified by bad stage management at Chicago and the people have turned from him temporarily. . . . And with him off the stage we have a leadership fit for discussion, an academic leadership— a leadership, wise and scholarly and cautious when we should have a leadership strenuous and certain and aggressive. The people are in the mood to follow, but alas, they are compelled to follow without knowing how miserable it is to follow the wrong kind of leadership. The more I read of the conditions in '58 and '59 and '60, the more I see them duplicated in our life today in America—fumbling, befuddled, idiotic optimism. Of course, when the flash of light does come, when the thing strikes, when the tragedy of our nation is dramatized, we will read the drama aright and will rise to take a noble part. But just now, we are having a period of national blind staggers. . . .

On February 26, President Wilson asked Congress for the power to arm American merchant vessels. Although Theodore Roosevelt, and even White in the past few months, felt that Wilson was struggling too much to maintain peace, Wilson's request was killed by a Senate filibuster. Wilson was in a difficult middle-of-the-road position, subject, on the one hand, to an attack from the group that believed war was necessary and inevitable and, on the other hand, from the last-ditch pacifists. White editorially denounced the senators who led the filibuster. When they succeeded in killing Wilson's request, he declared that the senators had disgraced the country. "They have done a dreadful and perhaps a tragic thing," he asserted.

After the Senate had adjourned, acting under his executive powers, President Wilson on March 12 ordered the arming of American merchant ships. Two days later White wired the President: "In your broad American leadership in this crisis I feel sure that the best opinion of the Middle West is solidly behind you. Do not fear to go forward decisively." But White was not sure, however, what effect the approaching war would have on American life. "I think the war will bring either a large forward jump or a large backward jump—I am not sure which," he wrote on March 13, 1917. "The great Civil War in America, it seems to me —was vastly more reactionary in its later influence than could have been imagined. The old soldier, as you may recall, formed a solid voting mass to whom ideas of progress were impervious and he was controlled for thirty years by a bad lot of property-minded politicians who used his patriotism as a bulwark behind which they built up a miserable system of privilege. This war in Europe may have a similar effect."

The sinkings of five American merchant ships in March finally led Wilson to ask Congress for a declaration of war on April 2. Twelve days before Wilson delivered his message to Congress, White had editorially asserted:

We have been in war for two years. When the *Lusitania* went down, after its destruction was advertised in the newspapers, war on America and American rights was declared by the German princes. But we have been longsuffering. We have turned the other cheek until it is calloused with blows. We need no longer wait for further provocation. We are at war. . . .

Having entered this war, we should not get out of this war until the German princes are so crushed and conquered that the emperor and the military autocrats of Germany will not hold back one single shred of their pretense that in war they have a right to coerce neutrals and to put the planet in a state of war.

This policy of the German rulers that her military need was paramount to the accepted rights of humanity in neutral nations, has set all neutral mankind against Germany. Germany must overthrow the ruling class which forced this hellish policy upon a kindly people. This country should so conduct her part in the war that when the surrender of Germany shall come, as it must come inevitably, the surrender shall not come from William the Kaiser, but from the German people through their republican representatives. With them we may treat. With William, treaties are scraps of paper, and America's entrance into the war should be the death knell of the ruling dynasty in the German Empire. With the Hohenzollerns, not with the German people, is our war. And it should be pushed to an everlasting defeat for that proud house.

By the time Wilson asked for a declaration of war, he was convinced that Germany threatened the destruction of the foundations of civilization. Her ruthless attacks on American neutral ships were a challenge to the honor and independence of the United States. Furthermore, if Germany won the war, the peace would be but a temporary settlement before she launched another war. Before Wilson sent his war message to Congress, the majority of the public seemed convinced that war was inevitable, imminent, and desirable. William Allen White's editorial policy in the weeks just before war came echoed this public sentiment.

Although during the 1930's it was charged that the United States went to war to protect the investments of American bankers in the Allied cause and to protect the business of American munitions makers, this point of view was then greatly overemphasized. At no time was it ever demonstrated that President Wilson or Congress was influenced by such forces. It was not loans or trade that led Wilson to ask for war; it was Germany's unrestricted U-boat warfare, which he held was an attack on humanity. The prevailing sentiment of the American people was for peace until the submarines sank American ships.

President Wilson could have kept the United States out of war had he and the public been willing to pay the price. The price required submission to German demands and the resulting loss of American honor. Moreover, it would have meant that Germany would probably have won the war. A triumphant Imperial Germany—not entirely dissimilar from Hitlerian Germany—would have dictated the peace. The peace terms that Germany forced on Russia early in 1918 furnish evidence that a German peace would have been far more punitive than what the Allies worked out at Versailles. With a German victory, the United States alone would have had to face the German colossus. This was the price of peace in 1917.

"We will not choose the path of submission and suffer the most sacred rights of our Nation and our people to be ignored or violated . . ." Wilson told Congress in his war message. "We have no selfish ends to serve. We desire no conquest, no dominion. We seek no indemnities for ourselves, no material compensation for the sacrifices we shall freely make. We are but one of the champions of the rights of mankind . . . It is a fearful thing to lead this great peaceful people into war . . . But the right is more precious than peace."

CHAPTER 13

HENRY AND ME

"IN THE largest measure the United States may be the factor in the war which will serve to deliver the world and Germany from the curse of militarism and the Hohenzollerns," White predicted the week following American entrance into the war. In the first feverish months after April, 1917, the Wilson administration had to mobilize an individualistic nation for total war. The federal government extended its control over industry and finance beyond the hopes of the most avid progressives. When White was asked in June, 1917, to express the opinion of the Middle West toward the wartime regulation of economic life, particularly the fixing of food prices, he was wholeheartedly for such controls. "Sentiment in Kansas is for the food control bill," he wired the *Literary Digest*. ". . . When the food control bill finally passes, the middle western farmer will demand that it shall remain after the war as a part of our national policy. Indeed most of the Socialistic devices now coming into our institutions as war measures will remain as a part of our national policy forever."

As the government increased its control of business, White continued to insist that such features as price fixing, government operation of the railroads, arbitration of labor disputes, and high income and inheritance taxes should be continued after the war. Believing in such a program, naturally the Emporia editor was going to be somewhat bewildered, perplexed, and mortified at what actually took place in the postwar decade under his own party's supervision.

One feature of wartime America that frightened White was the growing intolerance of the public. He warned in his paper that German art, music, and literature should not be banned in a frenzy of superpatriotism. But by June 16, 1917, he had to admit that an orgy of intolerance was sweeping the country. "The war has a throttle grip on our thinking," he sadly observed.

White was not only dismayed over the actions of intolerant patriots, but also irritated and angry at certain of his progressive friends who were denouncing the war as a Wall Street bankers' war. As he understood the conflict, it was essentially a struggle to prevent autocratic Germany from dominating Europe and eventually the rest of the world. Yet, back home in Kansas, his old friend Joseph L. Bristow was writing editorials in the Salina *Journal* opposing the pending selective service bill and sneering at the war effort. "If you know of a good, honest, two-legged man who believes in the Star Spangled Banner and the Bull Moose platform, who would run for the Senate as an American citizen and not as a granny-grunt or an assistant German, trot him out," White told Henry J. Allen. "But I am not going to support Joe for a minute on the grandmotherly program he outlines."

In the opening months of the war, White was enthusiastic in his praise of Woodrow Wilson's leadership. "He is a man of small enthusiasms, and of no personal following. He has not a charming or lovable personality to draw men to him," White editorialized on May 1, 1917. "Yet he has by force of sheer intellect drawn America about him in the leadership of a world combat for democracy as no other American leader has drawn America about him for years." White then sent the editorial to Wilson's secretary, Joseph Tumulty, observing that "Some time when the chief needs jollying along, kindly poke under his Presbyterian nose the editorial from yesterday's Gazette."

White's praise of Wilson infuriated Colonel Roosevelt, a faithful reader of the *Gazette*. Scornfully, Roosevelt wrote Henry Cabot Lodge that their Emporia friend had fallen for the belief that Wilson was the "great idealist of the war for Democracy." That summer, White admitted to Roosevelt that perhaps he had praised Wilson too much, but the reason he had done so was his anger at the attacks on Wilson and on the war effort by Robert M. La-

Follette and Joseph L. Bristow. Anyway, declared White, Wilson had done well after March 4. "He has got the declaration of war; he has got the conscription; he has got things moving, not rapidly, but I should say on the whole in the forward direction even if in more or less confusion, but still moving," White told Roosevelt. "And after all, he is about the only man who can act. So it has seemed to me wise to stand for whatever good he has done and stand rather vigorously for those things because there is a cult here in this country which wants to flunk out of the war, and is trying to make the war unpopular by calling attention to the mistakes of the administration. If we flunk out of this war, as I see it, we will have it to fight again. Only by fighting out this war can we hope to settle the issue with Germany for this generation and the next. And it has seemed to me that Bristow and LaFollette and Cummins and that group which is forever belly-aching around about the council of defense and the graft, and the favoritism at Washington are really making a sentiment not so much against graft and corruption and favoritism as they are making a sentiment against the war. And I have feared that too much anti-Wilson talk, now that we are in the war, would justify the pro-German pacifist and would not help matters at Washington."

Roosevelt agreed that one should stand with Wilson "against the LaFollette-German-socialism-pacifism combination" but that "Fundamentally our whole trouble in this country is due more to Wilson than any other one man, and his foes of the stamp you mention are able to attack him now only because of the weapons he himself forged for their use. Everything he has said since April 2nd can be justified only if we not merely unstintedly condemn, but treat with abhorrence what he has done before; and he has *done* badly. As Raymond Robins said to me, 'Wilson has spent two and one-half years dulling the conscience of our people and weakening their moral fibre, and then without any change in circumstance he reversed himself while running full speed; and naturally the machinery stops and an immense number of people are completely puzzled and find themselves wholly unable to get up any moral enthusiasm.'"

* * *

In July, 1917, the 49-year-old Emporia editor received an opportunity for direct participation in the war effort when the American Red Cross asked him to investigate their work in Europe. White eagerly accepted the offer, but insisted that he must be allowed to pay his own expenses. "It is more or less skittish crossing the pond and the submarines are still restless and peevish and I may end up in the harp party on the golden shore," White confided to Walt Mason on August 2, 1917. "If I should go down in glory, be good to the boys and girls in the office and sometimes drop in and write something for Mrs. White. She will run the paper while I am gone, whether temporarily or permanently."

White's good friend Henry J. Allen also was asked by the Red Cross to go to Europe and in mid-August the two roly-poly Kansas editors arrived in New York to embark for the war zone. "White and Allen Off to Win War," headlined the New York *Sun* on August 11. "Leaders of Kan. Will Kan Kaiser if They Don't Kan-Kan Among Sea Fish." The article then facetiously added: "The war is at last on its way to a definite settlement. This was the inference when it was ascertained yesterday that two Kansans were in town for a few days preparatory to sailing for France." The article related: "In the salon of Mr. White's sumptuous suite at the Vanderbilt there was secretly convened a notable gathering of seven ex-Bull Moosers, eleven magazine editors and a few score of leading New Yorkers formerly of Kansas." As the gathering broke up one person asked, "When'll I see you again, Bill?" White shook his head with a lugubrious smile and replied, "Perhaps in the fish market."

According to the *Sun* article, White discussed the revolutionary rumblings taking place in Russia and remarked: "I'm only sorry that they saw fit to send us to France instead of to Russia. I'd love to go to Russia just now." "Why?" asked the reporter. "It's my last chance to see a Bull Moose convention!" observed White. The Communist Revolution that broke out in Russia that fall was to excite White's interest and admiration. "I have faith in Russia," he wrote Victor Murdock on January 14, 1918. "I believe that the Russian revolution is the greatest net gain of this war so far." He told his readers a week later: "In a middle class world where, after all, business is business and profits are royal, what a specter of terror must the Bolsheviki be! They stand for something ahead of profit—humanity. . . . Today in Russia, all uniformed, all blind, all mad and tremendously stupid, stands a new man in the world. The worker. This will be his century. He is coming to his own! . . . For the first time since history dawned he is having an international say."

While White was overseas in the late summer and autumn of 1917, he wrote his wife voluminous letters relating his day-by-day impressions. When he returned he took these letters, added a fictitious love story to them, and wrote *The Martial Adventures of Henry and Me*. This book was loaded with humor, warmth, and sympathetic understanding. It had the rich mellow quality that was to be an outstanding characteristic of White for the rest of his life. By the war years, he had smoothed down many of his rough edges and he developed the charm and tolerance that would lead many people to seek advice from him in his role of the "Sage of Emporia."

The Martial Adventures of Henry and Me, based on White's daily experiences, furnishes an interesting although necessarily superficial view of Europe from a three months' visit. He did express his understanding of Europe, however, in the picturesque language that he used in commenting on the American scene. When White and Allen reached Paris, they discovered that the uniforms they had bought in New York made them look like "lilies of the valley and bright morning stars." The Red Cross thereupon sent them with a Mr. Hoppen to buy new uniforms. As White related the story in *The Martial Adventures of Henry and Me:*

Now Mr. Hoppen is related to the Morgans—the J. Pierpont Morgans—and he has small notion of Emporia and Wichita. So he took us to a tailorshop after his own heart. We chose a modest outfit, with no frills. We ordered one pair of riding breeches each, and one tunic each, and one American army cap each. The tunic was to conform to the recent Army regulation for Red Cross tunics, and the trousers were to match; Henry looked at me and received a distress signal, but he ignored it and said nonchalantly, "When can we have them?" The tailor told us to call for a fitting in two weeks, but we were going to the front before that. That made no difference; and then Henry came to the real point. "How much," he asked, "will these be?" The tailor answered in francs and we quickly divided the sum into dollars. It made $100. "For both?" asked Henry hopefully. "For each," answered the tailor firmly. There stood Mr. Hoppen, of Morgans. There also stood Wichita and Emporia. Henry's eyes did not bat; Mr. Hoppen wore a shimmering Sam Browne belt. Looking casually at it Henry asked:

"Shall we require one of those?"

"Gentlemen are all wearing them, sir," answered the tailor.

"How much?" queried Henry.

"Well, you gentlemen are a trifle thick, sir, and we'll have to have them specially made, but I presume we may safely say $14 each, Sir!"

Henry did not even look at me, but lifted the wormwood to his lips and quaffed it. "Make two," he answered.

The world should not be unsafe for democracy if Wichita and Emporia could help it!

While the two Kansans were in Paris, Dorothy Canfield Fisher, who had been serving in the war zone near Soissons, returned to Paris to act as their interpreter. She recalled years later about this experience with White that "he was wholly at home in the Hotel Crillon on the Place de la Concorde. Speaking no French, he was instantly on good and workable terms with the non-English-speaking French men of affairs with whom he was dealing. I was so proud of him as showing these provincially Parisian men an example of pure, native Americanism at its colorful, honest, savory first-rate best that I could scarcely bear it that my father was no longer alive to rejoice."

Allen and White traveled to various parts of the battle front inspecting Red Cross establishments. Many times they were under fire. The two of them spent weeks on their inspection tour. White enthusiastically praised the American Red Cross for having built many cantonments where French soldiers could get food, rest, and baths. It was the work of the Red Cross, he related, that had revived French morale from near a breaking point. He was also high in his praise of the contribution of the Y.M.C.A. huts in the various camps. These huts, equipped with writing tables, billiard and game tables, and a counter with gum, candy, and trinkets, were valuable as "safety valves." "No other nation in this war," he wrote, "is paying so much attention to keeping their men fit as the Americans are spending and no other nation is doing it so competently as America is doing through the Y.M.C.A."

White was deeply impressed by the distress, disease, and suffering that the war had brought to France. "That France has held so long under this curse proves the miracle of her divine courage!" he declared. Another aspect of the war that was stamped on his mind was the fact that at the outset the United States had been a debtor nation, but the Allied need for money had witnessed their selling of American securities and their borrowing heavily from the American people. "American capital must rebuild Europe," White wrote. ". . . American capital is tremendously on trial and . . . this European situation is going to take a tremendous lot of altruism on the part of men who control large sections of capital to work the thing out on lines of modern tendencies and to keep back precipitate and ill-considered revolutions which are in the political mind and heart of humanity and will come if normal economic and social development is throttled or is put up in front of a commercial gun and forced to hand over."

From France, White and Allen traveled to Italy in the company of Medill McCormick of Chicago to study the impact of the war on that country. When they visited the Royal Palace in Rome, they were dazzled by what they considered to be "the ornate impotent gorgeousness of a useless leisure class." "Henry nudged me," White related, "as our Kansas eyes bugged out at the Byzantine splendour and whispered: 'Bill, what this place needs is a boss buster movement. How the Kansas legislature would wallop this splendour in an appropriation bill! . . . Topeka,' sighed Henry, deeply impressed, 'never will equal this!' "

These "innocent" Americans, in the presence of decadent European royalty, had an extremely amusing experience with the King. White described the incident to Thomas Nelson Page, American ambassador to Italy:

. . . Did you ever hear about when Henry and Medill went to see the King? You may remember that I was sick in Rome when they pulled out for Udine. When I got there they had the cigars on Henry. It seems that when Henry saw the king crossing, and re-crossing his legs and swallowing his yawns, and when he heard Medill pulling his fingers and cracking his knuckles, Henry concluded to end a tiresome and uninteresting interview and spoke up and said, "Well, Medill, I suppose we might as well excuse ourselves to his Majesty and be going."

The Colonel who had them in charge nearly fell off his chair, and the King said, "O please" in his mild little voice, but Henry insisted on getting up and stalking out and dragging Medill with him. When they got into the anteroom, the Colonel, who was with them, fell on their necks and said, "O you Republicans—how you do like to put royalty in its proper place."

From Italy, Allen and White traveled to England. White's impression of England was a quite typical experience that many American visitors shared on visiting the mother country. "England, as one rides through it who lives beyond the seas, and uses the English tongue, always must seem like the unfolding of an old, old dream. England gives her step-children the impression that they have seen it all before!" White noted. "And they have; in Mother Goose, in Dickens, in Shakespeare, in Thackeray, in Trollope, in the songs of British poets, in the landscapes of British artists! At every turn of the road, in every face at the window, in every hedgerow and rural village is the everlasting reminder that we who speak the English tongue are bound with indissoluble links of our foster memories from the books and the arts, to ways of thinking and living and growing in grace that we call English. It is more than a blood or breed, more even than a civilization, is this spiritual inheritance that comes from this English soil; it is the realization in life of a philosophy, the dramatization of a human creed. It may be understood, but not defined, yet it is as palpable and substantial in this earth as any material fact."

While in England they lunched with H. G. Wells, dined with James Barrie, and had tea with Lord Bryce. In *The Martial Adventures of Henry and Me,* White jokingly described the many mistakes of social etiquette they made at these affairs. Many years later, this book with its humorous Kansas description of British society, played a major role in a debate on the floor of the United States Senate. Isolationist Senator Rush Holt attacked White for being chairman of the Committee to Defend America by Aiding the Allies and asserted that White was trying "to enlist the United States as a British ally in the European War." The reason, declared

Holt, was to be found in *The Martial Adventures of Henry and Me,* which was concerned with a glowing description of White's lavish entertainment by British society. Holt's conclusion was that the author was perhaps "seeking to return to those delightful fields as the hero who helped shove the United States for a second time into war as Britain's ally." White, wisely refraining from answering this demagogic attack, wrote a friend: "Holt is such a nut I can't think that anyone would seriously be affected by what he said and that particular story. Aren't they hard up for argument?"

This European trip left a number of significant impressions on White's mind. Everyone he met seemed to him to be longing for the dawn of peace. It should be remembered, he charged, when the time came to draft the peace that the Germans were "a breed apart—savage, material-minded, diabolic, unrestrained by fear or love of God." Moreover, it was clear in his mind that the Germans did not live according to Christian principles. They were not interested in reason but rather in unreasoning obedience. White recorded that in Italy, France, and England "the real thing we found was an awakening people, coming into the new century eager and wise and sure that it held somewhere in its coming years the dawn of a new day." The war, he declared, would bring vast social and economic upheavals. Caste and class interests, alike in the Allied powers as well as in Germany, would come out of the war with their special privileges lost. The war was a world-wide revolution that had destroyed the old social order. After the war, he predicted, "we shall have in a rather large and certainly in a keenly interesting degree a new heaven and a new earth."

After White's return to the United States in October, 1917, he gathered together his letters to Mrs. White and in April, 1918, published *The Martial Adventures of Henry and Me.* The book was received with tremendous enthusiasm. Theodore Roosevelt wrote White: "Not only have I read it but Mrs. Roosevelt has read it and now my daughter has read it, and we all think it one of the most delightful books that have been written since the war began. Indeed I think it a very remarkable book; for the humor, for the wisdom, for the deep tenderness, and for the kind of high Americanism, which makes me very grateful to you." Left-winger Max Eastman, whose *Masses* magazine had been suppressed by the government, told the Emporia author: "I am more grateful than I can very well say for your very charming book. There are two special reasons; one is that I sadly need something just now to make me take things not too seriously (yet seriously enough), the other is that I like especially to think that I have a few friends like you when our queerly promiscuous government is so unfriendly."

* * *

On his return from Europe in October, 1917, White plunged into the task of writing articles publicizing the work of the Red Cross in Europe. The Wheeler syndicate distributed these stories to such influential papers as the Kansas City *Star*, the St. Louis *Post-Dispatch*, the Cincinnati *Enquirer*, the San Francisco *Examiner*, the Philadelphia *Bulletin*, and the Chicago *News*. For weeks White devoted his evenings to speaking about the war to Kansas farmers at schoolhouses and country churches. He felt that the farmers did not understand the war. Europe was apparently remote from a Kansas farm. Furthermore, the farmer, a rugged individualist, reluctantly supported the socialization of control necessitated by the war. Farmers were irritated, too, that the price of their wheat had been fixed rather than permitted by inflation to rise sky-high. White tried to counteract their ignorance as to the meaning of the war and their hesitancy over accepting food and price regulation by telling them something of what he had observed on his European trip. "What I have been trying to do is to get this war to the farmer," he wrote Walter Lippmann on November 20, 1917. "Of course, he is the last man who socializes and as this war is the greatest social adventure, he is the last man in. But I think he is coming, though slowly . . ."

While the Emporia editor was engaged in publicizing the work of the Red Cross and talking to Kansas farmers about the war, his long-delayed novel, *In The Heart of A Fool*, was finally dispatched to the publishers. He had been working on this progressive book off and on for some eight years. The many distractions that had forced him to put it aside for long intervals took their toll on the novel. It was not so sprightly as *A Certain Rich Man*. The book reflected the fact that the author's mind was burdened with many problems and that he was tired while it was being written.

In The Heart of A Fool was published at a time when the American people had turned away from the progressive movement and were concentrating on the problems of war. As a result, the book never had so wide a popular acclaim and sale as did *A Certain Rich Man*. White was aware that the book was no longer timely. "I have tried to set forth a thesis," he told his publisher. "The thesis being that this is essentially a spiritual not a material world and that in this spiritual world only spiritual rewards and punishments come as a result of spiritual virtue or spiritual lapses and that material gains and losses are in no way connected with a man's spiritual attitude. Of course, it seems to me that the crux of the whole war is the struggle of the world away from the gross materialism of Germany to a certain higher spiritual standard of life contained in the word, Democracy. And in that the book is tremendously timely. But I fear that the average reader may not detect the trend of the book."

In The Heart of A Fool was the last novel White ever wrote. After the war he turned principally to biographical studies, feeling that he could more adequately put his messages across through this literary medium. Also, as he once jovially explained to Robert van Gelder, "Fiction is a matter of glands. When one is no longer personally interested in sex, and when anger has been succeeded by mellowness, then it is time to quit writing fiction."

The setting of White's progressive novel was a mining and iron-smelting town that grew out of the midwestern prairies. The hero of the book, Grant Adams, was a powerful labor leader who spurned love and money to fight for the cause of improving the conditions of the workingman. By the time that this book was written, the Emporia editor was far more tolerant and understanding of the reformer than he had been in his earlier writing. Adams was not treated as a harebrained fanatic, but as a great man who was trying to translate God's principles into social action. *In The Heart of A Fool* revealed that White had now acquired a much deeper understanding of the problems created by industrial America than he had had when he wrote *A Certain Rich Man*. His many trips to eastern cities, his experiences with labor leaders like Big Bill Haywood, whom he met at Lawrence, Massachusetts, during the great textile strike in 1911, and his contacts with men like

Ray Stannard Baker and Louis Brandeis, who were conversant with labor problems, had served to broaden White's own knowledge and understanding of society.

In The Heart of A Fool portrayed the development of America from the gilded age to the progressive era. White declared in the book that the progressive spirit of justice and fairness had triumphed over the spirit of greed and exploitation that had characterized America after the Civil War. Then with this accomplished, America in 1917 carried her own crusade for justice at home to the world stage. He concluded the book in the following tone:

So it came to pass that the riches of the continent were poured out for an ideal, that the genius of those who had seemed to be serving only Mammon was devoted passionately to a principle, and that the blood of those who came in seeming greed to America was shed gloriously in the high emprise which called America to this new world crusade. Moses in the burning bush speaking with God, Saul on the road to Damascus, never came closer to the force outside ourselves which makes for righteousness,—the force that has guided humanity upward through the ages,—then America has come in this hour of her high resolve. And yet for fifty years she has come into this holy ground steadily, and unswervingly; indeed, for a hundred years, for three hundred years from Plymouth Rock to the red fields of France, America has come a long and perilous way—yet always sure, and never faltering.

The novel received a mixed reception. Francis Hackett ripped into it, charging that the characters were subordinated to the moralizing of the author. "You are an artist," Hackett declared. "When you are not an ambassador or an editor or a reporter or a publicity man or a Progressive—you are an artist—sometimes, even, when you are one or all of these. But *In The Heart of A Fool* was not written with its eye honestly on the human object. It was written by the romantic Puritan, with propaganda behind it." White, who was in Paris reporting the Peace Conference when this review was published, readily admitted that the novel had its failings. But he wrote Hackett: "I find that you hold that when a moral or a purpose or propaganda of any sort comes into a novel art flies out of the window . . . I feel that a story is a good story only if it does have a purpose—some sort of moral purpose."

285

The Chicago *News* reviewer thought that the novel was "about the dullest and most unentertaining reading that I have done in two and one-half years reviewing for this department," while the Brooklyn *Eagle*, on the other hand, stated: "We have had much sage dissertation for years to the effect that there could not be 'a great American novel.' . . . But while the critics have been busy proclaiming that the thing could not be done William Allen White of Kansas has gone and done it. . . ."

* * *

While *In The Heart of A Fool* was being both praised and denounced by the critics, White was busy concentrating on his return to the Republican party. In February, 1918, he launched Henry J. Allen's campaign for governor of Kansas. Morton Albaugh, a personal friend of Allen's, swung the standpat element of the Republican party behind the Allen candidacy. The Wichita editor's candidacy was an excellent vehicle for White to re-enter the Republican fold, and he became the dominant figure behind the campaign. *The Martial Adventures of Henry and Me* was written partly to build up Henry J. Allen for the governorship. Throughout the primary and part of the election campaign, Allen was in France working for the Red Cross. This actually was a shrewd political move which undoubtedly won great sympathy for him. "I feel now that you should stay until after the August primary and so do the other fellows," White told Allen on March 5, 1918.

In pushing Allen's candidacy, White was quite definitely looking ahead to 1920. He told Allen on April 27, 1918, that he was "a fairly good white hope for the Presidency in 1920." Although White stated that he preferred Theodore Roosevelt to anyone else, Roosevelt had aroused too many animosities to be elected. Furthermore, no Republican member of Congress had been a constructive leader for the past year and no Republican governor was of large enough stature for the post.

One aspect of the political picture in the Middle West in 1918 that worried White was the activity of the Non-Partisan League. This group was preaching the need of vigorous social and economic reforms and, at the same time, was apparently disinterested in the war effort. White told his Democratic congressman, Dud-

ley Doolittle, that if the Non-Partisan League became too powerful and ran candidates for Congress, the two major parties should
get together and back just one candidate who was for the war
effort. In case the league ran a candidate against Doolittle, White
declared that the Republicans should withdraw their man and
back Doolittle.

White was not opposed to the League's demand for state-owned
elevators, mills, and packing plants; heavy taxes on the rich; and
the exemption of farm improvements from taxation. "If the Non-
Partisan League had hove in sight before or after the war," White
stated, "I would have been glad to have encouraged it, but I regard the winning of this war as the paramount issue in this world
at this time. I think it is the most righteous war ever started on this
planet, and the Non-Partisan League is so thoroughly tainted with
pacifism and pro-Germanism, that I should regard it as an enemy
to the country no matter what its economic doctrines were . . . I
do not believe that this is the time to foster movements having
for their prime objects any economic progress that is not distinctly
related to this war."

However, White cautioned his friends to attack only the war
stand of the league and not their economic program. He himself
was confident that these demands of the league were not far from
what had to come out of the war. Price fixing, government ownership of transportation and communication, state grain elevators
and packing houses were not at all impossible. He was sure the
United States was not going to return to an individualistic society
dominated by "entrenched capitalism."

That spring, in the midst of his Kansas political battles, a rather
amusing incident occurred. The Denver police wired him: "Are
you dead? Man of your name 35 died here of pneumonia. Relatives unknown." White avidly replied: "Your wire asking if I am
dead here. Opinions differ but my closest enemies feel that I am.
Personally, I doubt it, but have no conclusive evidence either way."
The most effective evidence that he was much alive was the increasing appeal of Henry J. Allen's candidacy to the people of
Kansas.

That summer, however, the Allen candidacy almost blew up.
Ivy Lee, head of Red Cross publicity, wrote White that the Red

Cross was so embarrassed by Allen's candidacy that Allen should resign from the Red Cross or withdraw as a candidate. White immediately suspected that Allen's primary opponent, W. Y. Morgan, was behind the entire affair. He was also certain that the Democratic party had a hand in it as well. Allen's gubernatorial candidacy was so popular that it was making it extremely difficult for the Democrats to re-elect their Kansas congressmen.

White quickly wired a number of people asking their help in preventing the ouster of Allen from the Red Cross until after the primary. White insisted that Henry P. Davison, head of the Red Cross, had sent Allen to France knowing that he was a candidate for office, and therefore should be willing to wait until after the primary. Hectic cables were sent from Emporia to Allen in Paris. Allen finally solved the problem himself. His Red Cross work was about completed, and when the Y.M.C.A. offered him the chance to leave Paris for field work at the front, he quickly resigned his Red Cross post. He wired White: "I think it was entirely the best thing to do. You are acquainted with the situation at Washington, and it was likely to become at any time an embarrassment to my friends here. The people here know that I have not worked any politics."

Morgan, Allen's opponent, tried to make political capital out of the affair. Just before primary day, he ran a large advertisement in the major papers asking "What Was the Reason Henry Allen Left the Red Cross? Investigate." White had expected this move and had a telegram from Davison of the Red Cross declaring that Allen left the Red Cross at his own insistence ". . . in order that he might render service with our troops which he thought would be of greater immediate importance than the work of which he had charge in Paris." This telegram was inserted in all the papers under the heading: "Here Is The Answer. We Have Investigated." The Red Cross incident did not adversely affect Allen's candidacy since he was nominated by a landslide in the August primary.

The future of the Republican party greatly concerned the *Gazette* editor during this last year of the war. He praised the selection of Will Hays in March, 1918, as chairman of the Republican National Committee and urged Hays to give the Progressives a square deal by assuring them adequate representation

on that committee. The big job ahead, White explained to Theodore Roosevelt, was "to convince the effective leaders of the Republican party that it must square itself with the times and with
the issues and forget the past and face to the future." The Republican party must be definitely radical in 1920 if it expected to
win.

"What is to be the attitude of the Republican party toward the
economic reconstruction of the war?" he asked Roosevelt. "Will
the emphasis on the property end of it be as heavy as the property
emphasis was in 1912 and again in 1916? Or will the Progressive
membership of the party soften and ameliorate the hard property-
minded conservatism which led the party to defeat in two campaigns? With the whole world being made over on new economic
foundations and into a new superstructure, it is unimaginable that
America will remain the same. Will the Republican party realize
that it is living in the changed world? Will men of great wealth
voluntarily give up many of the privileges that go to organized
wealth or will these privileges have to be strangled out of them
in a long hard political fight?"

All these were valid questions raised by a small-town Kansan
vitally concerned over the future of his country and of his party.
How was he to know in 1918 that in the decade to come the Republican party was to close its eyes to the problems of a changing
world? How was he to know that the Republican party would
serve as the vehicle for organized wealth to run the government
for a decade? All of this, of course, was carried out by the Republican party at the price of being defeated for four successive
terms by Franklin D. Roosevelt after the public had awakened to
its abuses.

White told Senator Charles Curtis on May 24, 1918, that the
Republican party must have a constructive policy of price fixing,
trust regulation, and a labor platform advocating the eight-hour
day, the minimum wage, and union recognition. Then he recommended General Leonard Wood as the candidate who would be
acceptable to both factions in the party. As to what the future
held for the nation and the Republican party in 1920, he proved
to be an exceedingly poor prophet. "I have no doubt of your
genuine desire to elect a ticket," he wrote Will Hays on August 6,

1918. "But on the other hand, don't ever think you can elect anybody who is an incrusted old reactionary—no one who thinks in terms of Lodge, Penrose, Lowden, Goodrich, Harding, and Watson, is going to get anywhere in this country."

On September 17, he warned Will Hays that he would drive the Progressives away from the Republican party if he continued "harping on the fact that after the war we are going back to the good old days." "I wouldn't stay with the Republican party over night," White asserted, "if I didn't believe that it was going to stand for a rigid unification of all the railroads . . . strictly controlled by the government and probably operated by the government if not owned by the government; and if I thought that price-controlling was to be abandoned; and if I thought the federalization of labor under labor conciliation boards was to be abandoned."

Although the national leadership of the party was firmly under the control of reactionary hands, White supported the straight Republican ticket that fall. He wanted to be a power again in state affairs. He had no desire to be a mugwump, shifting from party to party and thus sacrificing influence within party ranks. Except for his independent candidacy for governor in 1924, he was to support the Republican ticket until his death. At times it was to be stultifying to his professed beliefs, but he had made his decision against any further party bolts.

A week before election day in 1918, White demonstrated his reborn zeal for Republican victory by attacking President Wilson's public appeal for the election of a Democratic Congress. A Republican victory, Wilson warned, would mean divided leadership in the critical days ahead, and it would be considered by the rest of the world as a repudiation of his leadership. White joined with Theodore Roosevelt, Charles E. Hughes, William H. Taft, and Will Hays in denouncing Wilson's request. "The President violated the rules of good taste; he stooped to a low partisanship," White asserted in the *Gazette* on November 4, 1918. Actually, of course, appeals similar to Wilson's had been made by Republicans in 1864 and in 1898.

On election day the Republicans captured control of the United States Senate. White hailed this repudiation of Woodrow Wilson, claiming that it would make Wilson more humble and contrite. On the other hand, White maintained, this election did not mean that Wilson was not still a great world leader nor did it mean that the American people would not support his plans for world peace.

Actually this election of a Republican Senate was to prepare the way for the defeat of the Versailles Treaty and the League of Nations in the Senate the following year. A Republican Senate, led by Henry Cabot Lodge, who had become chairman of the Foreign Relations Committee by virtue of the Republican victory in 1918, was to wreck the chances for lasting peace. With a Democratic Congress, which probably would have followed Wilson's leadership, the United States would have joined the League, and thus have accepted its proper share of responsibility for international peace. White was to denounce Republican senators in 1919 for opposing the League, but he deserved a share of the responsibility for having helped create the senatorial situation that wrecked America's entrance into the League.

The serious significance of a Republican Senate dominated by Lodge was ignored in the jubilation that swept the nation over the signing of the Armistice on November 11, 1918. White hailed the Armistice as a great opportunity to bring about a new era of hope for the world. "If this great war," he editorialized on November 28, 1918, "which has overthrown the kings has also overthrown the selfishness and greed in human hearts—high and low (for alas, greed is not an upper class vice exclusively) then we shall be ready for the victory. But if the war has not purified us, we are not ready. For to make the world better we must conquer ourselves— our own greed, our own selfishness, our own tyranny . . . And unless the great war has made us all feel the pull of brotherhood in our hearts, unless we all feel that we are willing to compromise the vast differences which men must have living in civilization, unless we are willing to submit to some injustices for the larger justice to our neighbors, then we shall soon have the same old world."

CHAPTER 14

A KANSAN
AT THE PEACE CONFERENCE

"THE CONSERVATIVES of Europe are in the saddle," the Emporia editor wrote Mrs. White from Paris on January 2, 1919, "and they are Tafts, who know nothing and learn nothing." White was in Paris at the Peace Conference reporting the proceedings for a string of American newspapers. His newspaper dispatches and his letters home furnish an excellent insight into the hopes, fears, and disappointments of an average American over the peace that was forged at Versailles. Like Woodrow Wilson, William Allen White had little understanding of the forces that had molded European development and, like Wilson, he had little understanding that force would be necessary to maintain any peace. With very little knowledge of European traditions and problems, White expected too much too soon at the conference. He was to find his extravagant hopes shattered on the reality of an everyday world. Yet, like Wilson, he fought nobly for the League of Nations with full knowledge that another war would develop unless the Allied powers continued to work together.

On the day the Armistice was signed, White had wired Theodore Roosevelt, Henry Cabot Lodge, and Will Hays asking their aid in securing him a position on the American peace delegation. When this failed to materialize, he agreed to report the conference for the Wheeler syndicate and to serve the Red Cross in a liaison capacity. On the first of December, White and his son Bill, who accompanied his father in a secretarial capacity, traveled to New York en route to the conference in France.

While in New York they outfitted themselves with Red Cross uniforms, visited with Mr. and Mrs. John S. Phillips and Brock Pemberton, and attended a number of stage shows. On December 9, the Whites visited Joseph Tumulty at the White House, and talked over some of the problems that would arise at the Peace Conference. The day before they sailed they visited Theodore Roosevelt, who was seriously ill. When they reached the hospital, Roosevelt was so sick that the doctor would not allow White to see him. White returned to his room at the National Arts Club only to find the office in a panic. The hospital had been frantically calling because Roosevelt had demanded that he be permitted to see White. "One could feel the mounting pressure of emotion under that hospital roof," White has written. "It was teetering ready to blow off." When White reached the hospital, the staff was overjoyed to see him and the doctor said, "I'd rather see you than any other man in America right now; may be we can get that man's temperature down!" "He seems to have been raising Ned," White wrote his wife.

White and Roosevelt talked for an hour about presidential possibilities for 1920, the eight-hour day, old-age pensions, and platform planks for the Republican party. Roosevelt also discussed *In The Heart of A Fool* and told White that he did not like it. He felt that the book made heroes out of impractical reformers. This was the last time White saw Theodore Roosevelt. On January 6, 1919, while White was in Paris, Roosevelt died. The following day White wrote Sallie: "This is the day when we heard of Roosevelt's death, and all day I have been on the verge of tears . . . I am very sad. All the Americans are sad here; they feel that a great world loss has come. I don't feel that way so much; God will take care of this world I suppose, but where will we have such another friend! Did I write you that when I came away from him in the hospital I felt that I had seen the last of him—the last of the robust vigorous Roosevelt that I met way back there in the old days. . . . He was going very fast that day when I saw him at the hospital."

*   *   *

The Whites sailed for New York aboard the SS *Chicago*. On the ship with them were Willis Kerr, librarian of the Emporia State Teachers College, and Mrs. Kerr traveling to Paris to work in the American Library Association War Service. After a gay Christmas party aboard ship, White wrote Mrs. Kerr: "Having had this pleasant oKerrance, let's fondly hope for a pleasant ReKurrance." White played the piano for a portion of the Christmas Eve dancing party and wrote Sallie that Bill "danced like a wood nymph. He certainly looked like a young he gazelle in his uniform."

White struck up a pleasant friendship on the SS *Chicago* with Norman Angell, the British author. Angell was reading *In The Heart of A Fool* and rated it as an extremely important work. White was greatly impressed with Angell's intelligent and well-informed opinion on world problems. Angell told him that he was afraid the imperialistic forces would check Woodrow Wilson's plans at the conference. By the time that White arrived in Paris, he too was convinced that Woodrow Wilson would have a difficult time winning a peace based on the Fourteen Points and on a League of Nations.

In Paris, the Whites shared with Angell a suite of rooms at the Hotel Vouillemont. During the feverish days just before the conference formally convened, White and Bill attended plays and operas and had dinner parties with Ray Stannard Baker, Ida M. Tarbell, and Dorothy Canfield Fisher. In talking with the Americans in Paris, White found unanimous support among them for Wilson's project of a League of Nations. But they were pessimistic that his peace program could be achieved.

On January 3, White attended his first press conference with the American peace delegation. These conferences, he later wrote, always were solemn occasions. "There they stood—grand, gloomy and peculiar: Secretary [of State] Lansing with befitting iron-gray hair and mustache, decent gray trousers, two-buttoned cutaway, bound with aggravating proper black braid and his features to match in aggravating diplomatic composure. Back of him ranged General [Tasker] Bliss in regalia, Commissioner [Henry] White, immaculately respectable in conventional black, and Colonel House, generally sitting on the head of a lounge or the arm of a

fat chair—the only one in the group not prim, proper, and pris-
matical."

White particularly enjoyed his contacts with Colonel Edward
M. House. He appeared to White to be a sincere and resolute person. "I had a talk and half an hour's walk along the banks of the
Seine with the Colonel . . ." he wrote Mrs. White on January 8.
"I found House rather radical—more than one would expect. He
is the force that has kept Wilson abreast of the times. He is quite
candid; he says things in short direct sentences and is rather engaging in his manner. He told me that the weakness of Wilson is
his inability to get on with people who disagree with him."

By the end of the first week in January, the whole world seemed
to be in Paris. There were seventy-five leading American newspapermen reporting the proceedings. Walter Lippmann, David
Lawrence, Mark Sullivan, S. S. McClure, and Lincoln Steffens
were some of the friends White found there that first week. His
old friend Ray Stannard Baker had the difficult task of running
the press relations of the American Peace Commission. "Baker and
I had a long walk last night until bed time . . ." White wrote his
wife on January 18. "He says that the President at last has got his
draft of the plan for the League of Nations ready. . . . Baker will
tell me about it tonight, as we are going to the opera. . . . Every
Sunday night Baker and Billy and I go to the opera." Baker had
so many problems in handling the press that after the conference
was over he told White that if he, Miss Tarbell, and Auguste Jaccacci had not been there, "I don't know how I should have even
gotten through . . . You were a little oasis of sanity in a great
desert of dementia."

The major decisions at the conference were made by the United
States, France, and Great Britain. Newspapermen were admitted
to the General Sessions, but they were not allowed at the meetings
of the Big Three where the chief decisions were made. Such a
restriction was considered by the American newspapermen to be
an abrogation of Wilson's first point of open covenants openly
arrived at. Wilson, however, justified these secret meetings by
writing: "I am for all we can get, yet I must work with other men
of other nations whose ideas of publicity are different from ours.

. . . When we reach real decisions everything must be made known to the world."

The American reporters called a meeting to protest their exclusion from the meetings of the Big Three. To their astonishment, the French newspapermen backed the secrecy. The English and Italian reporters were persuaded to support the Americans in a plea for publicity. White played a leading part in this meeting. As he wrote Sallie: "The boys treated me splendidly deferring time and again to my opinion. . . . The whole American press, from the representatives of the Navy League to those of the Socialist dailies in New York were unanimous. It was fine to see that the American press so far as our vital life is concerned is free . . . The ethics of the reporting profession, its essential independence as a craft, was splendidly vindicated. Europe was puzzled. Here were men only hired to work for great papers acting freely without consulting their owners. . . . It was really enough to take the breath away from the Europeans to whom reporters are little more than high grade servants or clerks. They called us the Soviet. And that's exactly what we were."

Near the close of the conference, a meeting of the American newspaper "soviet" was called to demand that reporters be allowed to attend the session when Germany received the peace terms. White, who was in charge of this meeting, appointed a committee to present their request. Unless they were permitted access to the session, they warned that they would refuse to send any more news to America about the conference. As a result, three American reporters as well as reporters of other nations were granted admittance.

The first newspaper dispatch that White sent from Paris on January 10, 1919, stated that Wilson's peace program did not "stand a dog's chance." White was rather disillusioned to discover that Britain wanted to maintain its imperial position and that France desired the Saar coal fields and a demilitarized Rhineland. Years later White was to record in his *Autobiography:* "I could not co-ordinate my facts and integrate them on the thread of wide international political experience. After all, I was just Republican precinct committeeman in the Fourth Ward of Emporia, Kansas, who had been on the state committee and had been on the National Committee, and so walked with what I thought was a heroic tread. But the vast complexity of European politics, built on centuries of tradition, usage, prejudice and conflicting desires, was not even remotely in any corner of my consciousness."

Although he might be ignorant of the ways of international politics, his good practical common sense led him to write in a dispatch a few days after the conference opened: "All cannot be settled, indeed comparatively little may be settled by this peace Congress if it holds a year; but if the will to unite in a league based upon mutual help, is manifest genuinely, its political expression does not matter much. Time will work that out."

White rapidly acquired information about world problems and the social forces that were shaping decisions at the Peace Conference. He met many specialists and well-traveled people. One day White had lunch with "a most radical young man," he confided to Mrs. White, William Bullitt, who enlightened him on the changes taking place in Russia. Years later Bullitt wrote White about this luncheon: "I have never forgotten what a charming human being you are." Many of the social forces in the world were so alien to the experience of this Kansan that he frequently was greatly puzzled. At one particular luncheon with Jane Addams, Mr. and Mrs. Frank Simons, and Mr. and Mrs. George Rublee, the discussion "was too deep for me. They were all so profound and so clever that I felt like no one," he wrote Sallie on April 23. He was greatly flattered, however, when Lord Robert Cecil, after a meeting with American reporters, asked one of the men who White was and then said that White's questions went to the heart of world problems.

Late in January, Vernon Kellogg arrived in Paris. Kellogg was now working under Herbert Hoover's guidance for the American Relief Association. Before America entered the war, he had been associated with Hoover on the Commission for the Relief of Belgium, and during American participation in the war, he worked with Hoover in the American Food Administration. Kellogg had just been in Poland surveying their food needs. He told White that babies were dying in Warsaw from the lack of milk and that famine conditions were widespread in Central Europe. From his contacts with Kellogg and Herbert Hoover, White wrote a number of dispatches concerning the European food situation.

* * *

Since the reporters were not permitted to attend all the peace sessions, they had plenty of time to spare for trips to the battlefields and surrounding countries. The French authorities tried to keep them occupied with trips, banquets, and ceremonies. "The French must have regarded us American newspapermen as queer fish," White later wrote. "We did not respond reasonably to any sort of treatment. . . . They garrotted us with kindness; gave us concerts . . . banquets with exquisite chamber music afterwards . . . and otherwise insidiously flattered us."

During the last week in January, White and his son Bill and nine other newspapermen took a trip to Strasbourg with a French lieutenant, who had charge of their party. While there they were entertained at a formal lunch by the French general in charge, General Gouraud. White had to make a speech for the Americans. "I stood up and made a speech . . . to General Gouraud," White later recalled, "which he did not understand, and he made a speech at me which I did not understand, so we shook hands warmly and smiled as intelligently as if both of us did not know we were a brace of lying hypocrites for pretending to comprehend one another . . . The General might even have attacked the sacred Bull Moose platform in his speech to me, or questioned the divinity of the inspiration of prohibition for all I knew, and for all I could have done about it."

White, his son Bill, and a New York *World* reporter took a side trip to the countryside around Coblenz, Germany, in order to investigate the American Army of Occupation. They found that the army was on amiable terms with the people of the Rhineland. From village to village they heard the same reports of utter boredom on the part of the soldiers, and their fervent desire to return home. German villagers told White that they liked the way American officers played games with the men. In their army, the officers looked down upon the men as mere cattle. White explained to the Germans that American enlisted men did not fear their officers, a statement which seemed to bewilder the Germans.

The Whites, in company with Burge McPhall, former *Gazette* employee, spent two days visiting Cologne. They were greatly impressed with the beauty of the Rhine valley and the picturesque villages along its banks. At Cologne they had lunch with General Douglas MacArthur at his headquarters in a beautiful German home. "In this austere and formal situation flashes General Douglas MacArthur," White wrote Sallie, "aged 38, a bachelor, with a grace and charm of a stage hero! I never have met before so vivid a man, so captivating a man; so magnetic a man. He is all that Barrymore and John Drew hoped to be." In Germany, White and his son also toured through the sumptuous hunting lodge of the Krupp munitions family. The feudal splendor of the estate appalled their democratic minds.

White's trip to Germany was an eye-opener. He was tremendously stirred by the untouched condition of the country. En route to Germany they had passed through the devastated countryside of France, and he wrote in a dispatch: "In France the white scar of ruins stretches like a leprous scale from the mountains to the sea. Cities are wrecked, farms are bombed into wasteland, commerce is blighted, homes are ruined, civilization is blanched and dead. This blighted area is from fifty to one hundred miles wide. Then it stops as sharply as though some terrific fire had been checked, and at the German border we see another picture. There the cities are untouched, the farms fat and smiling, business is proceeding as usual, homes are comfortable and civilization functioning as though no great war had touched it."

The irony of victory, the Emporia editor realized, was that defeated Germany would emerge from the war more powerful than France. This, he declared, was tragically unfair. "The peace should not be written," he told his readers on March 6, "until the delegates to the conference see not merely the devastation that is France, but the unpunished Rhineland. These are parts of the same picture." With real insight he wrote Sallie that "Germany is the same Germany; changing government, sending the Kaiser to Holland is not enough. The fellows here along the Rhine, the Americans, feel that the whole democratic movement in Germany is a mere trusteeship for the autocracy which will come back in a few months or a few years as the exigency of the politics of Europe demand."

Tragically for the world, White's prediction was correct. The creation of the German republic served as a disguise under which the militarist forces were able to start rearming. The people of the western democracies unwisely assumed that a Republican Germany would throw off the strangle hold of the militarists, the Prussian landlords, and the industrialists. The Allies failed to occupy Germany proper or to control German industrial production. After the United States rejected the Versailles Treaty, the restrictions on the size of the German army and on military production were flagrantly violated. Long before Hitler became dictator, the German General Staff, the big industrialists, and the Prussian Junkers had begun preparations for World War II. After the United States had entered World War II, White recalled his visit to Germany in 1919 and remarked that American kindness to defeated Germany had been a tragedy for the world because the Germans mistook kindness for weakness. The United States had made a tragic error, he maintained, in believing that the German people wanted liberty and democracy.

After White had returned to Paris from this tour of Germany, he was infuriated when Oswald Garrison Villard, editor of the *Nation*, over a luncheon table poured out tears for Germany. Villard was so "full of sympathy for the poor Germans that I wanted to choke him," wrote White. ". . . Once a Dutchman always a Dutchman. He wants Germany let off from any penalty for the war. Wow! and I had to pay for his food while he talked that way." Villard's magazine, in opposing the Versailles Treaty and the League of Nations, reflected Villard's belief that the terms of peace were too severe. Yet, from the perspective of the events that led to World War II, the steps taken at the Peace Conference to curb Germany's military power were far too weak. German propaganda was extremely effective in persuading many Americans that the treaty was too severe. Actually fewer mistakes were made in the treaty than it became fashionable to claim in the United States and, of course, profitable for Germany to assert.

* * *

The Whites returned to Paris in time to celebrate the editor's fifty-first birthday on February 10, 1919. The old *McClure* staff— Ida Tarbell, Ray S. Baker, and Auguste Jaccaci—and Dorothy Canfield Fisher gave a dinner party in his honor. It was the first birthday he had spent away from Sallie since he was twenty-five, and, as he wrote her, "it is a long and dreary day." Just before this birthday celebration, President Wilson had appointed White a delegate to a proposed conference with Soviet Russia at Prinkipo. *The New York Times* correspondent declared that White "was chosen apparently as a hard-headed American with a great capacity for getting on well with all comers." Ray S. Baker had urged Wilson to appoint White, since, in spite of White's lack of knowledge of diplomatic affairs, he would be a good common-sense observer.

Russia was not represented at the Paris Peace Conference, and this projected meeting was designed to talk over the relations between the Allies and the new revolutionary Soviet government. A month earlier White had been approached by the American peace delegation to see if he would go to Russia for the government, to try to establish diplomatic recognition and intercourse. France at this point, he was told, was blocking any move toward the recognition of Soviet Russia. After watching French machinations, he explained to Sallie: "The difference between world politics and Kansas politics is not much. You simply play the same game on the same board with larger checkers. Topeka and Paris are the same kind of towns!"

The day after his appointment to the Prinkipo meeting, White declared that the Russian Bolsheviks should be allowed to develop their regime in Russia without interference from other nations. White was supported in this attitude by Colonel House, who told him that he did not care what kind of government the Russians had, if they did not try to disturb the peace of the rest of the world. Although White himself was not in agreement with Communist principles, he believed that Russia had the right to determine her own internal government and social organization. The capitalistic world, however, trembled at the thought of Russia. She was too greatly feared to be admitted into the League of Nations;

yet, when the country did enter the League in the 1930's, she proved to be an active supporter of collective security.

White was displeased at what he felt was sheer blindness in dealing with revolutionary Russia. "Russia is coming along all right in spite of the stupidity which seems to be inspiring the world in dealing with Russia," he wrote a friend late in 1919, "but the Russian is only suffering the martyrdom of birth which every new idea must suffer in the world, and like every other new idea in the world the Russian idea will be more or less modified by life and will take its place in relation to the philosophies of life on this planet in due course, in spite of the malice which greets it now."

George Creel, director of the American Committee on Public Information, was unhappy over White's appointment to the Prinkipo conference. He had been trying to persuade President Wilson to appoint a "deserving Democrat," "and now," Creel told Brand Whitlock, "he sends White, a good fellow, who is always for the President, except during the time of election." White was not very much pleased with the other appointed delegate, George D. Herron. After working with him for several weeks on the proposed conference, he told Mrs. White that "Herron is forever seeking ghosts and goblins and is so serious that I shall go mad if ever I am cooped up with him on a train or a ship." Some years later White wrote M. P. Briggs, author of *George D. Herron and the European Settlement*, that Herron's belief that he was playing a messianic role made him "one of God's pedestal dwellers, always moving about in bronze or marble . . . yet a kindly and some way sweet and gentle soul withal."

Herron's appointment evoked a storm of abuse from the American press and pulpit. Herron had had a remarkable career. In the 1890's he had attracted widespread attention for his preaching of the social gospel as the professor of Applied Christianity at Grinnell College. He joined the Socialist party and campaigned for the election of Eugene Debs in 1900. Herron's Christian socialism was attacked by the good Iowa farmers and businessmen as economic heresy. His economic unorthodoxy, however, could be tolerated, but when his wife divorced him in 1901 and he married the daughter of the woman who had endowed his professorial chair, that was too much for Christian Iowa. The Congregational ministers defrocked him, and he and Mrs. Herron went to live in Italy. When the war came, he served the American and Allied governments in many diplomatic negotiations.

The New York Times devoted a two-column editorial on February 10, 1919, to the Prinkipo appointments. They approved of White, since he had opposed the Populist movement, which they declared was "a milder form of Bolshevism"! But there was nothing in favor of Herron's appointment. "As a teacher of the extreme doctrines of socialism," declared the *Times*, "and of the loose views of the marriage relation which many Socialists hold, Mr. Herron has been in close sympathy with the principles which have guided Lenin and Trotsky in their war upon capitalism and upon society." Other newspapers and some preachers were even more violent in their reactions to the Herron appointment.

White was considerably disturbed by the unfavorable American attitude toward Herron. Although he did not share their views, he felt that Herron's presence at Prinkipo might seriously handicap the effectiveness of the American mission. He feared that the American delegation might have to disagree with the French and file a minority report. But Herron's name on a minority report would not secure a favorable backing from the American people. White therefore sent word through Charles R. Crane and Ray S. Baker of the American Peace Commission that he would resign if this step would make it easier for Herron to agree not to go to Prinkipo.

For days after their appointment, White and Herron busied themselves gathering information on Russia. They did their best to convince the anti-Soviet Russians that the delegates would not be pro-Soviet at the conference but would try to discover the truth about the Russian situation. In the midst of interviewing interpreters, stenographers, and diplomats who wanted to accompany them to Prinkipo, White wrote Mrs. White: "I'd give up all my hopes of Prinkipo for one minute of Emporia." He urged her to join them in Europe. "Come on," he wrote, "take the boat for Constantinople, bring Mary and join the show. It's once in a lifetime. . . . If you can't do that you can get the same reaction by inviting Frank Lloyd Wright to Emporia for a week."

Charles R. Crane, old Chicago friend and keen student of Russia, arranged meetings for White with prominent Russians. The Prinkipo conference, however, never took place. The French had been opposed to it the entire time. They wanted a Russian government that would recognize the czarist debt largely held by the French government. Not only did the French wreck the proposed conference, but they took the lead in sending troops to Russia to aid the anti-Soviet forces. White was always convinced that President Wilson had not abandoned the project, but that the French "craftily made it impossible."

In the summer of 1920, when a great wave of anti-Russian sentiment, much of it hysterical, swept the United States, White adopted an unflinching attitude toward Soviet Russia. He declared that he had a great deal of sympathy for the Russian revolution. "I believe," he wrote, "in the Russian revolution and that the Russian people through their revolution will be able to conquer themselves and to rise after their own manner, following their own star to a vastly higher civilization through revolution to democracy than they ever could have risen through autocracy." The American people, he stated, should try to understand the exploitation of the Czars, and that "Lenin and Trotsky represented the inexorable reaction of Russia to the age-long oppression of the old regime." He charged that the American people were extremely ignorant of Russian affairs and should take a more active interest in American policy toward that country.

*   *   *

"I first saw William Allen White . . . in a dining room, of the Hotel Vouillemont, in Paris, where during the peace conference he enjoyed much good French food, supplemented by tin boxes of Kansas cakes, made by the subtle hand of Sallie," a fellow reporter once remarked. "In this room full of eminent Americans, and of Americans who were trying to look more eminent than they were, the stout and sandy man from Emporia, whose rotund proportions fitted so ill into a Red Cross uniform, whose chin rolled so rebelliously over a stiff military collar, stood out as The American. A picturesque and salient individual, ambassador plenipotentiary of the tall and gawky Uncle Sam." White not only learned a great deal about world politics while in Paris, but had a good time doing it. He renewed friendships with Jane Addams, Lincoln Steffens, and Charles Crane; and he started friendships with Mr. and Mrs. Thomas Lamont; Frederick Whyte, young English journalist and member of Parliament; Felix Frankfurter; Mrs. Robert Herrick; Henry Kitchell Webster; and Dr. Morton Prince of Boston. He and Bill made a practice of finding the best French restaurants and eating the rich food that Paris could provide. But by March, 1919, he was tired of Europe and longed for the Kansas prairies. He was a bit lonely, too, since Norman Angell had left the conference. "He was a source of inspiration and of information," White wrote home on March 13. "And I have grown quite fond of him."

Late in March, White visited the American Expeditionary Force's university at Beaune, near Dijon, France. Here were some six thousand soldiers carrying on real university work. White lectured to some seven hundred students in the journalism class. He was tremendously impressed by the democratic aspects of the education the soldiers were receiving. Gold Coast boys mingled on the same plane with corn-fed farm lads. It was Jacksonian democracy at its best. The doughboy student, White wrote, "was from every academic institution in America, and from every state and territory in the Union. He was white, black, brown, and red in race and color, and with the neutral tints lying between the fast colors! But he was democratic to the core . . . in the student activities the university men knew no caste nor creed."

Back in Paris in April, White was disappointed at the attempts of the French premier, Georges Clemenceau, to drag out the peace negotiations and to block the League of Nations. White felt that the peace treaty should be speeded up, because the apparent indecision of the Big Three seemed to be stimulating confusion and uprisings all over Eastern Europe. The situation seemed so tense to him that he actually felt that a revolution might break out at any time in France. On May Day, White watched a crowd of from four to five thousand people parade in the Place de la Concorde. They marched past the balcony where he was standing, singing the International and crying "Viva Wilson and Boo Boo Clemenceau." That night White attended a dinner with Thomas Lamont and Lincoln Steffens in honor of Alexander Kerenski, who had been driven out of power in Russia by the Bolshevist revolution. White was unimpressed by Kerenski. He did not say anything important, and he was shifty and legalistic in his remarks. White observed that Kerenski had a voice "like the wrath of God. Speaking in that big room it sounded as if he were roaring in a bathroom."

On April 11, White enlivened the fourth open session of the Peace Conference. One big, bearded "Frenchman" insisted on standing in front of the press chairs. White had Ray S. Baker send for an attendant to make him sit down, but the attendant refused. Then White got a girl reporter who could speak French to tell him that if he didn't sit down, White would knock his "head off." She delivered the message and White followed quickly by grabbing the fellow and loudly crying, "Sit down, sit down or get out." The man quickly moved, and the crowd behind applauded. "The French policemen guarding the conference were aghast," White wrote, "the commissioners all turned to see who was being assassinated and I was discovered seated looking blandly at the ceiling." Imagine White's surprise when he discovered that the bearded "Frenchman" was Jo Davidson, the American sculptor!

In his regular dispatches to his American readers, White gave every encouragement to Woodrow Wilson's peace proposals. Like Wilson, White had realized that isolation from world affairs was no longer a safe road for the United States. "We have the closest possible relations to the world," he informed his readers; "we are the world's banker and the world's grocer. . . . Those are delicate jobs for a nation to hold. They are war-breeding jobs. We can have peace with our neighbors only by the establishment of laws—new laws under a League of Nations. . . ."

Although the Emporia editor continually reiterated his belief that America had to co-operate with other nations to maintain peace, he was quite aware that many Americans were bewildered and confused by their country's new position in world society. The United States had grown so rapidly that many people had been unable to adjust their thinking to the new conditions that America's overwhelming industrial strength had created. These bewildered Americans were thinking in terms of their country as it had been in its relatively isolated position in the mid-nineteenth century, whereas America now was the world's greatest industrial power. The idea that America must play a positive role in maintaining world peace was still beyond the ken of many citizens, particularly those from White's Middle West. "We have not preached the partnership of society to our people," he wrote Sallie on February 15, 1919; "we have not shown them the close relations between the Kansas hog-raiser and the Italian farmer who needs the Kansas meat; we have not taught our people to think in world needs or world markets."

White insisted that the United States must play a positive role in helping to decide major world policies. He urged, for instance, that the United States accept a mandate over Armenia, which was being carved out of the old Turkish Empire. Such a step, of course, was vigorously opposed by American isolationists, who were unable to see that the United States should assume world commitments. Yet the price of failing to be a party to the commitments was two wars for the United States in twenty-four years.

White wrote his wife in April that Wilson was having a difficult time with the old European traditions that were entering the peace negotiations. White was pessimistic because Wilson was not fighting hard enough for a real League of Nations. As the outline of the League began to take shape, however, he believed that it was "a good beginning but only that." He told Sallie on April 23: "While it is but a shadow it is indeed a shadow sent by the rising sun."

Professor James T. Shotwell, who was an important member of the advisory group attached to the American peace delegation, recorded in his diary that he had discussed the League and the proposed International Labor Office with William Allen White on April 30, 1919. "White," wrote Shotwell, "has not lost his head here in the whirl of conflicting emotions and sees possibilities for the future in the work already done."

The same day that he talked with Shotwell, White wrote Sallie that Wilson "really has done wonders here; and how he has done it is past me. I give him up. He is more mysterious than ever. All so vague and remote and impersonal and colorless; yet tremendously powerful. He has really dominated this situation—and that all alone. No one has helped him. His own delegation has helped him more by guiding him away from the blunders it made. He has no friends, no cronies, no advisors. I give him up."

Although the Versailles Treaty as finally drawn had its faults, Woodrow Wilson felt that the creation of the League of Nations would compensate for the mistakes. While agreeing to some concessions hostile to his Fourteen Points, he had forced many compromises from the Allied powers. William Allen White agreed with this belief of Wilson's and told the American people in the *Saturday Evening Post*, for August 16, 1919, that Woodrow Wilson had "achieved about a seventy per cent success in the realization of his ideals, high as they were."

The central structure of the peace settlement was the League of Nations. The League was supposed to execute certain parts of the treaty, unsettled issues were to go to the League, and the new mandate system over conquered areas was answerable to it. The League was the great dream of President Wilson for the preservation of world peace. White, the small-town Kansan, was inspired by Wilson's vision of a world based on collective security. "The Conference is almost over," he wrote Wilson on April 28. "I believe I have known something of the inside of almost every great movement—something of what you have done. And as one American belonging to the cynical profession of the press, it may hearten you to know that every great move you have made has seemed to me wise and just and strong. I shall go home to support your course here with enthusiasm and with what force I can command . . . I have the honor to subscribe myself in this splendid adventure of yours into world politics."

*　　*　　*

Although the Peace Conference was not quite over, White and his son Bill left Paris on May 14 for a stay in England on their way to the United States. On their last day in Paris, they had lunch with Ray S. Baker and Colonel E. M. House. White had boundless admiration for both men. Baker, he felt, gave the reporters their best impression of Woodrow Wilson, while Colonel House "always was candid, truthful and well-informed in his relations with the newspapermen."

Soon after White reached London, he sent the following poem

to Franklin P. Adams and Ray S. Baker for the bulletin board in the Paris pressroom:

AN INTERMEZZO FOR THE FOURTH ACT

If my peculiar pulchritude in Paris seemed to please
Upon the Champs Elysées 'mongst the blooming chestnut trees;
Or if along the Rivoli in hell's melange of men
Which bubbled in the war-brew, you observed me now and then;
Or if the picture rising, of my rolly poley form,
A-toddle down the boulevards, should make your heart grow warm—
O Phillys, wipe that picture from your mem'ry cold and flat—
    You should see me in my new straw hat!

For I'm in London now my dear, in London old and gray,
And spring is fading in the past, and summer's under way.
But London is a decent town, polite and smug and curt
It breaks her heart to frivol and you break her laws to flirt!
And how she works and how she frets, and yet she's always sweet;
So I am here in London for to give the town a treat.
And if I'm middle aged and bald and slow and rather fat—
    You should see me in my new straw hat!

Perhaps we're not immortal lass, but O I wish we were;
Though not to save some prudish saint or pale philosopher,
I want to find those lads whom life's sweet poignant beauty wracked,
Who had to duck and cut the show, before the second act—
Say Schubert, Keats or Phidias, those olden golden boys—
And tell them something of the play, and how it never cloys.
For I have seen three acts, and now I'm fifty, but at that—
    You should see me in my new straw hat!

The day he arrived in London, White wrote to Sallie that it seemed like home to be in England again. London was so much more like Emporia's Exchange Street than Paris was, that it made him happy. "The English language and English ways," he said, "and simple kind faced people more than make up for the English cooking!" His stay in London afforded him a chance to renew his friendship with Norman Angell, Frederick Whyte, H. G. Wells, and John Buchan. With Angell, White attended meetings of the Labor party called to protest certain provisions of the peace treaty.

"They certainly have a free speech over here that we don't have in America," he told Sallie on May 20. "Ten thousand people were present and the treaty denounced, Lloyd George was denounced, the government was denounced and speakers demanded that the Labor party, which is the socialists shall take over the government."

At another meeting, William Bullitt spoke on Russia, and White was prevailed upon to deliver a few comments. "The free frank incendiary way that these British radicals talk about Revolution would make your hair curl," he declared, "only they don't expect bloodshed. They expect to have a chatty revolution and then all go home to tea." White predicted in an article for *Collier's*, on September 27, 1919, that the Labor party would soon come into power in England and nationalize mines, railroads, power, and communications.

On June 7, the Whites left London for a visit to Ireland to investigate the Irish nationalist demands for freedom from Great Britain. This trip produced a significant article, "Through American Eyes," for the British weekly review, the *New Europe*, on June 19, 1919. White stated that England and the United States had to work together to keep the peace. "Co-operation in aims, in ideals, in peaceful competition for the world's business, is necessary. Jealousy is fatal," he wrote. "The United States and the United Kingdom and the British Empire have each learned the great necessary lesson of internal national co-operation. It is their great secret—this genius for large combination. They must now learn that lesson in internation co-operation. By its strength, it will save for humanity the ideals we fought for in the great war . . . If we fail, the League fails."

But, he pointed out to his British audience, the great obstacle to this Anglo-American co-operation was Ireland. The Republican party, White declared, was organizing the Irish-American vote against the League of Nations. Their plan was to defeat the League by demonstrating that it was a British device to rule the world. "To prove that," White wrote, "it becomes necessary to convince the Americans that Great Britain is a grasping oppressor of unwilling captive peoples. The Irish situation furnishes the example needed."

With extraordinary foresight, White stated:

And the Americans, thus aroused against England and persuaded that England is backing the League of Nations for British imperial aims, may lose their heads and permit partisan malice and jealousy to defeat the ratification of the League in the American Senate. If that is done, Wilson and his party are discredited for the 1920 elections, the Republicans will whoop it up against England to justify the slaughter of the League and incidentally to bag the Irish vote and the pro-German vote; and, while the demagogues triumph, humanity will suffer. Then, with the League of Nations abandoned, English-speaking peoples will have to spend their energies in wars and preparations for wars. The whole fabric of the plan to check the progress of humanity is based upon the fiction of England as the Cruel Stepmother. Destroy that fiction, prove that England is not oppressing Ireland, and America will ratify the League.

The way to take Ireland out of American politics, he remarked, was to grant it dominion status like Canada or Australia. The Irish and pro-Germans had sufficient votes to hold a balance of power in America. If they killed the League in the Senate, they would also have enough strength to force America away from close relations with the British Commonwealth of Nations. "Germany, resurrected in ten, twenty, or thirty years hence, will try to gather a group of nations about her," he predicted. "And America, while she might not be counted in the German group, would be no Ally of the English against the German group if the Irish continue to have a grievance and join with the Germans." This was a remarkable forecast of what took place in 1935 when the United States passed the Neutrality Law. Under this bill the United States refused to ally itself with England and France against the threatening power of Nazi Germany. By this time the American people had so succumbed to isolationism that they unwisely and incorrectly thought they could ignore the destruction of democracy all over the world. They wanted to believe in 1935, although from 1939 to 1941 they began to see that this was fallacious, that American democracy could exist in a world dominated by Fascist dictatorships with no danger to the security of the United States.

The Irish situation, as White had prophesied, was utilized by Republican isolationists as an argument against America's joining the League of Nations. Although Southern Ireland did receive her independence, it was not granted until after the issue had played a significant role in defeating the League. White's warning in this article was so forthright and shrewd that the London *Times* on June 23, 1919, reprinted his most significant statements and announced that this was "a striking article on the Irish question in its bearings upon Anglo-American relations."

The more White pondered over the peace terms, now that he was away from the hectic Parisian scene, the more he felt that France had been too materialistic and too full of revenge. The French had demanded steps to ensure the security of France and forever remove Germany as a menace. The French had wanted the Rhineland but had relinquished the demand when Wilson and Lloyd George pledged American and British aid against Germany in the case of future aggression, a pledge that was not carried out when Hitler reoccupied the Rhineland in 1936. France had also demanded an international force to carry out the peace terms, but England and the United States had refused. The Anglo-American world, less realistic than the French, refused in 1919 to face the fact that force was necessary to maintain peace. The French had further demanded adequate inspection of Germany to make sure that she did not rearm, but this too had been blocked by England and the United States.

White, a typical American in his fear of power, objected to the French belief that force was necessary to ensure peace and security. By simply applying the law of reason to Germany, he apparently believed, the Germans would cleanse themselves of all future predatory instincts. White thought that the French were being too revengeful in demanding control of the Saar and in their demands for heavy reparations for German destruction in France. It was not, White felt, that he was softening in his belief that Germany should be punished. The Germans actually deserved everything and even more than they received in the Versailles Treaty, he wrote his wife. But the whole point was that the United States had gone to war for a noble purpose; it had gone to war with no vengeance in its heart for the German people. Actually, in believing this, White was overlooking the fact that the United States had gone to war to protect its security, not to enforce the Fourteen

Points on the rest of the world. His naïveté about world politics was now bringing only confusion to his mind as to the terms of peace.

"I have another article in my head about the peace—the hard malicious French peace, full of revenge and of materialism that would shame the Kaiser," he wrote home on May 31. "When you think of what Grant and Lincoln did, this peace makes you ashamed. Not that the boche does not deserve it and more: not that he would not have done much worse; but we were supposed to be fighting in a noble cause, more interested in setting him and the world a good example than in following a wicked one."

Twenty-three years after he had expressed this feeling that the peace was too hard on Germany and that the French had been wrong in demanding force to maintain the peace, White was to admit that he had been wrong. The collapse of collective security from 1919 to 1939 and the rise of Adolf Hitler was to convince him that the great weakness in the League of Nations had been its lack of power to curb recalcitrant members. "Editorials on the League question in the United States were sadly uninformed," he recalled. "Newspaper editorial writers, who on the whole represent the best elements of the American popular mind, just didn't grasp the real truth. And newspaper leadership failed. It failed because, even though it had the facts, it could not disseminate the truth."

Although in the spring of 1919 White was disturbed by certain provisions of the peace, he realized that the inclusion of the League of Nations offered a method of ameliorating the mistakes in the document. He sailed for New York late in June, determined to fight for ratification of the Versailles Treaty and for American entrance into the League of Nations as the only sane procedure for bringing about the beginning of a "new heaven and a new earth."

CHAPTER 15

THE REPUBLICANS
AND THE PEACE

"FOR TWO generations the Republican party has attracted to its ranks men who are pleased and proud to be known as men of a 'constructive mind,' " White declared in the Emporia *Gazette* on September 13, 1919. "The Republican temperament is the constructive temperament. The Republicans are born, not made. They have been men who do things as politicians and statesmen, who achieve rather than criticize. . . . It is curious, therefore, to observe that Republican leaders, men from the Holy of Holies . . . have been chiefly engaged in turning the Republican party into a party of criticism. And their chief criticism has been directed toward the League of Nations."

The Emporia editor was horrified on his return to the country to observe the actions of some of his Republican friends. White warned that those Republicans who were opposing the Versailles Treaty out of an implacable personal and political hatred for Woodrow Wilson were "endangering the peace of the world." White was aware that senators like Henry Cabot Lodge had nothing but hatred for Wilson, that some senators were bitter because the President had not included any of their members on the Peace Commission, and that some over-partisan Republican senators did not want a peace treaty drafted by a Democratic president to pass, since it might ensure a Democratic victory in 1920.

White agreed that Wilson had made a mistake in not including any prominent Republican on the American peace delegation and had been unwise in not seeking help and advice from men like William H. Taft and Elihu Root. But he felt that the Republicans should rise above such petty prejudices and adopt a broader view of the situation. They should realize that Europe was seething with unrest. "Without some strong hand to suppress the instinct for war in the heart of Europe," White observed, ". . . war is bound to come."

From a political standpoint, the Emporia editor thought that Republican opposition to the League of Nations was exceedingly stupid. If the Republicans killed the League, and war was raging in the world by 1920, the Democrats would have an unbeatable issue. They could tell the people that the Republican party had rejected the device that would have maintained peace. White's prediction might have been carried out had the Republicans defeated the League in a clear-cut fashion. But Senator Lodge played a clever game that left the American public bewildered and confused as to who was responsible for the treaty's rejection.

When President Wilson presented the peace agreement to the Senate, the Senate did not divide into two groups, one for and one against. Instead, four groups were formed: (1) a protreaty group of 43 Democrats and one Republican, who were for ratification without any qualifications; (2) the "mild reservationists," composed of 15 Republicans, who were warmly for the treaty but desired slight reservations or changes; (3) the "strong reservationists," made up of about 20 Republicans, who favored ratification with strong reservations; and (4) the "irreconcilables," 12 Republicans and 3 Democrats, led by W. E. Borah, who as isolationists were opposed to ratification under any condition.

A majority of the Senate, then, although in varying degrees, wanted to accept the treaty and the League of Nations. A poll of American newspapers revealed that the press was overwhelmingly for ratification of the Versailles Treaty, and outstanding leaders like Henry Cabot Lodge, Theodore Roosevelt, William H. Taft, and Elihu Root had all endorsed the principles of a League of Nations prior to 1919.

Senator Lodge of Massachusetts, although he had publicly

favored the league principle in 1915, was the man who devised the method of killing the League and the Versailles Treaty in the United States Senate. Lodge was Republican majority leader and chairman of the Senate Foreign Relations Committee. He wanted to defeat Wilson, a man he deeply hated, and he wanted to bring his party back into power. The method, however, was not to launch a frontal attack on the League, because too many people had been enamored of Wilson's vision of world peace. The way to kill the League was to present the issue before the Senate in such a way that the three pro-League groups of senators would not be able to vote together.

The best way to accomplish this was to attach reservations to the Covenant of the League. Senator James E. Watson has written that Lodge told him, "I do not propose to try to beat it by direct frontal attack, but by the indirect method of reservations." In his book *The Senate and the League of Nations* (1925), Lodge admitted that he had told W. E. Borah that "any attempt to defeat the Treaty of Versailles with the League by a straight vote in the Senate, if taken immediately, would be hopeless . . ." and that the thing to do, therefore, was "to proceed in the discussion of the treaty by way of amendment and reservation." Senator Lodge's daughter also has stated: "My father hated and feared the Wilson League, and his heart was really with the irreconcilables. But it was uncertain whether this League could be beaten straight out in this way, and the object of his reservations was so to emasculate the Wilson pact that if it did pass it would be valueless."

When Wilson turned the Versailles Treaty over to the Senate, Lodge kept the treaty in the committee's hands for many months. This delay was necessary since Senator Moses, one of the irreconcilables, later said that if the rules of the Senate had permitted a quick vote, "the Versailles Treaty would have been ratified without reservation." While the treaty was in the hands of the committee, Lodge, in league with the irreconcilables, launched a publicity campaign to convince the public that the nation should not join the League of Nations.

Lodge was wise enough to know that the American people would not accept isolationist arguments against the League. The arguments he and his cohorts developed, therefore, were perfectionist arguments. The Versailles Treaty was held not to be good enough for America, and the American people were told that they should not join unless the imperfections were removed. Old emotional images also were utilized. "It impairs American Sovereignty!" and it "Surrenders the Monroe Doctrine!" the public was informed.

William Allen White lashed out at this concerted attack on the League of Nations. "Nine months after the Republican victory at the polls in November, 1918, the Republican party has not put forth one constructive measure upon which Republicans are united," White charged on September 13, 1919. "The Republican attitude toward the League of Nations is curiously unRepublican, in that it destroys without building up. . . . As a matter of party policy, it would seem to be the wise thing to take the League of Nations out of politics by ratifying it in such a manner that ratification would be acceptable, and then to go on into new issues of American reconstruction."

Late in July, after he had returned to Emporia, White wrote Senator Arthur Capper, urging him to support the League, although White said that he did not care for the rest of the treaty. "I believe you will very well play safe," White advised, "by taking the ground that we should have either the League of Nations, or the Treaty, but we should not have both." Apparently, however, White did not hold to this peculiar position very long. He was soon advocating Senate ratification of both the Versailles Treaty and the League, although he favored several minor reservations in the Covenant.

Nationally, White assisted in the fight to secure the Senate's ratification of the treaty by writing two *Saturday Evening Post* articles. In these articles, White declared that Wilson had played a great role at Versailles. Even though the treaty contained mistakes, the League of Nations was a device to rectify any evils. "Americans must always read with pride," White wrote, "that their president more than any other man in the world is responsible for giving the world its first draft of a real League of Nations . . . our American democracy may be honestly proud that it has raised up one who put into the hearts of all the world . . . the aspiration of our hearts for the coming of a peace of good will among men of good will."

The amazing thing, White contended, was that Wilson had succeeded in putting so much liberalism and democracy into the treaty, in view of the opposition to such principles at Versailles. The European statesmen were materialists, but Wilson had managed to win the greater part of his demands. Everyone at the Peace Conference, White asserted, was impressed by Wilson's sincerity, fundamental wisdom, and courage.

Wilson's greatest weakness, White noted, was his penchant for playing a lone game. He did not take advice well, particularly advice at variance with his own ideas. Years later White was to write George Fort Milton that Wilson "failed where he did fail because of his personal qualities—his aptitude to distrust his friends, his incapacity to do business with his enemies, and his fatal, deadly faith in his own judgment."

In August, 1919, White toured Wisconsin for a week, under the auspices of the League to Enforce Peace, to urge ratification of the League of Nations. From his contacts with midwestern people, he realized that the foes of the League had succeeded in stirring many latent suspicions. Irish-Americans were claiming that the League was a British device to rule the world and that the British dominions would vote with England and thus give England six votes in League affairs. White answered this anti-British argument by declaring that the dominions were free, and that they "will follow America much quicker than they will follow England." On October 2, 1919, White wrote Sir Horace Plunkett in Ireland that "America is in a sad state. The professional Irishman is raising hell over here about the League of Nations and the six British votes, and the oppression of Ireland. . . . I am doing what I can for the League, am talking and writing for it, but it is in pretty bad with the folks."

On September 3, President Wilson launched a tour of the West to arouse public sentiment for the League. At Minneapolis, on September 9, Wilson asked, "What are we debating in the United States? Whether we will take part in guiding and steadying the world or not. And some men hesitate. It is the only country in the world whose leadership and guidance will be accepted. If we do not give it, we may look forward, my fellow citizens, to something like a generation of doubt and of disorder which it will be impossible to pass through without the wreckage of a very considerable part of our slowly constructed civilization."

On this tour, Wilson collapsed. He returned to Washington, broken and paralyzed. Now the most powerful protagonist of the League could fight no more. In October and early November, the Senate debated the League with the reservations that Lodge's Foreign Relations committee had appended to the document. In Washington, White reported: "It is inconceivable that the League will be rejected. . . . The stars in their course are with it. . . ."

Perhaps realizing that Lodge was out to kill the League by adding reservations, White urged Wilson to accept the reservations. President Wilson, however, was opposed to the Lodge reservations. He felt that if the United States placed conditions upon its entrance into the League, other nations would do likewise, and the League would be reduced to a meaningless document. Just before the Senate voted on November 19, Wilson wrote to the Democratic leader, Senator Hitchcock: "I sincerely hope that the friends and supporters of the treaty will vote against the Lodge resolution of ratification. I understand that the door will then probably be open for a genuine resolution of ratification. I trust that all true friends of the treaty will refuse to support the Lodge resolution." Wilson advised the defeat of the League with reservations, expecting that then a vote could be had on the League as it stood in the Versailles Treaty. Lodge never permitted this vote to take place.

On November 19, 1919, the Senate rejected the League by a vote of 39 to 55. Ratification was supported by the reservationist senators (groups two and three), and was opposed by the irreconcilables in combination with the Wilson Democrats (group one). Lodge's strategy had succeeded. He had presented the question in such a way that the three pro-League senatorial groups did not vote together. Following the advice of Wilson, the Democratic senators had helped vote down the League with reservations.

Perhaps Wilson was right in believing that if the United States placed conditions upon its membership it would have weakened the League. On the other hand, William Allen White and the

League to Enforce Peace, of which he was a leading member, announced on November 18 that, although some of the reservations were harmful, the League still had enough power to preserve the peace. "The treaty, even with the reservations now adopted," their statement declared, "can accomplish the purpose and should be ratified." It was White's opinion that Wilson was too unyielding in this situation. His refusal to accept the reservations, White contended in the biography that he soon wrote of Wilson, was his "last great blunder."

The Senate's action in rejecting the treaty came as a shock to the nation. A demand for a compromise between the League Democrats and the reservationists swept the country. On February 7, 1920, the Senate voted to reconsider the treaty. Four days before this action was taken, White editorially asserted that everyone but President Wilson knew that the Allies would gladly accept America in the League upon America's terms. "The President's insistence upon no compromise is one of the saddest things Americans have had to witness in many years," wrote White. ". . . His intellectual vigor, his indomitable will, his great spiritual vision made him a great figure in Europe. But the same ruthless will, refusing sane and acceptable compromise, makes him a miserable figure today."

On March 19, 1920, the second vote was taken on the treaty with reservations. The question was whether enough Democrats would realize there was no alternative but to vote for reservations; otherwise the treaty would forever be lost. President Wilson, however, wrote another letter from his sickbed, urging his followers to oppose the treaty with reservations. He had faith that the public wanted the League, and he was willing to wait for the approaching presidential election to serve as a popular referendum on the subject. Moreover, Wilson told Ray Stannard Baker: "These reservations are not made by thoughtful men to improve the Covenant; they represent a dishonorable attempt, on the part of the leaders who do not speak for the people, to escape any real responsibility, so far as the United States is concerned, for world peace in future years. . . . These evil men intend to destroy the League."

The voting on March 19 followed the same pattern as in the preceding November. Enough administration Democrats voted with the irreconcilables to defeat the treaty with reservations. The manner in which the Senate defeated the Versailles Treaty was an indication of the validity of John Hay's remark: "A treaty entering the Senate is like a bull going into the arena. No one can say just how or when the final blow will fall. But one thing is certain—it will never leave the arena alive."

White always placed the blame for the defeat of the Versailles Treaty on Wilson's uncompromising attitude toward the reservations. Yet editorially before November, 1919, White had criticized the antics of Republicans opposed to the League. Possibly, since White was always a good Republican as election day approached, it was convenient to overlook his party's share in the defeat of the treaty. White's old friend Ray Stannard Baker always believed that the Emporia editor was not very penetrating on the question of ratification of the League with reservations. He never realized, added Baker, that the Lodge reservations would have so seriously crippled the League that the League would have been ineffective.

In 1924, when Wilson died, White still was convinced that Wilson's intransigent nature had wrecked the peace. When the news of Wilson's death came over the Associated Press wire, White sat down at his cluttered desk and wrote:

> God gave him a great vision.
> The devil gave him an imperious heart.
> The proud heart is still.
> The vision lives.

White not only was disturbed during 1919 by his party's obstructionist tactics toward the Versailles Treaty, but was appalled by the wave of reaction that was sweeping the country. All the ideals of the progressive era seemed to be in a complete eclipse. White battled against the oncoming tide of reaction. On July 23, 1919, he told his readers that justice was more important than business prosperity. "Our social and economic system is full of gross injustices which can be removed," he declared, "but only by making those who take what they do not earn give it back to those who earn what they do not get."

White wrote Leonard Wood, who was a candidate for the Republican presidential nomination in 1920, that he must not fail to attract the progressive followers of Theodore Roosevelt. The trouble with his candidacy so far, White asserted, was that he was too conservative toward labor. "The strike seems to be the only weapon which some men have to advertise their wrongs," White wrote Wood on November 12, 1919. "And so long as the strike is carried on decently and in order, a striker has his legal rights, and the danger of your candidacy is that you will get it hooked up with the type of man who calls every labor union man a socialist and every strike an attempt at revolution."

The year 1919 witnessed numerous and violent strikes aimed at forcing wages up to the inflationary price level. The strike that swept the steel industry from September, 1919, to the following January, attracted the widest attention. On October 6, White was in Washington for the Wheeler newspaper syndicate, reporting an industrial conference of businessmen, labor leaders, and public representatives, which had been called by President Wilson to help solve industrial conflicts. The conference failed because the industrialist group refused to accept the recommendations of the representatives of labor and the public. Labor desired the eight-hour day, union recognition and collective bargaining, the principle of the living wage, and a national board to conciliate labor disputes. White remarked that the employer class offered "nothing but a desire to stand upon its ancient rights and do battle for the order that has been for a hundred years." When the businessmen refused to accept the principle of collective bargaining, the conference collapsed.

White was strongly in favor of collective bargaining. His support of this essential aspect of employer-employee relations provoked an attack based on the argument that those who supported such steps were dangerous Socialists and visionaries. "I suppose all good men are socialists in the sense that they are interested in the orderly, evolutionary progress of society from the more simple form to the more complicated, as the human mind becomes broadened by a wider development," was his calm answer. "But to say that all men should be party socialists is silly. It seems to me that a lot of reactionaries are making blithering fools of themselves trying to scream their heads off about socialism. Whenever they disagree with a man, or anything, they call him a socialist."

To those who cried out that there was danger of a Communist revolution sweeping the country, White stated that the way to fight radicalism was by steady employment rather than by guns. The worker should be guaranteed a minimum wage large enough to maintain "a family of six in the enjoyment of all the comforts of our civilization, electric lights, central heat, and power, modern plumbing, convenient fuel for cooking, decent housing, good clothing, clean and exhilarating amusements, time for reading, and money to make profitable reading possible, some leisure for seeing his city, his state, and his country, and at least a high school education for all of his children and a college education for such of his children as desire it."

During 1920 the wave of emotionalism and reaction continued to sweep the United States. Led by Attorney General Palmer, superpatriots declared war on all spokesmen for unconventional doctrines. Palmer arrested a countless number of "radicals" and deported some of them. White denounced Palmer for "seeing Red," and charged that "every man who hopes for a better world is in danger of deportation by the attorney general. The whole business is un-American. . . . If a man desires to preach any doctrine under the shining sun, and advocates the realization of his vision by lawful orderly constitutional means—let him alone. . . . The deportation business is going to make martyrs of a lot of idiots whose cause is not worth it."

White was aware that a number of reactionary business forces were attempting to defeat liberal ideas by smearing these ideas as being un-American. These reactionaries were wrapping the mantle of Old Glory about themselves and insinuating that their opponents were unpatriotic. This technique did not fool the wise old Emporia editor. On February 25, 1920, shortly after his fifty-second birthday, he told his readers: "Probably more bigotry and reaction just now are hiding under the phrase 'Americanism' than ever hid under one word before. If Americanism means anything, it means freedom of speech, freedom of thought, freedom of press. Every wicked, greedy force in America today is trying to strangle discussion under the guise of promoting Americanism. . . . Americanism of the genuine sort fears no idea enough to suppress it. Americanism does not strangle the press or stop any debate. The man who talks about hunting them out, standing them up and shooting them down, is not 100 per cent American. He is 99 per cent coward who is afraid his creed won't stand the tests of free speech and a free press."

Politically White did his best to stem the tide of reaction in the Republican party. Will Hays appointed him to membership on the Committee on Policies and Platform for the 1920 campaign. As White confided to Victor Murdock, however, Hays "has about twenty or twenty-five former Bull Moose on that committee and about twenty-five others who are as near Progressives, as Cummins or Kellogg. . . . But he also has on Murray Crane and a lot of old high binder standpatters who haven't had an idea since the fall of Babylon and who, while they agree with the general justice of the fall of Babylon, think it was hasty and ill considered."

Working with Harold Ickes, White laid plans for a conference of progressive leaders before the convention, in order to draft their demands for submission to the Republican platform committee. Hays balked at this meeting, but when White and Ickes assured him there would be no publicity, he withdrew his objections. On April 30, the meeting was held at Ickes's home in Winnetka, Illinois. By wire, White urged many Bull Moosers to attend so that they might draft a progressive platform. Otherwise, he warned them, reactionaries like Lodge, Penrose, Watson, and Smoot would control the platform. As Ickes has written, the meeting "was a flop. . . . Our deliberations, so far as I could judge, had not the slightest effect upon the platform that was later adopted at the Chicago convention."

Possible candidates, too, occupied White's thoughts prior to the Republican convention. He was not to have any more success in this endeavor than with the platform. Late in 1919, White wrote a few editorials in favor of the candidacy of General Leonard Wood. As he explained to Wood, however, he was working with Governor Allen to secure a Kansas delegation pledged to Allen. In case the Allen candidacy made no progress, the delegation would be friendly to Wood. White's real candidate was neither Wood nor Allen; it was Herbert Hoover. In Paris White had become acquainted with Hoover through Vernon Kellogg. White now urged Kellogg to organize sentiment for Hoover. "Isn't there any-

one in New York who has the good of his country at heart sufficiently to take hold of this Hoover matter?" White inquired on
January 6, 1920. ". . . It would take some money. I should think
a million or so. . . . But it will yield a million per cent for humanity, if it is successfully handled."

White vigorously denounced a growing boom for Senator Warren G. Harding. He hadn't had an idea in thirty years, declared
White. "He is against every advance made in this country in a
dozen years . . ." White charged in the *Gazette* on March 24,
1920. "He has opposed every forward step that America has made
either in war or peace. His public declaration is stupid where it is
not crooked, sometimes both." To fight candidates like Harding,
White sought and won election as a delegate to the convention.

Just a few weeks before the convention met, White took the
type of step which, for the remainder of his life, made machine
Republicans distrust him and led independent citizens to listen to
and cherish his advice. In the May 29 issue of the *Saturday Evening Post,* in an article entitled "The Leaven of the Pharisees," he
explained that, although the Kansas machine had supported him
as a convention delegate, they were constantly afraid he would
criticize their actions. Governor Allen, for instance, had told him
to "be careful"! This is what party machines and regularity try
to do to people, White asserted, and then he added: "Party leadership in America is stone blind and stone deaf. . . . And here's the
trouble: It's the Pharisaism of the parties. We have become more
partisan than American." Such criticisms of the Republican party,
of course, was not too welcomed by the party moguls. When
Morton Albaugh, chairman of the Kansas State Republican Committee, was once asked about the possibility of winning a given
election, he replied: "Unless Bill White breaks loose between now
and election day, we've got it sewed up. I'm sitting on his coat-
tails. If the garment holds, we'll win."

Although the Emporia editor did denounce the hypocrisy of
political parties in his *Post* article, he remained regular to the extent of warning that a third party was no solution, and that "two
successive Democratic administrations constitute a national calamity, and the prospect of a third looms like a cataclysm before us."
As election day approached, the fact that he had previously sup-

ported both the domestic and international policies of the Wilson administration was conveniently forgotten.

* * *

White was unable to attend a preconvention meeting of the Republican platform committee in May because his doctor had forbidden him to do any work for a month. He was close to nervous exhaustion and was unable even to write editorials for the *Gazette*. "Mother and I are celebrating our wedding anniversary by going to the Country Club with grandma and Mary and the Finneys. We are all very well except me . . ." he wrote his son Bill at the University of Kansas on April 27. "My heart, lungs, kidneys and stomach are all working beautifully, but my head piece is no good." Then, foreshadowing the tragic death of Mary the next year, he added: "Mary's horse ran into an automobile the other day and cut her hind leg and the horse is in the stable for general repairs, otherwise Mary is all right. This is the regular monthly toot that Mary has."

White was well enough, however, to attend the Republican convention, which opened in Chicago on June 3, both as a delegate and as a reporter for a nation-wide syndicate. White was one of the twelve members of the subcommittee that drafted the party's platform. For three days and two nights they wrangled over the planks. The platform that was produced was a wholesale denunciation of Wilson's foreign and domestic policy. The gravest fight in the committee came over the issue of the League of Nations. Lodge prevented an endorsement of the League with his reservations and thereby tended to prove that he had always been an isolationist and had used reservations only as a technique to defeat the League. The platform committee adopted a meaningless plank on world co-operation. It was so vague that both isolationists and internationalists found comfort in it. "It was fearfully and wonderfully made," White once recalled. "It meant nothing except that it frankly did mean nothing."

Few of White's demands were incorporated in the Republican platform. He wanted planks calling for vigorous enforcement of prohibition, for federal aid to maternity centers, and for industrial arbitration. None of these were adopted. Shortly after the convention, he wrote to a close friend: "I never lie to you about politics so I am willing to admit that I am heartbroken about politics. . . . The platform, as you say, was a straddle, but the left leg was moved to the left by me more or less. Borah and McCormick and another man named Nylan of San Francisco were able assistants and we pulled the thing as far to the left as we could, otherwise it would not have been a straddle but would have been a reactionary document. As it is, it does endorse trading with Russia, it rebukes (informally) the New York legislature for throwing out the Socialists, it provides for collective bargaining, it gives women in industry all that they ask for . . . and takes steps toward several progressive measures. It isn't entirely reactionary."

That the Republican party of 1920 was clearly the organ of property and special privilege was revealed not only in the platform but in the candidate who was selected for the presidency. On June 11, the convention began balloting for its nominee. When the convention adjourned after a day of voting, General Leonard Wood and Governor Frank Lowden stood deadlocked on the fourth ballot. That night the leading reactionaries in the party— Henry Cabot Lodge, Reed Smoot, George Harvey, Joseph Grundy, Charles Curtis, Senator Brandegee, and Senator Wadsworth—planned the nomination of a fellow senator, Warren G. Harding. "This Senatorial conspiracy developed," White later wrote, ". . . because Republican Senatorial leadership wished to submerge the Presidential office. Under Theodore Roosevelt and Woodrow Wilson for fifteen years of the twenty years in the new century, the President had taken leadership, and Congress, particularly the Senate, was losing its prestige."

There was, however, still another great force at work for Harding at the convention. This force was the oil interests, which were to have great power during the Harding administration. At the convention, Harry Sinclair summoned possible candidates for president and vice-president to his room for cross-examination. Harding was the figure that satisfied both the oil interests and the senatorial cabal. Years later White wrote: "There can be no doubt in the mind of any one who reads the testimony in the numerous oil suits brought later by the government that oil controlled the Republican convention of 1920."

The senatorial plan for nominating Harding called for four more ballots to see if the Lowden-Wood deadlock would break. If it did not, the senators on the ninth ballot would lead their states in the bolt to Harding. The morning after this agreement, Charles Curtis explained the plan to the Kansas delegation, which had been casting the majority of its votes for Wood. White immediately stood up, denounced Harding, and warned that they would live to regret such a step. Curtis, however, controlled the delegation, and on the ninth ballot the members deserted both Wood and Lowden and cast a unanimous vote for Harding. White later explained his vote for Harding: "I felt that when there were nineteen other members of the delegation, friends of Senator Curtis going to Senator Harding, it would be rather mulish for me to stand off and not give them a unanimous delegation." Commenting on this vote for Harding in his *Autobiography*, he summarized his subsequent political career by observing: "I was torn, as I often am in politics, between the desire to jump in the fiery furnace as a martyr, and the instinct to save my hide and go along on the broad way that leadeth to destruction. In the end I toddled along."

Harding won the nomination on the tenth ballot. White refused, however, on this ballot to vote for the senator. He had allowed Curtis to have a unanimous delegation on the ninth and that was enough. For the first eight ballots, White had voted for Wood, but now he cast his last vote for Herbert Hoover. A few months after the convention, White confessed to Gifford Pinchot that Hoover "doesn't go as far as we do. He is not a well drowned liberal. But he has come a considerable way on the journey and I think, is moving, though slowly."

Writing to Leonard Wood, several weeks after Harding's nomination, White explained that he had stayed with him as long as he had had a chance for the nomination. "It is hardly necessary," White confided on June 21, 1920, "to say that Harding is not the type of man I desire for president, but I shall accept him because anything is better than the Wilson type. Neither do I think it is proper that the United States Senate should nominate the president. . . . I think it is a great mistake to elect the president from the Senate, by the Senate and for the Senate."

After Governor Coolidge of Massachusetts had received the vice-presidential nomination, Will Hays appointed White chairman of the committee that was to call on Coolidge and notify him of this honor. White refused to do it. He wanted to rest in Colorado before reporting the Democratic convention at San Francisco. Hays insisted. White continued to refuse. Later he admitted to W. L. Chenery of *Colliers* that in 1920 he had no great admiration for Calvin Coolidge. Not until Coolidge became president was White attracted by this Yankee politician. Then the New Englander so amazed and so fascinated the Emporia editor that White wrote two books about him!

Late in June, White hurried to San Francisco to report the Democratic convention for the Wheeler syndicate. The Democrats unequivocably endorsed the Versailles Treaty and the League of Nations. In domestic affairs the Democrats promised a lower tariff; endorsed woman suffrage, maternity and infancy pensions, and a child-labor law; and declared that "labor is not a commodity." Governor James Cox of Ohio was nominated for the presidency with Assistant Secretary of the Navy Franklin D. Roosevelt as his running mate. Although Cox was not a man of strong liberal tendencies, he did represent Wilsonian ideals.

In his newspaper stories, White agreed that the San Francisco platform was "the most liberal platform the Democrats ever have written." The labor planks, he wrote, were much better than those of the Republicans. The Democrats, too, were more favorable to government ownership of the railroads. Toward the League of Nations, White adopted an extraordinary attitude. "It is a thundering battle between tweedle-dee and tweedle-dum," he declared. "The League is safe, whatever happens. No one need agonize seriously over that." White explained to his readers: "The campaign opens with one party fairly liberal, but highly ineffective, and the other upon the whole conservative, with a record for efficiency." He predicted that the campaign would be fought on the issue of Democratic idealism versus Republican efficiency.

Actually it was not. The issue that won the election for Harding was his pledge of a "return to normalcy." A few weeks before his nomination he had said that "America's present need is not heroics but healing; not nostrums but normalcy; not revolution but restoration; . . . not surgery but serenity." Harding offered the United

States, tired by the efforts of the progressive era and the war, an escape from domestic and international responsibility. He offered America rest rather than a crusade for a better society. Harding was a commonplace Ohioan who worshiped McKinley. He longed for the good old days, before Theodore Roosevelt had vaulted into the presidency, when the government did not regulate business but supplied it with fat subsidies.

White knew that Harding was at best only a third-rater and that he had made no important record as senator. "He was," White later wrote, "at the height of his statesmanship, a mere bass drum, beating the time of the hour, carrying no tune, making no music, promoting no deep harmony; just a strident, rhythmic noise." Yet White supported Harding for the presidency. On June 14, the Emporia editor told his readers: "He is a clean, honest man. His Republicanism is unchallenged. . . . He will conform to Republican opinion when elected. And every man or woman who calls himself a Republican should vote for Harding. . . . Harding and Coolidge look good to me." Three days later, although admitting that Harding was a hidebound conservative, White wishfully asserted that Harding probably would listen to liberal advice after being elected.

"The case of William Allen White is a sad one," sorrowfully observed George Creel. "Here was a natural-born reporter, keen in his observation, photographic as to impression, a master in winnowing chaff from the wheat, and with an unerring instinct for facts. Inherited Republicanism was his trouble. White lives in Kansas, a Republican State; his friends are Republicans, and all of them have office, want to stay in office, or else are running for office. Even today William Allen White is a good reporter between campaigns, but where a Republican candidate has been decided upon he heaves a weary sigh, puts reporting by and takes up the burden of propaganda."

White's good friend Harold Ickes, who had been a fellow delegate at the Republican convention, protested against White's editorial that all Republicans should vote for Harding. Ickes insisted that Harding was not a fit man for the presidency. "I regard Senator Harding as a complacent instrument ready for manipulation by the big special interests," Ickes declared on June 30, 1920. "He is a platitudinous jellyfish whose election I would regard as distinctly detrimental to the best interests of the country." Ickes closed his letter of protest on a note that demonstrated White's commanding national prestige and influence, a prestige and influence that was to increase immeasurably from 1920 to 1944. "It is bad enough," wrote Ickes, "for you to have to argue with indignant constituents from your own district without having your friends, as far away as Chicago, harry you with such letters as this. But the trouble with you is that you aren't a local Emporia institution. In a very real sense I am one of your constituents too."

Politically White really was unhappy. Everything was in a terrible mess. When he poured out his heart to Victor Murdock, Murdock replied: "My dear Will: I am glad you are still able to feel pain." To Harold Ickes, White confided: "I have no more use for Harding than you have. He makes me see red when I think of him; I regard his nomination as a menace to the Republic." Why, then, did he support Harding? He carefully explained to Ickes that he thought Governor Cox and the Democrats were worse. This, of course, was a debatable question. From 1920 to his death, to the bewilderment of many of his progressive friends, White supported the straight Republican ticket, except the gubernatorial candidate in 1924. He supported, for instance, much that Franklin D. Roosevelt did, but opposed him in election years. President Roosevelt summed up the relations between White and himself when his special train stopped at Emporia during the 1936 campaign. "Bill White is with me three and a half years out of every four," he told the Emporians. No statement could have been more appropriate. For three and a half out of every four years, from 1920 to 1944, White saw America with an amazing clarity. He vigorously denounced, during each such period, the Republican party for its isolationist policy and for its intimate tie with reactionary business forces. Yet, as Elmer Davis has pointed out, in the spring of every election year a curious form of amnesia crept over him. Then he took up the cudgels in support of the Republican party.

Such a paradoxical situation was understandable only as part of the pattern of White's political behavior. In politics he was an eminently practical fellow. In a normally Republican state one had to support the straight ticket to have influence. He had bolted the party once and that was enough. One lost too much power as a state leader by bolting too often. White persuaded himself that in a realistic world he could best mold public opinion to work toward what he considered his purpose in life through the Republican party.

White would throw bricks at Republican leadership from within the ranks, not from the outside. He explained his attitude in the following letter:

. . . My contention is that while this is a government of parties, the people should not be party-minded. Let the party organizations be party-minded and let the independent vote decide between the two parties.

Heaven knows there will always be enough party-minded people too lazy to think and too indolent to move out of party lines and they will more or less furnish the momentum for parties.

But parties must be kept by the fear of God and the fear of God is the fear of the independent vote. And the more independent voters there are, and the more independent people hold the balance of power, the better the parties will be. This is my contention. Personally I am in the Republican party because I can break more windows and let in more light and air by throwing rocks from the inside than I can from the outside. But the average man is not equipped as I am and doesn't like to break windows and I do. So while I am a partisan, the average man, I think, who is intelligent and wants to get action on his vote, should get action as an independent rather than as a partisan, and let the men who care more for party than for country, run the party.

The Whites spent the summer of 1920 at their Colorado cottage far removed from politics. They had loads of company, an average of seven guests eating meals with them every day. By this time the children were grown up. Bill was to attend Harvard that fall, and Mary was studying hard to gain admission to Wellesley. She had been carefree about her studies in the past, but by 1920 she was reading a great deal. "She reads all sorts of tremendously serious highbrow stuff," her father told Edna Ferber. ". . . She is so rotten good that I'm always afraid that when she takes off her corset cover her wings will sprout and she'll fly away." While

332

Mrs. White was out of town that October, Herbert Hoover came to Emporia on a campaign tour for the Republicans. White held a dinner in his honor and Senator Capper was present along with a number of local dignitaries. Mary sat at the head of the table, and her father swelled with pride. "You should have seen your daughter," White wrote Sallie, ". . . dressed for her party—the sweetest thing in the world."

By mid-September, White was back in Emporia working for the Republican ticket. He played a prominent part in Governor Henry J. Allen's campaign for re-election. Editorial after editorial called for the election of the straight Republican ticket. Years later, White, dutifully chagrined, denied that he wrote more than one editorial for Harding, but he actually wrote a number. On September 3, for instance, he stated that every Republican should support the ticket, because the Democratic party was dominated by "the big booze bosses and the Solid South." The same charge he had used in 1912, but under Wilson the Democrats were far more progressive than the Republicans ever had been. "If the Harding administration," he told his doubting friends, "begins to grow reactionary, or if it is stupid and blind, an enlightened public sentiment can scare it into its senses."

Although he wrote editorials in favor of Harding, he refused to write any articles for nation-wide magazines. When Herbert Croly urged him to do a sketch for the *New Republic,* White refused because "I am so low in my mind that I wouldn't laugh at Charles Chaplin throwing a whole custard pie at Cox or Harding or both." White wrote Harding, during the summer, that the progressives did not like his talk about a return to normalcy, and that "they don't like you to be called a man of the McKinley type; because they feel that the McKinley day was the least satisfactory day in the history of the Republican party . . . they will want specific, progressive performance after the election and I feel sure that you will see the wisdom of their course."

Woodrow Wilson had hoped that the election of 1920 would serve as a mandate on the League of Nations. The Republicans, however, so muddied the affair that no mandate was expressed. Warren G. Harding in one speech was anti-League and in another pro-League. By election time he had the public highly confused.

"One half of the speeches were for the League of Nations if you read them hastily," Chester Rowell has written, "but if you read them with care every word of them could have been read critically as against the League of Nations. The other half were violent speeches against the League of Nations if you read them carelessly, but if you read them critically every one of them could be interpreted as in favor of the League of Nations."

In August, one of Harding's anti-League speeches prompted Herbert Hoover to wire White to join with him and many other prominent Republicans in protesting privately to Harding. White readily joined in this action. However, despite the fact that he and many other leading Republicans were privately disturbed over Harding's anti-League position, on October 15 White joined thirty eminent Republicans—men like Hoover, Taft, Hughes, Root, Wickersham, and Lowell—in declaring that a vote for Harding was a vote in support of America's joining the League of Nations. "We . . . believe," the statement asserted, "that we can most effectively advance the cause of international co-operation to promote peace by supporting Mr. Harding for election to the Presidency." This appeal was made to bolster Harding's flabby backbone, but more important, it was issued to stop pro-League people from voting the Democratic ticket.

For the rest of the campaign, White denied that the League was an issue. "There is absolutely no difference between the two parties," he wrote one rightfully suspicious person on October 27, 1920. If Harding is elected, he added, the United States would be in the League within sixty days. "He has written and told a number of men," White declared, "whose names are on that statement that the first thing he will do will be to try to straighten out the tangle. . . . Now by making this statement favoring his election we have shown him our good will. We have shown him that we are willing to play ball with him and are therefore in a position as Republicans, and we represent a pretty strong force and faction in the Republican party, that we have certain rights which he is bound to respect."

Probably thousands of doubtful Americans were persuaded to vote for Harding because of the public statement by the thirty-one Republicans. Yet White was shrewd enough politically to know that there was no way to hold Harding to any pledge once he was in office. H. N. MacCracken, president of Vassar, refused to sign the statement for that reason. He explained: "The names of those signing it will not in my opinion have any influence on Senator Harding's foreign policy after election. It seems to me that the same group of Republican Senators will control Republican policy who have controlled it in the past, and that nothing is to be expected from them in the way of international co-operation."

In the light of the statement by the thirty-one Republicans and of the occasional pro-League stand of Harding, many pro-League citizens undoubtedly voted for the Republican candidate. Vice-President-elect Calvin Coolidge remarked: "I doubt if any particular mandate was given at the last election on the question of the League of Nations and if that was the preponderant issue." Harding quickly forgot any promises about joining the League. Under his administration, the United States was to embark upon an irresponsible course of isolationism abroad and reaction at home. White told Gifford Pinchot several weeks after Harding's election: "The Republican party is married to Big Business. And until we annul the marriage by getting new men and new blood into the organization, all our fights will be more or less sterile."

Although White was to deplore many of the manifestations of "normalcy" in the decade ahead, the ironic fact was that at election time he thoroughly supported the Republican party—the party that was heavily responsible for America's isolationist policy, for America's turning away from progressive tendencies, and for a great deal of America's business and political corruption in the era of normalcy. He and the other thirty eminent individuals who signed the statement that Harding would take the United States into the League of Nations betrayed the country, in a sense, by vouching for Harding and then failing to force him to redeem the promise.

PART IV

NORMALCY AND REFORM

CHAPTER 16

THE HARDING ERA

LETTER after letter passed across the old roll-top desk of William Allen White as an ill-at-ease America sought to re-establish itself during the sad, gay days of the nineteen-twenties. Under the mask of careless hilarity, many thinking Americans were frankly troubled by the problems, as yet unsolved, which a postwar decade had brought. The shadow of the implications of an irresponsible era led many bothered minds to seek the homespun wisdom of the son of a happier generation. White, the genial editor of the Emporia *Gazette,* by now looked upon as the wise spokesman of middle-class America, became to many the symbol of sanity in the turmoil that was the 1920's.

White's desk sagged under the weight of letters which flooded the Emporia post office. Strangers, friends, acquaintances, politicians—the great and the unknown—all alike troubled by the problems of conservatism, isolationism, corruption, and their own inability to find happiness, turned to this small-town editor because he alone seemed stable in a world of chaos. The merry, blue-eyed, cherubic gentleman of Kansas, busy as he was as a newspaper editor and publisher, magazine writer, popular biographer, and political leader, found time to answer every one of his troubled correspondents and to offer a note of sanity and justice to a groping generation.

To Emporia's most distinguished citizen, the twenties were an ugly nightmare. They frightened him. He saw those foolish, roaring years which followed the first war as an unbelievable, irrelevant potpourri of speakeasies, Teapot Dome scandals, bathing beauty contests, Florida real estate booms, anti-Bolshevist scares, and Ku Klux Klans. In private letters, magazine articles, and editorials in his *Gazette*, White poured forth his misgivings and fears for the nation and his judgments on an America gone money-mad, isolationist, and supernationalistic. He saw the American conscience take a complete leave of absence—desert its world responsibility and ignore its own vital economic and social problems. This was not an era of "normalcy" to White; this was an age utterly abnormal.

It was an age of hate. A reign of terror—the great Red scare—resulting in the smashing of labor unions and the pinning of the label of Bolshevism on progressive-minded citizens swept the country. Outbreaks against the Jews, the Catholics, and the Negroes were frequent. This intolerant nationalism culminated in the Ku Klux Klan, which terrorized large areas of the nation and exerted a demoralizing influence on the community life.

The first Christmas of "normalcy" in 1920 found Kansas's most famous editor particularly unhappy. His mood over American apathy toward international co-operation and progressive legislation at home led him to write to his old friend Ray Stannard Baker, the biographer of Woodrow Wilson, in an almost prophetic tone: "What a God damned world this is! I trust you will realize that I am not swearing; merely trying to express in the mildest terms what I think of the conditions that exist. What a God damned world! . . . If anyone had told me ten years ago that our country would be what it is today, I should have questioned his reason."

Appalled by the collapse of moral idealism in the postwar years and puzzled by America's ingrown piety and concern only for America first, White tried to seek a plausible explanation for this strange state of the public mind. He came to the conclusion that the American people had hoped for too much to flow out of the war and from the Peace Conference. They had expected a new world to develop. They had not realized that the forces of the past would mold the postwar world. And when the age-old traditions of the Old World had asserted themselves in the peace,

America had become disillusioned. While fighting the war the United States was "en route to glory," White wrote. "President Wilson had Billy Sundayed us into a millennial ecstasy. He went to Europe—and exhorted the common people into a fine frenzy of hope— However, the actual governments and the real governing classes of Europe are and always have been realists. So when they sat down with the President at the peace conference—blooey went the dream of the world!—European greed had disillusioned us. Suddenly America became as materialistic as Europe. Our circular insanity ran from zenith to nadir. Our faith became a sneer; our generosity waxed into greed."

When the wave of uncritical reaction swept the country during the postwar period, it was probably not too surprising that many of America's great middle class became convinced that labor unions were un-American and "communistic," and that antiunion employers were able to smash union organization ruthlessly. "The country is reactionary—against labor, middle-class conscious," White explained to Gifford Pinchot, governor of Pennsylvania, on September 11, 1923. "The red-baiters have so thoroughly scared the people with the bogey of Bolshevism that any public man who takes any public attitude in favor of organized labor, or any other kind of labor as far as that is concerned, does so at his tremendous peril politically." When James J. Davis, Harding's secretary of labor, sought White's views on employer-employee relations, White significantly replied that the greatest problem was not the union organizer but the intolerant, somewhat money-mad boss. The real troublemaker, White added, was the "boss who feels that he has to hire spies to know what his men are doing, the boss who feels that the labor market is like the cattle market or the cotton market."

Reactionary businessmen utilized the fear of radicalism to push their pet measure, the open shop. When White was told by a well-meaning soul that Abraham Lincoln would be for the open shop were he alive, White's frank reply was: "Some way I feel that Lincoln would do no such thing. I feel very strongly that his deep sympathy and understanding for the man who is down and is trying earnestly and intelligently to rise, would impel Lincoln to realize that the unions have done more for labor than any other one force in the last hundred years, excepting, perhaps, universal education. I feel that the Christian view of Lincoln would try to encourage the unions to give them more and more power and make their membership more and more intelligent."

Closely allied with the antiunion phobia of the roaring twenties was the technique of labeling progressive-minded groups and individuals with the taint of communism or socialism. Reactionary forces deliberately smeared liberals as Communists or Socialists in order to discredit their proposals with the American people. White warned the public that they must not accept these reactionary stereotypes, because such beliefs played directly into the hands of those who did not want a social and economic democracy for middle-class America. In answer to a plea from a member of the American Legion for an editorial warning of the dangers of radicalism, the Sage of Emporia dictated a most vigorous reply:

I do not feel that we need much of a "line of defense against the advance of radicalism." The radical is a poor fish who doesn't get anywhere. The real danger is your conservative, your reactionary, and he is getting somewhere. He is liable to have this country by the throat, and if I was getting up a first line of defense, I would line it up against the highly respectable politician who bolsters up the big grasping profiteers of high finance, rather than against the poor simp, who rages around about overturning the country. The country will not be overturned, but it is liable to be put to sleep, and I wish the Legion would get a little more excited about the dangers of respectable conservatism and insidious reaction and run out a first line of defense against some of those ginks.

The same emotional climate which produced the Red scare aided the flowering of such "one hundred per cent American" movements as the Ku Klux Klan. The second Klan's terrorism toward Catholics, Jews, Negroes, and immigrant groups stirred White's wrath. Again and again his editorial pen flailed the vicious, undemocratic Klan beliefs. When the New York *World*, under the able editorship of Herbert Bayard Swope, began an exposé of the Klan, White immediately wrote Swope: "There are, of course, bad foreigners and good ones; good Catholics and bad ones and all kinds of Negroes. To make a case against a birthplace, a religion, or a race is wickedly un-American and cowardly. The whole trouble with the Ku Klux Klan is that it is based upon such deep foolishness that it is bound to be a menace to good government in any community. Any man fool enough to be Imperial Wizard would have power without responsibility and both without any sense. That is social dynamite."

Late in 1920, the National Security League, a superpatriotic group which was stirring the fires of excessive nationalism, asked White to write an article on "What Is One-Hundred-Per-Cent Americanism?" He refused, since, as he told them, "My idea of one hundred per cent Americanism is an American who has intelligent faith enough in his country and his ideals to allow any other American however stupid and however crooked and however malicious to say what he pleases, to think what he pleases and to do what he pleases and to print what he pleases in controversy of American ideals and then laugh at the fool rather than to put him in jail. I fear that the standard of Americanism of your league doesn't come up to that. You lack about fifty per cent of the faith in America that I do and so I fear that my article would not be acceptable."

* * *

Whatever the reactionary tendencies of the postwar decade in social and economic democracy, they were accompanied by remarkable technological changes in American industry. These changes were particularly significant in the journalistic and motion-picture industries and were pregnant with serious possibilities for the future of American democracy. White was disturbed by the failure which he saw in these two great organs of opinion to serve as real media of education and enlightenment for American democracy. He was also greatly concerned over the trend, in his own profession, toward consolidation and ownership of American newspapers by fewer and fewer men.

He saw one of his own novels, which concerned deep moral and social problems, made into a bitterly disappointing movie. After seeing the film based on *In The Heart of A Fool*, he wrote Mrs. White: "Well I saw it. . . . How they did it, how they could

343

take a story and so thoroughly mangle it is far, far, beyond my limited intelligence. . . . Mary White sat by me during the ordeal and chuckled and giggled and made the funniest running comment you ever heard. For instance, 'Father, why did you take their money? They haven't used your story.' Mary has been deliriously hilarious about it. She is a perfect dear. She knew I was plagued to death and she cheered me up. The picture is a mess."

After sadly watching the progress of the movie industry in the early twenties, the Emporia editor sat down one day and wrote to Will Hays, at that time the czar of filmdom's moral code:

. . . Until you grade the theaters very sharply you will not get very far reforming the movies. The spoken stage does grade the theaters very carefully. You know what kind of a play to expect in certain houses and from certain actors and certain producers, . . . but as it stands now in the moving picture business every picture has to appeal more or less to all kinds of people in the audience. So it doesn't rise very high. It cannot rise high, and as the result the high-brow avoids the movies, and they are given over largely to the lowbrows. If you would have a high-brow theater, a middle grade theater, and a lowbrow theater, the patron then would know where to go to get the kind of a show he wanted . . . The movie audience is obsessed by the moron, because every picture house expects a moron to be a patron. Until you can segregate your moron, and make plays, and consequently play houses, for the fifteen per cent of people whose intelligence scores over thirteen years old, you won't get very far purifying or uplifting the movies.

*   *   *

Although William Allen White was disgusted with the movie industry as such, he found some of filmdom's personalities fascinating individuals. In one of his happiest comments, he wrote to Franklin P. Adams about the Emporia visit of Mary Pickford and America's swashbuckling hero, Douglas Fairbanks:

The "Doug" was there but the "Pickford" was not, at least, she was invisible in her car, which was no great matter. I liked the "Doug" very much. Direct, casual sort of cuss, and as you say not professionally unspoiled. The professionally unspoiled is a sad lot, isn't it? It is like the absolutely pure. I have always had a low opinion of Royal Baking powder on that account.

In his own field of journalism, the small-town editor regretfully witnessed the consolidation of many independent papers and the resulting unemployment of thousands of reporters, editorial writers, and printers. Sadly, too, he watched the passing of the individualistic editor and his colorful outpourings. When "Marse" Henry Watterson, editor of the Louisville *Courier-Journal* died, White declared that the newspaper business was developing no more individualistic editors like Watterson. The reason was that the advent of improved machinery had greatly increased the cost of starting a newspaper. Since young men no longer had enough money to start their own paper, they went to work for big-moneyed newspaper entrepreneurs. "They are naturally not given the liberty in their hired men's jobs that they would have on their own papers," White asserted. "So they get into other work, or shrivel up and die mentally. The time was when the country printer or reporter could start his own paper with a little help and little nerve. That time has passed. The day of the big corporation-owned paper is here."

White saw the rise of great newspaper empires like Hearst and Munsey's. He saw newspapers become valuable only as purveyors of headline scandals or shares of stock; and he saw them fail as leaders of the people. To him, American democracy seemed the poorer for this change. It was in such a mood that upon the death of one of these "corrupters of the traditional press in America," Frank Munsey, he wrote the following obituary in the *Gazette:*

Frank Munsey, the great publisher is dead.

Frank Munsey, contributed to the journalism of his day the talent of a meat packer, the morals of a money changer and the manners of an undertaker. He and his kind have about succeeded in transforming a once-noble profession into an eight per cent security.

May he rest in trust!

To Nicholas Murray Butler, president of Columbia University, White wrote explaining this piece:

Probably I was a little rough on Frank Munsey but the whole tendency of the times in newspaper consolidation and standardization, I think, works badly. I would rather have the press as it was in John Milton's time, or Benjamin Franklin's time, when a man with the proverbial shirt tail full of type could express himself, air his views, and get it off his chest, rather than to have the mass production of newspapers owned by investment bankers and filled full of stupid syndicate matter and conventional opinions as they are today. It is a bad thing for the newspaper business and it is a bad thing for the people. And Munsey and his kind are getting halos for doing a bad thing. I have no quarrel with Munsey, personally, but I had to say what I said for the craft I loved.

Another publisher whom White heartily disliked was William Randolph Hearst. In all the major events which White covered for various newspaper syndicates during the twenties—and all the rest of his life—he would never permit his copy to be sold to the Hearst papers. Upon protest from the syndicates that he was losing a great deal of money, he sternly replied: "Hearst is my idea of a rattlesnake crossed with the smallpox. I do not like him or any of his works, and I would not work for him for any money on earth." When a Hearst editor protested White's refusal to have his syndicated articles carried by Hearst papers, White told him: "For you as a newspaperman I have the greatest respect. You are doing your job as it is given you to do it, and doing it well. The Hearst papers, considering their policy and their public, are consistent, and I have no quarrel with the men who make them. I just do not like their policy. I have a low opinion of Hearst as a man and as a newspaper publisher, and holding that opinion I do not want to write for him, and being free, white, and over twenty-one, I am not going to do it."

*　　*　　*

White's small-town America was shocked in October, 1920, to find its way of life impaled by Sinclair Lewis, a young redheaded novelist. With keen satire, Lewis in *Main Street* scoffed at the materialistic civilization of the small-town Rotarian and Kiwanian. The good life, for them, had degenerated into an insane scramble for money. Lewis's *Main Street* town of Gopher Prairie, located in the Middle West, had none of the wholesome, friendly, neighborly, democratic virtues that William Allen White claimed existed in small-town America.

Gopher Prairie was a dull, ugly town dominated by stolid, respectable citizens who had no ideas to offer except petty gossip. At their luncheon clubs and Country Club affairs, they expressed their profound belief, and would brook no disagreement, that union labor should be crushed and all agitators hanged. Self-satisfied and smug, the town bankers and businessmen talked about democracy but did not practice it. To them, democracy really meant the opportunity to exploit their fellow man. It did not mean generosity, aid to the downtrodden, and a sense of social responsibility. These molders of public opinion in Gopher Prairie, according to *Main Street*, were all for democracy and Christianity as long as these beliefs were not taken too seriously.

As soon as White finished reading *Main Street*, he wrote Sinclair Lewis, whom he had met the preceding fall at the Washington labor conference: "I hasten to tell you what a noble thing you have done. It has been years since I have read anything so splendidly conceived and so skillfully executed as *Main Street*. . . . If I were a millionaire, I should buy a thousand of those books and send them to my friends and then I would go and bribe the legislature of Kansas to make *Main Street* compulsory reading in the public schools. No American has done a greater service for his country in any sort of literature, than you have done." White advised his subscribers to read the book, remarking that any small town that felt it could be content with its progress needed this book.

Sinclair Lewis was extremely grateful for White's praise, coming as it did among the charges being hurled at him that he had not faithfully portrayed small-town midwestern life. "There is nothing (not even a good letter from John Galsworthy)," Lewis wrote him, "which has given me keener pleasure than your words." Although White enjoyed *Main Street*, he did feel that it told only half the story. "He does not tell the other side," White explained to Victor Murdock on December 20, 1920, "but at that, the side that he does tell is worth telling. It is the sort of thing that puts discontent into the hearts of folks. And I think that contentment is worse than 'red' any day."

A few months after the publication of *Main Street*, Victor Murdock brought out a chatty book about small towns called *Folks*. White sent copies of this volume to editors all over the country, with the message that here was a book that answered the new school of writers like Sinclair Lewis and Sherwood Anderson. In *Collier's* for July 30, 1921, White rallied to the defense of Main Street America. The American town, he maintained, breathed with "a spirit of mutual help, a spirit of militant altruism." "The *Main Street* of Mr. Sinclair Lewis is a great book," he declared, "but it is written in ignorance of the tremendous forces that make for righteousness in every American town. Dorothy Canfield's *The Brimming Cup* is a truer book because it takes account of those righteous currents that are moving—however muddily, however sluggishly—moving with the current of progress which is surely directing humanity from a barbarous past to a kindlier, broader, better way of life."

Two years after *Main Street*, Lewis published *Babbitt*, another satirical attack on the manners and hypocrisy of life in the average American town. White hailed this book too as an extremely significant contribution. "Most readers will hate the book. But the worse they hate it," he wrote in the *Gazette* on October 2, 1922, "the more they should read it. . . . It is not the truth any more than *Main Street* was the truth. But man! man!—it does assemble a lot of ugly essential and challenging facts about modern life. . . . Sinclair Lewis is one of the major prophets of our times, a Jeremiah probably, but Heaven sent. If we heed his lamentations, we are saved. If we ignore it, we are gone."

The major quarrel that White had with realistic writers like Lewis and Sherwood Anderson was their denial of the nobility of man. They reduced life to a mechanical process and thus denied that there was a spark of the divine in every man. Once you convince man that life is nothing but a mechanical process, "you rob him of his faith, hope, and love," White declared. White's fundamental belief in a benevolent evolution revealed itself when he added: "One thing has persisted through all man's journey in this wilderness ever since he came down from the trees. That is his inextinguishable optimism, his unswerving hope, his unfailing faith. . . . To keep man's faith in his destiny alive through the creation of beauty, and so to urge man on to the Kingdom of God, is the purpose of art." From his own experience of having seen the wilderness of mid-America transformed into the bustling society of the 1920's, White was convinced of the progress of mankind. True, there were aspects of life that were mean and cruel, but life was far better than it had been a century before.

The lack of beauty in small-town life that Sinclair Lewis described, White maintained, was not peculiar to the small town. What Kansas lacked, he once stated, was "a sense of beauty and the love of it." But this was not peculiar to Kansas. It was a tremendous American problem.

The small-town life that White was defending was undergoing rapid changes in the decade after World War I. The increasing use of automobiles was helping to destroy the provincial qualities of the isolated small town. As Kansans drove through New England or along the Pacific Coast, they tended to slough off their own peculiar qualities that had been developed in the relatively isolated Kansas of the past. Although in 1922 White was to describe Kansas as a Puritan survival, the uniqueness that had been Kansas was beginning to disappear. Not only the automobile, but the great popularity of motion pictures and the developing radio industry increased the trend away from uniqueness toward conformity with the rest of the country. White, in his "Kansas A Puritan Survival" in the *Nation* on April 19, 1922, explained that Kansas had been a center of such reforms as populism, prohibition, and progressivism because of its Puritan desire to achieve an equitable society. After World War I, however, Kansas failed to be the center of powerful reform movements. Kansas ceased to be the state of mind it once had been. Smugly satisfied by the state's material progress, many Kansans between the two World Wars settled down to protect the status quo. By the twenties, Kansas was prosperous, plutocratic, and reeking with automobiles. No longer was Kansas, as White had once claimed, the state where reform movements were bred and nurtured until other areas took them up. No longer was it true, as White stated, that the only way to stop progress in America was to destroy Kansas.

By 1934 White himself began to realize that Kansas was quite different from what it had been in the past. It seemed to him to have lost its state pride. "Have we, perhaps, being cosmopolitan, hooked on the air with everything this side of Mars, lost our sense of Kansas as 'a local habitation and a name'? . . ." he inquired.

"Probably our historical background does not thrill us with the pride that the story of Kansas—free-state Kansas in its struggle—thrilled those young men and women homesteading in Kansas in the grasshopper years, amid the drouths and hardships of a new, raw civilization."

*   *   *

White's fame as a common-sense interpreter of life was enormously increased in 1921 by a tragic event. Early in May, White left Emporia to deliver speeches in the East and to visit Washington to gather material for articles on the Harding administration. On May 11, he received the following telegram from Mrs. White: "Mary has had another tumble from horse. No scars but severe shock. Horse absolutely to go. Mary may stand it but I can't." Soon her condition became serious, and her father and brother Bill at Harvard hurried home. While making train connections in Chicago, White was told by Harold Ickes and Edna Ferber that Mary had died.

The day after the funeral, White, with Mrs. White at his side, shut himself in his office and wrote a beautiful tribute to his daughter. In the greatest emotional crisis of his life, he wrote a piece that has lived and been treasured far more than anything else he ever wrote:

MARY WHITE

The Associated Press reports carrying the news of Mary White's death declared that it came as the result of a fall from a horse. How she would have hooted at that! She never fell from a horse in her life. Horses have fallen on her and with her—"I'm always trying to hold 'em in my lap," she used to say. But she was proud of few things, and one was that she could ride anything that had four legs and hair. Her death resulted not from a fall, but from a blow on the head which fractured her skull, and the blow came from the limb of an overhanging tree on the parking.

The last hour of her life was typical of its happiness. She came home from a day's work at school, topped off by a hard grind with the copy on the High School Annual, and felt that a ride would refresh her. She climbed into her khakis, chattering to her mother about the work she was doing, and hurried to get her horse and be out on the dirt roads for the country air and the radiant green fields of the spring. As she rode through the town on an easy gallop she kept waving at passers-by. She knew everyone in town. For a decade the little figure with the long pigtail and the red hair ribbon has been familiar on the streets of Emporia, and she got in the way of speaking to those who nodded at her. She passed the Kerrs, walking the horse, in front of the Normal Library, and waved at them; passed another friend a few hundred feet further on, and waved at her.

The horse was walking, and as she turned into North Merchant street she took off her cowboy hat, and the horse swung into a lope. She passed the Tripletts and waved her cowboy hat at them, still moving gaily north on Merchant street. A Gazette carrier passed— a High School boy friend—and she waved at him, but with her bridle hand; the horse veered quickly, plunged into the parking where the low-hanging limb faced her, and, while she still looked back waving, the blow came. But she did not fall from the horse; she slipped off, dazed a bit, staggered and fell in a faint. She never quite recovered consciousness.

But she did not fall from the horse, neither was she riding fast. A year or so ago she used to go like the wind. But that habit was broken, and she used the horse to get into the open to get fresh, hard exercise, and to work off a certain surplus energy that welled up in her and needed a physical outlet. That need has been in her heart for years. It was back of the impulse that kept the dauntless little brown-clad figure on the streets and country roads of the community and built into a strong, muscular body what had been a frail and sickly frame during the first years of her life. But the riding gave her more than a body. It released a gay and hardy soul. She was the happiest thing in the world. And she was happy because she was enlarging her horizon. She came to know all sorts and conditions of men; Charley O'Brien, the traffic cop, was one of her best friends. W. L. Holtz, the Latin teacher, was another. Tom O'Connor, farmer-politician, and Rev. J. H. Rice, preacher and police judge, and Frank Beach, music master, were her special friends; and all the girls, black and white, above the track and below the track, in Pepville and Stringtown, were among her acquaintances. And she brought home riotous stories of her adventures. She loved to rollick; persiflage was her natural expression at home. Her humor was a continual bubble of joy. She seemed to think in hyperbole and metaphor. She was mischievous without malice, as full of faults as an old shoe. No angel was Mary White, but an easy girl to live with, for she never nursed a grouch five minutes in her life.

With all her eagerness for the out-of-doors, she loved books. On her table when she left her room were a book by Conrad, one by Galsworthy, "Creative Chemistry" by E. E. Slosson, and a Kipling book. She read Mark Twain, Dickens and Kipling before she was ten—all of their writings. Wells and Arnold Bennett particularly amused and diverted her. She was entered as a student in Wellesley in 1922; was assistant editor of the High School Annual this year, and in line for election to the editorship of the Annual next year. She was a member of the executive committee of the High School Y.W.C.A.

Within the last two years she had begun to be moved by an ambition to draw. She began as most children do by scribbling in her school books, funny pictures. She bought cartoon magazines and took a course—rather casually, naturally, for she was, after all, a child, with no strong purposes—and this year she tasted the first fruits of success by having her pictures accepted by the High School Annual. But the thrill of delight she got when Mr. Ecord, of the Normal Annual, asked her to do the cartooning for that book this spring, was too beautiful for words. She fell to her work with all her enthusiastic heart. Her drawings were accepted, and her pride—always repressed by a lively sense of the ridiculous figure she was cutting—was a really gorgeous thing to see. No successful artist ever drank a deeper draft of satisfaction than she took from the little fame her work was getting among her schoolfellows. In her glory, she almost forgot her horse—but never her car.

For she used the car as a jitney bus. It was her social life. She never had a "party" in all her nearly seventeen years—wouldn't have one; but she never drove a block in her life that she didn't begin to fill the car with pick-ups! Everybody rode with Mary White—white and black, old and young, rich and poor, men and women. She liked nothing better than to fill the car with long-legged High School boys and an occasional girl, and parade the town. She never had a "date," nor went to a dance, except once with her brother, Bill, and the "boy proposition" didn't interest her—yet. But young people—great, spring-breaking, varnish-cracking, fender-bending, door-sagging carloads of "kids"—gave her great pleasure. Her zests were keen. But the most fun she ever had in her life was acting as chairman of the committee that got up the big turkey dinner for the poor folks at the county home; scores of pies, gallons of slaw, jam, cakes, preserves, oranges and a wilderness of turkey were loaded in the car and taken to the county home. And, being of a practical turn of mind, she risked her own Christmas dinner to see that the poor folks actually got it all. Not that she was a cynic; she just disliked to tempt folks. While there she found a blind colored uncle, very old, who could do nothing but make rag rugs, and she rustled up from her school friends rags enough to keep him busy for a season. The last engagement she tried to make was to take the guests at the county home out for a car ride. And the last endeavor of her life was to try to get a rest room for colored girls in the High School. She found one girl reading in the toilet, because there was no better place for a colored girl to loaf, and it inflamed her sense of injustice and she became a nagging harpy to those who she thought could remedy the evil. The poor she had always with her and was glad of it. She hungered and thirsted for righteousness; and was the most impious creature in the world. She joined the church without consulting her parents, not particularly for her soul's good. She never had a thrill of piety in her life, and would have hooted at a "testimony." But even as a little child she felt the church was an agency for helping people to more of life's abundance, and she wanted to help. She never wanted help for herself. Clothes meant little to her. It was a fight to get a new rig on her; but eventually a harder fight to get it off. She never wore a jewel and had no ring but her High School class ring, and never asked for anything but a wrist watch. She refused to have her hair up; though she was nearly seventeen. "Mother," she protested, "you don't know how much I get by with, in my braided pigtails, that I could not with my hair up." Above every other passion of her life was her passion not to grow up, to be a child. The tomboy in her, which was big, seemed to loathe to be put away forever in skirts. She was a Peter Pan, who refused to grow up.

Her funeral yesterday at the Congregational Church was as she would have wished it; no singing, no flowers except the big bunch of red roses from her brother Bill's Harvard classmen—heavens, how proud that would have made her!—and the red roses from the Gazette force, in vases, at her head and feet. A short prayer: Paul's beautiful essay on "Love" from the Thirteenth Chapter of First Corinthians; some remarks about her democratic spirit by her friend, John H. J. Rice, pastor and police judge, which she would have deprecated if she could; a prayer sent down for her by her friend, Carl Nau; and, opening the service the slow, poignant movement from Beethoven's Moonlight Sonata, which she loved; and closing the service a cutting from the joyously melancholy first movement of Tschaikowski's Pathetic Symphony, which she liked to hear, in certain moods, on the phonograph; then the Lord's Prayer by her friends in the High School.

That was all.

For her pallbearers only her friends were chosen: her Latin teacher, W. L. Holtz; her High School principal, Rice Brown; her doctor, Frank Foncannon; her friend, W. W. Finney; her pal at the Gazette office, Walter Hughes; and her brother Bill. It would have made her smile to know that her friend, Charley O'Brien, the traffic cop, had been transferred from Sixth and Commercial to the corner near the church to direct her friends who came to bid her good-bye.

A rift in the clouds in a gray day threw a shaft of sunlight upon her coffin as her nervous, energetic little body sank to its last sleep. But the soul of her, the glowing, gorgeous, fervent soul of her, surely was flaming in eager joy upon some other dawn.

Franklin P. Adams reprinted "Mary White" in "The Conning Tower" in the New York *Tribune*, May 24, 1921, and then other papers all over the country carried the piece. "As nearly as I can figure it out," White wrote Walter Armstrong on June 3, 1921, "it has gone out in papers aggregating a total subscription of two and a half million, probably a wider circulation than anything that has ever been published in the Gazette. And I cannot help feeling that some place along the line her life has reached out and touched other lives through this article and I hope it has touched them for good. That immortality is sure. And it heals my sorrow some-what to know that I helped her to that wider influence."

A flood of letters poured into the *Gazette* office. Friends and strangers alike described how deeply they had been touched by the editorial. "It was really better than I thought," he wrote Bill, now back at Harvard. "And to tell the truth, Bill, it seems really better than it is. It was such a simple, inevitable thing to do that I see no grace and little merit in it."

McClure's Magazine reprinted the article with Mary's picture that summer, and Christopher Morley, realizing the classic quality of the editorial, included it late that year in the volume, *Modern Essays*, that he edited. In his foreword to the article, Morley observed: "This is not the sort of thing one wishes to mar with clumsy comment." By the time the Emporia editor died, "Mary

White" had grown in fame and circulation. It was reprinted in countless high school and college textbooks, and it was widely used on radio programs. Letters still poured into the *Gazette* office year after year asking for reprints. "Probably if her father has any sort of lasting fame beyond the decade following his death," he wrote in 1937, "it will come from this editorial. I shall go as far as I go, which very likely is only a little distance, along the path where Mary's hand may lead me. That also is enough fame for me."

For months following Mary's death, the Emporia editor was busy answering all the letters that had poured onto his desk. The most expressive and the most revealing of all the letters that he wrote was one to his old El Dorado playmate, Kate Redden Smith: "Mrs. White and I have none but joyous memories of Mary. She gave out humor and sunshine as beaten steel gives out sparks, and all of our recollections of her are merry ones. It is hard to think of her without smiling, and the shadow of her face across our hearts brings laughter. We are not deceiving ourselves about the blow. It was a terrible stroke and we are infinitely lonely. But we are not shaking the bars of this finite cage and asking unanswerable questions of fate. We know only that we do not know, and that it is all mysterious. Yet because our most uncommon lot of happiness for twenty-seven years has by this cruel circumstance been made the common lot, we are not dubious of the goodness of God and the decency of man. Mary is a net gain. To have had her seventeen years, joyous and rollicking and wise, and so tremendously human in her weaknesses and in her strength, is blessing enough for any parents, and we have no right to ask for more."

Five years after Mary's death, the Wellesley College class that she would have graduated with dedicated their class annual to her memory. Mary's high school, within a month of her death, set aside a room to serve as a rest room for colored girls in memory of Mary's struggle for such accommodations. Mrs. White furnished the room and had it done over at regular intervals. In 1926 the Whites gave the city of Emporia a park as a memorial to their daughter. Quietly over the years they had bought up fifty acres of land, and then suddenly they offered it to the city as a gift on the following terms:

First, that it shall always be used as a park, and that the park shall not be commercialized.

Second, that the name of White shall never be used in connection with the park.

Third, that we be allowed for five years to spend as much as we can afford, of our own money, probably something like a thousand a year in improving the park and bringing it up to a plan submitted by Hare & Hare, landscape artists of Kansas City.

Although the park was a memorial to Mary, it never carried her name. It has always been known as Peter Pan Park.

Mary's death left an indelible mark on the Whites' life. It was months before Mrs. White recovered from the shock, and for years afterwards she could not mention Mary's name without tears coming into her eyes. Throughout the years she kept Mary's room almost as Mary had left it. Mary's father, although less visibly affected than her mother, revealed in many ways the depth of the tragedy to him. In 1941, for instance, when Bill brought an orphan back from bombed London, all White's remarks about the little girl were in terms of comparisons with Mary. That same year Mrs. Grace Moore, an Emporia neighbor, took a widow with three children to see the *Gazette* editor. The widow had been unable to secure local relief. White looked at her and said, "You are about the age of my Mary, thirty-seven, aren't you?" She nodded, and he said, "I just robbed a man of a ten-dollar check; here you take it." He then called the proper authorities and had her placed on the relief rolls. During the two years before Mary's death, her father had been writing *A Friend's Chronicle*, a description of his relations with Theodore Roosevelt. While he was writing the book, Mary was in and out of his spacious study a great deal. He talked the book over with her many times. After she died, her father was never able to complete the manuscript.

Something of his deep sorrow he revealed in a letter to Mrs. White a year after the tragedy: "Bill is going to the dance at the Country Club tomorrow night. How my heart aches for her! She would be just coming into all that!! I miss her so."

* * *

A few months after Mary's death, *Judge*, a weekly humor magazine, invited White to conduct its editorial page. The owners of *Judge* also operated *Leslie's*, a serious weekly magazine. At first they urged White to write the editorials for *Leslie's*, but he preferred the humor magazine. "I doubt if the *Leslie* work would suit you or me," he wrote them on October 27, 1921. "I am eager to do the *Judge* thing because it will get me out of political discussion into a rather festive and hilarious discussion of life, society, and manners touching politics only satirically and lightly. That I could not do in signed articles for Leslie. I would have to be a Godsaker and a hell roaring progressive. I have those moods but they come on me rarer and rarer, and I am trying to get away from them."

Weekly, from December, 1921, to August, 1922, White wrote from fifteen hundred to two thousand words for *Judge*'s editorial page. *Judge* welcomed White to its pages by declaring: "Good news, folks! *good news*—William Allen White every week in Judge! Didn't we tell you—good news? Yes, every week he's going to write the Editorials. Not seriously, oh, no! Not on your *Judge*."

Although White had the knack of expressing himself in crisp earthy vernacular, he also was cosmopolitan enough to fit into the urbane humor of *Judge*. He demonstrated through these editorials that he could play the role of the smooth sophisticated New Yorker just as well as the more simple role of the country editor. His *Judge* editorials encompassed a vast range of subjects. The opening issue, for instance, discussed Woodrow Wilson, Tammany Hall, and the new federal tax bill.

Trying to be humorous all the time in his editorials must have been a severe chore. When he resigned his *Judge* position, one newspaper observed wisely: "In attempting to reason constantly in an ironical vein, Mr. White has been inclined to invert much of his sound philosophy for purely rhetorical purposes. It is not always possible to turn every serious topic into a joke and it is not always wise to treat humorously problems that merit sober political consideration. There is a tendency in publications of the *Judge* type to surround every subject treated with a background of persiflage. . . . William Allen White is not at home in that atmosphere."

A few months after he undertook this work, he found himself in conflict with *Judge* over the issue of prohibition. In a letter to White in June, 1922, the editor of *Judge* wrote that he wanted to favor light wines and beer. "For heaven's sake don't make that blunder," White advised him. ". . . There is no more hope for light wines and beer than there is for the return of the benevolent slaveholder . . . I should not feel comfortable working for a paper that advocated light wines and beer, unless I have the absolute freedom to make fun of the movement."

Shortly after this letter, White sent *Judge* an editorial charging that the brewers had been responsible for all the evils of the old saloon. "There is just one reason why there will never be light wines and beers in this country," White declared, "and that is because the brewers, when they had a chance, defied decent people all over the Middle West by making their saloons as crooked, as nasty and as wicked as they could be. The saloons were brewers' saloons, and it was the brewers' influence which made the saloons so intolerable that they never will come back; not even with light wines and beer."

Judge objected to printing this editorial. Douglas H. Cooke, *Judge's* vice-president, doubted that they could prove that the brewers were solely responsible for the saloons. Furthermore, prohibition as it was being practiced was hardly a benefit to the country. Cooke had powerful evidence to support this statement. Violations of the Eighteenth Amendment were on the increase. Gangsters were organizing powerful bootlegger rings to violate the law, and were using their rich profits in bribing politicians and police officers not to enforce prohibition. Instead of abolishing liquor, all that prohibition was accomplishing was the substitution of poor and often poisoned liquor for good liquor. As Bourke Cockran of New York told the Democratic convention in 1920, when he opposed William Jennings Bryan's advocacy of prohibition: "These ladies and gentlemen speak as if the use of liquor had been abolished by this amendment. It has not, but there is this difference: that formerly where the average drunkard was jolly, now he is paralyzed."

White allowed *Judge* to kill his editorial on the brewers. In July, however, Douglas Cooke told him that they had better end their arrangement. Cooke pointed out the insuperable difficulties arising from the fact that their editorial page was conducted from Emporia. The distance made it impossible to hold personal conferences in order to harmonize differences of opinion between White and the editors of *Judge*. White and *Judge* parted the best of friends. White's last editorial stated:

IN WHICH WE SAY GOOD-BYE

With this issue of *Judge* the editorial page passes from the writer whose name has been at the head of these columns for over eight months. When I took the job I knew what every good newspaper man knows, that a mailorder editor is bound to fail. Editing a paper or magazine is like loving a wife; one has to be on or near the spot to be successful. And as one wife is all a man can love successfully at one time, so one newspaper is about all a man can edit at one time. Long distance editing is impossible. Every week matters of policy come up which require conference and when the paper is published in New York and the editor lives fifteen hundred miles from New York, conference must be eliminated. And with conference eliminated, unhappy results are inevitable. It so happens that the other and responsible editors of *Judge* believe that "Life, Liberty and the Pursuit of Happiness" are curtailed by the lack of light lines and beer in our national life. I have grown up in a state where wines and beers are as unimportant in the social scheme of things as catsup and brown gravy—good enough condiments in their way but insignificant and not highly interesting. Doubtless the other editors of *Judge* could outtalk me if I were in New York for conference. But as I live out in prohibition Kansas, they can't do it. Either they would have to get along with a rabid, fanatical prohibitionist or I would have to take light wines and beer. And as I would not come to New York and they could not publish *Judge* in Emporia, they get their light wines and beer and with it goes my most hearty good wishes for their long lives, their unfettered liberty and their successful pursuit of happiness. It has been a joyous adventure editing *Judge* at long range. But it has lacked coherence and wisdom because they cannot be transmitted by mail or wire. They are born of intimacy, of daily communion and of loving attention. And so because a newspaper is so much like a home, the absentee must sacrifice his love for it, for its prosperity. But he goes with kindly memories and high hopes that his going may profit the work he has deserted.

White's resignation attracted widespread newspaper comment. He explained to inquiring reporters that he could not remain on a paper that advocated things he did not believe in. To the editors of *Judge* he jokingly observed that his resignation had attracted enough free publicity for *Judge* to compensate for his salary.

The loss of the *Judge* income was not a serious problem to White, since in May, 1922, he had started to write a weekly feature for the Sunday New York *Tribune*. White's feature "As I See It" brought him $15,000 a year plus fifty per cent of the gross return on syndicate sales. As the *Tribune* explained to him, what they desired was "a once-a-week series on any subject in the news that you may elect to handle in the half-humorous, half-satirical style for which you are famous. It may be anything from politics to the fad for bobbed hair." White described the offer to his son Bill at Harvard, adding proudly, "I want you to know the old man is not such a dead one yet."

"As I See It" ran in the *Tribune* for about a year. In the column, White treated as wide a variety of topics as he did in his *Gazette* editorials: prohibition, love, politics, food, the farm problem, free speech, H. L. Mencken, the Ku Klux Klan, and occasional books. White soon tired, however, of meeting a weekly deadline. Years later various syndicates tried to induce him again to write a nation-wide column. When Will Rogers died, White was offered ten thousand dollars and a commission to take Rogers's place. But he steadfastly turned down all such offers. "I do not well see how I can get into the regular syndicated story business," he wrote Frank Knox of the Chicago *Daily News* on July 3, 1934. "Whatever I do worth a tinker's dam is spontaneous. The minute I sign a contract I lose my spontaneity, which is the chief wellspring of my writing." When George Matthew Adams urged him to syndicate a daily editorial, White refused this offer too. "I am sure," he explained to Adams, "that if my stuff was syndicated I would begin to strut and soon I would be no better than the other self-conscious, preening peacocks and profound pundits who are tied to a daily column."

*   *   *

At the time when his resignation from *Judge* was being contemplated, White was plunged into one of the most dramatic struggles of his career. Governor Henry J. Allen and he came into conflict over the labor situation near the close of Allen's second term. Before this dissension, White had had a high opinion of Allen's administration. He had been impressed with Allen's work, despite the spirit of apathy and reaction that was dominating Kansas. "You have pulled a dead weight ahead, and done it well," he told the governor on October 15, 1921. "And if sometimes you get to using the terminology of the capitalists and the moss-back I do not blame you, because the good Lord knows if I had to wrestle as you have wrestled with the crazy radicals on one hand and the conniving employers on the other hand—both stinkers—I would probably use even a lower terminology than you have used."

The great wave of strikes that hit America in 1919 led Kansas, early in 1920, to pass a law substituting compulsory arbitration for industrial warfare. Organized labor was not well entrenched in Kansas, a predominantly rural state with no large urban center, except in the coal regions in the southeast. A severe strike there late in 1919 precipitated the creation of the Kansas Industrial Court. Governor Allen eagerly seized upon compulsory arbitration as a means of preventing strikes in key industries. At Allen's request, White's fellow townsman and political standpat opponent, W. L. Huggins, helped draft the bill creating the industrial court.

When the state legislature conducted hearings on the proposed bill, many labor leaders opposed the law as an attempt on the part of capital to shackle labor and kill all unions. White appeared before the legislature as a man representing the public interest, and advocated the passage of the law. White was interested not in breaking unions, as were some of the supporters of the bill, but in securing industrial peace. He declared: "When labor and capital engage in a brawl which threatens daily processes of civilization, we are taking away the right to that brawl and saying the quarrel must be settled in the public interest . . . We are not trying to throttle capital and labor in Kansas, but to emancipate them from their own strangle hold upon each other and to establish an equitable and living relation between them." When the industrial court was set up, Allen offered White an appointment as one of the three judges, but White did not accept.

After the Industrial Court had been in operation for a year and a half, White wrote: "The industrial court holds no hope for capital except an orderly process of progressive surrender to a continually enlightened labor force, taking a larger and larger share of the profits and a wider and wider control as the years file by, in the management of the 'back room.' The Court will be a fair umpire; it will keep down disorder. But it will not check labor in its inevitable forward movement." White feared, however, that the employer group would wreck the law before it had a fair trial. This fear led him to warn Allen that the employers' associations were more of a danger to decent society in Kansas than were the radicals.

On July 1, 1922, a nation-wide strike of railroad shopworkers occurred after the Railroad Labor Board had slashed wages. Since this strike involved interstate commerce, the Kansas phase of it was outside the jurisdiction of the Kansas Industrial Court. Governor Allen, however, issued an order based on the Industrial Court Act prohibiting the strikers from picketing. But under the federal law governing railroad problems, the workers had the right to strike and to picket. Governor Allen's action thus put the state of Kansas clearly on the side of the employers as a powerful antilabor force.

White believed that Allen had no right to interfere in a nation-wide strike. If the court tried to arbitrate the case, their decision could have no effect on the nation-wide settlement. As a result, the only effect of applying the law was to hamper the strikers. On August 22, 1922, White told a friend: "I think the trouble with the industrial court law is that Henry has an obsession that he wants to crush organized labor with it." Just before the strike took place, White asserted that the railroad workers had cause for complaint. They had been promised a living wage, but now the

Railroad Labor Board had violated this promise by the wage cut. In case a strike occurred, the public should remember that the workers had a legitimate cause for action.

Nine days after the strike had been called, White observed: "The Gazette feels that the men have a just grievance, and that they have been badly treated. They feel that they could do nothing but strike. While it was surely unwise to strike now, yet the right to strike is inalienable until the law guarantees that the railroad industry shall pay a living wage." Immediately Allen wrote him warning that certain strikers had "murder in their hearts," and that he should not support them too wholeheartedly.

"You say those men have murder in their hearts," White replied on July 11, 1922. "They didn't have murder in their hearts last week, but, on the other hand, they are ten days further from their jobs than they were then, and that contributes to their emotions and then to see troops rattling around with guns and equipment doesn't tend to make the men any sweeter. . . . If you and I felt the question of food for our children and felt justified in the strike—and they sure do feel justified—we might tip over a few cars and burn them and snipe at a few scabs. . . . I verily believe that if I were one of those men, I'd do all the devilment they're going to do when they begin, and they'll soon begin."

This letter elicited a long reply from Allen in defense of the use of state troops against the strikers. "If all labor sympathizers were like you," Allen told his old friend, "I wouldn't send any troops anywhere, because you would not be dangerous as a member of a mob. Your humanity would keep you from hurting anybody. You are only dangerous at a time like this when given a double action typewriter and the ability to play upon the same according to your emotions." Allen then candidly explained to White that he was really two people. "You have two sides to your nature—one the emotional side out of which you write at a time like this, and the other your hardheaded business sense out of which you do a mighty good job of carrying on business. . . . Emotion at a time like this is the spark that sets off the dynamite and I am pleading with you to get hardheaded because there is dynamite at Emporia. I write none of this in anger, but all of it in love and in confidence."

Actually, when White followed only his hardheaded business sense, he was a rather dull and mediocre individual. It was when he rose above this narrow setting, such as in a great emotional crisis like the death of Mary, or the progressive revolt, or this labor dispute, that he achieved distinction as a wise philosopher and keen interpreter of life.

The day after Allen's letter was written, White again stated on his editorial page that, although the strike was not wise, nevertheless the strikers were not dangerous radicals. Since the strikers were not permitted to picket, they printed posters reading: "We Are For The Striking Railroad Men 100 Per Cent. We Are For A Living Wage and Fair Working Conditions." Friendly merchants were asking to display these posters in their store windows. The attorney general held that this was just another form of picketing, and Governor Allen ordered all posters removed.

On July 19, White denounced Allen's order as an "infamous infraction of the right of free press and free speech. Certainly it has not come to such a pass in this country that a man may not say what he thinks about an industrial controversy without disobeying the law." White then placed the poster in the *Gazette* window, explaining: "Instead of 100 per cent, we have started it at 49 per cent. If the strike lasts until tomorrow we shall change the per cent to 50, and move it up a little every day. As a matter of fact, the Gazette does not believe that anyone—not even the Gazette— is 100 per cent right. But somewhere between 49 and 100 per cent the men are right. . . . If the Industrial Court desires to make a test case, here it is," White challenged. ". . . Either we have free speech and a free press in this country, or we have not. Now is the time to find out."

Judge McDermott of the industrial court denounced White's action, and Governor Allen stated that neither free speech nor liberty of the press was involved. White was free, said Allen, to discuss the strike in his paper, but he had violated the antipicketing law when he hung up the poster in the *Gazette* window. White continued to maintain that it was a question of free speech, and he refused to remove the poster. He told Albert Beveridge: "I felt that I should defy their demand to take it down in order to test the question whether or not in a state wherein no martial law had been declared, where not a gun has been fired, and where there has been no bloodshed, the utterance of any opinion about a strike temperately made and issued in an orderly manner, is not a citizen's right."

White's adamant stand prompted a sarcastic editorial in *The New York Times* on July 24: "The dearest friend of Man and Henry Allen, the Emporia darling of the Kansas and the human race, Mr. William Allen White, poet, novelist, sociologist, journalist, traveler, as well as a pin-prick in the solid sunflower heart, sits happy in his thought-boudoir, longing for the touch of a policeman's hand." The *Times* expressed surprise that White had advocated just 49 per cent sympathy since Kansans usually did things 100, 150, or 150,000 per cent. "He isn't a true Kansan," the *Times* taunted. "He has been cosmopolitanized and corrupted. . . . Not by compromise did Kansas make herself feared among the nations. Has the epicurean-stoic-pragmatist philosopher of Potato Hill [Ed Howe] darkened Emporia?"

When White refused to remove the poster, the governor reluctantly had a warrant sworn out for the arrest of his beloved friend, charging him with violating the antipicketing law and conspiring with the strikers to stop the trains. White received a tip on July 22 from Topeka that an officer was on his way from the state capital to serve the warrant. White then had his managing editor, Cal Lambert, take him for an hour's drive in the country; he explained that he did not want to be arrested early in the afternoon, since it was better to have the story break in the morning newspapers where it would have a greater circulation. When it was too late for the afternoon papers to cover the story, White had Lambert drive him back to the office to be arrested.

After his arrest, White ordered the poster taken down and asked the strikers to remove any others that they had on display in Emporia and to keep them down until the courts rendered a decision on his case. Praising Allen's brave and patriotic administration of the law, White declared: "The Gazette does not agree with him in the action which seems to suppress the fundamental right of free speech. . . . But the difference in opinion about the wisdom of suppressing the fundamental right of American citizenship while the courts are trying to get at the truth and the right, should not prevent the Gazette nor all good citizens from upholding his hands and giving him the earnest support which loyalty requires." White urged the strikers not to resort to force while the case was pending. "Force will win nothing," he advised them. "But the rights of free utterance through speech and a free press are fundamental." Although the governor held that White had broken a law, he announced: "The friendship of all these years cannot be broken by the differences in our opinion as to what constitutes a violation of the law."

Three days after White's arrest, Allen spoke at the "Governor's Day" celebration at the Emporia State Teachers College. When White introduced Allen to the student body, political enemies of the two men thought their dispute was a mere publicity-seeking scheme. Actually the two men differed fundamentally, but they refused to destroy their friendship over the issue. White wrote to Mrs. Allen:

. . . I believed deeply that it was wrong to forbid the posters and I knew that so long as Henry was my friend and everyone knew it, my protest would not be misunderstood; that is, no one would say I was protesting to embarrass a political foe. . . . I feel that I owe more to Henry than to any other man in the world. I could not pay—indeed I never can for all he has meant to me—but I can pay him less if I am less a man. If I had refrained from acting out of deference to Henry I would not have been worthy of all he has meant to me. If he had not acted as he did from first to last—a fine brave manly part—he would have been unworthy of the faith I have in him. The deepest friendship makes the firmest and fondest faith, not the closest agreement.

White's arrest attracted widespread newspaper and magazine comment. Outside of Kansas the press was overwhelmingly sympathetic to Editor White, but in Kansas he was subjected to severe attacks by property-minded journalists. The Lawrence *Journal-World* observed that White claimed he was upholding both the industrial court and the strike. "Nobody else," stated the *Journal-World*, "could be both for and against strikes and get away with it, but fortunately the Emporia editor has no very solid reputation for consistency that he must uphold." The Manhattan *Mercury* charged that "By his action, done because of the impulses of his great heart, Mr. White has encouraged the present tendency toward lawlessness," while the Abilene *Reflector* said, "It may be a lot of fun—but this is no time to rock the boat." To his support, however, came the Concordia *Blade-Empire*, the Independence *Free-Press*, and the Hutchinson *Gazette*. "To an unbiased mind, it must seem conclusive that White's stand is a laudible one," observed the Concordia *Blade-Empire*.

When the chorus of abuse continued in the Kansas press, particularly attacks in the Kansas City *Kansan*, which declared that he ought to be "hung, drawn and quartered," White sat down and wrote an editorial on July 27 entitled "To an Anxious Friend":

You tell me that law is above freedom of utterance. And I reply that you can have no wise laws nor free enforcement of wise laws unless there is free expression of the wisdom of the people—and, alas, their folly with it. But if there is freedom, folly will die of its own poison, and the wisdom will survive. That is the history of the race. It is the proof of man's kinship with God. You say that freedom of utterance is not for time of stress, and I reply with the sad truth that only in time of stress is freedom of utterance in danger. No one questions it in calm days, because it is not needed. And the reverse is true also; only when free utterance is suppressed is it needed, and when it is needed, it is most vital to justice. Peace is good. But if you are interested in peace through force and without free discussion, that is to say, free utterance decently and in order—your interest in justice is slight. And peace without justice is tyranny, no matter how you may sugar coat it with expediency. This state today is in more danger from suppression than from violence, because in the end, suppression leads to violence. Violence, indeed, is the child of suppression. Whoever pleads for justice helps to keep the peace; and whoever tramples upon the plea for justice, temperately made in the name of peace, only outrages peace and kills something fine in the heart of man which God put there when we got our manhood. When that is killed, brute meets brute on each side of the line.

So, dear friend, put fear out of your heart. This nation will survive, this state will prosper, the orderly business of life will go forward if only men can speak in whatever way given them to utter what their hearts hold—by voice, by posted card, by letter or by press. Reason never has failed men. Only force and repression have made the wrecks in the world.

The clarity and vision of this editorial won its author increased fame and prestige. The New York *World* reprinted it and called it "a model of kindly and devastating criticism." Franklin P. Adams declared in his column, in the same paper, that it should win the Pulitzer prize as the best editorial of the year. Other papers and magazines reprinted "To an Anxious Friend" and were as fulsome in their praise. The following May, White was awarded the Pulitzer prize because the editorial "excelled in clearness of style, sound reasoning and in its power to influence opinion in the right direction." Commenting on the award, the New York *World* wrote: "In the profession and to hosts of readers the high light of the year is the prize given to William Allen White. . . . In this famous, often-quoted editorial Mr. White made clear his title as one in the long line of courageous journalists who have championed freedom for their profession in the cause of the common good."

Within a few days of his arrest, White had offers of legal aid from such top-flight lawyers as Felix Frankfurter, W. G. McAdoo, W. E. Borah, and A. J. Beveridge. Although White was prepared to carry the case to the United States Supreme Court, the governor and the attorney general finally dropped the case and never brought the Emporia editor to trial. Later, when White heard rumors in November that the case was to be dropped, he vehemently protested to Allen, and then enlisted the support of some newspaper friends to tell Allen that it must come to trial. "I get so many letters from people abusing me for a 'frame-up,' who think we have done wrong in remaining on friendly relations after the arrest," he wrote Allen on November 28, 1922. "I believe that a regular legal adjudication is the necessary outcome for us both. A dismissal would give too much color to the frame-up theory."

Attorney General Richard J. Hopkins, who had originally opposed White's arrest, did not want to try the case. When the case came up in the district court on December 8, Hopkins and Allen were both out of the state. Hopkins's representative had the case dismissed over White's protests. The presiding judge, W. C. Harris, rebuked the state and declared: "The court is forced to the conclusion . . . by the conduct of the moving party, that this case was commenced maliciously, or recklessly, without investigation of the facts to ascertain whether a prosecution was justified, and in either event the action taken was equally reprehensible."

Although White held to his friendship with Allen, he was offended at Allen's dropping the case. "I was never so deeply hurt in all my career in politics as I was by his ruthless behavior at that time," he wrote Rodney Elward ten years later. Three years after this White-Allen incident, the Industrial Court became dormant. White's arrest cost the Court prestige, but more fundamental causes brought its downfall. Political interference with the court's work, Governor Allen's impetuous nature, the increasing anti-union bias of the court in preventing picketing but ignoring the employer violations of the law, and two adverse decisions from the United States Supreme Court ultimately wrecked the court.

* * *

"The early twenties," Senator George Norris once wrote, "brought the American people to their knees in worship at the shrine of private business and industry. . . . Great wealth took possession of the government. It was reflected in Mr. Harding's selection of a cabinet. It characterized all political utterances. The stock phrase 'less government in business, and more business in government' was, I recognize, a natural reaction against the necessary regimentation of people in wartime. But it brought into the places of high responsibility men who could not be expected to have a farsighted view of public service. . . . Reaction rushed eagerly forward to exploit its triumph to the fullest."

President Harding, whose political advancement had been the result of the work of Ohio bosses, took these politicians into the national government with him. Their leader, Harry M. Daugherty, was made attorney general. Harding's brother-in-law was awarded the post of superintendent of prisons, and a home-town lawyer was made comptroller of the currency. Harding's loyalty was not directed toward the best tradition of American democracy, but toward the bosses in his party and particularly toward the Ohio gang. Harding had no sense of technical fitness for technical jobs.

His inability to cope with the major problems of his day is revealed in a story that William Allen White wrote about him after his death. Harding remarked to his secretary over the question of tax reform: "John, I can't make a damn thing out of this tax problem. I listen to one side and they seem right, and then—God!— I talk to the other side and they seem just as right, and here I am where I started. I know somewhere there is a book that will give me the truth, but, hell, I couldn't read the book. I know somewhere there is an economist who knows the truth, and I don't know where to find him and haven't the sense to know him and trust him when I find him. God, what a job!"

White found himself in a peculiar position during Harding's presidency. He still insisted that he himself was a progressive. "I am a progressive," he wrote, "because I believe in the continuous orderly growth of human institutions; that the world is not bundled up for immediate delivery into the millennium; and that only as we give of our lives in the effort to replace human wrongs by human rights do our institutions grow." From time to time he visited Harding, and was impressed, he later wrote, by "his sincerity, his evident desire to rise above his political background. . . . I found him warmhearted and sincere. I don't know how brave he was. I know that he lacked academic and intellectual background."

White wanted to have influence with President Harding. He wanted to be close to the White House just as he had been in Theodore Roosevelt's day. Occasionally, however, he could not hold back criticism of Harding's actions. He objected to the cabinet appointments of Daugherty, and of Albert Fall as secretary of the interior. But soon after criticizing, he would again praise Harding. On August 8, 1921, he wrote an editorial filled with eulogies and sent it to the President with these words: "You are really doing a man's job, in a man's way, and I am tremendously proud to be an American citizen under your administration." Harding naturally was pleased with the editorial and flatteringly wrote White: "I have enjoyed reading it. . . . I am saying these pleasant things so that I may follow with the admonition that though the administration hungers for your support it never wants you to approve of anything that does not appeal to the Kansas conscience and the convictions of a busy and famous editor. It is all right to talk about taking the 'surge' out of your 'insurgency,' but I would not have you put aside your chief attraction for the world."

At the end of five months of Harding's administration, White told one person: "I have been thoroughly and happily surprised at the way the President is handling himself and fitting the situation. I believe he will make one of our great presidents." On March 4, 1922, *Collier's* published an article by White called "The Best Minds, Incorporated." Years later, when Samuel Hopkins Adams wrote the story of these years in *The Incredible Era*, he was amazed and startled at White's praise of Harding in this *Collier's* article.

According to White, Harding had gathered the best minds in America around the White House. "He plays no favorites," declared White. "Even his social friends have no political influence with him." "Daugherty, being an old Ohio crony, is supposed to have great power," White explained. "But probably when he got into the cabinet his power was considerably discounted." Placing himself out on a limb beyond recall, White observed that Harding was "doing a better than fair job." How badly White was fooled by Harding, or wanted to be fooled, was soon to be revealed by investigations of the corruption perpetrated by Harding's friends in the Ohio gang.

Actually White in his heart knew that Harding was beyond his depth in the presidency. In the middle of the great railroad strike in 1922, White declared that Harding was not the man to deal with labor problems. Employer-employee relationships required a statesmanlike vision which Harding did not have. "The whirlpool is ahead," White told his readers on August 1, 1922. "Someone must run the boat. Someone must lend a guiding hand and a directing brain to this country or America will feel the shock that is rocking the world. . . . President Harding is the head of our organized American civilization. Enough moral power lies in the presidential office to give him all the weapons he needs to restore orderly commerce and just relations among workers and employers . . . he must decide to turn back to abnormalcy and lead the people as their ruler."

After visiting Harding in the fall of 1922, White hailed the President as a gentle, sincere, fair-minded man, with courage. White denied that Harding was a tool for big business. But a month after this editorial, White felt called upon to attack Harding's attorney general for being antilabor and on the side of the employer group. The Emporia editor was having a difficult time reconciling his own ideals and his desire for influence with the President. When a *Gazette* reader assailed White for approving of Harding on one day and the next day jeering at him, White replied: "In a general way the Gazette is Republican; but if the Republican party gets in what seems to be a wrong position, the best duty of a good Republican is to call attention to what seems a wrong position. If a man is right today and wrong tomorrow, say so frankly in each case without malice, and yet heartily. A Newspaper has one obligation and one only, to print the truth as far as it is humanly possible, and to comment upon the truth as candidly and as kindly as is humanly possible, never forgetting to be merry the while, for after all the liar and the cheat and the panderer are smaller offenders than the solemn ass."

Just before the Whites left for a Mediterranean cruise with the Victor Murdocks in February, 1923, White declared in the *Gazette* that the Harding administration was "sweetly progressive." Cabinet members like Secretary Albert Fall, he declared, had a negligible influence on the President. Although White admitted in his correspondence that Harding was not so progressive as he desired, nevertheless Harding was "about one hundred per cent more progressive than the crowd that nominated him."

In Washington, by the spring of 1923, rumors were current of major scandals within the administration. The head of the Alien Property Custodian's office was suspected of stealing large sums of money. The attorney general's office, referred to as the "department of easy virtue" by Senator Ashurst, reached its lowest ebb in morale and morals under Daugherty. A Senate committee was later to find Daugherty guilty of illegally selling liquor permits and pardons. Whispers were also current about the sudden prosperity of Secretary Fall. It was later revealed that Fall had secretly leased to the Doheny and Sinclair oil interests valuable government oil reserves, and in return had received large sums of money.

Harding personally seems to have been innocent of participating in the orgy of corruption. But early in 1923 he had become aware of its existence, and of what it would mean to his reputation. In June, 1923, the President left Washington for a trip to Alaska. At the President's request, White spent some time with him at a Kansas City hotel. White noticed that Harding's "lips were swollen and blue, his eyes puffed, and that his hands seemed stiff when I shook hands with him." Shortly after White's arrival, Mrs. Albert Fall was suddenly ushered in and closeted alone with the President for an hour. When Harding emerged from this interview, Senator Arthur Capper, who was present, has reported that Harding was puzzled, distraught, and worried. What Mrs. Fall told Harding has never been revealed, but it may have been Harding's first warning that the corruption of Secretary Fall was about to be exposed.

The following day, as Harding was riding across Kansas with White, he told the Emporia editor: "In this job I am not worried about my enemies. I can take care of them. It is my friends who are giving me trouble." On this western trip, Harding's health broke. He died in San Francisco on August 2. Weeks before Harding died, W. L. White, working on the *Gazette* during his summer vacation from Harvard, wrote an editorial about Vice-President Coolidge, referring to him as "the little runt of a man" who "quacks when he talks." The editorial was filed to be used when copy was needed. As fate would have it, the night before Harding died, the editorial appeared. Immediately letters poured into Emporia denouncing this as an attack on the new President of the United States. "I have been around the newspaper office all my life, and one thing I know, the one place where deadly dynamite lies is always on the standing galley for the editorial page," White later confided to George W. Marble of the Fort Scott *Tribune*.

Three years after Harding's death, Brand Whitlock suggested to White that he should write a book about the dead President. By this time, White had regained his perspective on Harding. He told Whitlock:

You know I would give anything to do it. It has fairly tantalized me for a year and a half. It isn't Harding's story; it is the story of his times, the story of the Prodigal Son, our democracy that turned away from the things of the spirit, got its share of the patrimony ruthlessly and went out and lived riotously and ended it by feeding among the swine. God what a story! The story of Babylon is a Sunday School story compared with the story of Washington from June 1919 until July 1923, and so far as that goes, considerably later. We haven't even yet got back to our Father's house. He can't see us even from afar off. It's invisible. And the whole thing is epitomized by the rise of Harding. If ever there was a man who was a he-harlot, it was this same Warren G. Harding.

When Nan Britton, Harding's mistress, published her confessions in *The President's Daughter*, White wrote to Henry J. Allen: "I note that you report that Long believes that the Harding story puts 'Harding in the class of the early English Kings.' Possibly. My view of the face cards would be it puts him in the class of the late English Jacks."

CHAPTER 17

A KANSAN IN BABYLON

"I WANT to be governor to free Kansas from the disgrace of the Ku Klux Klan," the Emporia editor declared on September 20, 1924. ". . . The thought that Kansas should have a government beholden to this hooded gang of masked fanatics, ignorant and tyrannical in their ruthless oppression, is what calls me out of the pleasant ways of my life into this distasteful but necessary task." From the day in 1921 when the first Klan organizer arrived in Emporia, the *Gazette* mercilessly exposed Klan activities. Referring to the "kluxers" as "moral idiots," White had been forthright in declaring that "to make a case against a birthplace, a religion, or a race is wicked, un-American, and cowardly."

Whenever the *Gazette* discovered the names of Klan members, it ceremoniously printed them. However, in spite of White's vigorous assaults, a Klan member was elected mayor of Emporia. White did not realize that in many ways the Klan was in the American tradition, although it was, to be sure, undemocratic. It was the spiritual descendant of such antiforeign movements as the American party of the 1850's and the American Protective Association of the 1890's. The official Klan publications reflected the average middle-class mind in its assertions of "one hundred per cent Americanism," and in its exclusion of Jews, Catholics, Negroes, and immigrants from membership.

The Klan was essentially a village and small-town organization. Although White rose above the provincialism of the small-town

America that nurtured the Klan, it flourished in the very communities that he always contended were the backbone of American democracy. The Klan, with its mysterious signs, its queer names, and its fantastic costumes offered relief from the drabness of small-town life. Its cheap moral idealism filled a need not met by the business, social, or civic life of main-street America. White did not need this relief from the intellectual starvation of Emporia, since he was away from the town a great deal, but many of his neighbors sought their escape in the mumbo jumbo of the Klan.

The police office of Emporia was so thoroughly dominated by the Klan for a time that the *Gazette* reporters could not secure news items, and Frank Clough, who later became the *Gazette*'s managing editor, has related the incident of being sent to the Broadview Hotel to copy the names of the Klan delegates to a state-wide convention meeting at the hotel. Klansmen tried to take the list away from him, and after a struggle he finally turned it over to the hotel manager. When White heard the story, he sent Clough back to the manager with the following note: "If a copy of the Broadview Hotel register for today is not in our office by seven o'clock this evening, the name of the Broadview never again will be printed in the *Gazette* except in case of police raids and similar events."

An hour before the deadline, the manager delivered the register, and the *Gazette* printed the names of the Klan delegates. The same paper carried an editorial praising the Broadview as a fine hotel. When White handed this editorial to Clough, he said: "Always remember after you spank a child, you should give it a piece of candy. It makes everyone feel better."

White was convinced that the Klan members in Emporia were fourth-rate citizens. He doubted that leaders of town opinion had anything to do with the organization. His opinion was supported by the fact that all over America the Klan was generally the refuge of the mediocre man. The Emporia Klan was backed by a weekly paper edited by Elmer Garner, whose later activities in his Wichita paper were to lead to his indictment on the charge of sedition after the Japanese attack at Pearl Harbor.

On October 5, 1923, White told Charles F. Scott that he was convinced that "The Ku Klux have got to run their course.

They've got to pizen themselves to death; just lie themselves so full of absurd, malicious, and incredible stories that their credulity being gorged will paralyze their suspicion. No arguments you may use, no facts you may present, no logic you may array will in the slightest affect these people. They have no capacity for receiving argument, no minds for retaining or sifting facts and no mental processes that will hold logic. If they had any of these things they wouldn't be Kluxers." Scott replied that he believed that newspaper attacks on the Klan helped to check the movement. "I have no doubt the K.K.K. will die out," he told White, "but I kinda like to aid and expedite the dying process."

During the spring of 1924, White advised a nation-wide audience that the way to kill the Klan was by giving it every chance to disseminate its absurd charges. "If they are met by a kindly tolerance," he declared, "their own intolerance will wither and pale." On September 20, 1924, however, instead of following the path of kindly tolerance, White launched a frontal attack on the Klan by announcing his independent candidacy for governor on an anti-Klan platform.

The Republican primary had resulted in the nomination of Ben S. Paulen, a standpatter, over Clyde Reed, Governor Allen's former secretary, and over former Governor W. R. Stubbs. The Klan issue had been injected into the race, and Paulen was accused of having Klan support. The Kansas City *Times* charged that "the Cyclops, Kleagles, Wizards and Willopses-wallopuses began parading in the Kansas cow pastures, passing the word down to the shirt-tail rangers they were to go into the Kansas primaries and nominate Ben Paulen." Although Reed and Stubbs drew the anti-Klan vote, and their combined vote was greater than Paulen's, Paulen received the nomination. At the subsequent Republican party council, Paulen was named chairman of the committee on resolutions. An anti-Klan plank submitted by Charles B. Griffith, candidate for re-election as attorney general, obtained just one vote in the committee, and Paulen prevented Griffith from bringing a minority report denouncing the Klan before the party council.

The Klan was out to defeat Griffith for re-election since he had tried to prevent it from doing business in Kansas without a state charter. In addition, the Klan wanted to defeat Frank J. Ryan, a Catholic and a candidate for re-election as secretary of state, and Jess W. Miley, candidate for re-election as state superintendent of public instruction. From the actions of Paulen and many of the other leaders of the party, it was obvious to White that they had no intention of antagonizing Klan support of their ticket.

Before the party council convened, White had urged it to denounce the Klan in the platform. Just before the primary election, White warned one Republican that Paulen had the endorsement of the Klan. "If you don't know it," White declared on July 21, 1924, "come to Emporia and I shall show you his picture in the window of every store of a Klansman in the town. Paulen also represents the conservative crowd. . . . It is my business in politics to see that the Progressive crowd has a show for its White House . . . Paulen with the endorsement of the Ku Klux crowd, as governor will be under obligations to them. They are a bad lot."

After Paulen received the Republican nomination, White was inclined to support him, but actually was too involved in completing a biography of Woodrow Wilson to devote much thought to politics. However, when Paulen prevented the anti-Klan resolution from being discussed at the party council, White declared that the time had come for him to put on his war paint and for "this fat little bald-headed fellow from Emporia" to carry the Klan issue to the people. He believed that the Democratic candidate, Governor Jonathan M. Davis, was no better than Paulen. It was true that the Democratic platform contained an anti-Klan resolution, but Davis had made no statement against the Klan.

White tried to get Henry J. Allen or Joseph L. Bristow to run as an independent candidate. On September 2, White wrote a letter to Charles F. Scott of the Iola *Register*, one of the powers behind the standpat wing of the Republican party, observing that Paulen and the Klan needed to be opposed. "If I was dead sure that I wouldn't win I should be glad enough of the fun and to give a lot of fellows who want to vote for a man who is not a klansman a chance to vote," he wrote Scott. ". . . I am willing to agitate, I suppose I am a fairly good agitator, but I also fear for myself as an administrator and the darn thing might run hog wild and elect me."

Scott assured White that he would not be elected, but "I am for all the things you stand for . . . and I wish to goodness somebody would make a fight for them." On the other hand, Scott was convinced that White's candidacy would only split the Republican vote and elect Davis. "So I really think you ought not to run," Scott advised, "though to tell the truth I ain't carin' a lot if you do. The older I grow—and I'll be 64 tomorrow—the more I hate a rabbit. I don't want to be responsible for Paulen's defeat; but if it should happen in spite of me I wouldn't grieve a lot."

White quickly told Scott that he agreed entirely with the letter, but he was still not sure what to do. To test sentiment toward his possible candidacy, White wrote many other letters. One letter, which he received from a Jewish merchant, stirred him deeply. The merchant stated that the Klan was boycotting his store, that his wife was being snubbed socially, and that his children were being mistreated at school. In order to verify the story, White wrote to his young friend Alf Landon, who lived in the same town, and who confirmed the story. "The thing got me," White later remarked, "and I decided to run."

On September 16, when Edna Ferber invited him to attend the opening of her new play in New York, he wired: "Sorry but I am engaged in putting the lie in the vox populi running as an anti-Klan candidate for Governor." Four days later White wrote in the *Gazette:*

WHITE ANNOUNCES

I have filed my petition for governor and am in this race to win. It is the largest independent petition ever filed for an office in Kansas. Over three times more names were signed to these petitions for Carr Taylor and myself for lieutenant governor and governor than were needed. None of these petitions came from my home town or county. I wished honestly to test sentiment. There can be no doubt about the sentiment. The issue in Kansas this year is the Ku Klux Klan above everything. The Ku Klux Klan is found in nearly every county. It represents a small minority of the citizenship and it is organized for purposes of terror. Its terror is directed at honest, law-abiding citizens, Negroes, Jews and Catholics. These groups in Kansas comprise more than one-fourth of our population. They are entitled to their full constitutional rights; their rights to life, liberty and the pursuit of happiness. They menace no one. They are good citizens, law-abiding, God-fearing, prosperous, patriotic. Yet, because of their skin, their race, or their creed, the Ku Klux Klan in Kansas is subjecting them to economic boycott, to social ostracism, to every form of harassment, annoyance and every terror that a bigoted minority can use. . . .

I want to offer Kansans afraid of the Klan and ashamed of that disgrace, a candidate who shares their fear and shame. So I am in the race to stay and to win. Kansas with her intelligence and pure American blood, of all states should be free of this taint of bigotry and terror. . . .

I call to my support least of all those who are oppressed by the Ku Klux Klan. We must have no class issue here. I call to my support rather all fair-minded citizens of every party, of every creed, to stop the oppression of this minority of our people. It is a nation-wide menace, this klan. It knows no party. It knows no country. It knows only bigotry, malice and terror. Our national government is founded on reason, and the Golden Rule. This klan is preaching and practicing terror and force. Its only prototype is the Soviet of Russia. So I feel that I am walking the path of duty in going into this race. I ask my fellow Kansans to come with me and to stand with me for free government and the righteous guarantees of our constitution, to all its citizens.

White's campaign was nation-wide copy. Always excellent material for reporters, he excelled during his six weeks' tour of Kansas. As soon as the news of his candidacy reached the East, Ernest Gruening wired: "For a generation you have been identified with all that is best and finest in the American tradition . . . but nothing in your long career is as important, essential and far-reaching as your splendid stand." Hamlin Garland told White that he was "a brash adventurer." The New York *World* hailed him as a great American, and the Louisville *Times* said that he was truthfully following in the footsteps of Theodore Roosevelt. "His election," the Syracuse *Post-Standard* observed, "would have a refreshing influence upon American politics." "If the citizens of other states could participate in the Kansas election," the Boston *Post* prophesied, "Mr. White would walk away with the governorship."

The *Christian Science Monitor*, however, felt that he could have found "a more important question in both State and national

politics than the Ku Klux Klan," while the New York Evening
Post announced that the Klan was dying everywhere and that it
did not require a campaign. The Omaha *World-Herald*, fearing
that White's campaign would hurt the Democratic candidate, declared that "Mr. White is just a trifle delirious," while the Omaha
Bee could see "nothing a-tall the matter with Kansas, but there
must be something dreadful the matter with ol' Bill White." *The
New York Times*, which had ridiculed him over the industrial
court fight, sarcastically declared: "Mr. White is grand and peculiar. . . . Slow thinkers may hold that when misguided men
guide the Republican Party into the cow pasture, a well-guided
Republican could afford to vote the Democratic ticket. Mr. White
is not guided. He is guide. He neither knows nor cares where he
comes out."

Within Kansas the situation was embarrassing to White's editor
friends. They all respected White as a lovable personality, although they were confident that he was threatening to upset Republican supremacy without too much justification. This bolt of
White's from party regularity, his previous Bull Moose activities,
and his frequent editorial criticism of standpat Republican leaders
made White a frightening ogre to the party regulars. If he thought
the party was wrong, he would say so. He would not accept party
discipline. As a result, the Kansas Republican leaders were always
fearful of what might appear some peaceful afternoon in the
Gazette. After all, he was a discomforting person to have around.
He could perceive evil. And he could reach the public with his
views!

J. L. Stryker, chairman of the Republican State Committee, declared that White made up the Klan issue; other supporters of
Paulen charged that White was simply seeking publicity, and that
he was irked because the standpat wing dominated Paulen. The
Republican regulars added that White and the Kansas City *Star*
crowd had so dominated the governor's office from the days of
W. R. Stubbs to Henry J. Allen that nothing of importance was
done without their approval. Since White and the *Star* could not
dominate Paulen, they were now out to defeat him. Therefore,
according to Paulen's friends, White was running in order to split
the Republican ranks and to help elect Davis. Even some of

White's friends declared that he would rather have Davis as governor than the reactionary Republican Mulvane machine. White, however, denied that this thought had ever entered his mind.

Yet, a few days before he decided to run, he had written a friend: "I think Davis is no better than Paulen. But that leaves me in a quandary. Generally speaking, I am not above supporting a crook, but if I do support a crook I want him to be a Democratic crook so that my party will not be loaded with the blame of his crookedness. I think that is the best kind of partisanship." The Democrats, meanwhile, charged that White was running to split the progressive vote that ordinarily would go to Davis. When Paulen actually was elected that November, the Democrats declared that White had been responsible, and had run only to help defeat Davis.

Victor Murdock's Wichita *Eagle* was one of the few Kansas papers whose editorials backed the White candidacy. Standpatter Charles F. Scott, too, shook off party regularity, and courageously backed White. The Sabetha *Herald* also threw its support to White and declared on September 24: "White's candidacy comes as a hope for better things, a conviction that at last someone might be chosen to handle affairs with justice for the public." Revealing his political sagacity, White insisted that neither Henry J. Allen nor Clyde Reed support him publicly. There were going to be many more battles for control of the Republican party, and White did not want the political future of these men to be affected by his bolt. "Clyde Reed offered to come out for me the other day, but I wouldn't let him," he told Allen on October 20, 1924. "I have asked him to denounce the Republican State Central Committee, which does not affect his regularity, nor spoil him for a candidacy two years from now."

White received powerful aid from the Kansas City *Star*. Although printed in Missouri, the *Star* blanketed Kansas. The standpat opposition to the *Star* had for years attempted to discredit the *Star*'s influence by charging that it was trying to boss Kansas affairs. In an attempt to demonstrate that White was a "tool" of the "Missouri paper," some Republicans sank to a low level even for Kansas politicians. They concocted a letter that was supposed to have been written by White to Fred Trigg of the *Star:* "This is a rotten job you have wished on me . . . If by any chance I am elected governor, I will have to put a cross on the state house dome, and wire the K.K.K. to keep the niggers away from the state house. Catholics, Jews and niggers are about all the support I have got."

In Protestant areas, White's Republican opponents circulated rumors that he was for parochial schools, and in Catholic areas they said that he was opposed to them. White's Democratic foes circulated a pamphlet composed of extracts from his writings criticizing the Catholic Church. The editor of the Westphalia *Times*, author of the pamphlet, had torn phrases from their context and left the impression that these were White's complete views on the subject. For instance, when White was in Rome in 1909, he had written an article for the *Gazette* in which he had remarked that "the funniest place in the Vatican . . . is the Sistine Chapel—but by day when it is open to the public, not only in the Vatican, but in all Europe. Nothing but the New York Stock Exchange or the Chicago grain pit could be more weirdly ridiculous." This type of remark was incorporated in the article to prove that White was hostile to Catholicism. The *Bourbon News* [Fort Scott] even went so far as to declare that White's articles written from Ireland in 1919 were so anti-Catholic that they had stimulated the founding of the Klan in Kansas.

In spite of the mudslinging, White thoroughly enjoyed his campaign. He had always delighted in personal contacts, and the campaign gave him the opportunity of visiting people in all parts of the state. Also, there was nothing he relished quite so much as a good fight. For six weeks he toured Kansas in the family Dodge with Bill doing the driving and Mrs. White cheering him on. According to one reporter, Mrs. White and Bill after one of his speeches "regarded their crusader with affection, mixed with amusement, a twinkling recognition of that Eternal Boy which makes 'Old Bill' the delight of Emporia and the pride of Kansas." Although *The New York Times* ridiculed the campaign as White's "Solo Jazz performance," it sent Anne O'Hare McCormick to Kansas, and the London *Daily News* also dispatched a reporter to cover the campaign.

"He enchants the crowd because he is eloquent and uproarious in their own speech . . ." Anne O'Hare McCormick reported. "In Kansas marrowy nouns and fruity adjectives are not the treat they are to us of stingier souls. Anywhere else Bill White's vocabulary alone could elect him." It was not campaign oratory, however, that determined the outcome of the election. All White's colorful epithets and newspaper publicity could not overcome the Republican precinct organization whose workers made contact with the individual voters. White's campaign lacked organization. He knew, of course, the value of such a machine from his many years of political experience, but since he did not want to be elected, he did not try to build a precinct organization of his own.

White's total campaign expenses were $474.60. Every Monday morning, he drew $25 from the bank for the week's campaign. While on tour, he relied on his host of friends for bed and board. Even though they might not support him in their papers, his newspaper friends gave him free room and meals and devoted ample news coverage to his campaign. At Ed Howe's house at Atchison, just before White made a speech, he consumed two ducks at dinner and boasted that he was the only man in America of fifty-six who could "carry" that many ducks. Howe's advance notices in the *Globe* on White's speech stated that "old Bill White doesn't want to be elected Governor. He is running for fun, for notoriety, to get newspaper publicity. Attend his meeting tonight; pack the hall . . . give him notoriety, and vote against him. He didn't come here looking for votes, but for cheers. Give them to him tonight."

After White's visit, Howe remarked: "When he was at my house I heard him marvel that he was flying over the country as a candidate for Governor. He is equally strange to me when he flies over the country in newspapers and books, in angel robes." This led *The New York Times* to comment: "So Howe doesn't know White. White doesn't know White. We don't know either." In one speech, when White stated that he was "just a short, fat baldheaded man who has learned much in the last year and will learn a lot more in the next few weeks," the *Times* noted that a positive result of the campaign would be the thinning down of "his soft Campanian contours."

On November 2, the old Dodge pulled up before the White

house on Exchange Street with a tired but happy campaigner. The next day he told his readers that he was in better physical shape than he had been in years. "He is happy to be home, and has no anxiety about tomorrow. His job is done. He has gotten out to the people with the klan issue, kept that issue before them for six weeks, and has removed from scores of small towns the curse of silence which the klan had put upon the issue." And White added that now "He has on his oldest suit of clothes and a flaming red necktie and an old brown hat. This rig is my fiercest protest against six weeks of circumspection, Sunday clothes, punctilious conduct and the public life. The goldfish has flopped out of the aquarium back into the puddle and is having a gay and festive time."

On election night he went home to bed and did not know until the next morning that Paulen had won, that Davis had run second, and that he was third. He polled 149,811 votes to Davis's 182,861, and to Paulen's 323,403. The Emporian was proud of his fight. "The fact that I could get out and spit in the face of the Klan," he told one friend, "and had done it has cleared up the atmosphere." In every one of his speeches, White had asked the people to vote for the anti-Klan candidates on the Republican ticket—Griffith, Miley, and Ryan. These three men were re-elected by slender majorities, and Henry J. Allen told White: "The more I think about your campaign the better I feel about it and without doubt you did save Griffith, Miley, and Ryan. The important thing of course was Griffith and but for the work you did for him he would have been beaten by fifty thousand, possibly sixty thousand."

The re-election of Griffith and Ryan ensured that the majority on the State Charter Board would not issue a charter to the Klan. Even *The New York Times* agreed that White had made the Klan ridiculous through his feat of being at once savage and humorous. White's campaign probably hastened the end of the already dying Klan. After 1924, as middle-class America regained its balance from the wave of aggressive nationalism that had washed in since 1919, the movement rapidly declined.

*   *   *

The day that White filed his nomination for the governorship, he finished checking the proof of his biography of Woodrow Wilson. He had been working intermittently on this book since 1919. When he undertook the task he told Colonel House: "I have had no personal relations with the President and know him but slightly, yet I have felt a deep interest in, and at times an enthusiastic appreciation for, many of the things he had done since he had been in the White House . . . He is a queer, complex of a man. I have never understood him." A considerable share of White's time in 1923 and 1924 was spent in the East and South gathering material on Wilson's background and interviewing Wilson's friends and enemies. For many of the statements that appeared in the book he relied heavily on interviews with men like Joseph Tumulty, Walter Lippmann, and Colonel House. Above all, he depended on his own intuition and knowledge of the Wilson era. As a Bull Mooser, he had been in close contact with the campaign of 1912, his many friends in Washington had kept him in touch with Wilson's domestic program, and he himself had gathered large amounts of material at the Peace Conference.

While in New York in February, 1924, he told a Columbia University student group: "I have been asked whether I would be a candidate for President on the Republican ticket. I am a Republican, but I am writing a book about Woodrow Wilson, which I would rather do than run for President. I would make the world's worst President. I hope I will not be the world's worst biographer." White was not interested in writing a factual history of the Wilson administration. Instead, he wrote a portrait of Wilson, heavily emphasizing the President's personal characteristics. Among the many questions that he asked people about Wilson were:

What was the most human touch he ever gave to you or anyone in your presence . . . ?

Was the President a good feeder? That is, did he know what he was eating? Do you suppose it ever occurred to him to ask what any dish was made of, or did he just accept food as a gift of God and let it go at that? Personally I regard cooking as one of the high arts—one of the last refinements of men's spiritualization. . . .

I have an impression that he liked men of a soft and gentle approach. Why? . . . Did he simply dislike the boredom of a "he" man, and desire the quick, intuitive communication that one gets with highly intelligent spirits, or was he merely impatient with opposition? . . .

White placed great emphasis on Woodrow Wilson's Scotch-Irish southern background as the key to the man. "He is pure bred Irish on one side," White wrote a friend on April 10, 1924, "pure bred Scot on the other, and Presbyterian since the Druids. He gets his manners and his good brain from the Scotch and his engaging personality and vicious temper . . . from the Irish." Although professional biographers told White that they thought his emphasis on the Scotch-Irish Presbyterian influence and the southern upbringing was unsound, White once said that if he was to do the book over, he would alter only the material since Wilson's second election. This change, he felt, was required by the vast amount of new material that had been unearthed after his book was written.

The biography produced a remarkable variety of reactions. Colonel House hailed it as "the most brilliant thing you have done," but Brand Whitlock, Wilson's ambassador to Belgium, "thought it a rather poor thing—poorly conceived and poorly written." Book reviewers had mixed feelings about the book too. The reviewer in the *Nation*, in praising Josephus Daniels's *Life of Woodrow Wilson*, observed: ". . . We are spared the bombastic rhetoric and the fearful and wonderful home-brewed bio-psychology which ruins William Allen White's otherwise interesting and creditable book." Late in 1925, White admitted to a Kansas friend: "The Wilson book was a labor of love. I disliked the man tremendously, but was rather fond of his type. So in affection and trepidation and a certain amount of pious scorn, I wrote the Wilson book."

* * *

In June, 1924, White temporarily ceased writing the Wilson biography to report the Republican and Democratic conventions for the Bell syndicate. At the Republican convention, Calvin Coolidge was nominated, with Charles Dawes as his running mate. "The convention differed from any other Republican convention that ever assembled," White observed, "in that the business men who control Republican conventions generally from the inside moved two rooms out and were fairly visible. . . . Business was directly in charge of the ship. Coolidge was the captain, of course, and a man of importance with the crew." The soul of the convention, White added, "was consecrated to the salvation of business, Big Business first, but little business if possible . . . At its best, this party in its present expression, now wholly conservative with no liberal flaw, spot or blemish in its creed, represents the moral yearnings of a benevolent plutocracy."

Whereas the Republican convention had been a placid, business-like affair, the Democratic convention was filled with drama and clash. A fierce battle for the nomination raged between Alfred E. Smith and W. G. McAdoo. "A Democratic Convention," reported White, "has to smell the blood of a death struggle before it can decide whom it will honor." After tiresome days of balloting, the convention nominated a compromise candidate, John W. Davis, a Wall Street lawyer. The Democratic platform was slightly more liberal than the Republican. It denounced the scandals of the Harding administration, advocated scientific revision of the tariff, and promised relief to the depressed farmers.

In addition to his daily news stories, White wrote convention articles for *Collier's* and the *Woman's Home Companion*. Macmillan's collected all this material and published it in book form that September, under the title of *Politics: The Citizen's Business*. "I don't expect any sale," White remarked, "but it will be a blithe little thing, a sort of pre-prandial cocktail for the big mess."

Included in this book were two chapters on the growth of pressure groups in American life. Vast organized minority groups like the American Legion, the Klan, and the Chamber of Commerce, he declared, formed an uncontrolled, tremendously powerful, invisible government. "The Congress of the United States, and the legislatures of all the states," he wrote, "are used as Olympic bowls for these great contests between the powers of invisible governments." If citizens wanted to influence government, White advised them to join pressure organizations.

During the 1924 campaign, White's Middle West rumbled with discontent. Disgruntled with the lack of liberalism in the two major parties, Robert M. LaFollette helped launch a third party movement of farmers and workers. "The great issue before the

American people today," LaFollette's platform asserted, "is the control of government and industry by private monopoly." LaFollette advocated government ownership of water and power resources, judicial reform, and the protection of labor against the injunction. "He is a man of the highest personal character," White observed. "Personally he is incorruptible. Politically he is immovable in his determination to battle in a finish fight for what he deems a just and righteous cause. His intellectual processes are strong and sound. In no personal quality of heart or mind or soul is either of his adversaries his superior."

Senator George Norris, running for re-election on the Republican ticket, openly supported LaFollette's independent candidacy. His neighbor to the south in Kansas, who was customarily bracketed with Norris as the leading spokesman of midwestern liberalism, supported Calvin Coolidge in spite of the fact that he had written Vernon L. Kellogg on September 29, 1923: "I feel intensely that the innate conservatism of Coolidge would be unloosed if ever he were elected."

White publicly urged Coolidge to discredit the nickname "Cautious Cal" and to defy the wet senators by enforcing the Eighteenth Amendment in the urban centers. This plea prompted the Chicago *Tribune* to observe: "Here music gets its subsidies, art its home, science its laboratories. Here is where a million fires make the steam of the nation. Here are its dynamos, its achievements and its records. This is Mr. White's drunken half of the country. When the Kansas will has been successfully imposed upon this drunken energy, intellect and adventure, the greatest architectural monument of the land will be a silo, the greatest work of art a crazy quilt, and the greatest thrill in life a snooze in stocking feet by the base burner."

Unless Gifford Pinchot or W. E. Borah was on the Republican ticket, White had predicted in 1923, the party would be defeated. White's editorial inspired *The New York Times* to remark on October 10, 1923: "This might look like war to the knife, but it may prove to be only war to the definition. Everything will depend on finding the right formula. If blind reaction is but seen through properly adjusted spectacles, it may be pronounced satisfactory 'constructive liberalism.' William Allen White himself did some pretty clever political defining in 1916."

In summing up the qualities of the three candidates, for *Collier's* on August 9, 1924, White stated: "The honest, intelligent, efficient, and courageous conservative finds a haven after his own heart in the Republican party. The restless, confused liberal who is too intelligent to believe that the moon is made of green cheese . . . will find rest for his soul with Davis and the Democrats. The free, untrammeled, fearless, and disillusioned liberal of the Left Wing, the radical, the discontented, and the rebellious seeker for illicit booze will gather with enthusiasm around the banner of LaFollette."

White chose Coolidge. Two years earlier, White had taken "an oath" not to leave the party again. "We once went out of the Republican party, banging the door, and took a look at it from the outside," he told his readers. "The longer we looked the bigger it got, so we went in again, and again banged the door, and we have decided that we can do more good for the peculiar kind of deviltry that is in our heart inside the party than without." While running as an independent candidate for governor, White justified his support of Coolidge by stating that it would have cost him half his strength had he endorsed LaFollette. Actually, although White was liberal for a Kansan, he was not an advanced thinker like LaFollette or Norris. He enjoyed picturing himself to people as a flamboyant liberal, but he was seldom very far ahead of the main procession.

White's editorial support of Coolidge elicited from the President this statement: "I do want you to know how much it has pleased me to have the assurance of your support. I say this, not so much because of its importance in terms of votes, but because, knowing yourself, your work, and your attitude toward public questions, I feel that it is worth while to have won this testimony of your confidence." In November Coolidge won by an easy margin. LaFollette ran third, although he did poll five million votes. White believed that good crops that year turned the Kansas farmers away from LaFollette. "A good crop and a good price makes it impossible to talk politics," he told Walter Lippmann. "I believe that the average man only looks to politics when he is in trouble; when he is out of trouble he accepts the dictum of the parties."

Furthermore, White was convinced that LaFollette lost a heavy labor vote because labor in the Middle West was shot through with Klan sentiment. "Certainly nothing has hit labor such a smash in my memory in politics as the Ku Klux Klan," White explained to Oswald Garrison Villard on November 19, 1924. "All over this Ku Klux territory, labor was voting for Coolidge because he was against the Pope. It will be a decade before labor recovers what it has lost by flirting with the Ku Klux Klan."

* * *

Shortly after the election, White traveled to the East to collect information for a *Collier's* article on Calvin Coolidge. Dorothy Canfield Fisher drove White to Coolidge's birthplace at Plymouth, Vermont, and White devoted considerable time to interviewing Coolidge's friends at Northampton, Massachusetts. By this time the Whites had been the guests of the Coolidges at the White House. Both Mr. and Mrs. White became admirers of the President much to the bewilderment of Victor Murdock, who told them that Coolidge was neither a statesman nor a progressive thinker.

White was so fascinated by this vinegary New England Yankee that the one article stretched into six articles and into two books. "I went east . . ." White later wrote, "without much thought of him, merely to fill an order, got interested in him, was baffled by him, and bedevilled by his evanescent character." The Emporia editor was puzzled by Calvin Coolidge, a small-town American, who was rural to the core, and yet who was the servant of big business, but who nevertheless acted in that role with an honesty that was impeccable. Perhaps this small-town Yankee president could explain to the small-town Kansan the conundrum of reaction and reform in American life. Perhaps he also could explain why the party of Abraham Lincoln was no longer the party of the people.

On his return from his trip to gather information on Coolidge, White bemoaned in the *Gazette*, on January 26, 1925, the fact that "The world is in the black tunnel of reaction. . . . The sinister forces of conservatism, the manufacturers' associations and its kith and kind, now have a hearing. Ten years ago they would be laughed at; twenty years ago thrown out on their tin ear." White was of course aware that Coolidge was backed by these "sinister forces of conservatism." When the *Collier's* articles on Coolidge were published in book form that same year, Harold L. Ickes wrote White that he did not like the book. To this letter White replied:

I didn't expect you to like the Coolidge book and yet I do think the old man is a mystic. Old Scrooge was a mystic. He had faith in the divine character of wealth as much as Lincoln had in the divine character of man. He and Coolidge both believe that Commerce is a sacrosanct matter. They are whirling dervishes of business, just as blind in that faith as Roosevelt and LaFollette were blind in their faith in the people and in the nobility of Man and the righteousness of the judgments of God. The fact that I don't agree with this thesis doesn't blind me to the fact that he is crazy about it, sincerely, genuinely, terribly crazy.

Calvin Coolidge: The Man Who Is President was a hastily written book. It was primarily a study of Coolidge the man rather than of his times. As he had done in writing Wilson's biography, White placed great emphasis on background. Coolidge was a Puritan mystic, White explained, who had a deep faith in the moral government of the universe. He adhered to the fundamental Puritan principles of moderation, temperance, industry, and frugality. White recognized that the dour, dry, taciturn Coolidge was the ideal of his America. "He represents exactly the mood of the people," the Emporia editor declared. "In a different mood he would not represent them of course. In the Roosevelt days he would have been impossible and out of line. But he is an honest, courageous, cautious, kindly conservative, and that is what the people want."

* * *

In the spring of 1925, White's old Bull Moose friend, Chester Rowell, acting as publicity man for the Institute of Pacific Relations, invited White to attend a meeting in Hawaii that July. Among the other American delegates to this conference were Ray

Lyman Wilbur, president of Stanford University; Stanley K. Hornbeck, lecturer at Harvard University; Henry C. King, president of Oberlin College; Payson J. Treat, professor of history at Stanford University; and Mary E. Woolley, president of Mount Holyoke College. According to Rowell, White brought a greatly needed spirit of humor and freshness to the meeting. The other members, however, mistook this spirit for levity, and White was never invited to attend another meeting of the institute.

White had ample free time from the proceedings to eat the exotic food of the islands and to carry on an extraordinary amount of sightseeing. In his regular dispatches to the *Gazette*, he devoted very little space to the institute. Most of the stories described the variety and abundant quantities of food that he was consuming. After reading these dispatches, *The New York Times* remarked: "O breaker of bounds, O incorrigible! . . . He must have gained about eighty pounds." A few days later the *Times* exclaimed: "In measured language and with affectionate regret and admonition, we have followed Mr. William Allen White's pacific massacres of a thousand varieties of foods, Eastern, Western, savage, barbarous and civilized . . . He is the world's one pantophagist, the all-eater."

At a bookstore in Honolulu, White discovered a copy of his biography of Woodrow Wilson, and he wrote Mrs. White that "it was the grand and glorious feeling." On July 10, he wrote to her: "This has been a lovely day but all the time I am divided in my joy of it by a terrible yearning to have you see it all . . . Just a moment ago Carol Binder of the Chicago News said that in 1919 he was in Emporia and saw a little girl on a horse riding by and they said she was Bill White's little girl and when he read the piece about her he wept. At the luncheon today a little oriental girl—I couldn't tell which—came to me and said she wanted to shake hands with Mary White's father! Every day, over and over this comes."

One day while White was riding with Chester Rowell, in a small outrigger canoe, a large wave capsized it. White started to swim ashore but became exhausted. Just as he was about to drown, Rowell, who had remained with the canoe, came by on a surf-board with an experienced surf rider; they pulled White onto the surfboard. When they reached shore, and he had recovered, he told Rowell that it had taken him so long to swim the distance that he expected Coolidge had been elected for another term. "If Kansas is prudent," commented one paper on this incident, "she will never let him take his life and most of our hopes of progress in his rash hands again." .

When the conference adjourned, White wrote Ray Lyman Wilbur that the most valuable contribution the institute could make to peaceful Pacific relations was to provide information. "I should say that the practical thing that could be done through the Institute," he explained on August 15, 1925, "would be to inform public opinion in the various countries on the Pacific of the aims of their neighbors. This should not be done officially. The diplomats have to say what expediency of the moment requires them to say, but there are in each nation free, intelligent men. Those free, intelligent men should visit other countries than their own much as missionaries go forth."

The Emporia editor was impressed by the problems of the Pacific countries. Ten years after this institute, he and Mrs. White made an extensive tour of the Far East and saw evidences of Japanese imperialism at first hand. The Kansas editor knew that the destinies of his own region were intimately connected with the course of events in other areas of the world, and he learned from this trip in 1925 that the Pacific was one source of possible trouble that could not be ignored.

*   *   *

Back in Emporia during the fall of 1925, William Allen White continued to worry over the firm control that predatory business interests were exercising on the government. He was aware that the antitrust laws were not being enforced and that monopolies were flourishing and making a mockery of the competitive system. He saw that immense wealth and corporate greed, reeking with narrow-mindedness and selfishness, were in control of the nation and the Republican party—the party which he felt was essentially and historically a middle class, sound, and popular party. All the more bewildering to White was the fact that Calvin Coolidge, head of the nation and the party, was a small-town man who somehow had become president in an age of reaction and ballyhoo.

White was aware, however, that the public was in no mood to revolt and support progressive leaders. "I am pleased, greatly pleased, that you are unhappy and dissatisfied with the times," he told Theodore Roosevelt, Jr., on July 15, 1926. "The nation has not yet been shocked out of its materialism. And, of course, Coolidge is a tremendous shock absorber. His emotionless attitude is an anesthetic to a national conviction of sin which must come before a genuine repentance."

When Brand Whitlock confided to White that he could not be part of the spirit of the new day, White agreed and wrote him: "We are in an age of paternalism; possibly benevolent paternalism but still paternalism. The age of striving toward fraternalism has for the moment passed. Of course I can't function in this age. I feel as you do that 'my show is over. The lights are out.' But," he added in a prophetic fashion, "may be I am wrong, and may be you are wrong and possibly the pendulum will swing back, though a man in one generation rarely lives to see the pendulum of events swing twice in his own direction."

White could see no hope in 1926 for the revival of the progressive cause. This feeling of hopelessness determined his support of standpat Charles Curtis's campaign for renomination to the United States Senate. "My opinion is not changed about Curtis," he confided to one friend, "but the whole trend of public opinion in Kansas, in the country, and in the world has changed. They don't want progressives . . . The country is in a Coolidge mind, and it is no time to waste our breath to get them out of it. I shall support Curtis because he is the best of the reactionary crowd."

When White announced that the *Gazette* would support Curtis, "without retracting a single word it ever said about him," the Leavenworth *Times* made the happy comment that it was not a question of retracting a single word but of retracting "whole sentences and paragraphs." White readily admitted that he had frequently impaled Curtis for being an errand boy of vested interests and the proponent of aggrandized wealth, but that Curtis was personally honest and would, therefore, receive his support.

"To this complexion has the great Kansas Progressive Movement under Theodore Roosevelt come at last!" moaned the New York *Times* on January 31, 1926. "If a man is only personally honest, he may with impunity advocate the most vicious and harmful public policies. Provided the errand boy of Wall Street does not actually steal, he may be forgiven all and be taken to the manly and capacious Progressive bosom. This seems like milk-and-water doctrine compared with the rude diet which the editor of the Emporia Gazette used to prescribe for his fellow Kansans."

*   *   *

Although he had supported Harding, Coolidge, and Curtis, William Allen White was attacked during the twenties as a subversive radical. His vigorous assaults on the Ku Klux Klan, his ready criticism of Red-baiters, and his support of organized labor were enough to bring down the wrath of "one hundred per cent Americans." When White had the temerity to write Governor Fuller of Massachusetts urging him to stay the execution of Sacco and Vanzetti, the wrath of the reactionaries knew no bounds. In the midst of the great Red scare, these two labor organizers were sentenced to death, on extremely flimsy evidence, for the shooting of a paymaster and his guard. Public opinion forced Governor Fuller to review the case. After an investigation, Fuller refused a pardon, and the men died on the night of August 22, 1927.

At the suggestion of Felix Frankfurter, White sent a letter to Governor Fuller on June 1, 1927. "I have just returned from New England where I have been talking to college groups," White told the Governor, "and I was surprised beyond words to find the bitterness and hate which had sprung up in New England, particularly in Massachusetts among those who fear that Sacco and Vanzetti will not be executed. Until I went into Massachusetts, into the home of my ancestors in fact, I had no idea that men could let their passion so completely swamp their judgment into fears and hatreds; so deeply confuse their sanity. I now know why the witches were persecuted and hanged by upright and Godless people."

The charge that White was a dangerous "Red" was rather amusing and amazing to him in view of his support of the straight Republican ticket. His philosophy was far from radical. "As a matter of fact," he wrote Judge George McDermott, on July 9, 1927, "my interest in the underdog is slight . . . I take sides against the upperdog for the upperdog's own good; to bring him down a pace. He is a better dog than the underdog generally, but he's always a better dog to be kicked in the slats and not allowed to eat up his opponent . . . I have no Bolshevik philosophy; no delusion that anything other than good brains and a kind heart will run this country, and I think on the whole the successful people in this world have better brains and kinder hearts than those who are not successful. But just because this class is endowed by God they should be kept from swelling up and taking a Babylonian pride in their wealth and be brought down to earth for the common good."

About the time of the Sacco and Vanzetti affair, the Daughters of the American Revolution subjected themselves to an attack from White and many other editors for distributing a pamphlet called *The Common Enemy*, which labeled middle-class liberals like White as subversive radicals. White indignantly wrote one person: "Any social or economic objective like peace or justice which brings peace, or mercy, or loving kindness, or understanding, or intelligence in any of its remote manifestations, is the subject of repressive activity by the War Department or State Department, and all the flunkies of big business thereunto appertaining. The D.A.R. has recently been taken over as a sort of Cheka, and of course the National Defense Society, and the National Civic Federation, the Easley group, have been for years leering suspiciously at any kind of pacifist activity."

When Hugh Powell of the Coffeyville (Kansas) *Journal* accepted the D.A.R. indictment and wrote that the Emporia editor had stood for "socialistic and communistic measures," White was deeply hurt. "I am a Republican and have in my desk a letter from the President of the United States commending me for my Republicanism in 1924," he wrote Powell on July 1, 1927. ". . . I have bolted candidates no more frequently than the average man. I have just been nosier . . . And it hurts like the dickens when you, whom I admire and respect, use the words 'communistic and socialistic' about my political activities. Call me a liar if you will; crazy if you must; coy, uncertain, hard to please if you have to;

but my dear Hugh please don't stick that dirty phrase, 'communist or socialist' on my name. I value my patriotism as I value nothing else in this world."

The D.A.R. not only circulated *The Common Enemy*, but drew up a blacklist of important Americans including Dean Roscoe Pound and Felix Frankfurter of the Harvard Law School; Mary E. Woolley, president of Mount Holyoke College; Clarence Darrow; Rabbi Stephen S. Wise; and Editor White. In a *Gazette* editorial, White wrote: "One wonders whether it is the Daughters of the American Revolution or the Daughters of the American Tories who are speaking." When the *Nation* held a Blacklist Party for all those whose names were on the D.A.R. blacklist, White wired the magazine: "Unworthy though I am to stand before the kings and queens of courage in the true American aristocracy, yet because some fumbling fool has placed me there I none the less appreciate the great fortune I have had in this distinction. Some people have all the luck. I am one. If a good name is rather to be chosen than riches, a place on the D.A.R. blacklist is better than a license to steal in a mint, or to have a hand in the Continental Trading Company's jackpot."

On April 2, 1928, the Associated Press carried a story that one D.A.R. member had denounced the Massachusetts chapters for blacklisting individuals. Mrs. Alfred Brosseau, president general of the D.A.R., defended the blacklist and declared that it contained names of only those who opposed the Coolidge naval building program. "That is not a fact," William Allen White declared. "My name is on that list, and I have supported President Coolidge's naval program. . . . More than that, my name was on the list two years ago when there was no question of armaments." Then White sailed into the type of offensive he so dearly loved: "The nice old girls of the present D.A.R. administration have been hypnotized by the brass buttons of the retired army officers and lured into the red-baiting mania by the tea gladiators of Washington."

Mrs. Brosseau labeled White's editorial as an "absolute misstatement of facts," and then trapped herself by denying that the D.A.R. listed such organizations as the League of Women Voters, the Y.M.C.A., and the Y.W.C.A. as subversive or subservient to radical forces. White immediately sent the following release to the Associated Press:

I have before me the official list sent out by the D.A.R. in a D.A.R. envelope, to the Regent of the Emporia chapter of the D.A.R. giving the list of subservient organizations . . . I want to present the key of that list to the American people. It particularly picks out organizations affecting colored people, Jews, and Catholics . . . This list . . . goes out of its way . . . to pick out and include the peculiar enemies of the Ku Klux Klan. The D.A.R. has yanked the klan out of its cow pastures and set it down in the breakfast room of respectability, removing its hood and putting on a transformation, bobbing its shirttail uniform to knee lengths . . . Mrs. Brosseau is a lovely lady with many beautiful qualities of heart and mind, but in her enthusiasm to parade as the goddess of liberty she has allowed several lengths of Ku Klux nighty to show under her red, white, and blue . . . She can now have the last say. I am done.

Mrs. Brosseau refused to comment on this attack except to say that "I thank Mr. White for his gallant offer of the 'last word,' and I hope it will be the last word in the matter. I emphatically disclaim all responsibility for the alleged list." White carefully explained to Henry J. Allen that the only reason he had entered the controversy was to discredit the blacklist. "I started in deliberately to outnag her," he explained, "and bedevil her and I see by this morning's paper that she has entirely reversed her position, says she is not responsible for the list, throws her skirts over her head, and runs for cover. That is all I wanted her to do . . . I have had a lot of fun out of it and some fairly good advertising, all of which helps."

He was unhappy over just one thing. He had not been able to finish his book *Masks in a Pageant* in time to capitalize on all the free publicity from the episode. *Masks in a Pageant* was a compilation of the political sketches he had been writing for magazines for the past thirty years. The old *McClure's* series on Platt, Hanna, Cleveland, Bryan, Roosevelt, and others was refurbished, and his recent *Collier's* articles on Coolidge, Alfred E. Smith, and Big Bill Thompson were included to complete the book.

"I am getting old," White added in his letter to Allen. "I don't co-ordinate. I sent the manuscript for my book off last week. The book won't be out for six or eight weeks, and this darn thing is wasted on the desert air. Ten years ago my luck, or my hunch, or my guardian angel would have got that manuscript out in January and had the book on the market as fresh vegetables today. Age is a terrible thing."

CHAPTER 18

THE CRASH OF BABYLON

"THE POPULAR national institution known as William Allen White has two component parts," declared W. L. Chenery in June, 1928. "One is the editor of the Emporia *Gazette*, a country newspaper with a circulation much larger than you would expect, and an influence far exceeding that of many big city dailies. The other is a man of affairs whose sensitive and tolerant mind ranges over the activities of this complex age, frequently followed by the cherubic person of its proprietor. Both parts combine to produce the most sparkling personality in American journalism today . . . He is an observer of the show, eager for the next act, richly competent to criticize the actors. A journalist whose only rule is that he shall be 'honest according to his lights, brave without being cruel, and as wise as a man may be who peeps at the world through a crack in the door.' "

The presidential campaign of 1928 found White far more than "an observer of the show." He was one of Herbert Hoover's most ardent supporters and campaign speakers. Before Hoover had secured the nomination on the first ballot, the Kansas editor had been sounding the clarion call for Coolidge's secretary of commerce. On July 19, 1927, for instance, White gave a dinner in Emporia to introduce Herbert Hoover to the Kansas editors. This was part of a successful build-up that eventually won the nomination for Hoover.

As a result of his policy of encouraging and aiding business as secretary of commerce, Hoover had the confidence of business-men. During his campaign in 1928 he was to reveal that he was thoroughly in sympathy with the widespread belief that the Coolidge prosperity was permanent. "We in America today are nearer to the final triumph over poverty than ever before in the history of any land," Hoover declared. "The poorhouse is vanishing from among us. We have not reached the goal, but given a chance to go forward with the policies of the last eight years, we shall soon with the help of God be in sight of the day when poverty will be banished from this nation." The policies of the last eight years, of course, referred to the subsidization of business and little governmental regulation. There was no doubt that Hoover agreed with Harding and Coolidge that progressive regulation of the business world had gone far enough.

White, however, tried to make himself believe that Hoover was a progressive. He was even able to convince Senator Borah of the validity of this belief, but a Kansas friend seemed skeptical. "Hoover is the only man in the Cabinet or the only man in an official position in either the Harding or the Coolidge administration who has an acute and practical knowledge of what the Wall Street fellows are trying to put over," White asserted on July 14, 1927, "and more than any other man he has tried earnestly and sincerely and all the time to checkmate the Wall Street crowd. He is the only man who has been in the cabinet since Roosevelt walked out nearly twenty years ago, who has a scorn for big business as such, who knows its 'tricks and manners.' "

Although White might fool himself into accepting Hoover as a progressive, his fellow midwestern liberal, Senator George Norris, did not. When Hoover was nominated, Norris bolted and supported Al Smith, although Smith's "wetness" and religion were an anathema to protestant Nebraska. Norris, however, was aware that Hoover was backward and reactionary, and, when Hoover vetoed the TVA Muscle Shoals bill in 1931, Norris's belief was borne out.

There was a large degree of pride of discovery in White's support of Hoover. As early as 1919, before Hoover had become a political personality, White had advocated his election to the presidency. Moreover, if Hoover was elected, White undoubtedly reasoned that he again would have influence in the White House. Ever since the days of Theodore Roosevelt, he had missed his once-familiar contacts with the administration.

Hoover's visit to Emporia in 1927 to meet the Kansas editors was fruitful. After the meeting, innumerable editors devoted columns to explaining and publicizing Hoover to the Kansas public. "I know of no one for many years who has made such good copy in Kansas as your visit made," White commented to Hoover on August 2, 1927. To Hoover's close associate Vernon Kellogg—and Kellogg's intimate tie with both Hoover and White helps to account for White's support of Hoover—White wrote: "Hoover is riding very well. An editorial or two, a magazine article or two will help. I shall do my part. He can direct, he knows his needs better than anyone just now . . . Furnish me the facts and I shall do the rest."

Before Hoover's nomination, his political opponents circulated the rumor that, since Hoover was too closely allied to business forces, his candidacy would cost the Republican ticket the rural states. Hoover and Kellogg asked White, the spokesman of grass-roots America, to deny the charge. Over the months, White in editorials, letters, and speeches continually asserted that Hoover could carry Kansas. To the Young Republican Club of New York City, for instance, White announced that "Secretary Hoover was the strongest candidate in the West next to President Coolidge."

Until Senator Curtis decided to enter the race for the presidential nomination, White had been planning to manage Hoover's primary campaign in Kansas. Then, however, White and his fellow progressives, in order to secure harmony in the party's ranks, decided to support Curtis. In return, their candidate, Clyde Reed, was to run as the Republican candidate for governor. Curtis, of course, represented the ultraconservative sentiment of Kansas. To justify his action and still be able to claim the title of liberal, White wrote: "Isn't there something in politics more than the hard realities? Isn't sentiment worth while, gratitude worth while, decent neighborly association worth while? All these things are in the Curtis candidacy in Kansas, and they are a credit to human nature."

While the campaign for delegates to the Republican convention was in full swing all over the country, White's son Bill wrote an editorial for the *Gazette*, saying that James Watson of Indiana and Governor Lowden of Illinois were fighting like roosters and securing no delegates, whereas Herbert Hoover's attitude was that of aloofness from the fighting cocks in the bloody pit. Calmly standing by, Bill wrote, Hoover vaguely resembled "a timorous fat capon gobbling all the worms." During the subsequent Hoover-Smith campaign, certain Democratic papers were to make wide use of the descriptive phrase "a plump and timorous capon" and to attribute it, of course, to Bill White's father.

Just before the convention, White, a delegate pledged to Curtis, wrote a feature article on Herbert Hoover for *Collier's*. "I certainly will not write a piece which would relate itself in any way with the present presidential race . . ." he disarmingly told Curtis. "I would write it as I would have written it a year ago, purely an analytical study of an unusual figure in American life. Certainly if there ever was a queer duck, in American politics, Hoover is that duck." The closest that White came in the article to revealing that Hoover was a queer duck was the statement that Hoover was "a vestal virgin in politics."

The article could only have helped Hoover's cause. It traced his career as a mining engineer all over the world, and contrasted him favorably with the trained politicians who were in the race against him. White concluded the article with the following question: "Can a democracy afford to pass under the leadership of a man deeply democratic at heart, but essentially without the instinct for democratic leadership?" After 1929, as the depression was deepening in intensity and millions of Americans were seeking work, White was to urge President Hoover to take colorful and dramatic steps to reassure the faith of the people in the democratic process. But the undramatic Hoover, "without the instinct for democratic leadership," was unable to meet the crisis.

White reported the two conventions for the Bell syndicate and served in the Republican convention as a delegate from Kansas. He was a member of the small committee that drafted the platform. In the committee proceedings, he was able to thwart an attempt by Senator Borah to place the party on record against American entrance into the World Court. Then, with the aid of Borah, he succeeded in drafting a plank denouncing the use of injunctions in labor disputes. The chief task White accomplished, however, was the organizing of the Kansas delegation against the McNary-Haugen Bill calling for federal aid in raising farm prices. This bill had been vetoed by Coolidge the year before as socialistic in principle. Hoover also was opposed to the McNary-Haugen principle. In the platform committee, White supported instead a Hoover-sponsored plank calling for a Federal Farm Board to encourage co-operative marketing.

White's news dispatches were extremely critical of the platform committee. "It was conservative to the point of reaction in its consideration of all social legislation excepting prohibition," he wrote. ". . . Anything that looked like social change was rejected; any hark back to Rooseveltian progressivism was frowned upon." Nor was he any less critical of the potential candidate: "When a great party like the Republican party resolves to keep business out of politics and politics out of business, when it abandons the purpose of its founders to make government an agency of human welfare the best minds of the country go into business and party conventions are conducted by a lot of animated rubber stamps debating solemnly whether to bow down in worship to an adding machine like Hoover or a cream separator like Lowden, or a backfiring tractor like Dawes."

When White wrote these dispatches, he was acting in the role of interpreter of life; when he supported Hoover in the subsequent campaign, he was the matter-of-fact Kansas politician and businessman. Although the Republican platform and candidate were not progressive, White discovered his issue for the campaign and his justification for remaining Republican, since Hoover stood for the enforcement of prohibition. "The Emporia Gazette and its editor, once the most intractable wild Indian on the reservation, have become the most regular of the regulars," commented the Wichita *Beacon* on June 22, 1928. "Time has mellowed the spirit of Emporia's sage, and his politics has shown a corresponding softening. No longer does he yearn for insurgency, his heart beating furiously at the call of the Clan-na-Gael."

* * *

At the Democratic convention, Franklin D. Roosevelt placed in nomination the governor of New York, Alfred E. Smith, the "happy warrior." Al Smith represented a far different type in American democracy from Herbert Hoover. He was the first life-time city dweller and the first Roman Catholic to receive the nomination of a major party. As governor of New York, his record on power regulation and labor problems had won him the respect of liberal forces. On the issue of prohibition, he was a wet. He had openly supported the repeal of the Eighteenth Amendment and the return to state control of liquor.

During the campaign, each party dodged the major issues of international relations, tariff, farm relief, and the regulation of utilities. Instead, the issues that dominated the campaign centered around religion and prohibition. White played an important part in Al Smith's defeat. Although he did not subscribe to the charges of religious bigotry that were hurled at Smith, as the key spokesman of small-town, rural America his attacks on the New York governor were of great value to the Hoover campaign. White's opposition to Smith as a wet and as a product of Tammany Hall and city life helped to take the public's mind away from the more important social and economic questions and focus the people's attention upon highly emotional and personal issues.

White, in spite of his tolerant attitude toward most issues, was apt to be an extremist on prohibition. He was so emotionalized over the question of liquor—or "booze," as he called it—that he refused to view the problem of alcoholic consumption as a personal matter. White once carefully explained to H. L. Mencken, who was ridiculing the "blue-nosed" Puritanism of the "Bible belt," that the motive for prohibition was economic not moral. "There isn't any jealous feeling," stated White, "of the fellow who wants to soak his hide full of coffin varnish, and more or less diluted carpet tacks, but instead a feeling that when his hide is so saturated he does things which cripples him as a producer of worldly goods, and makes him a burden to the tax payers, either through his own desires to tear up sidewalks, or to take an axe and go home to make clam chowder out of the Children."

Speaking in Salt Lake City more than a year before the 1928 campaign, White declared that there were many bigots who would never vote for a Catholic candidate for the presidency. Although the official Catholic paper of that diocese criticized White for making the statement, the campaign substantiated its validity. Before the campaign started, when White was the interpreter not the Kansas politician, he had a high opinion of Al Smith. Two years earlier, he had written a laudatory article about Smith for *Collier's*. Smith, White had explained, was a new type in American democracy; he was not a backwoods product like Andrew Jackson and Abraham Lincoln. He was a "city feller." But White was quick to add: "There is no reason why the back alley cannot produce as good moral, spiritual, mental and physical timber for politics as the backwoods." Although Smith was the product of Tammany Hall, White in 1926 did not feel that to be a detriment. Tammany experience trained leaders to work with people, and to administer government with warmth and human feeling. Presidents without political experience, White pointed out, suffered grave handicaps. There was no question in White's mind that Al Smith was a friendly, affable personality, and that, "for all his happy Tammany regularity, he was becoming a free man."

Smith's major weakness, according to the Emporia editor, was his lack of understanding of rural peoples and rural habits. Although Smith had striking qualities of leadership, so far he was not a national statesman. "We may be facing new issues in our politics," White wrote, "based for the first time upon the conflicting interests, the conflicting morals, the conflicting aspirations of a rural civilization as those interests, morals and aspirations clash in a nation which is rapidly becoming industrialized and urban. . . . Hence Al Smith . . . He becomes the symbol of a mighty challenge to our American traditions, a challenge which, if it wins in the struggle which may ensue, will bring deep changes into our American life."

Two years after this article was written, on July 12, 1928, White, now in the role of the Kansas politician, opened the Republican campaign with a speech at Olathe, Kansas. After praising Smith's "unusual intelligence, splendid courage and rare political wisdom," he attacked Smith's Tammany Hall affiliation and charged that when Smith was a member of the New York legislature he had voted against laws prohibiting gambling and prostitution. Immediately Smith challenged White's facts. Bill and Mrs. White wanted him to drop the whole thing, because even if Smith did vote against such bills, no legislator would dare cast such votes without good reasons. They suggested that White did not know the entire background of the legislative vote, which might well explain the negative vote satisfactorily.

White, however, would not listen to them. He not only issued further statements attacking Smith's Tammany record and his wetness, but charged that "as President of the United States he will menace American ideals and threaten the institutions of our fathers. Smith must be beaten if America remains American." This, of course, was emotionalism. It was the mediocre Kansas politician speaking, not the man who had won fame as an interpreter of life. It was the statement of a provincial Kansan who had forgotten that America was a land of immigrants, and that Ellis Island was more important to the growth of the nation than was Plymouth Rock.

Heywood Broun quickly pointed out that White was actually asserting that, unless you were of early New England vintage, you were not American. "From down in the cornfields there comes a mournful sound," declared Broun. "If America remains American. It never has and should not. The greatness of this country does not lie in living on a leash tied 'round a stump."

The New York Times's interpretation of White's charges against Smith was that "William Allen White, sitting between 'Dave' Mulvane and 'Charley' Curtis, feels mighty uncomfortable. Star-eyed crusader, hast thou wandered there? His sleep is haunted by the reproachful shapes of the elder LaFollette and the Roosevelt of 1912. So he keeps the siren of the Emporia word-works bellowing horribly, seeking to drown the reformer's still, small voice."

There was so much criticism of White for his charges against Smith that White engaged two people to comb the New York legislative record to substantiate the charges. He had based his attack not on research, but on a statement that had appeared in a small paper in upstate New York. Faced with the necessity of proving his accusations, White persuaded the Republican National Committee to finance the work of the two researchers.

Late in July the Whites arrived in New York on the way to Europe. On July 29, White repeated the charges and declared that he had photostatic copies of Smith's votes to prove the truthfulness of the indictment. "He is honest, he is brave, he is intelligent," White declared. "I don't question his motives. To get where he is with his crowd he had to do what he did, and from his standpoint it probably was worth the price. But the real point of interest is that the record for the American people . . . is the picture of Tammany putting the pressure on fine, aspiring young men like Al Smith, forcing them to use their courage not upon the evils of Tammany but in behalf of the friends of Tammany."

At this point, Walter Lippmann visited White and explained that Smith had voted against bills to regulate gambling and prostitution because he had felt that these laws were unconstitutional, unenforceable, and that they would encourage police corruption. Immediately, White withdrew his two charges on prostitution and gambling, but maintained the charge that Smith had opposed the regulation of saloons.

On August 2, when White sailed for Europe, he left behind a great deal of trouble. Although the trip had been planned before the unhappy episode of the charges, there is no question but that the sailing came at an opportune time for White. A small-town paper, the Zanesville [Ohio] *Times Recorder*, praised White for rendering a great public service by exposing Smith's record, but the unfairness of White's attack prompted former Kansan Jay E. House to write in the New York *Evening Post* that New Yorkers did not understand him as Kansans understood him. "When Old Bill goes on a rampage—and he's nearly always on one," wrote House, "the people read about it in the papers and say, 'Well, I see where Bill White's broke loose again,' and as likely as not forget all about it. With unusual qualities of heart and mind, he is a strange mixture of generosity, fairness, kindness, good humor, inaccuracy, and hot-temperedness. Politically, Kansas, that has known him and loves him, writes him down as unstable as water and uncertain as the wind."

When White withdrew the charges of gambling and prostitution, Democratic papers declared that he had retracted his charges. Fearing that such a statement might be made, White left a letter with Henry J. Allen, who was in charge of publicity for the Republican National Committee, making it clear that he had withdrawn but not retracted the charges. On August 15, Allen released this letter to the press, but to increase its effectiveness he stated that it was a cablegram White had just sent from Paris. Declaring that he had not withdrawn the charges, White wrote: "On the prostitution issue I proved my case, got a conviction and suspended the sentence. I only did this because I felt that a debate on the subject of harlotry was not worthy of a presidential campaign."

The Democratic press now claimed that White had retracted his retraction. Being an experienced politician himself, White must have known that in the heat of campaigns there is little difference between withdrawals and retractions. On August 20, Al Smith denounced White for his "vile suggestions" and stated that his votes on these issues were dictated by a regard for public interest, or were based on sound constitutional grounds, and had intelligent and creditable reasons behind them.

Hoover and the Republican National Committee now began to fear that White's charges would boomerang and cost Hoover votes. Henry J. Allen told Bill White that Hoover had said, "I'm afraid White may have spoiled our best issue." Allen himself denied that the Republican party was behind the attack, despite the fact they had paid a portion of the expense incurred in investigating the legislative record. Bill wrote his father in Europe urging him to say nothing further lest the Republican National Committee publicly disavow him.

On September 29, White returned from Europe ready for the fray. He was welcomed with open arms by Hoover, who told him: "Do not let your mind be disturbed, we love you." White delivered campaign speeches in Kansas, Georgia, North Carolina, and Tennessee. In his speeches in the South, White hammered upon just one point—Smith's opposition to prohibition. White pointed out that Smith had voted to protect the open saloon. "It is bad enough," White charged, "to vote for an all-night saloon as a young man, but as governor of New York and as candidate for President to defend a vote for the after-midnight saloon shows a lack of moral intelligence that comes from the deadly blight of his Tammany associations."

The intensity of the presidential campaign and the hatred engendered by the issues of liquor and religion were thoroughly revealed in the hordes of letters that descended upon the Emporia editor. The type of Protestant who had been beguiled by the Klan sent White cartoons and handbills, which charged that Smith's election would mean that the White House would be under the Pope's power. The heat of these letters and their enclosed material was violent. One pamphlet, for instance, read:

The music of the sidewalks of New York becomes the battle cry of alienism as the gargled throats of the superstitious followers of the Pope swing into line for the march on the White House. . . . *The Pope of Rome raises on high his bloody baton of ignorant superstition to lead his battalions of death upon the Temple of Liberty* . . . Americans, this is not a political fight on economic questions. *This is war. A religious war to the Death between Americanism and Romanism.* . . .

In spite of the vigorous campaign put on by Smith, Hoover won by the decisive margin of twenty-one to fifteen million votes. Smith even lost the border states. He was defeated because the average American was repelled by his Catholicism, his wetness, and his city background. The main-streeters and the Babbitts, and the rural Southerners and Westerners of old American stock feared that Smith's election would bring new forces and new ways into dominance in American life. William Allen White contributed immeasurably to this belief. Although White did not sanction the religious bigotry of the campaign, as the recognized spokesman of small-town, Anglo-Saxon, rural America, he played upon the latent fears of his Babbitts that city dwellers were inherently evil and that the cosmopolitan mixture of ethnic stocks in the cities was threatening the older America.

Explaining the election returns to Justice Louis Brandeis on January 12, 1929, White declared that Smith "represented a strange, unfamiliar, and to many narrow minds, an abhorrent tendency in our national life. Partly it was religion that symbolized the distrust. But I think it was chiefly an instinctive feeling for the old rural order and old rural ways."

*   *   *

The state election was as satisfying to White as was the election of Herbert Hoover to the presidency. White's group within the Republican party swept into control of the governorship with the election of Clyde Reed. Since Senator Charles Curtis had now been elected to the vice-presidency, one Kansas senatorial seat was vacant. During Reed's campaign, charges were made that if elected he would appoint Henry J. Allen to succeed Curtis as senator. Since these charges were hindering Reed's campaign, Allen issued a public statement: "I am not to be considered a candidate for the United States Senate. . . . I would not be available for appointment . . . next March even if Mr. Reed, when elected governor, would be gracious enough to offer it to me."

After his election, Clyde Reed told White that he had received many votes from anti-Allen forces, and that he was, therefore, obligated not to appoint Allen to the Senate. At this juncture, Fred Trigg, the Kansas political correspondent for the Kansas City *Star*, began to create favorable publicity for the appointment of Henry J. Allen to the Senate. Soon the problem was how to arrange the situation so that Allen could be appointed without damaging Reed politically. Trigg's campaign in the *Star* stressed that Allen was badly needed in the Senate by President Hoover and thus was the logical appointment for Reed to make. Trigg and Allen now began to work on Herbert Hoover so as to create the impression that Hoover was personally asking Governor Reed to appoint Allen because he needed him as floor leader. At this point White was asked to urge Hoover to make the request of Reed. Unwillingly, White agreed to do this. He felt that the whole business was shady but to demonstrate his loyalty to his faction in the Republican party, he urged Hoover to request Reed to appoint Allen.

White hailed Allen's appointment by stating that he would "wear his toga like a Roman." Privately, however, beginning in 1930, White revealed that he had been shocked by Allen's appointment. He actually wrote in letters that he had opposed the appointment and was shocked that Reed had made it. White's reluctant request of Hoover had probably been important in securing the appointment. *Collier's* correctly asserted that White was Henry

J. Allen's press agent, "for it was Bill White who created the reputation that preceded Henry to Washington."

Herbert Hoover was soon to feel the pressure of these Kansas
leaders on another crucial issue. After taking office, Hoover announced that judicial appointments would no longer be made on
the basis of senatorial recommendations. Only proved ability would
be taken into consideration in selecting federal judges. A vacancy
happened to exist in the federal court in Kansas when Hoover
took office. Senators Capper and Allen, White, and the Kansas City
Star threw their support behind Richard J. Hopkins, a justice of
the Kansas Supreme Court. The Kansas Bar Association urged the
appointment of W. F. Lilleston, a corporation lawyer.

For months the fight occupied a large amount of White's time.
The Emporia editor charged that the standpat wing and the corporation attorneys were behind Lilleston's appointment, but he made
no mention of the Kansas State Federation of Labor's opposition
to Hopkins as antilabor. Lilleston's supporters objected to Hopkins
and charged that the Anti-Saloon League was behind him. The
Kansas situation attracted nation-wide attention, and large city
dailies like the Chicago *Tribune* and the Baltimore *Sun* attacked
Hopkins as a tool of the Anti-Saloon League forces. President
Hoover was in a difficult position. He desired to appoint judges
free of politics, but his powerful supporters White, Capper, and
Allen, now a White House intimate and a Hoover spokesman in
the Senate, were insisting on Hopkins.

White prevented Capper and Allen from accepting any third
person as a compromise candidate. He told Allen that Hoover
was being fooled by William Howard Taft, who was trying to
entrench plutocracy in the courts. White informed Hoover's
attorney general that Hopkins was being opposed by the lawyers
for the predatory interests. "If the Courts are named by the lawyers of this country without the veto of politics," White explained,
"you will remove the one check which the people have in their
fight for justice. . . . I quite agree with you that you should go
outside of politics to investigate your men. But I don't believe that
you can follow the leaders of the Bar in America as the Bar is now
organized . . . Go to the Bar surely, but beware of the high
salaried leaders who have interested litigants."

In August, 1929, White traveled to Washington to see Hoover concerning the Hopkins appointment. White refused to withdraw Hopkins's name, and now began to exert indirect pressure on Hoover through David Hinshaw, a former Emporian, now a White House intimate. At last Hoover succumbed and sent the Hopkins appointment to the Senate. The Chicago *Tribune*, the Baltimore *Sun*, and the New York *World* led the fight against confirmation.

While the Senate Judiciary Committee was investigating the appointment, White hurried to Washington in December, 1929, to talk to George Norris, the committee chairman, and to W. E. Borah, the chairman of the subcommittee that was handling the Hopkins affair. White convinced these old friends that an outrageous fight was being waged against Hopkins. After the Senate had followed the committee's recommendation that the Hopkins appointment should be confirmed, White wrote Borah: "I am under a thousand obligations to you in the Hopkins matter. Without you Hopkins would be busted."

Paul Jones, publisher of the Democratic Lyons *Daily News*, remarked the day after the favorable vote was taken that "Dick Hopkins leaves the State Supreme bench and goes to the Federal bench. But his appointment did not come quickly and easy. It was deferred for several weeks and twenty-two United States Senators bitterly fought his appointment . . . The only good thing that has come of the whole affair is that Hopkins and his record have been given a thorough airing. A typical Kansas politician of the saintly type who uses church pulpits for his political forum has had his halo pulled slightly awry. The fight on Hopkins came mostly from outside the state, from forces that are trying to preserve the decency and integrity of our republican form of government. . . . 'Dick' Hopkins is known as a 'good man,' he belongs to the Anti-Saloon League and the Methodist Church, and he goes to church, especially when he is in a campaign. He seems to fill the bill for Kansas."

* * *

On February 7, 1930, three days before his sixty-second birthday, White was appointed by President Hoover to serve on a Commission for the Study and Review of Conditions in Haiti. In the summer of 1915, when the European war necessitated peace in the Americas, the Wilson administration had landed marines in the Negro Republic of Haiti. On this island, conditions had been chaotic for years. Continuous revolutions and corrupt dictatorships had left Haitian society and economic life badly disorganized. The marines were landed to bring order out of the chaos, to protect and expand business opportunities for Americans, and to forestall any danger of Germany's seizing Haiti as a naval base.

The occupation of Haiti was only one step in the American expansion from 1898 to 1928 that led to the extension of the American sphere of influence over the Caribbean region, Central America, and a large section of South America. Under Theodore Roosevelt, American policy toward Latin America had been ruthless. He acquired the Canal Zone and made Panama a protectorate; he placed the customhouses of the Dominican Republic under United States supervision; and he established the right of the United States to regulate Latin America's relations with Europe through the Roosevelt corollary to the Monroe Doctrine. Under Woodrow Wilson, America's empire reached its greatest extent. Wilson added Nicaragua and Haiti as protectorates, and interfered in Mexican affairs.

Harding and Coolidge maintained the empire acquired by Roosevelt and Wilson, but were more avid than previous presidents in using marines to collect the dividends of American investors in Latin America. American public opinion near the close of the Coolidge presidency began to protest against American intervention in the domestic policies of Latin America. William Allen White was extremely critical of America's bad neighbor policy. "The deep and almost diabolical property-minded view of Coolidge and his force on all subjects," White told Senator Borah on May 6, 1927, "is going to affect our foreign relations with the rest of the world. We have either got to recognize that the flag does not follow the promoter or go to war with those countries which hold a different dollar view from ours."

Relations with Mexico were particularly tense during the 1920's. The Mexican Constitution of 1917 vested the ownership of subsoil mineral and oil deposits in the Mexican nation. Immediately, American oil investors clamored for American intervention to protect their property rights. American troops were stationed along the Rio Grande to bully Mexico. Editor White objected to outside pressure on Mexican affairs. "If Mexico wishes to nationalize oil, as Great Britain does, why not let her?" he wrote in the *Gazette* on June 14, 1921. "If we are fair with Mexico, she will be fair with us—even with our oil millionaires. Why not try the golden rule among nations?"

In 1927, Mexican-American relations nearly reached the breaking point. The Coolidge administration favored a policy of military intervention to prevent the nationalizing of Mexican oil and the confiscation of large landholdings. White told Dwight Morrow: "I wish I could take our dearly beloved President and persuade him that the friendship of the Latin nations is on the whole and in the long run vastly of more cash value to America than the money he could make in forcing our view of the Mexican situation upon Mexico." Early in January, 1927, White visited Senator Borah in Washington and urged him, as chairman of the Senate Foreign Relations Committee, to advocate the submission of the Mexican question to international arbitration. Working closely with Nicholas Murray Butler, who suggested arbitration to Coolidge, White persuaded a number of senators that arbitration, not military intervention, was the reasonable solution. On January 25, 1927, the Senate voted unanimously for arbitration, and the administration, thus rebuked, altered its tactics and soon dispatched Dwight Morrow as a goodwill Ambassador to Mexico.

Three months after the Senate vote, White became an honorary vice-president of a National Citizens' Committee on Relations with Latin America. What he most desired, he wrote Borah, was someone in charge of Latin-American relations who would change our entire attitude toward that area. White realized that the United States should not force its type of civilization on Latin America. "Our American civilization and that of Northern Europe generally, is based upon the proper emphasis of thrift, honesty, industry, punctuality and similar Puritan virtues . . ." he explained to Borah. "Civilizations to the south of us in Europe and South America do not stress those Old Testament virtues as we do. Other things are more important. They have built their civilization in which they have a right to live, even if they live back-wardly, upon virtues which please them. They view our over-emphasis of property with the same horror that we view their easy consideration for thrift, industry, punctuality."

By the time Herbert Hoover was inaugurated president, hatred of the United States was rampant in Latin America. The Mexican policy, armed intervention in Nicaragua under Coolidge, the presence of marines in Haiti, and the general policy of assuming that the United States should run Latin America's relations with European powers made the United States a greedy imperialist nation in Latin-American eyes. After his election, and before his inauguration, Hoover, in a goodwill tour of South America, wit-nessed some of Latin America's Yankeephobia at first hand.

The situation in Haiti became acute soon after Hoover took office, when a series of riots swept the island republic. General John H. Russell of the Marine Corps invoked martial law, and the marines fired upon a mob, killing ten Haitians. This agitation was stimulated by the Haitian opposition to American occupation, in order to bring the question to a head. It was evident to them that President Louis Borno, maintained in power by American marines, had no intention of calling an election to choose his successor. Four years before, he had violated the constitution and had re-tained the office of president or dictator.

Along with White, President Hoover appointed to the Haitian Commission to investigate conditions on the island the following: W. Cameron Forbes, former governor general of the Philippine Islands, as chairman; Henry P. Fletcher, former ambassador to Italy, Mexico, and Chile, delegate to the Pan-American confer-ences of 1923 and 1928, and Hoover's adviser on his goodwill tour; Elie Vezina, secretary of L'Union St. Jean Baptiste d'Amérique, a chevalier of the Legion of Honor, and a knight of the Order of St. Gregory, an honor bestowed only by the Pope; and James Kerney, editor of the Trenton [New Jersey] Times, a Democrat and a former adviser to Woodrow Wilson.

According to White, the only thing he could contribute to the commission was "a virgin mind." White was assured by a White House intimate that he had been included on the commission "as a guarantee to the public that the investigation wouldn't be a

White-washing affair." On receiving this diplomatic appointment, White reluctantly ordered his first swallowtail coat. He also borrowed his son Bill's plug hat. "I did this for the dignity of the West and the glory of Kansas," he explained.

While traveling to join the other members of the commission at Key West, Florida, White stopped at Palm Beach, scene of one of the wildest orgies of land speculation during the boom of the twenties. There he visited Edna Ferber and the Jerome Kerns. In the extravagance of Florida tourist society, White was truly the Puritan in Babylon. As he wrote home:

. . . Palm Beach is just a great big stinking bawdy house of the rich and pretended rich; all sham that should be shame! It has neither beauty nor distinction. . . . Such luxury I never saw before. . . . Of all the places on earth not to visit—this is it; and as for living here—it is beyond belief. . . . If you could only see it—deadly exotic wicked. . . . I wonder what's happening at home? . . . It all seems so far away; on such a different planet from this. I wonder which *is* the real America. Are these idlers and triflers the Americans of the end of the century? or are we left over from the nineteenth? Surviving Victorians? It's all a queer mess.

Before joining the other members of the commission, White and James Kerney spent a day together at Palm Beach planning their strategy. They feared that the other members of the commission would be too conservative and too cautious. Both of them were convinced that the commission should recommend definite steps to withdraw the United States marines from the island. They agreed to work together to ensure that such steps be included in the final report.

On February 28, the commission landed at Port-au-Prince. While aboard ship the commission had worked out a statement to be released on their arrival which pledged the United States to terminate American military occupation at the earliest possible moment, and to replace United States civil officials with Haitian personnel. The statement also announced that the commission would conduct hearings at which all people, whether for or against the incumbent government, would be heard. Fletcher, Kerney, and White were largely responsible for this statement, whereas the other two members were reluctant to use the phrase "to terminate American military occupation."

The State Department refused to allow this statement to be released. Instead, the department wired the commission an innocuous statement that said nothing about withdrawing from Haiti. White and Kerney refused to accept it. White maintained that it would offend the Haitians and disgust the civilized world. The commission then formally voted against releasing the State Department's suggested text. On the day of their arrival the commission issued a statement that differed from their original one but was not so weak as the State Department's. It did not, however, make any pledges as to the termination of American military occupation. As a result, the commission was faced with a boycott by the Haitian opposition. The commission had asked that all Haitian groups present their points of view, but the opposition boycott now brought about a stalemate.

It was at this juncture that White made a valuable contribution to the commission's work. Pierre Hudicourt, a leader of the opposition and a friend of Oswald Garrison Villard of the *Nation*, went to see White. Villard had explained that he could trust White's liberal tendencies, and after White had declared that the commission wanted to serve Haiti, the boycott was called off. The opposition now cultivated White, and he was a frequent guest at country club dances and at dinners at their homes. The Haitian correspondent for the *Nation* cabled: "The work of the commission has been superlative. The Commissioners themselves have been earnest, intelligent, thorough, unbiased, fearless, determined. By their tact and sympathy they have won the confidence and co-operation of the Opposition. Mr. White is the most influential member."

White was amazed and puzzled at what he saw in Haiti. Eighty-five per cent of the population of three million were illiterate. The vast mass of Negroes were dominated by a small mulatto group, which was French rather than African in culture. The lawyers, teachers, and doctors of this group had studied in Paris and were thoroughly French in point of view. After visiting in the homes of the mulatto leaders, he wrote Sallie: "These were not Negroes but French. . . . The manners of these people are exquisite. They are living in the eighteenth century and have the serious manners of the grandees . . . They seem to have faith in me and are giving me every social attention, which I frankly accept. They seem to feel that I speak their language. Anyway I'm going to play fair with them. . . ." The *Nation* reported that the Haitians were saying about White: "Already we love and trust him. . . . He has found our soul."

Shortly after the boycott was abandoned, the commission was faced with another crisis. The opposition had been banned from conducting a parade to protest the American occupation. The situation was tense, and violence was imminent. "The whole population feel that its liberties have been trampled down," White wrote to his son Bill. "They honestly feel that we are tyrannical and the fact that the occupation is honestly trying to serve the Haitians does not get to them, because we are not serving them in the Haitian way. However, we are trying to serve them after the manner of American civilization and American ideas which they loathe. We are in the 20th century looking toward the 21st. They are in the 18th century with the ideals of the Grand Louis always behind them as models."

A leader of the opposition explained to White that their parade had been prohibited by the incumbent President and the American marines. White worked through the commission, and the ban was removed. On the day of the parade, White had lunch at the home of Monsieur Hudicourt. "I never had so sophisticated and as beautiful a meal in my life," he once said. It was French food with delicious sausages, pickled fish, tomatoes in oil, garnished fish salad, breast of roast turkey, gravy with onions, potatoes, ice cream, cake, and coffee.

After the meal, White attended the church services at the starting point of the parade. Then, back at the hotel, he watched the parade pass by. Much to his embarrassment, at regular intervals the parade would halt and some leader would deliver a speech of gratitude to him for having permitted the parade. "It was a great day for the Hattons and the Kelleys," he told Sallie, "and not since Tom la Doola invaded Afghanistan have the Irish had such a triumph. But for us the parade would have been either squelched or started in spite of the police, which might have brought on a revolution. For these people are at the brittle breaking point."

As White was watching the parade, there suddenly appeared prostrated at his feet an old, gray-haired, black peasant woman wearing a faded blue calico dress. White reached down to help her up; and trying to place a Haitian flag in his hands, she spoke to him in a tongue he did not understand. The paraders halted and began to gather around them. White helped the peasant woman up, and the paraders began to threaten her for bothering their benefactor. In order to reassure the paraders that he was not embarrassed by the incident, he waved at the crowd and touched his fingers to his lips in as affectionate a gesture as he could make. The crowd was stilled with amazement that a white man from the United States and one of ambassadorial rank would do such a thing. After a few seconds of silence, the paraders broke out with a roar of applause. "After that it was pie for the commission," White explained to Roger Baldwin. "We could do anything we wanted to do with the Haitian opposition which had been teetering on the brink of revolution and bloodshed until that hour, having somewhat lost faith in all Americans."

Le Nouvelliste of Port-au-Prince hailed White's action by declaring on March 3 that "The people of Haiti . . . will be sincerely affected upon learning of this gesture by Mr. White," and W. Cameron Forbes, chairman of the commission, has observed: "There is no question but that Mr. White appealed greatly to the emotional people of Haiti for whom he evinced such sympathetic attachment."

After several days of listening to the Haitians enumerate their troubles, the commission discovered that a revolution might break out at any time. They wired President Hoover for power to handle the situation. Then the commission told President Borno that he would have to abide by the Haitian constitution, which prevented him from succeeding himself. The commission had no doubt that public sentiment was hostile to the continuation of Borno in power. "He is thin, tall, toothy and most disagreeable, and lives entirely apart from reality," White wrote home. ". . . He has a little sneering laugh. . . . I kept pinching myself—and Kerney said he did also—to realize that I was not listening to a stage melodrama. It just did not seem possible that any man should be so patent a stage villain."

Forbes and Fletcher conducted the negotiations with the Haitian opposition whereby its leaders drew up a list of five names of acceptable presidential candidates, and President Borno agreed to select one of these, Eugene Roy, to serve as temporary president. Soon after assuming office, Roy was to call an election of a legislative assembly, which would elect the permanent president. Borno had no choice but to accept this plan, since he was in power only with American support.

With this problem solved, the commission began to investigate the withdrawal of the marines and the appointment of Haitians to military and civil posts. They made a tour of the island, conducting hearings at the major towns. Outside the sophisticated town of Port-au-Prince, White was impressed with the pure African nature of the people. Instead of possessing a veneer of French culture, the people in the hinterland of Haiti were as African in point of view as had been their ancestors, who had been transplanted there to work as slaves on French plantations.

On March 16, the commission left Haiti. They had had some difficulty in persuading the State Department to accept their arrangements for the new president, but at the last minute the State Department concurred. The department insisted upon caution and that everything be in writing. So meticulous was the department in its wired instructions that White told the other commissioners: "The young men in the Department feel that control of this Commission has passed entirely out of the hands of Forbes and Fletcher into the hands of White!"

On board ship, the commission drew up its report for President Hoover. They recommended the gradual withdrawal of the marines; the replacement of American officers in the Haitian constabulary and in the civil service by Haitians; the replacement of General Russell, when the time came for his transfer, by a civilian high commissioner; and the recognition of the newly elected president. An appendix was added to the report. "Confidentially, let me tell you," White wrote Oswald Garrison Villard, "you can avoid the Appendix. It was done in the State Department by the oiled and curled Assyrian bulls that inhabit those stalls."

The President's Commission to Haiti rendered a valuable service toward the improvement of relations in the Western Hemisphere.

Although the marines were not completely withdrawn until the administration of Franklin D. Roosevelt, the avowed willingness of the United States to abandon its previous policy of intervention in the domestic affairs of its neighbors marked the launching of the Good Neighbor Policy. When Roosevelt took office, certain steps already taken, such as those concerning Haiti, made it easier for the Roosevelt administration to develop fully the role of the Good Neighbor.

White claimed that, since he did not understand the workings of diplomacy, he did not contribute much to the success of the Haitian commission. Actually his ability to win the confidence of the opposition helped pave the way for the commission's success. Hubert Herring, executive director of the Committee on Cultural Relations with Latin America, wrote him on February 20, 1932: "I am just back from seeing your special friends in Haiti. If you are ever inclined to feel dejected, you can always remember that the Haitians have installed you in the high places along with the Holy Trinity. . . ." *Le Nouvelliste* of Port-au-Prince remarked about White on March 6, 1930: "How well the name corresponds to and fits the character, White of soul and of heart . . . full of wise counsels and generous fervor, gay, lovable in his person."

Shortly after the commission left Haiti, White had reports from his friends in the opposition, Georges N. Leger and Charles Moravia, that President Borno was trying to sabotage the commission's plan for the election of Eugene Roy. White quickly wired the State Department, and he was assured that General Russell would receive orders to execute the proposal. White also had the other members of the commission insist upon the maintenance of their plan.

On May 15, Eugene Roy was inaugurated president, and six months later the National Assembly chose Stenio Vincent to serve the unexpired portion of the 1930-1936 term. The commission had stated in its report that it was "under no delusion as to what may happen in Haiti after the convocation of the elected legislative assembly and, to a greater extent, after the completed withdrawal of the United States forces . . . The educated public opinion and literate minority are so small that any government formed in these circumstances is liable to become an oligarchy." Until education could reduce illiteracy, the commission predicted that Haiti would be in danger of constant political upheavals.

Although the constitution forbade his re-election, President Vincent had such complete dictatorial powers by 1936 that he had his term of office extended for a five-year period. Haiti was far from democratic after 1930, but its political system was not to be dominated by the United States. If it was to have tyranny, it would be its own form. Summing up the Haitian situation, White declared that it was the "problem of the tropics, of course, a shrewd, ruthless, sophisticated but in Haiti culturally refined ruling class of bourbon French mulattoes with the ideals of Louis XIV aristocracy; beneath it an ignorant illiterate mass of fairly purebred Africans, and neither class either desiring stable self-government or with a tradition or understanding of stable self-government; that on the one hand, and the terrible impact of capital seeking investment, requiring self-government, pressing upon the people like the pressure of water on the ocean bottom. Cruel, relentless, hopeless! One hell of a mess—the century's problem in the hot, green ribbon that bands the globe."

*   *   *

By the time White returned from Haiti, a major depression was under way in the United States. On October 29, 1929, a catastrophic drop in prices had occurred on the stock market. In every city and town, families dropped from affluence into poverty. Day after day more and more people were thrown out of work. Europe was already in a depressed state. In the United States the depression had come as the result of many forces. There had been an overproduction of capital goods at the existing price level; a high artificial price level had been maintained by monopolies; the farmers for years had had low purchasing power; and there had been an excessive and an unsound stock market speculation. During the Coolidge era, the businessman, the grocer, the clerk, and the washerwoman were all hypnotized by the idea that prosperity was eternal. They squandered funds on stocks with no attempt to evaluate the soundness of their investment.

As early as April, 1929, William Allen White had deplored the widespread speculation on the stock market. He warned that too much money was being lent by corporations and investment trusts to stockbrokers for speculative purposes. "What about the day of reckoning?" he asked. "When will the sleeper awake? It is a house of cards. Step softly, breathe lightly and watch out. This condition cannot go on forever." Although Emporia directly lost very little when the crash came, White pointed out that "the loss which Emporia will feel will be the indirect loss; the loss which comes to a rural community when the wheels of industry slow down. That may come later and it may be serious."

Every day during 1930, thousands of men were being thrown out of work and a general spirit of unrest was spreading through the nation. White wrote an editorial on December 13, 1930, in which he declared: "Surely the need of the hour is for strong, dramatic leadership, together with the drama of a cause. For ordinary times an ordinary President will do. But President Hoover, who has some sort of a shrinking horror of connecting his office with causes, should be told by his advisers that in extraordinary times, times of turmoil and panic, the presidential office must take leadership in the country . . . Go to the people, Mr. President. They are dependable. Lincoln, Roosevelt and Wilson found the people a tower of refuge and of strength. Whoever is wise and honest and brave, they will follow to victory."

Through an intermediary, White urged Hoover to open a relief office in Cleveland or in Chicago, and spend part of his time at his office administering relief. This would be a dramatic step, White explained, which would encourage the public to believe that their president was a man of action. White was completely aware of Hoover's inability to stir people emotionally. "He can plow the ground, harrow it, plant the seed, cultivate it, but seems to lack the power to harvest it and flail it into a political merchantable product," he observed late in 1929. A year later, White confided to his former colleague on the Haitian commission, James Kerney: "There is no hope for the ineptitude of this administration . . . For a man who has high intentions and a noble purpose, our beloved President has a greater capacity for doing exactly the wrong thing at a nicely appointed right time than any man who ever polished his pants in the big chair at the White House."

In spite of the unfavorable situation for the Republicans, White again did his best to hold Kansas in the Republican column in 1930. His candidate, Governor Reed, however, was soundly defeated in the primary, a defeat attributed to his appointment of Henry J. Allen to the senatorship, to the hostility of organized labor and farm groups, and to the work of John Hamilton as campaign manager for Reed's opponent. In the subsequent election that November, Allen was defeated in his race for the senatorial seat and a Democrat, Harry H. Woodring, captured the governorship. White had some consolation, however, in the election of his son Bill to the state legislature and of his cousin Roland Boynton as attorney general.

The equanimity of the two major parties was upset during the 1930 campaign by the independent candidacy of Dr. John R. Brinkley for the governorship. Brinkley had been operating on men to revitalize them, and he had built a radio station to advertise his practice. Before long he had a tremendous following. The Kansas City *Star* charged that Brinkley was a quack. Soon the State Medical Board revoked Brinkley's right to practice. Six weeks before the November election, Brinkley decided to fight back by running for the governorship. The law, however, now required that an independent candidate had to file by June 20 in order to have his name printed on the ballot. Over his powerful radio station, Brinkley explained to the people that they would have to write in his name on the ballots and place a cross-mark in a square opposite his name.

Before election day, White tended to minimize the Brinkley campaign. He admitted to his friends that the two major parties were running weak candidates, and that a strong protest movement was basically sound. He did not think, on the other hand, that Brinkley would receive many votes since a write-in campaign required higher intelligence on the part of the voter than Brinkley's supporters had. White was convinced that Brinkley was "a dirty quack," but he warned the Kansas City *Star* that its scathing attacks on the man were making him a martyr.

White was amazed when Brinkley polled 183,278 votes. The Baltimore *Evening Sun* failed, however, to see why William Allen White was so startled and indignant that Brinkley should have amassed such a large vote. "Why should it surprise anyone?" the *Sun* asked on November 8. "Kansas voted for Sockless Jerry Simpson. Kansas voted for Pfeffer . . . Throughout her political history it has never entered the mind of Kansas to doubt the power of political ghosts, witches, alchemists and devil-dancers; and so she has steadily turned loose on the country a succession of apparitions such as has been conjured up by no other State in the Union."

Some Kansas political observers have felt that if many of Brinkley's supporters had not marred their ballots and thus lost their vote, or if Brinkley's name had been printed on the ballot, he would have been elected. White was appalled as he studied the meaning of the election returns. He believed that Brinkley was a serious menace, the more so because economic conditions were so desperate that the Brinkley candidacy could flourish on economic dissatisfaction. Likening Brinkley to Huey Long of Louisiana and Big Bill Thompson of Chicago, White observed: "He is, I think, the most perfect master of mob appeal I have ever seen in American politics . . . It is a type of fundamentalism like that which boiled over in Tennessee, and passed the fundamentalist law in Arkansas two years ago."

* * *

When the Democrats captured control of Congress in November, 1930, White knew there was no hope for the Republicans two years hence unless Herbert Hoover allied himself with such progressives as George Norris. All through 1930, White wrote to Henry J. Allen and other close advisers of Hoover urging them to persuade the President to surround himself with men like Norris and Borah rather than with the reactionary group. That Hoover was constitutionally unable to work with progressive forces was amply indicated in George Norris's campaign for re-election in Nebraska in 1930. Norris had refused to support Hoover in 1928 and Coolidge in 1924. On the floor of the Senate he had conducted the people's fight against Republican leadership on many issues vitally important to the nation. Robert H. Lucas, director of the Republican National Committee, led the fight against Norris's bid for re-election. White broke with the party's action and aided Norris by writing editorials and sending bundles of *Gazettes* into

Nebraska for distribution. He also wrote many letters on Norris's behalf. When Norris was re-elected, White editorially warned Hoover that Norris was on the right side of issues, and that Hoover should work with Norris rather than fight him.

White was convinced that Hoover had too much of the administrator's confirmed timidity to be a real leader of democracy in the increasingly grave economic situation. As Hoover's stock sagged with the public, the Democrats' chances for 1932 increased immeasurably. "These are great days for you Democrats," the Emporia editor wrote Governor Franklin D. Roosevelt of New York on December 17, 1930, "but don't be too cagey. If the old ship rights herself within the next year . . . the people will forget that she ever listed, and what I fear is that if she does not right herself soon, the crew will come storming out of the fo'c's'le and throw the whole quarter deck crowd into the sea . . . Unless the middle class has brains enough to curb the plutocracy and produce some approximation of justice for the underprivileged . . . we shall segregate on one ballot the credulous, the suspicious, the bigoted, the ignorant, led by the crafty and the fools."

To bolster public confidence in Hoover, White helped White House intimates like David Hinshaw launch a political tabloid in the fall of 1930. White was thoroughly aware by this time that Hoover was no progressive. But at the urging of Hinshaw, who was not above utilizing White's midwestern liberalism as a cloak for the reaction of the administration, White wrote for the first issue of *Washington* an article in which he hailed Hoover as a great idealist in the tradition of Theodore Roosevelt and Woodrow Wilson.

As the economic situation continued to deteriorate, President Hoover called commission after commission of businessmen to Washington to pledge to keep up wages and not lay off their workers. These voluntary agreements invariably broke down, but Hoover, a firm believer in co-operation among businessmen, was reluctant to increase the power of the government to meet the crisis. Since the Republican administrations before 1929 had subsidized but not regulated business, the Hoover administration was unwilling to admit that this policy had been an obvious failure. Hoover, in the gravest economic crisis of the nation, refused to increase the powers of the positive state to force business to serve the people. Over the protest of Editor White, Hoover vetoed government operation of the power plant at Muscle Shoals, which had been designed to serve as a yardstick to test power rates charged by private utility companies.

At the beginning of 1931, the Department of Labor made the conservative estimate that 4,500,000 people were out of work. During that year bread lines lengthened, and many people feared that violence might break out. Although President Hoover agreed that no one must go hungry, he was unwilling for the federal government to embark upon direct work relief. Private agencies and local governments were left to handle relief, even though they could not cope with the problem.

In March, 1931, while serving as chairman of Emporia's effort to secure jobs for the unemployed and to supply relief for the destitute, White's health broke down. For the next six months he was so nervously exhausted that he had to spend most of the time vacationing in New Mexico and Colorado. By August, however, he was well enough to serve as a member of President Hoover's Committee for Unemployment Relief. White brought to the President's Committee certain pronounced views. From his own experience, he knew that the problem of relief for the unemployed was not just a local problem. The national government alone had the resources to deal with the situation. The industrialization of the country and the organization of monopolies had taken control of industry away from local people and had lodged it in a few urban centers. As a result, local communities did not have the resources or the weapons of control to provide work. White also believed that "in this modern civilization under governments founded upon some semblance of the rule of reason the world does owe every man a living, who will work for it."

White further believed that the Hoover administration should take steps to reform the evils of private capitalism. "I have been wishing for some time," he wrote Chester Rowell on July 14, 1931, "that the President would find it in his heart to evangelize a little upon the duties of the great industrial leaders and teach them that duties go with rights." He thought that the worker should be guaranteed decent food, housing, and clothing; the education of his children until they were twenty-one; and security against poverty and old age. "The President has stood bravely and effectively for the privileges of the invested dollar," White added. "Now is the time for him to stand also for the duties of the invested dollar."

In addition to serving on the President's Committee for Unemployment Relief, White was appointed by Governor Woodring as a member of the Governor's Committee on Employment to coordinate its work with that of the President's Committee. After attending several of the meetings of the President's Committee, White was impressed with the fear that existed in the minds of the leaders of industry. They were afraid, he told Henry Haskell, that there soon would be barricades in the streets and bloody turmoil.

When the *Nation* asked White what he would do in the depression crisis, if he were a dictator, White answered that he would remove the fear motive from industry in order that the worker would have the feeling of security in his job; he would guarantee a minimum standard of living; he would support workers' insurance to cover sickness, accidents, and old age; and he would teach the powerful and the supercilious to be humble.

On the question of relief, White explained to Senator Capper that he did not agree with Hoover that the federal government should not appropriate money for public-works relief. The Reconstruction Finance Corporation, sponsored by Hoover and chartered by Congress in January, 1932, to lend money to banks, railroads, industry, and to farmers, did not satisfy White. "I do not hold with the President's theory that business is either wiser, more honest, or more effective than government, in its various phases . . ." he told Capper. "Jimmy Walker, Big Bill Thompson, Vare and their kind are better, wiser and more efficient than are Raskob with his inside pool manipulating the markets, the crooks whom La Guardia uncovered, Insull with his pyramid of larceny, and Kreuger with his till-tapping, bond snatching manipulations."

The country was faced with starvation amidst plenty. Unless the federal government took action to provide work, White warned, there would be serious trouble ahead. "I am not for giving any man a dole," he wrote Capper, "but I do believe that every honest man able to work should have work even if we have to stretch a point to give it to him. . . . We are faced with a condition of starvation, not with a theory of economics."

Although the effects of the depression were grim enough in Kansas, White was appalled by the impact of the depression on a great metropolitan center like New York. "I can see more evidence of depression in one block of a city street than in miles of countryside . . ." he told *The New York Times* on May 15, 1932. "In the West the effects of depression are not so evident. The corn is beginning to grow, so are the other crops. Remember that no matter how hard the times, food can never be so scarce in an agricultural center as in a metropolis. After all, a man can nearly always raise all he needs to eat . . . But here as I walk along I not only see a great increase in the number of down-and-outers, but even among those who are more or less prosperous, I notice a great preponderance of long faces. Everyone has the same tale of hard luck . . . Today New York is a busted Babylon."

CHAPTER 19

THE REBIRTH
OF THE PROGRESSIVE MOVEMENT

"ON THE whole and by and large, I am for the New Deal,"
William Allen White informed an audience at the University of
Kansas on June 11, 1934. "It is neither Communist nor Fascist.
Much of it is necessary. All of it is human. And most of it is long
past due." Although many of his Republican friends screamed that
the New Deal was un-American, White knew the deep roots that
the movement had in the American past. From his own intimate
experience with Theodore Roosevelt's Square Deal and the Bull
Moose party, the Emporia editor was quite aware that the New
Deal marked a resurgence of the prewar progressive era.

His tolerant attitude toward Franklin D. Roosevelt's reforms
and his unwillingness to join in the general Republican abuse of
the New Deal increased White's prestige as a mellow interpreter
of life and led many people to agree with a New York *Times*
remark that the Kansas editor was "as vital as the trees and sunshine. Years do not age him." Although he was to support a large
share of the New Deal laws, White did oppose Franklin D. Roosevelt's election in 1932, 1936, and 1940. Before the 1932 campaign,
he was displeased at President Hoover's support of the Smoot-
Hawley tariff, his veto of the Muscle Shoals Bill, and his inaction
on the relief problem. But he asserted that he was for Hoover for
having appointed Richard Hopkins to the federal bench in Kansas,

for not vetoing the Norris-La Guardia Anti-injunction Bill, and for appointing Benjamin Cardozo to the Supreme Court. At least a year before the election, however, White knew that Hoover was doomed to defeat in the Missouri and Mississippi valleys. "On a vote now with nobody running against him in Kansas," White declared, "Hoover would lose the state."

White covered both conventions in 1932 for the North American Newspaper Alliance. At the Republican convention, he asserted that the delegates were spending too much time on the prohibition question and too little time on the depression crisis. "It's funny when the country is teetering on an economic brink, that all the Republicans can think about is whiskey," he observed. "The group that is supposed to represent the brains of the country (Yes, I mean the Republicans) is shadow boxing on this rather irrelevant liquor problem."

The Republican platform that year advocated the extension of the protective tariff, acceptance of membership in the World Court, restriction on immigration, and the development of the St. Lawrence waterway; and pledged the party to support "any plan which will help to balance production against demand, and thereby raise agricultural prices, provided it is economically sound and administratively workable without burdensome bureaucracy." "It is a good platform," White declared, "but it is so badly couched in pernicious language that the voter never will see what it means."

The Democrats adopted a platform denouncing the Republican policy of isolation abroad and of fostering monopolies at home. Positively, the Democrats advocated reciprocal trade agreements, aid for the farmers, federal relief for the unemployed, the regulation of the stock exchange, and the reform of the banking structure. Governor Roosevelt, after being nominated on the fourth ballot, flew to the convention in Chicago to deliver his acceptance speech. In this speech he promised "a new deal for the American people."

Roosevelt explained that the problem was to restore control of the government to the people. "Let us now and here highly resolve to resume the country's interrupted march along the path of real progress, of real justice, of real equality for all of our citizens, great and small," he told the convention. "Our indomitable leader in that interrupted march is no longer with us, but there still survives today his spirit. . . . Let us feel that in everything we do there still lives with us, if not the body, the great indomitable, unquenchable, progressive soul of our commander in chief, Woodrow Wilson."

"I liked Roosevelt's speech," White wrote Harold Ickes on July 14, 1932. "I was in the Hall and heard it. It seems to me the most important acceptance speech we have had for twenty years. And if Roosevelt can make good with it, nobody will be happier than I. I wonder if he will go the distance, that is all that bothers me."

Roosevelt toured the country advocating farm relief, tariff reform, the regulation of utilities, and the economic reorganization of the business structure. The Democratic candidate explained that the problem facing America was that of adapting the existing economic organization of capitalism to the service of the people. Roosevelt did not propose to destroy capitalism, but in the tradition of the prewar progressives he urged the need of reforms to correct abuses and to head off revolutionary movements from developing.

Hoover countered Roosevelt's request for the positive state by reiterating his belief that the government should subsidize but not regulate business. "This campaign is more than a contest between two men," Hoover charged. "It is more than a contest between parties. It is a contest between two philosophies of government. . . . Our opponents . . . are proposing changes and so-called new deals which would destroy the very foundations of our American system." White, of course, knew that both Hoover's philosophy of rugged individualism and Roosevelt's proposal of the positive state were in the American tradition. The only real question was which was in the democratic tradition.

Although the Emporia editor believed that the positive state was the only road to a free and democratic society, he supported Herbert Hoover during the campaign. He knew that Hoover would be overwhelmed. He predicted that all the despairing, all the defeated, all the disgruntled, and all the underprivileged would vote for Roosevelt.

In late August, White visited those areas in Nebraska and Iowa where farmers had organized to prevent produce from being delivered to market unless they received a fair price for their labors. He saw barricades set up in the streets, market-going trucks overturned, and the sheriff and his deputies overwhelmed. "Faith in democratic institutions, in parliamentary government, is beginning to wane among certain despairing Western farmers," White warned. "The farmers across the country are grim and sad and sore. . . . When the American farmer comes out to the road with a club or a pitchfork, the warning flag is out. There may be danger ahead." The bitterness toward President Hoover that White saw among these farmers was unbelievable and, he felt, unreasonable; nevertheless, it meant that Hoover could not carry any state between the Rockies and the Mississippi.

White wrote editorials for Hoover and the straight Republican ticket, and he delivered a nation-wide radio speech that was recorded and widely rebroadcast. White asked for the re-election of the President on the grounds of Hoover's having led America wisely through the depression. Referring to Roosevelt as "a fair-spoken, amiable, adroit politician" and to the Democratic party as a "mercenary greedy partisan horde," White stated that to turn the government over to them "might easily throw America into chaos, financial, social, political."

White's support of President Hoover was partially the result of personal friendship, of pride of discovery, and a reluctance to desert a sinking ship. More important than these factors, however, was, as usual, the situation in Kansas. To bolt the Republican ticket would threaten White's power in the Republican party in his home state, where his candidate, Alf M. Landon, was running for governor; White did not want to take any steps that would endanger Landon's election.

In his campaign, Landon was fortunate in having Dr. Brinkley run as an independent candidate since Brinkley split the Democratic vote and made it possible for Landon to survive the Democratic tidal wave that swept the rest of the nation. White led the attack on Brinkley. With the aid of the Kansas City *Star*, Kansas was blanketed with White's blistering editorials. His most scathing denunciation of Dr. Brinkley appeared in an editorial entitled "Save Kansas." Written in the same cutting, biting language as "What's the Matter With Kansas?" the editorial declared that "a demagog threatens this State who may easily wreck our institutions and break down thirty years of progressive legislation." White charged that Brinkley as governor would "debauch our higher educational institutions and make Kansas a laughing stock from one end of the country to another. . . . Heretofore a Kansan has been able to walk the world with a high head. Are we going to bow our heads after the election; bow in shame that the intelligent, patriotic people of this State did not have the sense or the courage to avert this disgrace?" After reading White's vitriolic language, *The New York Times* facetiously remarked that "Kansas is bleeding from every pore of her vocabularium. Sharp's rifles are discharging from the well-known Emporium of White & Son, unlimited, and Bibles are closed until after election."

Although Roosevelt carried Kansas, Landon captured the governorship. White's newspaper friends were quick to tell him that his attacks on Brinkley were a major factor in the successful outcome of the gubernatorial election. "I had the same fun fighting Brinkley," White wrote Kansas stockraiser Dan Casement on November 12, 1932, "that I had fighting the klan and it was the same outfit, the organized moron minority, plus the despairing and the disgruntled who knew better."

*   *   *

Just before his friend Hoover left the presidency, White visited him in Washington and gathered material for an article on the titular head of the Republican party. White contended in the article that Hoover had been handicapped because he looked on the presidency as purely an administrative office whereas it was also a pulpit and a forum. To be successful, a president had to mobilize public opinion behind his administration, but White pointed out that Hoover lacked this talent. According to White's estimate, Hoover, never a plutocrat, did not have the knack of publicly scolding men of wealth. White believed, however, that by taking such steps as creating the Reconstruction Finance Corporation, Hoover had pointed the way toward recovery.

"He is a queer man," White confided to a Kansas friend. "He is tremendously middle class, hates plutocrats as much as he suspects proletariats, lives simply, despises luxury, tries to be efficient, has a flinty, repressed Quaker tenderness, easily wounded, grumbles where he should God damn, pouts and pets where he should grin and giggle, works like a horse, hates too much, fears too much, and loves too little. I like him for his loyalties. But he is a queer bird. Personally everyone whom I ever knew intimately and well is a queer bird. God only makes queer birds when you know them."

In the years that passed after Hoover left the White House, the Emporia editor insisted that Hoover was the scapegoat of the depression and that in time history would rescue him from an unjust oblivion. According to White, if Hoover had been re-elected in 1932, he would have placed many of the New Deal's laws on the statute books. "He has the most unfortunate mannerism based upon a habit of life which gives orders and cannot do teamwork," White wrote. "He would have been a swell dictator but a poor president. If the country ever wants a dictator, he is the white-haired boy."

By the time President Hoover left office, fifteen million men were out of work, the banking structure of the nation was tottering, and farmers had organized vigilante groups to prevent foreclosure of their farms. Everyone turned to Washington for aid. "Your distant relative is an X in the equation," White wrote Theodore Roosevelt, Jr., on February 1, 1933. "He may develop his stubbornness into courage, his amiability into wisdom, his sense of superiority into statesmanship. Responsibility is a winepress that brings forth strange juices out of men."

Roosevelt's inaugural address on March 4, 1933, gave hope to a disillusioned and embittered America. Asserting that "the only thing we have to fear is fear itself," he promised a new deal for the forgotten man. "We must act and act quickly." Roosevelt then supplied America with militant action. He pushed a bewildering and extraordinary number of laws through Congress. A month after Roosevelt's inauguration, White editorialized: "Strange things are moving across this American world of ours. The country seems to want action—dramatic action. Roosevelt is supplying the want."

White was immensely pleased with the appointment of his old

friend Harold L. Ickes as secretary of the interior, of Henry Wallace as secretary of agriculture, and of Frances Perkins as secretary of labor. One week after Roosevelt's inauguration, White told Ickes: "It doesn't matter much what your man Roosevelt says. It is what he is doing that is pleasing the American people. So far so good. If he would keep this up for four years I am ashamed to think what will happen to us poor benighted Republicans if there are any left."

"These are grand days, worth living for!" he wrote Ickes in an enthusiastic mood on May 23. "Your Big Boss is doing a splendid job. I am scared stiff about him. Every day, as he handsprings lightly over the first page, tossing the world on his toes, I am jostled by a fear that he will fall down, but he has not fallen down so far." Ickes assured White that Roosevelt had great qualities. "He has strength and power and imagination and political sagacity," observed Ickes, "and with it all, he is one of the friendliest and nicest human beings that I have ever been associated with." White's support of much of the President's program during 1933 was gratefully received by Roosevelt, who wrote him: "It gives me a great deal of pleasure to know that you are with us in these strenuous times."

*　　*　　*

Three months after the launching of the New Deal, the Whites sailed for London, where White reported the International Economic Conference for the North American Newspaper Alliance. Traveling with them was Henry Haskell, who was covering the conference for the Kansas City *Star*. From the conference, White reported that Europe was tremendously impressed with the New Deal's attempt to curb rugged individualism. He felt that, on the whole, the conference was a waste of time. Since the United States refused to stabilize the dollar, little could be accomplished. The New Deal, at this point, was lowering the value of the dollar to help stimulate an economic revival, and feared that any stabilization of its value would check hopes of American recovery. At the conference, White established a friendship with Secretary of State Cordell Hull and left with a lasting impression of his honesty, intelligence, and courage.

From London the Whites journeyed to Russia to gain firsthand information concerning the immense changes that had swept that country under the Soviet regime. They had "two gorgeous weeks" in Russia "and saw the world turned upside down," White wrote Erwin Canham of the *Christian Science Monitor*. The Whites spent most of their time in the company of American reporters— Walter Duranty, William Henry Chamberlin, Maurice Hindus, Eugene Lyons, and Louis Fischer. Russia, to the Whites, was the most fascinating country on the planet. They were impressed with the magnitude of the Soviet attempt to industrialize a country that had been dominated by feudal traditions up to 1918.

White told his American audience that Soviet Russia was "not the American kind of civilization which clicks with precision. It bumps and rattles. . . . But it stands up and marches." He discounted any rumors that Soviet leadership would be overthrown. Pointing out that each race or division of mankind was entitled to work out its own destiny, White wrote: "For the most part the present Russian State satisfies the Russians, however much it must irk and agonize Americans."

Although White made it exceptionally clear in his dispatches that he disliked the lack of a free press, trial by jury, and freedom of speech, the fact that he praised the accomplishments of the Soviets in transforming Russian society irritated the Russophobes in the United States. The additional circumstance of his favoring immediate American recognition of Russia, and of having favored it throughout the twenties, only embittered those Americans who found consolation in hating the Russian Revolution.

From Leningrad the Whites traveled to Warsaw and then to Vienna. They were shocked at the condition of this delightful city, threatened as it was by Nazi Germany on its border, and by the reluctance of the royalty and landlords of the old Austro-Hungarian Empire to accept a republican, democratic Austria. The month of September they spent touring Italy, revisiting many of the spots they had seen on their first European trip in 1909.

While in Italy, White had an interview with Benito Mussolini. To jolly Mussolini a bit, White told him that Soviet Russia was the most stable government on earth. When Mussolini blinked his eyes and belligerently exclaimed "What?" White, in a mischievous fashion, answered: "Because they are still shooting them in Russia. They are quicker on the trigger than you people are and are good for a long time."

By Armistice Day of 1933, White was back in Emporia, where he expressed in a *Gazette* editorial his acute distaste for the forms of government flourishing in much of Europe. He charged that Russia was ruled by "proletarian tyrants"; that Germany was governed by "paranoiac sadists"; and that Italy had given up her liberties "to fill her stomachs." Reflecting American disillusionment toward World War I, White added in a sarcastic mood: "What a glorious war! All wars are like that. The next one will be worse. War is the devil's own joke on humanity. So let's celebrate Armistice Day by laughing our heads off."

When his old friend Jacob Billikopf praised this editorial, White explained: "I was feeling sad that day, low in mind. Generally I am more optimistic. But the growth of fascism in Central Europe east of the Rhine and the foothills of Italy, and the growth of communism in Eastern Europe depressed me for I am a democrat and the age-long fight for liberty has seemed worth while. I cannot see it obliterated without heartbreak."

* * *

While the Whites were on their European tour, a great bond scandal rocked Kansas. Late in August, national bank examiners unearthed a million-dollar forgery of Kansas municipal bonds by Ronald Finney of Emporia. The investigation revealed also that Warren Finney, Ronald's father, had stripped his many banks of their real assets and filled them with forged securities. Some state officials were deeply involved in the scandal. The offices of state auditor, the state treasurer, and the attorney general had been manipulated by the Finneys for their own designs.

The bond scandal shook the White family. The Finneys and the Whites had been intimate. They had worked together in politics and in town affairs, and the two families had spent many vacations together. Whenever distinguished guests were visiting the Whites, the Finney family was usually invited to dinner. White had secured Warren Finney the post of Kansas chairman of President Hoover's antihoarding campaign. White had also written in

1931 an introduction for a pamphlet by Finney advocating a state income tax. Many times he had recommended Warren Finney to his friends as a fine, public-spirited citizen. W. L. White has written a revealing description of the relations of the two families, as well as the bond scandal, in his novel *What People Said* (1938).

When the bond scandal was exposed, the Whites had the Warren Finneys' daughter with them on their European visit. As soon as they reached New York, they hurried to Emporia, in case White was needed to testify at the trial. Although he had been on intimate personal terms with Warren Finney, he had not mixed business with this relationship. He had not deposited money in Finney's bank and was not involved in the financial manipulations of the Finney family.

"Our homecoming was one of the saddest of my life," White wrote one friend. "For twenty years and more . . . I have enjoyed the friendship of a man named Finney in this town. . . . I knew him as a fine, public-spirited, generous, intelligent, courageous and sometimes cantankerous man. But like all bankers he was leading some kind of a double life. What, I don't know. His son went wrong, probably so far as I can figure it out forged a million dollars' worth of municipal bonds. . . . There are two theories of the crash and the disgrace that followed. I can subscribe to either. One is that the son is trying to protect the father; the other is that the father is trying to protect the son . . . It is a hard life. When you get along in your sixties you like to feel the stability of your friends."

White was not called upon to testify at the trial that led to the conviction of the Finneys. The trial was front-page news for months. It was being conducted at the same time that Kansas Federal Judge Richard Hopkins was securing a divorce, and some observers felt that the overwhelming amount of publicity connected with the Finney trial was partially designed to take the minds of the citizens away from the divorce. Some observers felt also that Governor Landon was pushing for a heavy penalty on the Finneys—Ronald had been a friend of the governor's—in order to build himself for re-election and as possible presidential material.

The Finneys were sentenced to the state penitentiary, but the father committed suicide before he could be taken to prison. It is rumored that before Ronald Finney was sentenced his attorney, in the presence of the judge, worked out an informal agreement with the state's attorney whereby, in return for a confession of guilt by Finney, the state would ask for a fifteen-year sentence. It is reported by some that Landon objected to the plan and the judge then sentenced Finney to six hundred years.

The White family always felt that the 600-year sentence had been unjust and was only a political gesture to capture votes. In previous Kansas forgery cases, fifteen years had usually been the maximum sentence, and White felt that Finney should have received the same term. Later White was unsuccessful in trying to secure a pardon for Finney from Governor Ratner, but he did succeed in obtaining the promise of a parole from Governor Schoeppel just before he died in January, 1944.

The Finney case was not closed for White with the sentencing of Ronald Finney. At an extraordinary session of the legislature, the lower house voted to impeach White's cousin Roland Boynton, the attorney general. When the Senate sat as a court of impeachment, the House action was defeated. White played a major part in bringing about this decision, by leading the defense of Boynton. White's newspaper friends received innumerable letters asking them to reprint White's editorials on Boynton's behalf. White was convinced not only that Boynton was not guilty of any dishonest act, but that the impeachment proceedings had been instituted by White's own political enemies to humiliate him before the people of Kansas.

"Don't get the idea that I think Roland [Boynton] is God's perfect child," White told Rolla Clymer on December 28, 1933. "He has his faults and lots of them. So have we all. But he has done nothing or omitted to do nothing that Alf [Landon] hasn't done. The parallel is perfect between them. And certainly Alf doesn't deserve impeachment; neither does Rolie. But the wolves have got after Rolie and if they taste blood in Rolie they will turn on Alf in the election as sure as shooting. The Democrats are already gathering evidence for their campaign, and Rolie's impeachment means a Democratic governor, which doesn't please me any more than it does you because I want Alf."

White made contact with individual senators while the impeachment proceedings were being conducted. He asked the Democratic members to listen to the evidence rather than merely to consider the political implications of the impeachment of a Republican officeholder. In return for help from John Hamilton in securing the vote of five conservative Republican senators, White promised to support Hamilton's campaign for the national chairmanship of the Republican party.

When the impeachment was defeated, White felt partially victorious over his political enemies. But in order to demonstrate that the Finney scandal had not impaired his political power, White played an active part in 1934 in the re-election of Governor Landon and in the selection of Clarence Beck of Emporia for attorney general. Through a hot Kansas summer, while for sixty days the temperature ran above a hundred degrees, White wrote editorials and letters in the primary campaign for Beck. "The hoot owls of conservatism in Topeka thought they had me all laid out with lilies a year ago," he explained to Clyde Reed, on August 4, 1934, "and I had to kick off the top of the coffin and get into this fight! I felt it was a matter of life and death. If they kept me down I would be down and out."

* * *

On his sixty-sixth birthday—February 10, 1934—the Emporia editor turned away from the trial of Boynton to observe in an editorial devoted to Franklin D. Roosevelt: "He may make mistakes—loads of them. But the folks know that he is brave and honest, and that he is never going to be caught making the most terrific of all mistakes, hesitating in a crisis. No mistake in times of calm is so bad as hasty action. No mistake in time of crisis and calamity is so tragic as hesitation."

When asked if the Roosevelt administration was leading the country toward dictatorship, White answered emphatically "No." If, however, the New Deal failed in its attempt to extend progressivism, White feared that fascism might then threaten the nation. When the Liberty League, organized by the "economic royalists" who were being curbed by New Deal reforms, attempted to smear the President's program as dangerous communism, White was quick to challenge their statement. From his personal experience in the progressive era, he realized that vested business groups were only too eager to disguise their exploitation by claiming that it was the right and privilege of every American to go his own way unhampered by the government. Such a road, in a civilization dominated by monopoly capitalism, White knew could lead only to the economic enslavement of the masses by the few. Nor was White fooled by the reactionaries' clever use of the symbol "free enterprise." He had seen free enterprise in the McKinley era and in the Harding-Coolidge era degenerate into monopoly, and he well knew that monopoly and democracy could not exist together. "The right of every man to go his own economic way and play his own selfish, sordid or silly economic game according to the dictates of his own stupidity or his own ignorant cupidity—that day is gone," White declared in the *Gazette* on August 15, 1934. ". . . A larger economic liberty will be gained by the restriction of the men who now use their liberties for economic license."

Much as White sympathized with the progressive ideals of Franklin D. Roosevelt, he was convinced that there was no well-conceived plan behind the New Deal. "The President goes on one running board after another . . ." commented White. "It is obviously a case of trial and error all along, with the President the greatest hitchhiker since Andrew Johnson going a little piece down the road with anyone, backward and forward, zigzagging, covering and recovering. And yet I am persuaded he is earnest and honest in his endeavor to get us out of the mess, though not intelligent. . . . Essentially he has courage, but I fear courage without intelligent purpose, if it sticks, will become arrogance and if he wobbles as he may, assuming his honesty, his very courage can become devastating."

On April 19, 1934, while he was attending the annual meeting of the National Society of Newspaper Editors in Washington, White saw the President at a White House press conference. It had been ten years since he had last seen Franklin D. Roosevelt. "I was struck by the change that had come over him," White observed. "He shakes his head a good deal and gestures from the neck up when he talks. He is facile, and his facility under duress may become recklessness, but under normal conditions is somewhat the basis of his charm . . . He has a habit of generalization and simplification which is not scientific . . . Away down in my heart I am scared." Then, indulging in what might be termed Republican wishful thinking, the Emporia editor added: "He cannot stand the storm. This is, of course, the futile blundering that all gratuitous prophecy is."

White was not fearful of the fate of democracy under Roosevelt, nor did he think that the dangerous challenge to democracy would come from communism. It would come rather from the right—from entrenched economic power. He was distrustful, nevertheless, of the power that was being concentrated in the hands of the government at Washington. Although he wanted to curb Wall Street, he never knew a businessman or a politician whom he would trust with all the power that was centering in the hands of politicians. "They are liable to be as wicked, as ruthless, as greedy as those men were in Wall Street . . ." he explained to historian Allan Nevins. "They took us to hell and I doubt if the politicians would be much better."

But White realized that the answer to the problem of how much power could be concentrated in the government was not to be found in hating "that man in the White House" or in denouncing the New Deal as communistic. Democracy itself was in a period of crisis. Liberty and freedom, which had been the goal of mankind for centuries, were being repudiated by fascism and communism in Europe. In the United States, he saw great danger of fascism's developing under the aegis of the plutocracy that controlled the finances and industry of the nation. Under the cherished doctrine of laissez faire, these potential Fascist forces could destroy America's free speech, free press, and trial by jury.

On the other hand, he reasoned, it was not too wise to concentrate too much power in government. White honestly admitted that he did not know the answer to this dilemma. Speaking at the 1934 commencement at the University of Kansas, he expressed the baffling problem this way:

. . . Can freedom live in the machine age? A machine age presumes the mass production of things, goods, material service, things which formerly were produced by individuals for other individuals, chiefly neighbors. Mass production requires mass distribution. The individual worker and the individual consumer are thousands of miles apart. To make ends meet between the consumer and the producer requires channelling, stern and inflexible. If those who control the machine make the channels, they are ruthless. If society under government attempts the channelling, the channelling becomes regimentation. Even now, even in America, over large areas where capital invested in coal, in textiles, in steel, in sugar, in citrus fruits dominates a region, the democratic liberties always are threatened. Free speech, a free press, the right of assemblage, the writ of habeas corpus, these liberties wilt and wither as the owners of machinery control the courts and the police. Democracy languishes. Freedom disappears before the machines. Would freedom thrive more sturdily when politicians control the machine than it thrives now in those regions where the machine controls the politicians? I don't know. I check the question up to you, this challenge of the age: Can liberty survive in the machine age.

White was quite sure that the Republican party had no leadership to guide America out of this morass. Too many of its leaders were screaming that the Bill of Rights was being endangered by New Deal reforms, when White knew that these leaders were only using the Bill of Rights as a bulwark of privilege, not as a defense of democracy. After Herbert Hoover had paid a visit to Emporia, White told Senator Capper: "Naturally Hoover feels that our property rights are set in the cement of the bill of rights, which I do not feel. I believe we can give up a good deal of vested interest and still survive as a democracy. We wrangled a little about that."

When a reactionary group within the Republican party launched *The Republican Builders* to defend "American institutions and the American Constitutional form of government," White refused to have any relations with them. He told one friend that he would not permit himself to be identified with any such "bunch of frozen faces." Instead of talking "sublimated blah," the Republicans should, he thought, offer the nation a better program of social security, collective bargaining, and federal work relief than the Democrats were formulating. "The trouble with our beloved party," he wrote Chester Rowell, on September 11, 1934, "is that it is shot through with the plutocratic conquest. If it can get rid of that, the party can revive. But it cannot live with fatty degeneration of the heart."

446

Shortly after the Republican defeat in 1932, White, from his editorial pulpit in Kansas, had advised the Republican party that it had to become a liberal party or it would disappear. The party needed to be reorganized in order to afford a home for the people who had been voting for liberals like Norris, the LaFollettes, and Borah. The Republican organization was too smug and too self-satisfied, White charged. It appealed to the social register and to the upper income brackets, but not to the city directory. To win another election, the Republican party had to carry the great Middle West. Otherwise it was doomed. When the 1934 mid-term Congressional elections resulted in an overwhelming endorsement for the New Deal, White again publicly declared that his party had no future unless it shook off the blighting hand of the reactionaries.

Four months after this statement, Governor Landon announced that the Republicans of ten midwestern states were going to hold a convention to launch the rebirth of the Republican party, and that William Allen White would probably head the resolutions committee, which would draft the platform. As soon as Landon's announcement was released, the press besieged the Emporia editor for information. He denied any knowledge of the regional convention, but declared: "I fear that America may drift into fascism in the next two or three years unless we Republicans act with real courage and wisdom. The Republican party must meet the challenge to our ancient democratic liberties, not by denouncing the shortcomings of this administration but by guaranteeing the common man something specific. . . . If the Republican party has the courage to turn to the humanity of Lincoln and away from the property-minded leadership which has dominated it most of the time for 20 years, we can save America. But America cannot be saved by merely denouncing the faults of Roosevelt. We must make an iron-clad covenant with the people to do certain definite possible things which will relieve the pressure of want and the fear of approaching poverty."

White issued this statement as a warning to Kansas National Committeeman John Hamilton, that he did not want to have any connection with the proposed conference unless it was to be definitely liberal. The mere release of White's name as chairman of the resolutions committee evoked widespread newspaper comment. Raymond Clapper observed that, if White's views dominated the conference, it would adopt a platform somewhere between the Hoover conservatives and the New Deal. "Many persons think of Mr. White as Mid-West incarnate . . ." observed the *Literary Digest*. "He not only knows what whole chunks of the population think; he knows how to put their thoughts into words." *The New York Times*, in commenting on the attempt to give birth to a new Republican party, stated: "Henry Allen and William Allen White are in active circulation, the most suave men-midwives that ever were."

As the conference plans began to take shape, White realized that its organizers—men like John Hamilton—were trying to use White's liberal reputation to mask their own reactionary purposes. "I am fairly well satisfied that the attempt to liberalize the Republican party is going to be rather a sad bit of ersatz," he confided to newspaperman George Fort Milton a month before the conference opened. When White told John Hamilton and Harrison Spangler, Iowa national committeeman, that he would not attend the meeting, Spangler and Arthur Hyde, former cabinet member, traveled to Emporia to try to change his mind. But White was adamant. He declared that he wanted no part in a conference that merely indicted the New Deal. "I am willing to indict this administration," he wrote Spangler, on May 4, 1935, "but I would shudder at a victory accorded by mere indictment unless that victory was based upon a realistic progress toward which all Republicans could work. But merely to oust the Democrats and then try to return to 1929 would be impossible. It would be tragically wicked, for it would again deny the people what they yearn for—a stable, working, industrial rehabilitation."

White made it clear to John Hamilton that he was not interested in a party that tried to revert to the ideas of the Coolidge era. What he desired was a Republican promise to establish a new social order, which would control prices to prevent monopolies from maintaining artificial price levels.

When Hamilton insisted that White's refusal to attend the conference would label it as an Old Guard affair, White relented to the extent of sending a letter expressing his views. But he refused to attend or to sign a platform that merely indicted the Democrats. White told his reactionary friends that he was receiving mail from people all over the nation who were disturbed at the New Deal, but who did not want to return to 1929. These people believed in the ends of the New Deal but were dissatisfied with the methods used and the progress made. Only a truly progressive platform would persuade them, however, to vote as Republicans in 1936.

By midsummer, a year before the presidential campaign, White was convinced that Franklin D. Roosevelt could defeat any possible Republican candidate. This conviction disturbed White considerably. Although he sympathized with the aims of the President, by 1935 he felt that Roosevelt was trying to do too many things too fast. "As you know," he explained to Herbert Hoover on June 8, 1935, "about forty per cent of the objection to most of the economic objectives in the Roosevelt administration is the haste and inconsiderate and grotesque impracticability of the methods which they are using, and the plans they are putting forth to achieve what, on the whole and with a discount of sixty and ten, might properly be called a reasonable social program. They are speed mad. Probably their excuse is that they are racing with the deluge. But I would rather take a little deluge than a wrecked car."

By midsummer of 1935, Roy Roberts and Lacy Haynes, of the Kansas City *Star*, and Oscar Stauffer, operator of a string of Kansas papers, had a presidential boom for Governor Alf Landon under way. Letters inquiring about Landon began to pour into Emporia. White replied to all the letters in such a fashion as to spur the boom along its rocky pathway. "He has had almost as much political experience as Coolidge had when he was elected vice-president," White told everyone who asked about Landon. "And Landon is a bigger man than Coolidge was the day he went to the White House. . . . The impact of the job in the White House is tremendous. If a man has any latent subconscious powers they are aroused by the overwhelming responsibility. Few men fail to respond to this awful challenge . . . I am inclined to believe that Landon would rise to it . . . All I know about Landon is good. It is a question of size, and the Lord knows he outsizes most of the Republican aspirants."

Landon's father was an old Bull Moose friend of White's, and

Landon himself had supported White's campaign for governor in 1924. The Emporia editor was always intensely loyal to his Kansas political friends, even when his loyalty led to a conflict with his ideals. With his commanding national prestige White could have wrecked Landon's ambitions by opposing the boom, but White was fond of him, he believed that Landon actually was a true progressive, and the sponsors of the Landon movement were White's intimate associates. Roy Roberts was an old political friend, Lacy Haynes was White's brother-in-law, and Oscar Stauffer had been a former *Gazette* reporter.

*   *   *

While the Landon boom was gaining momentum, the Whites left the country to attend the inauguration of Manuel L. Quezón, the first president of the Commonwealth of the Philippine Islands, on November 15, 1935. White had long believed in the independence of the Philippines and in a nonimperialist role for the United States. But after this tour of the Far East with Mrs. White, he was gravely concerned over the Japanese menace. He feared that if the United States withdrew completely from the Philippines, the Japanese would quickly conquer the islands.

From the Philippines, the Whites spent two months traveling in China. They visited Hong Kong, Shanghai, Hankow, and Peking. "The trip to the Orient was the greatest adventure of our lives," White told Henry Haskell shortly after they had returned. "Russia paled a little before it." While in China and in the Philippines, White visited many of the hospitals and medical centers that the Rockefeller Foundation had been maintaining during the years when he had served as a member of the foundation's board of trustees.

The Whites spent an entire month in Peking, where they enjoyed the stimulating company of Nelson T. Johnson, the American ambassador. "Peking is one of the few places I have been for which I am a little bit homesick," White later wrote a friend there. "I didn't get enough. Some of these autumns Mrs. White and I are going to show up, if the pallbearers don't grab me too quick."

The Japanese attack on China in 1937 ended for White any hope that he might return to Peking. His own brief experience in the Orient, however, made him a passionate friend of the cause of China in the trying years after 1937. Although White went to the Far East with a commission from the North American Newspaper Alliance to file any story he thought was of interest, he did not write a line about the trip. It was such a different world from any he had known that he did not sufficiently trust his knowledge and judgment to describe or interpret the Orient.

The beauty and the culture of the aristocratic Chinese made a deep impression on this Middle-Western American. The poverty and ignorance of the masses, however, shocked his democratic sense of equality. From his own account of this Chinese trip, he and Mrs. White spent most of their time sight-seeing and shopping. A ricksha boy named Ling pulled White all over Peking. The human quality of White was well revealed when, after his return home, he sent some Chinese money to Ling with his thanks for showing him the city. White once described his ricksha experience in the following manner:

It was cold there during the winter we were there . . . and I wore a heavy overcoat and Ling, when he went to haul me, pulled off his heavy overcoat and wrapped it around my legs, and for $6 I had picked up a yellow Mongolian automobile rug which I wrapped around me, and it began to pile up pretty heavily. Of course, I was a holy show . . . because I could see people looking at me along the street as I rode in this ricksha with this little fellow carrying me along. I looked as though I weighed a ton . . . One day I went into a hotel and Ling parked himself with the other taxi men along a great rack where they all stood, and when I came back he was laughing. I said, "What are you laughing at, Ling?" He waited until he got me all tucked in . . . and he said, "Ricksha boy said Ling have got laughing Buddha."

CHAPTER 20

CONSERVATIVE LIBERAL

"HE is neither tight nor taciturn," William Allen White maintained when people called Governor Alf Landon the "Kansas Coolidge." By the time the Whites had returned to the country in February, 1936, the Landon campaign had assumed amazing proportions. The 68-year-old editor was so swept off his feet by the enthusiasm of the Landon followers that he even predicted Roosevelt could not carry Kansas against Landon.

On his return from the Orient, White discovered also that William Randolph Hearst had climbed aboard the Landon band wagon after a visit at the executive mansion in Topeka. "You can't take his aid without assuming his liability," White warned Landon on February 8. "He will beat you at any game you can play. The swift, well-placed kick is the only thing that will do the business for him." The Emporia editor had expressed his dislike for the Hearst type of journalism frequently over the years, but he reached the epitome of his characterization of Hearst when he told Morris L. Ernst on February 29, 1936, that "Hearst, to my notion, is the most vicious influence in American life—bar none. He is worse than Aimee McPherson, Father Coughlin, Huey Long, Cardinal O'Connell, Bishop Manning and Jim Reed all rolled in one. I would even add the Liberty League if I could throw in Arthur Brisbane into the Hearst scale."

When Hearst backed Landon in the California primary, Herbert Hoover and his followers took up cudgels against both Hearst and Landon. White confided to Hoover that over his protests the Landon advisers had made the tie with Hearst. "I am not as you presume," he explained to Frank Motz of the Hays (Kansas) *News,* on March 26, 1936, "anywhere near the inner councils of the Landon boom. I am just allowed to walk up and down the hall outside of the anteroom that leads to the parlor and lets in to the outer bedroom which goes into the inner bedroom off of the bathroom, where the work is done. But at least I am running such errands as I may be able to run when they squeeze the buzzer."

White announced that Landon should repudiate the Hearst support. When Harry Chandler of the Los Angeles *Times* and Chester Rowell of the San Francisco *Chronicle* deluged White with wires stating that California would be for Landon provided Hearst was rebuked, White carried the message in vain to the Landon advisers. He was in an extremely difficult position. Landon's most intimate adviser, Lacy Haynes, was White's brother-in-law. White felt that he could not go too far in objecting to the Hearst alignment without causing a rupture in the family. In May, the defeat of the Hearst-backed Landon ticket in the California primary confirmed White's warning that Hearst was a political liability.

Although unhappy over the Hearst situation, White continued to work for Landon. He wrote an introduction for a preconvention booklet, *Deeds Not Deficits—The Story of Alfred M. Landon,* by Richard B. Fowler. The introduction was, however, remarkably restrained for William Allen White. Usually, when he was *for* some candidate, his supporting editorials sparkled with colorful language. His closest approach to vigorous writing on Landon's behalf was in such statements as these: "Landon is a substantial person. He has his feet on the ground. He is no rabble rouser." "Today, he is the most interesting phenomenon in Republican politics."

Although such statements were lukewarm for political pamphleteering, it is certain that White's endorsement of Landon helped to sell the Kansas governor to the rank and file of Republican voters. The author of the Landon pamphlet explained to White that the Landon advisers "are counting strong on this booklet to win delegates; and we are all convinced that an introduction by you will do more to put it over than anything else we can do or say." Malcolm Bingay of the Detroit *Free Press* remarked on March 7, 1936: "I see that my old friend, William Allen White . . . will be in Alf Landon's corner. Half of any man's fight is to have ol' Bill White in his corner. Bill doesn't back 'em unless they are clean and fine, and carry a wallop." Innumerable letters poured into the *Gazette* office attesting to White's influence upon many Americans. "When ugly rumors are repeated to me about Landon," one letter observed, "I am glad to say 'That can't be so, because William Allen White is for him and knows him well.' So, all over the country, the people who know you, personally or through your writings, are judging Governor Landon favorably."

Well aware of the immense prestige that had gathered about his name during the last two decades, White began to suffer misgivings as to his support of Landon. When Landon asked him to serve on the Republican platform committee as his personal representative, White refused. He did not approve of some of the reactionary forces that were contributing to the Landon campaign fund; he did not like the fact that every time he wrote some vigorous liberal phrases for Landon's speeches, the Landon board of strategy removed them; and he did not believe that Landon would back him in a fight for a progressive platform.

Lacy Haynes and Roy Roberts told White that a refusal to serve on the platform committee would seriously hurt Landon's chances for the nomination. White was then placed in an unhappy and embarrassing position. Landon had loyally supported him for governor in 1924, and Landon's father had been a wheel horse in the Kansas Bull Moose party. White did not want to hurt these two good friends. Reluctantly he agreed to serve on the committee.

In April, 1936, White went East to attend the annual meeting of the American Society of Newspaper Editors and to develop sentiment for Landon and for a liberal platform. Landon's only chance for victory, White announced, was to convince the public that he was a "fighting progressive." While he was in Washington, the Kansas Congressional delegation assembled twenty midwestern congressmen to hear the Emporia editor speak about Landon. "The Kansas Congressmen were nice enough to say that I made a good impression," he wrote Landon. ". . . I talked before two or three groups of young New Deal radicals, newspapermen, Bill's friends, who think Bill and Kathrine are rich because they wash occasionally and I think I have made an impression on them."

White's old friend, Senator Borah, Landon's principal preconvention rival, proved difficult for White to handle. White wanted Borah to help him draft a liberal platform, but Borah refused, feeling that White was trying to use him to help picture Landon as a militant progressive. In New York City, White talked about Landon and the Republican platform to Thomas Lamont, to Winthrop Aldrich of the Chase National Bank, and to the Young Republican Club. "In these talks," he explained to Landon, on April 21, 1936, "I talk as honestly as God will let me about you, paint your warts and all, with no attempt to picture a messiah or a superman and yet I think this method is the most effective that I can use."

White also attended a two-hour press conference at the White House. "He is more and more sure of himself from year to year," White wrote of the President, and he added that no one could defeat Roosevelt unless he did it himself by some slip. Yet he dreaded the re-election of the President, he wrote to Ray Lyman Wilbur on May 11, 1936. "I am satisfied he will cut down the free area not alone of economic action, but the area of free expression of the individual," White asserted. "I fear he has the unconscious arrogance of conscious wealth, and that he will develop all the faults of . . . the Legion and the Liberty Leaguers in stifling free speech and its attendant rights by social and economic pressure, and at the same time I firmly believe he will curtail far beyond the need of curtailment the right of the individual to whatever honest return and emolument a citizen's qualities entitle him." On the other hand, White honestly admitted: "I have no illusions about the wisdom of the Republican party or its essential nobility. I am certainly 'standing in the need of prayer.' "

*   *   *

White covered both political conventions that summer for the North American Newspaper Alliance. In addition, he was the Kansas delegate on the Republican platform committee. The day before he left for the convention, he wrote Landon that he wanted to withdraw from the committee. An hour before traintime, on

June 3, Landon arrived in Emporia and urged White not to desert him at this crucial point. A few days before Landon's visit, the Supreme Court had thrown out a New York minimum-wage law for women. White had immediately sent a dispatch to both the United Press and the Associated Press, criticizing the court's action and declaring that the powers of government must be broadened to secure justice for all. "The Republican party cannot shut its eyes to the fact," White declared, "that somewhere in government, either in the hands of the states or in the hands of the federal government, some definite power should lie which will make this government an agency of human welfare and still avoid the totalitarian state, still leave men free to rise or fall by the exercise of their own judgments, their personal qualities, still preserve a political democracy, and still guarantee to the average man willing to work, his honest, well-earned share in the profitable income of society."

As soon as reactionaries like John Hamilton read White's release, they demanded that he be removed from the platform committee. Landon, however, insisted that the Emporia editor had to remain on the committee, and he told White that he agreed with the sentiments expressed in the release. At Landon's personal request, then, White went to the convention to serve on the platform committee.

At the convention, roly-poly William Allen White and scores of Kansans roamed the streets of Cleveland wearing yellow sunflowers inscribed with Landon's name, while Roy Roberts, Lacy Haynes, and John Hamilton planned the strategy necessary to capture the nomination. Convinced that there was no hope for victory, the Old Guard actually were only too eager to allow the Kansans to control the nomination.

With the backing of Landon, White tried to insert in the platform a plank calling for a constitutional amendment to allow the states to regulate the minimum wages of women; a plank advocating the placing of all federal employees up to assistant secretaries in the Cabinet under civil service; and a plank for sound money based on gold. The Landon platform, which had been prepared under the direction of Charles P. Taft, however, was badly mangled by the committee.

Before the platform was sent to the convention, White telephoned Landon and explained how his planks had been defeated. The Kansas governor urged White to bring a minority report to the convention hall, but White was too tired to undertake the fight that this would entail. White made one more attempt to persuade the committee to accept Landon's three planks. "I failed incontinently . . ." he wrote Clyde Reed on July 8, 1936. "They just gave me the horse laugh in subdued and gentlemanly tones. And I felt most sad. . . . When I came out of the Committee at half past seven I ran into young Charley Taft who is a gorgeous youth, as starry-eyed as you and I were a quarter of a century ago. And he was beaming like a full moon, or a cat that had swallowed an old fish. . . . I asked: 'Why so gay, Charley?' And he pulled from his pocket a copy of Landon's telegram and said: 'The governor insists on this being read to the Convention before the balloting begins so that if they don't want him they don't have to have him.' "

Before Landon was nominated, the telegram was read to the convention. It stated unequivocally that Landon was for a constitutional amendment on the minimum-wage question, for broad extension of civil service, and for sound money based on gold. White always maintained that this was a brave move on Landon's part to back up the fight that White had been waging in the committee.

Although it had been White's hope that Landon would appeal to the liberal vote of America, it was apparent to him from the first stages of the campaign that the Old Guard reactionaries were in control of the Republican campaign. Instead of a clear-cut avowal of progressive principles, the Republicans denounced the New Deal. "America is in peril," the Republicans charged. "For three long years the New Deal administration has dishonored American traditions." Landon's speeches reflected a continuous drift toward the reactionaries. Every time Editor White wrote a liberal speech for Landon, reactionary influences deleted the telling liberal phrases. "I glean from my own observations," White wrote Henry Haskell on August 11, 1936, "and from the gentlemen who are consulting the entrails around Alf, that he is having one hell of a time with speeches. As soon as the Magi get up a speech, the Shepherds come and tear it down." Charles Taft con-

457

firmed White's suspicions that the reactionaries were diluting Landon's remarks in order not to irritate the Liberty League type of Republican.

When Landon's manager, John Hamilton, began to cry Communist at Roosevelt, White wrote an editorial denouncing Hamilton for such tactics. After this editorial, *The New York Times* quite accurately described White's unhappy state of mind by observing: "No longer, crowned with green leaves, full of breakfast sausage, good hope and a bursting vocabulary, does Emporia William White, sitting in his word-works, carol and caper, finding everything good in Kansas and the rest of the world. His skies are overcast . . . October will soon be over, thank heaven. Mr. White, who scarcely knows which side he is on, will get his bearings and recover his tranquillity."

To Roosevelt's support rallied not only traditional Democrats, but many of White's old friends like Senator Norris, who had established the Progressive League for Roosevelt. White was in a difficult spot, and he knew it. After Landon's nomination, he refused to play a major part in the campaign. John Hamilton's attempt to keep him off the platform committee had convinced him that regardless of Landon's own views, he had no business in a campaign controlled by reactionaries.

Yet, in his own way, White continued to help Landon. He wrote articles for the *Saturday Evening Post* and *The New York Times Magazine* and published them, together with some additional material that September under the title *What It's All About; Being A Reporter's Story of the Early Campaign of 1936*. Although White declared that this was a partisan Republican book, it actually was remarkably restrained. When Harold Ickes pointed out to White that nowhere did he say "Vote for Landon," White's laconic reply was, "I know."

When Ickes said, "I could not for the life of me see, even on the basis of your deft portrayal of him, why anyone should vote for him for President," White explained that Landon was one of his boys. For years, White wrote, he and the older Kansas Republicans had been building up a young group to take over political power. It was therefore impossible for him to desert the leader of this younger group. "I feel bound to him," White told Ickes on

July 24, 1936. "And you have to go along with your friends and trust their vision if you trust their honesty and intelligence so long as they have been loyal to you."

Thousands of letters poured into Emporia during the campaign, asking if Landon was a drunkard. Had he balanced the budget at the expense of the schools? Had he married for money? White answered all these letters and wrote a nation-wide dispatch stating that Landon had not wrecked the schoolteachers' salaries to balance the budget. He also wrote for the "Washington Merry-Go-Round" a column in which he attempted to portray Landon as a progressive rather than as the conservative the campaign literature was depicting. This article he deleted from the *Gazette* on the day when it was to have appeared.

Yet in none of this material did White really ask anyone other than Kansans to vote for Landon. After the "Washington Merry-Go-Round" article had appeared, Marcellus Murdock of the Wichita *Eagle* wired to ask if White meant the last line in the column, which implied that it was "necessary for voters to shut their eyes to vote for Landon." White cagily replied: "If old John Public can't comprehend a little gay persiflage from me even in a hot campaign, I'll have to let him call me a traitor. It's happened before to my surprise and delight." The mere fact, however, that he was for Landon influenced many people. By this time, White had achieved the role of folk hero and father confessor to many bewildered souls. One person, for instance, wrote White from Scotland: "I have told everybody over here that has asked me about the election: 'I am all for Roosevelt, but, if Landon has at his side William Allen White no citizen of America honest with himself, but can rest assured that we need have no fear for America.'"

All the writing that White did for Landon, including *What It's All About*, he did without consulting either Landon or John Hamilton. Whenever Landon asked for advice, White gave it freely, but he did not travel on Landon's campaign train or visit his headquarters at Topeka. In the years after the fiasco of the campaign, White did his best to make it appear that he had taken little or no part in the campaign. Actually, although his role was not strategic, he did play a larger part than he enjoyed admitting.

Early in September, White warned Landon that he might lose
Kansas, and a week before election day he definitely told Landon
that he could not carry his own state. While he was in Boston
just before election, gathering additional material for the new
biography of Calvin Coolidge that he had been working on intermittently for several years, White made a campaign speech before
the Harvard Club. He spoke less about Landon than he did about
seeking the truth in the election. Everywhere in the East he found
that his old progressive friends had turned away from Landon
because of the increasing reactionary tenor of the Landon campaign.

The man responsible for this, White felt, was John Hamilton.
"John has a seven-devil lust to live and shine under the blessing
of the rich," White explained to Oscar Stauffer on July 29, 1936,
"and he has turned over what ought to have been a good middle-of-
the-road campaign to the hard-boiled political reactionaries . . .
and their financial supporters." As election day approached, the
North American Newspaper Alliance asked White to write a story
for release if Landon won. "You have a quaint sense of humor,"
the wise old Emporia editor wired back. "If Landon is elected I'll
write you a book about him, bind it in platinum, illustrate it
with apples of gold and pictures of silver, and won't charge you a
cent. Why waste good telegraph tolls on a possibility so remote
as the election of Landon?"

During the campaign, White also wrote editorials advocating
the re-election of Senator George Norris, who was fighting the
Republican machine in Nebraska. Although his support of Norris,
who nationally was working for the re-election of Roosevelt, might
have bewildered many people, it did not disturb William Allen
White. In order to keep the situation from becoming embarrassing,
however, he persuaded Senator Norris not to campaign for Roosevelt in Kansas.

Franklin D. Roosevelt did embarrass him, however. When
Roosevelt's train stopped at Emporia on October 13, White was
afraid that, if he went to the train, the President would make fun
of his support of Landon. On the other hand, Roosevelt was the
President of the United States, and it would be an affront for the
editor not to greet him, or so White reasoned. When the train

stopped, White was on the outskirts of the crowd, trying to appear inconspicuous. But Roosevelt picked him out and to the enjoyment of the crowd announced: "Bill White is for me three and a half out of every four years."

"The President got me on the spot yesterday," White confided to Roy Roberts. "I was standing in a doorway in the station as far back as I could get in the crowd. . . . He called for me, I made no response . . . I said nothing and tried to duck back into the doorway, but couldn't. Then the crowd told him where I was and he beckoned me up to the train, and I grinned and shook my head. Finally, after he had finished speaking, he said to the guards, 'Make a gangway there for Mr. White.' Then he again said, 'Come on up, I want to see you a minute.' And there was nothing for me to do but to come up unless I had been conspicuously rude to the President of the United States." After the Roosevelt incident, White went back to the *Gazette* office and dictated an editorial referring to Roosevelt as the "old American smiler" and "Mr. Smoothie," and declaring that he was for Landon because of the waste and extravagance that had accompanied New Deal measures. Some of Landon's managers, however, were furious at White. This type of incident, which was liable to happen at any time, caused considerable trouble for the rest of the campaigners. The managers had to keep explaining that really White *was* for Landon. After the Landon campaign had closed, White admitted that it "was a nightmare. It had neither logical sequence in its conception and execution nor any touch of reality."

The Emporia editor attributed Roosevelt's re-election, in the greatest landslide in American political history, to the taint of plutocracy on the Republican party. The election, he added in a newspaper release, was a clear-cut endorsement of the Roosevelt belief in the government as an agency of human welfare. "From this November day on," he wrote, "we should have a new America, an America in which at least for four years the federal government should be the strong coercive arbitrator between those who have and those who have not. Government has a mandate to curb cunning greed and to balk the antisocial plans of the strong. Under that mandate the American government should move into a position where it will do something about the obvious maladjustment of American income and a more equitable distribution of the products of American industry . . . We are walking down a strange highway but we have deliberately chosen to go that path. Our eyes are wide open. We know what we need and neither courts, nor Constitution, nor ancient tradition can hold us here at the turn of the road. We are going on a great new adventure."

In view of the overwhelming newspaper support for Landon, White was convinced that the election returns were a vivid indication that the editorial page had ceased to have the influence it had once had. "It seems to me fewer and fewer people are guided by editorials," he wrote a fellow editor. "In another generation when writing was more of a wonder than it is now, when straightway English composition was the gift of a favorite few, I can see how the editorial page commanded a certain deference which is lost today. More and more I am surprised, and more and more I have my vanity pricked like a bubble when I go into a miscellaneous crowd to find how few people have paid any attention to what I write. . . . I go on writing editorials probably because I'm a vain old fellow and once people paid attention to me."

* * *

As soon as Congress convened in January, 1937, President Roosevelt indicated that he looked upon his re-election as a mandate to extend New Deal policies. But, before new laws were passed, he felt that something had to be done to curb the Supreme Court. The court had declared unconstitutional the NRA, the AAA, the Farm Mortgage Act, the Bituminous Coal Act, the Municipal Bankruptcy Act, and the Railroad Retirement Act. In the President's opinion the court was nullifying the electorate's desire.

On January 6, Roosevelt told Congress that "means must be found to adapt our legal forms and our judicial interpretation to the actual present national needs of the largest progressive democracy in the modern world." The Supreme Court's power to block social legislation had long been a subject of bitter debate. It was charged that when conservatives were defeated at the polls they were able to enlist the support of the Supreme Court in fighting laws designed to regulate business in the interests of the people. Proposals had been made before 1937 that the court should not be allowed to annul a law by a 5-to-4 vote, and that Congress should be able to override court decisions just as it could override a presidential veto.

President Roosevelt, instead of taking either of these steps which would have really altered the court's power, maintained that the fault lay not in the court but in "some of the human beings on the court." Six of the nine court members were over seventy. Roosevelt asked Congress to empower him to appoint "additional judges in all federal courts without exception where there are incumbent judges of retirement age who do not choose to resign." In the case of the Supreme Court, the voluntary retirement act was to be seventy, and the President was to be allowed to appoint a new judge up to a maximum of six—for every justice who did not retire at that age.

For months the proposal was widely debated all over the nation. Reactionaries like Frank Gannett, New York State publisher, organized societies to fight the President's plan. In a fireside chat, Roosevelt explained that the court, in destroying social legislation, "has been acting not as a judicial body, but as a policy-making body." The President maintained that his plan would "bring to the decision of social and economic problems younger men who have had personal experience and contact with modern facts. . . . This plan will save our National Constitution from hardening of the judicial arteries."

William Allen White joined the opposition to the President's plan. He refused to accept the accusation that the court was a center of reaction. Three decades earlier he had not agreed, either, with the charges of reaction that the first Roosevelt had hurled at the Supreme Court. White was willing, however, to support amendments that would prevent the Supreme Court from declaring laws unconstitutional by a 5-to-4 vote, that would prevent lower federal courts from annulling acts of Congress, and that would grant Congress the power to repass, by a two-thirds vote of both houses, a law declared unconstitutional by the Supreme Court.

Although the Emporia editor sanctioned these steps to reform the court, he claimed that he had upheld the Supreme Court all through his life. "I believe on the whole it is the most liberal, indeed the most radical branch of our Government continuously through the generations," he wrote in 1935. Then, in the light of this remark, he added the following bewildering sentence: "But after all, the settled conviction of the American people expressed at three elections should be more potent than even the will and wisdom of the Supreme Court." If the court, as he maintained, was the most radical branch, it should have been abreast of the needs of the 1930's, which it obviously was not. Actually, during the court fight in 1937, White finally agreed that the court was reactionary toward social legislation.

White was afraid of the ramifications of President Roosevelt's proposal. Although the number of judges on the court had varied in the past, White feared that the passage of the Roosevelt bill would establish a dangerous precedent. He declared that he did not like the way the court annulled laws, but that no President should tamper with it. If he did, then someday the court would not be a bulwark against a Fascist-minded Congress. "Assuming," he wrote Felix Frankfurter on March 23, 1937, "which is not at all impossible, a reactionary President, as charming, as eloquent and as irresistible as Roosevelt, with power to change the Court, and we should be in the devil's own fix if he decided to abridge the Bill of Rights by legislation which he could easily call emergency legislation. And that is what bothers me—not Roosevelt in the White House today, but the weapon he may leave there if he wins this Court fight, for some other President in 1944 or 1948."

On February 6, White sent to the United Press a release in which he opposed the President's plan. In late March he wrote six articles for the North American Newspaper Alliance, and on April 25 a feature article for *The New York Times*. He also worked through his friends in Washington. He and Senator Norris carried on a long correspondence. White urged that the progressives form a bloc to submit an alternative proposal for a constitutional amendment, carefully defining the term "interstate commerce" in order to prevent the court from nullifying federal laws regulating business. "I think it extremely wise for the Progressive Bloc to offer an alternative solution," he explained to Norris on February 22, 1937, "rather than to be put in a position of mere opposition. Our group has not been opposers ever. We have been constructive and we should be constructive now."

Norris carried White's letter to the President, but Roosevelt would not abandon his project. White also tried to influence President Roosevelt through Harold Ickes. Ickes, however, insisted that the amendments White proposed would take too long to be passed. Although Ickes preferred amendments in the long run, the need of the moment was for immediate relief from the court's reactionary tendency. White contended that an amendment could be passed by the time of the Congressional elections of 1938 and that death soon would give the President occasion to appoint one or two members of the court.

White not only fought the President's plan through his liberal friends, but he joined Frank Gannett's reactionary committee as well. He cautioned his reactionary friends, however, from taking the lead in the fight. The way to defeat the proposal was to stimulate the liberals to attack it. "I hope," he wrote James E. Watson on February 16, 1937, "that the more evident representatives of his economic opponents will not be too prominent in this political fight; by which I mean the Liberty League, and the DuPonts and that whole crowd. They are black beasts in the popular imagination and if they rally against the President, they are liable to make him friends instead of enemies."

In the midst of the furor, the Supreme Court itself really decided the fate of the President's plan. On March 29, the court upheld a minimum-wage law of the state of Washington, thus reversing its decision in the New York case nine months before. Several weeks later the court upheld the Wagner Labor Relations Law, and on May 24 the Social Security Law. On June 1, Justice Van Devanter, a firm New Deal foe, retired from the court. The President now would have an appointment, and this vote would ensure a liberal court. Why, then, add any more justices? That summer the President's bill was defeated, and within the next two or three years so many of the old judges retired or died, that Roosevelt made six more appointments. After 1937, the Court reversed many of the trends of the preceding years, and the President was able to say that while he had lost the battle, he had won the war.

*　　*　　*

Although White was actively engaged in fighting Roosevelt's court plan, he was not too busy to ignore the need of reforming the Republican party. The only future the party had, he declared, was to move to the left. Reactionaries like John Hamilton had to be removed from control of the party.

Early in 1937, White mobilized his Kansas progressive friends to back Democratic Governor Huxman's effort to have the legislature ratify the child-labor amendment to the federal constitution. White, Senator Arthur Capper, and several others telephoned and telegraphed Republican members, asking them to vote for the amendment. Aware that the only way to accomplish an objective in a democracy was to be more powerfully organized than the opposition, White secured newspaper support for the amendment and persuaded women's clubs, labor organizations, and churches to apply pressure on their representatives. When this particular fight was won, he told Gifford Pinchot: "After a long and rather useless life in American politics, I have discovered that sentiment counts 25 per cent, organization 60 per cent, inertia of the other fellow 20 per cent, and if you succeed the rest of it is his blundering."

On July 20, 1937, the Emporia editor, appalled by the heat of the Kansas summer, decided that political conditions were too stagnant and that he had to lend a note of humor to the situation—but humor with a purpose. He dictated an editorial declaring that Mayor Fiorello LaGuardia was the one man who met the requirements of the Republican party in its quest for a leader. LaGuardia was the Republican's Modern Lincoln, observed White. Both the Associated Press and the United Press carried the editorial, and a storm of abuse immediately broke about White's head. The type of American Protestant of the old stock, who had fallen for the Klan, wrote White letters filled with vivid invective. The Portland *Oregonian*, on the other hand, realistically commented: "William Allen White had a large part in the selection of the last

Republican nominee for president. The adventure was, to be mild about it, not attended by conspicuous success." Then the paper added: "Phooey! for Mr. White's 1936 selection. Phooey! for his selection for 1940."

White thoroughly enjoyed the response to his proposal. It took his mind off the heat, and it was a diversion from the labor of completing his second biography of Calvin Coolidge. Most of all, the LaGuardia suggestion annoyed the reactionary Republicans, and White was hilariously happy whenever he could irritate this group. In a rather shrewd analysis of himself, he explained to Alf Landon on September 4, 1937: "I do many things like that purposely, not to attract attention to myself. I can get plenty of publicity any time I want it doing conventional things. But because it seemed to me that some one ought to knock a hot liner. . . . I don't want any rewards for my expressions, my explosions, my snorts of rage and joy. I have had my fun as I went along. And I suppose I have persisted politically, not in spite of what seemed to be bad breaks at the time, but because time has generally justified them."

White's boost for LaGuardia so incensed John Hamilton that he refused to appoint White as the Kansas member of a new policy committee on party affairs. The Kansas Congressional delegation, Alf Landon, and the New York Republican organization urged the White appointment, but Hamilton refused. White commented to Herbert Hoover: "It indicates the general idea of the Republican organization toward reasonably liberal Republicans. But maybe I am not reasonably liberal!"

Although the Old Guard might dislike him, the high regard in which White was held by many leaders in American life and by the general public was demonstrated in December, 1937, when he underwent an operation at the Mayo Clinic. A host of telegrams and letters descended upon Rochester expressing hope for White's early recovery. President Roosevelt wired that he hoped White soon would be back at his writing, "for we all need to jog people into speeding up their evolutionary process of thinking." During the next year, some of White's editorials on the New Deal especially delighted the President. He wrote White on June 14, 1938, after one exceptionally able editorial: "Can't you bribe the New York Times and Herald Tribune to run them occasionally?" At the annual White House press conference of the American Society of Newspaper Editors in 1938, President Roosevelt praised White's editorial "Not Fear of One Man" and berated the rest of the editors present for aggravating the nation's economic ills by fostering fear of that one man, himself.

An autographed picture of Roosevelt, which hung in White's study, attested to their friendship and to Roosevelt's mellow sense of humor. It was a picture of Roosevelt in a seersucker suit, and it was inscribed: "To William Allen White—from his old friend who is *for* him all 48 months." A letter appended to the picture read in part: "Dear Bill: Here is the seersucker picture, duly inscribed by the sucker to the seer." This friendly relationship which existed between the Emporia editor and the President was to be an important factor in White's successful role as chairman of the Committee to Defend America by Aiding the Allies in 1940.

*   *   *

Shortly after White's return home from the Mayo Clinic, a severe and dangerous wave of Red-baiting and of anti-Catholic and anti-Semitic outbursts swept through Kansas. This native American state, with a small number of Jewish people and peoples of Catholic stock, now furnished as fertile soil for these bigots as it had in the days of the Ku Klux Klan. Kansas Red-baiters tried to persuade the legislature to conduct an investigation of alleged Communist activities at the University of Kansas because a K.U. student had joined the Spanish Loyalists. White took a leading part in a newspaper campaign that ridiculed the bill into defeat. Not long after this victory, liberal Kansans were faced with the menace of Gerald B. Winrod, Wichita Fascist, who launched a campaign to secure the Republican senatorial nomination.

White was gravely worried. Winrod, he felt, was a natural product of Kansas. The state had produced an entire line of fanatics like John Brown, Carrie Nation, Dr. Brinkley, and now Winrod. Winrod was doubly dangerous in White's eyes because he was a revivalist preacher. He cloaked his anti-Semitic and pro-Hitler sentiments in Biblical phrases. Since he was a preacher of the gospel, bearing God's banner, many good Kansas Protestants could not believe that he could utter any but God's sentiments.

A capable revivalist orator, he was a master at arousing people's emotions. In 1938, he transferred his emotional appeals to the realm of politics.

Winrod was only one of the many native Fascists who, stimulated by the success Adolf Hitler was having in Germany, were blooming all over the nation. Winrod was in close collaboration with Elizabeth Dilling, author of *The Red Network*, Colonel E. N. Sanctuary, William Dudley Pelley, and Herman Max Schwinn, German-American bund leader on the West Coast. Winrod was pastor of the Defender Tabernacle and publisher of the *Defender*, the *Constitutionalist*, and the *Revealer*. After a trip to Germany in 1934, Winrod began to praise the accomplishments of the Nazi movement. He distributed the forged *Protocols of Zion*, and he founded the *Revealer* to describe the "World Jewish Conspiracy."

Fundamentalists in the Bible belt were deluged with Winrod's hate pamphlets. After his trip to Germany, he discovered that Roosevelt was a Jew and that the Sino-Japanese War was Jew inspired. The Catholic Church, too, he revealed was "the harlot woman" of the Bible. By 1938 he had a large following among the frustrated, bewildered Kansans of native American stock, who had been seeking some scapegoats upon whom to blame their economic troubles. Winrod apparently had an ample supply of funds for his various projects. Editor White always believed that native Fascists like Winrod were being financed by reactionary industrialists, who found these men convenient tools, since they preached against a democratic America.

"I deeply fear that the Fascist, raw and unashamed," White wrote on February 28, 1938, "stands a fairly good chance to go to the United States Senate from this state. . . . The situation is ripe for it. The idle mind of distressed people is turning, even if futilely and vainly, to any noise in the periphery . . . thinking that it is a call of succor."

White backed Clyde Reed in the primary against Winrod. White feared that the standpat Republicans, who disliked Reed, would support the Winrod candidacy. After talking to Landon, who did not like Reed either, White and Landon wrote letters to their personal friends all over the state, warning them that Winrod must be defeated because he would hurt the ticket that fall.

This plea probably contributed more to the defeat of Winrod than did the reaction against all of Winrod's anti-Semitic and pro-Nazi views.

White used his newspaper connection to the fullest to defeat Winrod. Not only did he utilize news columns and editorial space, but he inserted advertisements in thirty daily and twenty weekly papers. A good deal of this space was contributed by his newspaper friends, but the rest he paid for himself. In the advertisements, White warned Kansas Republicans that Winrod was a Fascist despite the fact that at the present moment "he is so tolerant and pious in his public utterances, so sweet and lovely that butter would melt in his mouth." "I feel deeply," White continued, "that the Republican party in Kansas this year should rise to its opportunity. But with Winrod on the ticket to defend—and we must defend him if we nominate him—our case is hopeless."

In addition to White's activities—and most other Republican leaders were conspicuously silent in their criticism of Winrod until the last days of the campaign—a group of preachers helped expose Winrod. These Protestant preachers urged that Winrod withdraw from the campaign for the honor of Kansas, for the sake of religious tolerance and racial goodwill, and for the sake of intelligent Americanism. Attached to the appeal of these preachers was a two-page document asking questions like the following:

If Winrod is not a Fascist, why all the articles in his publications praising Hitler and his regime? (See *Defender*, December 1933, page 5, and *Defender*, March 1935, page 15.)

If Winrod is not a Fascist, why have the pro-Fascist and pro-Nazi groups in Germany and in the United States listed him as friendly?

If Winrod is not a Fascist, why has he advertised for sale the "International Jew" by Henry Ford, repudiated years ago by Mr. Ford, but now reprinted by the Fascists and Nazis in Germany and England? (See *Defender*, March 1934, page 20.)

If Winrod is not a Fascist, why does he denounce all progressive Protestant groups as "the apostate Protestant hierarchy," "the Protestant Papacy," and why does he denounce Judaism as apostate and Roman Catholicism as pagan and assume that everybody is wrong but Winrod?

If Winrod is not a Fascist, why did he charge in the *Defender* of December 1935, page 6, that all sentiment against Nazi Germany and Hitler in the United States was inspired by Communists?

These preachers were led by L. M. Birkhead, for twenty years the crusading pastor of the All Souls Unitarian Church in Kansas City, Missouri. After a visit to Germany in 1935, where Birkhead visited Nazi propaganda headquarters and was told that the Nazis had friends in the United States who included Winrod, Pelley, and Sanctuary, Birkhead returned home and launched the anti-Fascist Friends of Democracy.

Birkhead carefully prepared a pamphlet of photostatic reproductions of Winrod's Fascist utterances and distributed it wholesale in Kansas. White aided Birkhead in the compilation of the pamphlet by advising Birkhead what material should be deleted. The pamphlet reproduced statements by Winrod under headings that read "Why Protestants Cannot Support Winrod," "Why Roman Catholics Cannot Support Winrod," "Why Kansas People Opposed to Nazi-ism Cannot Support Winrod," and "Why Winrod Is a Menace to American Democracy."

White played such a prominent role in the anti-Winrod campaign that the Winrod forces concentrated their fire on him. They circulated a pamphlet entitled *How Red Is White?* A few years before, Elizabeth Dilling also, in her *Red Network*, had classed White as a dangerous "Red," along with Sinclair Lewis, Harry Emerson Fosdick, and John Dewey. *How Red Is White?* charged: "He has associated with the reds, pinks, and yellows for years; he has 'joined up' with numerous communistic organizations." The pamphlet asserted that such organizations as the Civil Liberties Union, the National Save Our Schools Committee, and the American Association for Economic Freedom—White was a member of all these organizations—were "communistic."

White was not disturbed by the Winrod attack. "For forty years I have won whatever fights I have won in Kansas by directing the fire of my candidate's opponents to me, thus keeping it off my candidate," White explained in glee. His fight against Winrod attracted nation-wide attention. When President Roosevelt asked him to explain Winrod's appeal, White replied: "He has all the elements of danger. He was a tent evangelist and knows the tricks of Father Coughlin, Huey Long and Billy Sunday. He is a nice blend of the three, temperamentally, intellectually, morally . . . He speaks well, either on the radio or to an audience, and is a strapping, handsome, smooth-talking man much like a medicine vendor or a soap-peddler. His religious angle is interesting. He is a four degrees sub-Baptist, more fundamental than Bryan, believes in all the prophecies of Revelations . . . One cannot assume that he is dishonest. He really believes it." Roosevelt wrote back on June 14, 1938: "It sounds to me like a situation in which the President of the United States cannot help . . . at least for the moment. Knowing T.R. and F.D.R. you will realize what a momentous admission that is!"

Although Winrod was defeated, he did obtain 53,000 votes. Clyde Reed praised White's superb handling of his campaign. After White's death, Harold Hammond declared in the Great Bend [Kansas] *Herald* that all the eulogies overlooked what he had done in 1938 to prevent Kansas from the disgrace of Winrod as senator.

The hate spread by Winrod did not die easily. During the fall campaign, Payne Ratner, Republican candidate for governor, was subjected to anti-Semitic abuse on widely circulated cards which read:

Vote only for Gentiles
Who knows how much
JEWISH Money Republicans
Are Spending?
Ratner Is A Jew.

White immediately suggested that Governor Huxman and the Democrats post a reward of $100 for the arrest of persons circulating such scurrilous cards. When the Democrats followed his advice, White editorialized: "No one believes that Governor Walter Huxman was in any remote way responsible for the circulars . . . labeling Payne Ratner as a Jew. Of course he's a Jew. Also, his mother was Irish, and of course he's Irish. And neither blood hurts him. Nor does the fact that he's a deacon in the Christian Campbellite Church hurt him either. And Governor Huxman handed a stinging rebuke to the Ku Kluxers and Jew-baiters who peddled these circulars."

After war broke out in Europe, when William Allen White headed a movement designed to arouse America to the menace of a Hitler victory, Winrod carried on a scathing attack on White, President Roosevelt, and anyone who believed that America's security was tied up with the Allied cause. Winrod opposed all defense measures, fought Lend-Lease, urged the strictest type of isolationism, and was a bulwark of the America First Committee in Kansas. After Pearl Harbor, he was indicted for sedition, but continued his technique of playing upon old Biblical and native American stereotypes of a day that had passed, stubbornly refusing to face the inevitable situation that America as the greatest industrial power had to co-operate with other nations to maintain international peace.

*   *   *

Shortly after the defeat of Winrod, William Allen White published his second biography of Calvin Coolidge, *A Puritan in Babylon*. It was more than a mere biography of Coolidge; it was also an excellent autobiography of William Allen White. It was a well-written, sparkling history of the postwar decade and its culmination in the Coolidge bull market.

White had been gathering material and writing this book from time to time over a period of five years. He hired a researcher to go through valuable letter collections like those of President William Howard Taft, who was chief justice of the Supreme Court in the Coolidge era, and he himself interviewed a wide variety of people in his quest for the human substance of the decade of the twenties.

White portrayed Coolidge as a simple, bewildered American of the old rural age, amidst the Babylon that was America during the period of his presidency. Although White praised Coolidge for cleaning out the muck left by the Harding administration, he observed that Coolidge let into power men far more dangerous to American democracy than the Ohio Gang. The Insulls, the Mellons, and the Dohertys sat at Coolidge's council table and he, with his belief in the benevolent feudalism of money, let these men bring America to its doom.

A Puritan in Babylon, White's best work of nonfiction, was extremely well received. Within a month, it was in its fifth printing. Wisest comment on the book came from Walter Millis, who wrote in *Herald Tribune Books,* on November 20, 1938:

Why William Allen White should feel that uneasy attraction in Calvin Coolidge's prim, thin and legendarily successful personality is not difficult to understand. The man whose own abounding life reveals the greatness in small-town Kansas could not fail to be arrested by this apparent symbol of the greatness in small-town Massachusetts. The progressive, Western, agrarian Republican who has been buffeted by all the doubts and inconsistencies and strains of the age in which an agrarian America grew into the temple of finance capitalism, with the Republican party as its oracle, could not fail to be fascinated by the conservative, Eastern but also essentially rural Republican who rose so smoothly and steadily through all those storms to head the party and preside over the nation in the last quiet sunset of that age before the descent of economic—and political—night.

When the Emporia editor was writing *A Puritan in Babylon,* he had explained to a friend: "I want to make this Coolidge book a story of the development of our plutocracy from McKinley's administration into an organized, arrogant, self-conscious governing oligarchy in 1929, the span of Coolidge's political life." White was so successful in developing this theme that Charles A. Beard rated the book as one of the twelve most interesting histories written in that decade.

CHAPTER 21

SPOKESMAN FOR THE GRASS ROOTS

"FOR as long as I can remember when anyone wished to find out or was advising someone from abroad how to find out what was the American view at the heart of the Nation and in its purest form, he turned as a matter of course to William Allen White in Emporia," Walter Lippmann once remarked. Walter Winchell declared: "William Allen White assumed that, since Kansas is the geographical heart of America, he was specially equipped to interpret America's soul. In this he was largely correct."

During the last twenty or thirty years of his life, White was the folk hero of many middle-class people. He seemed to offer a sense of security to a group whose values were in a state of flux; he appeared to be a rock of stability in an America and a world that were undergoing epoch-making changes. Many people saw in this successful, mellow, small-town editor a justification for their type of civilization, which was subjected to attack for being mean and materialistic and was being altered before their very eyes.

White seemed a little wiser concerning the major problems facing society than did most of the people who began to worship him as a folk hero. They carefully read his widely reprinted editorials, his magazine articles, his syndicated news stories, and his books. Excellent editorials like "Mary White" and "To an Anxious Friend" first attracted many people to this small-town editor. "Mary White," alone, was the first really intimate tie that millions had with him. Until his death the *Gazette* received thousands of requests every year for reprints of this editorial.

The publication of two volumes of his editorials *The Editor And His People*, edited by Helen O. Mahin (1924), and *Forty Years on Main Street*, edited by Russell H. Fitzgibbon (1937), served to increase the number of people who were attracted to his human, tolerant, understanding point of view. During the three decades before his death, the amazing number of articles in major magazines and editorials in important newspapers devoted to the Emporia editor demonstrated his growing attraction for the reading public. In addition to this printed interest, a remarkable number of letters from all sorts of troubled people poured into Emporia. Many of them were from individuals whom he never had met, but who turned to him because of his folk-hero appeal. He answered all the letters that he received with a personal, not a form, letter. He loved to write letters. He did it with great zest, and his best writing frequently appeared in these letters in which he expressed himself even more freely than in his editorials. In a facetious mood, but nevertheless a mood revealing insight into the position he held in American life, he wrote Bruce Bliven of the *New Republic* on June 14, 1934: "I receive a lot of mail. It comes like the dew of Heaven and from the just and unjust. I seem to be some sort of papier-mâché Messiah to a lot of morons, rich and poor, who turn to me in trouble."

The following are some of the characterizations of White, in print or in letters, that demonstrate his unique position in American life:

William Allen White of Emporia: An American Institution is 70.—*Life*, February 28, 1938.

He is as Lincoln-like as a mortal can be, except in his style of architecture!—V. Y. DALLMAN, *Illinois State Register*, February 12, 1940.

White is my ideal of a typical American at his best.—EDGAR DEWITT JONES, Boston *Herald*, 1939.

His mouthpiece was no larger than most of ours, and yet he had made himself heard around the world. He was living proof—and in this there was infinite hope for all of us—that it is not the size of the job, but the size of the man that counts.—BEN HIBBS, *Saturday Evening Post*, February 26, 1944.

I honor him most for expressing our great American values.—PRESIDENT IRVING MAURER, Beloit College, March 19, 1935.

White stands out as one of the leading figures and builders of a prairie civilization that is gradually assuming the common American shape.—ELIZABETH S. SARGEANT, *Century Magazine*, January, 1927.

Along the crowded Main Street from Broadway to the Golden Gate, where daily a nation goes by—confused, complacent, angry, panicky, proud—a rotund man with a merry eye has for forty years gone up and down, talking . . . Main Street has been kindlier because of him, and safer; and his fellow citizens have understood better themselves, each other, their country and their dreams.—HERMANN HAGE-DORN, Roosevelt Memorial Association Award, October 27, 1934, to White as "an outstanding interpreter of the American mind."

White is the dean of literature in the Middle West; it would be a crime against him to so elect him; but that's what he is.—CARL SAND-BURG, May 24, 1924.

I always thought about him and Will Rogers as typical Uncle Sams of our generation.—JOSEPHUS DANIELS, December 6, 1944.

In one sense the late William Allen White may be taken as a composite grass roots thinker. On his regular visits to New York City, he was usually interviewed by reporters from the metropolitan press and they invariably interpreted his opinions as in contrast to the prevailing temper on the eastern seacoast.—E. C. LINDEMAN, *Survey Graphic*, June, 1944.

During the decade of the twenties, White cast himself, perhaps somewhat with his tongue in his cheek, as the defender of small-town, homey virtues from the attacks of highbrows like H. L. Mencken. He was the defender of Puritan civilization against the attacks of skeptics living in the vulgar, big city. After one of his assaults on the evils of urban life, *The New York Times* referred to him as the "head philosopher of the Bucolic School" and added that "In one sense it is a defeat of himself, for he too is an erring man, subject to the bond of iniquity. He can't keep away from Manhattan, but at a distance and as a Kansas moralist he views it with alarm."

White read with considerable amusement H. L. Mencken's charges that his small-town America was inhabited by "stupid yokels" and "uncivilized barbarians." "I am very fond of old Henry Mencken . . ." White remarked. "Henry is the top-sergeant of all the literary drillmasters. It is his job to hang up his

'Bible Belt' dummy and to smack and show his teeth and roar while he jabs his bayonet into the dummy's belly for the instruction and edification of the recruits." Publicly, White praised the accomplishments of Mencken's Bible belt in producing a civilization with more material comforts than were ever seen before in human history. White also contended that there was more neighborly kindliness, honesty, and diligence in the small town than in the urban center. Privately, however, he was willing to admit that a state like Kansas had its failings. He once declared that the population of Kansas could be classed as twenty to thirty per cent moron; thirty to forty per cent three cuts higher; ten to fifteen per cent capable of intelligent leadership; and only five to ten per cent who really knew what it was all about.

In 1922, White denounced the great urban centers and their variegated population as a menace to America. They were teeming with inefficiency in the city government, stuffed payrolls, and grafting public servants. All this he blamed on the recent immigrant groups. "We are filling our cities with men and women who lack the mental grasp of the colonists who fought our Revolution, who established our land, who wrote our Constitution and so made America," he declared. ". . . Another civilization has invaded these shores, one not reared to hold ardent opinions about the Anglo-Saxon political taboos." These attitudes were dangerously similar to the lofty "one hundred per cent American" doctrines of the Klan, which White was so vigorously denouncing in this same era. Columnist Heywood Broun immediately challenged White's statement. He pointed out that government in the big cities was as efficient as the state governments controlled by rural areas. Furthermore, Broun added that native American states like Mississippi sent far worse demagogues to Congress than the polyglot cities.

It was during the 1928 campaign that White assumed most completely the role of spokesman of the cornfields in rebuke of New York City. Even the Paris [France] *Times* was attracted by White's invective in this campaign and remarked that "as a crusader he is doing things which the 'tabloid' newspapers had not thought of doing." White charged that Herbert Hoover, reared on an Iowa farm, was a product of the American mind and the

American background, whereas Governor Smith was the product of a different civilization. The farm and small-town dwellers, added White, were the only ones with the true American ideals.

In the closing years of his life, disturbed at the supremacy of industrial-urban America over his small-town civilization, he explained his America and his lifelong experience in the Middle West in *The Changing West* (1939). This book was William Allen White in a mellow, humane, and realistic mood. "The settlement of the western United States offers a first and shining example of a free people, morally and intellectually literate, using their own devices, their own sense of justice, to develop the wealth of a region and distribute it as a common wealth," he declared. For his democratic nation to survive in an industrial era, he was convinced that wealth must be as equitably distributed as the wealth of the land had been in the West during the nineteenth century. "What man did with that fabulous increase in wealth that came with the settlement of the West," he wrote, "man can do now as he plunges into the new era. But he must carry in his heart the two things that made the wilderness blossom as the rose: first, a neighborly faith in the decency of man; second, a never faltering vision of a better world."

* * *

Although William Allen White consciously looked upon himself as a spokesman for the middle class, at the same time he would not stand for their support of such tomfoolery as the Ku Klux Klan, the great Red scare, and the generally illiberal philosophy of the standpat Republicans. He looked upon himself as a clarifier of the ideals and the aspirations of the middle class. He tried to explain to them why they should not be illiberal in their thinking; why the great Red scare was a mechanism used by the predatory forces to check progressive ideas; and why democracy with its belief in the dignity of human beings was worth defending.

This "incarnate voice of the American middle class," as *The New York Times* called him, was a very complex individual. His role as interpreter-philosopher of American life attracted millions; his role as the Kansas-Emporia politician and businessman gave him power in provincial politics. He was thus a strange mixture of broad, kindly tolerance and small, narrow provincialism—a composite American.

White was an excellent commentator on the passing scene, and a reflection of it as well. His was a snapshot judgment on men and issues, but expressed in colorful language. He interpreted men and events in terms of their immediate importance, seldom in terms of their long-run implications. "Actually White was not always the great leader he was supposed to be," commented the Washington *Post* on March 10, 1946. "He was rather a magnificent mirror of mid-America; a perfect facsimile of the best in middle-class culture as it developed toward self-expression and social consciousness. True, in later years he fought the Ku Klux Klan and isolationists, hated fascism and believed, at least intellectually, in most reforms which aided the underdog. But generally speaking he was the national thermometer rather than the penicillin."

White had a desire for political power and a loyalty to his personal friends similar to that of a machine politician. He was infatuated by men like Theodore Roosevelt and impressed by men of the caliber of Harding and Coolidge. Yet he was capable of growth. After a few years had passed—except in the case of T.R. —he could look back at some of the men he had admired and at his own views at that time and poke fun at his own naïveté. He could laugh at himself and make other people laugh, and he had a genuine sense of humor and an understanding of human weakness.

White was vain. He relished publicity and attention. He noted in his *Autobiography* that he was "a born exhibitionist." He was ambitious too. He enjoyed having a finger in local, state, and national politics, and he delighted in having friendships with eminent people. At the same time he could be warmhearted and generous. "Above all," commented the Iola *Register*, "he was an utterly irrepressible, bubbling spirit, a veritable fountain of youth."

There were in William Allen White the lovable warmth, the tolerance, and the fine human qualities of rural America. These traits were offset at times by blindness toward the greatness of men like William Jennings Bryan and Woodrow Wilson and by a superficiality in understanding the basic issues facing American life. But White was brave; he had courage; he wasn't afraid of a fight. On the other hand, he led too comfortable a life to plunge too deeply into a crusade to cure the miseries that beset America. He was moderately wealthy, and he was happy—too happy to venture too far out in front of the main body of troops to slay any dragons.

White's national reputation reached such a point that few enterprises of a public nature were launched without their sponsors seeking at least his moral support if not his active participation. For instance, when the Committee to Boycott Japanese Aggression was formed in 1938, William Loeb explained that the committee needed his name because people would rally to a cause that he supported. "Why pick on you?" Loeb asked. "Because, whether or not you realize it, you completely bridge all classes and factions in the United States." Charles R. Crane wrote the Emporia editor in 1936: "With the death of Will Rogers you are the only 'American' left whose voice has any carry."

* * *

During the many years that the Emporia editor looked upon himself as the spokesman for grass-roots America, he disdained descriptions of his middle class in terms of income statistics. To him, a member of the middle class was any person who had a sense of security in his work or profession and thus a feeling of self-respect. The plutocracy, or the upper class, on the other hand, were those who did no work and derived a living from interest on investments, or those who depended upon their predatory talents for a livelihood. The proletariat, to White, included any person who did not know where next week's food, board, and living expenses were coming from.

The middle class always flourished best, he contended, in the country and in small towns. As a group, it was class conscious, but, since this class included the vast majority of Americans, he felt that its type of class consciousness was not objectionable. But any class-conscious feeling on the part of the plutocracy or the proletariat was not to be tolerated. White enjoyed appearing before both labor and business groups to warn them not to trample on middle-class ideals and aspirations. Speaking from the consumer's viewpoint to the International Management Congress in

1938, he took capital on one knee and labor on the other and bashed their heads together with jovial impartiality. He criticized the employer class for shortsightedness in fighting the eight-hour day, old-age pensions, and unemployment insurance. Employers knew these reforms were coming, yet they put cotton in their ears and cried "communism." "If a dozen or twenty years ago you, Mr. Capitalist, had used the social sense of the average man in the street," White declared, "this problem of unemployment and old-age pensions would not be handing to your arch-enemies an organized subsidized class-conscious proletariat which can be voted to your destruction. By your sloth you created the particular head devil who is mocking you."

Before the Abraham Lincoln Club of Los Angeles, which he characterized as "the most conservative plutocratic group in an open-shop town," he declared in 1939 that labor must come into a new status in American life. The employer must bargain with union labor on the basis of mutual self-respect. "I am all for the rugged individual," he said, "provided the rugged individual has an understanding heart! But we must also demand freedom for the worker, freedom under law to organize, freedom under law to speak out even though he is wrong, legal freedom to assemble even for a misguided purpose so long as the worker keeps the peace."

Speaking to the National Association of Harvard Clubs in Chicago, on May 21, 1938, White warned that the continuation of large numbers of unemployed workers was a definite threat to the future of the middle class. If the unemployed did not have job security, they would soon cease to be middle-class citizens and form a class-conscious proletariat. If American democracy was to survive, he declared, the unemployed must have work and wages sufficient to establish a decent standard of living. "A little common sense, a little common pity, a little common justice then, twenty years ago in our land," he observed, "would not have made it necessary to turn workers hungry upon the street."

White summed up many of his views on the plutocracy in a series of lectures delivered at Harvard University and published as *The Changing West* in November, 1939. He declared that the reason why many workingmen lacked an adequate wage and the benefits of self-respect was the employer's fear and greed. The problem child in industrial relations was not the labor racketeer, bad as he was, but "rather the man in the front office, the man at the flat-topped desk, the capitalist, the owner, whether he be a soulless corporate entity or a finite man mildly mad with a delusion of the danger to his property rights."

Class-conscious labor activity also stirred his wrath. The sabotaging labor leader of the Industrial Workers of the World type must be curbed. Those labor leaders, however, who concerned themselves with collective bargaining and improved wages and conditions of work were carrying on a legitimate task. But, he observed in 1938, "for labor to say in effect: 'Down with all bosses! We'll run not only the shop but the whole country!'; for labor to go into the ballot box and emerge class-conscious against all bosses good and bad, that policy menaces the existing economic structure of American civilization. . . . The political labor boss . . . would turn a democracy into a contest between two class-conscious parties, a class-conscious proletariat and a class-conscious plutocracy. . . . The labor union militant and undefiled—yes; the vertical union and the closed shop? Yes. But a class-conscious labor party in a democracy—no!"

The middle class, White contended from his own political experience, was not interested in a definitely liberal and a definitely conservative party. They desired the existing situation, in which both elements lived side by side in each of the major parties. They would not accept political parties on an economic-class division. The industrial worker and the depressed farmer, White maintained, had only to convince the middle class of the justice behind their demands, and the middle class would help them achieve their ends and at the same time absorb them into their own ranks.

Middle-class democracy, to White, was the institutionalized philosophy of Jesus stripped of its theological terminology. The democratic process, he believed, should curb the egoistic, selfish instincts of men, but at the same time leave the exceptional man free to develop his talents commensurately with honest, neighborly, social conduct. Being a practical citizen, the Emporia editor was willing to concede that America had achieved only thirty or forty per cent of a true democracy based on the ethics of Jesus.

Yet the common man did have more benefits under democracy than under any other form of government; the government had partially curbed greed and had shortened the hours of labor; and the average citizen did have the opportunity through government to redress his wrongs. "The democratic order has upon the whole, admitting its faults," he wrote, "made more people happy, useful and decent than any other constitutionalized system ever established by man."

Having seen a democratic society take root in his own trans-Mississippi West, in spite of its obvious imperfections, he became a champion of a way of life that was being threatened by the spread of totalitarianism all over the world. Democracy might be slow, it might be wasteful, it might be clumsy, but it did leave men free, he argued. In 1939, when totalitarianism was at the zenith of its power, he predicted: "The totalitarian state is morally doomed . . . because it hampers, checks, tries to guide and control the man who under the free democratic process, by reason of his talents and power, would assume leadership and give the forward command to society. I mean the inventor, the enterpriser, the statesman, the financier, the great man who comes every decade in every generation to function in the human hive and hold democracy to its ideals as a human organism. I would keep the leader honest, of course. I would make the exceptional man give full social return for every privilege he enjoys. But after that, the leader should be free."

White always urged patience on those who wanted to achieve perfection in their day. Too much speed in reform might provoke a dangerous reaction. During the years from 1900 to 1939, he felt that considerable progress had been made toward a better society. "Patience is the first virtue of a democracy," he declared. He cautioned inquiring young men to be tolerant toward the delays of democracy. Dictatorship was no way to cure democracy's ills since "The gorgeous thing about a dictatorship is that it furnishes a damn fool a sure, quick way to take his country to hell and prove what a chump he is. Watch for the Hitler and Mussolini fireworks. Democracy has its checks and balances. We elevate dubs and boobs and tear them down because we are free to do so and never fail to do so. But the dub and boob of the dictatorship are permanent. They stick until they crash."

Every citizen in a democracy, he thought, had a responsibility —a moral obligation to fight for and to expand the benefits of freedom for the underprivileged. Freedom should not degenerate into license and the refusal to accept a social point of view. Lecturing his neighbors one evening in the *Gazette*, he wrote: "This town is the child of many prayers. This town is the ideal realized only after those who dreamed the ideal, laid them down to rest with the dream still a dream. This town is the fruit of great aspiration, and we who live here now, have a debt to posterity that we can pay only by still achieving, still pursuing."

*　　*　　*

White's fellow journalists readily admitted that in the years from 1919 to 1944 the Emporia editor held a unique position in the American newspaper world. "William Allen White restored the personality in journalism," remarked Robert Lincoln O'Brien of the Boston *Herald*. "He was the most colorful editor since the days of Horace Greeley, James Gordon Bennett, and Charles A. Dana." In 1922, a Philadelphia paper referred to him as the Peter Pan of journalism, and *The New York Times* regularly was amused by his colorful editorial language. "His 'vocabulary laboratories' . . ." the *Times* observed on August 17, 1925, "are producing their finest goods. He bubbles with fun and mischief." In 1938, *Time* referred to him as that "gusty old editor" and added that he was the "best-known and most respected small-town newspaperman in the United States." Just before his seventieth birthday the *Rocky Mountain News*, on February 6, 1938, declared: "This man is the greatest American country editor." A little over a year later Oscar Stauffer observed in the Arkansas City *Daily Traveler:* "Many persons living in Kansas fail to appreciate how William Allen White towers in the world." "The most joyous and resonant country editor in America," remarked Anne O'Hare McCormick in 1924. E. D. Canham declared in 1939 in the *Christian Science Monitor:* "He embodies everything that seems fine to his eversentimental profession; he is what American journalism ought to be."

Many young journalists were indebted to White for guidance and inspiration. The late Raymond Clapper, widely respected columnist, told White on February 8, 1938, that he had been a great influence on his career and Ben Hibbs, *Saturday Evening Post* editor, recalled that when he and other young men started newspaperwork in Kansas, "Bill White, who even then was known wherever in this world the English language was spoken, was the bellwether of the flock—our hero. I suppose, unconsciously, most of us tried to be like him, and we practically rolled over with happiness when our editorials were reprinted in the Emporia Gazette." To the journalism students at the University of Kansas, he was a legendary character in their profession. A Filipino wrote him in 1936: "As a young man aspiring to become a newspaperman I have looked up to you as my ideal journalist."

During the last thirty years of his life, White deplored the declining opportunity for a poor man to start his own paper. Expensive machinery required far too much capital for most young men. Furthermore, as the amount of money invested in newspapers increased, journalism was transformed into a six per cent investment. After Harold Ickes had debated the question of the freedom of the press with publisher Frank Gannett, in 1939, White told Ickes that he had missed one good point by not stressing the tremendous property sense of the owners of American newspapers. "That property sense biases editors and owners, and incidentally employees, so heavily that almost instinctively and automatically newspapers take the property side of every controversy," White declared. "They think they are fair, they try to be fair, but when in any town of over 10,000 it would take a $100,000 to establish a newspaper, and when an established newspaper in any town over 10,000 begins to be worth ten or fifteen thousand dollars for every thousand population you can see what the property sense does to newspapers."

As early as 1926, White regretted the passing of the free editor who had been able to express himself without worrying as to the attitude of his business office. "With all our tall talk about ideals we editors have only a contract status, and the more we emphasize our ideals, the more tenuous becomes our contract status," White asserted. ". . . To deliver our message, to create our ideal we must

486

have machinery—the tools of our craft. These tools cost tens of thousands of dollars, often millions. So the man who owns the tools, the man who owns the paper, owns us. . . . We are servants, that is what is the matter with the American editorial page."

When George Seldes published *Lords of the Press* (1938), an attack upon the newspaper tendency to color the news in favor of vested interests, White urged that the book be made compulsory reading for every American school of journalism. Although he did not agree entirely with Seldes's thesis, White did tell the American Society of Newspaper Editors on April 20, 1939, that American papers were unusually affected by a property interest. Too often, he charged, in the past few years of New Deal reform the press had published editorials hostile to all social progress. On the other hand, he felt that the press was "honest to its lights" and few editors "obviously and shamelessly defend malefactors of great wealth." Furthermore, most papers printed both sides of a controversy even though editorially they generally displayed a conservative bias. "Taken by and large on the whole the American newspapers are the most dependable source of public information," he declared. "In this country American journalism, with all its faults, and they are many, is the only free, unfettered, unbossed, unlicensed vehicle through which one way or another finally and surely the truth comes to the American people."

Every once in a while White was disturbed by certain antiliberal tendencies within the Associated Press, of which he was a member. Since the AP relied upon its local outlet to gather the local news for the entire system, the local publisher, tied in with the Chamber of Commerce, might naturally tend to color the news on a labor story to favor the employer side of the controversy. On war news or on local news like fires and crime the AP did excellent reporting, but their labor news, White felt, had to be read with care. "It is so easy for a reporter, a copy-reader, the city editor, and the staff of our prosperous papers to take the country club attitude, the boss' slant toward those who for one reason or another are whacking the established order," he told Kent Cooper, director of the AP on August 29, 1932. "But the easy thing must be avoided if we retain any value as a news agency except such value as may come to us as a purveyor of journalistic fodder for contented cows."

The great danger to the newspaper was not direct corruption by property-minded forces, but the fact that the publisher and editor absorbed the color of his environment. His association with the plutocracy of every community—in the country club, in the university club, in the Chamber of Commerce—White contended was what degraded a publisher and gave him a sense "of the eternal rightness of the established order." From this conservative environment, added White, the publisher gained his antilabor bias, his opposition to government regulation of the stock exchange, and his hostility to government control of public utilities. As a result, White wrote: "It often happens, alas too often, that a newspaper publisher, reflecting this unconscious class arrogance of the consciously rich, thinks he is printing news when he is doctoring it innocently enough. He thinks he is purveying the truth when much that he offers seems poison to hundreds of thousands of his readers who don't move in his social and economic stratosphere."

The correcting factor in this situation, White believed, was that if a publisher went too far in coloring the news, eventually he would wreck his paper. The publisher was influential only as long as the public believed in his integrity. When his readers deserted the paper, advertising would drop and the paper would be doomed. "The American press is as free as the American people," noted White. "Our press has the faults of our people and their saving virtues."

White was also gravely concerned over the power of national advertising agencies as a threat to the freedom of the press. In 1938, he observed that there was serious danger in the years ahead that these agencies would exercise an unbelievable pressure upon newspapers. "I am not afraid of consolidating newspapers, I am not afraid of a one-newspaper town," he wrote *Editor and Publisher.* "What I am afraid of is that advertising agencies who are also political and public-relations advisers to big groups of advertisers like steel, oil, copper, automobiles, and the like, may see the tremendous advantage they have by cutting down or cutting out advertisements from liberal papers."

In 1938, the American Society of Newspaper Editors, in electing William Allen White as their president, stated that his "newspaper service represents the highest example of the influence and leadership that may be exercised by an American writer and editor." As head of this society he devoted his efforts to raising the standards of schools of journalism. It was his firm conviction that aspiring journalists should acquire the degree of Bachelor of Arts before entering a journalism school. Whenever students asked him what courses they should take in college to prepare for a newspaper career, he warmly recommended broad courses in history, geography, economics, and literature. The better the background of information available, he explained, the quicker were the chances of going ahead in newspaperwork.

There were two kinds of journalism, White always carefully explained to journalism classes. There was the get-the-money type of paper that accepted no social obligations, held no moral scruples, and existed merely for financial returns. This type of paper appealed to the emotions of a moronic type of reader. The advertising columns of such a paper were open to every swindler, and the news columns could be perverted by money. "Sensational headlines, sensational language, appeals to fear, hate, envy and cupidity are the tools of this kind of journalist's workshop," he declared.

On the other type of paper, the news was printed carefully, without sensational headlines, and was interpreted without favor to any group. Although it was more difficult to make money in this type of journalism, there was more satisfaction and more ultimate happiness.

* * *

White's unique ability to express himself in highly colorful language was as characteristic of the last few years of his life as it had been of his earlier days. "There's Vitriol and Salt in his Editorials," remarked the *Literary Digest* on April 24, 1937. "I don't know of anyone who can say as much in a few words as you can . . ." Walt Mason told him after he had written his stinging editorial on Frank Munsey's death. White was a brilliant editorial writer, but he was only a moderately successful publisher.

His outside earnings made him a successful country journalist

Editing the *Gazette* furnished White an important byline to reach the American public, but it did not afford him the style of living to which he had become accustomed.

As White grew in stature, his influence nationally appeared to be greater than his influence in Kansas, and his influence in Kansas was greater than his influence in Lyon County. Although he had had considerable success in selecting winning candidates in Kansas politics over the years, during many years he was unable to carry Lyon County for his gubernatorial candidate. An Emporian was quoted as saying in 1924: "Bill has done a good many crazy political things . . . We love him . . . We're for Bill all right, but we just can't take his political advice. He is our greatest town asset, but he's also our bummest political adviser."

The New York Times rather satirically referred to him in 1928 as the "Playboy of Kansas" and stated: "Something may be the matter with Kansas, but nothing is wrong with the way in which it sizes up the humor of her most eminent citizen, Mr. White. Whether he is running for Governor himself in a joke campaign, or terrifying the East with his solemnity of mien as a reformer, Kansas knows that he invariably furnishes excellent entertainment."

During the twenties and early thirties, much of the burden of running the *Gazette* and writing the editorials was carried by son Bill. Many of the editorials from 1927 to 1934 that were credited to the father by the outside world were actually written by Bill. Bill was more of a liberal than his father. He too had the knack of expressing himself in forceful language. When Bill left Emporia in 1935 to become a free-lance writer in the East, the Iola *Register* observed: "He is a better writer than his father was at his age, and that is saying a lot. It is entirely possible that he will attain a place in literature that will equal or exceed that of his father."

The *Gazette* was a profitable paper in the twenties. In 1929, just before the stock market crash, White was offered $400,000 for the property. By now the paper had a circulation of slightly over seven thousand copies in a county of nearly thirty thousand people. The paper was democratically operated. The staff, for instance, persuaded the editor to add comic strips to the paper when he loathed the idea. On October 4, 1920, he wrote in the editorial column: "The boss is whipped . . . the force has beat him. He thinks that they [comics] make a low appeal; that their humor is broad, and their level of intelligence negligible. But the force maintains that they sell papers. Why they should sell papers is beyond the boss; except that the fact that people with low enough intelligence to read the 'funnies' do have money. . . . So with shame and apology to the Gazette readers who have brains in their noodles and not tripe or scrambled eggs, the Gazette begins its publication of the 'funnies.' From which the good Lord deliver us."

The labor turnover on the *Gazette* was remarkably low in view of the small salaries paid the employees. By 1939, the average tenure of employees was 17.8 years. The oldest printer, Conrad Jones, started in 1899 and worked on the paper until his death in 1941. White worked out a profit-sharing system that helped to stabilize employment. Each year at Christmas there would be a dinner for all the *Gazette* employees and their families, and each employee would receive a check for his share of the *Gazette*'s profits. The size of each person's check depended upon the *Gazette*'s total profits, the recipient's years of service, and the size of his salary. In 1920, when business was flourishing, each person received ten per cent of his annual wage as a bonus. This system was modified in 1937 and 1938 to conform with the social security law.

After the crash of 1929, the *Gazette* had difficult years, but the full force was maintained, subject to two wage cuts. White's outside earnings made it possible for him to continue to hire a full staff. These depression years found many ambitious young people unable to obtain their first journalistic position. Editor White, worried over their lack of opportunity, finally decided to allow a few of those who wanted to work on the *Gazette* without pay to come to Emporia and gain experience. In a five-year period, the *Gazette* had from twenty-five to thirty such volunteer workers, or, as the permanent staff called them, "students in the W. A. White School of Journalism." The "school," however, closed when the wage-and-hour law was enacted. The regular staff of Frank Clough, Paul Chandler, Russell Roberts, Roger Triplett, and Ted McDaniel supervised the training of these aspiring journalists. They never knew when the "boss" would add two or three additional apprentices to the already crowded newsroom.

During White's last few years, his birthdays were occasions for sparkling editorials and festive parties. By the time he had reached the age of sixty, he was no longer the redheaded, militant editor of earlier years. He was still rotund, but now he was white-haired and tending toward baldness. Although he was still vigorous in expressing his opinions, he was far more mellow in dealing with his opponents. When a person wrote objecting to some action or statement, he would dictate a personal reply emphasizing that honest men could have different points of view, and then close with the remark: "It's differences of opinion that make horse races profitable, marriages risky, and democracy work." His kindly, generous tolerance toward those with whom he differed was a significant factor in his growing influence with the public.

On February 10, 1933, when White reached the age of sixty-five, he wrote in a mellow mood:

I have been shaving this funny old face every Sunday, Tuesday, Thursday and Saturday for years and years. I have come to look on it as a mask behind which the reality that is I has to hide. It is getting a bit battered and shopworn. Perhaps it would not be such a bad idea to cast it off and let dust return to dust and if there is any salvage "with God be the rest."

In the meantime life has been good, a tremendously interesting adventure. I have never had a bored hour in my life. I get up every morning now wondering what new strange, gorgeous thing is going to happen and it always happens at fairly reasonable intervals. And generally, and this is a part of the unbending curve of my life, adventure comes from afar, from the outside, from things over which I have no control. Lady Luck has been good to me. I fancy she is good to everyone only some people are dour and when she gives them the come hither with her eyes they look down or turn away and lift an eyebrow. But me, I give her the wink and away we go.

* * *

Five years later, on his seventieth birthday, over a hundred of his fellow townsmen sent him flowers; birthday cards and letters poured in from the entire country; and when White arrived at the *Gazette* office that morning he was greeted by a thousand citizens and a forty-piece band. Just before his birthday, *Collier's* carried an autobiographical article by the editor; *Life* and *Look* magazines and Fox Movietone News photographed White, the *Gazette* office, and the town of Emporia; and newspapers devoted columns of news space and editorials to the 70-year-old editor.

John Finley in *The New York Times* explained that the newspaper profession was proud to claim White as a member. "It is impossible to think of the Middle West, or the American small city, or the homely virtues, or independent journalism, without thinking of William Allen White," Finley observed. "Mr. White is the great unbossed American . . . Will White is sound and sweet and humorous and sad. He is idealistic and poetic and practical enough to make a good property out of a once nearly worthless country paper—which was and is no slouch of a job . . . If we could believe that the whole Middle West was something like Will White, and that the rest of the country was something like the Middle West, one could be perfectly confident as to the future."

Although the citizens of Emporia greatly respected William Allen White, few of them were on intimate terms with him during the last two decades of his life. There were very few people left in the town who called him Bill or Will. There were more people who called him by his first name in New York City than in Emporia. When Lewis Gannett visited Emporia, he was struck with the fact that the editor was called Mr. White by Emporia's citizens. Gannett, in a friendly fashion, accused White of deliberately cultivating the impression that he was a simple country editor, when actually he no longer was the small-town editor who knew everyone by his first name.

* * *

From 1926 to 1944, in addition to editing the *Gazette*, writing books and articles, and mixing in politics, White served as a judge for the Book-of-the-Month Club. He was one of the original judges of this pioneer book club, and highly and seriously regarded his work of reading and selecting books for mass distribution. During the years in which White was a judge, the club membership increased from 4,000 to 600,000. This remarkable growth was ample evidence of a great need met by the Book-of-the-Month Club. The club clearly increased the public's interest in books and through its monthly selections exerted a powerful influence over American literary and cultural life.

Seldom before the club started had nonfiction books been best sellers. By selecting many works of nonfiction, the club helped to popularize this type of reading and gave publishers confidence of a potential market that never had existed in the past. Harry Scherman, president of the Book-of-the-Month Club, believes that the publishers accepted many nonfiction manuscripts, which they would not have published before the club's origin, because they thought the manuscript might interest the judges of the club.

In the last few years of White's work as judge, the club had become a significant mail-order book business. For every two selections purchased, the club gave its members a book dividend. The magnitude of the club's business could be seen in 1944 when the retail value of the book dividends was over $9,000,000.

To William Allen White the function of the judges who selected books was not chiefly a literary assignment. Their task, he believed, was to pick books that most exactly suited their customers. Twenty per cent of their membership, he believed, were highly sophisticated people who liked books well written, who were interested in the way the author said things rather than in what was said, and who did not mind a spot here and there of dirt provided it was applied artistically by the author. At the bottom of the scale were another twenty per cent who were primarily interested in snappy books, who wanted the hero and heroine to marry in the end, but who also liked to have a book a little too deep for them on the center table to impress their guests. The other sixty per cent of the membership he visualized as average intelligent Americans, who had had college training or the equivalent. These men and women knew something of the artistic currents of the day, were occasionally interested in politics, and were familiar with the classics. When White picked a book, he was aiming at this group. They wanted wholesome books, and were more interested in what was said than the way it was said provided the sentences were not too involved.

This analysis of the club's membership was pure fancy on White's part. The club never made any such breakdown of its members. Its subscription list followed the pattern of the best magazines, but beyond that the club had no data to back up White's offhand characterization of its membership. Harry Scherman has remarked that this analysis was an interesting example of White's enjoying writing something that was different and striking, whether or not it was actually factual.

As the Book-of-the-Month Club expanded, it followed a regular pattern in the selection of books. Every month leading publishers submitted in advance of publication their important forthcoming books. These books were read by employed readers who were chosen for their critical ability. From these readings emerged the books submitted to the judges for final consideration. Whenever the original readers reported that a given book would interest the judges, a copy was sent to each judge on the editorial board.

The original editorial board represented a catholicity of taste and experience. In addition to White—the only midwestern member—the judges were Christopher Morley, Dorothy Canfield Fisher, Heywood Broun, and Henry Seidel Canby, the chairman. Christopher Morley was widely respected as an essayist and novelist of unusual charm, and as a man with a wide knowledge of the book trade; Dorothy Canfield Fisher, old Kansas friend of White's, had established her reputation as a novelist; Heywood Broun was a vigorous New York columnist with a passionate interest in the underdog; and Henry Seidel Canby, once a professor at Yale, was the founder and first editor of the *Saturday Review of Literature*. Once a month these judges met and voted on the books. For a book to be selected as the book of the month, it had to be given first place by a majority of the judges.

The theory on which the judges worked was that when any book interested all of them—whether because of good writing or the nature of its material—it would also interest the membership of the club. For this theory to be successful, of course, the judges had to be broad in interests and endowed with good common sense. According to Harry Scherman, White was an excellent sounding board. He was exceptionally able in telling what he liked in a given book. When White was enthusiastic over a book, Henry Seidel Canby has remarked, that was a good indication that the book had real appeal. As a critic of the literary quality of a book, however, Canby felt that White was frequently unsound. In Christopher

495

Morley's opinion, White's judgment on books, five out of six times, was liable to be very bad. Yet he liked to read or hear White's comments since they were so witty and so well phrased. In the Book-of-the-Month Club circles, Morley felt that White was always a great big overgrown boy. He could be shrewd in analyzing books, but inevitably there was the humor and zest of a boy in his opinions.

As a member of the editorial board, White quite regularly appointed himself the unofficial judge of the public's taste. He would oppose or advocate a given manuscript on the basis of what he considered would be its public appeal. His judgment was frequently poor as to whether the public would like a given book. He objected, for instance, to the selection of Bruce Marshall's *Father Malachy's Miracle* on the ground that it would alienate their Catholic members. At his insistence, the editorial board decided not to select the book. Immediately after they rejected it, the Catholic Book Club adopted it.

Living in a small town, White thought, placed him in closer touch with the public's tastes than were the other judges. White's name immeasurably aided the initial success of the club. He brought the spirit of the midwestern rural area into the club's circles. It was important during the first few years that the club not be typed as too "highbrow" or too purely literary in the H. L. Mencken tradition. White's name on the editorial board served to prevent this typing. His name meant to the public that a common-sense Midwesterner, a great human being, was part of the Book-of-the-Month Club. He was neither too radical nor too conservative, and he did not belong to any small literary coterie.

Since White emerged during these same years as the spokesman, interpreter, and folk hero of the middle class, his name as a judge offered this group representation in the selection of books. To his work as judge of the Book-of-the-Month Club, White applied his lifelong policy of never being too far out in front of public opinion. The other judges felt that the club should be in advance of current tastes and promote good and different reading. But he would object that a given book was beyond the small-town reader. The other judges frequently adopted the book on the theory that they were thus stimulating the reading taste of the public. Although White disagreed many times with the selections made by the other judges, he was never unyielding. Canby would call him on the telephone and explain that they wanted the book he opposed, and he would tell them to go ahead.

White was held in high personal esteem by the entire Book-of-the-Month Club organization. Although they might disagree with his literary views and be skeptical of his judgment as to what the public would buy, they respected his common-sense attitude on life and his fine qualities as a human being. When he was in New York, he used the club offices as his own office, and the publicity and secretarial staff always looked forward to his visits with keen anticipation.

The affectionate regard in which William Allen White was held by his fellow judges and by the rest of the Book-of-the-Month Club was clearly evident in "William Allen White—In Memoriam" —a pamphlet which the club printed and distributed to its membership the month after White's death. The pamphlet contained tributes from Henry Seidel Canby, Christopher Morley, Dorothy Canfield Fisher, and Harry Scherman as well as a reprint of "Mary White" and a short autobiographical sketch written by White for the Emporia *Gazette* a year before. The pamphlet also contained an excellent selection of photographs of White and the town of Emporia which had appeared previously in *Life* magazine.

In the second month of the club's operation, White was instrumental in establishing a rule which was strictly adhered to in the future policy of the club. He and the rest of the judges agreed that none of their own books would ever be submitted to the organization as the book of the month. Frequently, their books were reviewed in the *Book-of-the-Month Club News*, but they were not chosen as the month's selection.

White's political friendships frequently were extremely valuable in his work as judge. Through his intimate tie with Herbert Hoover, for instance, he overcame Hoover's objection to having his book *The Challenge to Liberty* made a dual selection with Henry Wallace's *New Frontiers*.

Whenever White could not attend the monthly editorial meeting, he would wire his epigrammatic comments on the books under discussion. "All the solid Middle West would be in those tele-grams," Henry Seidel Canby has written, "—its background of Puritanism, cracking down on the flippantly indecent, surprisingly appreciative of frank honesty, scornful of piddling sophistication. All its liberalism, too, the liberalism of a man who hated equally reaction and the radical dogmatism of writers who had never tried to make politics or economics do useful work. When he found a book that seemed to him to do the job that good books should— please, and clarify, and lift the imagination of the reader, you could almost see his typewriter finger descend with a whoop on the key. His criticism was instinctive, and sometimes (so the others might think) it was wrong, and we told him so. But when it was right how right it was!"

Harry Scherman has remarked that they could always count on some hilarious critical slant in White's comments on books. His telegrams were "ebullient blowings-off; they were deliberately exaggerated, and he knew that his confreres knew it," Scherman has written. Yet, in those picturesque telegrams, one can glimpse White's extraordinary skill as an interpreter of the passing Ameri-can scene. As one reads his comments, one can visualize his alert blue eyes sparkling with humor.

The following are excerpts from a few of William Allen White's telegrams:

MARCH 1, 1939

FAR AND AWAY THE BEST NOVEL IS "THE GRAPES OF WRATH" BUT IT WOULD BE A MISTAKE TO BUY IT. THOUSANDS OF OUR READERS WOULD BE OFFENDED BY ITS NECESSARY BUT TO ME QUITE INOFFENSIVE INDECENCY. "BITTER CREEK" IS PURE SYNTHETIC ERSATZ WITH DIME NOVEL CHARAC-TERS. MOVIE PSYCHOLOGY AND ALTOGETHER PRETTY TERRIBLE. "WIND, SAND AND STARS" [it was selected] WOULD MAKE A SWELL SUPPLEMENTAL CHOICE. I LIKE "AMERICA IN MIDPASSAGE" [it was selected] AND WOULD REJOICE IN ITS SELECTION BUT FEAR TO RECOMMEND IT BECAUSE IT IS A LITTLE HEAVY FOR OUR BUYERS. TOO MUCH LIKE WALTER LIPPMANN'S SWELL BOOK THAT FLOPPED A FEW YEARS AGO.

DECEMBER 28, 1939

"GENTLEMAN FROM STRATFORD" MERE SYNTHETIC, BLOODLESS, ACA-DEMIC, LITERARY STRUTTING, A WAX VENEER ON BASSWOOD WITHOUT REAL GUTS.

JANUARY 25, 1940

IF WE TAKE "TROUBLE IN JULY" IT WILL BE OVER MY DEAD BODY AND PROTEST UNLESS [Erskine] CALDWELL CLEANS OUT THE ONE SCENE IN WHICH THE MAN AT THE LYNCHING PARTY TELLS HIS STORY OF HIS RELATIONS WITH THE NYMPHOMANIAC . . . AS TO "MRS. MINIVER," I WONDER HOW THAT GOT ON THE BILL OF FARE. IT HAS ALL THE CONSPICUOUS INCONSEQUENCE OF A LITERARY MEAT LOAF, OR A MOCK DUCK, A CHICKEN A LA KING AT A CHURCH SOCIAL, OR AN IMITATION CHARLOTTE RUSSE MADE OF MASHED POTATOES AND BROWN GRAVY [it was selected].

FEBRUARY 21, 1941

STILL THINK "CAPTAIN PAUL" IS A WASTE OF TIME EVEN IF THE LAST CHAPTER IS THE BEST TALE OF A SEA BATTLE I EVER READ, BUT NOT WORTH WADING THROUGH TWO HUNDRED THOUSAND WORDS OF BRACKISH DISH WATER. HOWEVER IF CHRIS [Morley] LIKES DISH WATER BECAUSE IT'S BRINY LET'S TAKE IT.

OCTOBER 15, 1941

I LIKED AMBASSADOR DAVIES' DIARY AND STATE PAPERS TREMENDOUSLY. IT IS AN IMPORTANT AND DISTINGUISHED BOOK BUT STANDING ALONE AS SINGLE CHOICE WOULD NOT SATISFY FORTY PER CENT OF OUR CLIENTS. IF IT IS USED SHOULD BE USED AS DUAL CHOICE. I DON'T LIKE "IVORY MISCHIEF" THE ADULTERIES BECOME TOO MONOTONOUS AFTER THE FIRST DOZEN THEY ARE REPETITIOUS AND ONE LONGS SOMEWAY FOR GOOD VIGOROUS CRIMINAL ASSAULT AND BATTERY. THE FACT THAT THIS STORY IS AS LONG AS ANTHONY ADVERSE DOES NOT SIGNIFY THAT IT WILL BE AS POPULAR. I SHOULD SAY SPEAKING BROADLY WHEN A WRITER MULTIPLIES HIS DIRTY LOVE AFFAIRS UNTIL THEY BECOME MERE BIOLOGICAL CASE RECORDS HE HAS LOST THE RABBIT'S FOOT OF HIS ART HAS BECOME A MERE CHRONICLER OF PATHOLOGICAL INCIDENTS [it was selected].

FEBRUARY 13, 1942

"THE LAST DAYS OF OFELIA" IS DELIGHTFUL STORY AND WE CERTAINLY CAN AFFORD TO BUY IT AND PUT IT IN BRINE [it was selected]. STILL THINK "SONG OF BERNADETTE" IS HACK WORK NOT UP TO OUR STANDARD [it was selected]. "LOVER OF LIFE" IS JUST A PAPER FROM A WOMAN'S CLUB ON FLEMISH ART DONE AS A CYCLORAMA. IT READS AS WELL FORWARD AS BACKWARD AND UP AS WELL AS DOWN. NOT HALF THE BOOK THAT "STAR GAZER" WAS.

JUNE 15, 1942

MY CHOICE ABOVE ALL OTHERS IS "THE RAFT" A STRAIGHTAWAY ADVENTURE STORY REAL SEA YARN. I AM GETTING SO WEARY WITH THE BOOKS OUT

OF BOOKS THE RESEARCH STUFF IN OUR LIST THAT AGAIN I CLAMOR FOR BOOK WITHOUT STYLE OR ANY ACADEMIC QUALIFICATIONS. IT HAS BEEN LONG TIME SINCE WE HAVE HAD THIS KIND OF STORY [it was selected]. . . . NIX ON "SEVENTH CROSS" BUT IN CHOOSING IT SEE IF I CARE [it was selected].

JULY 15, 1942

SEEMS TO ME BY ALL ODDS THE BEST BUY IS DE VOTO "THE YEAR OF DECISION" [it was selected] IT WILL STAND UP WITH "WASHINGTON REVEILLE" [selected the year before] ALTHOUGH NOT SO INTERESTING A PERIOD AND OF COURSE WITH NO GREAT FIGURE IN IT BUT STILL IT IS DIGNIFIED JOB OF WHICH WE CAN ALL BE PROUD. THE ITALIAN BOOK "SEED BENEATH THE SNOW" I FOUND TEDIOUS. THE DIALOGUE IS CARVED IN BASSWOOD AND THE CHARACTERS ARE PURE THEATER FOR ME AT LEAST THE INTEREST DOES NOT RISE. "RIVER ROGUE" IS THE DIRTIEST BOOK I EVER READ. NOT THAT I WAS SHOCKED BY IT. THE FENCES BARNS AND OUTHOUSE WALLS OF CHILDHOOD'S GOLDEN HOUR GAVE ME GREAT FAMILIARITY WITH GENERAL IDEA OF BOOK. I FEEL THAT IT WOULD OUTRAGE AT LEAST A THIRD OF OUR READERS, AND DON'T FEEL WE SHOULD RISK THAT WHEN WE HAVE REASONABLY ACCEPTABLE BOOK LIKE "THE YEAR OF DECISION." IF YOU DON'T TAKE IT AND THERE IS ANY SUPPORT FOR IT WHY CAN'T WE HOLD IT OVER. WITH OUR START IT MAY EASILY ATTAIN THE CENTERTABLE CHAMPIONSHIP FOR NINETEEN FORTY-TWO.

SEPTEMBER 15, 1942

PROBABLY THE MOST SALABLE ITEM ON THE LIST IS "THE VALLEY OF DECISION." WITH ALL ITS OBVIOUS FAULTS OF IMPROBABLE INCIDENT AND OFTEN AWKWARD WRITING, IT IS AN ANSWER TO PRAYER FOR AN AMERICAN NOVEL. I SHOULD SAY THAT THE FACT THAT IT IS AS TERRIBLE AS "GONE WITH THE WIND" OR "ANTHONY ADVERSE" SHOULD BE PROOF THAT IT HAS WHAT IT TAKES TO MOVE IN BOOKSTORES . . . I COULDN'T STAND CECIL BROWN'S "SUEZ TO SINGAPORE" BECAUSE HE HEROIZES HIMSELF ALL THE TIME. HE IS MORE INTERESTED IN HIS BATTLES WITH CENSORS THAN HE IS BATTLES OF JAPS. "WINTERS TALES" IS ONE OF THOSE BOOKS THAT BEWILDERED ME. AS I READ I THOUGHT "WELL MAYBE THIS IS SYMBOLISM" BUT I GOT TO THINKING "NO THIS IS ALCOHOLISM." MY FINAL CONCLUSION IS THAT IT IS GIBBERISH [it was a dual selection]. THE BOOK I ENJOYED MOST WAS HERBERT AGAR'S "TIME FOR GREATNESS" BUT I AM NOT SURE THAT WE WANT THAT KIND OF BOOK AT THIS TIME, THAT WOULD TAKE FOURTH OF OUR ANNUAL OUTPUT AND IT IS NOT FAIR TO RAM AMERICAN HISTORY DOWN THROATS OF OUR READERS . . . WHICHEVER ONE OF THIS LOT YOU TAKE YOU HAVE MY BENEVOLENT MALEDICTION.

PART V

A KANSAN LOOKS AT THE WORLD

CHAPTER 22

BETWEEN TWO WARS

"I AM deeply distressed to hear of the death of your husband," Secretary of War Henry L. Stimson wired Mrs. White on January 29, 1944. "I held for him the greatest affection and admiration and during the crisis leading up to this war he performed invaluable service to the nation."

As chairman of two powerful propaganda organizations, White in 1939 and 1940 climaxed his long career of molding public opinion by leading the argument over the foreign policy of the United States. Many people expressed bewilderment that a small-town editor from the traditionally isolationist Middle West should be heading committees urging aid to the Allied nations. White, however, knew that the destiny of his own prairie state was inexorably tied to events in Europe and in the Far East.

The irresponsible course in world affairs pursued by the United States during the days of Republican supremacy appalled Editor White. "We may think we can stand aloof; we tried that once. It won't work," he warned in the *Gazette* on May 24, 1921. "War is a disease of civilization from which no country is immune when it breaks out. . . . America's job is a world job. Our isolation is a fiction. We are in Europe now, no matter how we may feel that the Atlantic severs us."

In the fall of 1921, after the first shock of Mary's death had worn off, the Whites traveled to the East, where White reported the Washington Disarmament Conference for the United Press and for *Collier's*. Just before leaving for Washington, White wrote an article filled with disillusionment at European diplomacy. At the Versailles Peace Conference, he charged, the world had lost its faith and, as a result, "The terror of a vast unbelief is gripping mankind in some sort of spiritual glacial epoch, which threatens chaos." The evils in the Versailles Treaty, he believed, had developed because of the secrecy that had characterized the proceedings. The Washington conference, too, would be filled with intrigue, he asserted, unless publicity was insisted upon before the statesmen met to discuss world problems.

The month he spent reporting the conference revived his faith in the progress of mankind. When the American delegation, led by Secretary of State Charles Evans Hughes, proposed the limitation of armaments, White hailed this proposal as "the greatest blow to unjust privilege that has been delivered in the world since Cromwell's day." "The man who packs a gun soon wearies of irritating debate," White explained. "But disarm the gun toter and he is amenable to reason." Gradual disarmament by all major powers might have been a step toward ultimate peace if there had been international supervision to make sure that all countries lived up to their pledges. Over the years, when Japan failed to live up to her agreement while the United States dismantled many of her ships, the Washington agreements became dangerous to American security. White sensed this inherent danger and declared that as a result of Hughes's disarmament proposals, the United States would have to abandon isolation for international co-operation. "Isolation will have to be scrapped before we scrap any ships," he declared. Instead, however, successive Republican administrations continued the policy of isolation and at the same time scrapped American ships.

For the first time in history, White told his *Collier's* readers, great nations had agreed to discard the use of arms and force. He warned, however, that disarmament alone might not secure world peace. "Certainly our failure as Americans to assume our responsibilities," he explained, "may mark the downfall of European civilization, and in the crash America will not be unscathed." Since the disarmament proposals were America's idea, White urged his countrymen to accept the responsibility of making them work.

"The stars in their courses are with us," he wrote, "but only if we put our souls under the burden and move forward with it."

The pledge at the Washington conference to arbitrate problems arising in the Pacific over the conflicting aims of Japan, Great Britain, the United States, and France, White felt was a step toward a stable world order. "The agreement to settle Pacific problems by arbitration is something to set one's teeth in," he observed. "Japan is the dynamite which might wreck the rapidly cementing union of the English-speaking peoples." The chief product of the conference, he believed, was the goodwill engendered and displayed toward one another by the English-speaking peoples. Although the results of the conference were constructive from his point of view, before many months had passed, the deteriorating world situation convinced him that the golden moment when the United States should have entered the League of Nations had passed. The jealousies and suspicions that had arisen among the European nations now made participation in the League dangerous for the peace of the United States. Yet he never doubted that had the United States joined the League at the outset, the United States, England, and France could have guided the world into peaceful channels. The Big Three had failed to offer leadership and direction and now the world was in a tumultuous condition. But although White felt that the time had passed to join the League, he did advocate membership in the World Court. He urged Senator Henry Cabot Lodge to lead the Senate Foreign Relations into approving membership in the court. White told Lodge that the Republican platform in 1920 had pledged the party on this question, and "it is now time that the pledge should be redeemed."

*　　*　　*

During the twenties, White took an active part in a number of committees devoted to securing peace through international co-operation. He was a member of the board of directors of the League of Nations Association; he was a charter member of the American Association for International Co-operation; he was chairman of an Education Committee in the Interest of World Peace; and he served as a member of the Jury of Award of the Bok Peace Prize for the best proposal for international peace.

In 1928 he attended the signing of the Kellogg-Briand Pact designed to outlaw war. He wrote from Paris that this pact marked a new epoch in history, but that it was only a gesture and a register of good intentions since no machinery was created to take effective action against any nation that broke the agreement. The Kellogg-Briand Pact proved to be dangerous for America since it lulled many people into a deceptive sense of security. Many people thought that under the agreement war was now impossible and that therefore preparedness was unnecessary.

During the Hoover administration, White supported the London Naval Treaty limiting the respective navies of the major powers. He also upheld Hoover's moratorium on the payment of war debts. He objected, however, with all his power to the Republican high tariff policy. He denounced the Smoot-Hawley tariff as a disastrous step for the welfare of the American people and for the peace of the world. After the passage of this tariff, White's prediction was borne out, since the tariff served only to deepen the economic crisis of the world and led other nations to raise their tariff walls in retaliation against America's policy of economic isolation.

In 1931, Japan started the world on the road to war by overrunning Manchuria. Although Japan had signed the Nine-Power Pact at the Washington conference, thus agreeing to respect the sovereignty of China, she struck at China at a time when the rest of the world was torn by severe economic troubles. The United States, England, and France were too preoccupied with their domestic situations to take effective action to halt this first step of aggression in Japan's policy of domination of the Far East.

President Hoover denounced the aggression as "immoral" and declared that the United States would co-operate with the League in support of the Nine-Power Pact. But the President made it very clear that if the League efforts failed, the United States would not join the League members in war to halt Japan. "We will not go along on war or any of the sanctions either economic or military, for these are the roads to war," Hoover asserted. It was his opinion that Japan's action did not "imperil the freedom of the American people, the economic or moral future of the people."

This attitude on the part of the chief executive of the greatest industrial nation in the world naturally hampered effective steps by the League of Nations. England, too, was reluctant to embark on forthright action. As a result, Japan, although censured by the League, acquired Manchuria and established a valuable precedent that Hitler and Mussolini were not to overlook.

White's first editorial reaction to the Japanese onslaught in Manchuria showed no awareness of Japanese traditions or of Japan's desire to dominate the Far East and expel all Western influence from the sphere. "Probably the public opinion of the world will stay the warlike hand of Japan in looting China," he reflected. "The goodwill of mankind is a powerful weapon. It has been organized quickly and expressed in sharp disapproval of Japan's move in Manchuria." Within a few months, White realized that more than goodwill was necessary to check the designs of the Japanese militarists. When the Japanese attacked Shanghai in January, 1932, White advocated that the navies of the world stop the fighting and eject the Japanese from Manchuria. "Civilization will not stand passively by and see a weak nation bullied," White declared in an overoptimistic mood.

Although, by the time of the Shanghai incident, White was aware that united military action was necessary to check the aggressive designs of Japan, his attitude was not shared by the bulk of the American people. Deeply immersed in their own economic crisis, most Americans failed to see the relation of the Manchurian affair to America's own future security. The Philadelphia *Record* observed, for instance, that "the American people don't give a hoot in a rain barrel who controls North China." Only after the Japanese attack on Pearl Harbor did many Americans realize that back in 1931 Japan had started the chain of events which culminated in that disaster. It would have been cheaper in lives and money to have co-operated with military means in 1931 to check the outbreak of aggression than to wait until the aggressors were far more powerful. But the Allied world in 1931 was badly divided. The United States, England, and France steadfastly refused to assume their responsibility for world leadership.

Although there is no question that individual Republicans like Henry L. Stimson, Nicholas Murray Butler, Elihu Root, and William Allen White advocated United States co-operation with other nations to maintain peace, the Republican party between the two great wars was dominated principally by isolationists. The Democratic party, in contrast, still reflected the sentiments of Woodrow Wilson. From 1933 to 1939, the Democratic administration played a far bolder role in world affairs than its Republican predecessors had done. Its attempts to prevent the collapse of world peace, however, were carried on in a world characterized by increasing aggression. In 1933, Germany began to rearm under Hitler. Two years later Italy marched into Ethiopia. The next year Hitler fortified the demilitarized Rhineland. In 1937, Japan attacked China for the second time in six years. The following year Hitler conquered Austria and dismembered Czechoslovakia. In the opening months of 1939, Hitler annihilated independent Czechoslovakia and occupied Memel, and Mussolini captured Albania. On September 1, 1939, the world went to war when Hitler launched his armies at Poland.

President Roosevelt and Secretary of State Hull were in a difficult position in the years from 1933 to 1941. They realized that the Japanese aggressions in the Far East and the German and Italian aggressions in Europe threatened American security. They believed, too, that the aggressive policies of the Axis powers were directed toward an ultimate attack on the United States. Yet large segments of the American public refused to see any threat to America in the various warlike moves of the Axis nations. Gradually, however, after September, 1939, an awareness of the ultimate purpose of the Axis led increasing numbers of Americans to support a policy of aid to the nations endeavoring to check the march of Axis aggression.

From the very outset of the Roosevelt administration, William Allen White found himself in general agreement with Franklin D. Roosevelt's foreign policy. "Apparently President Roosevelt is preparing to cut away from the ancient tradition which provided for the isolation of America," White observed on May 23, 1933. ". . . The Gazette has believed for fifteen years that isolation is impossible for any nation that takes leadership in a modern world. . . . We welcome the Rooseveltian attitude."

When the Roosevelt administration recognized Soviet Russia, White was enthusiastic in his praise of a step he had long supported. He had no sympathy with the professional Russia-haters. As early as 1920 he had advocated reason rather than emotion in dealing with the new Russia. He had served on the executive council of the American Committee for Russian Famine Relief and on the advisory council of the American Society for Cultural Relations with Russia. His trip to Russia in 1933 had convinced him that it was absurd for the United States to refuse diplomatic recognition of a government that had been in power for fifteen years. He disliked the suppression of the individual in Russia, but he was tremendously impressed by the zeal of the young Russians for their government and for its social ideals.

White also found himself in complete agreement with the New Deal's Good Neighbor Policy. From his own experiences in Haiti, he had seen at first hand something of the hatred of the United States that existed in Latin America. Long before the United States had a Good Neighbor Policy, White was demanding respect for the rights of the Latin-American nations.

The reciprocal trade treaties were still another important ingredient in Roosevelt's international policy thoroughly backed by White. White's advocacy of the trade treaties as a means of checking economic nationalism and as a step toward real world peace elicited from President Roosevelt the following note on January 23, 1940: "At this critical time in world affairs it is fine to know that there are strong voices like yours which are willing and ready, irrespective of any partisan consideration, to speak out courageously in defense of constructive and farsighted policies—policies that seek to build the future welfare of our country." Secretary Hull, too, appreciated White's ardent support of the trade treaties. After White's death, Hull demonstrated the extent of his appreciation of the Emporia editor's support by telling Mrs. White that her husband's "service in the field of international relations was extremely valuable. . . . In his passing the community and the country have lost one of their finest citizens."

* * *

During the rise of aggression in the thirties, White was torn between two poles of thought. He wanted peace for the United States. "War is the devil's joke on humanity," he said on November 11, 1933. On the other hand, he knew that international co-operation was absolutely necessary for a real peace, although this internationalism meant the danger of war. There was no question in his mind that the rise of Hitler in Germany was a threat to American security. "The Germans have known the taste and feel of liberty and yet their minds and hearts reject it," he observed on July 22, 1934. "They are unwilling to die for liberty. Unless a nation is willing to die for liberty, if it is too cowardly to face the guns, its liberties always are in danger. America must learn this lesson."

The Japanese aggression in Manchuria in 1931 and Italy's attack on Ethiopia in 1935 convinced White that a world conflict would soon break out. When such a conflict came, he was sure that the United States could not stay out. We could not keep out of world troubles, he confided to his readers on July 20, 1935, because when "even one man's liberty is imperiled, all men's liberties are in danger." Yet his desire for peace led him to ignore the wisdom in his own statement. During 1935, instead of advocating the unity of the peace-loving nations as the only means of checking the aggressors, he vigorously supported the pending neutrality legislation.

In 1934, President Roosevelt had urged Congress to place an embargo on trade with any nation that violated the Kellogg-Briand Pact. The Roosevelt proposal would have left the United States free to throw its great industrial production behind the victims of aggression. The mere knowledge that the United States would do this, the President argued, might discourage the Fascist nations from wrecking world peace. Congress and the public, however, had succumbed to a great wave of isolationism and would not accept the President's proposal. The belligerent nationalism of Japan, Germany, and Italy had aroused fears of a new war, and the general American reaction was that the United States could remain aloof. There was no conception in this attitude that the United States might be the ultimate target of the Axis nations.

This American fear of a new war came at the very time the country was accepting the belief that American participation in World War I had been a mistake. A Senate committee investigating the munitions industry misled the public by stating that munitions makers and international bankers were heavily responsible for American entrance into the war. A number of books and articles were written with emphasis on the intrigues of these financial and business forces. By 1935, the American people were so confused and so forgetful that they demonstrated no awareness that the alternative to American participation in World War I would probably have been a German victory—a victory that would have been far more rigorous on the Allies than the Versailles Treaty was on Germany. Nor by 1935 did the American public show any realization that America's security had been at stake in 1917 and that a German victory would ultimately have been a threat to America's position in the world.

Naïvely and wishfully, a large part of the American public believed by 1935 that the United States could smugly withdraw from world affairs, protected by its two great oceans. An overwhelming demand arose for a law that would keep the United States neutral in the next war. Over President Roosevelt's protest, Congress passed a law that placed an embargo on the export of arms, ammunition, on implements of war to *any* belligerent nation. This bill did not discriminate between aggressor and victim. The aggressors thus were confident that, if they plunged the world into war, the United States would refuse to aid their victims—the natural allies of the United States. From 1935 to 1939, this Neutrality Act prevented the United States from playing a powerful role to maintain peace, and it actually encouraged the Axis to launch their aggressions.

It was one of the greatest acts of folly ever passed by an American Congress. It was based on two false assumptions. The first was that the United States had entered World War I because of munitions makers and international bankers; the second was that the United States could ignore with impunity the destruction of the other democracies by the Axis. A few people in 1935 pointed out the fallacies behind these assumptions. They particularly warned that American security would be endangered if no other democratic nations existed in the world. President Roosevelt's request for a law that applied an embargo to the aggressor only had been based upon the frank assumption that it was vital to American security to aid the nations opposing the Axis dictators. But Congress and the public were in no mood to accept this position in

1935. Yet after 1939, when Hitler's mechanized columns began to plow under one country after another, many Americans awakened from their lethargy and advocated aid to the remaining countries opposing Germany. It was not, however, until after war had broken out that the majority of Americans, now realizing how foolish the Neutrality Act was, supported steps to revise it.

The Emporia editor proved to be an excellent reflection of prevailing public opinion on the question of American foreign policy. In 1935 he mirrored the confusion of the average American by his ardent support of the neutrality law. His desire for peace overcame for a short time his more correct judgment that international co-operation was necessary to attain peace. His utterances in 1935 show little realization of what he himself had believed before 1935 —and was to believe after 1935—that the United States could not bury its head in the sand in the face of world troubles.

White actually urged steps beyond the Neutrality Act. He declared on October 9, 1935, that to keep out of war the United States should bottle up her entire export trade, not just her munitions trade, with belligerent nations. During this year, too, White talked in terms of wars being "foreign wars" and neutrality being a realizable fact in the modern world. Yet in the period after September, 1939, he was to take the lead in explaining to America that neutrality was impossible in a highly technological world; and the general public by that time was to be in general agreement with White's attitude.

The Emporia editor was no more sure of himself on the entire problem of peace and war than was the average American. When *Forum and Century* asked him in 1937 how the United States could stay out of war, he declared that although he still advocated the embargo on the shipment of munitions, he was not too sure that this was an intelligent attitude. He did feel, he added, that any belligerents having the money and the ships should be free to purchase munitions in the United States and transport them in their own boats.

Congress amended the Neutrality Act on January 8, 1937, to extend its provisions to the civil war now raging in Spain. This step, plus the refusal of England and France to aid the Loyalist government, made it impossible for the elected government to secure aid. At the same time, Germany and Italy were using the Spanish conflict as a dress rehearsal for the great conflict of the future. By a shortsighted policy, the powerful democracies permitted Germany, Italy, and General Franco to destroy Republican Spain. The American public, largely indifferent to the conflict, failed to realize that Franco's victory was just one more step toward Fascist domination of the world.

To stir the American public, the American Friends of Spanish Democracy launched an organization with the express purpose of creating sentiment for the lifting of the embargo on the shipment of munitions to the Loyalist cause. White refused to assist this group. "I do not know what to do," he frankly wired them on March 18, 1938. "I have all the natural feeling of indignation that any proper person must have at the rats of Spain. Yet, I hesitate to add one word that might influence America to go to war." He did, however, serve as a member of the Spanish Child Welfare Association, which worked for the relief of children in both Franco and Loyalist Spain.

The renewal of Japanese aggression in China in July, 1937, found the United States in a very unhappy diplomatic situation. The threat of Hitler and Mussolini in Europe so preoccupied England and France that the United States was left alone to oppose the Japanese action. The foolishness of the Neutrality Act was amply demonstrated in this crisis. The American public was overwhelmingly sympathetic to China. Yet if the Neutrality Act was enforced it would strike a heavy blow at China and hamper Japan but little. The President, realizing the state of public opinion, did not invoke the Neutrality Act since neither side had formally declared war. William Allen White was strong in his support of the President's action. He further demonstrated his revulsion against Japanese aggression by serving as honorary vice-chairman of the American Committee for Non-participation in Japanese Aggression and as a member of the American Boycott against Aggressor Nations.

By March, 1938, when the Germans invaded Austria, White had regained some of the perspective on international affairs that he had had prior to his support of the Neutrality Act. He was disturbed by the tendency of England and France to appease Hitler by winking at German aggressions. He realized that the United States would be in a highly insecure position if the appeasers in France and England should submit to some kind of Fascist rule. "If this country has one supreme duty," White declared on March 3, 1938, "it is to call the democracies of the world together and with their power before they crumble, to assemble a world peace conference. There demands of the underprivileged nations may be heard and considered. These underprivileged nations—Germany, Japan, Italy—are naturally motivating their hunger with a lust for war. America must either satisfy them in conference or on the battlefield."

That September at Munich when England and France acquiesced to the dismemberment of Czechoslovakia, White warned that the danger of war had been only temporarily averted. "America may breathe deeply now," he remarked, "but she should tighten up her belt for tomorrow, gird up her loins for the inevitable strife." The tottering structure of world peace led President Roosevelt to reiterate his belief that collective efforts were necessary to avert war. In October, 1937, the President had urged the quarantining of the aggressor nations. "There must be positive endeavors to preserve peace," he had declared. In January, 1939, he told Congress: "There are methods short of war, but stronger and more effective than mere words, of bringing home to aggressor governments the aggregate sentiment of our people." This method would be a Congressional revision of the Neutrality Act in order that the victims of aggression could secure equipment and munitions from the United States. By this time it was clear to farsighted people that the law had encouraged the aggressors to make their warlike moves. It was a dangerous law for America's future. The bill assumed that the United States would stand aside in a conflict between the Axis powers and the democracies. But if the Axis threatened to crush England and France and, together with Japan, seemed on the verge of dominating Europe, Africa, and Asia, the United States would be in a precarious position. If this situation occurred, the demand for American intervention to prevent Axis domination of the world would be irresistible and inevitable. The logical action to take, therefore, was for the United States to act to prevent war from arising.

The Senate Foreign Relations Committee refused, however, to report the revised neutrality bill to the Senate. The committee was not willing to free the President so that he could threaten the dictators and thus, as he hoped, prevent the war from being launched. "There was only one power on earth which could give Hitler and his associates pause," Sumner Welles discovered a few months later on his trip to Europe. "That would be their conviction that, in a war of devastation forced upon Europe by Germany, the United States in its own interest would come to the support of the Western democracies. Equally clearly, however, there was at that moment not the remotest chance that our government could tell the Nazi government that this would prove to be the case. The great majority of the American people were altogether confident that they could keep out of the war. No executive in Washington with any sense of his responsibility to the American electorate, or with any regard for his constitutional limitations, could assume the authority for bluntly informing the government of the Third Reich that the United States would support Great Britain and France should Germany persist in her policy of world conquest. And yet it was only that threat which would have the remotest chance of averting the greatest calamity that the modern world had known."

* * *

When war broke out on September 1, 1939, the Whites were at their cabin at Moraine Park, Colorado. Even this remote mountain hideaway was shaken by the impact of World War II. Within two weeks, the Whites were back in Emporia and the editor was soon supporting President Roosevelt's request of September 21 for the repeal of the embargo forbidding the sale of arms and ammunition to nations at war, and the substitution of a cash-and-carry plan instead. The Allies needed equipment for war, and it was vital to American security that Germany be defeated. Repeal of the embargo, therefore, was in order.

Although White in 1935 had stood for a complete embargo on all exports to warring nations, he had shifted away from this position by 1937 and had supported instead a cash-and-carry plan. He had, however, given no support to President Roosevelt's attempt to secure the revision of the Neutrality Act during the first six months of 1939. It was not until after the shock of war that he took a leading part in the controversy.

On September 26, Clark Eichelberger, director of the League of Nations Association and the Union for Concerted Peace Efforts, called White from New York and asked him to head a committee which would explain to the public the need for supporting President Roosevelt's request for the cash-and-carry law. The executive committee of the Union for Concerted Peace Efforts had decided to ask White to head the Non-Partisan Committee for Peace through Revision of the Neutrality Law because, as one member later explained to him: "For many years your name has stood for the highest ideals of honor and integrity in American politics . . . We knew that around your name would rally a large number of people who, anxious to promote the best interests of our country . . . would recognize in your leadership the answer to their difficulties."

When the members of the Union for Concerted Peace Efforts were discussing a possible chairman for their new committee, they had asked a number of influential men in Washington for suggestions. It was Secretary of State Cordell Hull who recommended the name of William Allen White. White was a logical choice for the committee. He was a Midwesterner. He was a vocal newspaper editor. He was a Republican who at the same time was on good terms with the President. By 1939, too, his name would attract a nation-wide following, and it would take the curse of New York leadership off the committee's work. As Drew Pearson and Robert S. Allen had stated in their "Washington Merry-Go-Round" column, on June 19, 1937: "Bill White is a significant and vital American leader because he is an enlightened, vibrant spokesman of the great farm belt of the nation, because he is an unrelenting foe of provincialism and because he keeps Main Street alert." With his background, White was just the man to carry the committee's appeal to mid-America.

At first, the editor of the *Gazette* refused to accept the chairmanship. He was seventy-one years old, and he wanted to devote his remaining years to writing his autobiography. Eichelberger and the members of his executive committee persuaded some of

White's intimate New York friends to urge him to head the committee. White finally agreed to undertake the task at the particular request of Dorothy Canfield Fisher, Irene Lewisohn, and Betty Gram Swing.

With White's acceptance, the Union for Concerted Peace Efforts dispatched a flock of telegrams to leading Americans asking them to join the Non-Partisan Committee for Peace through Revision of the Neutrality Law. Soon the new committee had a nation-wide membership of distinguished citizens, including Colonel Frank Knox, publisher of the Chicago *Daily News;* Freda Kirchwey, editor of the *Nation;* Chester Rowell of the San Francisco *Chronicle;* Monsignor John A. Ryan; Rabbi Stephen A. Wise; Henry S. Coffin; Marshall Field; Robert Sherwood; and Edward G. Robinson.

White had a twofold purpose in heading this committee. He wanted to keep the United States out of war if that was possible, but at the same time he wanted the United States to contribute to the defeat of Hitler. His other objective was to try to forestall the Republican party from making the question of foreign policy a partisan issue. As a leading Republican, he hoped that he could persuade Republican congressmen to discuss the President's cash-and-carry proposal on its merits.

White's Non-Partisan Committee functioned as a stimulator and a molder of public opinion. Before White reached New York, Eichelberger had sent instructions to the committee's membership, urging a letter-writing campaign to congressmen and to the newspapers. On October 15, White, now in New York, delivered a talk over the Columbia Broadcasting System. He declared that no law could keep us out of war, but he was convinced that involvement was less likely under the cash-and-carry principle. Under the existing law, nonwar goods could go to the belligerents in American ships, which entailed the danger of loss of American lives and ships. The proposed cash-and-carry revision, he pointed out, did not permit American ships to carry anything to belligerents. Instead, the Allied powers would have the right to come with their own ships and money to buy whatever materials they needed. On a more altruistic plane, he also pointed out that next to America's desire to stay out of war was her wish for an Allied victory. But the existing law severely handicapped the Allies. They should be permitted the privilege of acquiring needed war goods from the United States on the cash-and-carry principle.

After all, White asserted, the European struggle was "a clash of ideologies. In Germany and in Russia, the state is the master of the citizen. In the democracies of Europe—France and England, Holland and the Scandinavian countries, the citizens control the state. The struggle of two thousand years for human liberty has been wiped out east of the Rhine. . . . These European democracies are carrying our banner, fighting the American battle. These democracies west of the Rhine and north of the Baltic are digging our first-line trenches. We need not shed our blood for them now or ever. But we should not deny them now access to our shores when they come with cash to pay for weapons of defense and with their own ships to carry arms and materials which are to protect their citizens and their soldiers fighting for our common cause."

By late October, the Non-Partisan Committee had local units active in thirty states, distributing literature, organizing meetings, and directing a pressure campaign on Congress. The bulk of the funds to carry on this work was contributed by interested citizens in sums ranging from five to fifty dollars. The largest contributor was Frederick McKee, a Pittsburgh businessman. Among the other large donors were Henry R. Luce of *Time*, *Life*, and *Fortune*; Theodore Pitcairn, of Philadelphia; and William F. Cochran, of Baltimore.

The propaganda activities of the committee were reflected somewhat in the changing attitude of the public toward the war. In September, just before the committee launched its program, a public opinion survey revealed that 65.6 per cent believed that the United States should aid neither side. By the next month, however, only 24.7 per cent still held to this point of view. Of course, the rapid German success in destroying Poland largely accounted for this extreme shift in American attitudes, but the Non-Partisan Committee's work undoubtedly contributed somewhat to the change.

Working directly on Congress, White discovered that the vast majority of House Republicans were opposed to the President's bill. "I would hate to have my party put itself in a posture where it can be charged that we played Mr. Hitler's game in the matter of the embargo," he wrote Republican minority leader Joseph Martin on October 23. "We have no reason to fear the effects upon us of a French-British victory. We have a whole lot to fear in the case of a Hitler victory. If we fail to repeal the embargo and Hitler should win, we, as a party, will be vulnerable."

On October 30, White discussed his position with individual Republican members of the House. However, he ignored the Kansas Republican members, since all of them were hopelessly opposed to the repeal of the embargo. Four days later the cash-and-carry bill passed the House of Representatives. The work of White and other leading Republicans like Colonel Frank Knox and Henry L. Stimson was none too successful in persuading Republicans to vote for the bill. Only twenty House Republicans voted for the administration's measure. One hundred forty voted to retain a law which was operating against America's best interest; a law which was severely handicapping the country's natural allies and thus aiding Germany in its bid for world domination.

Some Republican congressmen refused to believe that Germany was a threat to the United States. Others contended that persecution by the British Empire was worse than the crimes of the Nazis. Representative Youngdahl of Minnesota charged that adoption of the cash-and-carry measure would make Roosevelt a dictator. "Repeal of the arms embargo," he contended, "is the first step towards the loss of freedom and democratic institutions on this continent." Many Republicans hated Roosevelt too much to support a bill championed by him. Other congressmen feared that the passage of the measure would lead to war. There was no conception on their part that in time the war would engulf the United States, and that therefore the wise policy was to keep allies in the fight so that after the inevitable blow struck the United States, this country would have support in the Gargantuan struggle ahead.

* * *

"This was the first time I had ever had hold of a lever that controlled a national current," White confided to his readers on November 6. "It was interesting—but scary! I had turned the juice off and on in Kansas many times for forty years and knew this switchboard fairly well. But I was so jittery, sitting before the big national switchboard that my mouth was dry and I kept licking my lips most of the time and batting my eyes. It was 'Dorothy' before the Scarecrow, and when the old Scarecrow, Major John Q. Public, if you must know his real name, came to life and began to walk, I was tickled pink—again like 'Dorothy.' "

When he reached Emporia, White found a letter from Secretary of State Hull thanking him for his valuable work as chairman of the Non-Partisan Committee. Soon a letter arrived from President Roosevelt: "Dear Bill: You did a grand job. It was effective and most helpful! I am writing this note just to say: 'Thank you, Bill.' " Both White's colleague, Clark Eichelberger, and Senator Claude Pepper told him that he had been a determining influence in securing the favorable Congressional vote. "It was a great fight," was White's characteristic reply to this praise, "but I fear that I am merely the rooster on the cow catcher who mistakes his crow for the engine's steam. But the rooster and I always have a lot of fun."

White, of course, was subjected to considerable abuse for his work as chairman of the Non-Partisan Committee. One person told him that his radio speech had been a "paradoxical hodge-podge of piffle," and added: "Of course, everyone except you and a few other slaves of defaulting France and England knows this is *not* our war." Many people wrote to him in denunciation of the British Empire in India. "I also have no illusions about British race pride in India," the Emporia editor replied. "Nevertheless, all those things considered, I feel that Hitler today is the more terrible menace."

Just a month before Congress adopted the cash-and-carry bill, Germany completed its conquest of Poland. The war then entered a quiet stage for the next six months. During this period White was severely concerned over the menace of Hitlerism. He felt that the Nazi idea of world domination had done irreparable damage to the progress of the world. He feared that a better-prepared Germany would soon launch a devastating blow at the Western European countries. If Germany succeeded in defeating France and England, the United States would be faced with a triumphant Germany in the Atlantic and a triumphant Japan in the Pacific.

Very disturbing, too, was the attack that Russia launched on Finland shortly after Germany's destruction of Poland. White's sympathies, like those of most Americans, were definitely with Finland. The *Gazette* lent editorial support to Herbert Hoover's Finnish Relief Commission, and White urged the American people to help Finland short of war. What was not clear in 1939, but became obvious after Germany attacked Russia in June, 1941, was that Russia desired strategic outposts in Finland for protection against a German assault. It is argued that had Russia not taken the Karelian Isthmus from Finland and constructed defensive positions, Leningrad would have fallen to the Germans and the course of the war might have been drastically altered. Finland was in an impossible position. Leaders like Baron Mannerheim had a passionate hatred of Russia, which once had controlled Finland. Most Finns naturally thought of Russia as their nation's most dangerous foe. When Russia asked for bases in 1939, Finland felt that it had no choice but to fight.

The Emporia editor was deeply concerned also over the complacency and apathy of the American people toward the epoch-making changes taking place in Europe. President Roosevelt was disturbed over this very same problem. "I need a few helpful thoughts from the philosopher of Emporia," he wrote White on December 14, 1939. "Things move with such terrific speed, these days, that it really is essential to us to think in broader terms and, in effect, to warn the American people that they, too, should think of possible ultimate results in Europe and the Far East. Therefore, my sage old friend, my problem is to get the American people to think of conceivable consequences without scaring the American people into thinking that they are going to be dragged into this war."

White's reply revealed a puzzled mind. He told the President he feared that the United States would enter the conflict. "Yet I fear to remain uninvolved," he quickly added, "letting the danger of a peace of tyranny approach too near. Finland seems to need us. . . . I suppose if we can help the Allies surreptitiously, illicitly and down the alley by night, we ought to do it."

From playwright Robert E. Sherwood also came a letter filled with concern over the international situation. Sherwood wrote White on December 11, 1939, that he thought it was necessary for the United States to intervene with force to save the world from the calamity of domination by the dictators. Sherwood's expressive letter stirred the editor. He thoroughly agreed that the dictators had to be defeated for the good of civilization. Yet he did not feel that he could raise his voice for military intervention. He felt that he had no right to tell young men that they had to lose their lives. On the other hand, the wisdom that he had acquired over seventy-one years told him that the aggressor nations had to be checked. "I have stood with you in spirit," White wrote Sherwood on December 27, 1939. "Always I have been constrained by an old man's fear and doubt when it comes to lifting my voice for war."

Although the future was to reveal that the Axis powers could not be defeated unless the military might of the United States was thrown into the conflict, White fervently hoped in 1939 and 1940 that the Axis could be defeated without American involvement. It was this hope of defeat for the Axis yet peace for the United States that in May, 1940, led White to chairman the Committee to Defend America by Aiding the Allies.

By the time of the Russian invasion of Finland, W. L. White was in Europe covering the war for both newspapers and radio. The Whites took immense pride in Bill's success. On Christmas Day he broadcast a memorable talk from the Russian-Finnish front called "The Last Christmas Tree." During that day he had visited front-line dugouts and had seen a Christmas tree laden with presents for the Finnish soldiers. He told his American audience of his experience in words that were glowing with praise for the Finnish spirit.

Robert E. Sherwood, who happened to hear the broadcast, was deeply moved by Bill's words. The next day he decided to write a play dealing with the totalitarian menace to democracy. "Bill White's Christmas broadcast galvanized in me the determination to try to put my unhappy, chaotic feelings into a play," he told Bill's father. The play, *There Shall Be No Night*, which opened on Broadway on April 22, 1940, was an immediate success. It later was awarded the Pulitzer prize as the best play of the year. Present at the opening performance as Sherwood's guests were Mr. and Mrs. William Allen White and Mrs. W. L. White.

During the opening months of 1940, White served on the Jury of Award of the Children's Crusade with Eleanor Roosevelt, Dorothy Canfield Fisher, and Monsignor John A. Ryan. The purpose of this crusade was to have American school children contribute money for the aid of the destitute children of Europe. White urged the state superintendent of the Kansas schools to encourage collections, and asked a number of newspapers to support the movement with favorable publicity. Most of the papers were quite willing to help, but dissenting words came from Robert R. McCormick of the Chicago *Tribune*. McCormick objected to the crusade as a type of sentimentalism that would arouse emotions and tend to get the country into war. White, who had a low opinion of the Chicago *Tribune* because, he charged, it violated newspaper ethics by editorializing in its news columns, replied to McCormick: "I have your letter about the Children's Crusade. I understand your position. It is that of the Priest and Levite who were distinguished characters and have lived long in history. And maybe they were right at that. Anyway, I have no doubt that the Good Samaritan when he got the hotel bill and the doctor bill and probably a suit for damages from the man who fell among the thieves wished that he had kept on his own side of the road."

An amusing incident involving White and the Chicago *Tribune* had occurred some time before this exchange of letters. A *Tribune* editor arrived in Kansas to speak at a meeting of the Kansas editors. White and this editor had never met before, and as the man stepped off the train, immaculate in spats and derby, he greeted White by saying: "Ah, the one and only William Allen White. Mr. White, I think I'd rather meet you than my creator."

"Well," said White, his eyes sparkling, "at least you'd be a damned sight safer."

*   *   *

Early in April, 1940, when Germany smashed into Norway and Denmark, the war entered a decisive phase for Europe. "The ruthless invasion of the northern democratic countries and the obvious design to enslave them," the Emporia editor later declared, "gave the people of the United States a sickening sense of the reality of Hitler's purpose. By early spring, it was obvious that Holland was in danger and America began to see what kind of a war it was, the fanatical conquest of a pagan ideology which justified slavery, which exalted cruelty, which banished chivalry, scoffed at the equality of men, and was aimed straight at the dignity of the human spirit."

Faced with the totalitarian challenge to his democratic way of life, White hurried to New York City, where he and Clark Eichelberger laid the plans for a new committee which would consolidate and crystallize public opinion and let Congress know that millions of Americans wanted aid to go to the democracies while the United States, at the same time, went ahead with its own defense program. White's pragmatic attitude was that it was necessary to keep the British navy afloat and to arm Great Britain, since behind the British fleet "we could have two years in which to prepare for the inevitable attack of the totalitarian powers upon our democracy, which must come unless Great Britain wins this war."

White and Eichelberger made contact with a wide variety of people in seeking support for the new committee. While he was in New York, White attended a luncheon in his honor at the Down Town Association. Frederic R. Coudert, the sponsor of this meeting, had gathered together a group of leading citizens from each political party. All the people present at this luncheon agreed to work through their respective parties to ensure the adoption, at the conventions that summer, of platforms that favored aid to the Allies.

Isolationists were later to charge that this Coudert luncheon "controlled by Wall Street" had drafted William Allen White to head the new committee. "The Committee to Defend America by Aiding the Allies," Father Coughlin's *Social Justice* asserted on June 24, 1940, "is a high-sounding name composed of high-handed gentlemen who are leaving no stone unturned to throw everything precious to an American to the dogs of war. Frederic R. Coudert organized this committee. Sneaking, subversively and un-Americanly hiding behind a sanctimonious stuffed shirt named William

Allen White, these men form the most dangerous fifth column that ever set foot upon neutral soil."

Actually, White and Eichelberger had planned their committee before this luncheon group met. What the isolationist and pacifist press never could comprehend was that White was no figurehead in the Committee to Defend America by Aiding the Allies. He was an active chairman until his resignation, and he played a decisive role in the formation of the committee's changing policy.

When the Germans smashed into Holland and Belgium on May 10, 1940. White and Eichelberger decided that the time had come to seek mass support for their new committee. On May 17, telegrams were sent from Emporia to many of the nation's leaders. Telegrams of acceptance quickly poured into Emporia from such leaders as President Seymour of Yale and President Conant of Harvard; Bishop Manning of New York City; Reinhold Niebuhr, of Union Theological Seminary; Catholic Bishop Lucey of Texas and Episcopal Bishop Sherrill of Boston; Thomas Lamont, New York banker; Robert Lincoln O'Brien, former editor of the Boston *Herald*; Judge Samuel Seabury, of New York; and Paul H. Douglas, professor of economics at the University of Chicago.

In the organization of a broad national committee, White as chairman and Eichelberger as executive director asked Hugh Moore, Easton, Pennsylvania, businessman, to be chairman, and Frederick McKee, Pittsburgh businessman, to be treasurer of the executive committee. Thomas K. Finletter, Frank G. Boudreau, and Lewis W. Douglas, all of New York City, and Mrs. Anita McCormick Blaine, of Chicago, completed the executive committee.

On May 20, the story of the formation of the Committee to Defend America by Aiding the Allies was released to the nation. The country was told of the huge number of acceptance telegrams that were swamping the Emporia telegraph office. "Public opinion as expressed by these telegrams from all parts of the country from people in all walks of life," White declared, "seems to be moving rapidly toward crystallizing every possible legal aid to the Allies."

CHAPTER 23

AID TO THE ALLIES

"HIS MARK on the United States was greater than a William Randolph Hearst's or a Col. McCormick's with his one million circulation in Chicago. For Mr. White's career showed justice everywhere to be his concern, that stirring up of narrow nationalistic feelings was injurious to welfare . . ." the Toronto *Globe and Mail* stated three days after William Allen White's death. White's activity as chairman of the Committee to Defend America by Aiding the Allies not only justified this praise but also revealed his commanding influence in American life. It is doubtful that the committee would have been so quickly accepted and supported by the majority of the American people had some other man been chairman. White's prestige as a mellow spokesman and elder statesman helped to sell the committee to the American people. The violent isolationist attacks on Chairman White and their joy over his ultimate resignation of this position would indicate that this group were keenly aware of his value to the aid-the-Allies movement. "I do not believe the people of this country realize how much they are indebted to Mr. White for his courageous stand in accepting the head of the Committee to Defend America," Marshall Stimpson later wrote to the Los Angeles *Times* on February 7, 1944. "No other man in the country, I think, would have had the public confidence which would have enabled him to so quickly get together so large and responsible a body of the citizens in every state into the Committee to Defend America Organization."

By July 1, 1940, six weeks after the public launching of the Committee to Defend America by Aiding the Allies, the committee had expanded to three hundred local branches all over the nation. From May to the middle of June, White guided the policy of the committee from Emporia. Day after day Eichelberger telephoned from New York to discuss problems and policy. White frequently revised statements suggested by the national headquarters in New York, and was clearly the principal force in deciding the policy of the committee.

The first month of the committee's existence witnessed epoch-making changes in Europe. On May 15, German mechanized divisions had sliced through the French line near Sedan. Within a week these German forces, racing to the English Channel, had cut off French and British forces in Flanders. On May 28, King Leopold of Belgium surrendered. During the next few dramatic days, more than three hundred thousand English and French troops were evacuated at Dunkirk. On June 5, Germany launched the Battle of France. Five days later Mussolini declared war. On June 22, France signed an armistice with Germany.

During these crucial days, the William Allen White Committee advocated that the United States government release airplanes to the private manufacturers, who in turn would sell them to England and France. The local branches of the committee stimulated the sending of letters and telegrams to Washington to demand this step. On June 10, the day Mussolini declared war, White wired President Roosevelt: "My correspondence is heaping up unanimously behind the plan to aid the Allies by anything other than war. As an old friend, let me warn you that maybe you will not be able to lead the American people unless you catch up with them."

That same day, President Roosevelt, in a speech at the University of Virginia, unequivocally declared that the United States was in favor of aid to the Allies. "Some indeed still hold to the now somewhat obvious delusion that we of the United States can safely permit the United States to become a lone island, a lone island in a world dominated by the philosophy of force," Roosevelt stated. "Such an island may be the dream of those who still talk and vote as isolationists. Such an island represents to me and to the overwhelming majority of Americans today a helpless nightmare. . . . We will pursue two obvious and simultaneous courses; we will extend to the opponents of force the material resources of this nation and, at the same time, we will harness and speed up the use of those resources in order that we ourselves in the Americas may have equipment and training equal to the task of any emergency and every defense."

During those June days when France was staggering under the German assault, the White Committee redoubled its efforts to mobilize American public opinion in favor of aid short of war. Radio talks, newspaper advertisements, and rallies were sponsored as a means of counteracting isolationist propaganda that German domination of Europe was no threat to the security of the United States. White's own attitude toward the German danger to the United States was expressed in a speech he delivered at the University of Kansas on June 10. "The two philosophies—the philosophy of force and tyranny, and the philosophy of neighborly kindliness that we call democracy—cannot meet and mingle on the same planet!" he declared. "The world has shrunken. Our great round earth with its vast ocean and high land has been drawn together with machinery until it is a little place, a veritable neighborhood that cannot live half slave and half free. I don't know in what form the dictator philosophy in the totalitarian state will meet you in your lives, dearly beloved. But it is out of bounds today. It stands just beyond our borders waiting. What your sacrifices will be, what hardships you may meet, what anguish you may know, I cannot prophesy. I only know unless that beast is chained upon the fields of France your lives will be maimed and mangled by its claws."

Ten days after this speech, White left Emporia to visit President Roosevelt, to report the national conventions, and to work at the New York office of his committee. Just before White started East, the President appointed Republicans Frank Knox and Henry L. Stimson to his Cabinet. Immediately Old Guard Republicans like John Hamilton denounced Stimson and Knox for accepting the positions. When White reached Washington the President told him that there was some danger that the Senate would not confirm the nominations. White immediately secured the names of doubtful senators and sent telegrams to their influential constituents asking that pressure be brought to assure approval of Stimson and Knox. Soon the telegrams deluged Washington and there was no longer any doubt that the two men would be approved. "I feel like Father Coughlin or Frankenstein," White told Charles P. Taft on July 5, 1940, "and I am duly and properly scared, humble and a bit ashamed that one man should have such power!"

In Washington, White discussed the work of his committee with President Roosevelt. "I knew I had his private support . . ." White once wrote concerning his relationship with the President. "I never did anything the President didn't ask for, and I always conferred with him on our program . . . He never failed us. We could go to him—any members of our executive committee, any member of our policy committee. He was frank, cordial, and wise in his counsel. We supported him in his foreign policy, many of us who voted against him in the election . . . He was broad-gauged, absolutely unpartisan, a patriot in this matter if ever there was one."

By July, White's committee had made a significant contribution in the molding of public opinion. The *Fortune* poll for that month revealed that 67.5 per cent of the people now favored aid to the Allies. Approximately two million signatures had been sent to the White House and thousands of telegrams and letters had gone to senators and representatives. Radio speeches, newspaper advertisements, and rallies had helped to crystallize public conviction that stopping Hitler at the English Channel was just good common sense. With the fall of France, White and the other leaders of the committee realized that the coming Battle of Britain might well decide the fate of the democratic world.

Late that June, in co-operation with Macmillan's, White and the committee published *Defense for America*, a book in which the arguments for aid to the Allies were presented in forceful articles by men in the academic, religious, newspaper, and business world. All the contributors agreed that the Nazis' triumph in Europe would be a menace to the security of the United States. The only possible way the United States could escape participation in the war, they contended, was to make sure that the Allies defeated Hitler. If the United States allowed the Allies to go down, the dictators would then turn their attack upon America. Edited with an introduction by White, free copies of *Defense for America* were sent to congressmen, teachers, governors, clergymen, and prominent businessmen.

* * *

Late in June, White reported the Republican convention at Philadelphia and worked with other influential Republicans to make sure that the platform favored aid to all peoples fighting for liberty. With this accomplished, White aided the presidential bid of Wendell Willkie through his dispatches to the North American Newspaper Alliance. White had met Willkie the previous fall during the Non-Partisan Committee campaign, and he had instinctively liked him. Willkie, to White, was a real man. He was forthright and courageous. Furthermore, he was unqualifiedly for aid to the Allies, whereas the other Republican possibilities—Robert A. Taft, Arthur Vandenberg, and Thomas E. Dewey—were either isolationist or very close to it.

After Willkie's nomination, White told his readers that Wendell Willkie was less of a stuffed shirt than any other presidential candidate he had ever known. "Of all the men as pre-presidential figures, I should say that Wendell Willkie and Theodore Roosevelt impressed me more deeply and favorably by their sincerity, by their wide intelligence and by their robust decent sense of humor," White declared.

Shortly after this editorial was written, White left for Chicago to report the Democratic convention. For months he had been writing feature stories trying to dissuade President Roosevelt from accepting a third term. The Emporia editor contended in these articles that Roosevelt could serve the country better as an elder statesman and philosopher than as president. At the convention both White and Eichelberger appeared before the platform committee to urge a clear-cut plank on aid to the Allies. They also asked members of their committee to wire the members of the platform committee and the convention delegates urging support of such a plank.

When the Democrats adopted a forthright plank for aid to the Allies, both parties were on record for the policy advocated by the White Committee. Throughout the campaign, White supported Wendell Willkie. His opposition to the President centered on the third-term issue. He argued that it was not wise to keep a party in power for twelve years, since the opposition party might disintegrate and leave the nation with a one-party system. From time to time during the campaign, however, White was warm in his praise of President Roosevelt's foreign policy. Many ardent Republicans were indignant at White for commending "That Man in the White House." T. A. McNeal of Capper's *Kansas Farmer*, for instance, wrote to White to protest against his praise of the President. "I read your letter from kiver to kiver, forward and back, lady in the center and six hands around!" White replied in a mellow mood. "I am willing to admit there is something in what you have to say. There always is. I am sorry that for well-nigh on fifty years, boy and man, my outgivings sometimes have got in your hair, indeed both hairs, but I am just built that way. I suppose I was all right until a mule kicked me. Come again when you can't stay quite so long."

White served Willkie as a trusted adviser. He had conferences with Willkie on August 1 and 2 in Colorado and encouraged Willkie to put into his acceptance speech a forthright statement of his desire for aid to Britain. After White's death, Willkie revealed his indebtedness to the Emporian when he wired Mrs. White: "He was a man whom I was proud and privileged to call a friend and his advice was invaluable. Bill White was one of the great men of his day . . . We are going to miss his common sense and farsightedness in the days ahead."

During the month following the conventions, White devoted a large amount of his time to attempting to bring Roosevelt and Willkie together on a common statement approving the sending of overage destroyers to England. German airplanes and submarines were playing havoc with the British Merchant Marine. In June, 1940, it was estimated that 269,000 tons of shipping went to the bottom, and in July, 290,000 tons. England needed a full fleet of destroyers to protect her shipping and to keep the supply line open to the United States. Many of her destroyers, however, were laid up for repair as a result of the damage inflicted at Dunkirk. President Roosevelt had suggested to White in their conference on June 29 that destroyers might be released to England in return for naval bases in the British possessions in the Western Hemisphere.

In July and August, the White Committee focused its attention upon arousing public support for the release of the destroyers. "If the President really wants to do it," White told his policy committee on July 26, "it can be done. But we must show him that the country will follow him in this matter." White did not succeed in bringing Willkie and Roosevelt together in a joint statement or even in a private agreement on the release of the destroyers, but he was able to advise the President that his opponent was for the plan.

On July 30, the White Committee ran an advertisement in major newspapers entitled "Between Us and Hitler Stands the *British Fleet!*" According to the advertisement, the British fleet served as a fortress "stopping the international gangsters from reaching the loot across the Atlantic Ocean." Britain, however, needed destroyers, and the public was urged to write or telegraph the President and congressmen that the destroyers should be released to England. Significant talks favoring the release of the destroyers were delivered by General John J. Pershing, and Admirals Harry E. Yarnell, William H. Standley, and Yates Sterling, Jr.

On August 22, White himself spoke to the nation over the Columbia Broadcasting System. After he had described the work of the now six hundred local chapters of the Committee to Defend America by Aiding the Allies, he made it clear that he wanted the defeat of Hitler and, at the same time, peace for the United States. The only hope for peace, he thought, was an Allied victory. If the Allies were defeated, the United States would be next on the dictator's list. The isolationists' position of doing nothing in the crisis was nonsense to White. To follow this policy meant the defeat of the Allies and war for the United States. The only hope for the United States to remain at peace, therefore, was to help make sure of an Allied victory. At that moment the last great Allied power, Britain, stood in grave danger. If Britain was conquered and the British fleet fell into Hitler's hands, White warned his listeners that the United States would be in deadly peril.

"How can we sleep comfortably in our beds," he asked, "until we know that for some just, honest, and legal return . . . those destroyers are on the high seas, manned with British sailors, hurrying to our first line of defense? . . . If Great Britain falls, a new phase of civilization will dominate Europe and will menace the United States and the Western Hemisphere. It is not a question of form of government between Great Britain and the European dictators. It is a way of thinking, a way of life, a social order, a slave economy that menaces the world, and the world cannot live half slave and half free."

By the middle of August a Gallup poll revealed that the majority of the American people favored the release of the destroyers to England. On September 3, President Roosevelt announced the release of fifty destroyers in return for naval and air bases in the English possessions in the Western Hemisphere. The White Committee hailed this step as a significant contribution to American defense. It is clear that the committee, functioning as a powerful vehicle through which the average citizen expressed his ardent desire for an Allied victory, had revealed to the President the widespread support for this transaction.

The British possessions that were soon turned over to the United States were immediately fortified and were extremely useful after Pearl Harbor in the American campaign against German submarines. The fifty overage destroyers performed invaluable service for Britain in the months following their transfer. They helped keep the Atlantic supply line open and were ready, too, for Channel fighting in case the Germans launched an invasion of England. "The cause of Anglo-American friendship and co-operation owes an unpayable debt to your husband for his generous and unsparing efforts to bring about a better understanding between our peoples," Lord Halifax wrote Mrs. White on the day William Allen White died.

* * *

After the completion of the destroyer-base exchange, the White Committee urged the release to England of twenty-five Flying Fortresses, as many fighter planes as could be spared, and twenty motor torpedo boats. White cabled General Douglas MacArthur, in charge of the defense of the Philippines, and asked his opinion as to further aid to Britain. "Such co-ordinated help as may be regarded as proper by our leaders should be synchronized with the British effort so that the English-speaking peoples of the world will not be broken in detail," MacArthur replied. "The vulnerability of singleness will disappear before unity of effort—not too late, not tomorrow, but today."

During the first two weeks of September, the Emporia editor worked on committee problems in New York and Chicago. These were tiring weeks for a man of seventy-two. When he returned to Emporia, he was confined to his home for ten days by a severe cold. His doctor would not allow him to return to New York until November. Even so, committee affairs were constantly on his mind, and hardly a day went by without innumerable telegrams and phone calls between Emporia and the New York headquarters.

By September, the committee had to concern itself with more than menace to Hitler. On September 27, Japan signed an alliance with Germany and Italy binding itself to enter the war on the side of the Axis in case the United States entered the European conflict. According to Forrest Davis and Ernest K. Lindley, in their semiofficial *How War Came*, a secret section of this alliance committed Japan to war against the United States and Britain when the circumstances were appropriate. Any doubt that such an agreement had been made was dismissed when the Tokyo *Asahi* newspaper said that as a result of the pact "a clash between Japan and America now seems inevitable."

This alliance of the Axis powers revealed that the United States had no freedom of action as to the question of peace or war. Whenever the Axis nations decided to strike, the United States would be at war regardless of the policy it was following. Rather than involving America in the war, the aid-to-the-Allies program kept allies fighting in this inevitable conflict while the nation launched its own defense efforts. Had the United States followed the isolationist policy, it might well have had no allies when the inevitable war came. Yet isolationist forces were so blind to the menace of the Axis nations and to the correctness of the defense steps being taken by the United States, that their most vocal newspaper, the Chicago *Tribune*. declared on June 5, 1940: "Under

Mr. Roosevelt our foreign policy . . . has been provocative. We have succeeded in irritating the Japanese by such proposals as the project to fortify Guam."

Despite his poor health, William Allen White was keenly aware of the meaning of the German-Japanese-Italian agreement. The duty of his committee was now, he felt, to arouse the nation to an awareness that a two-ocean war faced America. But while the people were perceiving the Japanese menace, they should not forget the need of aiding Britain, for, White said, "if Great Britain wins (and we are arming her to win) we shall have to fight no war. France will be free; so will Belgium, Holland and Scandinavia, and we need have no worry about Japan and her Axis. The Pacific fight will be won in the Atlantic."

White had nothing but scorn for those Americans who wanted the United States to appease the Axis. Charles A. Lindbergh, the darling of the isolationist cause, told the American people on August 4, 1940: "In the future, we may have to deal with a Europe dominated by Germany . . . An agreement between us could maintain peace and civilization throughout the world as far into the future as we can see." Lindbergh, White declared in a *Gazette* editorial on October 15, was "blind to the fact that the longer the United States can arm Britain and keep her fighting, the more time we shall have to prepare to meet Germany . . . All but France tried to be neutral, as Lindbergh advises. And what did it buy them? And our arming Britain will have nothing to do with the attack which Hitler will make upon this country. Why? Because Hitler's whole philosophy, his idea of government, his economic setup, his insatiable ambitions, all make it impossible for a free country and a free people to live beside Hitler's world enslaved. To that Charles Lindbergh shuts his eyes. So when he opens his mouth, he utters folly and people shake their heads and walk away."

During the weeks just before the presidential election, White and his committee were embroiled in politics. Although the committee officially was nonpartisan, White was for Willkie and Eichelberger was for Roosevelt. A number of committee members wanted the organization to publish the records of incumbent isolationists running for re-election to Congress. White refused to allow this. As White explained to Arthur J. Goldsmith, of the committee's New York City chapter, such a step would require the committee to oppose almost all the Republican members of Congress. This, argued White, would destroy the nonpartisan character of the committee and make it an adjunct of the Democratic party.

White's refusal to permit the committee to fight isolationist congressmen bewildered his followers, who did not understand his Kansas political background and connections. If he had allowed the committee to oppose all isolationists, White would have had to fight all the Kansas Republican incumbents and support their Democrat opponents! If he had done this, it might well have injured the re-election of Republican Governor Payne Ratner, White's friend and political ally. It might also have jeopardized a constitutional amendment permitting the state to have a civil-service system. White had spent years gaining support for this bill. For the last two weeks of the 1940 campaign, he suspended many of his activities for the Committee to Defend America by Aiding the Allies, and drove all over Kansas making addresses in favor of the constitutional amendment.

If White had led a nation-wide fight against isolationist Republicans, it would have required him to bolt the party in Kansas, but this, of course, he would not do. Much of the isolationist opposition to the committee's objectives in 1941, of course, might have been prevented had the Emporia editor allowed his committee to take an active part in the Congressional elections. The Kansas situation, however, deterred him from sanctioning steps which clear thinking about the security of America should have necessitated.

"This is the year when the independent voter in Kansas can afford, if he is a good citizen, to vote the straight Republican ticket," White informed his readers on November 1. "Because, taken by and large, man for man, from top to bottom, the men running for office on the Republican ticket in the nation, in this state and this county are men of high character and superior ability." A letter that White sent isolationist Hamilton Fish, containing views similar to this editorial, caused him many a trial and tribulation.

When White refused to sanction the action of his committee against isolationists, members of his New York City chapter organized a Non-Partisan Committee to Defeat Hamilton Fish. This new committee circulated Fish's record and pointed out that he had organized a committee to fight the repeal of the embargo in 1939; that he had been feted in Germany; that he had stated that German demands on Poland were just; and that he had opposed measures to aid the Allies.

White, for some reason, felt called upon to write Fish, on October 18, that no one had authorization to use against him the name of the Committee to Defend America by Aiding the Allies. "However you and I may disagree about some issues of the campaign," he told Fish, "I hope as Republicans we are united in our support of the Republican ticket from top to bottom in every district and every state." And, White added, this letter was not private. When Fish read this letter from White to public audiences during his campaign, the members of the Non-Partisan Committee to Defeat Hamilton Fish were indignant. They immediately telegraphed White that he had lent aid and comfort to an enemy of the program of the Committee to Defend America by Aiding the Allies. Hugh Moore and Frederick McKee, of the national executive committee of the White organization, urged White to stop Fish from using his name. The opponents of Fish were not using the White Committee in their campaign, they told White. Furthermore, if a poll of the committee were taken, White would discover that the members favored action against isolationists regardless of party affiliation.

White finally solved this unhappy dilemma brought about by his own partisan zeal, by wiring the opponents of Fish: "Our Committee is nonpartisan. As such we wish to see the Republicans and Democrats elected who support a program of aid to Great Britain. Our Committee naturally wishes to see appeasers, isolationists and pro-Germans defeated irrespective of party. You may make the widest use of this you wish." Fish, however, was re-elected and during 1941 continued to be a vigorous foe of the program for aiding Britain.

There is no doubt that the campaign was a source of continual grief to the Emporia editor. Ardent Republicans disliked his praise of Roosevelt's foreign policy, and equally ardent Democrats disliked his editorials urging the election of Willkie. White was not bitter or disillusioned with American democracy over the re-election of the President. But he was disturbed somewhat by the obvious urban support for Roosevelt and the rural support, outside the South, for Willkie. The domination of his rural society by urban America had long been a source of worry to him. He hated to see the passing of his simpler America, and to him a more intimate, friendly, and democratic America.

With the election completed, White wired every one of the committee's 750 local chapters: "I earnestly urge each chapter . . . to arrange immediately, for this week . . . a local mass meeting to appeal for national unity. The campaign will be over; we take off our political buttons and wear just one button 'Defend America by Aiding the Allies.' "

*   *   *

The White Committee carried out its program amid bitter protests from a vocal opposition. In spite of the cries and charges raised by this opposition, the polls of public opinion revealed that the committee had the support of an ever-increasing majority of the American people. White was subjected to considerable personal abuse for heading the committee. "Anyone who would stoop so low as you have done is a disgrace to Americanism," charged one person. Many correspondents characterized him as a cheap warmonger, and one critic declared: "In your mercenary reason for advocating help for the Allies it might be well for you to state that you and your friends are too old and physically unfit to serve in front-line trenches in France but you want to speak for the youth of our country to see that they are killed, maimed and crippled while you live in comfort and become a great dollar-a-year patriot."

White had a generous answer to all his critics. "I have your kind letter and have read it with great interest," he would reply. "There are, of course, two opinions held honestly by intelligent people in the United States. One is that to help the Allies keeps the war away from America by letting them fight the war in Europe rather than wait until the Germans conquer Europe and turn their greedy eyes westward. The other opinion is your opinion and many fine, wise people hold it. There being two sides, perhaps the best thing each of us could do is to respect the honesty and integrity of each other's opinions and realize that there must be differences if there is to be progress in the world."

Isolationists frequently charged that White was a tool of Wall Street and that his committee was financed by international bankers and munitions makers. These people were always informed by White that the committee's books were open for their inspection. The White Committee, unlike the isolationist committees, was not secretive about its funds. It published a list of its chief contributors, which was in sharp contrast to the policy of the America First Committee.

The American Fascists went further than their isolationist allies in their attack on the White Committee. Frank Woodruff Johnson charged in *The Octopus* that White was a stooge for the Reds and the Jews. The White Committee, insisted *The Octopus*, was "working with Jewry to propagandize us into the World War holocaust."

The Chicago *Tribune* and the Hearst papers were among the chief newspaper foes of the White Committee. On September 5, 1940, the *Tribune* declared: "William Allen White's Committee to Defend America by Aiding the Allies keeps repeating the statement that 'the British fleet is our present defense.' That is a monotonously chorused untruth." White's low opinion of the *Tribune's* policy of editorializing in its news columns was expressed in a vigorous editorial in the *Gazette* on October 22, 1940. "Another funny thing about going to Chicago," he told his readers, "is to read the papers, the Hearst paper and the *Tribune*. In policying of the news they are the worst offenders in the United States. No matter what form of paranoia the editors and owners have, their passing screwballia is reflected in the first pages of the papers and the readers are poisoned with the insanity of the owners. . . . These morning papers reek with unfairness. It is papers like that that make the freedom of the press a joke. There are precious few of them, but enough to give many dumb readers the notion that the freedom of the press is a private snap to make money or arrogate power to the editors and owners. Which is too bad."

The isolationist camp contained a peculiar variety of groups. In addition to the pure isolationists and the American Fascists, it consisted of members of the Communist and Socialist parties, the perfectionists of the *Christian Century* type, and many reactionary businessmen who congregated in the America First Committee. Three isolationist committees—the War Debts Defense Committee, the Make Europe Pay War Debts Committee, and the Islands for War Debts Committee—were inspired by George Sylvester Viereck, a Nazi agent who was put in jail after Pearl Harbor. Viereck's committees utilized the Congressional franking privileges of isolationist senators like Ernest Lundeen and Robert Reynolds, and of isolationist congressmen like Martin L. Sweeney and Stephen A. Day, in mailing tons of isolationist propaganda to the public.

The chief foe of the White Committee was the America First Committee headed by General Robert E. Wood of Chicago. This committee distributed a great deal of isolationist propaganda that originated from the office of Viereck's committees. Ralph Townsend and Laura Ingalls, later to be indicted as Axis agents, were featured speakers at America First rallies. The America First Committee's publications displayed no realization of the Axis menace to American security. "We have nothing to fear from a Nazi European victory," their New York chapter bulletin declared in September, 1941.

The German Propaganda Ministry hailed the America First Committee in January, 1941, as "truly American and truly patriotic." Although the America First Committee repudiated the support of the German-American Bund, it did not reject the support of Fascist organizations like William Dudley Pelley's Silver Shirts, Father Coughlin's Christian Front, the Ku Klux Klan, and the American Destiny party. By October, 1941, the American Legion in California discovered that Axis agents had infiltrated into the California America First organization so thoroughly that America First "has not only confused the minds of the people it attracts, but also has poisoned the minds of persons of outstanding community reputation who have participated in its activities."

In November and December, 1940, the various isolationists groups, spearheaded by the America First Committee, launched a widespread attack on the Committee to Defend America by

Aiding the Allies, charging that it was a warmongering committee. Many of the abusive letters received by Chairman White were undoubtedly stimulated by the isolationist committees. Over the air and in the press, isolationists charged White with leading America into war. "William Allen White, who once was a good country editor . . . is sending up senile thunder for American entry," asserted Guy Fowler in the Whittier [California] *Reporter* on December 12, 1940. Attacks like these disturbed the 72-year-old editor. These charges formed one of the chain of events that eventually led to White's resignation as chairman of the Committee to Defend America by Aiding the Allies.

*   *   *

On November 11, 1940, White left Emporia to work on committee matters in Chicago and New York. For the next several weeks his time was completely occupied with conferences and luncheons dealing with committee problems. White's concentrated work, however, was beginning to take its toll on his health. "I'm having a busy time," he wrote his managing editor. "Every hour seems to be scheduled. This committee job is both getting my goat and renewing my youth. . . ." One problem that caused him great concern was the increased sinking of English supply ships by Nazi submarines. "I fear," he wrote his old friend Helen Sutliff on November 18, 1940, "that Great Britain needs help on the sea. I don't know how we can give it to her without taking a step nearer to severance of relations with Germany. It's a serious thing and I'm greatly puzzled."

Another vexing problem concerned the New York City chapter of the committee. He confided to Eichelberger: "The New York Committee is my hair shirt." White felt that this group was demanding too much influence on the national committee's affairs. They were, also, he believed, running off on side issues and not keeping the sole focus of the committee upon the general program of aid to Britain. It was more than just the New York City chapter, however, that worried him. There were a number of individuals in the New York, Washington, and Baltimore chapters who had realized that aid to Britain was not enough to defeat Hitler. They believed that Hitler was such a threat to American security that the United States should enter the war at once and do its share in defeating the menace of the Axis.

Some of these individuals met from time to time at the Century Club in New York to discuss the international situation. For a time they maintained a New York headquarters under the direction of Francis P. Miller, author and organization director of study groups formed by the Council on Foreign Relations. At times the policy of this "Miller Group" or "Century Club Group," was similar to that of the White Committee; and at other times it was more advanced. White did not agree with the belief held by many of the members of this group that the United States should go to war. He was heading the movement to aid Britain in the hope that Britain alone could defeat Hitler. If Britain failed and the United States was plunged into war, White would reluctantly support this inevitable development. He would not, however, sanction steps to speed up the inevitable. During November and December he began to fear that the Miller Group might push the policy of his own committee too far toward intervention. "I am worried all the time about that Century Club crowd," he wrote Eichelberger on December 3, 1940. "They are probably more nearly right than I am. They are young men and of course are impatient with my leadership . . . I realize that probably my leadership is crippled by my slow judgment, by my desire to keep fairly abreast of public sentiment and not to get out too far in front. That has been a life technique and I cannot readjust my years to a new technique. I am writing to you frankly because it is a most serious matter which concerns my relations with the Committee . . . it is beginning to assume the form of a crisis."

While he was in New York in November, White and his policy committee agreed on a new statement of policy. The committee suggested that the President declare a state of national emergency in order to mobilize industrial resources for maximum production; that the United States give all possible material and financial help to China and place an embargo on all war materials for Japan. Toward the European situation, the new policy released on November 26 stated: "The life line between Great Britain and the United States is the sea route to the Western Hemisphere.

Under no circumstances must this line be cut and the United States must be prepared to maintain it . . ." The second significant announcement of the new policy declared: "We favor through Congressional action a revision of our international policy. This would include a repeal or modification of restrictive statutes which hamper this nation in its freedom of action when it would co-operate with nations defending themselves from attack by nations at war in violation of treaties with the United States."

Although these two statements did not explicitly advocate American convoys to Britain and the repeal of the Neutrality Act, there is no question that such steps were implied in the policy release. According to Clark Eichelberger, everyone at the meeting including the Emporia editor knew that this implication was inherent in the statement.

On November 28, on behalf of the Committee to Defend America by Aiding the Allies, White received from H. A. Bruno the annual award of the National Association of Accredited Publicity Directors for "the most distinguished service in the whole field of public opinion formation." After receiving this award, White took the train for Emporia. Back in Kansas, he began to worry. The isolationist accusations that he was a warmonger, added to the fact that he was excessively tired and concerned over the Century Club Group and the New York City chapter, heightened his nervous condition.

On December 10, he wrote his old friend Thomas Lamont, who was in general agreement with White on committee matters, that he was frightfully disturbed over the Century Club Group. If they were not careful, White declared, the advanced demands of this group would wreck the White Committee. "We are getting in Dutch with the country," he observed. He then implied that his worry over this situation might lead him to relinquish his post as chairman of the committee. A few days after this letter was mailed, White received a note from Frederic R. Coudert, warning him that the Scripps-Howard newspaper chain was planning to launch an attack on the committee.

On December 20, White dictated this personal letter to Roy Howard, head of the chain:

Look now Roy, you and I have been buddies more or less and I hope I have deserved the honor of your friendship these twenty years and more and why I am sending this is on account that a friend in Washington says you are preparing to strafe our outfit and particularly me because we are heading HB for war. All right only this:

The only reason in God's world I am in this organization is to keep this country out of war. I don't go an inch further or faster than Wendell Willkie or the American Legion or the American Federation or the National Grange; nor an inch further or faster than you went this month in the Filipino magazine on the Eastern question. I am abreast of you and no further and I haven't changed since we talked in Chicago last July. The story is floating around that I and our outfit are in favor of sending convoys with British ships or our own ships, a silly thing, for convoys unless you shoot are confetti and it's not time to shoot now or ever. Another thing: The America First crowd keeps insisting that we are in favor of repealing the Johnson Act, a stupid thing to do because it would not help Great Britain and there are half a dozen other good legal ways to get aid to Great Britain. The President is following his own way. But the Johnson Act should not be repealed and we are not for it. Still one more charge: It is not true even remotely that we favor repealing [the Neutrality Law] to carry contraband of war into the war zone.

That would be leading us to war and our organization and I personally am deeply opposed to it. If I was making a motto for the Committee to Defend America by Aiding the Allies, it would be "The Yanks Are Not Coming." We could not equip them and feed them if they went. We have less than two hundred thousand ready and we need them worse at home on the assembly belt than we need them in Europe. War would defeat the end for which our Committee is organized to defend America by aiding Great Britain and would bring on a thirty year conflict. The Yanks are not going because if they went to war they would lose our cause. That is my firm unshakeable belief. And to strafe me because some members of our organization who are not officially representing us are martial-minded is as foolish and unfair as it would be to call the Knights of Columbus appeasers because Joe Kennedy gave Roosevelt the Judas kiss. Not one official utterance of our organization has anything remotely suggestive that we feel the only alternative for American defense through aid to Great Britain is war. Moreover I have sat in all executive councils, all policy making committees and I have never heard war seriously discussed in any official group of our organization at any time. I hope you know that I am not a liar and I hope you feel I am not a sucker and I trust you will believe what I am writing.

Howard immediately requested permission to publish the letter and White agreed—without consulting Eichelberger or the members of his executive and policy committees—provided the end be changed to read: "never heard war as an alternative objective seriously discussed by an official group of our organization at any time. America will go to war or stay out of war not because we make Hitler mad but only when, as and if Hitler thinks he can win the war."

White permitted this letter to be published for a variety of reasons. He wanted to show his "fanatic opponents"—the America First Committee and other isolationists—that he was not for war; he wanted to warn the Century Club Group and the eastern members of his committee that they should not move too fast for the Middle West; and he wanted the public to understand his own attitude toward the war. There seems to be little doubt that White was worried that committee affairs might jeopardize his prestige with the American people. He had achieved his status of interpreter and folk hero by never being too far ahead of public opinion. If he did not check the policy developments sponsored by the more alert Easterners, he and his committee might be ahead of public feeling. The Century Club Group obviously wanted to lead and form public opinion, but White could not abandon his lifetime practice of being just slightly ahead of his middle-class America. He was willing to head a committee that channeled public sentiment and gave it expression, but he was not willing to be the head of a committee that was far ahead of prevailing public attitudes.

When White had been in the East and helped formulate the policy statement of November 26, he had been acutely conscious of the critical international picture. At that time he had agreed on a policy that implied the repeal of the Neutrality Act and sanctioned convoys to Britain. When he returned to the Middle West, he discovered that the necessity for such steps was neither understood nor appreciated. Not desiring to be out of step with his region, he repudiated the policy statement of November 26 in his letter to Roy Howard. Yet many times over in the past few months, White had remarked that it really did not matter what steps the United States took to aid the Allies since Hitler would attack whenever it suited his purpose. "If Hitler finds it advantageous at any time to make war on us he will find a reason; make an incident a cause of war," White had told a group of writers on November 18. "We shall not be attacked because of our moral attitude, whatever that may be. Did it help Czechoslovakia to capitulate, or did it help Norway to carefully guard her neutrality? Make no mistake we shall not be attacked, if we are attacked, because of an attitude—it will be because of our worldly goods."

As long as the committee merely advocated the release of destroyers, torpedo boats, and airplanes, it was only expressing the sentiment of the majority of the public. By December, 1940, these steps were not enough. There was no question that it was foolish to allow American goods going to England to be sunk. Supplies on the bottom of the ocean were not aiding the defense of either England or America. Since the majority of the public agreed that Hitler should be defeated, logic should have required support for convoys and a repeal of the Neutrality Act which barred American ships from war zones. The public, however, shrank from this step. When White had returned to Kansas, he recognized this situation and acted accordingly. White and the general public wanted mutually contradictory ends. They wanted the defeat of Hitler, but they also wanted peace for the United States. Few Americans were willing to face the fact in December, 1940, that they could have peace only at the price of a Hitler victory or that the defeat of Hitler required intervention by the United States. White was a faithful reflection in December, 1940, of this confused American attitude toward the war.

*   *   *

The publication of the White letter to Roy Howard created an enormous furor. Isolationist spokesmen General Robert E. Wood and Charles A. Lindbergh capitalized on it by claiming that White agreed with them. Within the ranks of the White Committee, the letter set off a number of explosions. Henry Sloane Coffin, president of Union Theological Seminary, threatened to resign if White opposed steps that were essential to aiding Britain. Other members charged that White was an appeaser, since he had written that "the only reason in God's world I am in this organization is to keep this country out of war." What White meant by this statement, he later explained to Frederic R. Coudert, was "only so long as that was a possible course." He was not for peace at any price nor was he an appeaser, but the Howard letter actually did not make this clear.

A large number of letters and telegrams poured into the committee's New York office threatening wholesale resignations unless White was repudiated. These complaints came from people all over the country, not only from the East. White's executive committee, headed by Lewis Douglas, tried to persuade White to issue a statement to clarify his position. White refused. On December 27, Major General John F. O'Ryan resigned because White's policy was "pallid and ineffective." Two days later Mayor LaGuardia denounced White for his words and accused him of "doing a typical Laval."

On December 26, Eichelberger wired White that his Howard letter threatened to wreck the committee. White then tendered his resignation as chairman, to take effect early in January. On January 1, 1941, before the executive committee had formally accepted the resignation, Lewis Douglas sent White a telegram in behalf of the executive committee urging him to come to New York to quiet the rebellion and to direct the fight to secure Congressional approval of President Roosevelt's recent proposal to lend or lease goods to the Allies. White looked upon this as an ultimatum—an ultimatum that he could not carry out. Mrs. White had been ordered to the desert country for the winter by her doctor, and he was going with her. That same day White telegraphed to Eichelberger, Douglas, and Hugh Moore his resignation, to take effect immediately.

On January 3, 1941, White told the home folks: "The job was too big a one for me, and after all, I have my own life to live, and again after all I wanted to celebrate my 73rd birthday in peace and devote the year or two or three that may be left to me to writing some books and helping with some chores around the house here in Emporia and Kansas." Then he added: "After the election,

I had a definite sense that the war fever was rising and I didn't like it. All of my life I have been devoted to peace, to the belief that war is futile and in this particular case to the conviction that if we could keep Great Britain fighting for our cause, this would never become our war." Possibly, although this thought was not expressed in either his editorials or his personal letters, by the time of his resignation he had realized that war was inevitable. Aid to the Allies had been the only hope of averting war when the committee was launched, but by December, 1940, it may have been clear to him that England alone could not defeat Hitler. Eventually the United States would have to help with military force. White possibly reasoned that he simply did not want to be chairman of the Committee to Defend America by Aiding the Allies when this inevitable war occurred. "I honestly hoped, while I was at the head of the internationalist group, that we could hold on and keep Britain afloat until Hitler went down," he wrote Paul Hutchinson of the *Christian Century*, on March 5, 1942. "But by the end of 1940 . . . I felt that my job was done as far as it could be done . . . Even if I held them back [those members clamoring for war], as I tried to by a letter to Roy Howard protesting against convoys and declaring that the Yanks were not coming and protesting against other offenses of the ghost dances for war, even then the inevitable was fairly obvious."

The personal letters that White wrote in the weeks following his resignation demonstrate that he was worried over the danger of approaching war, and the identification of himself and his committee as warmongers. He resigned, he told Secretary of War Stimson, chiefly "because a group of radical warmongers in New York City is confusing our national organization with the New York City chapter and making my chairmanship a source of endless contention." The situation, however, was more complex than this. Many members from outside of New York had protested his Howard letter. But, as a matter of fact, White's resignation would have occurred anyway, even if the Howard incident had not taken place. He was exhausted from the hard work involved. Mrs. White was ill. And he had mentioned to Eichelberger and others in November that he would soon have to resign. Involved, of course, in White's conflict with the New York chapter of his committee was the Midwesterner's antagonism toward New York City. Many times he had expressed his indignation at the New Yorker's peculiar provincial view that they were the entire nation and at their lack of understanding of midwestern attitudes toward the war.

Best comment of all on White's resignation was an editorial in *The New York Times* on January 4, 1941:

. . . Mr. White is, as he says, earning "a living running a country newspaper"—a newspaper, it may be added, that comes like a sane, kindly breath of the Kansas prairie into metropolitan New York and is read with respect by newspapermen everywhere. He is 72 years old. Though he is still in some respects a cherubic and hopeful young man, his friends know that his health has not been too good recently. After doing a magnificent job he has earned a vacation.

No one who knows him doubts his fervent and courageous love for democracy. As much as any one man in the United States he helped win public support for the "arsenal of democracy" policy which the President proclaimed last Sunday evening. His name and personality made the White Committee a going concern in its first difficult days. In carrying on, as it intends to do, the Committee will still benefit by the prestige given it by William Allen White and by the trust and affection which he has inspired in millions of Americans.

Like the rest of us he has no doubt been pulled two ways—toward doing everything possible to beat Hitler and toward doing nothing that will get us into war. In this conscientious facing of a difficult problem, as in his hatred of stupidity, tyranny and injustice, we would like to think that he is a representative American. We do know that this would be a poorer, more cynical, less generous country without Will White of Emporia.

Shortly after his resignation as chairman, the Whites left Emporia for a winter in the warm Arizona desert. Just before their departure, President Roosevelt in his annual message to Congress warned the nation of the dangerous world situation. "In times like these it is immature—and incidentally untrue—for anybody to brag that an unprepared America, single-handed, and with one hand tied behind its back, can hold off the whole world," the President declared. The answer to America's peril was to furnish maximum aid to Britain under a lend-lease program. "Let us say to the democracies," Roosevelt told Congress: "We Americans are vitally concerned in your defense of freedom. We are putting forth our energies, our resources and our organizing powers to give you the strength to regain and maintain a free world."

The Emporia editor praised the speech as a "New Magna Charta," and remarked: "This flaming message of President Roosevelt encircling the globe, will kindle the fire of faith in men, freemen and bound men over the whole round earth . . . It will give to aspiring men everywhere new hopes . . . It was a great day, a great occasion, a great man—all three united—that spoke to the world today."

From time to time while on his vacation, White sent editorials to the *Gazette* supporting the pending lend-lease proposal. He praised Wendell Willkie's support of the President's measure, and vigorously criticized the solid Republican opposition to the bill in Congress. Only thirty-five Republicans in the House voted for the measure and only ten in the Senate. The Republican record in Congress, White believed, was about the record Adolf Hitler would have made had he been the Republican leader.

On February 25, White went to New York to accept the annual award of the *Churchman* to the person who had rendered the greatest service to his country during the previous year. All the speakers—Dr. Hu Shih, Mrs. J. Borden Harriman, Clarence Streit, Clark Eichelberger, and Wendell Willkie—were united in their praise of White. White's acceptance speech was a masterful plea for America to assume its world responsibilities. After the gangster nations were defeated, it would be necessary to police them "until they see that goodwill on this earth pays better than the ruthless use of force." "You ask me," White remarked, " 'Why should we police the world?' And I tell you there is something hard and practical in duty . . . We are indeed and in truth our 'brothers' keepers.' Would it not have been cheaper twenty years ago in cold dollars and cents to take our place in the League of Nations than to spend the billions we are spending today for defense? If we shirk our duty now we shall have to spend another national treasury twenty years from now."

After this speech, White returned to Arizona. When Mrs. White's health did not improve, they left for the Mayo clinic. The doctors ordered them both to slow down and conserve their strength. During April and May, although White wrote editorials for the *Gazette*, he appeared at the office only an hour or two each day. In spite of his poor health, White watched the changing panorama of the war with something of his old-time vigor and interest. During March the sinking of Allied shipping in the Atlantic reached a critical point. Then on March 25 Germany announced that it was extending the zone of war operations to Greenland. This was a direct threat to American security; the United States occupied Greenland to forestall a German attack on that area. Isolationists, however, were unable to see that German operations in Greenland were a threat to the United States. Oswald Garrison Villard, for instance, several years after this step still charged: "There can be no pretense that any such occupation was necessary for the safety of the United States."

In late April, the Committee to Defend America by Aiding the Allies unequivocally urged that the United States convoy merchant ships to England. Lewis Douglas pointed out that British shipping losses placed that nation in a desperate position—"so desperate that we may be left alone, dangerously alone to face a hostile world ruled by force and dominated by the Axis powers whose ambitions, so they openly declare, are to recast the world, including ourselves, in their own evil image." This committee position aroused the ire of the isolationists, who still were unable to realize that war was inevitable for the United States.

Letter after letter poured into Emporia, denouncing White, who was now honorary chairman of the committee. "You have nearly put us into war," declared one writer. "Hurray! Aren't you happy and tickled to death? . . . The death of all the young men that will follow on the trail of what is now going on, will fall on your shoulders when you face the 'Guardian of the Threshold.'" On April 3, White wrote Eichelberger that he must resign as honorary chairman. He was tired of controversy, and he was not physically able to answer all the abusive letters he was receiving. White still did not believe that the committee should advocate convoys. Until the administration declared that convoys were necessary, the committee should not take a stand on the question. When the President felt that convoys were necessary to protect American security, then, White warned, he would support convoys. He was not against convoys, but was opposed to the committee's advocating them before the administration felt they were necessary. "When the President is for them, I'm going to support them, of course," he explained to one committee member. "But I do not believe that our organization should keep nagging him and needling him while he is hesitating . . . I don't think our organization is doing any service to the President in building up public sentiment that will force his hand."

Many times in his April and May editorials, White expressed the opinion that war now seemed inevitable for the United States. If Hitler defeated England, we would certainly be in the war. Since Vichy France was completely under Hitler's domination, the Emporia editor advocated American occupation of the French West Indies. "This may mean war," he wrote. "But if it does mean war, it is the inevitable war which would come if we let the Nazi masters of France establish air bases a few hours by air from our Panama Canal."

To those people who charged that the President was a scheming, malevolent, and ambitious dictator who wanted to drag the United States into war, White declared: "It is wickedly unfair to say that he is conniving and intriguing to be the great war leader . . . he will not gain greatly in fame when war comes to this hemisphere. . . . Ahead of him, no matter which turn he takes, calamity immeasurable rises across his path. Is it any wonder he hesitates? Is it any wonder that he seems baffled and bewildered?" White, furthermore, observed on the second anniversary of the outbreak of the war that after every move the President had made in the past two years, the isolationists had croaked that he was leading us to war. Yet he had been able to keep us out so far. Had Roosevelt listened to the isolationists, we would be in the war at the moment and with no allies to assist us. "I think if we ever had an American statesman who has been firm and foresighted in his conduct of the foreign policy to keep us out of war," White told Clark Eichelberger on July 29, 1941, "Roosevelt has been the man and that statesman."

*   *   *

The course of the war was decisively altered on June 22, 1941, when Germany suddenly attacked Russia. Acting Secretary of State Sumner Welles immediately declared: "Any defense against Hitlerism, any rallying of the forces opposing Hitlerism, from whatever source these forces may spring, will hasten the eventual downfall of the present German leaders and will therefore redound to the benefit of our own defense and security." Isolationist senators like Taft and Wheeler, however, led the fight to exclude Russia from lend-lease aid. These isolationists completely misjudged the attitude of the public. Although the people disliked the Soviet system, they knew that a German defeat of Russia would increase the Nazi threat to America.

On June 23, 1941, White pointed out that the course Germany followed in attacking Russia, when the time seemed to be propitious for Germany, was just the course Germany would follow with the United States. Although he made it clear that he did not like the Soviet system and had opposed the Finnish war, he observed that it did make a difference which nation won. He was not too ardent toward Russia, however. He charged that both Stalin and Hitler were "conspicuous international liars." "Both have betrayed and murdered their best friends. Both are tyrants, ruthless of human life, utterly impervious to the claims of dignity for the human spirit. So both hate democracy with a craven hate."

Yet White did realize that the German-Russian conflict afforded the United States more time to prepare for this inevitable war. The United States should therefore send lend-lease aid to Russia. His distrust of Russia continued in spite of this attitude. The world would never be safe until Hitler was defeated, he wrote an old Kansas isolationist friend, "and, if you ask me, this world won't be safe even then . . . unless Joe Stalin is shoved back in his corner."

During the summer of 1941, while the future of the world was being decided on the plains of Russia, in the air over Britain, and on the Atlantic Ocean, White was depressed at the lack of alertness on the part of the American public. Two-fifths of the people were more interested in the baseball scores than in the foreign news. One-fifth of the public was pro-German for ethnic reasons or as partisan Republicans and "Roosevelt-baiters" or for family reasons, because they had relatives of war age. Only the remaining two-fifths understood the meaning of the war. "Roosevelt could not take this country into war today if he tried to do so by proclamation," White explained to Julian Street on August 30. "We must be attacked before we will fight. And what you and I regard as attack—the menace of the totalitarian power—does not get into the noodles of the great plain people."

The Republican members of Congress, White felt, were greatly responsible for the sluggish nature of public opinion. The Republicans that July had overwhelming voted against the continuance of the Selective Service Act in the gravest crisis the nation had faced since the Civil War. White wrote a letter to Wendell Willkie on August 16 suggesting a general movement among Republicans to protest the "copperhead record" the party was making. "We just can't let Landon and Hoover and Taft and Lindbergh carry the Republican banner without a fight for it," he told Willkie. Three weeks before, on July 21, White had written an editorial addressed to the Kansas Republican congressmen. In this editorial he warned them to stop playing a partisan Republican game with national security. "You have gone as far as you can on the Quisling route " he told them.

* * *

On September 11, 1941, America First spokesman Charles A. Lindbergh asserted: "The three most important groups which have been pressing this country toward war are the British, the Jewish, and the Roosevelt Administration." "Shame on you, Charles Lindbergh, for injecting the Nazi race issue into American politics," White editorialized. "You can pillory the Jews if you will, or the Methodists or the Catholics if you dare, but alas in defending your inalienable right to speak your mind the Gazette cannot hold its silence at the moral treason of your words—at your unkind, unneighborly, dishonest words."

All that fall White continued to tell his subscribers and his correspondents that Roosevelt was not a warmonger; that if his policy had not been followed, we would have been in the war sooner. In October, he began to warn his readers of the danger of an attack by Japan. If Germany succeeded in defeating Russia, the United States and Britain would have to concentrate their strength to meet a triumphant Hitler. Japan would then be free to establish her "New Order" all over the Far East.

During October, while Japan was making threatening gestures in the Far East, a number of American ships were sunk in the Atlantic. President Roosevelt told the country that the Neutrality Act should be revised to permit the arming of American merchant ships. He also pointed out that lend-lease material was being sunk by German submarines. For the protection of American security, the provision of the Neutrality Act that banned American ships from belligerent ports should be repealed.

White supported the President's request for neutrality revision, as did Wendell Willkie. On November 11, White warned House Republicans that Japan would consider a close vote an indication that the United States was badly divided. "A big affirmative vote on modifying the neutrality law will give Japan notice that the United States is a united country, that the Congress will support the President in his policy toward Japan," White predicted. "And it's Japan that will start this war, not Germany!"

The isolationists in and out of Congress, however, with no comprehension of the inevitable conflict that was approaching, opposed the President and talked as though the United States had a choice between peace or war. The revision of the Neutrality Act passed the House on November 13, by the narrow margin of 212 to 194. "Here we are as Republicans in Congress," declared White on November 28 after only 22 Republicans had voted for the bill, "following a national leadership that is provincially partisan and has even skated close to the thin ice of treason to our flag and our government in its times of stress and peril."

Less than a month after this vote, the United States was attacked at Pearl Harbor by the Japanese. In the debate that raged after Pearl Harbor, the old isolationists, or nationalists, accused President Roosevelt of being responsible for the American defeat at Pearl Harbor. These were the same forces that had denounced him before Pearl Harbor as being a warmonger for every warning he had issued and for every step that he had taken to prepare America for the war. The Chicago *Tribune*—the most vocal organ of isolationism and excessive nationalism—in its bitter charges against

Roosevelt, conveniently overlooked one of its own editorials written on October 27, 1941. The President had just issued a warning against the Japanese danger in the Pacific. The *Tribune*, as an authority on national security, asked: "What vital interest of the United States can Japan threaten? She cannot attack us. That is a military impossibility. Even our base at Hawaii is beyond the effective striking power of her fleet."

Even before 1939, Roosevelt had warned the country of the impending danger of war. Many citizens just did not wish to face reality. William Allen White observed, nine days after Pearl Harbor, that a court-martial of the general and the admiral in charge at Pearl Harbor would be a mockery. The American people and Congress were basically to blame for the disaster.

On the day following Pearl Harbor, while Americans were still reeling from the shock of the Japanese attack, White dictated a long editorial assessing the situation and analyzing those responsible for it:

The Japanese sudden, violent, treacherous and unprovoked attack proved that the President's foreign policy was right. Japan has justified those who have supported this policy. . . . The Sunday attack of Japan was exactly like the attack of Hitler on Poland, Norway, Holland, Denmark and Belgium. . . . The mind of the aggressor flouts the decencies and amenities of international life whether the aggressor be one dictator or another . . . Thus it was obvious that sooner or later the United States would have to fight that spirit in the world. So when Japan attacked the United States, Japan proved to the various Quislings in this country, to the earnest, honest pacifists and to those tender souls who thought they could appease Germany by denying that she menaced us or by ignoring our danger, how deeply, deadly wrong they had been. They kept calling warmonger to those who were frantically trying to keep us out of war by helping the other democracies in their struggle and by aiding anyone who would fight Hitler and wear him down. . . .

The United States has entered the World War and will not sue for peace or listen to appeals for peace until the tyrants are overthrown and until aggression has been made so expensive that what Mussolini did to Abyssinia, to Albania, to Greece, what Germany did to Poland, to Norway, to Denmark, to Holland, to Belgium, to Central Europe, and what Tojo did Sunday to Hawaii and Manila will never be repeated on this earth again. This is the new order which America must set up and police for a hundred years if peace shall come to men of good will.

It was inevitable sooner or later that war should come. No plan could guarantee peace . . . The dictators, not we, have led us into this war. They have brought war to us because they thought the United States was divided. . . . The recent Congressional votes of Congressmen who registered disapproval of arming our ships, leaders who would tear down our national guard army in the face of the enemy, gave Japan the idea that this country was divided. Under that delusion Japan dared to strike. Those who cast those appeasing Quisling votes are more directly responsible for this war today than any other one force in American politics. We are at war now instead of later because the Republican leadership in Congress fooled the Japanese into thinking they could attack a divided country. The shame of that vote now is obvious to all.

CHAPTER 24

A FIRST-CLASS FUNERAL

"WAR has been in the air for twenty years," William Allen White explained to his readers on February 17, 1942. "The maladjustments of national economic advantages, the lust to dominate, the insanity of race superiority, the poison of supernationalism in the German people and the Japanese, would have made war inevitable even though we had tried appeasement and had let Great Britain fall and China go down." It was clear to the Emporia editor that the steps he had helped persuade America to adopt before Pearl Harbor had had little or nothing to do with American involvement in the war. The Japanese attack had revealed, he believed, that the United States was the ultimate objective of the Axis nations.

During the first months after Pearl Harbor, as Japan conquered island after island and reached closer and closer to Australia and India, White pointed out that the American defeats could be explained in terms of America's reluctance to prepare for the war. The public had been peace-loving; nothing that the President could say had been able to arouse them to the Axis menace. No American, declared the Emporia editor, could fail to respect President Roosevelt's heroic qualities, his demonstrated ability to lead the nation through the crisis of war, and his statesmanlike vision on the world situation ever since he had taken office. When isolationist Senator Taft, in March, 1942, criticized the government's failure to be ready for war, White remarked that one look at Taft's voting record was ample indication where the responsibility for unpreparedness actually belonged.

For the good of mankind, White declared early in 1942, the Allied powers should unite in a world organization and be ready to police the world after the defeat of the Axis. To win the war each nation, he asserted, had to sacrifice its own immediate interest for the common good. When some of the old isolationist forces criticized the administration for shipping troops and equipment to England rather than fighting only the Japanese war, White pointed out that the war was indivisible. "When you hear a voice in this country complaining, whining, protesting that we should look to out interests first, then and there spot a Quisling, conscious or unconscious," White editorialized, "a traitor to the world-wide democratic cause. If the Quislings win, freedom falling pays the price of their narrow viewpoint."

Just before the annual Associated Press meeting in the spring of 1942, Will T. Beck, editor of the Holton [Kansas] *Recorder* and brother of a Chicago *Tribune* editor, wrote to ask White to vote against the application of the Chicago *Sun*, the *Tribune*'s newly launched rival, for an Associated Press franchise. White's answer was forthright. "I would do most anything that you or Ned would ask, but for Colonel McCormick—No," he told Beck. "I think the Chicago *Tribune* is potentially the most dangerous newspaper in the United States. . . . I happen to have no use for the rich man who, like Marshall Field, because he has money, thinks he can start a newspaper. Neither do I want to appear to stand for the Chicago monopoly of Colonel McCormick who before this war is over will either be in jail or wreck the country." On June 29, White warned his readers that when peace came the United States would have to look out for men like Charles A. Lindbergh, Joseph M. Patterson, Merwin K. Hart, and Robert R. McCormick. These individuals, White charged, had no love for democracy.

In spite of the outpourings of the discontented elements, by the spring of 1942, White was convinced that the bulk of the citizens of his home town were war-conscious. Even though they had been lethargic up to December 7, 1941, now they were ready to accept higher taxes, restrictions on luxuries, and even the loss of their sons. "But the thing that puzzles me is this," he wrote in the *New Republic* for April 13, 1942: "with all our literacy, with all our college graduates, shall we be able to see the fundamental causes that make for wars? Shall we be able to understand that only as the United States takes leadership in some kind of a world association, union, alliance or treaty-making organization to promote economic justice on a world scale will we be able to reduce the likelihood of war? I repeat, will Emporia see it? Will the Middle West see it? For Emporia is just another name for the Middle West."

* * *

In the early summer of 1942 the Whites went to the Mayo clinic for a checkup. White's health was beginning to fail, and his doctor tried to persuade him to lighten the load he was carrying. Actually, by that time, the *Gazette* had lost some of the ablest members of its staff, and White was having to devote more time to the paper's affairs than was customary.

One eager desire was uppermost in his mind during these last years of his life. He was writing his autobiography, and he wanted to complete it. Yet he was so much a part of his world that he could not shut himself away and devote full time to this task. His schedule while he was in Emporia was to arise early, and every morning at half past seven dictate his autobiography for an hour and a half before going to the *Gazette* office to answer his letters and supervise newspaper matters. After lunch and a short nap, he would dictate his editorials for the next day's paper and stop work about half past five.

Even though he was none too well and though he wanted to complete his autobiography, he could not keep out of local and state politics. For a lifetime he had been carrying on the career of newspaperman, literary figure, and politician; in his seventy-fourth year he could not change. "Just now I am helping to nominate a governor," he wrote his old friend Edna Ferber on July 21, 1942, "and am busier than a man falling out of a balloon without a parachute. But it would be pretty terrible not to be a part of things. . . . I am state chairman of the War Bond drive and one of the national directors of the Red Cross and what with one thing and another, manage to keep the moss off the north side and the mildew off my brain and the cobwebs out of my eyes."

The gubernatorial campaign of 1942 was to be the last major political undertaking for the Emporia editor. At seventy-four he displayed a remarkable vitality in politics. The Kansas Republican party, White decided early in 1942, needed a house cleaning. There were too many "doddering old septuagenarians" who were holding third, fourth, fifth, and seventh terms. If he were a young man, he told Jack Harris of the Hutchinson *News*, he would launch a rebellion to clean out the State House.

White's own contribution to the rebellion was to support the gubernatorial candidacy of Andrew Schoeppel, a veteran of World War I, instead of the candidacy of Lieutenant Governor Carl Friend, who was in his seventies. Schoeppel had been unknown to White until Henry J. Allen had called him to White's attention in February, 1942. White decided to support Schoeppel in April after Schoeppel told White that he would maintain the merit system, safeguard the primary law, and stand by the income tax.

The primary attracted considerable attention when Senator Clyde Reed also decided to run for governor. He made his campaign on the issue of curbing heavy union initiation fees for workers in war industries. White refused to support his old ally. White told Reed on July 17 that, although labor racketeering was a grave evil, it was a federal and not a state problem. Reed could fight it more successfully in Washington as senator than in Topeka as governor. "The whole plan and scheme of Senator Reed to kill the blackmailing labor racketeers with a pop-gun emplaced on the golden dome of the State House would seem to give Clyde a chance not for statesmanship but for a halo along beside Simple Simon who tried to catch a whale in his mother's pail," White editorialized on July 30. "If Clyde wants the whale, and it's a desirable whale all right, why doesn't he go back to the United States Senate with the harpoon that Kansas has put in his hand, and tackle the whale where it lives?"

Reed, White felt, was running for governor with more than the labor issue in mind. He was running to humiliate Alf Landon. Schoeppel was looked upon as Landon's candidate, and Reed hoped

561

to break Landon's political power in Kansas. White denied that Schoeppel was controlled by Landon. Schoeppel's candidacy, according to White, had been backed by the Willkie supporters weeks before Landon decided to support him. "Alf may be as bad as you think he is, even that is debatable," White wrote one friend, "but he isn't half as smart as you think he is and that's the God's truth."

Although White might deny that Landon was controlling Schoeppel, it was rather significant that White carried on his campaign efforts for Schoeppel independent of the state headquarters at Topeka. In addition to writing editorials, which the Kansas City *Star* frequently reprinted, White raised money for page advertisements which he inserted in forty daily and forty-five weekly papers in Kansas. After Schoeppel's primary victory, White campaigned for the straight Republican ticket. His ancient ally, Arthur Capper, was running for re-election. In spite of Capper's isolationist record, White supported him. The editorial that White wrote for Capper was read into the *Congressional Record* and reprinted by the senator as his major piece of campaign literature. "Arthur Capper is more than a senator," declared White. "He is an influence. He is a sort of incarnate institutionalized voice of the farm and the small town. . . . In his way Arthur Capper is the peer of any leader this State ever has known."

Kansans began at once to point out to White that he had recently objected to seventy-year-olds in the Kansas State House. Capper was seventy-seven, and here White was supplying the chief ammunition for Capper's re-election! White denied that he was inconsistent. Capper was in a legislative office, and long terms were desirable there, White asserted, whereas long terms in administrative offices were undesirable. Best comment on the affair came from Rolla Clymer, who knew his old boss very thoroughly: "If Mr. White had hewed to his line, he would have put Capper into the state house category with the 'old boys.' He didn't. . . . It's only Mr. White's way—and what a way! He's in a class by himself and Kansas wouldn't change him one whit for all the dreams of empire."

Although Capper was renominated, White failed to carry Lyon County for him. The *Gazette's* advertising manager, C. C. Alexander, ran the county campaign for Capper's opponent and thus helped in the defeat of his boss's candidate by two hundred votes.

White supported not only Capper and Schoeppel that fall, but all the Kansas Republican congressmen who were running for re-election. He had denounced these men a year before for their iso-lationist record, but when campaign time arrived White was back in the family fold. "If I, being as I am a leader in our Progressive group in this State, had bolted . . . I would have started a row that would have defeated my candidate for Governor," White declared. "Also I would have ended my leadership which would not make much difference except that it would have busted the Kansas merit system by busting me, and it would in effect repeal the income tax law for which I am standing by discrediting me, and it would have killed me for any other further use and activity along lines on public policy, in Kansas, and for what? For nothing! The calves' eyes are set. . . . There is a drift against the President. The drift could not have been stopped in Kansas. All I would have done would be to commit hara-kiri for nothing . . . You must remember as your tears splash upon the pavement that poli-tics is always the choice between evils. I think I have chosen the lesser."

The editorials and letters that White devoted to the political situation in 1942 revealed, so far as Kansas politics were concerned, that he was just one more Kansas machine politician; those which he wrote on the national situation demonstrated his clarity and vision as an interpreter of American life. The two groups of writ-ings seem almost to have been written by two different human beings, except that for many years White had been this peculiar blend of interpreter and philosopher and provincial Kansas busi-nessman and politician.

While he was acting as an interpreter of American life, the Emporia editor had asserted on February 12, 1942: "If only the Republican party that gave us Lincoln would forget its hatred of Roosevelt, get rid of its bias toward plutocracy, get back to the grass roots and the hearts of the people . . ." and he had confided to his old friend Josephus Daniels that he feared "that the Repub-lican leadership outside of Willkie and Jim Wadsworth and per-haps Tom Dewey—(they come with say fifteen to forty per cent discount for cash)—are all sitting around waiting for some reverse in the American armed forces to break out with an isolationist itch and begin yelling, 'Why are we fighting England's battles?' . . . They are forever clamoring about patriotic unity and then ending with a note beginning 'but.' It is but, but! Revealing, it seems to me, a very small, mean mind. In fact I am forced to the conclusion their 'butts are bigger than their brains.' "

White thoroughly enjoyed Wendell Willkie's courageous defiance of Old Guard Republicans like Hamilton Fish, Joseph Martin, and Robert Taft. In his attacks on reactionary Republicans, Willkie was just like Theodore Roosevelt, White stated. While the Republican party was following the blind and stupid leadership of the Old Guard, White observed that the President was making a great record as a war leader. He was unconsciously making himself inevitable for a fourth term. To elect him again, however, would put an unbearable burden on nerves and blood. Yet, White added, to reject him might involve great dangers. The great hope of the world rested on Franklin D. Roosevelt.

During the 1942 campaign White called for the defeat—outside of Kansas—of isolationists of the Hamilton Fish type since their election would be a menace to the nation. White was extremely depressed when the primaries revealed that Fish had won in New York and that Pappy O'Daniel had won in Texas. The Fish election could be explained, he decided, in terms of a greedy plutocratic reaction, and the O'Daniel triumph in terms of the moron minds of the ignorant and underprivileged Texans who fell for the demagoguery of O'Daniel. "Perhaps this world war and another and another will be required to get the truth to Dutchess County and rural Texas," he wrote in a despairing tone.

As election day approached, White urged Nebraska to re-elect their great senator, George Norris. On election day, however, Nebraska turned its back on this famous leader. In various other parts of the nation isolationists were sent back to Congress. "On the whole it was an 'anti' vote, not a 'pro' vote," White explained, "and because public opinion before Pearl Harbor was not ready for war, millions of voters were not willing to punish members of Congress for voting as the voters themselves would have voted in 1939, in 1940 and in most of 1941. . . . The fact that the Congress is fairly well filled with last-ditch isolationists can't be helped. We had to go into the war with a rush before public opinion was soundly formed. And we will pay the price, I fear, when it comes to the peace. I shouldn't wonder if it would need another war and maybe another to get the kind of peace that will work."

Although the Emporia editor deplored the return of many isolationists to Congress, in Kansas he helped immeasurably to elect Senator Capper and the entire Congressional delegation. As far as the Kansas Republicans were concerned, White was willing to waive their isolationist record as irrelevant. In the heat of the campaign, he completely dismissed their record on foreign policy and advocated their re-election to "show the Democrats that this country is overwhelmingly two-party minded, anti-New Deal, anti-third term, anti-war fumbling, anti-boondoggling." The Emporia editor, once more in the familiar pattern, frankly justified his support of the straight Republican ticket on the basis that party regularity gave him power in Kansas affairs.

Yet nationally White was aware that an isolationist vote was not irrelevant but terribly relevant to the question of peace. After the elections had returned so many isolationists to Congress, White told Paul Hutchinson of the *Christian Century* on November 17, 1942: "I am scared to death that after the war the country will go isolationist, possibly over the settlement of the peace with Russia. For Russia will have to be taken into the council—God or no God. And it will be so easy to pound the drum and gather a crowd and march out on any peace treaty that puts any responsibility upon this country—economic or political—to guarantee the peace of the world or try to keep that peace."

* * *

Although William Allen White did support the straight Republican ticket in Kansas in November, 1942, he quickly reassumed the role of interpreter of American life as soon as the election had passed. When, for instance, President Roosevelt returned home early in 1943 from the Casablanca Conference with Winston Churchill, the Emporia editor dictated an editorial replete with pungent phrases, wit, and humor:

Well, it is now 60 hours since the Old Smiler returned to the White House from his great adventure. He saw more of an amazing world than Marco Polo. He saw in North Africa alone as much conquered land as Alexander saw when he wept for new worlds to conquer. He performed a feat so strange even in modern war, so amazing and unbelievable, that if it had been prophesied 50 years ago men would have stoned the prophets for impiety!

Biting nails—good hard, bitter, Republican nails—we are compelled to admit that Franklin Roosevelt is the most unaccountable and on the whole the most enemy-baffling president that this United States has ever seen. He has added a certain vast impudent courage to a vivid but constructive imagination and he has displayed his capacity for statesmanship in the large and simple billboard language that the common people can understand; moreover, that the people admire even when it is their deadly poison. We have got to hand it to him.

Well, darn your smiling old picture, here it is! Here, reluctantly amid seething and snorting, it is. We, who hate your gaudy guts, salute you.

This editorial inspired the President to wire White on his seventy-fifth birthday celebration, on February 10, 1943: "Congratulations on reaching the three-quarter mark. I hope that during the next twenty-five years you will be with me all the time instead of only three and one-half years out of every four. I think that in a quarter of a century the firm of White and Roosevelt might be able to bring the Four Freedoms at least to this nation of ours."

At 8:30 A.M. on his birthday White strolled into the *Gazette* office with a cherubic expression on his round, apple face. As he entered the door, the *Gazette* staff lined up to greet him, and at 9:30 the Junior Chamber of Commerce called to pay its respects. At the Rotary Club luncheon that noon he was presented with seventy-five American beauty roses. All day long, letters and telegrams of congratulation poured in the *Gazette* office. That afternoon as he dictated his birthday editorial, for just about the first time in his busy writing career, he was at a loss for words. After describing the events of the day, he groped for words and wrote: "It has been a gay 75 years."

"Americans wished the U.S. had more editors like him," remarked *Time*. And Oscar Stauffer's Topeka *State Journal* declared: "Today William Allen White, of Emporia, is 75 years young; a week ago Friday Kansas was 82. How does it happen that they are not the same age for Kansas is William Allen White and Mr. White is Kansas. . . . Somehow when we think of William Allen White, we see him sitting in the Gazette office at Emporia, distilling a philosophy of common sense and sound living."

*   *   *

After his birthday supper, White took a train East to spend a week in Washington and New York. He marveled at Washington, now the commercial, political, and spiritual capital of the world. "It is hardly the time to carp about a global economy," he declared. "We must either lead it, direct it and be the guiding star, or some other nation will take the job. For a global economy is necessary—either under our leadership or Joe Stalin's."

With the other members of the American Society of Newspaper Editors, he attended a Roosevelt press conference at the White House. "He talked for twenty minutes, glowing with gracious vitality," White reported of Roosevelt. "He seemed to be gay, sure of himself, a bit festive at times, informative, indeed illuminating and he seemed full of 'wim, wit, and wigor'! I was astonished, perhaps amazed is a better word, at the abounding vigor of the man after 10 years in the White House."

This Washington visit convinced White that those Republicans who charged that the New Deal was using the war to put through social reforms did not know what they were talking about. Representatives of the great steel, iron, coal, copper, automobile, and railroad combines, not New Dealers, were running the war effort. These industrial leaders were doing a superb job of production. "They have great talents," White observed. "If you touch them in nine relations of life out of ten, they are kindly, courteous Christian gentlemen. But in the tenth relation, where it touches their own organization, they are stark mad, ruthless, unchecked by God or man. . . . These international combinations of industrial capital are fierce troglodyte animals with tremendous power and no social brains."

The average citizen, White reflected, not only had to face the menace of the Axis, but had to check the greed of the domestic monopolies. It would be a tragedy if, after the war, American society should allow this group to regain the political power it had had in the days of Harding and Coolidge! If America went back to the spirit of the 1920's, back to Republican normalcy, "God help the world!" White wrote in a caustic editorial on April 10, 1943.

His visit to New York City actually frightened him. He discovered that the Old Guard leadership of his party could do nothing but deliver bitter, raucous diatribes against the President. "Which is all right. Everyone knows the New Deal is not heaven sent . . ." White remarked. "But the trouble with the Republican leaders in Congress and such as I found in the more violent wards of the New York bedlam is that . . . they are 'agin' everything and 'for' nothing." Instead of leading the fight against major mistakes of the President, all the Republican leadership concerned itself with was stirring demagogic emotions about such unimportant issues as Communists employed in government offices. "The country," declared the Emporia editor, "faces this real danger: that in rallying the boys in the pool hall, those cheap morons who are easily excited by specious issues, the Republican party may be the center of a Fascist movement. The Republicans will go forward, howling 'Down with the Nazi New Deal'; and prove themselves to be Fascist to the core and reactionary at heart . . . It's all cheap! Cheap! Cheap!!! . . . Beware of the Republican who has no argument except hatred and denunciation of the White House."

As White looked forward to the Republican campaign in 1944, he was convinced that Wendell Willkie was the only Republican who could be elected. Yet he knew that the Republican National Committee was trying to destroy Willkie. Mentions of General MacArthur's name as a potential standard-bearer he deplored. Remember the miserable administration of General Grant, White warned. When the reactionaries and isolationists began to rally around the candidacy of Governor John Bricker of Ohio, White began to sizzle. On March 17 he boiled over in an editorial that was filled with pungent phrases and fighting language. It was just about the last editorial White would write in his vigorous editorial style, and the Emporia "word-works" were full that March day. "The same forces in the Republican party that gathered about

Taft in 1912 and nominated Harding in a smoke-filled room in 1920—namely the Republican National Committee, a group of hard-boiled politicians—seems determined to force the nomination of Bricker," declared White. "And who is Bricker? Alice Roosevelt is said to have defined him in five words: 'Bricker is an honest Harding.'" Bricker's failure to speak out on the international situation prompted White to declare: "A man who can stand in American politics, aspiring for high office without even the intelligence, without the courage or sheer honesty to make some declaration upon the most important issue ever faced by this old earth, certainly is not the kind of a man for the Republicans to rally around. Surely the Republican party cannot be so craven as to conspire to sneak into victory with no issue but Bricker and a bellyache. Bricker is an honest Harding—thumbs down."

"I am enclosing an editorial about Bricker which I wrote and which has raised hell clear across the continent," he wrote Wendell Willkie in a jovial mood on March 29, 1943. "I have a stack of letters as big as a hired girl's leg. I just had to take a sock at that bird and hope this will find you the same." When a fellow Rotarian protested to White that Bricker was a good Rotarian and quite different from White's description, the Emporia editor replied: "His statement to the New York Times about our foreign policy after the war was a perfect masterpiece of blah. It just didn't mean anything and could be interpreted both ways. It was exactly the sort of statement that Harding issued twenty-four years ago on the same issue when he was in Bricker's place. I have no doubt that he has made a good governor. I have no doubt that he is an honest man. But I do think that in the presidency he would be a menace to the peace of the world."

*   *   *

Early in April, 1943, the Whites visited New York City for the monthly meeting of the Book-of-the-Month Club judges. While there they were both stricken with influenza. "We go hand in hand, Mr. White and I, even in influenza," Mrs. White told reporters. The editor's influenza deepened into double pneumonia. He had not recovered sufficiently to leave the hospital to celebrate their golden wedding anniversary on April 27. They had planned to repeat their honeymoon by traveling first to Santa Fe, New Mexico, and then to Estes Park, Colorado. Instead they spent the day in the hospital, where mail from all over the nation swamped their room.

On May 5, they were back in Emporia but had to remain at home for their convalescence. Only occasionally during the next few weeks did White write any editorials. He was not in the mood. He no longer jested and joked about the house. He was slipping physically, and he knew it. He did, however, have the energy to write a few letters to influential Republicans. What he wanted, he carefully explained, was to have the party take an unequivocal stand for international co-operation. He closed a long letter on this subject to Mr. and Mrs. Roger Straus, by noting: "This started out to be a note of gratitude. And here it is, an old man babbling about those years when he will be merely a ripple under the daisies."

Late in June the Whites left for Colorado to recuperate at their cabin in Moraine Park. Day after day they sat on the porch of their cabin and watched Longs Peak as it towered 5,255 feet about them. "I've got lead in my pants and I love to sit down and look nature squarely in the face without batting an eye," White told a reporter. "These mountains you see are always different—they are moody; they always tell a different story, and you can watch them by the hour and learn—it's good for you."

Political matters from time to time continued to occupy the editor's attention. Letters of advice went to Wendell Willkie and Governor Thomas E. Dewey. White made it clear that he wanted the rank-and-file Republicans to be told that after the war the United States had to put the world back on its feet. It was not being utopian, he insisted, to advocate that American energies, American production, and American credit help rehabilitate the world.

President Roosevelt, White felt, was no longer offering the nation vigorous leadership. "F.D.R. is, if you ask me—which you don't—an old bull who is losing his cud," White wrote George Fort Milton on August 12, 1943. "He is not the man that he was in 1936 and the job has multiplied by ten. I don't fear that he will lead us into Fascism. What I fear is that he cannot lead us all.

I feel that his political impotence is the great danger that we face as a nation, because there is no other leader in sight with the tremendous world prestige which Roosevelt enjoys, who once could have guided us into and through the turmoil that lies ahead of us after the surrender." Either Willkie or Dewey, or in fact anyone but Bricker, White was confident, could defeat Roosevelt in 1944.

Early that September, when Thomas E. Dewey advocated an Anglo-American military alliance, the Emporia editor praised the New York governor's courage and common sense. White had been thinking for some time that an Anglo-American understanding had to be the core of whatever peace was established. Russia and China, too, should be included in the agreement, but the basis had to be an understanding between the two English-speaking nations. Concerning the question of whether Russia and the United States could live at peace in one world, White declared: "It is possible for two ideals, the ideals of Washington and Jefferson on the one hand and the ideals of Lenin and Stalin on the other, to live on this globe if they both aim to secure justice among men and establish a fair, honorable and self-respecting life for humanity."

After Dewey's support of an Anglo-American alliance, White asked a friend for a copy of Colonel McCormick's Chicago *Tribune* editorial on the Dewey statement. "I'll bet he turned flip-flops," remarked White. "The old Colonel ought to read the answer in the stars. The world is moving toward understanding and a deep realization that unless we create some sort of a world tribunal to keep the peace, the boys in the pool hall are going to take the show and run the earth." After reading the *Tribune*'s bitter attack on Dewey, accusing the governor of being "Anti-American" and of having been taken in by Wall Street and No. 10 Downing Street, White observed with his old-time sense of humor: "I have to go to New York two or three times a year and I pass through Chicago, and the old Colonel's editorials are always a source of joy. How he can do it without throwing Chicago into convulsions of laughter, I don't know."

Early in October, 1943, White wrote his last two dispatches for the North American Newspaper Alliance. They were also the last utterances on politics and on world affairs by this small-town interpreter who had made such a deep impression on American life.

Even in these final newspaper stories, White expressed his thoughts in his characteristic, colorful language. Although the Republican platform in 1944 would contain "chloroforming phrases stressing 'constitutional methods' and 'no loss of sovereignty' to appease the isolationists," White predicted that it would be a platform advocating world collaboration. He also asserted that the candidate would be either Willkie or Dewey. Just in case the Republicans wanted to re-elect President Roosevelt, all they had to do, White advised, was to nominate an isolationist. White's words of advice to the Republican party, advice which he had been dispensing in prolific but seldom accepted amounts for the past few decades, prompted the San Francisco *Chronicle* to remark, after his death: "The Republican party at a critical time loses the benefit of White's liberal influence and sound practical sense."

* * *

Late in October, when the Emporia editor underwent an operation at the Mayo clinic, it was discovered that he had a cancer which would probably cause his death in the next four months. Although the news of the operation, as befitted a lifetime policy, rated only a brief mention on page two of the *Gazette*, it attracted major attention in most American newspapers. An amazing number of letters and telegrams poured into Emporia and Rochester, Minnesota, expressing hope for the quick recovery of America's most famous editor. Perhaps the most touching note came from Kansas Democratic leader W. H. Burke. "Kansas Republicans need you to maintain a semblance of respectability and Kansas Democrats have long needed a hell raiser of your kind," Burke wrote. "Take care of yourself, come home and start life over."

Before White underwent the operation, he told his son Bill that if he failed to recover, there were several projects he wished Bill would carry out for him. He wanted Governor Schoeppel to pardon Ronald Finney, now having spent almost fifteen years of imprisonment for the Kansas bond scandal. White also hoped that his unfinished autobiography would be published. Before his father died in January, 1944, Bill had persuaded the governor to grant the parole to Finney. The autobiography, which Bill edited for publication, was released two years after his father's death.

A month after the operation, Mrs. White brought her husband back to their comfortable home at 927 Exchange Street. During December, 1943, the editor was able to visit the *Gazette* only once or twice. At Christmastime, since he was not well enough to greet the employees at the office, they came in groups of two or three to pay their respects to the "boss."

In the weeks just before his death, the *Gazette* carried no mention of the famed editor's serious condition. Meanwhile, Bill moved into his father's office and began to write the editorials and to supervise business affairs. Soon, for the first time since June 3, 1895, the phrase "W. A. White—editor" would have to be removed from the masthead of the paper.

Two weeks before his death William Allen White displayed a flash of the old White who had achieved fame for his sparkling sense of humor. As Bertha Colglazier, the Whites' cook, chauffeur, housekeeper, and person extraordinary, came into the room where he was lying, he asked, "Bertha, do you think I will ever get well enough to accomplish anything again?" Bertha lied that of course he would. The editor's blue eyes began to sparkle, and he replied, "Bertha, you'll suffer in purgatory for that." Only once did he show that he knew he was soon to die. One day he said to Dr. Frank Foncannon, with tears brimming in his eyes, "I would like to have just two more years to finish my autobiography."

On the morning of January 29, 1944—Kansas Day—the Emporia editor died. The man who was the symbol of the greatness of small-town America succumbed to a heart attack twelve days before his seventy-sixth birthday.

"He lived out his span," wrote Henry Seidel Canby in the *Saturday Review of Literature*, "and there has been no better and no more rewarding life for friends and country than the career of this editor and man-of-letters and public voice of democracy, who has been for a generation the symbol of the great Middle West."

To the *Gazette* office and to the home came messages of condolence from all over the United States and from many other areas of the free world as well. President Roosevelt wired Mrs. White: "My heart goes out to you and Bill in the loss of a beloved husband and friend. The newspaper world loses one of its wisest and most beloved editors in the death of William Allen White. He made the Emporia Gazette a national institution. As a writer of terse, forcible and vigorous prose, he was unsurpassed. He ennobled the profession of journalism which he served with such unselfish devotion through more than two score years. To me his passing brings a real sense of personal loss for we had been the best of friends for years. Mrs. Roosevelt joins me in this assurance of deepest sympathy."

Eulogistic editorials appeared in paper after paper and Harold Laski wrote from London: "White seemed to me to be part of that America of which the supreme representatives were Jefferson and Lincoln; the America which is concerned first of all with the ordinary people and their lot in life; the America which is simple, kindly and proud to think that an humble man can there become a significant man . . . White was a noble representative of the average American at his best."

A *Life* magazine photographer, whom White had invited in 1941 to return someday to Emporia and attend a "first-class" funeral, took pictures of the funeral procession and the Book-of-the-Month Club quickly issued a memorial pamphlet to their editor-judge. Shortly after White's death, B'nai B'rith, a Jewish men's organization, created the William Allen White Inter-Faith fellowship at the University of Kansas in memory of White's lifetime crusade against bigotry and intolerance. In April, 1944, the American Society of Newspaper Editors gave a medal to Bill White in honor of his father's distinguished contribution to their profession —the first time such an award had ever been made by the society to one of its own members. Several months later the Pulitzer Prize Board, on which White had served for seven years, sent Mrs. White a special scroll bearing a gold metallic reproduction of the Pulitzer public service medal in posthumous tribute to the Emporia editor—the first time in the history of the Pulitzer Prize Committee that such an honor had been awarded.

Citizens of the state which White had done so much to glorify organized two foundations to memorialize the life and service of their most famous editor. The William Allen White Foundation, with Henry J. Allen as chairman, was established to raise funds in a nation-wide campaign to endow a William Allen White School of Journalism at the University of Kansas. "The purpose of our foundation," Allen declared, "is to enlarge his life into the history of Kansas. Some folks called him loose-minded. He changed his convictions. But he was always honest, strong and expressive. We want to keep alive the spirit of 'small' journalism which Will White personified—the weeklies and the small town dailies, the honest type of country journalism, colorful, friendly, humorous, just and imaginative."

The William Allen White Emporia Memorial Foundation was organized by White's home-town neighbors to establish a shrine in Emporia in memory of the late editor. Their plans were to have Jo Davidson make a bronze statue of White and erect with it a bronze tablet of the "Mary White" editorial in a suitable location. The local foundation planned also to establish a loan fund for needy students, maintain a memorial room at the Emporia State Teachers College library, and make a contribution to the William Allen White School of Journalism.

*　　*　　*

Amid grief and great pride, White's Kansas neighbors on January 31, 1944, buried the man who had kept them before the nation's eyes for fifty years. "America has lost a truly noble and useful citizen at a time when she has none such to spare," declared Harold L. Ickes, while the *Daily Oklahoman* remarked: "This western area without William Allen White is going to be different. . . . It was a large place in our American life that William Allen White had come to fill."

The Emporia editor's funeral was "first class," as he had predicted. Regardless of convention, Mrs. White conducted the funeral as her husband would have wanted it. His body lay on his own lounge in his spacious study where he had written so many of his books and articles. Mrs. White had Bertha Colglazier pass the word around town for his friends to come. And they did, both colored and white. On the day of the funeral out-of-town friends—Governor Schoeppel, Senator Capper, Henry J. Allen, Alf M. Landon, Victor Murdock, and many others—called at the home.

The funeral procession started from the White home, with all the out-of-town notables and all the *Gazette* employees following,

575

and moved to the chapel of the College of Emporia, where the *Gazette* carrier boys formed a guard of honor along the steps and raised their arms in salute as the coffin was carried into the chapel.

President Dan A. Hirschler played Tschaikovsky's "Symphonie Pathétique," William Allen White's favorite piece which he had selected to be played at the funeral of daughter Mary in 1921. The Reverend Stephen J. Williams, pastor of White's church, the First Congregational, recited the Twenty-third Psalm and closed with a prayer expressing thanks for a life that "has done so much to make life better for so many of us."

The spirit of Mary White was in the air. The red roses that her father had described in the editorial were there, and Henry J. Haskell discussed the editorial in his funeral talk. Haskell described William Allen White's accomplishments and read from some of his writings. He quoted some choice selections, and there was a ripple of laughter several times through the audience.

"This chapel seems empty without him," Haskell declared. "Yet, in a larger sense, it is not empty. It is crowded with memories that are more than memories, with achievements that live on in the lives of the generation that has been affected by him. When we met William Allen White in person or on the printed page, we came like Bunyan's Pilgrim to the interpreter's house. For he was a great interpreter of the human spectacle, be it comedy or tragedy. He was a great preacher of righteousness, of sane and wholesome living. But he preached through the medium of interpretation, by appealing to us through the hearts of men, our own hearts and of others."

A crowd of eighteen hundred persons attended the services at the grave in Maplewood Cemetery, where the editor's body was placed beside that of his daughter. "They buried him, near sundown, in Maplewood cemetery, while a tremendous silent crowd looked on and a Welch choir sang the Resurrection Hymn in their own language—as once they sang it at the grave of Mary," wrote a reporter for the Chicago *Sun*. ". . . In the cemetery, in the dying sun, under the dead trees, William Allen White was only a tired editor gone home to greet his little girl."

NOTES

The numerals at the left refer to pages and lines in this book. The bibliographical note that follows each page and line number explains the source of the quotation or of the reference which ends at that point in the text.

PART I: THE END OF THE FRONTIER ERA

Chapter 1

NATIVE AMERICAN

10:10 "How Kansas Boarded the Water Wagon," *Saturday Evening Post*, July 11, 1914, p. 5.

10:20 White to the writer, interview, Nov. 13, 1941; see "Long Marches and Hard Bivouacs," speech delivered at the University of Kansas, June 10, 1940; printed by the Emporia *Gazette*. "It's Been a Great Show," *Collier's*, Feb. 12, 1938.

10:37 Wichita *Eagle*, March 31, 1907.

11:7 All the source material quoted in this book is in the William Allen White files—most of which now are at the Library of Congress—unless otherwise specified.

11:17 White to M. Moll, June 21, 1934; to Mrs. W. R. Irwin, Aug. 5, 1936.

11:33 White to V. P. Mooney, April 5-Sept. 26, 1916, letter book; to Judge Branson, March 1, 1938; Jessie P. Stratford, *Butler County's Eighty Years* (El Dorado, 1935), p. 143; El Dorado *Times*, May 27, June 1, July 8, 1941.

12:3 Emporia *Gazette*, May 7, 1924.

12:16 White to V. P. Mooney, April 5-Sept. 26, 1916, letter book.

12:31 White, "Memoirs of a Three-Fingered Pianist," *Woman's Home Companion*, September, 1927, p. 12.

14:7 See "Address of the President," *Kansas Historical Quarterly*, VIII (1939), 77; "Fifty Years of Kansas," *World's Work*, VIII (June, 1904), 4872; "The Glory of the States, Kansas," *American Magazine*, January, 1916, p. 41.

14:15 C. D. Clark and R. L. Roberts, *People of Kansas* (Topeka: Kansas State Planning Board, 1936).

15:8 "Kansas, A Puritan Survival," *These United States*, ed. by Ernest Gruening (New York: Boni and Liveright, 1923), pp. 9-11. See Carl Becker, *Everyman His Own Historian* (New

York: F. S. Crofts & Co., 1935), p. 2.

15:21 See James C. Malin, John Brown and the *Legend of Fifty-Six* (Philadelphia: American Philosophical Society, 1942), pp. 504 ff.; Avery Craven, *The Coming of the Civil War* (New York: Charles Scribner's Sons, 1942).

16:18 Much of the material about Mary Hatton comes from Laura M. French's story in the Emporia *Gazette*, May, 7, 1924, and William Allen White's recollections in the same issue. See also *The Recorder*, Bulletin of American-Irish Historical Society (1934).

16:27 Emporia *Gazette*, May 7, 1924.

17:27 T. F. Doran, "Kansas Sixty Years Ago," *Kansas Historical Collections*, XV, 490.

18:6 Emporia *Gazette*, May 7, 1924.

18:34 White to P. H. Coney, July 22, 1924.

20:8 White to V. P. Mooney, April 5-Sept. 26, 1916, letter book.

21:3 White, "What Music Has Done for Me," *Etude*, LVI (December, 1938), 779-780; "Memoirs of a Three-Fingered Pianist," *op. cit.*, p. 84.

21:21 White, *Boys—Then and Now* (New York: The Macmillan Co., 1926), pp. 18-19.

22:1 See J. C. Malin, "An Introduction to the History of the Bluestem-Pasture Region of Kansas," *Kansas Historical Quarterly*, XI (February, 1942), 3-28.

22:10 *The Real Issue* (Chicago: Way and Williams, 1896), p. 22.

22:22 White, "Bill's School and Mine," *Journal of Education*, 75 (March 7, 1912), 257; J. M. Satterthwaite, reprinted in the Emporia *Gazette*, Feb. 26, 1943; White to Dale Messman, June

1, 1908; *Western Butler County Times*, Sept. 21, 28, Oct. 5, 12, 1944.

23:10 Wichita *Eagle*, March 31, 1907.

23:14 O. E. Olin, "Will White—Boy and Man," *Western Homes*, I (October, 1897), 12-14.

23:18 Anna Myers to White, April 27, 1940.

23:25 Topeka *Capital*, July 20, 1902, p. 11.

23:30 Victor Murdock to the writer, interview, Oct. 19, 1941.

24:20 White to Joe Emerson, July 19, 1935.

24:32 White to Eugene Bryan, Nov. 29, 1914.

25:4 *Boys—Then and Now*, p. 16.

25:25 White, "Memoirs of a Three-Fingered Pianist," *op. cit.*, p. 25.

26:5 Emporia *Gazette*, Feb. 22, 1943.

27:8 *Forty Years of It* (New York: D. Appleton & Co., 1914), p. 27.

30:20 O. E. Olin, "Will White—Boy and Man," *Western Homes*, I (October, 1897), 12-14.

30:24 White to the writer, interview, Feb. 28, 1941.

30:28 Wichita *Eagle*, March 31, 1907.

Chapter 2

COLLEGE DAYS IN KANSAS

32:14 This diary is in the possession of Mrs. Robert L. Jones of Emporia, Kansas, who kindly permitted the writer to quote from it.

33:4 White to W. T. Foster, Aug. 10, 1934.

33:10 See Gene A. Howe, "My Father Was the Most Wretchedly Unhappy Man I Ever Knew," *Saturday Evening Post*, Oct. 25, 1941.

33:17 *History of Kansas Newspapers*, ed. W. E. Connelley (Topeka, 1916), p. 120.

34:9 "Mr. White Interviews Himself," *Proceedings*, American Society of Newspaper Editors, 1929, p. 79.

34:19 *Ibid.*, p. 80.

35:2 White, "Newspapermen at Work," *New Republic*, Dec. 28, 1942, pp. 862-863.

35:8 In 1910, White lent Fulton money to stop a foreclosure on his weekly paper in Arkansas.

35:22 "William Allen White," *Kansas Newspaperdom*, April, 1894, p. 2.

35:37 "Mr. White Interviews Himself," *op. cit.*

36:21 Emporia *Gazette*, July 26, 1917.

36:32 White to A. J. Carruth, Jr., Sept. 11, 1935.

37:7 Speech delivered at a K.U. anniversary dinner, November, 1938. White MSS.

37:31 White to Gladys Williams, May 15, 1929.

38:5 These papers are preserved in the University of Kansas library.

38:17 *William Allen White In Memoriam*, written and published by the Book-of-the-Month Club, Inc., 1944.

38:27 *Sunflowers* (Lawrence: Journal Publishing Co., 1888).

39:11 John A. Rush to the writer, June 20, 1941.

39:13 T. F. Doran to White, Jan. 2, 1935.

39:15 Quoted in Helen Sutliff to White, July 28, 1937.

39:22 Speech delivered at a K.U. anniversary dinner, November, 1938. White MSS.

39:37 "Reminiscences of Kansas University," *Kansas Magazine*, April, 1909, pp. 12-15.

40:8 "Brigadier General Fred Funston," McClure Syndicate, Pittsburgh *Leader*, May 21, 1899.

40:33 White to Claudius O. Johnson, July 3, 1934.

41:10 Jan. 29, 1940.

41:35 White to G. O. Foster, July 14, 1934.

42:2 March 5, 1940.

42:11 White to Vernon Kellogg, Jr., Feb. 23, 1938.

42:23 White to Dale O'Brien, Feb. 12, 1937.

43:2 Cited in the Topeka *Capital*, Aug. 11, 1887.

43:22 Emporia *Gazette*, Nov. 5, 1909.

43:28 Morse to the writer, June 22, 1941.

44:8 "Two Recent Kansas Books," *University Review*, March, 1889. See also *University Review*, December, 1888; September, 1888; March, 1888.

44:23 Quoted in Frank C. Clough, *William Allen White of Emporia* (New York: Whittlesey House, 1941), pp. 56-57.

44:35 Lawrence *Journal*, Aug. 3, July 31, 1888.

45:22 White to Jack Harrison, Feb. 13, 1922.

45:28 Dorothy Leibengood, "Labor Problems in the Second Year of Governor Martin's Administration," *Kansas Historical Quarterly*, V (1936), 191 ff.

46:26 Letter in possession of Helen Sutliff, Stanford University.

Chapter 3

YOUNG CONSERVATIVE

48:29 Emporia *Gazette*, Nov. 5, 1909.

48:37 *Ibid.*

49:9 F. L. Pinet, "William Allen White—Kansan," *Kansas Magazine*, July, 1909, pp. 1-7.

49:14 Emporia *Gazette*, Jan. 8, 1930.

49:19 Murdock to the writer, interview, Oct. 19, 1941.

50:2 This speech written on El Dorado *Republican* copy paper

is in the Huntington Library.
50:9 Emporia *Gazette,* Jan. 8, 1930.
50:15 White to M. M. Downing, Feb. 24, 1938.
50:34 May 1, 1891.
50:36 White to Paine, Sept. 10, 1891. All the White letters to Paine are in the Huntington Library. White wrote: "You are very good to praise my work, and I am proud to have your approval."
51:30 White to Jennie Sutliff, Jan. 21, 1891. Letter in possession of Helen Sutliff, Stanford University.
52:31 See R. C. Miller, "The Populist Party in Kansas" (unpublished Ph.D. dissertation, University of Chicago Libraries); John D. Hicks, *The Populist Revolt* (Minneapolis: University of Minnesota Press, 1931); C. McA. Destler, "Western Radicalism, 1865-1901: Concepts and Origins," *Mississippi Valley Historical Review,* XXXI (December), 1944.
54:4 Elizabeth N. Barr, *The Populist Uprising. History of Kansas and Kansans,* ed. by W. E. Connelley, Vol. 11, p. 1122.
54:21 *Stratagems and Spoils* (New York: Charles Scribner's Sons, 1901; later, The Macmillan Co.), pp. 207-208.
55:6 *Masks in a Pageant* (New York: The Macmillan Co., 1929), p. 230.
56:20 It is reprinted in White's *The Real Issue* (Chicago: Way and Williams, 1896), pp. 168-179.
57:17 "The Man Who Made the 'Star,'" *Collier's,* June 26, 1915.
58:14 Ethel F. Fisk, ed., *The Letters of John Fiske* (New York: The Macmillan Co., 1940), p. 618.
58:22 White to Albert Beveridge, Nov. 25, 1922.

58:37 "The 'Confederate Colonel' As a Political Issue," *Agora,* II (July, 1892), 27-31.
59:21 *Stratagems and Spoils,* viii-ix.
60:2 White to S. P. Aber, March 9, 1933; Walter Armstrong to writer, Sept. 18, 1944.
62:14 White to Harold Denny, August 8, 1931; see also "Mr. White Interviews Himself," *op. cit.,* pp. 84-85.
62:26 Exhibit C, special section of letter file box marked "January-February, 1929." This is a portion of a letter but the recipient's name and the date are not on the carbon.

Chapter 4

BIG-CITY JOURNALISM

63:18 White to the writer, interview, Oct. 21, 1941; Emporia *Gazette,* April 13, 1915; Kansas City *Star,* Sept. 18, 1930.
64:10 Emporia *Gazette,* Jan. 26, 1901.
64:20 April 27, 1893; May 13, 1893; June 3, 1893; Nov. 9, 1893.
65:17 "Mr. White Interviews Himself," *op. cit.,* pp. 85-86. White is in error over the mention of typewriters. The *Star* had no typewriters in this period.
66:15 Emporia *Gazette,* Nov. 17, 1923.
67:7 "Some Personal Glimpses of Early Kansas Editors," *Kansas Editor,* March, 1933, pp. 1-4.
67:17 White to the Kansas City *Star,* Aug. 14, 1930.
67:35 May 16, 1895.
68:6 White to the Kansas City *Star,* Aug. 14, 1930.
70:11 "Concerning 'Art For Art's Sake,'" *Agora,* III (April, 1894), 290-295.
71:13 Jan. 22, 1893.
71:19 Green Bay (Wis.) *Press-Gazette,* Jan. 16, 1925.

73:23 Quoted in Clough, *William Allen White of Emporia*, p. 67.

74:3 White to Paine, no date.

74:15 "Rhymes by Two Friends," *Kansas Magazine*, September, 1909, pp. 65-66. See also F. L. Pinet, "William Allen White—Kansan," *Kansas Magazine*, July, 1909, pp. 1-7.

74:20 White to Paul Lemperly, Aug. 16, 1900.

74:27 June 29, 1934.

74:31 Several of his poems from *Rhymes by Two Friends* were reprinted in *Sunflowers: A Book of Kansas Poems*, selected by Willard Wattles (Chicago: A. C. McClurg & Co., 1916), and *Some Emporia Verse*, compiled by J. H. Powers (Emporia, 1910).

74:36 O. E. Olin, "Will White—Boy and Man," *Western Homes*, I (October, 1897), pp. 12-14.

75:6 White to H. O. Mahin, April 15, 1929.

75:10 D. A. Latchaw to writer, June 17, 1941.

75:36 Sallie White to writer, interview, Sept. 15, 1945.

76:12 *Flowing Stream—The Story of Forty-Six Years in American Newspaper Life* (New York: E. P. Dutton & Co., 1939), p. 556.

76:34 White to J. E. House, Aug. 21, 1929.

77:4 White to G. W. Watt, Nov. 15, 1939.

Chapter 5

COUNTRY EDITOR

79:11 Rowell to the writer, interview, Jan. 14, 1944.

79:34 New York *Herald Tribune*, Feb. 1, 1944.

80:23 White to C. M. Vernon, Nov. 29, 1907.

81:10 Emporia *Gazette*, May, 31, 1935.

82:2 A. D. Read to the writer, May 8, 1944.

82:10 Topeka *Capital*, June 20, 1902, p. 11.

83:2 June 4, 1895.

83:23 Emporia *Gazette*, Dec. 7, 1895.

84:7 White to George Clark, Aug. 9, 1900.

84:11 White to W. R. Greason, Nov. 20, 1912.

84:16 May 21, 1895.

84:22 White to A. W. Coons, Feb. 9, 1938.

85:13 G. A. Nichols to White, Dec. 15, 1931.

85:20 White to A. W. Coons, Feb. 24, 1938.

86:27 Emporia *Gazette*, Oct. 10, 1900.

87:1 *Ibid.*, July 20, June 4, Sept. 5, 1895.

87:6 *Ibid.*, Oct. 12, 1895.

88:32 *Ibid.*, June 20, 1895.

89:3 *Ibid.*, June 16, 1896.

89:15 *Ibid.*, June 17, 1896.

89:23 *Ibid.*, June 19, 1896.

89:38 "Bryan," *McClure's*, July, 1900, p. 234; *Masks in a Pageant*, p. 250.

90:11 Avery Craven, *Democracy in American Life* (Chicago: The University of Chicago Press, 1942), pp. 137-138.

91:7 Emporia *Gazette*, Aug. 11, 1896.

91:19 White to R. F. Sullivan, April 13, 1931.

92:37 Emporia *Gazette*, Aug. 11, 1896.

94:14 *Ibid.*, Aug. 15, 1896. This is reprinted in R. H. Fitzgibbon, ed., *Forty Years on Main Street*, and H. O. Mahin, ed., *The Editor and His People*. The following tell how it was written: Emporia *Gazette*, Aug. 15, 1904; Aug. 16, 1926; Feb. 1, 1944; "Personal Notes," *Harper's Weekly*, Feb. 1, 1902, p. 155; Kansas City *Times*, Aug. 15 and Aug. 25, 1926.

94:19 Aug. 29, 1896. All White's letters to Way & Williams Company are in the possession of Mrs. C. L. Williams. Copies are in the Newberry Library, Chicago.

94:23 One critic of White's has charged: "At that time William Allen White was just coming into the full vigor of his young manhood. He, too, faced a crisis. Endowed by nature with bubbling energy and an enthusiastic love of life, inspired by upsurgings of the poetic emotions of a passionate soul, his was the opportunity to become a great leader of a great liberty-loving people. He had a chance that few men of his endowments have been given to take up the fight for economic justice—to battle with the people for realization of their democratic ideals. But he was also goaded by his love of the fleshpots to gain immediate material rewards—to try to climb to the top of the existing social order—to become a leading light among the *Overlords*. It was, on that fateful day of Aug. 15, 1896, the time for him to make his choice; it was the time to choose whether he would cast his lot with the people or join in the embattled defense of their exploiters. He

chose the latter and left the crossroads behind, proceeding on the course which has shaped his career and played such an important part in moulding the destiny of the nation." See W. G. Clugston, *Rascals in Democracy* (New York: R. R. Smith, 1940), pp. 97-98.

95:7 To White, Sept. 25, 1896; *Harper's Weekly*, Feb. 1, 1902, p. 155.

95:23 Oct. 23, 1896.

96:24 March 20, 1896.

98:2 Dec. 9, 1896. Garland collection, the University of Southern California Library.

98:8 XXII (January-June, 1897), p. 24.

98:15 Dec. 6, 1896. See also Springfield (Mass.) *Republican*, Jan. 24, 1897; *Outlook*, December, 1896; New York *Sun*, Nov. 17, 1896; St. Louis *Globe-Democrat*, Nov. 29, 1896; *Nation*, March 11, 1897.

98:26 Jan. 7, 1897, pp. 6-7. The review was written by Droch (Robert Bridges).

98:37 Oct. 29, 1896.

99:7 February and March, 1897; Emporia *Gazette*, Jan. 31, 1944.

99:22 Sidney Kramer, *A History of Stone & Kimball and Herbert S. Stone & Co., 1893-1905* (Chicago: N. W. Forgue, 1940).

99:37 Reprinted in the Emporia *Gazette*, Feb. 13, 1897.

PART II: REACTION AND REFORM

Chapter 6

THE MC KINLEY YEARS

104:28 *Masks in a Pageant*, p. 215.

105:6 Dec. 16, 1901.

105:26 I am indebted to Mrs. C. L. Williams for the poem and the

details on the meeting with McKinley.

106:2 Nov. 30, 1897.

106:6 Mrs. Jones to the writer, interview, Feb. 21, 1941.

107:18 Oct. 27, 1934. Roosevelt Memorial Assn. MSS., Harvard

University Library, and in White MSS.

107:30 Speech Oct. 27, 1936. Roosevelt Memorial Assn. MSS.

108:14 See Henry Pringle, *Theodore Roosevelt* (New York: Harcourt, Brace & Co., 1931).

108:29 Oct. 27, 1934. Roosevelt Memorial Assn. MSS.

109:7 *All in the Day's Work* (New York: The Macmillan Co., 1939), pp. 259-260.

109:19 See the New York *Tribune*, July 29, 1897, for comment on an article of White's in the *Atlantic Monthly*, August, 1897.

109:28 Oct. 26, 1897. Roosevelt Memorial Assn. MSS.

110:9 White to Rebecca Sewell, March 18, 1933.

110:25 Emporia *Gazette*, Feb. 18, 23, March 5, 1898.

111:2 Fitzgibbon, ed., *Forty Years on Main Street*, p. 248.

111:16 Emporia *Gazette*, June 12, 1898.

111:38 April 7, 1899.

112:19 T. R. to White, May 25, 1899. Roosevelt Memorial Assn. MSS.

113:3 July 1, 1899. Roosevelt Memorial Assn. MSS.

113:6 White to W. E. Umor, June 29, 1899.

113:18 July 6, 1899.

113:25 July 5, 1899.

113:34 August, 1899.

114:4 White to Leland, Aug. 1, 1899.

114:12 Aug. 15, 1899.

114:23 Laura M. French, *History of Emporia and Lyon County*, pp. 71-72.

115:10 Clipping in letter from E. F. Brown to White, Oct. 12, 1899.

115:21 Sept. 22, 1899.

115:32 Dec. 29, 1899.

116:8 White to W. G. Clugston, March 10, 1938.

116:16 To Robert Bridges, July 25, 1899.

116:26 Oct. 28, 1899. Roosevelt Memorial Assn. MSS.

116:29 "Psychological Counter-Current in Recent American Fiction," *North American Review*, CLXXIII (December, 1901), p. 877.

117:33 Emporia *Gazette*, March 3, 1937.

118:18 See "Bryan," *McClure's Magazine*, July, 1900, pp. 232-237.

119:4 Feb. 6, 1900.

119:15 Emporia *Gazette*, April 14, 1900.

119:28 May 9, 1900.

120:2 June 23, 1900.

120:8 *Ibid.*

120:12 White to Mrs. T. W. Johnston, June 27, 1900. See the Emporia *Gazette*, Jan. 31, 1944.

120:21 Emporia *Gazette*, Aug. 10, 1900.

121:23 *Ibid.*, Dec. 5, 1940.

122:5 *William Allen White In Memoriam*, published by the Book-of-the-Month Club.

122:20 White to Walker, Oct. 24, 1901; to C. S. Gleed, Nov. 16, 1901.

122:26 White to McClure, Dec. 17, 1901.

122:30 Sept. 1, 1937.

Chapter 7

EXPANDING HORIZONS

124:8 March 22, April 10, 1901.

124:29 Hamlin Garland, *Roadside Meetings* (New York: The Macmillan Co., 1930), p. 342.

124:35 See issues for May 18, March 30, April 6, 1901.

125:5 May 9, 1901. See issues of the *Post* for four weeks beginning with Sept. 21, 1901.

126:2 "Lawton—the Metropolis of the Wilderness," *Saturday Evening Post*, Sept. 7, 1901, Vol. 174, p. 388.

126:12 White to F. S. Wood, Nov. 27, 1923; F. S. Wood, *Roosevelt as*

We Knew Him (Philadelphia: J. C. Winston Co., 1927), p. 71.

127:8 Aug. 21, 1901.

127:14 Aug. 27, 1901.

127:22 Aug. 29, 1901.

127:35 Emporia *Gazette*, Sept. 7, 1901.

128:7 Sept. 10, 1901.

128:31 Quoted in Kenneth Heckler, *Insurgency Personalities and Politics of the Taft Era* (New York: Columbia University Press, 1940), p. 21.

129:10 *Masks in a Pageant*, p. 265.

130:26 Speech before Roosevelt Memorial Assn., Oct. 27, 1934.

131:2 *The Autobiography of Lincoln Steffens* (New York: Harcourt, Brace & Co., 1931), p. 503.

131:14 Pp. 214, 289.

131:29 "Psychological Counter-Current in Recent Fiction," *North American Review*, December, 1901, CLXXIII, pp. 876-878.

131:34 W. S. Culbertson to White, March 31, 1934; Springfield (Mass.) *Republican*, Dec. 22, 1901, and Seattle *Times*, Dec. 28, 1901, praised the book, as did the New York *Tribune*, Jan. 29, 1902.

132:3 Nov. 1, 1901.

132:19 Oct. 30, 1901.

132:22 Nov. 6, 1901.

132:27 Nov. 6, 1901.

132:32 Nov. 16, 1901.

132:38 Nov. 14, 1901.

133:7 Dec. 19, 1901.

133:13 T. R. to C. S. Gleed, Dec. 7, 1901. Roosevelt MSS., Library of Congress.

133:24 Dec. 17, 1901.

133:37 *McClure's Magazine*, December, 1901, pp. 145-153.

134:20 White to George B. Cortelyou, Dec. 18, 1901.

134:28 Dec. 20, 1901.

134:32 Dec. 24, 1901.

135:6 Jan. 6, 1902.

135:14 Claude Bowers, *Beveridge and the Progressive Era* (New York: Houghton Mifflin Company, 1932), p. 175.

135:23 John S. Phillips in the Goshen (N. Y.) *Democrat*, Feb. 10, 1939.

135:36 Emporia *Gazette*, Feb. 11, 1937. Speech at Roosevelt Memorial House, Oct. 27, 1936.

136:16 White to Angelo Scott, Sept. 26, 1916.

136:35 Roosevelt to White, June 23, 1903.

137:2 White to W. F. Ewing, Aug. 8, 1910.

137:17 White to Keith Clevenger, Nov. 13, 1912.

137:37 See also "Cuban Reciprocity—A Moral Issue," *McClure's Magazine*, September, 1902.

138:20 Tarbell, *All in the Day's Work*, p. 200.

139:2 Elmer Ellis, *Mr. Dooley's America* (New York: A. A. Knopf, 1941), p. 216.

139:11 See *Saturday Evening Post*, March 14, 21, 28, April 4, May 2, June 27, 1903.

139:18 April 14, 1903.

139:26 May 28, 1903. See Emporia *Gazette*, Nov. 30, 1903.

139:29 *Selections from the Correspondence of Theodore Roosevelt and Henry Cabot Lodge* (New York: Charles Scribner's Sons, 1925), Vol. II, p. 26.

139:32 White to Roosevelt, July 11, 1903.

139:38 Oct. 31, 1903.

140:3 Kansas City *Times*, April 20, 1929.

141:8 March 16, 1904. See Eric F. Goodman, *Charles J. Bonaparte: Patrician Reformer* (Baltimore: Johns Hopkins Press, 1943), pp. 50-66; Bishop, *Theodore Roosevelt and His Time*, Vol. I, pp. 252-255.

141:16 Lindsay to White, April 5, 1904;

Roosevelt to White, April 12, 1904.

141:19 He also wrote an article on the postal investigation, "Grafting and Things," for May 7, 1904, issue of *Saturday Evening Post*.

142:7 Folk to White, April 25, 1904.

143:2 White to Hadley, Oct. 4, 1904.

143:4 White to Folk, Oct. 19, 1904.

143:28 "The Dollar in Politics," "Seconding the Motion," *Saturday Evening Post*, July 2, July 23, 1904.

143:37 White to Mildred Reeves, Jan. 8, 1940.

144:14 "The Great Political Drama at St. Louis," *Collier's*, July 12, 1904.

145:27 Chicago *Daily Inter-Ocean*, Oct. 31, 1904; Emporia *Gazette*, Nov. 2, 1904.

145:32 White to Harry Bone, Oct. 12, 1904.

146:27 Dec. 2, 1904.

147:35 Nov. 25, 1904.

Chapter 8

FULL-BLOWN PROGRESSIVE

148:20 White to Mr. Black, Santa Fe Railroad, March 2, 1905.

149:8 Mark Sullivan, *The Education of an American* (New York: Doubleday, Doran & Co., 1938), pp. 188-191.

149:26 Tarbell, "Kansas and the Standard Oil Company," *McClure's Magazine*, September and October, 1905; J. J. McLaurin, "The Oil Situation in Kansas," *Outlook*, June 17, 1905.

149:38 "The Kansas Conscience," *Reader Magazine*, October, 1905, pp. 488-493.

150:20 "The Golden Rule," *Atlantic Monthly*, October, 1905, pp. 433-441. See also "Political Signs of Promise," *Outlook*, July 15, 1905, pp. 667-670; "Why the

Nation Will Endure," *Saturday Evening Post*, March 4, 1905, p. 12.

151:17 White MSS. Article on Strong.

151:30 White to Mrs. T. W. Johnston, March 1, 1905.

152:38 June 24, 1906.

153:11 See also New York *Tribune*, April 22, 1906.

153:19 White to C. M. Harger, Feb. 7, 1938. See C. C. Baldwin, *The Men Who Make Our Novels* (New York: Dodd, Mead, 1924), pp. 556-557, for a criticism of White as "a provincial with a provincial's prejudice and a provincial's qualms."

154:37 May 23, 1906.

155:5 White to W. A. Harris, May 24, 1906.

155:15 Emporia *Gazette*, June 5, 1906.

155:23 July 5, 1906.

156:22 Aug. 16, 1932.

156:31 Emporia *Gazette*, May 1, 15, 22, 1906.

157:5 White to D. A. Valentine, July 6, 1906.

157:28 Aug. 9, 1906.

158:7 Aug. 8, 1906.

158:12 Henry F. Pringle, *The Life and Times of William Howard Taft* (New York: Farrar & Rinehart, 1939), Vol. I, p. 317.

158:15 Aug. 11, 1906.

158:35 Aug. 11, 1906.

160:2 *American Chronicle* (New York: Scribner's Sons, 1945), pp. 223-224.

160:14 *American Magazine*, October, 1906, p. 573.

160:31 Oct. 11, 1906.

161:4 *Collier's*, Oct. 20, Nov. 10, and Dec. 1, 1906.

161:36 Jan. 2, 1907.

162:25 March 15, 1907.

162:32 Feb. 16, 1907.

163:11 White to Robert Stone, June 14, 1907.

164:5 Roosevelt to Bonaparte, Aug. 2,

15, 23, 24, 1907. Library of Congress. See C. O. Johnson, *Borah of Idaho* (New York: Longmans, Green & Co., 1936), pp. 84-87.

164:34 Jan. 21, 1908.

165:4 Jan. 19, 1908.

165:11 White, *Masks in a Pageant*, Vol. I.

166:1 White to Victor Murdock, Jan. 22, 1908.

166:20 White to T. W. Johnston, April 29, 1908.

166:24 May 4, 1908.

166:30 White to K. W. Heckler, Nov. 26, 1938; Heckler, *Insurgency Personalities and Politics of the Taft Era*, p. 89.

167:16 Long to Morton Albaugh, May 23, 1908. Kansas Historical Society.

167:30 White to W. F. Allen, July 13, 1908.

167:36 Shultz to the writer, interview, Dec. 8, 1941.

168:11 Sept. 8, Aug. 13, 21, 1908.

168:22 White to H. Lonergan, Feb. 13, 1930; Chicago *Record Herald*, June 13-19, 1908.

168:31 Pringle, *The Life and Times of William Howard Taft*, pp. 354-355.

168:34 White, "A Brief for the Defendant," *Collier's*, July 4, 1908, pp. 9-10.

169:15 Oct. 10, 1908.

169:30 Nov. 6, 1908.

Chapter 9

INSURGENT YEARS

170:25 "It's Been a Great Show," *Collier's*, Feb. 12, 1938, p. 64.

172:29 Harry Kemp, *Tramping on Life: an Autobiographical Narrative* (New York: Boni and Liveright, 1922), pp. 245-246. White encouraged this young poet to continue his writing, and he urged him particularly to study American life and write American folk poetry. White gave Kemp money from time to time to help defray his living expenses at K.U., and White also persuaded millionaire Charles Crane to send Kemp a weekly subsidy for an entire year. Some of Kemp's poetry appeared in the *American Magazine* and some in book form. As regent of K.U., White frequently had to protect Kemp from being dismissed. Kemp did not conform to the ways of a midwestern state university, and when one professor charged that he was crazy and a detriment to the school, White told Kemp he had replied, ". . . no doubt you were crazy, you starry young tramp, you! . . . but that I wished some of the professors shared a little of your virus . . . it might make them more alive and interesting." *Ibid.*, pp. 301, 323-324, 329-330.

173:11 March 21, 1909.

173:22 Sept. 25, 1909.

174:8 White to Mrs. T. W. Johnston, Aug. 22, 1909.

175:1 Aug. 4, 1909.

175:7 September, 1910, pp. 680-681; years later historian John D. Hicks in *The Populist Revolt* (Minneapolis: University of Minnesota Press, 1930), p. 461, wrote: "A novel that includes much that is true about the history of Kansas and the pioneer west."

176:2 White to the writer, interview, Sept. 19, 1939.

176:18 White to L. D. Ratcliff, March 20, 1910.

176:29 Dec. 10, 1909.

177:22 The more intimate details are from interviews with Laura M. French and Mrs. R. L. Jones. See also Kansas City *Star*, Hutchinson *Daily News*, Kansas City *Times*, Aug. 28, 1909; Emporia *Gazette*, Aug. 27, 1909, Jan. 31, 1944.

177:26 Sept. 18, 1909.

178:8 See Heckler, *Insurgency Personalities and Politics of the Taft Era*, pp. 11-26.

179:4 White to Dr. Babie, September, 1909.

179:18 Nov. 13, 1909.

180:35 Sept. 9, 1908.

181:9 White to A. A. Roe, Jan. 17, 1910.

181:37 March 21, 1910.

182:1 March 21, 1910.

182:19 See Pringle, *The Life and Times of William Howard Taft*, Vol. I, pp. 472-474; also A. T. Mason, *Bureaucracy Convicts Itself* (New York: Viking Press, 1940), and Harold Ickes in *Saturday Evening Post*, May 25, 1940.

184:26 The writer is indebted to Laura M. French, who was at the party, for the details and a copy of the poem. See also Emporia *Gazette*, Feb. 1, 1944.

184:34 Allan Nevins, ed., *The Letters and Journals of Brand Whitlock*, Vol. II, pp. 131-132.

185:2 March 12, 1910.

185:24 White to Helen Clapesattle, April 10, 1940.

185:37 Dec. 31, 1910.

186:12 White to J. C. O'Laughlin, June 7, 1910.

187:11 *Papers of Edward P. Costigan Relating to the Progressive Movement in Colorado, 1902-1911*, ed. by G. B. Goodykoontz (Boulder: University of Colorado, 1941), p. 144.

187:19 Lindsey to J. N. Dolley, June 29, 1910.

187:32 White to Dante Barton, June 20, 1910; Barton to White, June 23, 1910; White to Barton, June, 1910.

188:2 Jan. 13, 1901.

188:19 March 11, 1910.

188:24 Aug. 5, 1910.

188:36 Topeka *State Journal*, Feb. 16, 1909.

189:8 Myer Lissner to White, Oct. 17, 1910.

189:13 Sept. 22, 1910.

189:37 White to S. A. Smith, Sept. 7, 1910.

190:9 Sept. 2, 1910; Sept. 27, 1910. See the Joliet (Ill.) *News*, Dec. 28, 1910.

190:30 Nov. 28, 1910.

191:6 White to Gifford Pinchot, Sept. 21, 1910.

191:14 Dec. 12, 1910.

191:16 White to Gifford Pinchot, Dec. 29, 1910.

192:6 White to Roosevelt, Jan. 17, 1911.

192:23 May 5, 1911.

193:5 Feb. 23, 1911.

193:9 April 15, 1911.

193:31 June 16, 1911.

194:13 White to Fred Trigg, May 29, 1911.

194:28 Denver *Post*, Sept. 10, 1911.

195:13 Oct. 24, 1911.

195:18 Lodge, ed., *Lodge-Roosevelt Letters*, Vol. II, p. 417.

195:33 David Leahy to White, Dec. 7, 1911.

195:36 Dec. 19, 1911.

196:7 Jan. 8, 1912.

196:34 Jan. 18, 1912.

197:2 Bristow to White, Jan. 11, 1912.

197:28 White to Charles Van Hise, May 24, 1912.

197:38 White to Walter Olin, April 30, 1912.

198:23 Jay House in the Wilson County *Citizen*, May 1, 1914.

Chapter 10

BULL MOOSE DAYS

199:14 Wilson County *Citizen*, May 1, 1914.
200:35 White to J. S. Phillips, May 15, 1912.
201:20 New York *Times*, June 15, 16, 1912.
201:22 *Ibid.*, June 17, 1912.
202:8 Pringle, *Theodore Roosevelt*, p. 562.
202:29 Pringle, *The Life and Times of William Howard Taft*, I, p. 802.
203:4 Emporia *Gazette*, June 24, 1912.
203:11 Hadley to White, July 6, 1912; W. T. Miller, "The Progressive Movement in Missouri," unpublished master's thesis, University of Missouri, 1927; H. T. Long, "The Political Career of Herbert Spencer Hadley," *ibid.*, 1939.
203:19 Chicago *Tribune*, June 8, 1912.
203:28 Bowers, *Beveridge and the Progressive Era*, p. 435.
203:33 See p. 345.
204:35 *A Peculiar Treasure*, p. 198.
205:9 See Matthew Josephson, *The President Makers* (New York: Harcourt, Brace & Co., 1940), pp. 446-447; George E. Mowry, *Theodore Roosevelt and the Progressive Movement* (Madison: University of Wisconsin Press, 1946).
205:13 White to Roosevelt, July 27, 1912.
205:15 White to E. E. Soderstrom, Aug. 23, 1912.
205:24 Chester Rowell to White, Nov. 29, 1919.
205:29 Charles E. Merriam to writer, interview, Oct. 19, 1939.
205:35 Nov. 29, 1919.
206:10 White to Perkins, June 3, 1914.
206:15 White to Claude Bowers, July 11, 1932; to writer, interview, Sept. 29, 1941.

206:17 Kansas City *Times*, Aug. 7, 1912.
207:32 July 26, 1912. Mr. Stanley was Kansas Republican national committeeman.
208:11 Emporia *Gazette*, July 3, 1912.
209:11 White to W. L. Cunningham, July 23, 1912.
209:18 Martha Caldwell, "The Woman Suffrage Campaign of 1912," *Kansas Historical Quarterly*, XII (August, 1943).
209:30 White to the writer, interview, March 27, 1941.
209:35 Open letter by J. E. Crider, no date.
210:20 Charles Vernon, "A Panegyric on Emporia," Emporia *Gazette*, May 14, 1927.
210:25 White to J. A. Burnette, Nov. 18, 1912.
210:37 Nov. 15, 1912.
211:13 Nov. 25, 1912. Compare this with White's *Autobiography*, in which he claims that he never supported Perkins.
211:32 Pringle, *Theodore Roosevelt*, p. 571.
212:10 Dec. 6, 1912.
212:15 Nov. 22, 1912.
212:31 "The Schools—The Mainspring of Democracy," *American Magazine*, August, 1909, pp. 376-383; *The Old Order Changeth*, p. 176; A. E. Winship, "The Critics of the School," *Journal of Education*, LXX (Sept. 9 and 16, 1909).
213:11 White to H. S. Pritchett, June 6, 1911.
214:26 July 19, 1939.
215:5 May 11, 1912.
215:15 White to J. W. Hanna, May 13, 1911.
215:23 June 27, 1910.
215:36 Emporia *Gazette*, April 15, 1899.
216:11 *Ibid.*, March 5, 1938.

216:14 White to Willis Gleed, Nov. 23, 1908.

216:17 White to Perlee Burton, May 7, 1910.

216:21 White to W. H. Anderson, Dec. 28, 1910.

217:2 Speech at K.U. Alumni Dinner, November, 1938. White MSS.

217:9 *Ibid.*

217:14 Dec. 5, 1912.

217:16 Dec. 8, 1913. K.U. Library MSS.

218:5 June 9, 1913.

218:30 June 6, 1913.

218:34 March 25, 1913.

219:14 Sept. 24, 1913.

219:16 Oct. 8, 1913.

219:23 White to Robert Bridges, Dec. 29, 1913.

220:3 June 30, 1913.

220:10 "How Kansas Boarded the Water Wagon," *Saturday Evening Post*, July 11, 1914.

220:15 Los Angeles *Times*, Sept. 20, 1914.

221:7 Bristow to L. A. Lockwood. Kansas Historical Society MSS.

221:11 White to S. Ingalls, Nov. 1, 1913.

221:14 Nov. 1, 1913.

221:25 Bristow to J. R. Harrison, Aug. 12, 1914; see also Bristow to L. W. Bloom, Aug. 14, 1914. Kansas Historical Society MSS.

221:32 White to V. Murdock, June 12, 1914.

221:35 White to W. R. Stubbs, April 24, 1914.

222:12 Roosevelt to White, July 6, 1914.

222:17 White to G. Pinchot, April 20, 1914.

222:23 July 6, 1914.

222:34 *Fighting Liberal: The Autobiography of George W. Norris* (New York: The Macmillan Co., 1945), p. 148.

222:38 Nov. 17, 1914.

225:3 Courtesy of Cecil Howes.

Chapter 11

SMALL-TOWN JOURNALISM, 1897-1914

226:5 The *Advance*, Nov. 27, 1913, p. 403.

226:23 "William Allen White," *Saturday Evening Post*, June 15, 1907, p. 22.

227:2 White to Helen Mahin, Oct. 7, 1926.

229:27 Emporia *Gazette*, Dec. 6, 1911.

229:33 White to Frank Buxton, Dec. 22, 1938; to writer, interview, Nov. 27, 1941.

230:14 Emporia *Gazette*, Dec. 27, 1902; Oct. 21, 1901.

230:27 White to the Success Company, Oct. 9, 1903.

230:34 Emporia *Gazette*, Dec. 19, 1913.

231:11 S. G. Blythe, "William Allen White," *op. cit.*

232:33 March 21, 1914.

233:9 May, 1916, p. 888.

233:18 Emporia *Gazette*, Oct. 12, 1903.

233:29 *Ibid.*, June 2, 1911.

233:33 *Ibid.*, Jan. 9, 1909.

234:4 White to F. W. Ives, Feb. 3, 1914.

234:28 White to E. C. Franklin, Nov. 19, 1909.

234:33 Sept. 19, 1912.

234:38 Oct. 29, 1905.

235:14 Feb. 5, 1903. Two collections of White's editorials have been published: *The Editor and His People*, edited by H. O. Mahin, and *Forty Years on Main Street*, edited by R. H. Fitzgibbon.

235:24 Fitzgibbon, ed. *Forty Years on Main Street*, p. 50 n.

235:30 Feb. 11, 1911.

235:38 Feb. 25, 1911.

236:16 May 5, 17, 1897.

237:22 "Emporia and New York," *American Magazine*, January, 1907, p. 261.

237:33 *The Education of an American*, p. 116.

238:22 Sept. 15, 1911.

238:27 Kansas Historical Society *Scrap Book*, Vol. X, p. 438.

239:9 Emporia *Gazette*, Feb. 1, 1944.

239:30 White to B. W. Crone, July 19, 1935; to Charles Scott, May 8, 1926.

239:36 W. E. Connelley, ed., *History of Kansas Newspapers* (Topeka, 1916), p. 114; "What Happened to Walt Mason," *American Magazine*, September, 1918, p. 19.

240:6 White to Charles Driscoll, April 5, 1932.

240:13 "Down and Out at Forty-Five," *American Magazine*, September, 1918, p. 20.

240:30 James Lawrence of the Lincoln (Nebr.) *Star* to writer, interview, Dec. 29, 1944.

240:33 "Down and Out at Forty-Five," *op. cit.*, p. 82.

241:22 June 24, 1908.

242:19 Emporia *Gazette*, March 29, 1897.

242:27 *Ibid.*, Feb. 1, 1944.

243:22 F. L. Pinet, "William Allen White—Kansan," *Kansas Magazine*, July, 1909, pp. 1-7.

243:35 *Tramping on Life*, pp. 250-251.

244:7 Fred Lockley to White, Nov. 8, 1935.

244:34 Topeka *State Journal*, Dec. 10, 1938.

245:5 *A Peculiar Treasure*, p. 227.

245:10 Goshen (N. Y.) *Democrat*, Feb. 10, 1939.

246:22 Jan. 9, 1912. See "What Music Has Done for Me," *Etude*, LVI (December, 1938), pp. 779 ff.

247:12 Kansas City *Times*, March 17, 1915. Contributors' column.

PART III: WAR AND PEACE

Chapter 12

WAR IN EUROPE

251:5 White to George Perkins, April 25, 1914; to W. R. Stubbs, April 24, 1914.

251:24 Emporia *Gazette*, Jan. 28, 1903.

253:6 See G. P. Morehouse, "Kansas as a State of Extremes and Its Attitudes During the World War," *Kansas Historical Collections*, XV, 20-22, which tends to support this statement.

253:15 May 24, 1915.

253:19 White to T. E. Leupp.

253:28 "The Republican Party," July, 1915, pp. 14 ff.

254:3 Aug. 3, 1915.

254:8 Aug. 27, 1915.

254:16 White to Annie L. Diggs, Oct. 12, 1915; to Roosevelt, Oct. 28, 1915.

254:25 See *League to Enforce Peace.*

Independence Hall Conference, Philadelphia, June 17, 1915 (New York: League to Enforce Peace, 1915).

254:29 Dec. 31, 1915.

255:10 White to the National Education Association, Jan. 8, 1916.

255:24 White to F. D. Smith, Jan. 5, 1916.

256:9 March 6, 1916.

256:14 March 9, 1916.

256:21 White to Frank Dale, March 13, 1916.

258:4 Courtesy of P. M. Benjamin, librarian, Allegheny College, Tarbell MSS.

258:8 *Post*, March 6, April 24, 1915; *Collier's*, March 4, 11, 18, 1916.

258:15 March 31, 1916.

258:22 March 27, 1915.

258:28 Aug. 24, 1916, p. 179.

259:13 White to W. E. Bobbs, April 16, 1915.

259:17 Emporia *Gazette*, April 23, 1915.

259:34 June 4, 1915.

260:3 "A Poet Came Out of Tailholt," *Collier's*, Dec. 25, 1915, pp. 3-4.

260:8 *My Friendly Contemporaries*, pp. 78-79.

260:17 Pemberton to writer, interview, April 14, 1945.

260:30 Nov. 30, 1915.

261:6 See Harold Ickes, "Who Killed the Progressive Party?" *American Historical Review*, XLVI (January, 1941), 314-315, for a discussion of this point.

261:12 White to Frank McLennan, Dec. 2, 1915.

261:37 White to A. R. Kinkel, Feb. 3, 1916.

262:5 White to J. M. Dolley, March 14, 1916.

262:13 Ickes, *op. cit.*, p. 323.

262:29 White to Ickes, May 17, 1937; White to Garfield, June 16, 1937.

262:36 White to Garfield, June 16, 1937.

263:10 May 17, 1937.

263:31 See N. M. Butler, *Across the Busy Years* (New York: The Macmillan Co., 1939), pp. 269-271; G. E. Mowry, *Theodore Roosevelt and the Progressive Movement*, pp. 348-352.

264:35 White to J. A. Kingsbury, Jan. 28, 1924; Gifford Pinchot to White, Feb. 20, 1917.

265:3 July 11, 1932.

265:14 White to Ickes, June 29, 1937.

265:28 White to Rodney Elward, June 24, 1916.

266:7 June 15, 1916.

266:30 Oct. 10, 1916.

267:2 Oct. 27, 1916; Emporia *Gazette*, Oct. 26, 1916.

267:19 White to W. H. Williams, Nov. 17, 1916.

268:2 Nov. 28, 1916.

268:7 Nov. 14, 1916. I am indebted to W. T. Hutchinson, who is

writing a biography of Lowden, for this letter.

268.28 Feb. 1, 1917, pp. 139-140.

269:19 Jan. 1, 1917.

270:26 Feb. 19, 1917.

270:38 Emporia *Gazette*, March 5, 1917.

271:17 White to Effie Franklin.

272:16 Ray Stannard Baker, *Woodrow Wilson: Life and Letters Facing War, 1915-1917*, Vol. V, pp. 492-501.

272:23 *Ibid.*, p. 493. See also Charles Seymour, *American Neutrality* (New Haven: Yale University Press, 1935).

Chapter 13

HENRY AND ME

274:21 White to Mark Sullivan, Jan. 28, 1918.

275:20 May 10, 1917.

275:35 Lodge, ed., *Roosevelt-Lodge Correspondence*, Vol. II, p. 526.

276:21 July 30, 1917.

276:36 Aug. 3, 1917.

279:26 *William Allen White in Memoriam.*

280:2 "The Y.M.C.A. Huts 'Safety Valves' for Our Boys in France," *Touchstone*, January, 1918, p. 350.

280:18 White to C. H. Sabin, Nov. 16, 1917.

281:9 Dec. 15, 1917.

282:9 See Walter Johnson, *The Battle Against Isolation* (Chicago: University of Chicago Press, 1944), pp. 166-167.

282:37 May 24, 1918.

283:6 May 6, 1918.

284:16 White to George Brett, June 29, 1917.

284:23 Robert Van Gelder, "Spring Books," New York *Times Book Review*, March 26, 1944.

285:32 *New Republic*, Feb. 15, 1919, pp. 91-92.

285:38 *Ibid.*, May 17, 1919, pp. 84-85, 88.

286:8 Nov. 20, 1918; Nov. 23, 1918. See Boston *Post*, Nov. 30, 1918; Washington *Star*, Dec. 1, 1918.

286:18 White to Allen, April 24, 1918. White wrote: "Apropos to the book I had a lot of half tone plates of your picture and mine in our uniforms which I am spreading over the state . . ."

287:6 Dec. 5, 1917. See H. W. Gaston, *The Non-Partisan League* (New York, 1920) and C. E. Russell, *The Story of the Non-Partisan League* (New York, 1920).

287:19 White to R. M. McClintock, Feb. 23, 1918.

287:27 White to Elmer Peterson, May 17, 1918.

287:33 April 13, 1918.

288:7 White to Theodore Roosevelt, July 1, 1918.

288:12 White to Davidson, June 29, 1918. Henry J. Allen told the writer on Sept. 16, 1945, that White's statement was not correct.

288:21 June 28, 1918.

289:1 March 4, 1918.

289:6 White to Theodore Roosevelt, March 25, 1918.

289:19 March 29, 1918.

Chapter 14

A KANSAN AT THE PEACE CONFERENCE

293:16 Speech before Roosevelt Memorial Association, Oct. 27, 1934.

293:20 Dec. 14, 1919. All of the material in this chapter is based on letters to Mrs. White unless otherwise specified.

294:7 Kindness of Willis Kerr.

294:25 See Tarbell, *All in the Day's Work*, pp. 336-358.

295:2 "Tale That Is Told," *Saturday Evening Post*, Oct. 4, 1919, pp. 19 ff.

295:18 See Baker, *American Chronicle*, pp. 375-456; Baker, *Woodrow Wilson and World Settlement* (New York: Doubleday, Page & Co., 1923, 3 vols.).

295:28 Nov. 13, 1919.

297:4 *The Autobiography of William Allen White* (New York: The Macmillan Co., 1946), p. 558.

297:11 Emporia *Gazette*, Feb. 13, 1919.

297:19 April 26, 1933.

297:34 See Vernon Kellogg, *Headquarters Nights* (Boston: Atlantic Monthly Press, 1917).

298:11 "Tale That Is Told," *op. cit.*

298:25 *Ibid.*

298:36 See "The Doughboy on Top of the World," *Red Cross Magazine*, June, 1919, pp. 45 ff.

299:10 See "In Germany with William Allen White," *Literary Digest*, April 26, 1919, pp. 64-66.

299:26 Emporia *Gazette*, March 15, 1919.

300:28 White to Mrs. White, March 21, 1919.

301:11 Feb. 9, 1919.

301:35 New York *Times*, Feb. 9, 1919.

302:17 Allan Nevins, ed., *The Letters and Journal of Brand Whitlock*, Vol. I, pp. 551-552.

302:27 Aug. 15, 1929; Briggs, *George D. Herron and the European Settlement* (Stanford: Stanford University Press, 1932), pp. 10, 50, 141-148.

303:25 White to Mrs. White, Feb. 13, 1919.

304:9 White to M. P. Briggs, Aug. 24, 1929; "What Happened to Prinkipo," *Metropolitan Magazine*, December, 1919.

304:24 "Litmus Papers of the Acid Test," *Survey*, June 5, 1920, pp. 343-346. Introduction to *Russian-American Relations, March, 1917-March, 1920.* Documents and Papers Compiled and Edited by C. K. Cumming and W. W. Pettit, under the direction of John A. Ryan, J. H. Scattergood, William Allen White (New York: Harcourt, Brace & Howe, 1920).

304:35 E. S. Sargeant, "The Citizen from Emporia," *Century Magazine*, January, 1927, p. 308.

305:25 "The Highbrow Doughboy," *Red Cross Magazine*, August, 1919, pp. 19-24.

305:33 White to Mrs. White, March 23, 1919.

306:6 *Ibid.,* May 2, 1919.

306:18 *Ibid.,* April 12, 1919.

307:13 *Ibid.,* May 15, 1919.

307:32 *At the Paris Peace Conference* (New York: The Macmillan Co., 1937), p. 301.

308:35 "Tale That Is Told," *op. cit.*

309:33 May 17, 1919.

310:12 *Ibid.,* May 31, 1919.

313:24 "Editors Live and Learn," *Atlantic Monthly*, August, 1942, p. 58.

Chapter 15

THE REPUBLICANS AND THE PEACE

315:9 Emporia *Gazette*, Sept. 13, July 11, 16, 17, 24, 1919.

315:30 See Clarence A. Berdahl, "Myths About the Peace Treaties of 1919-1920," Carnegie Endowment for International Peace Pamphlet #383, October, 1942; Walter Johnson, "Senatorial Strategy, 1919-1920: Will It Be Repeated?" *Antioch Review*, Winter, 1943.

315:37 See D. F. Fleming, *The United States and the League of Nations, 1918-1920* (New York: G. P. Putnam's Sons, 1932), pp. 3-26.

316:3 See Karl Schriftgiesser, *The Gentleman from Massachusetts: Henry Cabot Lodge* (Boston: Little, Brown & Co., 1944), pp. 331-351.

316:15 *As I Knew Them* (Indianapolis: Bobbs-Merrill, 1936), pp. 190-191.

316:26 New York *Herald Tribune*, March 7, 1930; T. A. Bailey, *Woodrow Wilson and the Great Betrayal* (New York: The Macmillan Co., 1945), denies that Lodge utilized reservations merely as a technique to defeat the League.

317:30 "The Peace and President Wilson," August 16, 1919; "Tale That Is Told," *op. cit.*

318:16 Aug. 12, 1943.

318:26 White to D. B. Taylor, Dec. 2, 1919.

319:34 Emporia *Gazette*, Oct. 8, 1919. See New York *Times*, Oct. 23, 24, 1919.

320:9 *Woodrow Wilson* (Boston: Houghton Mifflin Co., 1924), p. 440.

320:36 Baker, *American Chronicle*, p. 474.

321:6 See Kenneth Colegrove, *The American Senate and World Peace* (New York: Vanguard Press, 1944), for a discussion of the Senate's treaty-wrecking history.

321:9 See *Woodrow Wilson*, pp. 455-456.

321:17 Baker to the writer, interview, July 24, 1945.

321:25 Emporia *Gazette*, Feb. 4, 1924.

322:26 See White, "First Shot in a New Battle," *Collier's*, Nov. 22, 1919, pp. 5 ff.

322:38 White to R. M. Easley, Nov. 17, 1919.

323:12 White to Paul Kellogg, Dec. 2, 1919.

323:24 Emporia *Gazette*, Jan. 8, 1920.

324:14 Feb. 4, 1920.

324:19 Ickes, *The Autobiography of a Curmudgeon*, pp. 223-224.

324:24 April 7, 1920.

324:27 *Op. cit.*, p. 225.

324:35 White to Wood, Nov. 12, 1919; to F. Moore, Dec. 1, 1919.

325:32 Topeka *State Journal*, Oct. 24, 1921.

327:12 White to Rodney Elward, June 15, 1920.

327:28 *A Puritan in Babylon, The Story of Calvin Coolidge* (New York: The Macmillan Co., 1938), pp. 188, 207.

327:33 White to W. E. Borah, March, 1928.

327:38 *Masks in a Pageant*, pp. 404-405.

328:14 White to E. V. Duffield, July 14, 1920.

328:24 White to W. R. Carter, June 16, 1920.

328:28 Dec. 3, 1920.

329:7 March 13, 1925.

329:33 "A Progressive Republican at San Francisco," *Review of Reviews*, August, 1920, pp. 198-

199, for a summary of his dispatches.

330:12 *Masks in a Pageant*, p. 402.

330:32 *Collier's*, May 15, 1920, p. 20.

331:14 White to Murdock, July 12, 1920; to M. Lissner, Sept. 3, 1920.

331:19 July 12, 1920.

331:35 "Bill White's Emporium," *Saturday Review of Literature*, May 8, 1937.

332:3 White to Neil C. Brooks, May 28, 1940.

332:6 White to the writer, interview, Feb. 12, 1940.

332:28 White to H. S. Roberts, April 25, 1921.

332:38 Sept. 14, 1920.

333:13 Fitzgibbon, ed., *Forty Years on Main Street*, p. 107 n.

333:27 Sept. 11, 1920.

333:33 July 10, 1920.

334:7 *The Problems of Peace* (New York: Oxford Press, 1927), p. 177.

334:20 New York *Times*, Oct. 15, 1920.

335:9 New York *Times*, Oct. 15, 1920.

335:22 Dec. 22, 1920.

335:33 See Bailey, *Woodrow Wilson and the Great Betrayal*, pp. 351-355.

PART IV: NORMALCY AND REFORM

Chapter 16

THE HARDING ERA

341:11 "Why I Am a Progressive," *Saturday Evening Post*, April 23, 1921, pp. 3-4.

341:30 June 18, 1921.

342:4 White to C. H. Howard, Feb. 10, 1921.

342:28 White to C. T. Start, Oct. 7, 1921.

342:34 See Emporia *Gazette*, Jan. 6,

March 14, April 22, June 1, June 2, 1921.

343:7 Sept. 17, 1921.

343:21 White to C. B. Orth, Nov. 1, 1920.

344:7 Sept. 23, 1920.

344:26 June 28, 1922; Emporia *Gazette*, May 11, 1922; "Are the Movies a Mess or a Menace?" *Collier's*, Jan. 16, 1926, p. 5.

345:18 Emporia *Gazette*, Dec. 23, 1921. See F. L. Mott, *American Jour-*

nalism (New York: The Macmillan Co., 1941), pp. 635-650.

345:31 Dec. 23, 1925.

346:8 Jan. 6, 1926.

346:17 White to G. T. Visniskki, Sept. 9, 1921.

346:26 White to Bradford Merrill, Sept. 20, 1921.

347:21 Nov. 23, 1920.

347:29 Nov. 27, 1920; later White hated Lewis's *Elmer Gantry* utterly and decided that Lewis had become an evil fellow. Lewis to writer, June 6, 1946.

348:13 See also "We Who Are About to Die," *New Republic*, March 9, 1921.

348:37 "This Business of Writing," *Saturday Review of Literature*, Dec. 4, 1926, pp. 355-356. See also White, "The Country Editor Speaks," *Nation*, June 12, 1929, p. 714.

349:8 "Kansas a Puritan Survival," *Nation*, April 19, 1922, pp. 460-462. Reprinted in *These United States*, ed. Ernest Gruening (New York: Boni and Liveright, 1923).

349:33 Emporia *Gazette*, April 25, 1922.

350:5 "Just Wondering," *Kansas Magazine*, 1934, pp. 86-88.

355:8 Fitzgibbon, ed., *Forty Years on Main Street*, p. 24 n.

355:27 No carbon was kept of this letter. Mrs. Smith graciously sent it to the writer.

355:30 Emporia *Gazette*, June 14, 1926.

356:8 To the City Commissioners, Oct. 28, 1926.

356:14 Laura French to the writer, interview, Nov. 26, 1941.

356:31 White to Theodore Roosevelt, Jr., July 15, 1926.

358:2 Pontiac (Mich.) *Daily Press*, Aug. 14, 1922.

358:26 D. H. Cooke to White, June 20, 1922.

359:7 July 11, 1922.

360:9 See New York *Times*, Aug. 11, 12, 14, 1922; New York *Tribune*, Aug. 11, 14, 1922.

360:18 May 12, 1922.

360:20 Feb. 25, 1922.

361:3 Jan. 5, 1939.

361:28 See W. L. Huggins, *Labor and Democracy* (New York: The Macmillan Co., 1922).

361:31 See Domenico Cagliardo, *The Kansas Industrial Court* (Lawrence: University of Kansas, 1941), for an excellent history of the court.

362:5 Kansas City *Star*, Jan. 12, 1920; H. J. Allen, *The Party of the Third Part* (New York: Harper & Brothers, 1921), pp. 89-90.

362:15 Emporia *Gazette*, June 3, 1921.

362:19 Oct. 29, 1921; to W. Y. Morgan, Aug. 3, 1921. See "Industrial Justice—Not Peace," *Nation's Business*, May, 1922, pp. 14-16.

362:29 Cagliardo, *op. cit.*, pp. 167-169.

362:33 White to M. D. Woolf, June 30, 1922.

363:3 June 22, 1922.

363:11 No date. Marked instead "Blue Monday."

363:38 July 12, 1922.

364:34 Wichita *Beacon*, July 21, 1922; H. J. Haskell, "Further Martial Adventures of Henry and Me," *Outlook*, Aug. 2, 1922, pp. 559-560.

365:4 July 25, 1922.

365:27 Emporia *Gazette*, Feb. 1, 1944.

366:9 New York *Times*, July 23, 1922.

366:28 August, 1922.

367:8 See "New Martial Adventures of Henry and Me," *Literary Digest*, Aug. 5, 1922, pp. 17-18.

368:7 Aug. 1, 3, 1922. See *Motion Picture News*, Aug. 19, 1922; *Literary Digest*, Aug. 19, 1922, p. 32.

368:12 New York *Times*, May 14, 1923.

368:18 Quoted in the *Literary Digest*, June 9, 1923, p. 30. The editorial has been reprinted in many books and the *Gazette* has regular requests for copies of it over the years. White, himself, served as a judge on the Pulitzer Prize Board the year before the award and some years after it as well.

368:27 White to Ralph Stout, Nov. 22, 1922; Topeka *Capital*, Nov. 19, 1922.

368:37 Topeka *Capital*, Dec. 8, 9, 1922; see *New Republic*, Dec. 27, 1922, p. 106; New York *Times*, Oct. 7, 9, Dec. 10, 20, 1922.

369:16 Cagliardo, *op. cit.*, pp. 236-245.

369:27 *Fighting Liberal* (New York: The Macmillan Co., 1945), pp. 215, 245.

370:11 *Masks in a Pageant*, pp. 422-423.

370:18 "Why I Am a Progressive," *Saturday Evening Post*, April 23, 1921, pp. 3-4.

370:23 White to S. Clemens, June 3, 1939.

371:4 Aug. 11, 1921.

371:8 White to Bishop W. F. Anderson, Aug. 6, 1921.

371:13 P. 299.

371:29 Emporia *Gazette*, July 19, 1922.

372:6 *Ibid.*, Oct. 5, Nov. 3, 1922.

372:19 *Ibid.*, April 25, 1923.

372:20 Jan. 12, 1923. Judge E. H. Gary of the Steel Trust was on the same Mediterranean cruise. The Philadelphia *Public Ledger* was prompted by this fact to remark: "Time was when 'Old Bill' White, of Emporia, and 'Vic' Murdock, of Wichita, would have been regarded with suspicion in the short-grass country for so much as walking down Wall Street. Had they been caught rubbing elbows with the Big Cinch, the Social Register and Big Business, they might have been hunted through the sunflower and kaffir patches and swung by their political necks until dead from the limb of the nearest cottonwood in the Arkansas or Neosho bottoms . . . And now, lo and behold! here they are on the S.S. *Mauretania's* million-dollar cruise with Judge Gary, who keeps the Steel Trust for a pet. Other names on that passenger list drip money and smell of Social Register, and for sixty-six summery, sleepy days the two Kansas pilgrims are to be exposed to the insidiousness of Big Business and will be cheek to jowl with Mammon."

372:21 White to C. W. Helstrom, July 9, 1923.

373:19 White to C. C. Magee, June 17; *Masks in a Pageant*, pp. 431-432; *A Puritan in Babylon*, pp. 238-239; Adams, *The Incredible Era*, p. 340.

373:31 July 15, 1926.

374:10 Aug. 10, 1927. See also *A Puritan in Babylon*, p. 230; "It's Been a Great Show," *Collier's*, Feb. 12, 1938, p. 64.

Chapter 17

A KANSAN IN BABYLON

376:6 See John M. Mecklin, *The Ku Klux Klan, A Study of the American Mind* (New York: 1924), for a penetrating study of the Klan's appeal.

376:28 Clough, *William Allen White of Emporia*, pp. 151-153.

377:11 Oct. 7, 1923.

377:16 "Patience and Publicity," *World Tomorrow*, March, 1924, p. 7.

377:28 Sept. 23, 1924.

378:8 New York *Times*, Aug. 26, 1924.

378:24 J. M. K. Abbott, "Bill White and the Shirt Tail Rangers," *Outlook*, Nov. 5, 1924, p. 360.

379:19 White to J. A. Harzfeld, July 29, 1926; to A. E. Holt, Nov. 11, 1924.

381:7 "William Allen White's War on the Klan," *Literary Digest*, Oct. 11, 1924, p. 16.

381:14 Sept. 15, 1924.

381:36 Charles F. Scott to White, Sept. 21, 1924; mimeographed letter in White files. "Montgomery County Republican Central Committee to the Republicans of Montgomery County"; no date.

382:9 White to Orris Dawson, Sept. 5, 1924.

382:14 See Clugston, *Rascals in Democracy*, p. 109.

382:18 There is some evidence that Scott's bolt cost him the appointment of secretary of agriculture in Coolidge's Cabinet. See *Congressional Record*, LXXXIV, No. 749, 13937-38.

383:5 Topeka *Capital*, Oct. 15, 1924.

383:8 See M. F. Amrine to W. W. Bieler, Oct. 2, 1924. White MSS.

383:18 June 5, 1909.

383:23 Oct. 9, 1924.

383:33 New York *Times*, Oct. 5, 1924.

384:4 *Ibid.*

384:12 White to the Secretary of State, Nov. 3, 1924.

384:37 Nov. 9, Oct. 15, 1924.

385:20 White to A. E. Holt, Nov. 11, 1924.

385:28 Nov. 11, 1924.

385:32 Oct. 28, Nov. 5, 1924.

386:9 Dec. 29, 1919.

386:25 New York *Herald Tribune*, March 1, 1924; New York *Times*, March 1, 1924.

387:15 White to the writer, interview, March 28, 1941.

387:20 Brand Whitlock to White, Nov. 12, 1924; Nevins, ed., *The Letters and Journals of Brand Whitlock*, Vol. II, p. 525.

387:25 April 15, 1925.

387:29 White to James Troutman, Dec. 31, 1925.

388:8 *Politics: The Citizen's Business* (New York: The Macmillan Co., 1924), pp. 28, 36, 43-44.

388:21 *Collier's*, Aug. 9, 1925; *Woman's Home Companion*, November, 1924.

388:25 White to Ferris Greenslet, July 22, 1924.

388:36 See White "Why All This Rumpus?" *Collier's*, Aug. 25, 1923, p. 5; "Farmer John and the Sirens," *Saturday Evening Post*, Nov. 12, 1921, pp. 10-11.

389:10 *Politics: The Citizen's Business*, p. 122.

389:30 Oct. 21, 1923; New York *Times*, Oct. 17, 1923.

390:19 Aug. 18, 1922.

390:22 White to O. G. Villard, Nov. 19, 1924.

390:33 Aug. 15, 1924.

391:2 July 31, 1924.

391:18 To writer, interview with Victor Murdock, Oct. 19, 1941.

391:23 White to James Troutman, Dec. 31, 1925.

392:18 March 19, 1926.

392:31 White to W. S. Fitzpatrick, Nov. 24, 1925.

393:8 To writer, interview with Chester Rowell, Jan. 14, 1944.

393:21 Aug. 23, Sept. 3, 1925.

393:24 July 6, 1925.

394:3 Rowell to the writer, interview, Jan. 14, 1944.

394:6 New York *Times*, Aug. 5, 1925.

394:19 See "Last of the Magic Isles," *Survey*, May 1, 1926, pp. 176-179.

395:20 Oct. 26, 1926; see "End of an Epoch" *Scribner's*, June, 1926, pp. 561-570; "The Confessions of a Politician," *New Republic*, Nov. 24, 1926, pp. 9 ff. This was unsigned: "Where Are the Pre-War Radicals?" *Survey*, Feb. 1, 1926, p. 556.

395:29 White to Lamont De Camp, Jan. 23, 1926.

395:37 See White, "Man Who Rules the Senate," *Collier's*, Oct. 3, 1925, p. 10.

396:8 Jan. 31, 1926.

397:27 White to Whiting Williams, June 18, 1927; Emporia *Gazette*, July 27, 1927.

398:11 April 3, 1928.

398:20 May 4, 1928.

398:34 Emporia *Gazette*, April 2, 3, 1928; New York *Times*, April 3, 1928.

399:16 Emporia *Gazette*, April 5, 1925; Topeka *Capital*, Apr. 5, 1928; New York *Times*, Apr. 6, 1925.

399:20 Topeka *Capital*, April 5, 1928.

400:5 April 6, 1928.

Chapter 18

THE CRASH OF BABYLON

401:14 "The Sage of Emporia," *Collier's*, June 9, 1928, p. 33.

402:17 C. O. Johnson, *Borah*, p. 408.

402:34 *Fighting Liberal: The Autobiography of George W. Norris*, p. 287.

403:15 Aug. 11, 1927.

403:20 Kellogg to White, Aug. 10, 1927.

403:24 New York *Times*, Oct. 27, 1927. See also White to Charles Baldwin, May 28, 1928.

403:36 Emporia *Gazette*, March 7, 1928.

404:9 White to G. C. Allen, Nov. 10, 1928.

404:17 April 9, 1928.

404:26 *Collier's*, June 9, 1928, p. 44.

404:37 White to E. E. Lape, July 5, 1928.

405:8 White to Herbert Hoover, June 18, 1928.

405:22 Emporia *Gazette*, June 11, 14, 1928.

406:36 April 29, 1922; "A Dry West Warns the Thirsty East," *Collier's*, Sept. 2, 1922, pp. 3-4. See also White "As Kansas Sees Prohibition," *Collier's*, July 3, 1926; "Anti-Saloon League," *Saturday Review of Literature*, June 16, 1928; New York *Herald Tribune*, Dec. 11, 1927, Magazine Section.

407:3 *Intermountain Catholic*, March 19, 1927.

407:31 "Al Smith, City Feller," *Collier's*, Aug. 12, 1926, pp. 8-9.

408:11 *Christian Science Monitor*, July 16, 1928.

408:23 New York *Telegram*, July 18, 1928.

408:31 July 14, 1928.

409:11 New York *World*, July 30, 1928.

409:18 New York *Times*, Aug. 1, 1928.

409:24 Aug. 1, 1928.

409:35 Quoted in "What's the Matter with White?" *Outlook*, Aug. 15, 1928, p. 611.

409:37 See, for instance, the Cleveland *News*, Aug. 3, 1928.

410:9 New York *Herald Tribune*, Aug. 15, 1928.

410:24 New York *Times*, Aug. 21, 22, 1928.

410:29 Oct. 1, 1928.

411:29 "Battle Hum of the Republic," *Collier's*, Aug. 18, 1928.

412:15 White to Henry Haskell, Nov. 20, 1928.

412:32 Emporia *Gazette*, March 30, 1929.

412:35 White to G. W. Hanna, Nov. 7, 1930; to R. A. Elward, Aug. 9, 1932. According to Allen, White and Hoover were the ones who persuaded Reed to make the appointment. To the writer, interview, Sept. 16, 1945.

413:2 "Kansas Cut Ups," Aug. 10, 1929, p. 49.

413:29 May 15, 1929.

413:38 May 4, 1929.

414:5 White to David Hinshaw, Aug. 24, 1929; to W. L. White, July 13, 1929.

414:17 Dec. 23, 1929.

414:33 See Clugston, *Rascals in Democracy*, pp. 207-220.

415:8 Ludwell Lee Montague, *Haiti and the United States, 1714-1938* (Durham: Duke University Press, 1940), pp. 210-211.

416:16 Feb. 4, 1927.

417:4 May 17, 1927.

417:36 White to Thomas Butcher, Feb. 12, 1930.

418:1 According to Augusta W. Hinshaw: "He was chosen for his sensitive nose for truth and to assure the public of getting all the truth—speaking out what might be needed." "Haiti Takes a Day in Court," *World's Work*, July, 1930, p. 40.

418:20 Feb. 22, 24, 1930.

418:28 White to Sallie L. White, Feb. 23, 24, 1930.

419:7 White to Sallie L. White, Feb. 27, 1928. Copies of the statements are in the White files. Unless otherwise specified, the source for the following material is White's letters to Mrs. White.

419:12 The text is in *Report of the President's Commission for the Study and Review of Conditions in the Republic of Haiti.* Publication of the Department of State. Latin-American Series, No. 2, 1930, pp. 2-3.

419:29 H. H. Weed, "Fresh Hope for Haiti," *Nation*, March 19, 1930, pp. 342-344.

421:18 April 26, 1930; "Haitian Experience," *Proceedings* of the American Society of Newspaper Editors, 1930, pp. 103-108; New York *Herald Tribune*, March 9, 1930.

421:25 W. Cameron Forbes to the writer, Nov. 2, 1945.

422:4 W. Cameron Forbes kindly supplied the author with a detailed description of these negotiations.

422:36 April 1, 1930.

424:20 White to Roger Baldwin, May 5, 1930.

425:10 Emporia *Gazette*, April 19, Nov. 20, 1929.

425:28 White to Allan Nevins, Nov. 15, 1934.

425:32 White to David Hinshaw, Dec. 3, 1929.

425:38 Dec. 5, 1930.

426:33 White to G. W. Hanna, Oct. 20, 1930.

426:35 White to G. B. Longan, Aug. 16, 1930.

427:11 See Clugston, *Rascals in Democracy*, pp. 141-160, for a vigorous defense of Brinkley.

427:20 White to F. T. Busch, Nov. 20, 1930.

428:4 Dec. 23, 1930.

428:7 White to Edward Keating, Nov. 22, 1930.

428:28 See New York *Times*, Oct. 19, 1930.

429:31 Emporia *Gazette*, Aug. 3, 1931.

430:14 Oct. 1, 1931.

430:21 Dec. 2, 1931, pp. 596-598.

431:3 May 23, 1932.

Chapter 19

THE REBIRTH OF THE PROGRESSIVE MOVEMENT

432:16 May 15, 1932.

433:2 White to Judson King, March 13, 1931.

433:6 White to George Akerson, June 2, 1931.

433:15 New York *Herald Tribune*, June 14, 1930.

433:24 White to David Hinshaw, July 9, 1932.

434:37 White to Margaret Deland, Sept. 22, 1932.

435:10 "The Farmer Takes His Holiday," *Saturday Evening Post*, Nov. 26, 1932, p. 7.

435:13 White to George Akerson, Sept. 8, 1932.

436:14 Oct. 24, 1932.

436:33 "Herbert Hoover the Last of the Old Presidents or the First of the New?" *Saturday Evening Post*, March 4, 1933, pp. 6-7.

437:8 White to F. D. Warren, Jan. 25, 1933.

437:18 White to the writer, Feb. 29, 1940; Emporia *Gazette*, May 7, 1936; Feb. 19, March 1, 1940.

437:37 April 6, 1933.

438:17 May 25, 1933.

438:33 See New York *Times*, June 13, 24, 29, 30, July 11, 1933.

438:36 White to George F. Milton, March 8, 1934.

439:27 See New York *Times*, Oct. 1, 2, 4, 5, 1933. See also K.U. *Graduate Magazine*, December, 1933.

439:32 White to Erwin Canham, Oct. 27, 1933.

440:3 White to Harold Ickes, Nov. 14, 1935.

440:20 Dec. 2, 1933.

441:26 White to Erwin Canham, Oct. 27, 1933.

442:22 See Arkansas City *Traveller*, Nov. 15, 1933.

442:26 White to Henry Haskell, Dec. 26, 1933.

443:7 White to Lacy Haynes, Feb. 13, 1934.

443:33 White to Clyde R. Faris, June 26, 1934.

445:5 White to Allan Nevins, May 24, 1934. See also White, "On Our Way—But Where Are We Going?" *Saturday Review of Literature*, April 14, 1934.

446:15 "Fifty Years Before and After" (printed by the University of Kansas, 1934), pp. 9-10. See also "American Youth and the American Spirit," speech over Columbia Broadcasting System, July 27, 1934 (printed by The Crusaders, Inc.).

446:25 April 2, 1934.

446:34 White to David Hinshaw, March 9, May 25, 1934.

447:10 "Liberalism for Republicans," *Review of Reviews*, January, 1933, p. 27.

447:14 Washington *Star*, Nov. 8, 1934, New York *Times*, Nov. 11, Dec. 9, 1934.

447:34 Wire to the Associated Press, March 27, 1935.

447:38 White to H. B. Johnson, April 11, 1935.

448:4 Washington *Post*, March 27, 1935.

448:11 April 6, 1935, p. 6; April 20, 1935.

448:35 White to John Hamilton, May 11, 1935.

449:1 White to U. S. Guyer, June 1, 1935.

449:7 White to Theodore Christensen, July 22, 1935.

449:10 New York *Times Magazine*, June 2, 1935.

449:37 White to E. B. Johnson, Aug. 19, 1935. See David Lawrence in the Washington *Star*, Oct. 11, 1935, for a reprint of White's statement on Landon.

450:19 White to Emilio Aguinaldo, April 3, 1937; speech before the Commonwealth Club of San Francisco, Jan. 24, 1936.

450:34 Feb. 19, 1936.

451:7 "I Cover the Pacific War Front," *Proceedings*, American Society of Newspaper Editors, April 16-18, 1936, p. 40.

Chapter 20

CONSERVATIVE LIBERAL

452:7 White to David Hazen, Feb. 20, 1936.

453:11 New York *Herald Tribune*, April 14, 1936.

453:18 White to Herbert Hoover, April 16, 1936.

454:1 March 3, 1936.

454:16 March 2, 1936.

454:18 White to Geoffrey Parsons, May 29, 1936.

454:21 White to W. L. White, March 2, 1936.

454:33 "In Kansas, the Landon Home State," *Review of Reviews*, April, 1936.

455:7 White to Harlan F. Stone, April 29, 1936; *Newsweek*, May 2, 1936.

455:18 White to H. F. Stone, April 29, 1936.

456:20 White to Harold Ickes, July 24, 1936.

457:23 White to the writer, interview, Nov. 14, 1941.

458:14 Oct. 12, 1936.

458:22 White to Marion Ellet, Nov. 9, 1936.

459:9 See Richmond *Times-Dispatch*, Sept. 24, 1936; New York *Times*, Sept. 26, 1936.

459:22 Sept. 28, 1936.

459:35 White to Colonel Henry Breckinridge, Aug. 15, 1936; to Raymond Clapper, Aug. 19, 1936.

459:37 See White to Russell Whitman, May 25, 1939.

460:3 White to Landon, Sept. 16, 1936; to Marion Ellet, Nov. 9, 1936.

460:11 White to Henry Haskell, Nov. 31, 1936.

460:17 See John Hamilton, "What the G.O.P. Needs," *Liberty*, Aug. 18, 1945, in which Hamilton urges the Republicans to be the conservative party.

460:32 White to Norris, Sept. 30, 1936; Norris to White, Nov. 9, 1936.

461:19 Oct. 14, 1936; Kansas City *Star*, Oct. 15, 1936.

461:23 A. L. Shultz to the writer, interview, Dec. 8, 1941.

461:26 White to T. J. Norton, Feb. 19, 1940.

461:29 White to Alf Landon, Nov. 5, 1936.

462:6 Emporia *Gazette*, Nov. 4, 1936; New York *Times*, Nov. 5, 8, 1936.

462:19 White to Ray Breitweiser, Nov. 17, 1936; *Literary Digest*, Dec. 19, 1936, p. 42.

463:31 See *The Old Order Changeth* (1910) and p. 180 of this biography.

464:8 White to D. J. Michelson, June 6, 1935.

464:19 White to Ed Rees, Jan. 19, 1937; to Freda Kirchwey, June 9, 1937.

465:11 Ickes to White, Feb. 13, March 15, 23, 1937.

465:14 White to Ickes, March 11, 1937.

466:8 White to Hamilton Fish, Dec. 4, 1936; to M. L. Requa, Jan. 1, 1937.

466:23 March 30, 1937.

467:4 July 21, 1937. See Staten Island *Advance*, July 21, 1937.

467:26 Jan. 18, 1938.

467:34 Jan. 17, 1938.

468:12 March 4, 1938.

468:25 Emporia *Gazette*, March 5, 1938.

469:9 See John R. Carlson, *Under Cover* (New York: E. P. Dutton & Co., 1943), pp. 165 ff.

469:19 *Defender*, March, 1936.

469:26 White to W. E. Sheffer, Sept. 1, 1939.

470:3 L. M. Birkhead to writer, interview, Feb. 28, 1945. See White to Dean Ackers, July 7, 1938; to Ira Faurot, July 26, 1938.

471:3 Friends of Democracy files. The preachers who signed the appeal were: J. C. Cleveland, M. D. Brown, D. E. Donaldson, B. E. Mills, S. D. Ogden, O. R. Powell, A. W. Roth, B. H. Smith, E. E. Tillotson.

471:35 White to Arch Jarrell, Jan. 29, 1938.

472:9 June 10, 1938.

473:10 *Defender*, November, 1940, p. 18.

473:15 See St. Petersburg (Fla.) *Daily Times*, Sept. 28, 1943, and Winrod's comments in the *Defender*, October, 1943, pp. 18-19.

474:2 Pp. 78-79, 294.

474:27 "Books of the Decade," *Yale Review*, XXIX (December, 1939), 422.

Chapter 21

SPOKESMAN FOR THE GRASS ROOTS

476:3 Some of the editorials in this volume attributed to W. A. White were actually written by W. L. White.

477:33 July 4, 1932.

478:3 "Savory Sage," *Literary Digest*, April 24, 1937; Emporia *Gazette*, Dec. 12, 1922; New York *Herald Tribune Magazine*, Feb. 11, 1923; Emporia *Gazette*, May 24, 1920; "The Challenge to the Middle Class," *Atlantic Monthly*, August, 1937, p. 198.

478:13 White to Olin Templin, Nov. 14, 1933.

478:23 "What's the Matter With America," *Collier's*, July 1, 1922, pp. 3-4.

478:31 *Ibid.*, p. 18.

478:37 Aug. 2, 1928.

479:7 See also "Solid West," *Collier's*, Dec. 30, 1922; "The Average American," New York *Times Magazine*, Jan. 4, 1931.

479:21 *The Changing West* (New York: The Macmillan Co., 1939), pp. 136-137.

481:27 White to the writer, interview, Nov. 8, 1941.

482:12 Printed by the Emporia *Gazette*.

482:23 White to Josephus Daniels, March 3, 1939; speech printed by Emporia *Gazette* and by the Los Angeles Lincoln Club.

482:34 Printed by the Emporia *Gazette*.

483:6 *The Changing West*, pp. 130-135.

483:21 Speech to the International Management Congress, Sept. 20, 1938.

483:26 "Yip from the Dog House," *New Republic*, Dec. 15, 1937, pp. 160-162; L. H. Robbins, "White Hails a Revolt of the Middle Class," New York *Times Magazine*, Nov. 20, 1938.

483:30 *Ibid.*; to C. E. Morgan, Nov. 26, 1930; White, "The Challenge to the Middle Class," *Atlantic Monthly*, Aug., 1937, p. 201.

484:8 *The Changing West*, pp. 116-117; "What Democracy Means to Me," *Scholastic*, Oct. 23, 1937; "Cheer Up, America!" *Harper's*, March, 1937.

484:25 "What Is the Democratic Process?" Commencement Address, Indiana State University, June 5, 1939, printed by the Emporia *Gazette; The Changing West*, p. 125.

484:30 *The Changing West*, p. 104; White, "The Blood of the Conquerors," *Collier's*, March 10, 17, 1923.

485:2 White to Whitley Austin, June 13, 1934; "Advice to a Young Communist," sent to *Editor and Publisher*, Oct. 5, 1935.

485:12 Feb. 27, 1911.

486:11 Feb. 26, 1944, p. 100.

486:12 Kenneth Kitch to White, Nov. 12, 1940.

486:20 "How Free Is Our Press?" *Nation*, June 18, 1938, p. 693.

487:4 "The Passing of the Free Editor," *American Mercury*, May, 1926, pp. 111-112; "Good Newspapers and Bad," *Atlantic Monthly*, May, 1934, pp. 581-586.

487:8 White to *Newsweek*, Nov. 25, 1938.

487:23 New York *Times*, April 21, 1939.

487:32 White to the writer, interview, Nov. 4, 1941.

488:9 White to Harold Ickes, Jan. 28, 1939.

488:18 Chicago *Times*, July 2, 1939; quoted in Marshall Field, *Freedom Is More Than a Word* (Chicago: University of Chicago Press, 1945), pp. 80-81.

488:26 "How Free Is the Press?" *Collier's*, April 8, 1939, pp. 16 ff.

488:31 *Time*, May 16, 1938, pp. 42-43.

488:37 Quoted in Silas Bent, *Newspaper Crusaders* (New York: Whittlesey House, 1939), p. 248; Harold Ickes, *America's House of Lords* (New York: Harcourt, Brace & Co., 1939), p. 37; White, "The Ethics of Advertising," *Atlantic Monthly*, November, 1939, pp. 665-671.

489:12 See "Journalism—Its Good and Its Gray Side," *World Review*, March 18, 1929, p. 104.

489:27 White to Drake Students of Journalism, Feb. 5, 1932.

489:34 Jan. 20, 1926.

490:9 B. E. Lyman, "Voting Behavior of Kansas Counties, 1862-1936," master's thesis, University of Kansas, 1937.

490:13 New York *Times*, Sept. 25, 1924.

490:20 *Ibid.*, July 31, 1928.

491:33 See Clough, *William Allen White of Emporia*, pp. 94-100.

493:4 See New York *Times*, Jan. 26, Feb. 11, 12, 1938; Kansas City *Star*, Feb. 10, 1938; *Life*, Feb. 28, 1928; *Look*, Feb. 15, 1938; *Christian Century*, Feb. 16, 1938; *Scholastic*, March 26, 1938.

493:17 Feb. 12, 1938.

494:11 Harry Scherman to the writer, interview, July 17, 1945.

494:35 White to *Saturday Review of Literature*, Sept. 27, 1935.

495:5 Harry Scherman to the writer, interview, July 17, 1945.

495:38 H. S. Canby to the writer, interview, July 18, 1945.

496:7 Christopher Morley to the writer, interview, July 17, 1945.

496:28 H. S. Canby to the writer, interview, July 18, 1945.

497:4 H. S. Canby to the writer, interview, July 18, 1945.

497:30 White to R. K. Haas, May 15, 1926.

497:35 White to Meredith Woods, Aug. 13, 1934.

498:13 *William Allen White In Memoriam*, prepared by the Book-of-the-Month Club.

PART V: A KANSAN LOOKS AT THE WORLD

Chapter 22

BETWEEN TWO WARS

504:10 "Will They Fool Us Twice?" *Collier's*, Oct. 15, 1921, pp. 5-6.

504:28 "Tinting the Cold Gray Dawn," *Collier's*, Dec. 17, 1921, pp. 5-6.

505:2 "Those Heartbreaks in Washinton," *Collier's*, Dec. 31, 1921, pp. 7-8.

505:11 "Will America's Dream Come True?" *Collier's*, Feb. 18, 1922, pp. 9-10.

505:21 See Emporia *Gazette*, Aug. 16,

Sept. 15, Dec. 6, 1922; Jan. 17, 30, Sept. 8, 1923.

505:28 April 25, 1924; New York *Times*, Jan. 31, 1926.

506:5 Emporia *Gazette*, Aug. 28, 1928.

506:16 See *People's Business*, May 21, 1930.

507:13 Emporia *Gazette*, Sept. 28, 1931.

507:18 *Ibid.*, Feb. 3, 1932.

508:22 *Peace and War: United States Foreign Policy, 1931-1941* (Washington: Government Printing Office, 1942), p. 3.

509:11 "Moscow and Emporia," *New Republic*, Sept. 21, 1938, pp. 177-180.

512:21 Emporia *Gazette*, May 7, 1935.

514:17 Emporia *Weekly Gazette*, Oct. 6, 1938.

515:22 *The Time for Decision* (New York: Harper & Brothers, 1944), pp. 119-120.

516:17 Charles G. Fenwick to White, Nov. 16, 1939.

517:14 For fuller details on the membership and operation of this committee see Walter Johnson, *The Battle Against Isolation* (Chicago: University of Chicago Press, 1944).

520:19 White to Frank Knox, Nov. 10, 1939.

520:29 Oct. 18, 1939.

521:8 Nov. 29, Dec. 8, 14, 16, 1939.

521:38 Dec. 22, 1939.

522:37 Dec. 29, 1939.

523:24 March 9, 1940.

523:33 Ben Hibbs, "Up Yonder the Trumpets Blew . . ." *Saturday Evening Post*, Feb. 26, 1944.

524:8 "The Story of a Democratic Adventure," unpublished MSS. on the Committee to Defend America by Aiding the Allies.

524:15 For detailed information on the formation of this committee see Walter Johnson, *The Battle*

Against Isolation (Chicago: University of Chicago Press, 1944).

Chapter 23

AID TO THE ALLIES

528:29 Printed by the Emporia *Gazette*.

529:18 "The Story of a Democratic Adventure."

530:23 Emporia *Gazette*, July 5, 1940.

530:29 See Chicago *Daily News*, July 6, 1940.

531:5 See Emporia *Gazette*, July 23, Aug. 26, 1940.

531:18 July 11, 1940.

532:12 For the details on the destroyer transaction see Johnson, Walter, *op. cit.*

535:13 Emporia *Gazette*, Oct. 11, 1940; White to Eugene Meyer, Oct. 10, 1940.

536:6 Sept. 30, 1940.

537:27 Oct. 26, 1940.

538:9 See "Thoughts after the Election," *Yale Review* (Winter, 1941), 217-227.

539:13 For further details see Johnson, Walter, *op. cit.*

539:19 Frank Woodruff Johnson was a pen name for Elizabeth Dilling, author of *The Red Network*.

540:13 For further details see J. R. Carlson, *Under Cover* (New York: E. P. Dutton, 1943); Michael Sayers and Albert E. Kahn, *Sabotage* (New York: Harper & Brothers, 1942); Henry Hoke, *Black Mail* (Reader's Book Service, 1944).

545:17 White to Raymond Clapper, Dec. 26, 1940; to J. N. Wheeler, Dec. 28, 1940.

546:11 White Committee *Progress Bulletin*, Dec. 2, 1940.

547:6 Jan. 7, 1941.

547:18 For more details see Walter

Johnson, *The Battle Against Isolation.*

550:19 Emporia *Gazette*, March 12, 1941.

550:36 Emporia *Gazette*, Feb. 26, 1941; New York *Times*, Feb. 26, 1941. See also White, "Choose Ye This Day," speech delivered at the University of Chicago, March 28, 1941, printed by the *Gazette.*

552:9 White to Roger Greene, April 5, 11, 1941; to O. G. Villard, April 12, 1941.

552:18 Emporia *Gazette*, May 17, 20, 1941.

552:26 *Ibid.*, May 27, 1941.

552:32 New York *Times*, Aug. 31, 1941.

553:26 Emporia *Gazette*, June 24, 26, 30, July 9, 31, Oct. 7, 1941.

553:31 White to William A. Smith, Sept. 21, 1941.

554:2 White to F. J. Hall, Aug. 25, 1941.

554:21 Interesting in view of this was a *Gazette* editorial on July 10, saying that Senator Capper should be re-elected in spite of his foreign policy.

554:31 Sept. 24, 1941.

Chapter 24

A FIRST-CLASS FUNERAL

559:2 Emporia *Gazette*, Jan. 2, 7, Feb. 18, March 21, 1942.

559:15 *Ibid.*, Jan. 12, 13, 15, 26, Feb. 17, June 12, 1942.

559:28 Feb. 23, 1942.

561:10 March 10, 1942.

561:19 White to Henry Haskell and Roy Roberts, May 16, 1942; to Schoeppel, April 22, 1942.

561:27 Emporia *Gazette*, June 18, July 17, 1942.

562:1 White to Fred Brinkerhoff,

Sept. 24, 1942; Emporia *Gazette*, Aug. 5, 1942.

562:7 White to Frank Motz, July 13, 1942.

562:23 Emporia *Gazette*, April 23, 1942.

562:30 *Ibid.*, May 29, 1942.

562:36 El Dorado *Times*, reprinted in the Kansas City *Star*, May 4, 1942.

563:21 White to the writer, Nov. 4, 1942.

564:7 Feb. 20, 1942.

564:11 Emporia *Gazette*, Jan. 13, June 20, Oct. 3, 7, 1942.

564:18 *Ibid.*, Feb. 28, July 10, 11, 1942.

564:29 *Ibid.*, June 16, 1942; to Clark Eichelberger, Aug. 28, 1942.

565:5 White to the writer, Nov. 30, 1942; Emporia *Gazette*, Nov. 4, 6, 1942.

565:10 White to Charles Sessions, March 16, 1942.

565:14 Emporia *Gazette*, Oct. 21, 1942.

567:33 See also White's speech, "Between the Devil and the Deep Sea," delivered to the Chicago Executives Club, March 19, 1943. Reprinted by the Emporia *Gazette*; *Rotarian*, July, 1943; Executives Club *News*, March 30, 1943.

568:25 Emporia *Gazette*, Feb. 25-27, 1943.

568:32 *Ibid.*, Feb. 11, 1942; Kansas City *Star*, Feb. 10, 1943.

569:29 White to Harry Hansen, April 8, 1943.

570:16 May 15, 1943; to Thomas Lamont, May 17, 1943.

570:24 Philadelphia *Record*, Aug. 31, 1943.

570:32 White to George Field, May 25, 1943; to Willkie, July 20, 1943; to Dewey, Aug. 19, 1943.

571:6 White to Alf M. Landon, June 24, 1943.

571:19 Emporia *Gazette*, Sept. 6, June 19, 22, Oct. 9, 1943.

571:27 White to Will Beck, Sept. 13, 1943.

571:34 White to P. Boettcher, Sept. 25, 1943.

572:9 New York *Times*, Oct. 10, 11, 1943.

ACKNOWLEDGMENTS

MANY PEOPLE contributed to this book. Without William Allen White's generosity in allowing me to have unrestricted access to all his letter material, the biography never could have been written. He also patiently answered all my impertinent questions about his life and did everything to make my work easier. After his death Mrs. White and Mr. and Mrs. W. L. White co-operated with me to the highest degree. At no time have they interfered in my research, and they have not prevented me from quoting from any manuscript material. Although the book could not have been written without the White family's co-operation, it is in no sense an official biography.

Many of William Allen White's old friends have assisted me by granting interviews, writing me letters, and some have allowed me to quote from their letters to Mr. White. I am particularly grateful to Victor Murdock, Mr. and Mrs. Howard Fleeson, Henry J. Allen, Henry Haskell, Lacy Haynes, Roy Roberts, Alf M. Landon, Oscar Stauffer, Mrs. Katherine Smith, Albert Ewing, Brock Pemberton, Charles E. Merriam, Harold L. Ickes, A. L. Shultz, W. G. Clugston, Irita Van Doren, Robert Van Gelder, Henry S. Canby, Dorothy Canfield Fisher, Christopher Morley, Harry Scherman, Ray Stannard Baker, Raymond Fosdick, Cecil Howes, Arthur Capper, Mrs. Vernon L. Kellogg, Walter Armstrong, Fred Ellsworth, Julian Street, Jacob Billikopf, Dr. S. J. Crumbine, Irving H. Morse, George Fort Milton, Arthur D. Read, John S. Phillips, Neil C. Brooks, Mrs. C. M. Sterling, Edna Ferber, Chester Rowell, Willis A. Parker, Henry E. Riggs, M. L. Izor, Rose Morgan, and Maude Smelser.

ACKNOWLEDGMENTS

The staff of the Kansas State Historical Society, particularly Kirke Mechem, Nyle Miller, and Mrs. Lela Barnes have been most helpful. My indebtedness to Paul Chandler, who microfilmed the White letters and allowed me to use some of his photographs in this book, is indeed great. Among the other members of the Emporia *Gazette* staff who were helpful during my lengthy stay in Emporia are Frank Clough, Roger Triplett, Russell Roberts, Mary Hughes, and Martha Klein. Bertha Colglazier was a rich source of information and Mrs. Frederick Bright was most co-operative. Laura M. French, formerly managing editor of the *Gazette* and historian of Emporia, supplied me with invaluable material, as did Mrs. Robert L. Jones of Emporia.

Nora Cordingley, in charge of the Theodore Roosevelt Collection at Harvard University, was most helpful with the Theodore Roosevelt material. P. M. Benjamin, librarian of Allegheny College, sent me material from the Ida M. Tarbell Collection, and Miss C. R. Dick, librarian of the University of Southern California, sent me material from the Hamlin Garland Collection.

Willis Kerr, librarian of the Claremont Colleges, kindly secured me copies of early White letters in the Huntingdon Library. Mrs. Chauncey L. Williams sent me White's letters to his first publishers and Miss Helen Sutliff sent me the earliest White letter in this book. I am also indebted to The Macmillan Company for allowing me to quote from Mr. White's published works; to publishers of magazines and newspapers for permission to include excerpts; and to the following publishers who allowed me to use quotations from their copyrighted material: D. Appleton-Century Co., E. P. Dutton & Co., Inc., Harcourt, Brace and Company, Inc., Harper & Brothers, Houghton Mifflin Company, Longmans, Green & Co., Oxford University Press, Rinehart & Company, Inc., Charles Scribner's Sons, Whittlesey House. Whenever such a quotation was used, credit was given in the notes.

William Sloane, formerly of Henry Holt and Company, offered valuable advice on this book, as did Charlotte Yarborough and Louise Frankenstein of Henry Holt, but above all I am indebted to Joseph A. Brandt, president of Henry Holt. It was his constant aid and encouragement that helped bring this biography to completion. He alone knows how much this sentence is an understatement. Through the generosity of the Newberry Library of Chicago, particularly through the kindness of my good friends Stanley Pargellis and Lloyd Lewis, I was granted a Newberry writing fellowship in 1945 which freed me from teaching and furnished me with the time to complete this book. I shall always be indebted to the Newberry Library for this grant and to the

Rockefeller Foundation, which supplied the funds to the Newberry Library.

Although I am, of course, solely responsible for the opinions expressed in this book and for any errors of fact, many people read all or a portion of the manuscript for me. First of all, my thanks to Avery Craven, stimulating teacher and good critic, for what he did to make the book. James C. Malin, of the University of Kansas, Cecil Howes, of the Kansas City *Star*, and Nyle Miller, of the Kansas State Historical Society, read the manuscript and saved me from many errors in Kansas history. W. T. Hutchinson kindly checked the finished draft and the following people read portions of the manuscript: W. Cameron Forbes, Christopher Morley, Dorothy Canfield Fisher, Henry S. Canby, Harry Scherman, Carl Hess, Milton Mayer, Ward Halstead, and L. M. Birkhead.

Mrs. Johnson aided me in the research that went into this volume, and the Social Science Research Foundation of the University of Chicago helped pay for part of the typing expense involved in this project. Mrs. Mary Louise Lavery was most helpful, as was Miss Esther Kirchhoefer.

BIBLIOGRAPHICAL STATEMENT

THIS BOOK is based on the unpublished letters *to* and *by* William Allen White. In addition, it contains excerpts from some of the letters that I included in my edition of *The Selected Letters of William Allen White* (Henry Holt & Co., 1947).

Mr. White saved carbons of almost everything he wrote from 1899 to 1944 and the originals of the letters that he received. In addition, I unearthed letters which he wrote prior to 1899, the location of which is mentioned in the notes in the back of the book when any such letter is cited. I have also examined the Theodore Roosevelt and William Howard Taft letters in the Library of Congress; the Joseph L. Bristow, Chester I. Long, and Charles Gleed letters in the Kansas State Historical Society; and the Frank Strong letters and James Canfield manuscripts in the University of Kansas library.

The notes and the statements in the text reveal the newspaper sources used in this study. It would be tedious to repeat the entire list here. Most useful were the Emporia *Gazette*, the Topeka *Capital*, the Topeka *State Journal*, the Wichita *Eagle*, the Wichita *Beacon*, the Kansas City *Star*, and *The New York Times*. Valuable press clippings on Mr. White are to be found in the Kansas State Historical Society and the University of Kansas library.

William Allen White was such a prolific writer that to list all his published articles and speeches here would make this book altogether too long. With the collaboration of Miss Alberta Pantle, of the Kansas State Historical Society, I have published in the *Kansas Historical Quarterly*, February, 1947, a bibliography of Mr. White's writings. I have a limited supply of reprints of this bibliography, and as long as my supply lasts I will send a copy to anyone who writes me for it. The notes in this biography indicate the White articles that I considered most valuable to this study.

WILLIAM ALLEN WHITE'S BOOKS

Rhymes By Two Friends. Fort Scott, Kansas: M. L. Izor & Sons, 1893. In collaboration with Albert Bigelow Paine.

The Real Issue; A Book of Kansas Stories. Chicago: Way and Williams, 1896.

The Court of Boyville. New York: Doubleday & McClure Co., 1899.

Stratagems and Spoils: Stories of Love and Politics. New York: Charles Scribner's Sons, 1901.

In Our Town. New York: McClure, Phillips & Co., 1906.

A Certain Rich Man. New York: The Macmillan Company, 1909.

The Old Order Changeth; A View of American Democracy. New York: The Macmillan Company, 1910.

God's Puppets. New York: The Macmillan Company, 1916.

The Martial Adventures of Henry and Me. New York: The Macmillan Company, 1918.

In The Heart of A Fool. New York: The Macmillan Company, 1918.

The Editor and His People; editorials by William Allen White. Selected from the Emporia *Gazette* by Helen O. Mahin; introduction and footnotes by Mr. White. New York: The Macmillan Company, 1924.

Politics: The Citizen's Business. New York: The Macmillan Company, 1924.

Woodrow Wilson, the Man, his Times, and his Task. Boston: Houghton Mifflin Co., 1924.

Calvin Coolidge, The Man Who Is President. New York: The Macmillan Company, 1925.

Some Cycles of Cathay. Chapel Hill: University of North Carolina Press, 1925.

Boys—Then and Now. New York: The Macmillan Company, 1926.

Masks In A Pageant. New York: The Macmillan Company, 1928.

What It's All About; Being A Reporter's Story of the Early Campaign of 1936. New York: The Macmillan Company, 1936.

Forty Years on Main Street. Compiled by Russell H. Fitzgibbon from the columns of the Emporia *Gazette;* foreword by Frank C. Clough. New York: Farrar & Rinehart, Inc., 1937.

BIBLIOGRAPHICAL STATEMENT

A Puritan In Babylon, the Story of Calvin Coolidge. New York: The Macmillan Company, 1938.

The Changing West: An Economic Theory About Our Golden Age. New York: The Macmillan Company, 1939.

Defense For America, edited with an introduction by William Allen White. New York: The Macmillan Company, 1940.

The Autobiography of William Allen White. New York: The Macmillan Company, 1946.

INDEX

Adams, Franklin P.: 239, 245, 354, 368
Adams, Samuel Hopkins: 143
Addams, Jane: 205, 297, 305
Aldrich, Nelson: 181
Aldrich, Winthrop: 455
Allen, Henry J.: 35, 161, 179, 222, 277, 286, 333, 361-369, 412, 426-427, 574
America First Committee: 540-541
American Federation of Labor: 189
American Magazine: 159, 165, 179
American Red Cross, White and Allen in (World War I): 277-283
American Society of Newspaper Editors: 488-489
Anderson, Sherwood: 348
Angell, Norman: 294, 305, 309
Anthony, Susan B.: 16, 26
Atchison *Globe:* 155

Babbitt: 348
Baker, Ray Stannard: 109, 138, 159, 295, 308
Ballinger, Richard A.: 182
Barrie, James: 281
Beard, Charles A.: 474
Beck, Clarence: 443
Beck, Will T.: 559
Beveridge, Albert: 221, 368
Bliven, Bruce: 476
Book-of-the-Month Club: 493-500

Borah, William E.: 163-164, 259, 315, 368, 389, 404, 427
Brandeis, Louis: 206
Bricker, John W.: 569
Brinkley, Dr. John R.: 426-427, 435
Bristow, Joseph L.: 124, 140, 157, 161, 163, 165-167, 179, 189, 220, 275
Britton, Nan: 374
Brosseau, Mrs. Alfred: 398-399
Broun, Heywood: 408, 495
Bryan, William Jennings: 89-92, 95
Bryce, James: 270, 281
Buchan, John: 309
Bull Moose party: 204-211, 217-225, 258-267
Bullitt, William: 297, 310
Burton, J. R.: 119, 123, 139
Butler County Democrat: 34
Butler, Nicholas Murray: 129, 416

Canby, Henry Seidel: 495, 573
Canfield, James H.: 37, 38
Cannon, Joe, 178, 181
Capper, Arthur: 155, 193, 220, 222, 373, 562-563, 565
Cardozo, Benjamin: 433
Century Club Group: 542-543, 545
Certain Rich Man, A: 61, 163, 174-176
Changing West, The: 479
Chenery, W. L.: 401

Chicago *Tribune:* 523, 534-535, 559, 571
Christian Science Monitor: 380
Clapper, Raymond: 486
Clemenceau, Georges: 305
College of Emporia: 31-33
Collier's Weekly: 143, 160, 167, 258, 310, 371, 390, 399
Committee to Defend America by Aiding the Allies: carries on amid protests, 538-541; crisis in, caused by White's letter to Roy Howard, 544-547; destroyer-base exchange approved by, 532-533; expansion of, 527; F. D. Roosevelt supports, 529; influence of, 528-529; launching and White as chairman of, 524-529; urges U. S. to convoy ships to England, 551; White resigns as chairman of, 547-549; White vexed by New York City Chapter of, 541-542
Coolidge, Calvin: 328-329, 335, 387-392, 473-474
Cosmopolitan: 122
Coudert, Frederic R.: 524, 543
Coughlin, Father: 524
Court of Boyville, The: inspiration for, 22; publication of, 115
Crane, Charles R.: 303, 305
Croly, Herbert: 333
Curtis, Charles: 156, 161, 221, 395, 403, 408, 412

Daniels, Josephus: 387
Daugherty, Harry M.: 369
Daughters of the American Revolution blacklist: 398
Davidson, Jo: 306, 575
Davis, Elmer: 331
Davison, Henry P.: 288
Dawes, Charles: 387
Debs, Eugene: 302
Democratic party: 25-27, 143-144
Dewey, John: 471
Dewey, Thomas E.: 530, 570-572
Dilling, Elizabeth: 469, 471
Doubleday and McClure: 115

Eastman, Max: 282
Editor and His People, The: 476

Eichelberger, Clark: 516, 524
El Dorado *Republican:* White as reporter on, 47-56

Fairbanks, Douglas, Sr.: 344
Fall, Albert: 370, 372-373
Ferber, Edna: 204, 244, 379, 418
Field, Marshall: 559
Finland: 521-522
Finley, John: 493
Finney, Ronald: 440-443, 572
Finney, Warren: 440-443
Fish, Hamilton: 536-537, 564
Fisher, Dorothy Canfield: 37, 279, 348, 391, 495
Fletcher, Henry P.: 417
Folk, Joseph: 141-143
Forbes, W. Cameron: 417
Forty Years on Main Street: 476
Fosdick, Harry Emerson: 471
Frankfurter, Felix: 305, 368, 396
French, Alice (Octave Thanet): 109
French, Laura M.: 81, 92, 239
Fuller, A. T.: 396
Fulton, T. P.: 33, 34
Funston, Frederick: 124

Gannett, Frank: 463, 465, 486
Gannett, Lewis: 78, 79, 493
Garland, Hamlin: 260, 380
Gary, E. H.: 186
Gazette, Emporia: becomes a local, state, and national force (1897-1914), 226-247; increasingly progressive tone of, 156; as local and national political organ, 144, 145; and "Mary White" editorial, 475; as profitable paper, 490-491; purchase and launching of, 76-77, 80-84; removes White's name from masthead, 573; run by W. A. White's son, 490; White's editorial style on, 118
German aggression: 513-515, 525, 527, 551
Gibson, Charles Dana: 186
God's Puppets: 258
Gouraud, General: 298
Greenback-Labor Party: 29

Hadley, Herbert: 142
Haiti, Commission for Study and Review of Conditions in: 414-424
Halifax, Lord: 533
Hamilton, John: 447-448, 456, 458, 460, 466
Hanna, Mark: 89, 103-104, 120, 123
Hapgood, Norman: 160, 167, 206
Harding, Warren G.: 325, 327-331, 333-335, 369-374
Hardy, Thomas: 173
Harper's Weekly: 95
Haskell, Henry: 438
Hatton, Mary Ann: 16-19
Haynes, Lacey: 453, 456
Hays, Will: 288
Hearst, William R.: 233, 346, 452
Herbert, Ewing: 59, 60
Herrick, Mrs. Robert: 305
Herron, George D.: 302-303
Hitler, Adolf: 469
Hoch, E. W.: 144, 149, 154-155, 165
Hoover, Herbert: 297, 324, 401-431, 478
Hopkins, Richard J.: 187, 368, 413-414, 432, 441
House, Edward M.: 295, 308, 386
Howard, Roy: 543-544
Howe, Ed: 19, 33, 384
Howells, William Dean: 109, 116, 117
Hughes, Charles Evans: 261-269, 334
Hughes, Walter: 239
Hull, Cordell: 438, 508-509, 516

Ickes, Harold: 262, 438, 486, 575
In the Heart of a Fool: 61, 217, 283-286, 343-344
In Our Town: 151-153
Institute of Pacific Relations: 392-394
International Economic Conference (London): 438
Isolationism: 251-254, 433, 508, 534-536, 555, 565

Jaccacci, Auguste F.: 109
James, Henry: 173
Jones, Robert: 31-33
Judge: 357-360
Judicial appointments: 413

Kansas: 14-15, 349
Kansas City *Journal:* 56-57, 59, 61-62
Kansas City *Star:* 56, 61, 63, 75-77, 121, 145, 157, 435
Kansas Day Club: launching of, 58
Kansas *Republican:* 83-85
Kellogg, Vernon L.: 31, 37, 39, 42, 44, 297
Kellogg-Briand Pact: 506, 510
Kelly, Florence Finch: 76
Kelly, Tom: 147
Kemp, Harry: 171, 173, 243
Kerenski, Alexander: 305-306
Kern, Jerome: 418
Kerney, James: 417
Kerr, Willis: 294
Knox, Philander C.: 124
Kohlsaat, H. H.: 94
Ku Klux Klan: 340, 342-343, 375-381, 391

Labor: 322, 361-369
Lamont, Thomas: 305, 455, 543
Laski, Harold: 574
Latin-American relations: 416-417
LaFollette, Robert M., Sr.: 157, 167, 191, 194-198, 388-389
LaGuardia, Florello: 466-467
Landon, Alfred M.: 435, 441, 443, 447, 449-450, 452-462, 561-562
Lawrence, David: 295
League of Nations: 291, 294, 306-308, 313-335
Leland, Cyrus: 126, 132, 133, 167
Lewis, Sinclair: 346-348, 471
Liberty League: 443
Life magazine: 574
Lindbergh, C. A., Sr.: 178
Lindbergh, Charles A., Jr.: 535, 554, 559
Lindsey, Ben: 168, 187, 205
Lippmann, Walter: 295, 386, 409, 475
Lissner, Myer: 217
Lodge, Henry Cabot, Sr.: 107, 139, 291, 314-315
London *Daily News:* 383
London *Times:* 312
Long, Chester I.: 139, 166-167
Lords of the Press: 487

Luce, Henry R.: 518
Lusitania: 253

MacArthur, Douglas: 299, 533-534
MacCracken, H. N.: 335
Machens, August W.: 140
Macmillan Company: 174, 529
Madison, E. H.: 193
Main Street: 346-348
Mark Twain: 74, 152
Martial Adventures of Henry and Me, The: 278, 282, 286
Masks in a Pageant: 399
Mason, Walt: 169, 184, 238-241, 489
Mayo Clinic: 467, 550, 560, 572
Mayo, William: 185
McAdoo, W. G.: 368, 388
McClure's Magazine: 105, 108-109, 113-114, 120-121, 133, 138, 149, 354, 399
McCormick, Anne O'Hare: 383, 485
McCormick, Medill: 280
McCormick, Robert R.: 523, 559, 571
McKinley, William: 89, 91, 95, 104-105, 127-128
McNary-Haugen Bill: 405
Mencken, H. L.: 406, 477
Mexico: 415-417
Monopoly: 29, 52, 137, 149, 394, 433
Moraine Park: 72, 570
Morgan, Anne: 184-185, 244
Morgan, W. Y.: 76
Morley, Christopher: 354, 495
Morrow, Dwight, 416
Muckraking: 138-139
Mulvane, David: 123, 408
Munich appeasement: 514
Munsey, Frank A.: 197, 205, 345
Murdock, Bent: 25, 43, 48
Murdock, Marsh: 25
Murdock, Victor: 25, 189, 222

Nation, The: 258, 268, 300, 387, 419
Nelson, William R.: and advocation of third party, 187; and Payne-Aldrich tariff, 178; as publisher of Kansas City Star, 63-69
Neutrality Act: 311, 511-515, 555
Nevins, Allan: 445

New Deal: 432, 438, 443-449, 457
New Republic: 333, 476, 560
New York Evening Post: 218
New York Herald Tribune: 474
New York Times, The: 303, 365, 383-384, 408, 458, 464, 477, 479, 490
New York Tribune: 354
New York World: 142, 266, 342, 380
Non-Partisan League: 286-287
Norris, George: 369, 389, 402, 427, 460, 464, 564
North American Newspaper Alliance: 433, 438, 455, 464

Paine, Albert Bigelow: 50, 60, 70, 72-74
Parker, Alton B.: 144
Parrington, Vernon L.: 91
Patterson, Joseph M.: 559
Paulen, Ben S.: 377-378, 385
Payne-Aldrich tariff: 177-178, 189
Pearson, Drew: 516
Pemberton, Brock: 239
Perkins, Frances: 438
Perkins, George: 205, 209, 211, 222
Phelps, William Lyon: 176
Phillips, John: 159, 184, 245
Pickford, Mary: 344
Pinchot, Amos: 211, 222
Pinchot, Gifford: 182, 389
Platt, Thomas: 119, 133-135
Plunkett, Sir Horace: 318
Politics: 25, 86-93, 132-137, 141, 144-145, 165-169
Populist party: 29, 52-55, 86-87, 90-93, 103-104, 161
Prinkipo: 301-304
Progressivism: clarified by Theodore Roosevelt, 128-129; and conservatism fight (1909), 177-180; forges ahead with Woodrow Wilson, 218-219; in 1912 presidential campaign, 191-198; publicized by White, 179; success of (1908), 168; symbolized by Bull Moose party (1912), 199-225; and Theodore Roosevelt, 170; wanes in 1914, 220-225
Prohibition: 219-220, 358-359
Protocols of Zion: 469
Puritan in Babylon, A: 473-474

Railroads: criticism of, by Populists, 53-54; in politics, 154-157, 162-163; White recommends government ownership of, 222

Real Issue, The: 69, 97-99

Reed, Clyde: 377, 382, 403, 412, 426, 469, 561

Reed, John: 258

Reed, Thomas B.: 107

Regeneration of Colonel Hucks, The: 55-56, 58

Republican party: 25-27, 29, 58, 86, 103, 120, 154-155, 169, 189-190, 259-268, 288, 290, 314-335, 446, 466, 508

Rhymes by Two Friends: 69-70, 73

Riley, James Whitcomb: 260

Robins, Raymond: 221

Roosevelt, Franklin D.: appreciates White's support, 438; congratulates White on 75th birthday, 566; discouraged by White from third term, 530; foreign policy of (1933-1941), 508-509; inaugural address of (1933), 437; methods of, criticized by White, 449; nominates Alfred Smith (1928), 406; opposed by White, 432; praised by White for leadership in World War II, 552, 558; praises White, 467-468; presidential campaign of (1932), 434; re-election of (1936), 461-462; sends sympathy on White's death, 573; speaks at University of Virginia (June, 1940), 527-528; visit of, to Emporia (1936), 460-461; White writes to, 428

Roosevelt, Theodore: death of, 293; defeat of (1916), 259-266; as leader of Bull Moose party, 199-211; and muckraking, 138-139; negotiations of, for presidency, 126-127; as N. Y. governor, 112; in 1904 presidential campaign, 143, 145; and progressivism, 128-129; on running for president (1912), 191, 194-198; and vice-presidential nomination, 119; White's early meeting with, and admiration for, 107-108; as White's ideal statesman, 170

Root, Elihu: 107, 315

Rowell, Chester: 79, 217, 392

Sacco and Vanzetti: 396

Saturday Evening Post: 95, 117, 124-125, 137, 146, 223, 258, 317, 458, 486

Saturday Review of Literature: 495

Scherman, Harry: 495, 498

Schoeppel, Andrew: 561-562, 572

Scott, Charles F.: 378, 382

Scribner's: 95, 113, 116, 118, 131

Seldes, George: 487

Sherwood, Robert E.: 522

Shotwell, James T.: 307

Smith, Alfred E.: 388, 402, 406-408, 479

Spanish-American War: 110-112

Spanish Civil War: 512-513

Standard Oil Company: 149

Steffens, Lincoln: 109, 138, 159, 295, 305

Stimson, Henry L.: 503

Story of a Country Town, The: 19

Stratagems and Spoils: 59, 116, 131

Straus, Oscar: 205

Strong, Frank: 151

St. Louis *Post-Dispatch:* 78

Stubbs, W. R.: 157, 161-163, 165-169, 179, 188-189

Sullivan, Mark: 148, 295

Supreme Court: 180, 462-466

Swope, Herbert Bayard: 342

Taft, Charles P.: 456-457

Taft, Robert A.: 530, 558, 564

Taft, William Howard: 158, 163-165, 168, 177-179, 182, 186, 192, 194, 200, 202, 315, 413

Tarbell, Ida M.: 108, 113, 138, 149, 159, 244

Topeka Capital: 155

Trusts: 145-146, 394

Tumulty, Joseph: 275, 386

TVA Muscle Shoals Bill: 402

University of Kansas: 37-46, 150-151, 212, 468

Vandenberg, Arthur: 530

Versailles Treaty: 291-292, 308, 313, 504

Villard, Oswald Garrison: 300, 551

Wallace, Henry: 438
Way and Williams: 96-99
Welles, Sumner: 515
Wells, H. G.: 281, 309
What People Said: 441
"What's the Matter With Kansas?"
  (editorial): 93-96
White, Allen, Dr. (father of W. A.
  White): 11-15
White, Mary: 144, 245, 326, 332-333,
  344, 350-356
White, Sallie Lindsay: 70-72, 125, 209,
  212, 222, 243-244, 260, 550
White, William Allen: active in international co-operation, 505-525; as ad-
  vocator of League of Nations, 306;
  on Anglo-American co-operation,
  310, 311; as ardent follower of progressive cause, 148-169; appraisal of
  Hoover by, 436, 437; attacked as radical, 396-399; attacks Al Smith, 406-
  410; attacks press and AP, 486-488;
  attacks Winrod, 468-473; attempts to
  reform Republican party, 466; as big
  city editor, 63; birthday celebration
  of (1910), 183; as Book-of-the-Month
  Club judge, 493-500; as booster for
  Emporia, 241, 243; as "Boss Buster,"
  144; and Calvin Coolidge, 391; as
  chairman of Committee to Defend
  America by Aiding Allies, 525-529;
  as champion of Bull Moose party,
  199-225; changing political attitude
  of, 141-144; chosen chairman of Non-
  Partisan Committee, 517; death of,
  573; defines types of journalism, 489;
  and depression of 1929, 424-431;
  early conservatism of, 47-62; early
  life of, 9-13, 22-25; early newspaper
  experience of, 34-36; editorial policy
  of, and views on function of newspapers, 228-236; editorial qualities of,
  118, 123; editorializes on Casablanca
  conference, 565, 566; editorializes on
  Pearl Harbor attack, 556; on education, 212-216; efforts of, to maintain
  progressivism, 258-268; fails in health
  (1942), 560; fights Ku Klux Klan, 375-
  383; first European tour of (1909),
  172-174; first newspaper job of, 25;
  and F. D. Roosevelt, 432-438, 443-450,
  570, 571; funeral of, 3, 4, 575, 576; as
  grass-roots spokesman and liberal,
  475-485; higher education of, 30-46;
  and impressions of Germany (1919),
  299, 300; influenced young journalists,
  486; as insurgent, 170-198; in Kansas
  politics, 165-169; and Labor, 322, 341;
  and the Landon campaign, 449-450,
  452-462; lauded as colorful editor,
  485; and League of Nations, 313-335;
  looks forward to 1944 Republican
  Campaign, 568; makes last trip East,
  567; marriage of, 71; and Mary
  White's death, 350-356; as member
  of Haitian commission, 414-424; and
  moving pictures, 344; operated on
  (1937), 467; opposes F. D. Roosevelt's
  court plan, 463-466; in the Orient,
  450, 451; parental influences on, 18-
  20; at Paris Peace Conference (1919),
  292-313; personal appearance of
  (1909), 243; poetic efforts of, 60; and
  postal frauds, 139-141; and preference
  for small town journalism, 237; prestige of, in state and national politics,
  187-198; and progressivism, 128, 129;
  and purchase of "Red Rocks," 244;
  in rail strike controversy, 361-369;
  and reactionary twenties, 339-374; receives awards, 543, 550; receives honorary degree, 185; in Red Cross
  (World War I), 277; as regent,
  Kansas University, 150-151; as Republican, 29; resigns as chairman of
  Committee to Defend America, 547-
  549; résumé of life of, 6-9; and Russian recognition by U. S., 508, 509;
  seventy-fifth birthday of, 566; as
  small town symbol, 4-6; and street
  fair (1899), 113-115; supports Hoover
  (1928), 401-431; supports Wendell
  Willkie (1940), 530, 531, 535-537; and
  Theodore Roosevelt, 107, 108; as
  trainer of future editors, 238-240;
  travels in Russia (1933), 439; under-
  goes serious operation, 572; views of,

on Russian Revolution (1917), 277, 278; warns Republicans about national security, 554; Woodrow Wilson biography by, 386; and World War I, 251-256; and World War II, 525-529; writes last two dispatches for N.A.N.A., 571-572.

White, William Lindsay: 120, 245, 292-293, 332, 403, 441, 490, 522

Whitlock, Brand: 184, 373, 387, 395

Whyte, Frederick: 305, 309

Wilbur, Ray Lyman: 393

William Allen White Emporia Memorial Foundation: 575

William Allen White Foundation: 574

William Allen White School of Journalism: 491

Willkie, Wendell: 530-531, 535, 537-538, 550, 564, 570

Wilson, Woodrow: 192, 203, 206-208, 211, 218-219, 253, 269-273, 275, 307-308, 314-321, 386

Winchell, Walter: 475

Winrod, Gerald B.: 468-473

Wood, Leonard: 289, 321, 328

Woodring, Harry H.: 426

Woolley, Mary E.: 393

World War I: 251-273

World War II: 515, 520-521, 523-525, 527, 551-556